THE IRISH CRIMINAL LAW SERIES

General Editor: Patrick MacEntee, SC, QC

Offences Against the Person

P E T E R   C H A R L E T O N,   BA (Mod)

of the Dublin Circuit, Barrister at Law,
formerly lecturer in law at Trinity College, Dublin

THE ROUND HALL PRESS

The book was input by
Gilbert Gough Typesetting and
output by Typeset Origination Services Ltd for
THE ROUND HALL PRESS
Kill Lane, Blackrock, Co. Dublin, Ireland.

and in North America by
The Round Hall Press
c/o International Specialized Book Services
5804 NE Hassalo Street, Portland, OR 97213

First published 1992, reprinted 1994

A catalogue record for this book is available from the British Library.

ISBN 0-947686-85-1 hbk
0-947686-89-4 pbk

Printed in Ireland by
Colour Books Ltd, Dublin

Peter Charleton

OFFENCES AGAINST THE PERSON

IN MEMORY OF

EVELYNE

Foreword

Peter Charleton's book on the substantive law relating to offences against the person in Ireland is the first of what we hope will be a series of works by various authors which eventually will cover the whole field of Irish criminal law both substantive and procedural. It is a tribute to his enthusiasm, diligence and learning that he has completed this volume ahead of schedule.

A result of the application of constitutional principles to our criminal law and of the different pace of legislative change between Ireland and England has been that Archbold, for all its great learning, is no longer an adequate *vademecum* for the Irish criminal lawyer.

Peter Charleton's work will supply a substantial and important part of what we lack.

This volume is intended to be primarily a practitioner's book, setting out the Irish law clearly but fully in the text and providing copious comparative material and suggestions for possible reform in the footnotes. The author's range of knowledge of comparative criminal law, particularly from Canada and Australia as well as the neighbouring jurisdictions, should be a useful antidote to legal provincialism. One can only hope that his suggestions for legal reform will not go unnoticed.

Mr Charleton is clearly a born teacher and I have no doubt that his book will be a great help to all those learning the law—at whatever stage of our legal education. Specimen indictments will be of particular assistance to practitioners.

I confidently trust that this work will meet with the support of all those interested in our criminal law and that it will have set a standard of accuracy and stimulation for the rest of the projected series.

Patrick MacEntee, SC, QC
Law Library
Four Courts
Dublin 7

Contents

Preface

The aim of this work is to discuss the criminal law relating to offences against the person. Further volumes in this series will consider the bulk of the substantive criminal law including what is termed the "general part". Some aspects of the fundamental theory are essential to the subject matter which follows. Intention in murder and defences specific to homicide occupy considerable space in this book as does recklessness in rape and criminal negligence in manslaughter. In other places a sketch of basic principle has been either inescapable or was thought to be useful in the final result. Similarly whilst an explanation of substantive criminal law is the purpose of this series, aspects of criminal procedure and evidence are mentioned in passing. Sometimes these are impossible to avoid in an attempt to explain the elements of an offence; an example of this occurs in the law relating to rape and sexual assault.

My starting point has been the law as it stood on Independence in 1922. Where no clear answer in this jurisdiction has emerged on a point since that time I have referred to the law in other common law countries.

I have tried to keep this text simple, feeling that unclear exposition is of no assistance to anyone, particularly if any portion of this book ever comes to be used in jury trials.

The help of friends and colleagues is noted overleaf. My wife Fiona is deserving of all my gratitude, as ever.

I must record that I am deeply indebted to Patrick MacEntee for his continual encouragement and the assistance he gave by suggesting both the content of this work and the manner in which it should, ideally, be written.

I have tried to state the law in accordance with the materials available to me on 13 June 1991.

Peter Charleton

Feast day of St Anthony of Padua, 1991

Acknowledgements

The author owes a debt of gratitude to the following: Mrs Kathleen Moylan who typed the entire manuscript with commendable skill and efficiency; Eugene Smart, Trinity College, Dublin, Tim Harley, of the King's Inns and Bill Schiller, of the University of London, who acted as research and proofing assistants; Tim Harley, again for preparing the index; Francis Hackett for providing much useful information on Australian law; the Staff of the Law Library in the Four Courts, the Berkley Library in Trinity College, Dublin, the Library of the Institute of Advanced Legal Studies, in London and the Library of the King's Inns, Dublin; my family and friends for their support; the various law journals and law reports who gave permission to publish the extracts cited or quoted in this volume; ICL for computer assistance; my publishers, especially Michael, Bart and Terri; and those not mentioned through inadvertence.

Works referred to and their Abbreviations

Archbold (1922)
Criminal Pleading, Evidence and Practice
by John Frederick Archbold, 26th ed,
by H.D. Roome and R.E. Ross

Archbold (1954)
Criminal Pleading, Evidence and Practice
by John Frederick Archbold, 33rd ed, 1954
by T.R.F. Butler and M. Garsia

Archbold (1966)
Criminal Pleading, Evidence and Practice
by John Frederick Archbold, 36th ed, 1966
by T.R.F. Butler and M. Garsia

Bl Com
Commentaries on the Laws of England
by Sir William Blackstone, 17th ed, 1830
by E. Christian

Brett Waller & Williams
Criminal Law, Text and Cases
by L. Waller, C.R. Williams, 6th ed, 1989

Burchell & Hunt
South African Criminal Law and Procedure,
1983, by E.M. Burchell, J.R.L. Milton and J.M. Burchell

Charleton
Controlled Drugs and the Criminal Law
by Peter Charleton, 1986

Clarkson
Understanding Criminal Law
by C.M.V. Clarkson (1987)

Co Inst
Institutes of the Laws of England
by Sir Edward Coke, 1797

Cross
Evidence
by Sir Rupert Cross and Colin Tapper, 7th ed, 1990

East PC
A Treatise of the Pleas of the Crown
by Edward East, 1803

Fost
A Report on Crown Cases and Discourses on The Crown Law
by Sir Michael Foster, 3rd ed, 1792
by M. Dodson

Gillies
Criminal Law
by Peter Gillies, 1985

Hale PC   *The History of the Pleas of the Crown*
                         by Sir Matthew Hale, 1736

Hogan & Walker   *Political Violence and the Law in Ireland*
                         by Gerard Hogan and Clive Walker, 1989

Howard   *Criminal Law*
                         by Colin Howard, 4th ed, 1982

Kelly   *The Irish Constitution*
                         by J.M. Kelly, 2nd ed, 1984

Kelly—*Supplement*   *Supplement to the above*
                         by G. Hogan and G. White, 1988

Kenny (1922)   *Outlines of Criminal Law*
                         by C.S. Kenny, 11th ed, 1922

MACL   *The Modern Approach to Criminal Law*
                         edited by L. Radzinowicz and J.W.C. Turner, 1948

McMahon & Binchy   *The Irish Law of Torts*
                         by Brian McMahon and William Binchy, 2nd ed, 1990

Phipson   *Evidence*
                         by M.N. Howard, Peter Crane, Daniel Hochberg, 14th
                         ed, 1990

Russell   *Russell on Crime*
                         by Sir W.O. Russell, 12th ed, 1964 by J.W.C. Turner

Ryan & Magee   *The Irish Criminal Process,* 1983

Sandes   *Criminal Law and Procedure in the Republic of Ireland*
                         by Robert Lindsey Sandes, 3rd ed, 1951

Stephen—*Hist*   *A History of the Criminal Law of England*
                         by Sir James Fitzjames Stephen, Vol. 1, 1883

Street   *The Law of Torts*
                         by M. Brazier, 8th ed, 1988

Stuart   *Canadian Criminal Law*
                         by Don Stuart, 2nd ed, 1987

Williams—*CLGP*   *Criminal Law: The General Part*
                         by Glanville Williams, 2nd ed, 1961

Williams—*TBCL*   *Textbook of Criminal Law*
                         by Glanville Williams, 2nd ed, 1983

Tables

STATUTORY INSTRUMENTS

UNITED KINGDOM ACTS

OTHERS

CASES

Tables

Tables

CHAPTER ONE

Homicide

1.01 The purpose of this chapter is to serve as an introduction to Chapters 2 and 3. Within that context the principles fundamental to a criminal trial will be explored.

Classification

1.02 Homicide is a broad categorisation of the various wrongs in criminal law whereby the life of a person is terminated. Life is most obvious from birth. Prior to that point the development of human life is protected by Article 40.3.3 of the Constitution.[1] Being political and directive in its nature the Constitution does not, of itself, define criminal offences.[2] It is the Oireachtas which is charged with the task of implementing the will of the people. Too often this responsibility has been ignored. Continuing neglect is explicable only on the basis of sloth or ignorance. Whereas English common law has been largely reformed, and is now in the process of codification, Irish law has developed through judicial activism. Unfortunately, in the realm of criminal law this has been least evident. Notwithstanding that, the people enacted a clause of the Constitution specifically guaranteeing life prior to birth. The problems which should have been solved by legislative intervention have been left untouched. The result is that the legislative code for the protection of life must be sought in a varied body of statutory and judicial interpretations which together comprise the law on abortion.[3]

Regrettably the structure of Irish criminal law is not built on clear fundamental concepts. Offences are not defined in terms of explicit elements. There has been no attempt to codify or reform the law in a coherent and self-consistent fashion since it was inherited from the United Kingdom in 1922. The law stated in this work has been extracted from a multitude of sources. We have attempted to state Irish law by reference to the legislation and decisions which are available. Additional comparative materials have assisted in the identification of the law, especially where no Irish authority exists.

A person who is born alive enjoys the protection of the law. If that person is unlawfully and intentionally killed by another the killing is murder.[4] Exceptionally, even an intentional killing may be completely justified where it was reasonably necessary for a person to defend himself, or otherwise lawfully use force even to the extent of deliberately taking life. There are two situations in which a charge of murder is reduced to manslaughter by reason of a defence. A person who loses self-control, usually due to some act on the part of the deceased, and kills may avail

---

1   This is due to the 8th Amendment which was introduced on 8 September 1983.

2   For a possible contrary view see *A-G (SPUC) v Open Door Counselling Ltd* [1988] IR 593 at 610, 617 and 622-23 HC & SC.

3   See ch 5.   4 See par 2.18-2.29.

of the limited defence of provocation.[5] This defence is a legal concession to human frailty operating in circumstances where the accused has ceased to be master of his own actions. The second situation is excessive self-defence. Here, the law recognises that a real mistake as to the degree of lawful force which a situation of self-defence requires, means that the accused lacks the moral culpability normally associated with murder.[6] In consequence his liability is also reduced to manslaughter. The defences of duress, necessity and infancy retain strong objective elements. Situations may occur where one or other of these defences fails due to circumstances which leave the accused objectively culpable but where, due to his subjective perception of events, he lacks the moral culpability normally associated with murder. Apart from provocation and excessive self-defence the defences general to the criminal law result, if they are successful, in a complete acquittal. Arguably, the rigid objective criteria inherent in other defences might justly be eased by allowing for a reduction of criminal liability from murder to manslaughter in certain defined circumstances.[7] An intoxicated killing amounts to manslaughter, and not to murder, through the application of the less satisfactory reasoning which artificially divides offences into those of basic and specific intent.[8]

Apart from these defences experience indicates that it is not uncommon for a killing to have occurred while the accused was suffering from mental disease or some lesser form of psychological imbalance. The effect of a finding of insanity is to place the offender outside the scope of punitive measures and to place him instead within a regime where society attempts treatment.[9]

The defences of provocation and excessive self-defence are peculiar to the law of murder and will be addressed in detail in due course. Completeness necessitates a brief sketch of other defences which are relevant to the crimes considered in this volume.

Where a person kills another, Garda investigations tend to focus on the crime of murder. It is a major part of Garda investigations to discover whether the killing was perpetrated deliberately. If the material from which a purposive killing could reasonably be established is absent, the investigation will focus on whether criminal liability for manslaughter can be established. The element common to both murder and manslaughter is that the accused is required to have caused the death of the victim. Where it cannot be proved that the accused did so intentionally other lesser culpable mental states may be present. Manslaughter may be committed either by criminal negligence, by an unlawful and dangerous act, or by an assault.[10] An intentional killing is difficult to prove. The varied fault elements in the three species of manslaughter ensure, in practice, that where the element of intentional killing is absent a degree of culpability consistent with manslaughter can usually be established.

The penalty for murder is life imprisonment. There is no discretion to impose a lesser sentence.[11] The penalty for manslaughter can vary, and in practice does vary,

---

5   See par 4.02-4.29.   6 See par 4.30-4.37.   7 See par 4.39-4.48.   8 See par 4.43-4.45.

9   See par 4.45-4.46.   10 For a full classification see ch 3.

11   Criminal Justice Act, 1964, s 5, repealed by the Schedule to the Criminal Justice Act, 1990. The 1990 Act retains mandatory life imprisonment for former capital murder cases, but defines it in s 4 as a minimum of forty years. Sentence cannot be commuted or remitted below this minimum period (less good behaviour remission).

from a fine or suspended sentence to a maximum penalty of life imprisonment. The circumstances under which manslaughter is committed vary widely in gravity. The historical development of manslaughter from the concept of an unlawful killing to the three current categories of wrong partially explains the wide range of sentences which may be imposed. In choosing a sentence judges will focus on the blame to be attached to the accused. A cursory sight of the categories of manslaughter indicates that blame will usually be present in a high degree where the accused has caused the death of the victim through a criminally dangerous act or omission or by an act which is, in itself, criminal and dangerous. The third category, of assault manslaughter, may occur in circumstances where only slight blame could reasonably be attached to the accused. Of itself, therefore, assault manslaughter explains the wide disparity in sentencing for this crime.[12]

1.03 Serious crimes are defined in terms of an external element (the visible wrong committed) and a mental element (the culpable mental state which accompanies that wrong). Generally, these must coincide.[13] It is useful to categorise these mental states in descending order of gravity. There are four relevant mental states: intention or knowledge, recklessness, criminal negligence, and negligence. Apart from fault crimes, where blame is ascribed due to a coincidence of external element with mental fault in the accused, certain regulatory offences proscribe conduct absolutely. In these offences where the accused brings about the external elements comprised of the illegal situation it is no answer that he was neither aware of what he was doing nor foresaw that the forbidden situation might occur. These are crimes of strict or absolute liability. The author believes that there are no such crimes relating to offences against the person.

A person acts intentionally when it is his purpose to bring about a particular result.[14] A person acts recklessly when he consciously takes a substantial and unjustifiable risk that a situation exists, or that a consequence will occur, as a result of his action.[15] In criminal negligence a person fails to exercise foresight, and thus to use necessary prudence, with the result that he places others in a situation of serious risk of injury.[16] Simple negligence involves a failure to exercise the foresight and prudence of a reasonable or ordinary person. Murder is an example of a crime of intent.[17] Rape is an example of a crime of recklessness.[18]

Manslaughter is the only current example of an indictable offence which can be committed by criminal negligence. As will be apparent from the definitions given in the text, most crimes can be committed by either an intentional or a reckless mental state. Intent or knowledge, recklessness, criminal negligence and negligence are categorised in descending order of gravity. Intention or knowledge is the most grave mental state which the law can ascribe to a particular crime. Recklessness, involving the conscious taking of an unjustifiable risk, is of a less serious order of culpability. The prosecution are not required to prove that the accused foresaw any risk where criminal negligence is the mental element of a crime. Criminal negligence is similar in conception to negligence but more grave in the culpability that is

---

12 See par 3.04. 13 See par 4.30. 14 See par 2.19. 15 See par 2.37. 16 See par 3.08.
17 See ch 2. 18 See ch 8.

attached where, due to a lack of foresight or application the accused places others in serious risk. Where a crime is defined in terms of a mental element of intention, recklessness by an accused will not suffice to make him criminally liable. Where recklessness is the mental element of a crime an intentional act, as a more culpable mental state will suffice. Similarly, an accused who kills another intentionally or recklessly is at least guilty of murder where the required mental element of the crime is criminal negligence. Less culpable mental states in the definition of a crime therefore include those of greater culpability. The scheme does not work in the opposite way. In murder, for example, the accused must have intended to kill or cause serious injury to the victim.[19] It is not enough that he merely took a substantial risk that his conduct could result in serious injury to the victim. Similarly, an act of criminal negligence does not amount to recklessness unless it can be proved that the accused foresaw the risk that his conduct, by way of act or omission, might occasion. In that situation his conduct will amount to recklessness.

Voluntary Conduct

1.04 Before the accused can be found guilty of a criminal offence his action must be voluntary.[20] Actions are not voluntary when they are directed by influences over which a person has no conscious control. Exceptionally, involuntary actions may be culpable where the accused, through his own criminal negligence, has put himself in a situation where he may suddenly lose control.[21] For example, a person driving a car may realise that he is growing extremely tired. He may accept the risk of falling asleep. A person who is asleep has lost consciousness and ceases to be responsible for his actions. In the example given, however, if the driver fails to stop and rest his negligence may suffice to convict him of manslaughter.[22] Similarly, it may be a sufficient act of criminal negligence for a person about to undertake a responsible task to intoxicate himself through drinking or drug-taking.

Subjective Test

1.05 Where the definition of a crime requires proof of intention or recklessness the accused must foresee the occurrence of the external elements of the offence.[23] Criminal negligence and negligence are, in contrast, judged or evaluated by objective standards. Consequently the prosecution need not prove that an accused foresaw the harm in question.[24] However, in manslaughter the test of criminal negligence has been defined by such a high standard of objective fault that few ordinary people would fail to foresee their act or omission resulting in a risk of serious harm.[25] In choosing an objective test, for one of the more serious indictable crimes the law has been influenced by the general tendency towards subjective fault as the correct basis

---

19   Criminal Justice Act, 1964, s 4.   20 See par 4.07.
21   For an analysis see Goode, "On Subjectivity and Objectivity in Denial of Criminal Responsibility: Reflections on Reading Radford" (1987) 11 Crim LJ 131; *Radford* (1985) 20 A Crim R 388 CCA SA.
22   *Pemble* (1971) 124 CLR 107 HC. Further see par 3.02.
23   Intent is discussed at par 2.19. Recklessness is disussed at par 2.37.
24   See par 3.10.   25 See par 3.08.

of criminal liability. The test, nonetheless, remains objective. An element of criminal negligence or negligence does no more than relieve the prosecution of the burden of proving the element of foresight.

Where intention or recklessness are elements of an offence the prosecution must prove that an individual accused acted intentionally or recklessly. These states of mind are judged or evaluated by a subjective standard. Criminal liability does not depend on the perception of a hypothetical reasonable man, but on the actual state of mind of the individual accused. As we have already noted, the requirement of intention or recklessness is common to all the crimes considered in this work, manslaughter excepted.

Proof of a subjective state of mind casts a heavy burden on the prosecution. The element of intention can, nonetheless, be proved. People are broadly similar in their mental processes. The shared perceptions and experience of mankind will allow a jury to draw a legitimate inference of a mental state. In criminal law a person is taken to have intended the natural and probable consequences of his action.[26] People generally transact important business, or do significant acts, knowing the nature of what they are doing and the consequences which experience tells them will or may ensue. The subjective approach in crime takes account of the fact that this principle is not of universal application.

A person is entitled to defend himself by pointing to evidence on the prosecution case, or by offering evidence, which may reasonably indicate that, despite the circumstances, the accused acted without the mental state which the crime requires. In considering whether this material raises a reasonable doubt as to guilt, the jury is collectively entitled to compare their view of the perceptions of an ordinary individual, in the circumstances proved by the prosecution, with the mental state claimed by the accused.[27] Such factors as age, tiredness and emotional state can, and do, contribute to the accuracy of perceptions. The extent of a person's information as to the consequences of his action will also have influences on his action. In a murder case, for example, where the prosecution must prove that the accused killed the deceased while intending to kill or cause serious injury, the jury may be asked to believe that, while evidently doing one thing, a person intended to do another. In rape,[28] the external element of the offence is defined as an act of sexual intercourse by a man with a woman who does not consent. The mental element of that crime requires that the accused intended so to do, or was reckless as to whether his victim consented or not. The accused may claim that he was under a misapprehension which changed the nature of his action from one which, viewed objectively or externally, was rape to one where he was innocent according to his own state of mind. In practice, it is more usual in rape cases for the accused to argue that the external elements of the crime have not been proved; either that he was not the person who committed the crime or that the woman consented to sexual intercourse and, for reasons of her own, later decided to lie. In murder cases, in contrast,

---

26 In homicide this is specifically provided for in the Criminal Justice Act, 1964, s 4. Further see par 2.23–2.28.

27 This is cast in statutory form by the Criminal Law (Rape) Act, 1981, s 2. For a further discussion see ch 8.

28 See ch 8.

intention is frequently the only issue in dispute. As a matter of practice it can be stated that the vast majority of criminal trials tend to focus on the external elements of the crime, that is to say whether the accused has been correctly identified as the assailant, and rarely focus on the issue as to whether the mental element was present. Excusing arguments, based on the perceptions of the accused, can be raised and are frequently a central issue in a murder case. It is for the jury, alone, to say whether such excusing arguments as to mental state amount to invention by the accused or whether, on the other hand, they raise a reasonable doubt and therefore entitle the accused to be acquitted.

Approaching a Criminal Case

1.06 In a criminal case it is the duty of the prosecution to prove, beyond reasonable doubt,[29] all of the external and mental elements of the offence. A crime should first be approached by defining these elements. The prosecution, having selected the appropriate charge or charges for a given set of facts, will then seek to prove the accused guilty of these charges. The external elements of the offence will be proved by what others saw or heard, or by what the accused admits to having done. The mental element of the offence can be proved by the jury inferring from the circumstances proved, including the motivation of the accused,[30] that he acted purposively or with the appropriate degree of foresight. Alternatively, he may simply admit that he had the requisite mental state.

The law of evidence proceeds on the theory that the burden of proof is on the prosecution to prove all the elements of the crime beyond reasonable doubt. No burden is cast on the accused. In practice, an accused will seek to raise a reasonable doubt as to one or more elements of the offence. He may do this, for example, by denying that the act or omission complained of was voluntary. Where the requisite mental element is knowledge he may claim that he was unaware of the fact which made his action criminal or he may claim that he was under a misapprehension, due to an honest mistake which, if correct, would have made his actions innocent. For example, a person accused of possessing a firearm may deny that he knew he had it in his house.[31] Where intent is the mental element of the crime the accused may deny that his actions were done purposively or that they were committed under the control of his conscious mind. He may say that he was drunk, or that he acted in a blind fury not knowing what he was doing. Where recklessness is the mental element

---

29   The Court of Criminal Appeal in *The People (A-G) v Byrne* [1974] IR 1 indicated that in charging the jury at a criminal trial the judge must inform them that to support a conviction they have to be satisfied of the guilt of the accused beyond reasonable doubt and that it is helpful if the judge contrasts that degree of proof with the standard of proof on the balance of probabilities applicable in a civil action. The accused is entitled to the benefit of any doubt where two views on a matter are justified and the jury should adopt the view which is favourable to the accused unless the prosecution has established the conflicting view beyond reasonable doubt. The practice in the Dublin Circuit is to follow this direction and to explain a reasonable doubt as the kind of doubt which would cause a person considering a very important business or domestic decision to hesitate and seek further information before finally deciding the matter.

30   See par 2.29.

31   See par 10.44-10.49. The prosecution must prove that knowledge for there to be any case against the accused in the first place.

of a crime, the accused may deny that he appreciated the serious risk which the prosecution claim was unjustifiably taken by him. An assault may be committed by recklessness. For example, a person dropping a rock from the top of a house may say that he expected nobody to be underneath. It would be easier to accept this excuse if the rock were dropped in an isolated area. If, in fact, the rock killed someone then lack of foresight would be no answer as the appropriate charge in these circumstances is manslaughter. The prosecution would be required to prove criminal negligence which, as we shall see in greater detail in chapter 3, does not require subjective foresight. In that case the accused may argue that a person of ordinary foresight might have done as he did, or that his failure to act carefully is not sufficiently blameworthy as to be criminal.

Furthermore, a person accused of a crime may also assert a defence. He may seek to establish his defence by calling evidence. Insanity excepted, the prosecution bears the burden of disproving, beyond reasonable doubt, any defence raised by the entire of the evidence, including both the prosecution and defence cases. In practice an accused will defend himself by either giving evidence raising a specific defence or by pointing to some factor in the prosecution case on which such a defence may fairly rest.[32]

1.07 Practice indicates that in the vast majority of criminal cases the issue which the jury has to decide is whether or not the accused was the person who committed the crime. An accused may claim he was mistakenly identified,[33] or that he was elsewhere, in other words, that he has an alibi.[34] Where the defence amounts to a denial of involvement the prosecution is still required to prove the mental element. That task is generally straightforward. Evidence sufficient to prosecute the person for involvement in a criminal act will frequently suffice, on a commonsense basis, to prove the existence of the appropriate mental element. For instance, a masked person who is armed with a gun may hold up a filling station and make away with a large amount of cash. An individual might be charged with that crime on the basis of a fingerprint found at the scene. The facts, once proved, give rise to an obvious inference that the masked man intended to steal and was aware that, in the process, he was threatening to use force on the station attendant.[35]

The Supreme Court have indicated[36] that it is the function of the appellate courts to examine appeals from the point of view of correctness in law and not to substitute their verdict for that of the jury.

---

32   *The People (A-G) v Quinn* [1965] IR 366 SC. Quoted at par 4.01.

33   Which is an extremely common defence. The judge, in addition to warning the jury not to convict if there is a reasonable doubt must also warn them of the dangers of a mistake where a case depends wholly or substantially on visual identification; *The People (A-G) v Casey (No. 2)* [1963] IR 38, 1 Frewen 521. The practice of bringing witnesses to informally identify suspects, without holding an identification parade, has also been held a discretionary ground for excluding evidence, in the exercise of judicial discretion; *The People (DPP) v O'Reilly* [1990] IR 415; [1991] ILRM 10 CCA.

34   The Criminal Justice Act, 1984, s 20, requires the accused to give notice of where he was and a statement of the witnesses to be called in support of that defence.

35   Par 6.31 discusses the crime of robbery.

36   In *The People (DPP) v Egan* [1990] ILRM 780.

The Course of a Murder Case

1.08 The function of a criminal trial is to prove that the accused perpetrated the act and did so with the mental state requisite for the particular offence. Frequently, the nature of the offence will indicate the available defence. It would be unusual, for example, in a burglary case,[37] where a person is found in the middle of the night taking property from someone else's house, to assert that he did not intend to deprive the owner of this property permanently, but only to borrow it. It might seem equally futile for a person who has admitted to having stabbed another to death to claim that this was not done deliberately. In cases of domestic killing it is often the case that the defence will concede manslaughter as the inevitable minimum verdict.[38] It is not necessary for the prosecution to prove the element of intent in murder by leading evidence from which it must be inferred that the accused set out deliberately, purposively and coldly to kill the deceased. The requisite mental element is simply an intention to kill or cause serious injury. This intent may be formed at any time coincidental with the acts or omissions which cause death.

People are usually hard driven before they kill. In order to show an absence of intent the defence may canvass in evidence almost the entirety of the relationship between the accused and the deceased prior to the killing. In order to prove a purposeful, as opposed to an accidental or unconscious killing, the prosecution may refer to prior incidents of a violent nature and to prior threats to kill.[39] Defence evidence may be led, to counter these allegations, that although the accused actually killed the victim he did not intend to do so. Acts which would seem to a dispassionate by-stander to be deliberate may be explained by the accused stating that prior to the fatal blow being delivered his mind went blank, leaving his body to act without any conscious direction from his mind.[40] He may assert that when he recovered a realisation of what he was doing it was too late to prevent what happened.[41] An example is *Falconer*[42] where the accused, who was married to the victim, following a violent marital history, had discovered the sexual abuse by her husband of their daughters. Following his unexpected return home and an assault on her she claimed to have remembered nothing until she found herself on the floor with the shotgun and the deceased close by. The Court of Appeal of Western Australia indicated their approach to this problem thus:

> In the context of automatism, if the accused did not know the nature and quality of his act because of something other than a defect of the reason from disease of the mind, then his act may not properly be described as voluntary. In such a case he would be entitled to be acquitted on the ground that the Crown had failed to prove beyond a reasonable doubt that the relevant act was voluntary. This is the significance of non-insane automatism. If the failure to realise the nature and quality of the act was

37 See par 8.23.

38 The circumstances in which manslaughter may be returned on a murder charge are discussed in par 3.03.

39 It is submitted that evidence as to other crimes should only be admitted where it is so logically probative of the crime as to outweigh prejudice: see further par 8.86.

40 This kind of evidence is frequently heard in cases of domestic killing.

41 On this see par 2.26.

42 (1989) 46 A Crim R 83 CA WA.

due to a defect of reason from disease of the mind then, according to the M'Naghten Rules, the accused would not be guilty, but insane. . . .[43]

The defence may also approach a murder case by positively asserting a defence. The accused may have stabbed the victim, killing him, and intending to cause him serious injury because the deceased had subjected him to a murderous attack. In the circumstances, he will argue, homicide was a reasonable choice.[44] If the accused was mistaken in viewing the attack upon him as potentially murderous and upon that basis killed the deceased, his crime is reduced to manslaughter by the special defence of excessive self-defence.[45] A voluntary and intentional killing is manslaughter, and not murder, where the actions of the accused resulted from provocation which caused the accused to lose self-control.[46] A killing may also occur by accident, as where a person shooting game mistakenly kills a person.[47] S 7 of the Offences Against the Person Act, 1861 provides:

> No punishment shall be incurred by any person who shall kill another by misfortune, or in his own defence, or in any other manner without felony.

Less frequently other defences, related to the age of the accused,[48] his state of intoxication,[49] mental disease,[50] the pressure and necessity which led him to commit the crime,[51] or a mistake[52] may be advanced as an answer to the charge.

Other Answers to the Charge

1.09 A case may also be contested by a claim that the evidence as presented by the State is insufficiently cogent to allow a jury to reach the conclusion beyond reasonable doubt that the accused is guilty.[53] For instance, a fingerprint may prove that the accused was present, at some stage, at the scene of the crime. If the fingerprint was found in a public area to which he might reasonably have had resort, prior to the offence, it may be of little or no probative value. If it was found on a piece of silver inside a private house, which the accused never visited, an inference of guilt might be drawn from the fingerprint alone.

Evidence may be either direct or circumstantial. Direct evidence indicates that the accused either admitted or was seen by a witness committing the crime. Circumstantial evidence consists of a set of concurrent facts which are explicable either on the basis of coincidence or on the basis of the guilt of the accused. An inference of guilt from circumstantial evidence is possible only where the circumstances proved by the prosecution are consistent only with the guilt of the accused and are inconsistent with any other reasonable hypothesis based on the same set of circumstances and consistent with innocence.[54]

---

43   At 88 per Malcolm CJ.   44 See par 4.47.   45 See par 4.30-4.37.   46 See par 4.02-4.29.
47   If such an accident occurs due to criminal negligence, it is manslaughter.
48   See par 4.48.   49 See par 4.43.   50 See par 4.05-4.06.   51 See par 4.39 and 4.42.
52   See par 4.38.
53   *The People (DPP) v O'Shea (No. 2)* [1983] ILRM 592.
54   *The People (A-G) v McMahon* [1946] IR 267 CCA.

Generally, all evidence which is relevant is admissible. Criminal trials involve frequent absences by the jury, while the judge rules on the admissibility of evidence. Clearly, the more damaging the evidence which the accused can manage to have excluded by arguing that, for legal reasons, the jury should not be allowed to know of its existence, the weaker the prosecution case will become. Sometimes these rules appear to lack justification. For example, an obviously accurate document cannot be produced in evidence, for the purpose of proving a fact therein stated, unless the person who brought the document into existence is also called.[55]

An admission made by the accused can only be accepted in evidence if it is proved by the prosecution not to have been the result of any hope of advantage or fear of prejudice excited or held out by a person in authority, or of oppressive conduct.[56] A voluntary confession may be excluded if it was taken in breach of the judges' rules.[57] Finally, the accused may call for the exclusion of evidence against him on the grounds that it had been obtained in conscious and deliberate violation of his constitutional rights, or that the trial Judge should, in the exercise of his discretion, exclude evidence obtained by an illegality.[58]

---

55   *The People (DPP) v Prunty* [1986] ILRM 716 CCA.

56   Generally see *The People (A-G) v Galvin* [1964] IR 325 CCA and *Ryan & McGee*, 121-35.

57   *The People (DPP) v Farrell* [1978] IR 13, 1 Frewen 558 CCA. The rules as set out in *The People (DPP) v Cummins* [1972] IR 312 SC are: I. When a police officer is endeavouring to discover the author of a crime there is no objection to his putting questions in respect thereof to any person or persons, whether suspected or not, from whom he thinks that useful information may be obtained. II. Whenever a police officer has made up his mind to charge a person with a crime, he should first caution such a person before asking him any questions, or any further questions as the case may be. III. Persons in custody should not be questioned without the usual caution being first administered. IV. If the prisoner wishes to volunterr any statement, the usual caution should be administered. It is desirable that the last two words of such caution should be omitted, and that the caution should end with the words 'be given in evidence'. V. The caution to be administered to a prisoner when he is formally charged should therefore be in the following words: 'Do you wish to say anything in answer to the charge? You are not obliged to say anything unless you wish to do so, but whatever you say will be taken down in writing and may be given in evidence'. Care should be taken to avoid the suggestion that his answers can only be used in evidence against him, as this may prevent an innocent person making a statement which might assist to clear him of the charge. VI. A statement made by a prisoner before there is time to caution him is not rendered inadmissible in evidence merely because no caution has been given, but in such a case he should be cautioned as soon as possible. VII. A prisoner making a voluntary statement must not be cross-examined, and no questions should be put to him about it except for the purpose of removing ambiguity in what he has actually said. For instance, if he has mentioned an hour without saying whether it was morning or evening, or has given a day of the week and day of the month which do not agree, or has not made it clear to what individual or what place he intended to refer in some part of his statement, he may be questioned sufficiently to clear up the point. VIII. When two or more persons are charged with the same offence and their statements are taken separately, the police should not read these statements to the other persons charged, but each of such persons should be given by the police a copy of such statements and nothing should be said or done by the police to invite a reply. If the person charged desires to make a statement in reply the usual caution should be administered. IX. Any statement made in accordance with the above rules should, whenever possible, be taken down in writing and signed by the person making it after it has been read to him and he has been invited to make any correction he may wish.

58   *The People (DPP) v Kenny* [1990] ILRM 569 SC. Generally see Charleton, 44-57.

Parties

1.10 Criminal liability[59] for an offence is not limited to the obvious perpetrator.[60] The policy of the law requires that those who assist in the commission of a crime in other capacities, whether by encouraging it or aiding in its commission, will equally be guilty.[61]

Presence at the scene of a crime is not an offence; nor is failing to intervene. In order to secure a conviction the prosecution must prove that the secondary party, by his presence, intended to assist in the crime or encourage its commission. This may be done by showing that the presence of the accused was due to an understanding with the principal that the crime was to be committed, or that on coming onto the scene of the crime he joined in it by assisting or encouraging its commission.[62] Provided an element of assistance or encouragement is present a person may be criminally liable even where his presence at the crime has not been previously arranged. For example, a person who comes on the scene of a rape and expresses encouragement to the rapist to continue with his action will be liable from that fact alone.

A doctrine much used in the courts is that of common design. Judges have, in practice, expressed this by indicating to juries that even a person who is not physically present at the scene where the crime is being perpetrated can be guilty if he has a role in the overall design of the commission of the crime. A popular phrase can convey the meaning by stating that a person who is not present at the scene of a crime is guilty if he is "in cahoots" with those who commit it. Where, for example, two people, A and B, set out to rob a bank using the car of C, all the parties will be guilty of the crime, despite B remaining with the car while A robbed the bank, and C staying at home though knowing of the general purpose to which his vehicle was to be put.[63] Robbery necessarily involves actual or threatened violence. Where A carries a loaded gun, to the knowledge of B and C and encountering a heroically resisting customer, kills him, the liability of B and C will depend, as it does with A, on their subjective mental state. However, the situation awaits rigorous analysis in case law.[64]

While some authorities base liability on participation in a common design,

59 A full discussion of this problem is reserved to Volume 2. Relevant statutory provisions relating to homicide are the Accessories and Abettors Act, 1861; the Offences Against the Person Act, 1861, s 67. See further the Piracy Act, 1837, s 4; the Treason Felony Act, 1848, s 8; the Petty Sessions (Ireland) Act, 1861, s 22; the Larceny Act, 1861, s 98; the Malicious Damage Act, 1861, s 56; the Forgery Act, 1861, s 49; the Explosive Substances Act, 1883, s 5. Further for a general discussion see Smith & Hogan, 148-50; Howard, 258-68; Stuart, 511-19. Generally see Giles, "Complicity—The Problems of Joint Enterprise" [1990] Crim LR 383.

60 But there must be some act of participation; *Dunlop & Sylvester* (1979) 99 DLR (3d) 301 SC.

61 *Maxwell* [1978] NI 43 CCA, *Maxwell* [1978] 3 All ER 1140, [1978] 1 WLR 1350, 68 Cr App R 128, [1978] Crim LR 40 HL. Killing through an innocent agent, such as a madman, is homicide in the principal; *Cogan & Leak* [1976] 1 QB 217, [1975] 2 All ER 1059, [1975] 3 WLR 316, 61 Cr App R 217, [1975] Crim LR 584 CA; *Matusevitch* [1977] 15 ALR 117 HC.

62 *Clarkson* [1971] 3 All ER 344, [1971] 1 WLR 1402, 55 Cr App R 445 Court-Martial AC.

63 *The People (DPP) v Egan* (1989) 3 Frewen 42.

64 The traditional rule is stated in *Anderson & Morris* [1966] 2 QB 110, [1966] 2 All ER 644, [1966] 2 WLR 1195, 50 Cr App R 216 CCA. See also *Calderwood & Moore* [1983] NI 361 CA.

including the unexpected consequences thereof, this, it is submitted, can no longer be accepted as accurate.[65] Each individual must be judged by his actual state of mind. There is no authority in Irish law which allows intent or recklessness to be implied constructively on the basis that the accused must be taken to have committed a crime because he participated in a different crime.[66] Since intentional conduct requires that the accused act with the purpose of causing the external elements of the offence[67] and since proof of recklessness requires that the accused foresee that his conduct carries a high risk of a particular criminal consequence,[68] the subjective mental states, as integral to the definition of the crime, must be fulfilled before the accused can be found guilty. Where a person participates in a crime and in the course of it another offence is committed, that other offence can only be ascribed to the accused if his conduct and mental state fit within the definition of the offence. The original offence cannot imply or import a mental element which the accused, in fact, did not have. If the prosecution is unable to prove the accused guilty of an element of the offence he must be acquitted. The problem of unexpected or unhoped for events occurring in the course of a crime requires separate analysis.

Tentatively it may be stated: where the mental element of the crime is recklessness then if those who assist the principal knowingly take a substantial and unjustifiable risk[69] that a further or ancillary crime may be committed, they are as guilty of the crime as the principal; where the mental element of the crime is intent those who assist the principal must, at least, tacitly accept that this further crime will, if necessary, be committed.[70] In the above example for B and C to be held liable for murder they must expressly, or tacitly, intend death or serious injury to anyone who may oppose their purpose. If they do not intend the death of the customer but voluntarily embark on a dangerous and criminal act, or act with criminal disregard for the safety of others they may be guilty of manslaughter.[71] If they foresee the risk of another crime being committed but proceed with their original criminal enterprise notwithstanding then that decision is sufficient to ground liability for any crime, which may be committed by recklessness. An example would be where A carried a baton to the robbery and hits a customer over the head, knocking him out. In those circumstances B and C will, by their participation in the robbery, have taken the risk of such an occurrence. They will therefore be liable, on the basis of recklessness, for assault.

Except in the case of what are called inchoate offence (incitement, conspiracy and attempt), the liability of the secondary parties depends on the principal actually completing the offence.[72] Where a person has embarked on the commission of a crime withdrawal serves to extinguish liability only if it is clear, unequivocal and timely.[73]

---

65   See the authorities at fn 63.

66   Clearly the law is otherwise where the mental element of the offence is criminal negligence or negligence. See further ch 3.

67   See par 2.19.   68 See par 2.37.

69   A justifiable risk could hardly exist in these circumstances.

70   A modern analysis of liability is to be found in *Slack* [1989] QB 775, [1989] 3 All ER 91, 89 Cr App R 252 CA. But see *Hyde* below.

71   See par 3.08 and 3.25.

72   Generally see Smith & Hogan, 130–76; Howard, 250–86; Stuart, 501–33.

1.11 The liability of secondary parties was discussed by the Court of Appeal in England in *Hyde and Others*.[74] The victim had died as the result of an assault. The prosecution proved that all three accused had attacked the victim, knocking him to the ground and kicking him. The blow which caused the death was probably delivered by the accused Collins. He was described as running back for five yards and then kicking the victim on the head in the same way as a football might be struck. The issue was whether it was necessary for the prosecution to prove the intent required for the offence of murder for any person, other than the one who had actually inflicted the fatal injury, to be guilty of murder. Lord Lane CJ stated:

> There are, broadly speaking, two main types of joint enterprise cases where death results to the victim. The first is where the primary object of the participants is to do some kind of physical injury to the victim. The second is where the primary object is not to cause physical injury to any victim, but, for example, to commit burglary. The victim is assaulted and killed as a (possibly unwelcome) incident of the burglary. The latter type of case may pose more complicated questions than the former, but the principle in each is the same. [The actual killer] must be proved to have intended to kill or to do serious bodily harm at the time he killed. As was pointed out in *R v Slack* [1989] 3 All ER 90 at 94, [1989] QB 775 at 781, [the secondary party], to be guilty, must be proved to have lent himself to a criminal enterprise involving the infliction of serious harm or death, or to have had an express or tacit understanding with [the actual killer] that such harm or death should, if necessary, be inflicted. . . . If [the secondary party] realises (without agreeing to such conduct being used) that [the actual killer] may kill or intentionally inflict serious injury, but nevertheless continues to participate with [the actual killer] in the venture that will amount to a sufficient mental element for [the secondary party] to be guilty of murder if [the actual killer], with the requisite intent, kills in the course of the venture. As Professor Smith points out, [the secondary party] has in these circumstances lent himself to the enterprise and by doing so he has given assistance and encouragement to [the actual killer] in carrying out an enterprise which [the secondary party] realises may involve murder.[75]

It is respectfully submitted that the latter part of this judgement is incorrect. If the secondary party merely proceeds with a crime knowing that an accomplice may inflict serious injury he is taking a serious and unjustifiable risk that such may occur. That, we suggest, is not intent. Intent cannot be manufactured by a combination of an accused proceeding with a risk and encouraging another in the commission of a crime which may result in that risk.[76] That is no different from the accused himself taking the risk. For murder to be committed the accused must intend to kill or to cause serious injury.[77] This does not require an actual agreement between the party

---

73   *Jensen* [1980] VR 194-201 SC; *Becerra & Cooper* (1975) 62 Cr App R 212 CA; *Whitefield* (1984) 79 Cr App R 36, [1984] Crim LR 97 CA. For an analysis of the law under the Griffith Code see O'Regan, "Complicity and the Defence of Timely Containment or Withdrawal" (1986) Crim LJ 236.

74   [1990] 3 All ER 892, 92 Cr App R 131.

75   At 895-96. This line of reasoning was adopted by the Privy Council in *Hui Chi-ming v R* [1991] 3 All ER 897.

76   In *Hamilton & Wehi* (1985) 9 Crim LJ 308 the New Zealand Court of Appeal accepted that a party who does not actually kill must contemplate that the actual killer might act with the intention of causing bodily injury. This analysis is, however, more equivalent to recklessness, than intent, under Irish law.

77   For an analysis which focuses on the mental state of the individual charged rather than the scope of the common purpose see *Britten & Eger* (1988) 37 A Crim R 48 CCA S Aus.

who kills and the party who is merely a participant in a different criminal enterprise. It does require a purpose which includes the killing of, or causing serious injury to, a victim if such a necessity or eventuality arises. The conditional nature of such an intent, or the fact that the accused may actively desire that the necessity for killing or causing serious injury will not arise, does not alter its nature.[78] The Supreme Court of Canada has applied a constitutional standard, arising from fundamental justice, that an accused charged with murder may only be convicted upon proof of subjective foresight.[79]

Where a person has a duty to interfere and protect a dependant, a common design may occur by a failure to intervene resulting in a crime being committed on the dependant.[80]

Where the law is designed to protect a particular class of persons, such as girls below the age for sexual intercourse, they cannot generally be parties to an offence despite their willing participation.[81]

Common Principles in Homicide

1.12 The external elements of homicide are common to murder and manslaughter. In both crimes the accused kills the victim. Murder is committed where the accused kills the victim intending, by his act or omission,[82] to kill or to cause serious injury to the victim.[83] Murder is reduced to manslaughter where, despite the elements of the foregoing definition being fulfilled, the accused has a defence of provocation[84] or excessive self-defence.[85] Manslaughter[86] is committed where the accused kills the victim; (1) by an assault intending to cause the victim pain or injury which is less than serious,[87] (2) by a criminal and dangerous act,[88] (3) or by criminal negligence.[89] It is also arguable, since the abolition of the felony-murder rule, that manslaughter can be constructively committed by a killing in the course of a felony. This argument is not, it is submitted, valid.[90]

Structure of the Discussion

1.13 Murder and manslaughter will be treated separately. In law, the issue of whether the accused has killed the deceased is resolved by the principles of causation. If the accused acted with intent to kill or cause serious injury and caused the death of the victim he is guilty of murder, not manslaughter. The elements of murder are

---

78   For a further discussion of intent see 2.18.

79   *Logan* (1990) 58 CCC (3d) 391 SC; PLJ (1990) 59 CCC (3d) 1 SC and see *Kirkness* (1990) 60 CCC (3d) 97 SC.

80   *Russell & Russell* (1987) 85 Cr App R 338, [1987] Crim LR 94 CA. There must be proof of presence or assistance or an inference thereof; *Lane & Lane* (1985) 82 Cr App R 5, [1985] Crim LR 789 CA. Further on the situations in which such a duty will arise see par 3.15-3.20.

81   *Whitehouse* [1977] QB 868, [1977] 3 All ER 737, [1977] 2 WLR 925, 65 Cr App R 33 CA. A discussion of this offence is to be found in ch 8.

82   3 Co Inst 47. This definition is the basis of the discussion of homicide in both Archbold (1922) 860-912 & *Kenny* (1922) 112-42. Further see par 3.15.

83   See par 2.19.   84   See par 4.02-4.29.   85   See par 4.30-4.37.   86   See ch 3.

87   See par 3.04.   88   See par 3.23-3.33.   89   See par 3.08-3.22.   90   See par 3.34-3.35.

therefore (1) causing the death of the victim and (2) an intention to kill or cause serious injury. These two elements form the basis of chapter 2. The discussion on causation in this chapter is equally applicable to chapter 3, which will consider the history and elements of the different forms of manslaughter. Chapter 4 will deal in detail with the two defences which reduce murder to manslaughter and will discuss briefly the other relevant defences in general criminal law. Chapter 5 deals with the other offences associated with homicide: infanticide and concealment of birth. Abortion is also considered in this chapter.

Coke's Definition

1.14 Lord Coke, writing in 1797, gave this definition of murder:

> Murder is when a man of sound memory, and of the age of discretion, unlawfully killeth within any county of the realm any reasonable creature in rerum natura under the king's peace, with malice aforethought either expressed by the party or implied by law, so as the party wounded or hurt, etc. die of the wound or hurt, etc. within a year and a day after the same wound.

Malice aforethought is peculiar to the crime of murder. It is now expressed in statutory form in s 4 of the Criminal Justice Act, 1964 as an intent to kill or cause serious injury to any person whether the person is actually killed or not.[91] This element is discussed under the heading "Intent".[92] For a person to be capable in law of being guilty of either murder or manslaughter he must be "of sound memory and of the age of discretion". In modern language this means that he or she does not have a defence of infancy,[93] insanity,[94] or that his action was involuntary.[95]

Jurisdiction

1.15 Murder and manslaughter constitute an exception to the general principle that criminal jurisdiction is territorial. The courts have jurisdiction over murders and manslaughters committed outside Ireland, provided the accused is an Irish citizen. S 9 of the Offences Against the Person Act, 1861, as adapted,[96] provides:

> Where any murder or manslaughter shall be committed on land outside the area of application of the laws of the State, and whether the person killed were a citizen of Ireland or not, every offence committed by any citizen of Ireland, in respect of any such case, whether the same shall amount to the offence of murder or manslaughter, or of being accessory to murder or manslaughter, may be dealt with, inquired of, tried, determined, and punished in any county or place in the area of application of the laws of the State in which such a person shall be apprehended or be in custody, in the same manner in all respects as if such offence had been actually committed in that county or place; provided that nothing herein contained shall prevent any person from being tried in any place out of England or Ireland for any murder or manslaughter committed out of England or Ireland, in the same manner as such person might have been tried before the passing of this act.[97]

---

91 Quoted at par 2.18.   92 See par 2.18–2.35.   93 See par 4.48.

94 See par 4.45–4.46.   95 See par 4.47.

96 By the Offences Against the Person Act, 1861, s 9, Adaptation Order, 1973, SI 356 1973.

97 In *Helsham* (1830) 4 C&P 394, decided under the predecessor of this s 9 Geo 4 Ch 31 s 1, it was held that if a murder took place abroad the accused must be described as a British subject, now an

Under s 10 jurisdiction is conferred where the accused is attacked in Ireland but dies abroad or is attacked abroad and dies in Ireland. Normally jurisdiction is limited to criminal offences committed within the territory of the State[98] regardless of the nationality or domicile of the accused.[99] An offence committed on an Irish ship is committed within the jurisdiction of the State.[1] An act taking place on board an Irish controlled aircraft also takes place within the jurisdiction of the Irish courts.[2]

1.16 Exceptional jurisdiction is given also under the Criminal Law (Jurisdiction) Act, 1976[3] and the Explosives Act, 1883.[4] The Extradition (European Convention on the Prevention of Terrorism) Act, 1987 gives an extremely wide jurisdiction relevant to our discussion. It is an offence contrary to s 5 of the 1987 Act to do or attempt an act in a convention country which if done in Ireland would have constituted an offence (in the case of (1) a serious offence) involving either (1) an attack against the life, physical integrity or liberty of an internationally protected person, (2) involving kidnapping, the taking of a hostage or serious false imprisonment or (3) involving the use, to the endangerment of persons of an explosive or automatic fire arm. The nationality of the offender is not relevant. Where the accused is a national of a convention country it is an offence to do or attempt an act, anywhere in the world, which would have constituted an offence in his own jurisdiction and, if he had been an Irish citizen, would have been an offence of murder or manslaughter, or an offence under s 2 and 3 of the Explosive Substances Act, 1883[5] involving either (1), (2) or (3) above. Under s 6 this jurisdiction can only be exercised in proceedings taken by or with the consent of the DPP. The DPP may not take or consent to proceedings except, in the case of the United Kingdom, where a warrant has not been endorsed for execution in the state or extradition proceedings have failed, or, in the case of a convention country, a request for extradition has been finally refused, whether in court, or otherwise. Proceedings may be taken in anticipation of a failure.[6]

Where a person does in Northern Ireland an act which, if done in Ireland, would constitute an offence scheduled under the Criminal Law (Jurisdiction) Act, 1976 he is guilty of an offence contrary to s 2 of that Act and is liable to the same penalty as

---

Irish citizen. But see *De Mattos* (1836) 7 C&P 458, 173 ER 203; *Jameson* [1896] 2 QB 425; Archbold (1922) 863.

98   Which includes internal waters and territorial seas (3 miles from the low water mark and a line across enclosed bays). A certificate by the Minister for Foreign Affairs is required if an alien is to be prosecuted for an offence on a foreign ship; Maritime Jurisdiction Act, 1959. Generally see Ryan & Magee, 25-34.

99   Aliens Act, 1935, s 4, Criminal Law (Jurisdiction) Act, 1976, s 20(3), Ryan & Magee, 25.

1   *Gulf Oil* [1973] ILRM 163 HC. Generally see Air Navigation & Transport Act, 1973.

2   Air Navigation & Transport Act, 1973, s 2.

3   These offences are noted in individual chapters and precedent indictments are included in ch 2, 3, 6, 7, 9 and 10.

4   See ch 9.   5   See generally ch 9.

6   S 6(3)(c). On these provisions see generally Hogan & Walker, 297-307; Ryan & Magee, 34-54; Campbell, "Extradition to Northern Ireland: Problems and Perspectives" (1989) 52 MLR 585; Charleton, "Extradition from Ireland to the United Kingdom" (1989) 53 J Crim L 235; Warbrick (1988) 52 J Crim L 414; Warner, in Wilkinson (ed.), *Contemporary Research on Terrorism* (Aberdeen, 1987) 486.

if the act had been committed in the State.[7] The offences which are scheduled are the common law offences of murder, manslaughter, arson,[8] kidnapping and false imprisonment. In addition the offences of wounding or causing grievous bodily harm or shooting with intent to maim, and malicious wounding or causing grievous bodily harm contrary to s 18 and 20 of the Offences Against the Person Act, the offences contrary to s 2, 3 and 4 of the Explosive Substances Act, 1883, robbery and aggravated burglary contrary to s 23 and 23B of the Larceny Act, 1916,[9] offences contrary to s 15 of the Firearms Act, 1925, s 26, 27, 27A and 27B of the Firearms Act, 1964,[10] and the unlawful seizure of aircraft and vehicles contrary to s 11 of the Air Navigation & Transport Act, 1973 and s 10 of the Criminal Law (Jurisdiction) Act, 1976 are also scheduled.

The King's Peace

1.17 Coke's phrase "under the king's peace", apart from declaring the limitations of jurisdiction, confirms that every person within that jurisdiction is subject to the protection of the law[11] and the Constitution.[12] An alien enemy can lawfully be killed in battle.[13]

Birth

1.18 Homicide is possible only where the victim has been born.[14] A person is born when his body is completely extruded from the body of his mother,[15] alive[16] even though the umbilical cord remains attached.[17] A child is alive when it exists, even for a very short time, independently from its mother after birth.[18] The old cases on

---

7   References to doing an act include references to the making of an omission under s 1(2). Liability does not depend on the accused being a national of any particular state. For an analysis of the working of the Act see *The People (DPP) v Campbell & Others* (1983) 2 Frewen 131 CCA.

8   Other arson offences under s 1-7 and s 35 of the Malicious Damage Act, 1861 are also included.

9   As inserted by s 5 and 7 of the Criminal Law (Jurisdiction) Act, 1976.

10   As inserted by s 8 and 9 of the Criminal Law (Jurisdiction) Act, 1976. See generally ch 10.

11   Archbold (1922) 867, Kenny (1922) 130-32.

12   Kelly, 433, 434.

13   *Page* [1954] 1 QB 170; [1953] 2 All ER 1355; [1953] 3 WLR 895, 37 Cr App R 189 C-M AC.

14   Archbold (1922) 873-4, Kenny (1922) 128-30. Generally on this topic see Atkinson, "Life, Birth & Live Birth" (1904) 20 LQR 134; Davies, "Child Killing" (1937) 1 MLR 203; Winfield, "The Unborn Child" (1942) 8 CLJ 78; Waller, "Any Reasonable Creature in Being" (1987) 13 Monash LR 37; Keown, "The Scope of the Offence of Child Destruction (1988) 104 LQR 120; Williams, "The Sanctity of Life and the Criminal Law", ch 1, TBCL ch 11; The Criminal Law Revision Committee, "Offences Against the Person Report", par 32-36.

15   *Poulton* (1832) 5 C&P 329, 172 ER 997.

16   For a modern analysis see *Rance v Mid-Downs Health Authority* [1991] 1 All ER 801; *Pritchard* (1901) 17 TLR 310; *Izod* (1904) 20 Cox 690.

17   *Crutchley* (1837) 7 C&P 814, 173 ER 355; *Reeves* (1839) 9 C&P 25, 173 ER 724; *Trilloe* (1842) 3 Mood 260, 169 ER 103; *Pritchard*, fn 3.

18   Thus attacking an obviously pregnant woman with intent to harm her renders the assailant guilty of manslaughter, at least, if the foetus being subsequently born alive dies from injuries or disease caused by the attack; *Prince* (1988) 44 CCC (3d) 510 Manitoba CA.

this topic are concerned with then contemporary ideas and medical practices and, it is submitted, that in the absence of evidence that the child was alive, the matter is one for expert testimony. The old authorities establish that it is not necessary that the child should have breathed.[19] The fact of breathing[20] assists in establishing an independent existence but is not necessarily determinative. The test which is generally accepted is that which requires the baby to have a circulation independent from its mother.[21] Barry J of the Supreme Court of Victoria put the matter thus in *Hutty*,[22] in charging a jury on a case of infanticide:

> Murder can only be committed on a person who is in being, and legally a person is not in being until he or she is born in a living state. A baby is fully and completely born when it is completely delivered from the body of its mother and it has a separate and independent existence in the sense that it does not derive its power of living from its mother. It is not material that the child may still be attached to its mother by the umbilical cord; that does not prevent it from having an independent existence. But it is required, before the child can be victim of manslaughter or of infanticide, that the child should have an existence separate from and independent of its mother, and that occurs when the child is fully extruded from its mother's body and is living by virtue of the functioning of its own organs.[23]

It follows that, at common law, the killing of a child in the womb is not homicide, but may amount to the statutory offence of abortion,[24] and that the child emerging from the womb has no legal protection.[25]

19   *Brain* (1834) 6 C&P 349, 172 ER 1272.

20   *Enock* (1830) 5 C&P 539, 172 ER 1089. Parke J: "The child might breathe before it was born; but its having breathed is not sufficiently life to make the killing of the child murder; there must have been an independent circulation in the child, or the child cannot be considered alive for this purpose"; *Sellis* (1837) 7 C&P 850, 173 ER 370; Crutchley, fn 4.

21   *Enock*, fn 7; *Wright* (1841) 9 C&P 754, 173 ER 1039; *Handley* (1874) 13 Cox 79, Brett J (jury charge): "A child is born alive when it exists as a live child, breathing and living by reason of breathing through its own lungs alone without deriving any of its living or power of living by or through any connection with its mother". The test is medical nonsense as independent circulation can be established, by foetal heart-beat, as early as the 6th week of pregnancy through ultra-sound scanning.

22   [1953] VLR 338 SC. Thus a child not born alive does not constitute a person and therefore a midwife causing death through criminal negligence cannot be guilty of manslaughter; *Sullivan* (1988) 43 CCC (3d) 65 BC CA.

23   At 339. A similar decision was reached in *Rance v Mid-Downs Health Authority* [1991] 1 All ER 801, 817-18, where Brooke J accepted that a foetus which had reached a stage in development where it was capable, if born, of living and breathing through its own lungs without any connection to its mother was a child which was capable of being born alive. Consequently, it was entitled to the protection of the Infant Life (Preservation) Act, 1929. See further *C v S* [1988] QB 135; [1987] 1 All ER 1230; [1987] 2 WR 1108 CA.

24   See ch 5.

25   Hence the passing in England of the Infant Life (Preservation) Act, 1929. The Australian Statutes are set out in Howard, 25. Stephen *Hist* III 2-3: ". . . the line must obviously be drawn either at the point at which the foetus begins to live, or at the point at which it begins to have a life independent of its mother's life, or at the point when it has completely proceeded into the world from its mother's body. It is almost equally obvious that for the purpose of defining homicide the last of these three periods is the one which is most convenient to choose. The practical importance of the distinction is that it draws the line between the offence of procuring abortion and the offences of murder and manslaughter, as the case may be. The conduct, the intentions and the motives which usually lead to the one offence are so different from those which lead to the other, the effects of the two crimes are also so dissimilar, that it is well to draw a line which makes it practically impossible to confound.

Protection under the Constitution

1.19 Since the 8th Amendment to the Constitution on 5 September 1983, it is submitted that the rule of common law which confines the protection of the law, through the offences of murder and manslaughter to children fully extruded from the womb is abrogated.[26] Equal treatment of unborn and born life is explicit in the Constitution which acknowledges the right to life of the unborn and guarantees to respect and protect it with due regard to the equal right to life of the mother. In civil law a constitutional wrong is enforceable in an action for damages despite the absence of a previously recognised remedy at common law or by statute.[27] There is, it is submitted, an absolute constitutional prohibition against the State passing, or carrying over under Article 50, unjust laws. Where the assistance of the state is sought in aid of a constitutional right its assistance need not be absolute in defending and vindicating that right but is limited, of necessity, by resources.[28] In this instance it may be unnecessary to seek to extend the limited judicial power, under the Constitution, to provide procedures for the award of damages for violation of constitutionally guaranteed rights into a power to create criminal offences.[29]

The criminal law withdraws its protection from the unborn child in the course of birth. There is no ready or compelling argument[30] to justify such a law.[31] Where a person solicits another to murder an as-yet unborn child when it is born the offence of soliciting to murder contrary to s 4 of the Offences Against the Person Act, 1861 is committed if the child is subsequently born alive.[32]

1.20 If a child is born alive but dies of an injury received before birth the person

---

The line has in fact been drawn at this point by the law of England: but one defect has resulted which certainly ought to be remedied. The specific offence of killing a child in the act of birth is not provided for, as it ought to be. It was proposed by the Criminal Code Commissioners to remove this defect [see s 212 of the Draft Code] by making such an act a specific offence punishable with extreme severity, as it borders on murder, though the two should not be confounded."

26   The text of the Amendment is set out at 5.01.

27   *Meskell v CIE* [1973] IR 121 SC. Generally see Kelly, 443-45.

28   This is a personal view on the language of the text. The matter is discussed but not resolved, in relation to the similarly framed Article 40.3 by the Supreme Court in *Pine Valley Ltd v The Minister for the Environment* [1987] IR 23.

29   In *A-G (SPUC) v Open Door Counselling*, fn 26 at 610, Hamilton P: "Though ordinarily it is no function of the courts to extend the criminal law, it may well be that where there is a breach of or interference with a fundamental personal or human right, they may be under a constitutional obligation so to do in order to respect, and, as far as practicable, to defend and vindicate that right". But see *Norris v A-G*, fn 1 at 53 (cited by Hamilton P).

30   It may be that this is the critical time for the occurrence of injuries to both mother and child to which a special rule should apply. The Oireachtas has however left the matter scrupulously alone.

31   In *The People (DPP) v T* (1988) 3 Frewen The Court of Criminal Appeal, in an incest prosecution struck down as unconstitutional the rule of common law which prevented the spouse giving evidence against another as being inconsistent with the constitutional protection afforded the family under Article 41. For reviews see Jackson, "Competence and Compellability of Spouses as Prosecution Witnesses" (1989) DULJ 149; Charleton (1990) ILT 140; O'Connor (1989) ILT 95.

32   *Shepherd* [1919] 2 KB 125, 14 Cr App R, 26 Cox 483 CCA.

who inflicted that injury may be convicted of murder or manslaughter.[33] In *West*[34] the act leading to death was a felony thereby grounding liability for murder onto the now abolished felony-murder rule.[35] More broadly, in *Senior*[36] a negligent mid-wife who severely injured a child in the course of delivery so that it died immediately after birth was convicted of manslaughter. The Court for Crown Cases Reserved rejected an argument that as the child was in the womb when the injury was received the crime could not be committed. More recently, Williams notes,[37] a case occurred in New Jersey where a murder conviction was recorded against a man who shot a pregnant woman whose twin sons were then delivered by caesarian section and died shortly afterwards.

The legal duty to care for a child begins at birth. Homicide by omission can only be committed as and from birth. So it has been held that a woman cannot be convicted of manslaughter by neglect of her new born child merely on evidence that knowing that she was near the time of delivery she failed to take the precautions necessary to care for the baby after birth.[38] The constitutional duty to protect life begins before birth. Consequently an omission by criminal neglect on the part of the child's parents, may give rise in Irish law to liability for manslaughter. The common law rule is otherwise.[39]

Death

1.21 Homicide cannot be committed[40] or attempted[41] if the victim is already dead. The Conference of Medical Royal Colleges and Faculties in the United Kingdom in a memorandum of January 1979[42] states that a person is truly dead on brain death

33   Archbold (1922) 873; Kenny (1922) 129. See Further 3 Co Inst 50; 1 Hawk ch 31, s 16; 1 East PC
      277; 4 Bl Com 198; contra 1 Hale 433. Turner accounts for the disagreement: "It must be
      remembered that disparity on the views held on these topics by writers of different periods can
      usually be explained by changes in the conceptions of *mens rea* which have occurred". Russell, 4011.
34   (1848) 2 C&K 784, 175 ER 329, 2 Cox 500. See par 3.34-3.35.   35 See par 3.35.
36   (1832) 1 Mood 346, 1 Lewin 183, 168 ER 346, 1005 CCR; Brown (1898) 62 JP 521.
37   Anderson, *The Times,* 17 July 1975, noted in TB 289. See also *Kwok Chak Ming* [1963] HKLR 349
      CA; discussed by Cannon [1963] Crim LR 748. And see *Sullivan* (1988) 43 CCC (3d) 65 BC CA;
      Prince (1988) 44 CCC (3d) 510 Manitoba CA.
38   Knights (1860) 2 F&F 46, 175 ER 952; Handley (1874) 13 Cox 79, Brett J (jury charge): "But
      supposing that the prisoner had not made up her mind that the child should die, yet had determined
      that none but herself should be present at its birth, without intending final concealment, but only
      for the purpose of hiding her shame for a time, and had to that intent delivered herself, she would,
      in the eyes of the law, have invested herself with a responsibility from the moment of birth, that of
      the care and charge of a helpless creature; and if, after having assumed such care and charge, she
      allowed the child subsequently to die by her wicked negligence, that would make her guilty of
      manslaughter . . ."; followed and explained in *Izod* (1904) 20 Cox 690.
39   Thus Walsh J in *McGee v A-G*, fn 26 at 312; ". . . any action on the part of either the husband or
      the wife or of the State to limit family sizes by endangering or destroying human life must necessarily
      not only be an offence against the common good but also against the guaranteed personal rights of
      the human life in question"; and in *G v An Bord Uchtála*, fn 1 at 69: "It lies not in the power of the
      parent who has the primary natural rights and duties in respect of the child to exercise them in such
      a way as to intentionally or by neglect endanger the health or life of the child or to terminate its
      existence." Further Walsh J in *SPUC v Grogan*, fn 1, at 767: "Such rights also carry obligations the
      foremost of which is not to endanger or to submit to or bring about the destruction of that unborn
      life."

being identified, whether or not the function of some organs, such as the heart, is still maintained by artificial means. Brain death occurs when all the functions of the brain have permanently and irreversibly ceased.[43] The procedure followed in this jurisdiction is that two consultants will certify a patient on life-support to be brain stem dead prior to a ventilator or other life-support machine being switched off. When this is done a non-consultant hospital doctor will certify that the patient is clinically dead. In *Green & Harrison*[44] the victim, Roche Frie, had been killed by three bullets fired into his brain. Green argued that as one bullet would have been enough to cause death, and since Harrison had already shot the victim once in the head, that when Green "pumped two bullets into him" he was already dead. Wood J rejected the suggestion of the Canadian Law Reform Commission that death be judged by the irreversible cessation of brain function. The trial judge ruled:

> The criminal law seeks to deter the incidents of . . . violent crime by holding
> accountable those whose conduct endangers the lives and safety of others. The civil
> law, in the context under discussion, seeks to ensure that societies' moral and personal
> values are not compromised in the pursuit of bona fide efforts to prolong or save
> meaningful life. In *R v Kitching & Adams* (1976) 32 CCC (2d) 159, [1976] 6 WWR
> 697 (Man CA) the Manitoba Court of Appeal considered the issue from the opposite
> perspective. . . . In my view the criminal law should, wherever possible, strive for
> certainty and simplicity in its approach to such definitional problems. The traditional
> criteria described by Mr Justice O'Sullivan at p 172 of the Report has both virtues:
> "Traditionally, both law and medicine have been unanimous in saying that it is not
> safe to pronounce a man dead until after his vital functions have ceased to operate. The
> heart has always been regarded as a vital organ". I adopt that traditional approach in
> this case. I propose to tell the jury that as a matter of law Mr Frie was alive so long as
> any of his vital organs—which would include his heart—continued to operate.[45]

Where a doctor decides to cease artificial support where the victim is already brain dead he does not kill the patient.[46] In *Malcherek and Steel*[47] severe injuries were inflicted on two separate victims who were treated by being put on life support apparatus. Tests showed brain death.[48] On the mechanical support being withdrawn

---

40 On this topic see generally Williams, *The Sanctity of Life and the Criminal Law*, ch 1; Hogan, "A Note
    on Death" [1972] Crim LR 80; Skegg, "Irreversibly Comatose Individuals—Alive or Dead?" [1974]
    CLJ 130; Kennedy, "Switching off Life Support Machines" [1977] Crim Lr 444; Skegg, "The
    Termination of Life Support Measures and the Law of Murder" (1978) 41 MLR 423; Bennyon,
    "Doctors as Murderers" [1982] CLR 17.

41 *Haughton v Smith* [1975] AC 476; [1973] 2 All ER 1109; [1974] 3 WLR 1, 58 Cr App R 198, [11974]
    Crim LR 305 HL. As to conspiracy see *Nock* [1978] AC 979; [1978] 2 All ER 654; [1978] 3 WLR
    57, 67 Cr App R 116 HL.

42 *British Medical Journal* and *The Lancet*, 3 February 1979. Further see CLRC, Offences Against the
    Person Report, par 37.

43 This is established by tests that none of the vital centres of the brain stem is still functioning. The
    decision to cease artificial support should be taken by two doctors; [1976] 2 BMJ 1187. Further
    Williams TBCL 281.

44 (1988) 43 CCC (3d) 413 SC BC.   45 At 416.

46 It could, however, be argued that a mercy killing was inspired by a loss of self-control. See the
    discussion of the unreported case of *Cocker*, by Taylor, "Provocation and Mercy Killing" [1991]
    Crim LR 111.

47 [1981] 2 All ER 422; [1981] 1, WLR 690, 73 Cr App R 173; [1981] Crim LR 401 CA.

48 Four of the six tests were carried out.

the victims died. The Court of Appeal refused to admit evidence that the tests were insufficiently stringent, both in themselves and in the way they were applied, holding that no such evidence would alter the jury's conclusion that the assailants had legally caused the death:

> Where a medical practitioner, adopting methods which are generally accepted, comes bona fide and conscientiously to the conclusion that a patient is for practical purposes dead, and that such vital functions as exist (e.g., circulation) are being maintained solely by mechanical means, and therefore discontinues treatment, that does not prevent the person who inflicted the initial injury from being responsible for the victim's death. Putting it another way, the discontinuance of treatment in those circumstances does not break the chain of causation between the initial injury and the death . . . it is perhaps somewhat bizarre to suggest, as counsel have impliedly done, that where a doctor tries his conscientious best to save the life of a patient brought to hospital in extremis skilfully using sophisticated methods, drugs and machinery to do so, but fails in his attempt and therefore discontinues treatment, he can be said to have caused the death of the patient.[49]

Proof that a person killed another involves a consideration of the legal rules as to causation. These are examined in chapter 2.

Extending Life

1.22 There is, it is submitted, no legal obligation on a doctor to take extraordinary measures to extend life. Where life appears to be doomed a medical practitioner may, in accordance with accepted medical practice, take a decision not to commit extraordinary resources to prolong its existence. Medical facilities are necessarily limited. The law does not require that a gravely ill patient should be treated by being given medical attention grossly disproportionate to the expectation of a recovery. Costello J has expressed the view, extra-judicially, that the right to privacy might evolve so as to allow a still lucid patient to decide to discontinue life prolonging treatment.[50]

In *Adams*[51] Devlin J, in the course of a jury charge, in a case where a doctor was alleged to have killed his patients for the purpose of gain,[52] stated that a doctor was not entitled, by prescribing drugs, to shorten life "by weeks or months" in the case of severe pain. Where the restoration of health was impossible the giving of pain killing drugs, which might have the effect of shortening life, "in minutes or hours, perhaps even in days or weeks" was not unlawful. Little guidance is thereby provided.

In terms of general principle no one is entitled to deliberately take life, not even a doctor with a patient's consent. Extraordinary efforts to preserve severely

---

49   All ER at 429, WLR at 697, 73 Cr App R at 182. See the remarks of Costello J reported in the *Irish Times*, 9 September 1987 which broadly agree in reasoning with that of the Court. For a further analysis see Lanham, "The Right to Choose to Die with Dignity" (1990) 14 Crim LJ 401 where the author argues that the law favours self-determination. Further see *Re Karen Quinlan* (1976) 355 A 2d 647; *In re Conroy* (1985) 486 A 2d 1209; *Re Farrell* (1987) 529 A 2d 117 All SC N Jersey.

50   *The Irish Times*, 9 September 1987.

51   [1957] CLR 365, *The Times*, 9 April 1957.

52   Devlin, "Easing the Passing" (1985). For a full account of the trial Bedford, *The Best We Can Do* (1989), and see [1987] Crim LR 365.

endangered life are not required where its early decline is inevitable or, it is submitted, where the quality of life will be gravely impaired or where such an effort will divert medical resources from where they may be better used.[53] The medical profession has set standards as to what quantities of drugs and what types of treatment can be safely tolerated by patients. If a doctor does not exceed those limits it would be difficult to make any case that he has acted in a criminal manner even though he thereby causes death. Clearly it is the nature of the illness that determines the treatment to be given. Extreme suffering in a patient in the throes of a fatal complaint may justify treatment which extends the accepted limits beyond those applicable to patients with a reasonable chance of recovery. Where those limits are manifestly exceeded, to the extent that medical science would indicate that they carry a substantial risk of fatality, the doctor authorising such treatment is putting himself at risk of an inference being drawn that he thereby intended to cause the patient's death.

In every case where life is shortened by treatment a doctor, in reality, causes death. He will have no criminal liability if he acts without criminal negligence and without intent to kill or cause serious injuries. The legal theory of causation in homicide looks to the question of cause and effect. Questions of blame for death are decided by reference to the mental element in murder and in manslaughter, by reference to the circumstances in which the voluntary action took place. A doctor prescribing a treatment to ease terminal suffering may realise that a risk of an earlier death is thereby created. His purpose is not to kill but to comfort his patient. That cannot be murder. Nor can liability for an offence of recklessness be grounded on those circumstances provided the risk is justified by the need to ease pain. Liability for manslaughter by criminal negligence is tested by the accepted standards of the medical profession.[54] If the course adopted is an accepted one, it cannot be negligent unless it is obviously defective.[55]

Conviction for Attempt

1.23 It is a general principle of the common law that a person charged with the commission of a felony could be found guilty of a misdemeanour where the misdemeanour is contained within the felony. S 9 of the Criminal Procedure Act, 1851 provides:

> . . . if, on the trial of any person charged with any felony or misdemeanour, it shall appear to the jury upon the evidence that the defendant did not complete the offence charged, but that he was guilty only of an attempt to commit the same, such person shall not by reason thereof be entitled to be acquitted, but the jury shall be at liberty to return as their verdict that the defendant is not guilty of the felony or misdemeanour charged, but is guilty of an attempt to commit the same, and thereupon such person shall be liable to be punished in the same manner as if he had been convicted upon an indictment for attempting to commit the particular felony or misdemeanour charged in the said indictment; and no person so tried as herein lastly mentioned shall be liable to be afterwards prosecuted for an attempt to commit the felony or misdemeanour for which he was so tried.[56]

53 For an example see *Re J* [1990] 3 All ER 930 CA and for further authorities see the cases therein cited.
54 See par 3.14.   55 See par 3.14.

Inchoate Offences

1.24 The law has never punished mere intention. The law of attempts carries with it a requirement that what is done by the accused is sufficiently proximate to the commission of a crime. This rule ensures that the accused, if he is to be convicted, must translate his intention into overt action. The law of attempt is discussed in the context of attempted murder.[57]

It is a criminal offence to agree with another to commit an unlawful act. Again, a mere intention is insufficient; it must be manifest in a conscious understanding of a common design with another party to perpetrate an unlawful act. The parameters of this crime are gravely uncertain. Again, a mere intention is insufficient, the intention must be manifest in a conscious understanding with another party of a common design to perpetrate an unlawful act. Two persons acting in combination may be considered to be more dangerous than one person acting alone. The true object of a conspiracy, however, is to bring within the net of the criminal law those persons who have taken care to guard themselves against liability for the commission of criminal offences by ensuring that their will is done through the hands of other and often less powerful parties. In the absence of a confession indicating an agreement to commit a criminal offence, which is unlikely unless the Gardaí have cause to investigate someone, a conspiracy is usually proved by acts and declarations of the conspirators consistent only with the existence of the agreement alleged by the prosecution and inconsistent with any other innocent explanation. In other words a conspiracy is most often proved by circumstantial evidence. The conspirators need not be expressly aware of one another once they are conscious of the fact that they are part of a larger design which has, as its object, or as one of its means, the perpetration of an unlawful act. Where conspiracies are advanced through various parties communicating with one central figure the law refers to them as "wheel conspiracies". Where they are perpetrated by each party communicating with his immediate superior or inferior, towards the commission of a criminal offence by further unknown persons, these are referred to as "chain conspiracies".[58] The law of conspiracy is briefly discussed in the context of ancillary offences to murder.[59] Neither conspiracy nor attempt merge in the completed offence. Both are subject to similar rules relating to the impossibility of a crime arising from the object sought to be achieved by the accused.[60]

Conspiracy, attempts and incitement are all indictable misdemeanours. Incitement consists of an effort to encourage or persuade another to commit a criminal offence.[61] The accused must know of, or be wilfully blind as to, all the circumstances which constitute the crime in question. He must intend the consequence of the crime.[62] It is of the essence of incitement that the accused intend to bring about the

---

56　Further see Archbold (1922) 215; Ryan & Magee, 365. It is outside the scope of this work to discuss criminal procedure beyond what is strictly integral to the offences discussed.

57　See par 2.40–2.41.

58　See *Meyrick* (1929) 21 Cr App R 94 CCA; *Griffiths* (1965) 49 Cr App R 279 CCA.

59　See par 2.38.

60　See *Nock* [1978] AC 979; [1978] 2 All ER 654; [1978] 3 WLR 57, 67 Cr App R 116 HL.

61　*The People (A-G) v Capaldi* (1949) 1 Frewen 95 CCA.

62　*Whybrow* (1951) 35 Cr App R 141 CCA.

criminal result. He must intend that the person commit the crime in question and the person solicited must know that what he is being solicited to do is an offence.[63] The essence of the crime is that the accused attempt, by persuasion or duress, to get another person to commit a crime. Merely causing another person to bring about the external element of an offence is insufficient. It is therefore necessary for the accused to intend the person incited to commit a crime. It is also necessary that such party be capable of committing the crime in question and that he not be, for example, in the category of the persons whom the crime is designed to protect.[64]

Where the inciter is successful in his object he becomes a party to the crime under the normal principles mentioned in this chapter. It is irrelevant to guilt that his incitement had no effect.[65] If the accused is "tongue in cheek" about his apparent incitement, and there is evidence to support such a defence, it may be accepted that he did not intend to incite another to commit a crime.[66]

63   *Curr* [1968] 2 QB 944; [1967] 1 All ER 478 CA.
64   *Whitehouse* [1977] QB 868; [1977] 3 All ER 737; [1977] 2 WLR 925, 65 Cr App R 33 CA.
65   *The People (A-G) v Capaldi*, fn 5.
66   *McLeod* (1970) 12 CRNS 193 BC CA; Stuart, 591.

CHAPTER TWO

Murder

2.01 This chapter deals with causation and with intent. The principles of causation are common to murder and manslaughter and are those generally applied throughout the criminal law.[1] Murder is a crime of intent. In the context of murder, intent is discussed in detail. The principles enunciated are the same as will apply to any other crime in which intent is an element of the offence. Ancillary offences to murder are also considered.

Murder is an offence contrary to s 2 of the Criminal Law (Jurisdiction) Act, 1976. Where that offence is committed in Northern Ireland it constitutes an offence contrary to that section.[2]

Causation

Homicide will be attributed to the accused where his act or omission substantially contributes to the death of the victim, notwithstanding that another cause or factor has also substantially contributed.[3] Where another act intervenes between that act or omission and the death of the victim it must be overwhelming, and such as to render the original act or omission merely a part of the history in which the death occurs, before the accused is thereby relieved of liability.[4] In general, the ordinary operation of natural causes has never been regarded as interrupting causation in law.[5] At common law the accused is not responsible for deaths occurring due to perjury and the consequent execution of the victim. Deaths occurring a year and a day after the conduct complained of are not attributable to the accused, notwithstanding causation.[6]

The Law Reform Commission of Canada have suggested a general principle which, when examined in the light of the authorities which follow, appears to conform with the existing law.[7] It has the virtue of being cast in simple and modern language:

1   In *Lesogoro & Another v The State* [1986] LRC (Crim) 814 the Court of Appeal of Botswana held that if causation was not found in murder it could not be found for manslaughter.
2   For a form of indictment see par 2.47 and for analyses see *The People (DPP) v Campbell & Others* (1983) 2 Frewen 131 CCA.
3   *Blaue* [1975] 3 All ER 446; [1975] 1 WLR 1411, 61 Cr App R 271; [1976] Crim LR 648 CA. Materials include Williams, "Causation in Homicide" [1957] Crim LR 429, 510; Camps & Harvard, "Causation in Homicide—A Medical View" [1957] Crim LR 576, Hart & Honoré, "Causation in the Law (1959); Elliott, "Frightening a Person into Injuring Himself [1974] Crim LR 15; Williams, *TBCL*, 374-401; Frankel, "Criminal Omissions: A Legal Microcosm" (1965) 11 Wayne LR 367; Gegan, "A Case of Depraved Mind Murder" (1975) 49 St Johns LR 417.
4   *Smith* [1959] 2 QB 35; [1959] 2 All ER 193; [1959] 2 WLR 623, 43 Cr App R 121 CCA.
5   1 Hale 431; 1 Hawk ch 31, s 6; 1 East PC 226; Hallett [1969] SASR 141 S Ct SA.
6   See Kenny (1922) 125-128; Archbold (1922) 868 2869.
7   Recodifying the Criminal Law 24.

Everyone causes a result when his conduct substantially contributes to its occurrence and no other unforeseen or unforeseeable cause supersedes it.[8]

It is the function of the judge to assess whether there is any evidence of causation and for the jury to find as a fact whether the accused caused the death of the victim.[9] A specific direction is not necessary unless the issue of causation is raised at the trial.[10]

2.02 It will usually be perfectly obvious that the accused has killed the victim. It is, nonetheless, standard practice in homicide cases to present a forensic pathology report to the jury by oral evidence. Where the conduct complained of did not directly or immediately bring about death, expert evidence will be needed to trace its cause.

Distinguished from the Mental Element

2.03 Causation has nothing whatever to do with the mental element of the crime or the fault to be ascribed to the accused. It is a completely separate and objective part of the trial enquiry. Its purpose is to determine whether the accused caused the death of the victim. That is essentially a scientific question which must be divorced from any question of blame. The accused may cause the death of the victim without intention, recklessness or criminal negligence and in so doing commits no crime. For the accused to be convicted of murder, or manslaughter, it must also be proved beyond reasonable doubt that in addition to causing the death of the victim he acted with a coincident mental fault appropriate for the crime.[11]

In *Hallett*,[12] the victim died of drowning when unconscious. Following an assault by the accused he was left in a position where the incoming tide might reach him.[13] The Supreme Court of South Australia responded to an argument that as the accused had fallen asleep after the fight he could not be said to have caused the subsequent death of the victim, by restating the law that these elements were separate and should not be confused:

> Foresight by the accused of the possibility or probability of death or grievous bodily harm from his act, though very relevant to the question of malice aforethought has nothing to do with the question of causation. The death of the deceased is the material event. The question to be asked is whether an act or series of acts (in exceptional cases an omission or series of omissions), consciously performed by the accused is or are so connected with the event that it or they must be regarded as having a sufficiently substantial causative effect which subsisted up to the happening of the event without being spent or without being in the eyes of the law sufficiently interrupted by some other act or event. It does not matter on the question of causation whether the accused after the commission of the act fails to appreciate or takes unavailing steps to avoid its probable consequences or mistakenly thinks he has taken such steps or fails to take such

8   See also Law Commission of the United Kingdom—Recodifying Criminal Law (1988, Cmnd 60); Model Penal Code s 213.
9   *Blaue*, fn 1. Departure from this principle leads to disturbing results: see par 2.09.
10 *Pagett* (1983) 76 Cr App R 279, 288; [1983] Crim LR 394 CA.
11 The mental element in murder is discussed in par 2.18, of the former offence capital murder at par 2.36. The circumstances in which manslaughter can be committed are discussed in ch 3.
12 [1969] SASR 141 S Ct SA.
13 The facts given are greatly simplified.

steps through some supervening factor unless that supervening factor so interrupts the effect of the original act as to prevent the original act from being in the eyes of the law the cause of death. In this case if the deceased was drowned and violent acts consciously performed by the accused had a causal effect which continued up to the moment of drowning it does not matter, so far as causation is concerned, whether he was unconscious on the beach until the tide covered him or whether while unconscious he rolled down the slope into the water or even whether in a state of insufficient consciousness he staggered into the water. Only if he consciously entered the water would it, in our view be even arguable that the chain of causation had been broken. ... The only question ... which can be raised in that connection is whether the action of the sea on the deceased can be regarded as breaking the chain of causation. We do not think it can. In the exposure cases the ordinary operation of natural causes has never been regarded as preventing the death from being caused by the accused.[14]

The remoteness of the conduct of the accused from the death of the victim can be relevant to fault. The prosecution must prove beyond reasonable doubt the fault element appropriate to the offence. Little assistance is to be expected from the suspected offender in explaining his own state of mind as culpable. Guilt is inferred from the circumstances. The more obvious the inference of the presence of a particular state of mind the easier will be the proof of fault. Such an inference becomes more compelling the closer in time and in sequence of events the death of the victim is to the conduct of the accused.[15]

Indispensable Condition

2.04 The first consideration in deciding causation is whether the conduct in question was an indispensable pre-condition[16] to the result complained of. This is not of itself sufficient. For example, if an employee is sent on an errand by his employer to a particular place and is murdered there the indispensable condition test is fulfilled. His employer could not have had any foresight of what was to happen. Even discounting this element, the death of the victim must be attributable[17] to the employer. In the example given the death of the victim occurs in a manner which cannot reasonably be regarded as the product of the employer's actions. There is no causative connection between the events. The real cause of the murder is the murderer. There is no proximity between the actions of the murderer and the request to do the errand.[18] To adopt the language of the Canadian Law Reform Commission,[19] the death was caused by an unforeseen and unforeseeable cause.

---

14 Bray CJ, Bright & Mitchell JJ at 145. Smith & Hogan 324 disagree with the proposition that intended consequences cannot be too remote.
15 Intention, in this context of murder, is discussed at par 2.19. The mental element in manslaughter is discussed in ch 3.
16 The sine qua non test.
17 An expression used by Hart & Honoré, 23. Williams prefers the expression "imputability" in his *Textbook of Criminal Law*.
18 See the discussion by Lord Sumner in *British Columbia Electric Railway v Loach* [1916] 1 AC 719 PC.
19 See par 2.01.

Intervening Cause

2.05 Where the accused sets in train a chain of events they may be interrupted by a new intervening cause.[20] If this is such as to make the original event relatively insignificant in the context of the eventual result the accused is not to blame.[21] So the accused may assault the victim who then rests himself on a seashore but is engulfed by a tidal wave.

A new intervening cause cannot destroy a chain of consequences if it occurs in the ordinary course of natural events.[22] A natural event is not unforeseeable; the use of that word does not import a requirement of foresight but is an objective way of testing the legal validity of a connection. Thus a series of early cases proceed on the assumption that the accused causes the death of the victim by moving a sick man against his will,[23] by moving a child in a neglectful manner,[24] by leaving a child in a pig sty[25] or in an orchard at a time when kites were common in England.[26] The reasoning in Hallett displays a common underlying reasoning imposing liability where, in the ordinary course, happenings in nature are accepted as continuing an event to which they are connected by the conduct in question.[27] Where police officers instinctively return fire and thereby kill a girl used by the accused as a shield, this action does not amount to an intervening cause.[28] Good sense demands, however, that the intervening cause test will protect the accused against liability from causation where death is caused by a freak occurrence which could never be fairly attributed to his action.

Degree of Contribution

2.06 The law recognises that death can be caused by a combination of circumstances and events. Legal causation is satisfied by the accused making a contribution to the death of the victim which goes beyond what the law would regard as minimal. Thus the Court of Appeal have spoken both of "a substantial cause"[29] and a cause more than a mere "de minimis".[30] The Court has denied that the cause needs to be substantial at all to render the accused liable.[31] In *Hallett*[32] the test used was "a

20   Novus actus interveniens.
21   *Smith* [1959] 2 QB 85; [1959] 2 All ER 193; [1959] 2 WLR 623, 43 Cr App R 121 CCA. Further discussed par 2.06.
22   Hallett [1969] SASR 141 S Ct SA, quoted par 2.03.
23   1 Hale 431; 1 Hawk ch 31, s 5; 1 East PC 225.
24   1 East PC 226.
25   1 East PC 226.
26   1 Hawk ch 31, s 6; 4 Bl Com 197; 1 East PC 226.
27   Fn 22.
28   Pagett (1983) 76 Cr App R 279; [1983] Crim LR 394 CA. The court rejected the proposition that self-defence or an act done in the execution of a legal duty could operate in law as an intervening act.
29   *Smith* [1959] 2 QB 35, 42-43; [1959] 2 All ER 193, 198; [1959] 2 WLR 623, 43 Cr App R 121 CCA, quoted at par 2.02.
30   *Cato* [1976] 1 All ER 260, 265-66; [1976] 1 WLR 110 at 116, 62 Cr App R 41 at 45 CA.
31   *Malcharek* [1981] 2 All ER 422, 428; [1981] 1 WLR 690, 697, 73 Cr App R 173, 181 CA.
32   [1969] SASR 141 S Ct SA; see also *Bingapore* (1975) 11 SASR 469, 480 S Ct SA.

sufficiently substantial causative effect which subsisted up to the happening of the event". The Supreme Court of Canada in *Smithers*,[33] where the victim died after a kick to the stomach by asphyxiation with vomit, used a formula of "a contributing cause . . . outside the de minimis range". This confusion in terminology is unhelpful especially in a jury issue. It is submitted that a substantial contribution to a cause does not have to be a major one but only one that could fairly be said to have mattered as events eventually transpired.[34]

In *Annakin & Others*[35] a traditional analysis of causation was upheld by the New South Wales Court of Criminal Appeal. The extraordinary circumstances of that case involved a "swap-meet" by motorcycling enthusiasts which turned into a battle with bats and guns between two rival gangs eventually causing the death of seven people. The direction to the jury was that it was sufficient if the accused's act was a cause of death, in the sense that it contributed to the death in more than what was merely a negligible or minimal way; if there was an intervening factor the jury should consider whether this could have been reasonably foreseen. If it was, it might be regarded as a natural consequence of the accused's act. The Court of Criminal Appeal accepted this direction. They stated that it was open to the jury to find that it was the unlawful fighting of the participants in the affray which caused the death in each case, notwithstanding that the immediate, direct cause of death was the act of one of the participants in pulling the trigger of a gun. Even if the accused had participated in the unlawful fighting as an aider and abetter, as he was present for the purpose of assisting or encouraging his "side" he was thereby a party to the conduct which caused the death. The Court emphasised that this process of reasoning had, as an essential component, the existence of a fight involving guns; otherwise there would be no potential for death by shooting. It was held to be correct in principle that causation exists if an act creates a real potential for a particular result and that event subsequently occurs (partly as a result of a reasonably foreseeable intervening factor). It would not be necessary for the accused to have foresight of this potential or the intervening factor for him to be liable in causation. Such foresight is, of course, necessary if the accused is to be found liable for an intent to cause death or serious injury. Liability for criminal negligence manslaughter is not dependent on foresight.

Any shortening of life is murder. Even causing the death of a condemned man a few hours before his execution[36] or of a terminally ill patient.[37] Where accused A

---

33 (1977) 34 CCC (2d) 427, 435, reviewed (1979) 11 Ottawa LR 234.

34 Further see Smith & Hogan 316; Howard 29: "The law attributes homicide to D if his act substantially contributed to the subsequent death of V, taking into account the actual time at which and the manner in which the death occurred"; Gillies, 484; Stuart, 106-16. A tacit application of this reasoning is to be found in a series of cases in which the courts have found causation from such an act as pointing a loaded firearm or pointing a knife onto which the victim runs; *Butcher* (1985) 16 A Crim R; (1986) 10 Crim LJ 185 CCA Vict.

35 (1987) 37 A Crim R 131 CCA NSW.

36 *Commonwealth v Bowen* (1816) 13 Mass 356.

37 1 Hale 428; Russell on Crime, 416; Archbold (1922) 868-69. Thus Parke J in summing up in *Martin* (1832) 5 C&P 128, 172 ER 907 charged the jury: "It is said that the deceased was in a bad state of health, but that is perfectly immaterial, as if the prisoner was so unfortunate as to accelerate her death he must answer for it". Approved in *Dyson* [1908] 2 KB 454, 21 Cox 669, 1 Cr App R 13 CCA. Further see *Hayward* (1908) 21 Cox 692.

delivers a fatal blow to the victim but, before death results, the victim receives a further injury from accused B which accelerates his death, accused B would be regarded as having caused his death. Accused A being guilty of attempted murder if his intention was to kill.[38]

It has been held that where accused A exhorts accused B to kill the victim and it is not possible to say if the fatal blow was struck before or after death, it does not effect causation if the victim died from the totality of the wounds inflicted.[39]

Common Law Exceptions

2.07 In 1755 three persons, MacDaniel, Berry and Jones were convicted of perjury with the purpose of having a person condemned and executed; a venture in which they were successful.[40] On their conviction judgment was arrested to allow a motion in arrest of judgment to be argued. The Attorney General declined to argue against the proposition that there could be murder by perjury[41] and the prisoners were discharged. Although of doubtful validity[42] no such reported prosecution has taken place in the common law countries since that date. The death penalty has been abolished in this jurisdiction.[43]

2.08 The death of the victim, according to traditional common law authority,[44] must take place within a year and a day[45] of the blow or other wrong done by the accused.[46] A delay of eleven months, within that time limit, does not bar a prosecution.[47] The rationale behind the rule is that if death occurred a year and a

---

38   *Mamote Kulang* [1964] ALR 1046, 111 CLR 62 HC.

39   *Askin & Carranceja* (1989) 42 A Crim R 402 CCA Vict.

40   19 St Tr 745; Fost, 121, 131, 364; 1 Leach, 44; 1 East PC 333. Apparently he did not want witnesses to be deterred from giving evidence in capital prosecution for fear of a later prosecution for murder; 4 Bl Cm 196.

41   Smith & Hogan, 327; Hart & Honoré, 405.

42   See Russell 426 and the authorities therein cited. Both Turner and Kenny (1922) 126 point out that in 1685 the lawyers of James II did not prosecute Titus Oates for the murder of the "Popish Plot" conspirators he had killed by perjury, although he was sentenced to a dreadful flogging; 10 St Tr 1079. Stephen *Hist* II 9 was of the view that the fact that the judges and juries acted on his testimony broke the causal link. The analysis by Stephen of the causation does not accord with the established authority. He puts forward the view: "that in the case of killing by an act the act must be connected with the death directly, distinctly and immediately".

43   Criminal Justice Act, 1990.

44   3 Co Inst 52, upheld in Dyson par 2.06.

45   So if the poison was taken or the injury inflicted before midnight today the death would have to occur before midnight on the same calendar date next year.

46   Smith & Hogan 312 consider, correctly it is submitted, that time runs from the infliction of the injury. Thus a bomb on a long set time fuse which explodes four weeks hence fulfils the intent to kill or cause serious injury at that time and not when it was placed. Further the crime of murder is only committed when the victim dies and the process is only begun by the accused when the bomb explodes. Arguably the fact that the accused could take steps to avert his crime up to the moment of commission continues his intent up to that time where the external and mental elements of the crime coincide. See further Criminal Law Revision Commitee Offences against the Person (1980 Cmnd 7844) par 39-41.

47   *Evans & Gardiner (No. 2)* [1976] VR 523 SC.

day after the injury it could not be discovered whether the victim died of that cause or in the course of nature.[48]

The exactitude of modern forensic pathology has rendered the rule obsolete.[49] No such rule bars a prosecution for attempted murder. An argument in favour of its retention is that a person should not have to wait indefinitely to know if there is to be a murder charge against him.[50] A form of attack has now evolved which makes nonsense of the common law time-scale. A person stabbed with an AIDS infected needle may live for years before even becoming sick.

It is submitted that constitutionality of the rule is dubious; it is a rule of law without a foundation in reality and unsupported by policy considerations which could specifically apply to murder. Arguably, the rights of the victim[51] require vindication even after death. The right to life guaranteed by Article 40.3 and the constitutional aim of "true social order" set out in the Preamble require that a person proved to have caused the death of a citizen, and against whom an arguable case of fault exists should not be protected from a murder conviction by outdated science. In this context the concept of the victim may extend beyond the deceased to his family under Article 41 and to society in general in the Preamble.

The Supreme Court of Pennsylvania, in *Commonwealth v Ladd*,[52] considered the year and a day rule to be one only of procedure or evidence which could be supplanted by adequate proof of causation. The Court held that "modern conditions had moved beyond it and left it sterile".[53] As a rule of common law it does not apply to the statutory forms of homicide; infanticide,[54] concealment of birth[55] and dangerous driving causing death.[56]

Vulnerability of the Victim

2.09 Experience indicates that a high proportion of homicide victims are disclosed, on postmortem examination, as having less than perfect health. Homicide is the hastening of the inevitable termination of life in death. Consequently even the fact that the victim was terminally ill and due to die within a short period is no answer to the charge.[57] The law has adopted a rigid standard in dealing with arguments by attackers that their victim might have survived but for a peculiar vulnerability: those who use violence on other people must take their victims as they find them.[58]

---

48   3 Co Inst 52.

49   Criminal Law and Penal Methods Reform Committee of South Australia—The Substantive Criminal Law (1977) 52–53.

50   Criminal Law Revision Committee, fn 46 par 39.

51   These were argued and considered for the first time by the Court of Criminal Appeal in *The People (DPP) v JT* (1988) 3 Frewen. In this case the common law rule that spouses could not give evidence against one another was held inconsistent with the Constitution where the charge amounted to an attack against the integrity of the family. See review by Jackson (1989) 11 DULJ 149 and Charleton (1990) 8 ILT (ns) 140.

52   (1960) 402 Pa 164, 166 A (2d) 501.

53   402 Pa 164, 171, 166 A (2d) 501, 507. Statutory interpretation led to a similar result in *Brengard* (1934) 265 NY 100, 191 NE 850 CA.

54   See par 5.16–5.18.   55   See par 5.19–5.20.   56   See par 3.35–3.45.   57   See par 2.06.

58   *Smithers* (1977) 34 CCC (2d) 427 S Ct Can; *Blaue* [1975] 3 All ER 446; [1975] 1 WLR 1411, 61 Cr

In *Smithers*[59] the accused caused the victim to be held by others while he kicked him in the stomach. The victim died because of aspirating vomit. This would not have occurred but for a malfunction of his epiglottis which had allowed entry of the vomit into the lungs. The Supreme Court of Canada held that the prosecution need only prove that the kick had caused the vomiting. It was unnecessary to go further and show that the kick had caused the aspiration. The malfunction of the epiglottis was not material as "one who assaults another must take his victim as he finds him".[60]

A pre-existing condition (for example, age or intoxication by drink or drugs) which hastens death or causes it to occur, when in a healthy individual recovery might have been expected, does not operate to sever a causal connection.[61] In *Blaue*[62] the Court of Appeal held that the vulnerability of the victim is not limited to a physical condition but extends to the whole person. In that case a girl received four serious stab wounds. She would have recovered but for her refusal, on religious grounds, to accept a blood transfusion. It was argued that because her decision was unusual the chain of causation was broken due to an unreasonable occurrence.[63] This contention was rejected on authority[64] and on policy grounds. The absence of reasonableness in the victim's conduct might weaken the proof of the accused's intent but it did not break the chain of causation. The accused was not entitled, having assaulted the victim, to insist on her abiding by his own precepts:

> It has long been the policy of the law that those who use violence on other people must take their victims as they find them. This in our judgment means the whole man,

App R 271; [1976] Crim LR 648 CA. A similar principle applies in the law of tort: If the damage which occurs is of a kind which ought to have been foreseen it is immaterial that its extent was unforeseeable; *Smith v Leach Brain* [1962] 2 QB 405; [1961] 3 All ER 1159; [1962] 2 WLR 148 CA, approved in *Burke v John Paul Ltd* [1967] IR 277 SC. Further see McMahon and Binchy 69.

59   Fn 58. Criticised in Stuart 112.

60   Fn 58 at 435-37. See further Archbold (1922) 869; *Martin* (1832) 5 C&P 128, 172 ER 907; *Cheeseman* (1836) 7 C&P 455, 173 ER 202; *MacDonald* (1844) 8 JP 138; *Murton* (1862) 3 F&F 492, 176 ER 221; *Hayward* (1908) 21 Cox 692; *The State v Frazier* (1963) 98 SW (2d) 707.

61   In *The People (DPP) v Flynn*, Circuit Court, unreported June 1986, a trial judge directed a jury to acquit the accused of the manslaughter of Niall Molloy who died after being hit a number of blows to the head. Post mortem examination revealed a slight heart abnormality. The case was withdrawn from the jury on a theory put forward by the defence that he had died spontaneously as a result of a heart attack due to excitement. There was no pathological evidence to support the heart attack theory. The pathologist had said that it was possible for heart failure to occur due to excitement. He did not say that such heart failure could have caused death in this particular case. The actual cause of death was brain swelling, a phenomenon that cannot occur unless the heart is functioning. At a later Coroners Inquest held on 24-26 July 1986 the jury returned a verdict as to cause of death of "acute brain haemorrhage consistent with having received serious injuries to the head". They were expressly invited by counsel for the family of the deceased to find such a verdict only if satisfied beyond reasonable doubt. For an account see *Magill*, August 1986. The rulings of the trial judge were, it is submitted, in error. The state of the victim was irrelevant to causation. A fantastic possibility does not amount to a reasonable doubt, the responsibility for finding which lay, in any event, not with the judge but with the jury.

62   Fn 58.

63   Applying the Canadian Law Reform Commission's proposed test the decision to refuse medical assistance on religious grounds is not, on an objective view, unforeseeable.

64   See par 2.19.

not just the physical man. It does not lie in the mouth of an assailant to say that his victim's religious beliefs which inhibited him from accepting certain kinds of treatment were unreasonable. The question for decision is what caused her death. The answer is the stab wound. The fact that the victim refused to stop this end coming about did not break the causal connection between act and death.[65]

This approach is, it is submitted, correct. Increased intercultural contacts have widened the foreseeable response to a critical situation. The aim of social order[66] requires that decisions made on the basis of a reasoning or a belief system, not held by the majority, should be treated respectfully. It does not assist social cohesion for a murder or manslaughter charge to fail due to the victim adhering to the cultural norms of the group to which he or she belongs. The unreasonable behaviour of the deceased has never been held to break the causal link with the wrongful act of his assailant.[67]

Contributory Negligence

2.10 Where the victim could have avoided death by taking some precautionary step or alleviating course of action, even one which any reasonable person would have taken, but fails to do so thereby making the effect of his injury worse than was necessary, the accused will not be relieved of responsibility provided his original act substantially[68] contributed to the victim's ultimate death.[69] In *Flynn*[70] the victim was, after the conclusion of a fight, struck on the forehead with a stone. Instead of resting he walked two miles to a police barracks, in order to make a complaint and returned home the following morning on horseback, a distance of four miles. The medical evidence was that the reaction caused by walking would have accelerated his death and that but for such exertion the deceased would have had better chances of recovery. The trial judge directed the jury that there should be a finding of guilty despite uncertainty as to whether or not the deceased might have died from the

---

65   Fn 62. All ER at 450.

66   Bunreacht na hÉireann, Preamble.

67   In contrast neglect inspired by religious motives, where the accused is under a duty to act to protect life, does not relieve the accused of liability for manslaughter; see par 3.20. A rare example of a break in causation occurred in *Mokgethi & Others* [1990] 1 SALR 32 SC where the victim was shot between the shoulder blades and then hospitalised where he was prescribed a wheelchair. Six months later he died of pressure-sore septicaemia due to failing to shift his position in the chair, as advised. The Supreme Court held that in general a perpetrator's action which is a *sine qua non* for the death of the deceased is too remote from the result to give rise to criminal liability in respect thereof if (a) a failure on the part of the deceased to obtain medical or similar advice, to undergo treatment or to follow instructions as to his treatment is the immediate cause of his death; (b) the wounding was not in itself lethal and was no longer lethal at the relevant time; and (c) such failure was relatively unreasonable, that is, unreasonable also taking into account the characteristics, convictions etc. of the deceased.

68   See par 2.06.

69   *Blaue* [1975] 3 All ER 446; [1975] 1 WLR 1411, 61 Cr App R 271; [1976] Crim LR 648 CA; Archbold (1922) 869; Hale PC 427-28. In contrast the tortfeasor can expect the person he wrongs to take reasonable steps to mitigate his loss; McMahon and Binchy 63-64. The same function of ensuring that unexpected consequences are not visited unreasonably on a wrong-doer is fulfilled in criminal law by the requirement of a mental element which is rarely an element in the law of tort.

70   (1867) 16 WR 319 CCR Ir.

effects of the blow had he immediately rested. The Irish Court for Crown Cases Reserved upheld the conviction. Pigot CB stated:

> . . . if a man who has received a serious blow or hurt does not alter his ways on that account, but continues to go through the ordinary course of life which he has been accustomed to pursue, that shall not exonerate the giver of the blow from his liability if such conduct has had the effect of causing death. But if, on the other hand, his acts subsequent to the blow have been so far out of the ordinary course as to give rise to a distinct set of circumstances causing a new mischief, there the new mischief will be regarded as the causation, and not the original blow.[71]

2.11 Similarly in *Wall*[72] consumption by the victim of much brandy after an illegal flogging did not break the causal link. In *Holland*[73] a similar result was reached on the victim refusing to have his finger amputated following an attack; this ultimately resulted in tetanus.

These situations have occurred more recently. So in *Bingapore*[74] the victim was injured in the head by an attack and was hospitalised. He discharged himself but was brought back to hospital six hours later requiring urgent attention and died subsequently. The Supreme Court of South Australia held there was no rupture in the causal connection because the injured party acted to his detriment or because some third party was negligent. Howard[75] comments on the foregoing cases:[76]

> In none of these cases could it be said that D's action amounted to more than a factor which contributed substantially to the victim's death. Indeed they go further and suggest by their width that D takes the risk that anything at all that the victim does whilst under the influence of D's attack may accelerate his death; but it is probable that at the present day the law would not be pushed so far because the spread of communications, education and medical science have made people in general more aware of the secondary dangers of serious injury and the facilities for treating them.[77]

In general, negligence by the deceased does not excuse the accused in criminal negligence manslaughter.[78]

---

71 At 320. The second sentence is in archaic language. The modern rule is that the new act must be so overwhelming as to render the original act merely part of the history in which death occurs; see par 2.01.

72 (1802) 28 St Tr 51, MacDonald LCB instructed the jury: "I apprehend that there is no apology for a man if he puts another in so dangerous and so hazardous a situation by his treatment of him that some degree of unskilfulness and mistaken treatment of himself may possibly accelerate the fatal catastrophe. One man is not at liberty to put another into such perilous circumstances as these, and to make it depend on his own prudence, knowledge, skill, or experience, what may hurry on or complete the catastrophe or on the other hand may render him service . . . and a murder may be committed, though unskilful treatment or misuse of himself, may have accelerated the death of the deceased".

73 (1841) 2 M&R 351, 174 ER 313.

74 (1975) 11 SASR 469, 480 S Ct SA.

75 Criminal Law 32.

76 *Flynn*, fn 70; *Holland*, fn 73; *Blaue*, fn 69; *Wall*, fn 72 and *Bunney* (1894) QLJR 80 SC.

77 Similarly in *Evans & Gardiner (No. 2)* [1976] VR 523, 525, The Supreme Court of Victoria commented on a review of the relevant authorities: "However we have seen no criminal case in which an omission to give or undergo treatment has been held to break the chain of causation between the felonious act and the death".

78 See par 3.21-3.22.

Medical Treatment

2.12 A supervening cause may so dominate a chain of events as to render the original cause which set them in motion of historical, as opposed to of material, significance. A wounded person may be confined to hospital and so will have to face the ordinary hazards of whatever treatment is deemed necessary. An inadequacy of diagnosis or treatment only becomes material where it is so abnormal and of such significance in the sequence of events as to cause death of its own impetus in circumstances where the original cause of treatment can fairly be discounted. So in *Bush v Commonwealth*[79] the deceased was shot by the accused and wounded to a degree where the injuries were "neither necessarily nor probably mortal". Her attending doctor negligently infected her with scarlet fever as a result of which she died. The murder conviction of the accused was reversed by the Kentucky Court of Appeal.

2.13 Different considerations apply where both the wound and the subsequent treatment contribute significantly to death.[80] Concurrent causes do not displace the liability of a person who has made a substantial contribution to death.[81] In *Davis*[82] the accused had broken the victim's jaw in two places. The victim later died in the course of the administration of an anaesthetic for the purpose of an operation. Matthew J[83] held that since the anaesthetic had been properly administered by a regular medical practitioner the fact that the death had primarily resulted from it did not affect criminal responsibility. He instructed the jury that if an injury was inflicted by one man on another, which compelled the injured man to take medical advice which necessitated an operation, then if death ensued in the course of, or from, the operation the assailant was responsible in law. He said that the jury must be satisfied that the accused injured the victim, who rightly consulted a competent medical practitioner, that an operation was recommended which involved an anaesthetic and that he died from that administration.

The reference of the correctness of the recourse by the victim to medical advice and the competence[84] of that advice leaves open the possibility that incompetence

---

79   (1880) 78 Ky 268.

80   *Davis & Wagstaffe* (1883) 15 Cox 174. Generally see Hart & Honoré, *Causation in the Law* (2nd ed., 1985) ch 12.

81   See par 2.05.

82   Fn 80.

83   After consulting with Field J.

84   In the earlier case of *Pym* (1846) 1 Cox 339, the accused was indicted as a principal in the second degree following a duel. A tumour developed on the site of the wound and an operation ensued to remove it in the course of which the injured party died. It was sought to introduce medical evidence that the wound would not inevitably have caused death. Erle J after consulting Rolfe B refused to admit it: ". . . where a wound is given, which in the judgment of competent medical advisers, is dangerous, and the treatment which they *bona fide* adopt is the immediate cause of death, the party who inflicted the wound is criminally responsible, and of course those who aided and abetted him in it. I so rule on the present occasion; but it may be taken, for the purpose of further consideration, that it having been proved there was a gunshot wound, and a pulsating tumour arising therefrom, which, in the *bona fide* opinion of competent medical men, was dangerous to life, and that they considered a certain operation necessary, which was skilfully performed, and was the immediate and proximate cause of death; the counsel for the prisoner tendered evidence to show this opinion was

in treatment could break the chain of causation by operating as a supervening cause. It appears that it can. In law the treatment will be required to be grossly abnormal, causing death where the victim should have recovered.[85]

Just as the accused is required to run the hazard of the victim behaving unreasonably on receiving an injury, he is also fixed with the responsibility for the hazards of medical treatment, the standard of which may vary enormously depending on location,[86] facilities and personnel. If the basis of this rule were only a public policy of not permitting wrong-doers to question the medical treatment of their victims, it would be unsupportable. Such evidence is, however, allowed.[87] The law in this area conforms with the principle that causes only cease in their effect when rendered immaterial by other events.

In *Jordan*[88] the accused stabbed the victim in a brawl. The knife wound penetrated the intestine in two places. At the time of his death the wound had almost healed. The injured man died of pneumonia resulting from pulmonary oedema. His assailant was convicted of murder. In the Court of Criminal Appeal two eminent specialists were called. They testified that a dose of the antibiotic terramycin had been properly administered but, on the deceased being found intolerant to it, that treatment was wrongly resumed. It was further claimed by them that the intravenous intake of the patient was grossly excessive. This, they said, led inevitably to bronchial pneumonia. The Court was not disposed to hear contradictory evidence from the prosecution as this was properly a matter for a jury. They allowed the appeal quashing the conviction. On the question of the principle to be applied the Court said:

> ... death resulting from any normal treatment employed to deal with a felonious injury may be regarded as caused by the felonious injury but we do not think it necessary to examine the cases in detail or to formulate for the assistance of those who have to deal with such matters in the future the correct test with regard to what is necessary to be proved in order to establish causal connection between death and the felonious injury. It is sufficient to point out that this was not normal treatment. Not only one feature but two separate and independent features of treatment were, in the opinion of the doctors, palpably wrong and these procured the symptoms discovered at the post-mortem examination which were the direct and immediate cause of death, namely, the pneumonia resulting from the condition of oedema which was found.[89]

wrong. . . . To admit this evidence would be to raise a collateral issue in every case as to the degree of skill which the medical men possessed." In *McIntyre* (1847) 2 Cox 379 a jury convicted of manslaughter, not murder, where after the accused had kicked the deceased in the stomach a surgeon attempted treatment by giving her brandy. Some went into the lungs and it was possible that it caused her death.

85   It is difficult to say in any situation if death is inevitable. In terms of causation if death was inevitable after the injury no issue as to causation arises.

86   So death which ensues due to the absence of medical facilities is caused by the accused; *Lee* (1864) 4 F&F 63, 176 ER 468; *Lockley* (1864) 4 F&F 155, 176 ER 511; *The People v Fowler* (1918) 178 Cal 657, 174 P 892; *HM Advocate v McPhee* [1935] SC 46; *Bradley* (1957) 6 DLR (2d) 385; *Popoff* (1959) CCC 116. [Taken from Howard].

87   Smith & Hogan 323.

88   [1956] 40 Cr App R 152 CCA.

89   At 157-58. The judgment was not well received by the medical profession in England. A subsequent hospital enquiry exonerated the treatment; *The Times*, 14 September 1956; *Williams* [1957] Crim LR 249.

2.14 This decision was subsequently confined to its own facts. In *Smith*[90] the deceased received two bayonet wounds, one in the arm and one in the back which, unknown to anyone, had pierced the lung causing a haemorrhage. Unfortunately the fight in which he had received his injury was between two regiments. The limited army facilities were overstrained by a number of other cases including two other serious stabbings. The deceased was twice dropped on the way to the medical bay. His treatment, because of a misdiagnosis of the lung injury, was "thoroughly bad and might well have affected his chances of recovery". There were no facilities for blood transfusion which would have given him a seventy five per cent chance of recovery. It was argued that the law on causation required death to result naturally and solely from the wound and that if anything else happened, which impeded the chances of recovery, another cause supervened. The Courts Martial Appeal Court rejected this contention:

> . . . if at the time of death the original wound is still an operating cause and a substantial cause, then the death can properly be said to be the result of the wound, albeit that some other cause of death is also operating. Only if it can be said that the original wounding is merely the setting in which another cause operates can it be said that the death does not result from the wound. Putting it another way, only if the second cause is so overwhelming as to make the original wound merely part of the history can it be said that the death does not flow from the wound. . . . A man is stabbed in the back, his lung is pierced and haemorrhage results; two hours later he dies of haemorrhage from that wound; in the interval there is no time for a careful examination and the treatment given turns out in the light of subsequent knowledge to have been inappropriate and, indeed, harmful. In these circumstances no reasonable jury or court could, properly directed, in our view possibly come to any other conclusion than that the death resulted from the original wound.[91]

The decisions in *Jordan* and *Smith* were followed in *Cheshire*.[92] The accused shot the deceased in the leg and stomach. While in intensive care the deceased developed respiratory problems and a tracheotomy tube was placed in his windpipe. Two months after the shooting, and following chest infections and other complications, the deceased died of cardio-respiratory arrest because his windpipe had become obstructed due to the narrowing where the tracheotomy had been performed. This condition was rare but it was not an unknown complication arising from the operation. The trial judge directed the jury that causation was only interrupted where the medical treatment had been reckless, in the sense that the doctors "could not care less". The Court of Appeal disagreed with the direction but held that no injustice had been done as it was more favourable to the accused than the law required. Bedlim LJ indicated the model direction thus:

> In a case in which the jury have to consider whether negligence in the treatment of injuries inflicted by the accused was the cause of death we think it is sufficient for the judge to tell the jury that they must be satisfied that the Crown have proved that the acts of the accused caused the death of the deceased, adding that the accused's acts need

90 [1959] 2 QB 35; [1959] 2 All ER 193; [1959] 2 WLR 623, 43 Cr App R 121 CCA; *Martiall* and in
    Malcherek [1981] 2 All ER 422, 428, [1981] 1 WLR 690, 696 CA.

91 Fn 90. QB at 42, All ER 198, WLR at 628, Cr App R at 13. Approved in *Bristow* [1960] SASR
    210, 217 S Ct SA and *Evans & Gardiner (No. 2)* [1976] VR 523 SC.

92 [1991] 3 All ER 670 CCA.

not be the sole cause or even the main cause of death, it being sufficient that his acts contributed significantly to that result. Even though negligence in the treatment of the victim was the immediate cause of his death, the jury should not regard it as excluding the responsibility of the accused unless the negligent treatment was so independent of his acts, and in itself so potent in causing death, that they regard the contribution made by his acts as insignificant. It is not the function of the jury to evaluate competing causes or to choose which is dominant provided they are satisfied that the accused's acts can fairly be said to have made a significant contribution to the victim's death. We think the word "significant" conveys the necessary substance of a contribution made to the death which is more than negligible.[93]

In summary: medical treatment is one of the hazards which the wrongful act of the accused may bring about. When the treatment is competent no question of the interruption of the chain of causation arises. Where death would inevitably have resulted despite such treatment a complaint of incompetence cannot be material. If the treatment is incompetent and causes death of its own impetus the assailant will be relieved of the responsibility of causing death where his original wrong did no more than provide the opportunity for that incompetence and where that wrong no longer makes any substantial contribution to the ultimate cause of death.

Mental Trauma

2.15 Whilst it may be difficult to prove death by shock or depression brought on by a criminal act,[94] no legal principle confines homicide to physical trauma.[95] In *Towers*[96] the accused assaulted a girl holding a baby. The reaction of the girl caused the baby such shock that it developed convulsions from which it later died. In *Hayward*[97] the accused quarrelled violently with his wife. He chased her from the house and when she fell kicked her on the arm. When the victim was picked up she was dead. Medical evidence showed an enlarged thymus gland and evidence was adduced that a person in this condition might be frightened to death. Ridley J directed the jury that if the evidence was accepted there was a sufficient chain of evidence to support a conviction for manslaughter.

2.16 Where the actions of the accused lead the victim to take some dangerous step leading to death, causation cannot be established by merely proving that the

---

93   At 677.

94   Elliott, "Frightening a Person into Injuring Himself" [1974] Crim LR 15. For a further discussion see par 6.03–6.05.

95   1 Hale PC 529: "If any man either by working on the fancy of another, or possibly by harsh or unkind usage, puts another into such passion or grief or fear that the party either dies suddenly or contracts disease whereof he dies. . . . This may be murder or manslaughter in the sight of God yet in *Foro Humano* it cannot come under the judgment of felony because no external act or violence was offered, and secret things belong to God and hence it was that before the statute of 1 James 1 ch 12 witchcraft or fascination was not felony . . .". This idea has not been acted on in recent times: Archbold (1922) 869; Kenny (1922) 126; Russell 413–16; Stephen *Hist* III 5; see also 1 East PC 225. Damages for nervous shock are recoverable in tort; McMahon & Binchy 305–13.

96   (1874) 12 Cox 530. The accused was not convicted. Denman J directed the jury in terms of the actual cause of the child's death.

97   (1908) 21 Cox 692. See also *Dugall* (1878) 4 QLR 350; *In re Heigho* 18 Idaho 566, 110 P 1029 (1910) SC.

behaviour of the accused led the victim to act in a particular way. Human reactions are so varied that the rule imposing liability for natural consequences is not apposite. The accused cannot be made liable for an extreme reaction based on a mistake. Therefore causation is only established where the victim dies while acting to evade actual violence or from a well-grounded apprehension of violence.[98]

It is arguable that the reaction of the victim need not be reasonable and that the accused, by his conduct, hazards the wide range of reactions that a grave or frightening situation may draw from people. His argument against liability is properly founded on the absence of the appropriate mental element.[99]

2.17 In *Stephenson v State*[1] the victim was raped by the accused in extremely brutal circumstances which included severe biting. She took a large dose of mercury bichloride tablets. The accused refused her medical aid but kept her in a hotel for some time before leaving her back on her doorstep. The girl died a month later from poisoning due to the tablets, possibly contributed to by an abscess as a result of a bite. On being convicted of murder the accused appealed, arguing that death was caused by the intervention of the victim herself, in a suicide bid, the injuries caused by the accused not being in themselves fatal. The Indiana Supreme Court rejected the appeal holding that the victim had been "distracted by pain and shame", as a result of the attack and that when she took the tablets the act was properly attributable to him:

> When suicide follows a wound inflicted by the defendant his act is homicidal, if deceased was rendered irresponsible by the wound as a natural result . . . we do not understand the rule laid down by Bishop *supra*, that the wound which renders the deceased mentally irresponsible is necessarily limited to a physical wound. . . . We therefore conclude that the evidence was sufficient and justified the jury in finding that

---

98   In *Evans* (1812), Russell 414, it was alleged that the victim threw herself out of a window in consequence of the accused's actions. The judgment was that if she acted from a well grounded apprehension of such further violence as would endanger life the accused was as answerable as if he had thrown her. In *Pitts* (1842) C&M 284, 174 ER 509, the jury was charged that where the victim slipped into a river to escape robbery or murder that such an act might be involuntary where done from a well grounded apprehension of immediate violence and that they might convict if there was no other way of escape and a reasonable man might so act. In *Curley* (1909) 2 Cr App R 109 CCA, the victim sought help on a balcony and fell. The jury was charged that the accused was responsible if the victim feared violence and went to the balcony for assistance without any intention of jumping. In *Beech* (1912) 7 Cr App R 197, 23 Cox 181 CCA the victim jumped out of a window because the accused was making repeated attempts to enter, having entered her home, to break into her bedroom. The jury was charged that if the conduct of the accused amounted to a threat of injury and the action of the victim was a natural consequence of that he was answerable for the consequences. See further *Coleman* (1920) 84 JP 112; *Lewis* [1970] Crim LR 647 CA; *Mackie* [1973] Crim LR 54; *Boswell* [1973] Crim LR 307; *Royall* (1989) 41 A Crim R 447 CCA NSW.

99   Smith & Hogan 327, in contrast, suggest that the accused must take his victim as he finds him on the authority of *Blaue* [1975] 2 All ER 446; [1975] 1 WLR 1411, 61 Cr App R 271; [1976] Crim LR 648 CA.

1   (1932) 205 Ind 141, 179 NE 633, SC Indiana, reviewed in "Legal Cause and Criminal Responsibility" (1933) 31 Mich LR 659. See also *People v Lewis* (1899) 125 CAL 551, 57 Pac 470 SC where the victim committed suicide after a fatal injury; *State v Angelina* (1913) 73 WVa 146, 80 SE 141 SC; *Jones v State* (1942) 20 Ind 384, 43 NE (2d) 1017 SC; Morris & Howard, "Studies", 20; Howard 32; *Pigney v Pointers Tranport Services* [1957] 2 All ER 807; [1957] 1 WLR 1121 where suicide was caused by an acute mental illness following an accident.

the appellant by his acts and conduct rendered the deceased distracted and mentally irresponsible and that such was the natural and probable consequence of such unlawful and criminal treatment, and that the appellant was therefore guilty of murder in the second degree. . . .[2]

It is uncertain if this decision would be followed here. Suicide remains a crime in this jurisdiction.[3] It involves a voluntary taking of one's own life. Continuing a chain of causation through the voluntary commission of a criminal offence simply because it was inspired by an original wrong seems inappropriate. A later voluntary act can be argued to amount to a supervening cause.[4] Unlike the fear cases the victim is not fleeing from the accused. As we have noted, causation by fear has been limited to ordinary or predictable reaction. Further the law seems to impose no condition that the suicidal act be either a natural product of the accused's action or reasonable in the circumstances. Such a condition is arguably impossible where the law has adopted a policy stance that suicide is a crime and therefore, by definition, an avoidable wrong. In *Stephenson* the particularly savage assault had caused the deceased to be in a suicidal state; that is less than a normal frame of mind. The suicide may have been a voluntary product of that mind and would not have occurred but for the attack. Tentatively, it may be stated that where the actions of the accused are such that, judged objectively, they are such as may precipitate an ordinary person into an unbalanced state of mind, the accused is responsible for any action that an ordinary person might take whilst in that condition. To apply the Canadian Law Reform Commission test[5] suicide is an unforeseen and unforeseeable consequence unless the accused by his conduct puts the victim into a condition where it might occur. The same principle would apply to any lesser form of self-injury inspired by the accused's actions.

The Mental Element in Murder

2.18 S 4(1) of the Criminal Justice Act, 1964 provides:

(1) Where a person kills another unlawfully, the killing shall not be murder unless the accused intended to kill, or cause serious injury to, some person, whether the person actually killed or not.

(2) The accused person shall be presumed to have intended the natural and probable consequences of his conduct; but this presumption may be rebutted.

The section contains a number of distinct concepts each of which require separate discussion.

---

2   At Ind 145, NE 637.

3   See par 2.40.

4   See the discussion in *Roberts* (1971) 56 Cr App R 95 CA: "Was it the natural result of what the assailant said and did, in the sense that it was something that could reasonably have been foreseen as the consequence of what he was saying or doing?"

5   See par 2.01.

Intent

2.19 The concept of intent has caused unnecessary confusion in criminal law. A basic discussion of fundamental principle will be followed by a detailed analysis of the relevant cases.

Basic Meaning

One can only mean something to happen when one realises that one's conduct, or the consequences of one's conduct, involves its occurrence. Intent necessarily involves a conscious choice to bring about a particular state of affairs. If one consciously chooses not to bring about a state of affairs one cannot intend it. In all but the rarest circumstances choosing to do something will mean that one also actively desires it. That rare exception may occur where the desire of the accused is to bring about a result knowing, albeit with regret, that another consequence will, in the ordinary course of events, follow from it or necessarily involve it. That state of mind is nonetheless intent.[6]

Probability and foresight are relevant to the decision as to whether intent exists but they do not, of themselves, amount to intent. It has never been an ingredient of intent that it must be possible for the accused to bring about the result that is his purpose. No matter how unlikely the success of the object which it is his purpose to achieve, once he is engaged on a course of conduct in order to bring about that particular result, he intends it. He will not normally engage in such conduct unless his object is achievable. It is a separate matter that an objective bystander will find it difficult or impossible to realise or infer from a person's conduct what his particular intent is. As a matter of practicality it follows that the less likely it is that the accused can achieve an object the less easily one can infer that he intends it.

A person cannot intend anything unless his mind activates him towards a purpose. That can only happen where there is foresight of what his purpose is, or what his purpose involves. Foresight causes differing mental states which vary almost infinitely from an inkling to a clear realisation as to a result or consequence. When the result or consequence is contemplated the mind may categorise what is foreseen from a possibility, through a probability, up to a certainty.

Intent is not recklessness; it is not the conscious taking of an unjustifiable risk. The line of distinction must not be blurred. It follows that although mental states may vary intent will involve a realisation that it is virtually certain or at least highly probable that a result will be achieved or a consequence will follow as a result of an action or an omission to act. Complete certainty is as difficult a state of mind to achieve in the commission of a crime as in other human endeavours; it is thus not necessary to form intent. A state of mind which can, in ordinary language, be categorised as risk-taking does not suffice. That state of mind is recklessness and will fall to be dealt with, as criminal negligence, within the ambit of the crime of manslaughter.

6   *Mohan* [1976] QB 1; [1975] 2 All ER 193; [1975] 2 WLR 859; [1975] RTR 337, 60 Cr App R 272; [1975] Crim LR 283 CA; *Pearman* (1984) 80 Cr App R 259; [1984] Crim LR 675 CA; Smith & Hogan 288; *Williams* [1987] CLJ 417 at 432; (1989) 105 WLR 387 at 388.

Intent is thus present where the purpose of the accused is to engage in conduct (which includes omissions), or to achieve a result, or when the accused acts in order to achieve some purpose which he knows, or of which he is virtually certain, if he is successful, involves a resultor consequence in the ordinary course of events.

The effect of s 4 of the Criminal Justice Act, 1964 was stated in *The People (A-G) v Dwyer*[7] to be that an unlawful homicide was not murder unless the necessary intent was established; the onus of establishing this beyond a reasonable doubt remains at all times on the prosecution, as also does the onus of proving beyond a reasonable doubt that the presumption that an accused person intended the natural and probable consequence of his action was not rebutted.

Definitional Analysis

2.20 The definition of intent approved by the Court of Criminal Appeal, in the context of intent to kill, in *The People (DPP) v Douglas & Hayes*[8] is that of Asquith LJ in *Cunliffe v Goodman*:[9]

> An "intention" to my mind connotes a state of affairs which the party "intending"—I will call him X—does more than merely contemplate: it connotes a state of affairs which, on the contrary, he decides, so far as in him lies, to bring about, and which, in point of probability he has a reasonable prospect of being able to bring about, by his own fruition.[10]

There is no requirement in criminal law that the accused have a reasonable prospect of achieving his intention. Where a person shoots at another from a great distance, intending to kill him, and striving to ensure the accuracy of his aim for that purpose, it is not any the less his intent because the death of the victim is extremely unlikely. Nor is it any the less intent, in the example given, that death resulted from exceptionally favourable wind conditions, or the missile striking a particularly vulnerable spot, or the absence of medical attention for hundreds of miles. However, it may be unlikely for a person to be engaged in conduct which cannot reasonably achieve a desired result. That is a question of evidence and proof by inference and has nothing to do with intent. Intent is a purpose peculiar to the individual mind of the accused.

In Canada the courts have colloquially construed intent as being an actual desire, end, purpose, aim, objective or design[11] without settling on a particular definition. In Victoria it has been held that the trial judge need not explain the meaning of intent to a jury where the prosecution case is simply that the accused acted with the purpose of bringing about the criminal wrong.[12] After much dithering the House of Lords have agreed that in a case of straightforward intent, as opposed to oblique intent (where the accused is trying to achieve an object knowing it involves another

7   [1972] IR 416, 420, 108 ILTR 17 SC.
8   [1985] ILRM 25 CCA.
9   [1950] 2 KB 237; [1950] 1 All ER 720 CA—later adopted by Hailsham LJ in *Hyam* (1975) AC 55 HL, other ref. fn 4.
10 Fn 9, 28.
11 Stuart 128
12 *Tait* [1973] VR 151, 153 SC.

consequence or result) it should be left to the jury to apply this ordinary word without further assistance from the judge. In *Moloney*[13] Lord Bridge explained:

> The golden rule should be that when directing a jury on the mental element necessary in a crime of specific intent, the judge should avoid any elaboration or paraphrase of what is meant by intent, and leave it to the jury's good sense to decide whether the accused acted with the necessary intent, unless the judge is convinced that, on the facts and having regard to the way the case has been presented to the jury in evidence and argument, some further explanation or elaboration is strictly necessary to avoid misunderstanding.[14]

It is difficult to see sense in that view. The jury is entitled to have the defence and prosecution cases put to it. A proper jury charge requires an explanation of the burden and standard of proof and an elucidation of the elements of the crime but not, apparently, an explanation as to a subject the House of Lords itself has tackled with a singular lack of clarity.[15] A jury hearing an ordinary word in a legal context are likely to wonder as to its meaning. Their puzzlement may increase with the elaboration of so many other matters peripheral to what they are attempting to decide in a murder trial. It is submitted that even in a simple case of intention the jury are entitled to be instructed as to its meaning in law; a sufficient explanation is given if they are told that they must give the word its ordinary meaning of a purpose or objective. That exercise may be further elucidated by the judge contrasting conscious risk taking with intention. The standard of proof in a criminal trial is, similarly, often explained by comparing the criminal standard of proof beyond reasonable doubt with the civil standard of probability or likelihood.

2.21 Intention cannot exist where the accused purposely acts in order to ensure that the result or consequence charged does not happen. The fact that he does not succeed in stopping the result or consequence can be evidence, where it was extremely unlikely that he would be successful, that he intended it to happen, notwithstanding his protestations to the contrary. While the running of a substantial risk does not amount to intent it has been proposed that the classic example of the person who sets off a bomb in a crowded public street should inspire a broadening of the mental element in the crime of murder into a form of recklessness to correspond to "wicked" recklessness.[16]

For example, a criminal leaves a time bomb in the foyer of a hotel and then telephones a warning, which is not acted upon, and thereby causes a number of

---

13   [1985] AC 905; [1985] 1 All ER 1025; [1985] 2 WLR 648, 81 Cr App R 93; [1985] Crim LR 378 HL. This point was not overruled in the cases which follow in the text. See further *DPP for NI v Lynch* [1975] AC 653, 690; *Lord Simon* [1975] 1 All ER 913; [1975] 2 WLR 641, 61 Cr App R 6; [1975] NI 35; [1975] Crim LR 707 HL.

14   AC at 926, All ER 1036, WLR at 664, Cr App R 106.

15   See Goff, "The Mental Element in the Crime of Murder" (1988) 104 LQR; Williams, "The Mens Rea for Murder: Leave it Alone" (1989) 105 LQR 387. For a similar view see *Tait* [1973] VR 151, 153-54 SC.

16   As in Scottish Law: Gordon, *The Criminal Law of Scotland* (2nd ed., 1978); McDonald, *Criminal Law* (5th ed.); Scottish Law Reform Commission Report No. 80 (1983) par 2.14-2.15. This view is held by Lord Goff, fn 8, 57.

horrific deaths. He knowingly takes a substantial risk of that occurrence. He can plead, and it may be correct, that he intended to cause damage to property and intended to avoid death or serious injury.[17] Similarly, the accused may have left a time bomb in a public place intending that it should go off when the place is likely to be deserted. In such a case the culpability of the accused may be thought to be higher because he has consciously initiated a substantial risk of death or serious injury and failed to take any step to ensure that the risk was kept to the minimum. Finally, the accused may plant a bomb where it is likely to kill or cause serious injury and express his defence in terms of a hope that no one would be injured. In each case it is a jury function to analyze the evidence, assisted by the presumption that the accused intended the natural and probable consequences of his action,[18] in order to decide whether there was an intention to cause death or serious injury. If they are left in a state of reasonable doubt on the evidence, which may include the explanation by the accused that he did not intend to kill or cause serious injury,[19] they must acquit.

The three examples given direct the mind towards the conclusion that in the third one the bomber intended to kill or cause serious injury. That is because, in the ordinary course of events, a bomb in a public place brings about that consequence. The considered object of the terrorist's intention is not distracted, as in the other examples, by a contrary purpose, such as damage to property, or a conscious attempt to divert that prospect.

Intent and Recklessness

2.22 If a person were to be a murderer for taking a substantial risk the law would define the mental element of the crime, as in the case of rape, in terms of recklessness.[20] Whether a crime is defined in terms of recklessness or intent, in each case the accused must be aware of, or foresee, the result or consequence of his act or omission. It could thus be argued that intent involves a mere foresight of a greater probability than recklessness.[21] That is not correct. Foresight is not intent but is evidence from which intent may be inferred.[22] Recklessness requires conscious risk

17   See the facts of *McFeely* [1977] NI 149 which was decided on the basis of an analysis of the law as it stood after *Hyam* [1975] AC 55; [1974] 2 All ER 421; [1974] 2 WLR 607, 57 Cr App R 91 HL.
18   See par 2.23.
19   It has yet to be decided in this jurisdiction how far the self-serving statements of A are admissible or the extent to which they must be adduced by the prosecution. *Pearce* [1979] 69 Cr App R 365 CA.
20   See par 2.36-2.37. Recklessness, in the context of rape, is considered in ch 8.
21   In *The People (DPP) v Murray* [1977] IR 360, 387 SC Walsh J: "Even if the specified and specific intent can be established not only when the particular purpose is to cause the event but also when the defendant has no substantial doubt that the event will result from this conduct, or when he foresees that the event will probably result from his conduct, the test is still based on actual foresight. Even on that basis, foresight of probable consequences must be distinguished from recklessness which imports a disregard of probable consequences. The essential difference between intention and foresight on the one hand and recklessness on the other is the difference between advertence and inadvertence as to the probable result". This analysis, it is submitted, is incorrect, as the test of intent proposed by the judge is indistinguishable from the test of recklessness proposed by the majority judgment from which he dissented on this point.
22   *The People (DPP) v Douglas & Hayes* [1985] ILRM 25, 28 CCA.

taking. Intent as a purposive mental state cannot be satisfied merely by running a risk. The accused must intend to happen what a reckless person merely risks happening.

Ordinarily, the different concepts will cause little difficulty, as where the assailant stabs the injured party, or throws him off a high balcony. In such cases the House of Lords, as we have seen, would leave it to the good sense of the jury to decide if the accused intended to kill or to cause serious injury to the victim without further explanation of the central concept.[23]

Oblique Intention

Where a man burns his house, knowing that a person is sleeping inside, or bombs an army barracks, knowing that a warning will not cause its abandonment, foresight of the death or serious injury to the victim becomes crucial and further elucidation of the concept of intention is essential in these circumstances.[24] In these circumstances the defence may try to divert the conclusion of an intended death or serious injury to the victim by explaining that the accused intended only the destruction of property and hoped that the victim might escape. As a matter of legal definition where the accused acts for a purpose, foreseeing as certain a consequence that the victim will suffer death or serious injury, he acts intentionally.[25] Martin J, for the Ontario Court of Appeal, so concluded in *Buzzanga*[26] where the accused was charged with wilfully promoting racial hatred:

> I agree, however, (assuming without deciding that there may be cases in which intended consequences are confined to those which it is the actor's conscious purpose to bring about), that, as a general rule, a person who foresees a consequence as certain or substantially certain to result from an act which he does in order to achieve some other purpose, intends that consequence. The actor's foresight of the certainty or moral certainty of the consequence resulting from his conduct compels a conclusion that if he, nonetheless, acted so as to produce it, then he decided to bring it about (albeit regretfully) in order to achieve his ultimate purpose. His intention encompasses the means as well as the ultimate objective.[27]

This aspect of intention may be called oblique intention.[28] It is nonetheless intention despite the name. The questions arise whether, in doing what he said he intended to do (1) did the accused foresee death or serious injury, and (2) how strongly must he foresee it before he can be said to have intended it?

As in an ordinary case of intention the forbidden result or consequence must be present in the accused's mind otherwise he cannot intend it. But foreseeing

---

23   Clarkson 62: ". . . juries have a free hand to convict where they feel it to be appropriate. They can expand or contract their definition of intention to meet the justice of the particular case. This is an intolerable position inviting prejudice, discrimination and abuse. It involves the abandoning of all standards in an area of law where it is crucial that standards be laid down. The principle of legality insists that people be informed in advance about what is acceptable or unacceptable conduct".

24   *Nedrick* [1986] 3 All ER 1; [1986] 1 WLR 1025, 83 Cr App R 267; [1986] Crim LR 792 CA.

25   Williams, "The Mens Rea for Murder: Leave it Alone" (1989) 105 LQR 388; Howard 41-42; Smith, "Intention in Criminal Law" (1974) Current Legal Problems 93 at 108-11.

26   (1979) 49 CCC (2d) 369 Ont CA.

27   At 384-85.

28   Williams, TBCL, 84-87.

something is not intending it, though it may be the most powerful material or evidence from which an intent may be inferred. It is not the law that probable consequences are always to be regarded as intended consequences. That infers intention constructively and s 4 requires actual intention. An occurrence foreseen as a probability is not necessarily intended though a consequence foreseen as a certainty is. If a result is certain in the mind of the accused he already embraces, by his action, the result of his action. Whereas, in the case of foreseeing a probability, he merely risks its occurrence. That is recklessness. In oblique intention purpose and desire may diverge.

In exploding a bomb in a plane, in order to collect insurance money on the wreck, the accused may desire the passengers to survive but know that they will not.[29] He is willing for them to die and knows that only the most extraordinary circumstances will save them. The pub bomber relies on a foreseeable possibility of his warning being heeded to forestall the death or serious injury he does not desire. The airplane bomber can rely on no sane mental process to categorise his action as merely taking a risk of death or serious injury and so successfully argue that his state of mind is under the ambit of recklessness or negligence. In the latter circumstances intent is a compelling inference.

Intention and the Presumption

2.23 S 4 of the Criminal Justice Act, 1964 states that the accused is presumed to have intended the natural and probable consequences of his action but that such a presumption may be rebutted. The presumption, unlike for example those under s 15 or s 19 of the Misuse of Drugs Act, 1977 or s 4 of the Explosives Substances Act, 1883,[30] places no burden of proof on the accused. In practice, every person accused of a crime will try to adduce sufficient evidence to raise a doubt.[31] Once sufficient evidence is adduced, either on the prosecution or defence case, it is for the prosecution to rebut any defence raised beyond reasonable doubt.[32] The presumption that the accused intended the natural and probable result of his action applies to all criminal law offences.[33] It means that the jury can infer that the accused acted with the mental process of an ordinary person where what he has done would not have been done by an ordinary person, unless he intended to do what he did. The Court of Criminal Appeal in *The People (DPP) v Douglas and Hayes*[34] put the matter thus:

> In the circumstances of any particular case evidence of the fact that a reasonable man would have foreseen that the natural and probable consequence of the acts of an accused

29 Smith, "A Note on Intention" [1990] Crim LR 85.
30 Which may place a burden of proving innocence on the balance of probability on the accused, once the prosecution prove certain preliminary facts; see par 9.18-9.19.
31 *The People (A-G) v Quinn* [1965] IR 366 CCA.
32 *Moore* [1987] AC 1578; [1987] 3 All ER 825, 86 Cr App R 324; [1988] Crim LR 177 HL; *Parker* (1963) 111 CLR 610, see [1963] Crim LR 569 HC.
33 *Martin* (1881) 8 QBD 54; [1881-5] All ER 699, 14 Cox 633 CCR; *Meade* [1909] 1 KB 895, 2 Cr App R 54 CCA; Archbold (1922) 396-402, 867-869.
34 [1985] ILRM 25 CCA.

was to cause death and evidence of the fact that the accused was reckless as to whether his acts would cause death or not is evidence from which an inference of intent to cause death may or should be drawn, but the court should consider whether either or both of these facts do establish beyond reasonable doubt an actual intention to cause death [or serious injury].[35]

2.24 A knife does not get into a person's heart unless someone puts it there. If that someone is proved to be the accused then, because the range of circumstances whereby the accused could stab the victim accidentally or unintentionally are improbable and unusual, the jury may conclude, firstly, that it was a voluntary action and secondly because of the nature of the act and the injury it is likely to cause, that there was an intention to kill or to cause serious injury. However, the facts of an individual case may indicate otherwise. To take another example; where the accused, in attempting to escape from a Garda intent on arresting him, sees an injured pedestrian lying on the road but nonetheless drives over the person in his car, an ordinary person would regard the death or serious injury to the victim as an inescapable or virtually certain consequence of the action of the accused. The jury may so infer and thus the accused will be proved to have acted with intent. He may nonetheless have an explanation inconsistent with intent and it is to the assessment of such an explanation that we now turn.

History of the Presumption

2.25 In England, up to the Criminal Evidence Act, 1898 and in Ireland, up to the Criminal Justice (Evidence) Act, 1924, the accused could not give evidence. The mental state of the accused was nonetheless to be assessed. The process was difficult for a jury which did not hear the accused explain his conduct from his own mouth. They were obliged to judge his mental state in the absence of any assistance from the accused as to how his mind was working at the time he was alleged to have committed the offence. More importantly in practice this was done in the absence of an opportunity to see the accused in the witness box and, by hearing and seeing him answer questions, consider his personality and temperament. The need to assess mental processes was met by assuming that the accused was a reasonable and ordinary person and that he acted as such.[36] In the crime of murder the law presumed intention, or as it was then called, malice aforethought, from the act of killing,[37] the only mitigation of that rule, up to 1898, illogically occurred where the body of the victim was not recovered.[38] Foster stated the presumption of malice thus:

> In every charge of murder the fact of killing being first proved, all the circumstances of accident, necessity, or infirmity are to be satisfactorily proved by the prisoner unless they arise out of the evidence produced against him, for the law presumeth the fact to have been founded in malice, until the contrary appeareth.[39]

35   At 28   36 See *Devlin* [1954] Crim LR 661 at 679.   37 Fost 255; 1 East PC 340.

38   2 Hale PC 290. This rule was not applied in the case of a murder occurring at sea; *Armstrong* (1875) 13 Cox 184; *Kersey* (1908) 1 Cr App R 260, 21 Cox 690 CCA and was finally laid to rest by the Court of Criminal Appeal in *The People (A-G) v Kirwan* [1943] IR 279; see Delaney, "The Irish Court and Corpus Delicti (1952) 68 LQR 460.

39   Fost 255.

Nonetheless the accused was presumed to be innocent until he was proved, beyond reasonable doubt, to be guilty. If the prosecution were to rely on circumstantial evidence in the case of murder or manslaughter the case had to be proved to the jury with "such certainty as they would act on in a matter of great consequence".[40] In 1935 in *Woolmington*[41] the House of Lords laid to rest the idea that the accused was required to prove a defence.

The notion of the reasonable man continued, however, unabated. In *Smith*[42] a policeman was killed. Smith, instead of pulling into the kerb as he was requested to do in order to investigate stolen property he was carrying, drove away in a panic with the policeman hanging on while the car swerved violently. A hand was seen punching the officer who was eventually dislodged under an oncoming vehicle. Smith said, on his arrest, "I do not mean to kill him but I did not want him to find the gear". Viscount Kilmure elevated the presumption that a person intends the natural and probable consequences of his action to an inescapable inference of law. Where a reasonable man would, in the circumstances proved, have intended either death or grievous bodily harm. . . .

> It matters not what the accused in fact contemplated as the probable result or whether he ever contemplated at all, provided he was in law responsible and accountable for his actions. . . . On the assumption that he is so accountable for his actions, the sole question is whether the unlawful and voluntary act was of such a kind that grievous bodily harm was the natural and probable result.[43]

Intent is Subjective

2.26 The Criminal Justice Act, 1964 makes it clear that the subjective test is operative when considering whether the accused acted with an intent to kill or cause serious injury. Even though a reasonable or ordinary person may, in the circumstances proved against the accused, have intended death or serious injury, yet the accused may not have done so. The reasons may vary infinitely. The observations of Denning J in *Hosegood v Hosegood*[44] erroneously rejected in *DPP v Smith*, are apposite:

> The presumption of intention is not a presumption of law but a proposition of ordinary good sense. It means this: that, as a man is usually able to foresee what are the natural consequences of his act, so it is, as a rule, reasonable to infer that he did foresee them and intend them. But, while that is an inference which may be drawn it is not one which must be drawn. If on all the facts of the case it is not the correct inference then it should not be drawn.[45]

40 *Franz* (1861) 2 F&F 580 Blackburn J.

41 [1935] AC 462; [1935] All ER 1, 30 Cox 234, 25 Cr App R 72 HL, adopted and explained in *The People (A-G) v Oglesby* [1966] IR 162 CCA.

42 [1961] AC 290; [1960] 2 All ER 161; [1960] 3 WLR 546, 44 Cr App R 261 HL.

43 AC 327, All ER 167, WLR 554, Cr App R 282. It is outside the scope of this work to discuss the storm of protest this decision generated. Suffice it to say that in New Zealand the Crimes Act, 1961 was amended to ensure that an objectively guilty mental state would not suffice for murder and the Australian High Court refused to give precedence to the decisions of the House of Lords; *Parker* (1963) 111 CLR 610, see [1963] Crim LR 569 HC. In England the rule was at first ignored and then repealed by s 8 of the Criminal Justice Act, 1967 which restored subjectivity to the presumption.

44 (1950) 66 TLR 735 CA.

45 738; see also *Buzzanga* (1979) 49 CCC (2d) 369 ONT CA.

A presumption can never be used to allow the prosecution to escape from the burden of proving guilt beyond reasonable doubt.[46] If an inference is not capable of being made, the presumption cannot assist the prosecution.

In any human action clarity of perception and foresight will vary from person to person. If the accused does not admit that he intended to kill or cause serious injury or, as is more usual, actively denies it, intent may still be inferred from all the circumstances. For example, if prior to shooting the victim it is proved that the accused left the place where they were together and returned with a gun he may explain this on the basis that he wished to make some such dramatic display as shooting into a building or killing an animal. This explanation need not necessarily be believed even to the extent of leaving the jury with a reasonable doubt. Where the accused stabs the victim in the presence of witnesses who testify that he spoke words clearly indicating that he knew what he was doing, the explanation of the accused that his mind went blank, prior to the speaking of the words and the act of stabbing, need not be regarded by the jury as evidence raising a reasonable doubt as to whether he acted with intent. The jury must make up their own minds as to whether this explanation raises a reasonable doubt or whether they are sure that even if the evidence may reasonably be true, it is explicable on the basis of a subsequent loss of memory. The evidence may also be a lie or a subsequent rationalisation of his conduct which he genuinely believes. Objective circumstances can be such as to outweigh any explanation of an absence of the requisite mental state given by the accused:

> A man's own intention is for him a subjective state, just as are his sensations of pleasure or of pain. But the state of another man's mind, or of his digestion, is an objective fact. . . . It is to be proved in the same way as other objective facts are proved. A jury must consider the whole of the evidence relevant to it as a fact in issue. If an accused gives evidence of what his intentions were, the jury must weigh his testimony along with whatever inference as to his intentions can be drawn from his conduct or from other relevant facts. References to a "subjective test" could lead to an idea that the evidence of an accused man as to his intent is more credible than his evidence of other matters. It is not: he may or may not be believed by the jury. Whatever he says, they may be able to conclude from the whole of the evidence that beyond doubt he had a guilty mind and a guilty purpose. But always the questions are what he did in fact know, foresee, expect, intend.[47]

Inference of Intent

2.27 It is impossible to accurately answer in advance the question of what evidence allows the jury to infer intent beyond reasonable doubt.[48] In cases of oblique

---

46   *Morisette v US* (1951) 342 US 246.

47   *Vallance* (1961) 108 CLR 56, 83, Windeyer J. Similarly see the approach of the Australian High Court in *Olasiuk* (1973) 6 SASR 255, 263: ". . . in inferring a man's intention from what he said or did, the jury are entitled to take into account their experience of life and to consider what intention would normally be inferred from such words or actions, but . . . they must realise it is the intention of the particular accused which is an issue". See further par 2.37.

48   If the circumstances are such as to leave the appeal court in a state of reasonable doubt the High Court of Australia have held that the accused should be acquitted; *Chamberlain* [1985] LRC (Crim) 285. For the contrasting English approach see O'Connor, "The Court of Appeal: Retrials and Tribulations" [1990] Crim LR 615. See also par 3.03.

intention the consequence caused by the accused's conduct will allow an inference of intent only where the consequence is virtually certain to occur in the ordinary course of events if the accused succeeds in his purpose and foresees that consequence.[49] In *Hyam*[50] the House of Lords treated foresight of a high probability as equivalent to intent.[51] This position was reversed by the House in *Moloney*[52] where the House emphasised that foresight was not intent but material from which intent could, but need not necessarily, be inferred. Lord Bridge[53] in Hyam was of the view that the probability of the consequence taken to have been foreseen must be little short of overwhelming before it would suffice to establish the necessary intention. Unfortunately he miscast the question to be asked of a jury in terms of death or really serious injury being a natural consequence of the accused's action and the accused foreseeing that natural consequence. In *Hancock and Shankland*[54] the House of Lords held that the correct jury question, in cases of oblique intent should refer not to natural consequences but to probable consequences. Natural consequences could be taken as meaning an occurrence as a result of the accused's action, which could be possible or probable. Lord Scarman[55] emphasised that in assessing the evidence, in order to determine whether the accused acted with intent, the jury should have it explained to them that the greater the probability of a consequence the more likely it is that the consequence was foreseen, and that if that consequence was foreseen, the greater the probability that the consequence was also intended. Finally in *Nedrick*[56] the Court of Appeal crystallised the law on the role of foresight and probability in intention thus:

> When determining whether the defendant had the necessary intent, it may therefore be helpful for a jury to ask themselves two questions (1) How probable was the consequence which resulted from the defendant's voluntary act? (2) Did he foresee that consequence? If he did not appreciate that the death or serious harm was likely to result from his act, he cannot have intended to bring it about. If he did, but thought that the risk to which he was exposing the person killed was only slight, then it may be easy for the jury to conclude that he did not intend to bring about that result. On the other hand, if the jury are satisfied that at the material time the defendant recognised that death or serious harm would be virtually certain (barring some unforeseen intervention) to result from his voluntary act, then that is a fact from which they may find it easy to infer that he intended to kill or do serious bodily harm, even though he may not have had any desire to achieve that result.[57]

49   *Nedrick* [1986] 3 All ER 1, [1986] 1 WLR 1025, 83 Cr App R 267; [1986] Crim LR 792 CA.
50   [1975] AC 55; [1974] 2 All ER 41; [1974] 2 WLR 607, 59 Cr App R 91 HL.
51   A position adopted by Walsh J in *The People (DPP) v Murray* [1977] IR 360, 387 SC.
52   [1985] AC 905; [1985] 1 All ER 1025; [1985] 2 WLR 648, 81 Cr App R 93; [1985] Crim LR 378 HL.
53   With whom Lord Frazer, Lord Edmund-Davies and Lord Keith agreed, Lord Hailsham delivering a brief concurring speech.
54   [1986] AC 455; [1986] 1 All ER 641; [1986] 2 WLR 357, 82 Cr App R 264; [1986] Crim LR 400 HL.
55   With whom Lord Keith, Lord Roskill, Lord Brighton and Lord Griffiths agreed.
56   Fn 49.
57   All ER 3, WLR 1027, Cr App R 270. In *Walker & Hayles* (1990) Cr App R 226, [1990] Crim LR 44 CA: "very high degree of probability" was accepted by the Court of Appeal as being correct. Similarly to the approach in *Nedrick* in *Ward* (1987) 85 Cr App R 71 CCA, judges were instructed to make it clear to the jury, in discussing foresight of consequences, that such was no more than

Inconsistent Decision on Intent

The effect of a defence on intent may be to excuse it or remove it altogether. If the accused, a doctor, cuts off the leg of the victim in order to allow his rescue from a collapsed building, the doctor will intend to cause a serious injury but may be excused by the defence of necessity.[58] Another way of regarding this example is to consider that the accused had no intention to harm the victim at all but rather to save his life. A direct intention can be regarded as a purpose or "a decision to bring about a certain consequence".[59] Thus considered the doctor's decision is to bring about the consequence of the victim being rescued. Despite this, it is obvious that he decided to remove the victim's leg, although rescue was his motive.

English law has forced itself into inconsistent reasoning principally as a result of a refusal to acknowledge the existence of a defence of necessity.[60] So the general who orders his men to defend their country, knowing that some of them will die, and the doctor in the example just quoted, both decide to bring about death or serious injury. It is more logical to regard their acts as having being done with that intention. Any criminal offence thereby committed would be negatived by reference to an overwhelming and immediate need to act in apparent contravention of the law where the accused was placed in a situation where he had no real alternative.[61] Article 40.3 of the Constitution expressly forbids the State to infringe the personal rights of the citizen. Unjust laws are contrary to the Constitution.[62] There are obvious circumstances where notwithstanding a breach of the criminal law the stigmatisation of the accused as a criminal or the enforcement of a punishment would be wrong. It is perhaps better to leave the definition of intent alone and deal with the accused, in the unlikely event of prosecution, as having a complete answer in the defence of necessity.

evidence of intent. The emphasis on English authorities results from a coincidence between our law of murder and English law. The Australian High Court in *Crabbe* (1985) 58 ALR 417 accepted that "a person who, without lawful justification or excuse, does an act knowing that it is probable that death or grievous bodily harm will result, is guilty of murder if death in fact results". In Canada an objective test for murder is written into s 212 of the Code providing for culpable homicide to be murder "where a person, for an unlawful object, does anything which he knows or ought to know is likely to cause death". This is an objective test and consequently a comparative analysis does not help us; Stuart 216-39. For a further discussion on proving intent see par 2.41.

58 See par 4.42. The matter is discussed in greater detail in volume 2.

59 *Mohan* [1976] QB 1; [1975] 2 All ER 193; [1975] 2 WLR 859; [1975] RTR 337, 60 Cr App R 272; [1975] Crim LR 283 CA.

60 For example in *Steane* [1947] KB 997; [1947] 1 All ER 813, intent to assist the enemy was negatived by the necessity to escape punishment. This was not the reasoning of the decision of the Court of Criminal Appeal however. In *Gillick v West Norfolk Health Authority* [1976] AC 112; [1985] 3 All ER 402; [1985] 3 WLR 830; [1986] Crim LR 113, the House of Lords excused contraceptive advice to girls under the age for sexual consent on the basis that the intent of the doctors was to prevent unwanted pregnancy. Clearly this advice aided the offence of unlawful sexual intercourse; see generally Smith & Hogan 57-61. Perhaps the cases were examples of what Lord Goff refers to as the judge's "educated reflex to facts"—"The Mental Element in the Crime of Murder" (1988) 104 LQR 30. Perhaps it is more clear to say that the judge liked the accused or what he did.

61 See par 4.42 where the matter is further discussed and the analysis of the Canadian Supreme Court in *Perka* (1984) 42 CR (3d) 113, 14 CCC (3d) 385, 386 and the Victoria Supreme Court in *Loughnan* [1981] VR 443.

62 *McGee v A-G* [1974] IR 284, 109 ILTR 29 SC.

Summary

2.28 The role of foresight and probability in intent may be summarised. Intent is an aspect of criminal guilt apart from recklessness. Ordinarily, intent involves the accused acting with a purpose of bringing about a result.[63] Where the accused acts to bring about a result knowing that, if he succeeds, a consequence of death or serious injury will ensue in the ordinary course of events, that also is intent.

Unless the accused admits his mental state it will have to be inferred from what he did and said. If the actions of the accused would naturally and probably cause death or serious injury the jury may infer that he acted with intent, unless there is contradictory evidence, which may include evidence from the accused. Where the accused challenges an inference of intent by contradictory evidence, or where material exists from which such a contradiction may be inferred, the jury may also consider it together with the inference that arises from the circumstances proved in the trial.

On the whole of the evidence the jury should consider whether the accused foresaw what he did. This is assisted by asking how probable the result of his actions was. If he failed to foresee a consequence he cannot have intended it. If he foresaw it he may have intended it, but he may not. It is not required that the accused be absolutely certain that he would cause death or serious injury. What is required is that he intended to cause death or serious injury. The more likely death or serious injury was in the circumstances proved, the more likely it was that the accused foresaw that. Where foresight is proved beyond a reasonable doubt intent may be inferred where the accused foresaw the consequence as virtually certain or as highly probable.

Foresight and probability are not intent. They are not even mental states equivalent to intent, they are only evidence from which intent may be inferred. As the question for the determination of the jury is the mind of the particular accused when he killed the victim, it remains possible that the accused may have foreseen death or serious injury as virtually certain yet not have intended it. This circumstance is, however, in the ordinary course of human events, unlikely.

Motive

2.29 Crime and moral wrong generally coincide.[64] The purpose sought to be achieved by a crime can be referred to as its motive. Crimes do not have to be committed from a bad motive.[65] Similarly, a good motive for committing a crime will not excuse. A person may enter into a suicide pact from motives of despair, or out of a desire to relieve suffering, but the survivor of such a pact will nonetheless be guilty of murder.[66]

---

63   *Mohan* [1976] QB 1; [1975] 2 All ER 193; [1975] 2 WLR 859; [1975] RTR 337, 60 Cr App R 272; [1975] Crim LR 283 CA.

64   See White, "Intention Purpose Foresight and Desire" (1976) 92 LQR 569, Howard 352-53.

65   The word maliciously, in statute, refers not to ill will but to the alternative ingredients of intent or recklessness; *Cunningham* [1957] 2 QB 396; [1957] 2 All ER 412; [1957] 3 WLR 76, 41 Cr App R 155 CCA.

66   *Abbott* (1903) 67 JP 151 CCA, further see par 2.40-2.42.

The criminal law generally ignores motives and focuses its enquiry on whether the actions of the accused correspond to the pre-defined elements of an offence. Good or bad motives may induce the accused into these actions; once he does the forbidden act with the requisite mental element he commits the offence. This is practical. The alternative of making motive an element of an offence would mean that the accused's guilt would depend on whether he could be proved to have acted under the influence of emotions such as envy, anger, pride or greed. Certainty demands that conduct be proscribed clearly in advance as wrongful leaving motive as a question in aggravation or mitigation of sentence. In the most exceptional circumstances the courts will grant an absolute discharge to an offender where a crime has been committed from the highest motives.

Confusingly, the words intent and motivation can be used interchangeably. Legally, intent has a specific meaning which does not necessarily correspond with motive. It is more correct to speak of intent as being the specific mental state with which the act or omission was done or not done. Motive may usually be described as the state of mind which causes that mental state to exist. For example, a desire to recover life insurance will make the accused wish to kill the insured person. The accused acts with intent to kill or cause serious injury, his ulterior purpose or motive is greed. Some crimes require two separate intents. A wilful entry onto property and an intent to steal is required, for example, for burglary; the accused must intend to enter and also intend to steal on entering.[67]

In proving the accused's intent, motive may be cogent evidence for the prosecution. The absence of motive, such as the unpleasant consequences for the accused of the victim's death, are similarly relevant as showing an absence of intent.[68] In *Lewis*[69] the accused was charged together with one Tatley with the murder of the latter's daughter and son-in-law. The murder was committed by Lewis posting to the victims a bomb in the form of a kettle rigged with dynamite which exploded on being plugged in. The issue on appeal to the Supreme Court of Canada was whether the trial judge should have admitted evidence that Tatley was angry that his daughter had married without his consent and whether the jury should have been instructed that Lewis had no motive for the bombing. Dickson J identified six propositions as to the place of motive in a criminal trial:

(1) As evidence, motive is always relevant and hence evidence of motive is admissible.

(2) Motive is no part of the crime and is legally irrelevant to criminal responsibility. It is not an essential element of the prosecution's case as a matter of law.

(3) Proved absence of motive is always an important fact in favour of the accused and ordinarily worthy of note in a charge to the jury.

(4) Conversely, proved presence of motive may be an important factual ingredient in the Crown's case, notably on the issue of identity and intention, when the evidence is purely circumstantial.

---

67 Similarly to be an accessory after the fact to felony the accused must act to ensure that the offender evades justice. While broader, this remains an intent.

68 Cross, "The Mental Element in Crime" (1967) 83 LQR 215 at 221.

69 (1979) 68 Cr App R 310, 47 CCC (2d) 24. The decision is discussed in Stuart 129-33.

(5) Motive is therefore always a question of fact and evidence and the necessity of referring to motive in the charge to the jury falls within the general duty of the trial Judge "to not only outline the theories of the prosecution and defence but to give the juries matters of evidence essential in arriving at a just conclusion."

(6) Each case will turn on its own unique set of circumstances. The issue of motive is always a matter of degree.[70]

Lewis had not proved an absence of motive for the killing and this fact became relevant in the trial. His identity as the person who posted the bomb was un-challenged. Consequently the trial judge had exercised his discretion correctly not to charge the jury on motive in respect of his case. Tatley's identity as a participant in the killings was, conversely, a live issue in the case and his motive assisted in proving his identity.[71] On this Dixon J commented as follows:

> The necessity of charging a jury on motive may be looked upon as a continuum at one end of which are cases where the evidence as to identity of the murderer is purely circumstantial and proof of motive on the part of the crown so essential that reference must be made to motive in charging the jury. The Crown's case against Tatley was such a situation. It was essential to establish motive and the trial Judge properly referred to motive in charging the jury in relation to Tatley. At the other end of the continuum, and requiring a charge on motive, is the case where there is proved absence of motive and this may become of great significance as a matter in favour of the accused. Between these two end points in the continuum there are cases where the necessity to charge on motive depends upon the course of the trial and the nature and probative value of the evidence adduced. In these cases, a substantial discretion must be left to the trial Judge. In *Imrich* (1974) 21 CCC (2d) 99, 6 OR 496, 39 CRNS 77, for example, the evidence of exclusive opportunity was such that motive receded into the back-ground.[72]

The decision accords with traditional interpretations of the role of motive in criminal law[73] that as evidence motive is a relevant factor.[74]

Coincidence of Fault

2.30 Generally the mental element and the external elements of a crime must coincide in point of time.[75] If the law were otherwise a person who had an intention of assaulting another would commit the crime of assault on accidentally knocking against that person. It would be wrong for the person who caused an accidental death to be guilty of homicide merely because he later felt good about the demise of the victim. Exceptionally, if the mental element of the crime becomes present during the course of a continuing external act,[76] such as an offence of possession, or where

---

70 At p 34-38, support of authorities may be found in the judgment.
71 See further *McKay* [1957] VR 560; [1957] ALR 648 SC.
72 At 38.
73 Stephen *Hist* III 18; Starkie, *Evidence* (4th ed., 1853) 849.
74 Williams (1986) 84 Cr App R 299 CA; Derry (1986) 83 Cr App R 7 CA.
75 *Fowler v Pagett* (1798) 101 ER 1103, 7 TR 509 KB. See generally Smith & Hogan 76-78, Howard 46-49; Stuart 306-9.
76 *Fagan* [1969] 1 QB 439; [1968] 3 All ER 442; [1968] 3 WLR 1120, 52 Cr App R 700 DC.

the accused fails to take reasonably possible measures to counteract a danger which he has created[77] such coincidence suffices.

As a matter of policy the absence of the relevant mental element at the time of perpetrating the external act makes no difference to liability where the accused has voluntarily weakened or extinguished his mental processes by voluntary intoxication in order to carry out his intention. This was explained by Lord Denning in *Attorney General for Northern Ireland v Gallagher*[78] thus:

> If a man, whilst sane and sober, forms an intention to kill and makes preparation for it, knowing it is a wrong thing to do, and then gets himself drunk so as to give himself Dutch courage to do the killing, and whilst drunk carries out his intention, he cannot rely on this self-induced drunkenness as a defence to a charge of murder nor even as reducing it to manslaughter.[79]

Continuous Event Doctrine

2.31 Controversy has been created by the situation where an accused person sets on a victim with the intention of killing, does not succeed in that purpose, but not being aware of that fact later goes on to dispose of what he thought was a corpse, thereby administering the *coup de grace*.[80]

The celebrated case is *Thabo Meli*.[81] The four accused decided to kill the victim and then arrange matters to look like accidental death. They hit him over the head. They believed they had achieved their purpose. The victim, whilst still alive, was rolled over a cliff when, it was later assumed by the Privy Council, the accused thought that he was already dead. It was argued that the external and mental elements of the crime had not coincided when the victim had met his death; when the accused persons had the intention of killing they had failed but when they had succeeded they lacked the intention to kill because they thought they were disposing of a corpse. This argument was brushed aside on the basis that the judges considered it "impossible to divide up what was really one transaction in this way".[82]

Causation Solution

The brevity of the reasoning in *Thabo Meli* makes it difficult to state a principle. It is submitted that where the accused embarks on a course of conduct, the ultimate purpose of which is to kill or cause serious injury to his victim, that intention suffices notwithstanding a later mistake which renders the intention inoperative.[83] The

---

77   *Miller* [1983] 2 AC 161 [1983] 1 All ER 978; [1983] 2 WLR 539, 77 Cr App R 17; [1983] Crim LR 466 HL.

78   [1963] AC 349; [1961] 3 All ER 299; [1961] 3 WLR 619, 45 Cr App R 316 HL.

79   AC at 382, All ER at 314, WLR at 641, Cr App R at 341.

80   Adams, "Homicide and the Supposed Corpse" (1968) 1 Otago LR 278; Hunt, "Hunt—Murdering a 'Body', by Disposing of It" (1968) 85 SALJ 383; Marston, "Contemporaneity of Action and Intention" (1970) 86 LQR 208; Turpin, "The Murdered Corpse—Thabo Meli Extended" [1969] CLJ 20; White, "The Identity of Time and of the *Actus Reus*" [1977] Crim LR 148.

81   [1954] 1 All ER 373; [1954] 1 WLR 228 PPC. See also *Shoukatallie* [1962] AC 81; [1961] 3 All ER 996; [1961] 3 WLR 1021 PC; *Moore* [1975] Crim LR 229 CA.

82   All ER at 374, WLR at 230.

83   See *Ramsay* [1967] NZLR 1105 where the New Zealand Court of Appeal, on construing the Crimes

principles of causation, discussed above, applied to the facts of a case like *Thabo Meli* would put the accused in a situation where he had done an act, with intent to kill or cause serious injury, which through the carrying out of that intention had led to the victim's death. It would be wrong for the law to distinguish between situations where the accused has done the victim a serious injury and left him to die by exposure and one where the accused has acted similarly but by disposing of what he believed to be a corpse, achieved his original purpose.[84]

In *Church*[85] the accused severely beat a woman and threw her body into a river. In so doing he claimed to believe that she was already dead from her injuries. In point of fact, she died by drowning after entering the water. At the trial the judge directed the jury that the accused should not be convicted of murder if, on throwing the victim into the river, he already believed she was dead. On being acquitted of murder and appealing a manslaughter conviction the Court of Criminal Appeal commented on the judge's direction thus:

> We venture to express the view that such a direction was unduly benevolent to the appellant, and that the jury should have been told that it was still open to them to convict of murder, notwithstanding that the appellant may have thought his blows and attempt at strangulation had actually produced death when he threw the body into the river, if they regarded the appellant's behaviour from the moment he first struck her to the moment he threw her into the river as a series of acts designed to cause death or grievous bodily harm.[86]

In general the courts have shown little sympathy for arguments advanced in such circumstances. It is submitted that the application of the general principles of causation is the correct answer to such arguments.

Intent in Attempted Murder

2.32 The accused can only attempt to commit a crime if it is his conscious endeavour to do the acts which constitute the crime. Murder occurs only where the victim dies. Where the charge is of attempted murder the accused must intend to kill. An intent to cause serious injury is insufficient.[87] In general, one cannot attempt to

---

Act, 1961, s 167, held that where the mental element of a crime requires knowledge this cannot be supplied by proof of an intention earlier in point of time.

84   See the criticism of the Zimbabwean Case of *Chiswibo* (1960) 2 SA 714 FC, cited in Stuart 308.

85   [1966] 1 QB 59; [1965] 2 All ER 72; [1965] 2 WLR 1220, 49 Cr App R 206 CCA. A similar decision was reached, on similar facts, in *Manuel & Grant* (1986) 10 Crim LJ 110 CCA NZ.

86   QB at 67, All ER at 74, WLR at 1224, Cr App R at 210.

87   *Whybrow* (1951) 35 Cr App R 141 CCA; *Mohan* [1976] QB 1; [1975] 2 All ER 193; [1975] 2 WLR 859; [1975] RTR 337, 60 Cr App R 272; [1975] Crim LR 283 CA. In *Jones* [1990] 3 All ER 886 the Court of Appeal decided that an attempt had been committed where the accused had got into a car driven by his ex-mistress's new lover and pointed a loaded sawn-off shotgun at him. There was no proof that the accused's finger had ever been on the trigger but there was evidence that the safety catch of the gun was on at the time of the attack. The court held that the accused's actions in obtaining the shotgun, shortening it and going to the victim's car were merely preparatory while his actions in getting into the car and taking the loaded gun and pointing it at the victim with the intention of killing him provided sufficient evidence for the jury to consider whether these acts were more than merely preparatory. Attempt is further discussed at par 2.41. For the test in England see *Gullefer* [1990] 3 All ER 882 CA.

commit manslaughter.[88] In *The People (DPP) v Douglas and Hayes*[89] the Special Criminal Court had found both accused guilty of attempted murder by shooting, contrary to s 14 of the Offences Against the Person Act, 1861. They had fired shots into a Garda car, the bullets striking the front of the car in close proximity to its driver. The Court held that the accused were guilty of murder because if a Garda had died murder would have been committed. The accused clearly intended[90] to kill or cause serious personal injury. The Court of Criminal Appeal reversed the convictions holding that an intent to commit murder required an intent to kill when the victim had not died.[91] Intent, in this context, will mean that the accused acts with a purpose to kill or a purpose of doing an act foreseeing that it would be a virtual certainty, in the ordinary course of events, that the victim will die if that purpose is accomplished.[92] Recklessness as to the external elements of a crime cannot amount to an attempt notwithstanding that intent or recklessness may suffice if the accused succeeds in his purpose.[93]

Transferred Intent

2.33 At common law[94] for the accused to intend to kill victim A but to succeed in killing victim B was nonetheless murder. This principle has been expressly retained by the wording of s 4 of the Criminal Justice Act, 1964 which makes a killing murder where the accused intended to kill or cause serious injury to a person "whether the person killed or not".[95] Thus where the accused wanted to kill his wife by handing her a poisoned apple but she gave it to their child who consequently died, the accused was found guilty of murder.[96] Similarly a random intent to kill or cause serious injury suffices, as where the accused discharges a gun into a crowd.[97] The doctrine is equally applicable to manslaughter[98] and is of general application throughout the criminal law save for where the actual wording of statutory provisions excludes it.[99]

88   *Creamer* [1966] 1 QB 72; [1965] 3 All ER 257; [1965] 3 WLR 583, 49 Cr App R 368 CCA. See the discussion at par 4.28.

89   [1985] ILRM 25 CCA. See also *Walker & Hayles* (1990) 90 Cr App R 226; [1990] Crim LR 44 CA.

90   The meaning of intent in murder is discussed above par 2.19–2.28.

91   Similarly the Canadian Supreme Court have held that an attempt to murder requires an intent to kill notwithstanding the much wider definition of the mental element for murder in ss 212 and 213 of the Code; *Ancio* (1984) 39 CR (3d) 1.

92   See above par 2.19 and subsequently.

93   Smith & Hogan 287–91; Howard 288–93; Stuart 536–39 who disagrees that intention in the context of intent should include an extension to indirect intention or foresight of certainty or near certainty of a consequence occurring as a result of the accused's purpose.

94   *Saunders & Archer* (1575) 2 Plowden 473, 75 ER 706; *Gore* (1611) 9 Co Rep 81, 77 ER 853. Generally see *Kenny* (1922) 133–34.

95   For the full text see par 2.18.

96   *Saunders*, fn 94. Generally see Ashworth, "Transferred Malice and Punishment for Unforeseen Consequences", in Glazebrook (editor), *Reshaping the Criminal Law* (London, 1978) 77 and subsequently.

97   1 Hawk ch 29, s 12; ch 31, s 8; 4 Bl Com 200–1.

98   *Mitchell* [1983] QB 741; [1983] 2 All ER 427; [1983] 2 WLR 938, 76 Cr App R 293 CA.

99   Generally see Smith & Hogan 73–78; Howard 40; Stuart 203–7.

Intent to Kill or Cause Serious Injury

2.34 S 4 of the Criminal Justice Act, 1964 requires that for the accused to murder the victim he must act with intent to kill or cause serious injury. Only where attempted murder is charged must the accused have expressly intended to kill. The only recorded discussion in Irish law of the effect of this alternative intent in murder is that by Henchy J in *The People (DPP) v Murray*.[1] Having accepted that each external element of a crime requires a corresponding mental element he commented:

> It accords with the mens rea or malice required for the act of non-capital murder, i.e. an *intention* to cause death or serious injury. If the less serious intention of causing serious injury is proved, it is no defence to a charge of murder for the accused to say that he had no *knowledge* that death would occur. While the type of constructive malice or intention exemplified by *The State v McMullen* [1925] 2 IR 9 is no longer recognised since the enactment of s 4 of the Criminal Justice Act, 1964, the offence of murder is basically one of intention which need not encompass the resulting death.[2]

In *Hyam*[3] the House of Lords was evenly divided on this question. Lord Diplock and Lord Kilbrandon held that an intention to cause grievous bodily harm was insufficient for murder unless the accused realised that his act was likely to endanger life. Lord Hailsham and Lord Dilhorne held that a simple intention to do grievous bodily harm was sufficient. Lord Cross expressed ignorance on the topic of criminal law but cast his vote with the latter faction. In *Cunningham*[4] the House of Lords upheld the earlier decision of the Court of Criminal Appeal in Vickers[5] and decided that the mental element in murder encompassed an intention to cause grievous bodily harm, meaning really serious bodily harm[6] to the victim. There was no requirement that the act done by the accused to the victim was either contemplated as being, or was, likely to kill.[7] No such requirement is specified in s 4.

It is proposed to reform the corresponding English[8] rule by requiring the accused to be aware of the risk of causing death. The revised rule is expressed in the draft Criminal Code, clause 54 (1) which clearly adds an additional element onto that required by the wording of the Irish Act:

> A person is guilty of murder if he causes the death of another (a) intending to kill or (b) intending to cause serious personal harm and being aware that he may cause death.

1   [1977] IR 360 SC.
2   At 401-2.
3   [1975] AC 55; [1975] 2 All ER 41; [1974] 2 WLR 607, 59 Cr App R 91 HL.
4   [1982] AC 566; [1981] 2 All ER 863; [1981] 3 WLR 223, 73 Cr App R 253 HL.
5   [1957] 2 QB 664, [1957] 2 All ER 741; [1957] 3 WLR 326, 41 Cr App R 189 CCA.
6   Smith [1961] AC 290; [1960] 3 All ER 161; [1960] 3 WLR 546, 44 Cr App R 261 HL. The decision on this point was not over-ruled. Further see par 6.22.
7   This point was not decided by the High Court of Australia in *La Fontaine* (1976) 136 CLR 62, 11 ACR 507. In *Solomon* [1980] NSWLR N/Av the New South Wales Court of Criminal Appeal decided, as a matter of statutory construction, that the injury must be likely to cause death. In contrast to s 4, s 166 of the Crimes Act of New Zealand provides that the bodily injury, from which death results, must be, in itself, of a dangerous nature. For an example see *Kirikiri* (1983) 7 Crim LJ 168 CCA NZ.
8   House of Lords, "Report of the Select Committee on Murder and Life Imprisonment" (session 1988-89, House, HL Paper 78). The Criminal Law Revision Committee reached a similar conclusion in 1980 – 14th Report, Offences Against the Person par 31 (cmnd 7844). See Ashworth (Reforming the Law of Murder) [1990] Crim LR 75.

Defining Serious Injury

The undefined phrase "serious injury" in s 4 gives rise to the possibility of a flexible approach. The purpose of s 4 was to abolish the constructive murder rules, exemplified in the abortion-murder case of *The People (A-G) v Cadden*,[9] and arguably[10] to retain in a codified form the concept of malice aforethought at common law. At the foundation of the State in 1922 it was by no means clear that malice aforethought, expressed as an intent to kill or cause grievous bodily harm, did not also require in the particular case of an intent to cause grievous bodily harm, that the act done by the accused to the victim was likely to kill.[11] The persuasive authority was *Vamplew*[12] in which Pollock CB, on the trial of a thirteen year old child for murder by poisoning, held that no one would commit murder unless he was conscious that the act done was one which was likely to cause death.

Suggested Solution

2.35 The gravest moral culpability attaches to a conviction for murder. The absence of that culpability has led to the creation of the special defences of provocation and excessive force in self defence.[13] As a matter of policy the Oireachtas is entitled, conversely, to decide that where the accused causes death by the intentional infliction on the victim of a serious injury, that he should not be allowed to argue his innocence of murder on the basis of a distinction between serious injury and death. There can be injuries which, though serious, are not usually life endangering, such as breaking a limb or a severe laceration of the face.[14] In both these instances death may occur from a combination of the wrong of the accused and the subsequent misfortune of the victim. There is no authority for the proposition that "serious injury" means harm inherently likely to cause death. The only argument for such an interpretation would be the state of the common law in 1922. The best analogy is with the law of causation which, although it is completely separate from the mental element in homicide, requires that the actions of the accused be a substantial and

---

9   (1957) 91 ILTR 97 CCA, further see par 3.34-3.35.

10   The difficulty with this argument is that the standard textbooks of the time, see fn 3, also encompassed recklessness as a species of murder at common law, a form upheld by the Australian High Court in *Crabbe* (1985) 58 ALR 417. Howard 50 argues that an attempt to cause grievous bodily harm may only be murder where the injury is such as to be likely to cause death.

11   Thus Stephen in his Draft Code (quoted in *History* III at 80-82) requires an "injury known to the offender to be likely to cause death" and an illustration to Article XXIV of his *Digest* (4th ed., 1887) 166, which he says in the *History* exactly corresponds to the common law, clearly requires the acts of the victim perpetrated on the accused to "be likely, according to common knowledge, to cause death". The Article which is 264 in the first edition (1877) at 211-13, and remains unaltered in all subsequent editions, makes no such requirement. Although Lord Hailsham in *Cunningham* [1982] AC 566; [1981] 2 All ER 863; [1981] 3 WLR 223, 73 Cr App R 253 HL, disagrees with him, he was not an experienced criminal judge whilst Sir James Stephen certainly was. Kenny (1922) clarifies this species of malice aforesight as "intention only to hurt"—and not to kill—but to hurt by means of an act which is intrinsically likely to kill". Archbold (1922) 870 makes a similar requirement.

12   (1862) 3 F&F 520, 176 ER 234.

13   See ch 4.

14   Lord Goff instances an acquittal where such an injury severed the jugular vein of the victim causing him death—"The Mental Element in Murder" (1988) 104 LQR 30 at 48.

operating cause of death; substantial, in this context, meaning more than merely trivial.[15] Hence it is possible to interpret the phrase "serious injury" as meaning an injury which creates a more than merely trivial risk of death. It is submitted that the accused must intend such an injury. It seems impossible to read into the words of s 4 a requirement that the accused need have contemplated a risk of death to the victim on perpetrating the act or omissions which led to the serious injury. Such a requirement would ensure that the accused could only be convicted of murder where he has, subjectively, shown a disregard for the victim's life, which, though a worthwhile law reform, requires an amendment to the current law.[16]

The Mental Element in Capital Murder

2.36 The penalty for capital murder was, up to the abolition of the death penalty in the Criminal Justice Act, 1990, death by hanging.[17] The penalty for any form of murder is now a mandatory sentence of imprisonment for life under s 2 of the Criminal Justice Act, 1964 as amended by the Criminal Justice Act, 1990.[18] The essential difference between the two forms of murder and capital murder, prior to reform, was that in the latter a further aggravating circumstance existed, being the special occupation of the person killed or the activity in which the accused was engaged when the killing took place. Up to the Criminal Justice Act, 1964 the death penalty had to be imposed in all cases of murder. The treatment of the distinction between the two by the Supreme Court is of importance in establishing judicial attitudes to two questions. Firstly, as to whether there is a requirement in Irish law for each external element of an offence to have a corresponding mental element and, secondly, whether that mental element is to be tested as being subjective (personal to the accused) or objective (mental element to be expected of a hypothetical reasonable or ordinary man or woman).

In *The People (DPP) v Noel and Marie Murray*[19] the accused were a husband and wife. They were part of an armed gang of four persons who robbed a bank. On their

15 Smithers (1977) 34 CCC (2d) 427 S Ct Can; see par 2.01-2.18.

16 The House of Lords in *Cunningham* [1982] AC 566; [1981] 2 All ER 863; [1981] 3 WLR 223, 73 Cr App R 253 HL, did not consider that either the institutional writers or the authorities established a requirement that the grievous bodily harm element be likely to cause death. Further, Lord Hailsham found that the felony-murder rule was never used to convict for murder, e.g. on an unlawful wounding, where the accused did not intend to commit grievous bodily harm. The best argument for the requirement in law of a likelihood of death being encapsulated into an intent to cause grievous bodily harm is that it represented the common law in practice, though never declared by any case, that acted upon by judges, of whom Sir James Stephens was the most authoritative.

17 Ss 1, 2 & 3 of the Offences Against the Person Act, 1861, as amended by s 5 of the Criminal Justice Act, 1964.

18 For the former categories of capital murder the sentence is a minimum term of forty years and it applies to (1) murder of a member of the Garda Síochána acting in the course of his duty, (2) murder of a prison officer acting in the course of his duty, (3) murder done in furtherance of an offence under ss 6, 7, 8 or 9 of the Offences Against the State Act, 1939, or in the course or furtherance of the activities of an unlawful organisation within the meaning of s 10 (other than paragraph (f)) of that Act, (4) for murder committed within the State for a political motive, of the head of a foreign State or of a member of the government of, or a diplomatic officer of, a foreign State; Criminal Justice Act, 1990.

19 [1977] IR 360 SC.

departure they were spotted by Garda Michael Reynolds, an unarmed officer then in plain clothes, who was driving in a car with his wife and small child. He gave chase. The gang stopped their car and ran. Garda Reynolds pursued the person whom he thought was the driver, Noel Murray. As this accused had just been captured or was about to be captured by Garda Reynolds, Marie Murray screamed "let go my fellow" and shot him dead at short range with a hand gun. Notwithstanding that s 3(2) of the Criminal Justice Act, 1964 provided for an alternative verdict of murder on a charge of capital murder and that s 3(4) of the same Act permitted the substitution, on appeal, of a murder or manslaughter verdict for a capital murder verdict, the Special Criminal Court held that no new offence had been created by the act. The Court of Criminal Appeal agreed. Capital murder was, the reasoning went, simply the remnant of the old murder sentence of death, imposed in all cases, but limited to more specific instances by the 1964 Act. In this case the fact of the victim being a Garda was one of those instances. As no new offence had been created by the 1964 Act, it was reasoned to be irrelevant to the guilt of Marie Murray on a charge of capital murder that she did not know or suspect that the pursuer of her husband was a Garda acting in the course of his duty.

On appeal the Supreme Court disagreed. Capital murder was a new offence created by s 1 of the 1964 Act. The primary reasoning was that murder and capital murder encompassed different elements and varying consequent punishments. The Court held that where an additional element was incorporated into an offence it was to be presumed that the Oireachtas intended that before the accused could be guilty of that element he should have acted with a guilty mind. In approving the rule of statutory interpretation, as stated by Lord Reid in *Sweet v Parsley*,[20] Henchy J said:

> . . . the basis for the presumption is . . . to avoid the unjust or oppressive application of the section to those who have not merited the guilt and punishment envisaged by the section, either because they are totally blameless or because their blameworthiness is only such as to attract guilt for a lesser offence.[21]

All the members of the Court rejected the reasoning drawn from the analogous crime of assault on a police officer in the execution of his duty, that the only mental element to be proved by the prosecution was an assault. The fact that the person assaulted was a policeman was an external fact for which it was necessary to support guilt by a mental element.[22]

The Court was willing to ordinarily define the mental element for an offence, or an element of an offence, in terms of intention or recklessness. An intention to kill or cause serious injury was necessary under s 4 of the Criminal Justice Act, 1964 for a killing to be murder. Where the killing took place in the circumstances of aggravation defined by s 1 of the Act, the Court held that the intention of the Oireachtas could not be fulfilled by requiring knowledge[23] as to those circumstances.

20 [1970] AC 132; [1969] 1 All ER 347; [1969] 2 WLR 470, 53 Cr App R 221 HL.
21 At 399.
22 McLeod (1954) 111 CCC 106, 20 Cr App R 281 S Ct Canada. For a further discussion see par 6.34-6.40.
23 Henchy J at 403, Griffin J at 415, Kenny J at 421, Parke J with Henchy and Griffin J at 424. The head note is incorrect.

Such a mental element would work against the intention of the Oireachtas. There were few cases in which such a mental element could be proved. Further, where the accused had considered or adverted his mind to that possibility, real culpability was occasioned by his disregard of that risk. Hence the mental element required to support guilt for the external circumstances stated in s 1 was recklessness.

The policy statement by the Court that in serious offences the external element of guilt must be supported by a culpable mental state is to be welcomed. Griffin J expressed difficulty in accepting that the Oireachtas could have intended a serious offence to be distinguished from a less serious one by the "accidental or fortuitous" occurrence of external circumstances.[24] This theme is common to all the judgments.[25] It is a statement of the correct basic approach to defining the elements of a crime. As such it is followed in this work.

Recklessness

2.37 The definition of recklessness remains a problem. All the members of the Court agreed that recklessness occurs unless the accused had foreseen at least a possibility of the element existing.[26] Henchy J adopted the formulation in s 2.02(2)(c) of the Model Penal Code:

> A person acts recklessly with regard to a material element of an offence when he consciously disregards a substantial and unjustifiable risk that the material element exists or will result from his conduct. The risk must be of such a nature and degree that, considering the nature and purpose of the actor's conduct and the circumstances known to him, its disregard involves culpability of high degree.[27]

Walsh J dissented holding that intention or knowledge must exist in respect of the aggravating circumstance but defined intention as foresight of probable consequences.[28] Griffin J, with whom Parke J agreed, defined recklessness in terms of the conscious taking of a risk.[29]

Degree of Risk

While there is no clear statement by the Court that recklessness involves the taking of a substantial risk it is submitted that this is the correct approach. By a majority of three to two the Court ordered a retrial on the issue as to whether Marie Murray was reckless as to the occupation of Garda Reynolds. It seems inconceivable, on reviewing the facts of the case, that the gang, pursued across a city and into a park by a motor vehicle, and thereafter on foot, would not have thought of the possibility that their pursuer, in showing such tenacity and courage, was a Garda. Both Henchy J and Walsh J were resolved to apply tests of guilt based on more than a bare possibility

---

24 At 412.

25 See particularly Walsh J at 390, Henchy J at 397, Kenny J at 421, Parke J at 424.

26 Walsh J at 387, Henchy J at 403, Griffin J at 413, Kenny J at 421, 422 leaves open the possibility of recklessness being treated as objective. Parke J agrees with the judgment of Henchy J and Griffin J at 424.

27 At 403.

28 At 387.

29 At 413, and see his subsequent analysis of the facts, applying this test at 416-19.

as to circumstances. Further the test in Irish law for criminal negligence, which suffices for the commission of manslaughter, involves a risk "in a high degree" of substantial personal injury to the victim.[30] Almost any act involves a risk of another occurrence or another concurrent circumstance. A risk giving rise to criminal liability, it is submitted, must be of sufficient weight to involve the accused in real culpability. The requirement in the Model Penal Code of a substantial risk and a high degree of moral culpability accords with this principle. This conclusion is supported by the fact that the Code definition approved by Henchy J has been recommended as the basic test for recklessness in Irish law in all the papers of the Law Reform Commission where the subject has arisen.[31]

All the members of the Supreme Court proceeded with their analysis of the case on the basis that the mental element of the crime was to be judged subjectively.

Criminal Justice Act, 1990

The Criminal Justice Act, 1990 abolished the death penalty for murder. A more severe punishment, in terms of restricted remission, was imposed for those convicted of certain categories of murder. The new legislation incorporates the decision in *Murray* by making it clear that the accused can only be found guilty of murder in such a situation if he was aware of this. The relevant legislation is as follows:

> 1. No person shall suffer death for any offence.
> 2. A person convicted of treason or murder shall be sentenced to imprisonment for life.
> (1) This section applies to —
> (a) Murder of a member of the Garda Síochána acting in the course of his duty,
> (b) murder of a prison officer acting in the course of his duty
> (c) murder done in the course of or furtherance of an offence under s 6, 7, 8 or 9 of the Offences Against the State Act, 1939 or in the course of furtherance of the activities of an unlawful organisation within the meaning of s 18 (other than paragraph (f)) of that Act, and
> (d) murder, committed within the State for a political motive, of the head of a foreign state or of a member of the government of, or a diplomatic officer of, a foreign state and to an attempt to commit any such murder.
> (2)(a) Subject to paragraph (b), murder to which this section applies, and an attempt to commit such a murder, shall be a distinct offence from murder and from an attempt to commit murder and a person shall not be convicted of murder to which this section applies or of an attempt to commit such murder unless it is proved that he knew of the existence of each ingredient of the offence specified in the relevant paragraph of subs 1 or was reckless as to whether or not that ingredient existed.
> (b) save as otherwise provided by this Act, the law and procedure relating to murder and an attempt to commit murder shall apply to the offence.
> 3. In this section—
> "diplomatic officer" means a member of the staff of a diplomatic mission of a foreign State having diplomatic ranks;
> "prison" means any place to which rules or regulations may be made under the Prisons Act, 1926 to 1980, s 7 of the Offences Against the State (Amendment) Act, 1940, s 233 of the Defence Act, 1954, s 2 of the Prisoners of War and Enemy Aliens Act, 1956, or s 13 of the Criminal Justice Act, 1960;

30 See par 3.08-3.09.
31 See Law Reform Commission Report on Rape par 24; Receiving Stolen Property par 130; Malicious Damage par 30 and page 42.

"prison officer" includes any member of the staff of a prison or any person having the custody of or having duties in relation to the custody of, a person detained in a prison.
4. Where a person (other than a child or young person) is convicted of treason or of a murder or attempt to commit murder to which s 3 applies, the court—
(a) in the case of treason or murder, shall in passing sentence specify as the minimum period of imprisonment to be served by that person a period of not less than forty years
(b) in the case of an attempt to commit murder, shall pass a sentence of imprisonment of not less than twenty years and specify a period of not less than twenty years as the minimum period of imprisonment to be served by that person.

Under s 6 persons indicted for murder to which s 3 of the Criminal Justice Act, 1990 applies may, if the additional element is not proved, be found guilty of murder, or, in the usual way, of manslaughter. Remission for good conduct is earned as if the sentence were a definite one of forty years' imprisonment for murder, or twenty years' imprisonment for attempted murder. Under s 5(3) the power of temporary release from a prison is restricted to grave reasons of a humanitarian nature.

Ancillary Offences to Murder

2.38 Several ancillary offences to murder are created by the Offences Against the Person Act, 1861. By s 4 of that Act:

> All persons who shall conspire, confederate, and agree to murder any person, whether he be a subject of Her Majesty or not, and whether he be within the Queen's dominions or not, and whosoever shall solicit, encourage, persuade, or endeavour to persuade, or shall propose to any person, to murder any other person, whether he be a subject of Her Majesty or not, and whether he be within the Queen's dominions or not, shall be guilty of a misdemeanour, and on being convicted thereof shall be liable, at the discretion of the court, to be kept in penal servitude for any term not more than 10 and not less than 3 years,—or to be imprisoned for any term not exceeding two years with or without hard labour.[32]

Conspiracy

Conspiracy is an indictable misdemeanour at common law consisting of an agreement of two or more persons[33] to do an unlawful act or to do a lawful act by unlawful means.[34] A conspiracy is complete once the agreement is entered into and whether the substantive crime is thereafter committed is immaterial.[35] It is gravely uncertain as to what unlawful acts can give rise to a criminal conspiracy. Certainly it is an indictable offence to conspire to commit a summary offence.[36] Probably the law extends a criminal conspiracy into any agreement, which, if done alone, would support a civil action for damages or which would effect a public mischief or would

---

32 Central Criminal Court Jurisdiction; powers of arrest and search only where given by statute.

33 Apparently a conspiracy cannot exist between husband and wife; 1 Hawk ch 72, s 8 but this principle may not have survived the enactment of the Constitution: *The State (DPP) v Walsh and Conneely* [1981] IR 412 SC

34 Archbold (1922) 1416-28; Kenny (1922) 287-92.

35 Carusi (1990) 45 A Crim R 165 CA NSW.

36 *Blamires Transport Services Ltd* [1964] 1 QB 278; [1963] 3 All ER 170; [1963] 3 WLR 496, 47 Cr App R 272 CCA.

result in the perpetration of a fraud.[37] The criminal offence of conspiracy to corrupt public morals has been expressly recognised in this jurisdiction.[38] In *The People (A-G) v Keane*[39] Walsh J, for the Court of Criminal Appeal, indicated that charges of conspiracy ought not, in practice, to be allayed when a substantive offence can be proved.

Solicitation

It is an indictable misdemeanour at common law to solicit or incite another to commit a crime even though the solicitation or incitement has no effect.[40] The words or acts used in solicitation must go beyond the expression of a mere desire and constitute an effort to encourage or persuade another to perform a criminal offence.[41]

Jurisdiction

A conspiracy or incitement to commit the murder of a person outside the jurisdiction is within the section, whether the accused is a citizen of Ireland or not. Where a conspiracy takes place outside of Ireland to murder any person it is indictable in any place within the jurisdiction where an overt act is done in pursuance of it within the jurisdiction.[42]

Elements of the Offence

It is unnecessary under this section to prove any effect by the accused by his solicitation, encouragement or persuasion, on the person solicited. In *Most*[43] the accused published an article in a German language newspaper circulating in London approving the murder of the Emperor of Russia and commending it as an example to revolutionaries. The Court for Crown Cases Reserved upheld a direction to the jury that the crime was made out if it was proved that the accused intended to, and did, encourage any person to murder any other person and that such encouragement was the natural effect of the article. It was unnecessary that the encouragement be addressed to any person in particular.

The external element of the crime consists of some act which has the effect of soliciting, encouraging, persuading or endeavouring to persuade another person to commit a murder and the mental element is an intention so to do. The external element of the crime cannot be committed unless the person to be murdered is

---

37   No other aspect of Irish law is in more urgent need of reform. Generally see Smith & Hogan 256-87; Howard 271-86; Stuart 562-90. For a discussion on impossibility in the law of conspiracy see *Nock* [1978] AC 979; [1978] 2 All ER 654; [1978] 3 WLR 57, 67 Cr App R 116 HL.

38   *A-G (SPUC) v Open Door Counselling Ltd* [1988] IR 593 HC and SC; a discussion of conspiracy is reserved to volume 2.

39   (1975) 110 ILTR 1, 1 Frewen 392 CCA.

40   Archbold (1922) 1428; Kenny (1922) 79-80.

41   *The People (A-G) v Capaldi* (1949), 1 Frewen 95 CA. Further see Smith & Hogan 252-56; Stuart 590-92.

42   Russell 613.

43   (1881) 7 QBD 244, 14 Cox 583 CCR.

evidence in proving an intent then the rule to be applied is the same for any other fact in a criminal trial; a conviction is only possible if the circumstantial evidence points unavoidably to the guilt of the accused and is inconsistent with any other rational hypotheses based on the same set of facts and consistent with innocence.[72] Drawing a loaded revolver from a coat pocket and shouting at the victim during a subsequent struggle "you have got to die" amounts to an attempt.[73]

At common law it is not a criminal attempt to endeavour to do something which, if completed, would not be a criminal offence. Neither is it a criminal attempt to endeavour to do something which, if achieved, would not be a criminal offence. In this context it could not be a criminal attempt to stab a corpse. However, it is a valid attempt for the accused to endeavour to commit a crime by choosing a means which makes it impossible of commission. In this context were the accused to shoot a bullet from a high-powered rifle into a person's apartment and at an object he thought was his intended victim, but which turned out to be a stuffed bear, he would be guilty of the criminal offence of attempt.[74]

Administration

2.42 The concept of administration in ss 11 and 14 have been given an extended meaning.[75] The inclusion in the sections of the words "cause to be administered to or to be taken by any person" renders such distortion unnecessary.[76] It is submitted that these words cover any voluntary act or omission by the accused, done with the necessary intent to murder, leading to the victim taking the poison or other destructive thing.[77]

Scope

The meaning of the concepts of "wound" and "grievous bodily harm" are discussed in Chapter 6.[78] "Explosive substance" is not defined by the Act because it was previously defined by the Explosive Substances Act, 1851. This definition should be applied where it occurs throughout the Offences Against the Person Act, 1861.[79] S

---

72 See Taylor on Circumstantial Evidence (1920) 69-74. For a further discussion on intent see par 2.19 to par 2.37.

73 *Linneker* [1906] 2 KB 99; [1904-7] All ER 727, 21 Cox 186 CCR; see White, fn 65.

74 The law in criminal attempts is set out by the House of Lords in *Haughton v Smith* [1975] AC 476; [1973] 3 All ER 1109; [1974] 2 WLR 1, 58 Cr App R 198; [1974] Crim LR 305 HL. In *Britten v Alpogart* (1987) 11 Crim LJ 182, the Supreme Court of Victoria rejected *Haughton v Smith* as incorrect. The Court held that impossibility was never an answer to a charge of attempt unless it was the accused's intention to commit an imaginary crime. The accused was to be judged on the facts as he believed them to be. In *Kristo* (1989) 39 A Crim R 36 the Court of Criminal Appeal of South Australia followed *Haughton v Smith*.

75 *Harley* (1830) 4 C&P 369, 172 ER 744; *Michael* (1840) 9 C&P 356, 2 Mood 120 CCR. See further Archbold (1922) 909; Dale (1852) 6 Cox 14.

76 For further cases on the meaning of administration within s 58 and 59 see par 5.05.

77 For a discussion on the meaning of "poison" and "noxious" see par 7.15-7.16. The word "poison" was given an extended meaning on the facts in *Clauderoy* (1849) 4 Cox 84, 2 C&K 907, 175 ER 381 CCR. It is submitted that "destructive" is an ordinary word implying that the substance administered to or caused to be taken by the victim is injurious to health or mental wellbeing.

78 See par 6.20-6.28.

79 See ch 9.

12 is confined to explosives which destroy or damage buildings and thus does not extend to motor vehicles. Ships and boats of all kinds are covered by s 13 and since explosives often result in fires the circumstance of such occurrence are covered by s 13. S 14 was the subject of a number of inconsistent decisions with regard to the meaning to be ascribed to the clause dealing with an attempt to shoot[80] but these can be understood as failing to take proper account of s 19 which clarifies the main section.[81]

The words "drown, suffocate, or strangle any person" in s 14 are ordinary words which have not been the subject of any interpretation qualifying them. Where the victim meets with any harm covered by s 11 to 15 due to his own action caused by the accused frightening him or her into taking that action it is submitted that such harm is attributable to the accused under normal causation principles.[82]

It is clear from the complications inherent in ss 11 to 15 that they are urgently in need of reform. It is perhaps better to charge attempts to murder at common law. As a common law misdemeanour there is no limit on the penalty which a court may impose.[83] The question as to whether provocation reduces an intent to murder to an intent to commit manslaughter, under the sections, or at common law, is discussed in chapter 4.[84]

Suicide

2.43 It is a crime[85] at common law to kill oneself,[86] if the killing is done with the same mental element as would make the crime murder.[87] While the common law regarded suicide as self-murder and therefore a felony[88] the perpetrator was beyond the reach of the law. Custom established a gruesome superstitious practice in place of punishment. The deceased's remains were buried at a cross-roads with a stake driven through the body.[89] As a felon the deceased, through his estate, suffered forfeiture until the abolition of that penalty in 1870. Religious rites of burial were forbidden up to 1882.[90]

---

80   *Browne* (1883) 10 QBD 381 at 386, 15 Cox 199 at 204 CCR.

81   *Duckworth* [1892] 2 QB 83, 17 Cox 495 CCR. S 19 is quoted in fn 59. For further discussion on the inconsistent decision see *Archbold* (1966) par 2570.

82   *Halliday* (1889) 61 LT 701 [1886-90] All ER 1028 CCR. But see *Donovan* (1850) 4 Cox 401. For a discussion of this see par 2.15-2.17.

83   *The People (A-G) v Giles* [1974] IR 422, 110 ILTR 32.

84   See par 4.28.

85   Generally see Barry, "Suicide and the Law" (1965) 5 Melbourne LR 1; Williams, *The Sanctity of Life and the Criminal Law* (1968) ch 7; St John Stevas, *Life, Death and the Law* (1961) ch 6; Lanham, "Murder by Instigating Suicide" [1980] Crim LR 215; Criminal Law Revision Committee (UK)—Second Report—Suicide (1960 Cmnd 1187); Smith & Hogan 358-61; Howard 117-18.

86   4 Bl Com 118; Russell (1832) 1 Mood 356, 168 ER 1303 CCR; *Gaylor* (1857) D&B 288, 7 Cox 253, 169 ER 1011 CCR.

87   Stephen *Digest* (6th ed.) Article 248; *re Davis* [1968] 1 QB 72. The mental element in murder is discussed at par 2.18.

88   *Kenny* (1922) 122 and the authorities cited at fn 85.

89   Stephen *Hist.* III 104-7.

90   Stephen, fn 88.

The doctrine of transferred malice, when applied to this crime,[91] causes an accidental killing occasioned in the course of attempted suicide to be murder. Thus in *Hopwood*[92] the accused shot and killed a girl. His defence was that he was in the course of committing suicide when the victim had tried to stop him but was accidentally killed. The Court of Criminal Appeal regarded this defence as equivalent to an admission of murder.[93]

It is arguable that a person who accidentally kills another in the course of attempted suicide lacks the moral culpability ordinarily associated with murder, and is more appropriately to be convicted of manslaughter by criminal negligence.[94] S 30 of the Coroners Act, 1962 prevents a coroner's court making any finding of civil or criminal liability consequent on a death. Accordingly a verdict of death by suicide can no longer be returned at an inquest.[95]

Attempted suicide is a misdemeanour at common law.[96] It follows that since the common law regards suicide as self-murder that only an intention to kill, as opposed to an intention to cause serious injury, is sufficient to commit the crime.[97]

Participant

2.44 A person who participates as a secondary party[98] in a suicide, or attempted suicide, is treated as a principal offender for procedural purposes.[99] A person is guilty of participating in suicide, or attempted suicide, where he encourages another to commit, or attempt, suicide, or where he intentionally so assists.[1] It has been argued

91   S 4 of the Criminal Justice Act, 1964 provides: "Where a person kills another unlawfully the killing shall not be murder unless the accused person intended to kill, or cause serious injury to, some person whether the person actually killed or not".

92   (1913) 8 Cr App R 143 CCA. See further Kenny (1922) 114 and *Spence* (1957) 41 Cr App R 80; [1957] Crim LR 188 CCA.

93   See the facts of *The People (A-G) v Feehan* (1968) 1 Frewen 333, where the accused initially told the Gardaí that she had emptied poison into the victim's glass and later, at the trial, said that the victim had done this himself.

94   *The People (A-G) v Dwyer* [1972] IR 416, 108 ILTR 17 SC, further discussed 4.33-4.35.

95   *The State (McKeown) v Kelly* [1986] ILRM 133. Such verdicts were rare in any event; Kenny (1922) 113.

96   Kenny (1922) 114; *Burgess* (1862) L&C 258, 9 Cox 247, 169 ER 1387 CCR. This does not amount to the felony of attempting to commit murder as provided for by s 11-15 of the Offences Against the Person Act, 1861; *Mann* (1914) 2 KB 107.

97   *The People (DPP) v Douglas & Hayes* [1985] ILRM 25 CCA, further discussed at par 2.25.

98   See the analysis of the extent of liability of participants and the mental element required of secondary parties in *The People (DPP) v Egan* (1989) 3 Frewen 42. With particular reference to participation in suicide by culpable acquiescence see *Russell* [1933] VLR 59; [1933] ALR 76 SC. The law as to parties is briefly sketched in ch 1 and is more fully discussed in Volume 2.

99   Accessories and Abettors Act, 1861.

1   *A-G v Able* [1984] QB 795; [1984] 1 All ER 277; [1983] 3 WLR 845, 78 Cr App R 197; [1984] Crim LR 35. This case was decided under s 2 of the United Kingdom Suicide Act, 1961. The Act abolished suicide but retained secondary liability for aiding, abetting, counselling or procuring the suicide of another. The elements of the offence are set forth in the judgment of Woolf J: "Before an offence can be established to have been committed it must be proved (a) that the alleged offender had the necessary intent, that is, he intended the booklet to be used by someone contemplating suicide and intended that the person would be assisted by the booklet's contents, or otherwise encouraged to take or attempt to take his own life; (b) that while he still had that intention he distributed the booklet to such a person; and (c) in addition, if an offence under s 2 of the Act is to

that it should not be a criminal offence to assist another to take their own life,[2] in cases of incurable illness or severe suffering.[3] This view does not represent the current law.[4] Suicide attempted or committed whilst insane does not amount to a crime.[5]

Suicide-Pact Survivor

2.45 The survivor of a suicide pact is guilty of the murder of the party who dies. By his consent to kill himself in the presence of the deceased, he is regarded as encouraging him in suicide.[6] In *Abbott*[7] a husband and wife had taken poison. Shortly afterwards the accused, the husband, sought help from his landlady. They were both treated but the wife died. The husband told the police that due to unemployment and worry the poison had been procured for the purpose of suicide. The wife had given some to her husband and then taken the rest. Kennedy J instructed the jury in the Central Criminal Court:

> The law is quite clear. If two parties mutually agree to commit suicide, and only one accomplishes that object, the survivor is guilty of murder. Was there such an agreement here? If so there can be only one verdict. A person who administers poison to another with the intention of killing him is guilty of murder if that person dies, and if two persons agree that they will each take poison, each person is a principal and each is guilty. A case has been cited by the learned counsel for the prisoner which is said to warrant the statement that a consideration for such agreement must be proved, but I have no hesitation in saying that this is not the law of the land. The entering into the agreement to kill themselves was illegal. It is contrary to the law of the land to commit suicide, and if two persons meet together and agree to do so, and one of them dies, it is murder in the other. . . . If you think there was such an agreement it is your duty to find a verdict of wilful murder.[8]

The necessity to find encouragement in a pact for mutual suicide, or in supplying the means of suicide,[9] thereby making the accused liable as a secondary party, does

---

2   be proved, that such a person was assisted or encouraged by so reading the booklet to take or attempt to take his own life, otherwise the alleged offender cannot be guilty of more than attempt". QB at 812, All ER at 288, WLR at 858, Cr App R at 208.

2   See the judgment in *Able*, fn 1.

3   Most recently by Kennedy, *Euthanasia: The Good Death* (1990). At the time of writing Euthanasia is reported to be widespread in the Netherlands and the Dutch parliament is considering regulatory measures.

4   See further Williams, "TBCL" 578; Criminal Law Revision Committee Report on Offences Against the Person par 379.

5   4 Bl Com 190; Russell 560-1.

6   *Croft* [1944] 1 KB 295; [1944] 2 All ER 483, 29 Cr App R 169 CCA. See however Williams, *The Sanctity of Life and the Criminal Law*, 265. Further see Russell 146. In *Schneidass v Corrective Services Commission & Others* (1983) Crim LJ 353 the Supreme Court of New South Wales refused an injunction to stop the force-feeding of a dangerous prisoner on hunger strike on the grounds that to do so would amount to aiding and abetting his attempt to commit suicide. The Court did not hold that there was a common law power in a prison authority to force-feed a prisoner.

7   (1903) 67 JP 151 CCA.

8   At 151-53, quoting Field J in *Jessop* (1887) 16 Cox 204 at 206. See further *Dyson* (1823) R&R 523, 168 ER 930 CCR; *Allison* (1838) 8 C&P 418, 173 ER 366; *Stormonth* (1897) 61 JP 729.

9   *A-G v Able* [1984] QB 795; [1984] 1 All ER 277; [1983] 3 WLR 845, 78 Cr App R 197; [1984] Crim LR 35, quoted par 2.43.

not arise if the accused kills the other party. The accused is then guilty of murder on normal principles, subject only to an argument that the law does,[10] or should,[11] allow for the conviction of the lesser offence of manslaughter.

Reform

2.46 In the Suicide Act, 1992 the crime of suicide was abolished. A person who attempts suicide is guilty of no crime. By s 2 a person who aids, abets, counsels or procures the suicide of another, or an attempt by another to commit suicide, is liable to a penalty of 10 years' imprisonment. Consequently, where, for example, a chemist supplies a person with poison knowing it is to be used to commit suicide he is guilty of an offence under s 2. A suicide pact survivor is also guilty of an offence as encouraging the suicide of another. A person who assists another in suicide by killing them is guilty of murder. A suicide pact survivor who actually has killed the deceased, is also guilty of murder. An example of this latter situation would be where two people mutually agree to inject poison into the other, but only one dies. An offence under s 2 can be found as an alternative verdict to murder or manslaughter.

Draft Indictments

2.47 There follow the appropriate forms of indictment for the offences considered in this chapter:

MURDER

Statement of Offence
Murder contrary to s 4 of the Criminal Justice Act, 1964.
Particulars of Offence
AB on the   day of   at   murdered CD.

Statement of Offence
Murder contrary to s 2(1) of the Criminal Law (Jurisdiction) Act, 1976.
Particulars of Offence
AB on the   day of   at   Northern Ireland murdered CD.

Statement of Offence
Murder contrary to s 4 of the Criminal Justice Act, 1964, and s 3 of the Criminal Justice Act, 1990.
Particulars of Offence
AB on the   day of   at   murdered CD a member of the Garda Síochána acting in the course of his duty (or prison officer, etc.).

---

10   "The lack of moral culpability normally associated with murder" argument; Butler J in *The People (A-G) v Dwyer* [1972] IR 416 at 428, 108 ILTR 17 SC.
11   As in the United Kingdom Homicide Act, 1957, s 4. See further Smith & Hogan 360-1. If the accused is the survivor of a suicide pact who has not killed the other he is liable as a secondary party under s 2 of the Suicide Act, 1961.

ANCILLARY OFFENCES TO MURDER

Statement of Offence
Conspiracy to murder contrary to s 4 of the Offences Against the Person Act, 1861.
Particulars of Offence
AB and CD together with persons unknown between the   day of   and
the   day of   , within the State, conspired together to murder XY.

Statement of Offence
Proposing to murder contrary to s 4 of the Offences Against the Person Act, 1861.
Particulars of Offence
AB on the   day of   at   , proposed to CD that he should murder
another person, that is to say XY.

THREAT TO MURDER

Statement of Offence
Causing a letter to be received threatening to kill contrary to s 16 of the Offences
Against the Person Act, 1861.
Particulars of Offence
AB between the   day of   and the   day of   at
maliciously caused CD to receive (or sent, delivered or uttered) a letter (or writing)
threatening to kill (or murder) the said CD.

ATTEMPT

Statement of Offence
Attempted murder.
Particulars of Offence
AB on the   day of   at   attempted to murder CD.

ASSAULT WITH INTENT

Statement of Offence
Wounding with intent to murder contrary to s 11 of the Offences Against the Person
Act, 1861.
Particulars of Offence
AB on the   day of   at   wounded CD with intent to commit
murder.

Statement of Offence
Shooting with intent to murder contrary to s 14 of the Offences Against the Person
Act, 1861.
Particulars of Offence
AB on the   day of   at   shot at CD with intent to murder.

SUICIDE

Statement of Offence
Complicity in suicide contrary to s 2 of the Suicide Act, 1992.
Particulars of Offence
AB on the   day of   at   aided CD to kill himself.

CHAPTER THREE

Manslaughter

Introduction

3.01 S 5 of the Offences Against the Person Act, 1861 provides:

> Whosoever shall be convicted of manslaughter shall be liable, at the discretion of the
> Court, to be kept in penal servitude for life, or to pay such fine as the court shall award
> in addition to or without any such discretionary punishment as aforesaid.[1]

Manslaughter is a scheduled offence under the Criminal Law (Jurisdiction) Act,
1976. Where the offence is committed in Northern Ireland it therefore constitutes
an offence contrary to s 2 of that Act.

There are three categories of manslaughter. Manslaughter may be committed (1)
by an assault, (2) by criminal negligence and (3) by a criminal and dangerous act. It
is arguable that manslaughter may also be committed where the accused causes death
in the course of the commission of a violent felony. This work does not accept that
viewpoint.

Murder cannot be committed unless the accused intends to kill or cause serious
injury;[2] mere awareness by the accused that he is taking a risk of the victim being
killed or being caused serious injuries is insufficient.[3] Taking such a risk, outside
such circumstances as, for example, major construction works or surgery where it
is justifiable, is clearly wrong. It would be surprising if the law did not impose a
penalty where a life has been lost in circumstances where it is clear that someone is
morally culpable. Parallel with the need to stigmatise and punish such offenders is
the idea that the intentional taking of a life is an act of an especially culpable kind.

Experience indicates that a person may take another person's life intentionally
and yet not have acted in a sufficiently culpable way to require conviction for the
ultimate crime of murder and the consequent punishment of incarceration for life.
Sometimes no stigma attaches as, for example, where the accused executes the victim
in sentence of law, or where the victim attempts to kill or seriously injure the accused
and is killed in necessary self-defence.

Circumstances of intermediate culpability do not require a murder conviction.
These have been identified where death occurs due to the victim by words or
conduct severely provoking the accused, causing momentary loss of self-control, or
where the accused, under attack by the victim, mistakenly supposing the attack to

---

1   The sections are quoted, as are all other sections from the Offences Against the Person Act, 1861,
    in accordance with the amendments introduced by the Penal Servitude Acts of 1864 and 1891 and
    by the Statute Law Revision Act, 1908.

2   Criminal Justice Act, 1965, s 4. Manslaughter is a scheduled offence under the Criminal Law
    (Jurisdiction) Act, 1976 which means that the offence committed in Northern Ireland will be an
    offence contrary to s 2 of that Act. A precedent indictment is to be found at the end of the chapter.

3   See par 2.19.

be extremely serious, retaliates appropriately to his judgment killing the victim. Finally the stringency of the test for murder leaves the prosecution, in many instances, unable to prove beyond reasonable doubt, an intention to kill or cause serious injury. In those circumstances it may nonetheless be clear that the accused was culpable in a high degree. The reports abound with cases where the accused attacks the victim with deadly force, but because of the absence of witnesses, the State can go no further than to prove a death and must rely on the accused's own statement admitting the killing but claiming an intent merely to frighten or postulating that he was acting in self-defence. So, for example, in *The People (A-G) v Mohangi*,[4] the accused killed the victim after a confession of infidelity. He destroyed the body in such a way that a medical opinion as to how death was caused was impossible. The accused recounted in a statement "I got hold of her and put my hands around her neck and before I knew anything it was the end". The accused was initially convicted of murder and on a retrial, ordered by the Court of Criminal Appeal, was found guilty of manslaughter.

The disparate nature of the incidents in which a killing occurs in circumstances where the killer is morally culpable could usefully be dealt with, as in some American states, by a graded solution to homicide. In this jurisdiction the answer is to divide the crime of homicide into murder and manslaughter. Manslaughter is the lesser offence. It carries a purpose apparently independent of rational definition. This is well expressed by Stuart:[5]

> Two separate purposes of the crime of manslaughter emerge. . . . One is to maintain a niche for murder under extenuating circumstances, while the other is to have an independent offence of killing where the state of mind is culpable, but less so than for murder.

Core Elements

3.02 It can be misleading to speak of a state of mind for manslaughter.[6] The elements of manslaughter do not require that the accused foresee the victim's death. No one can be convicted of a true crime unless they intend to do the act which constitutes the crime.[7] In the instances of provocation and excessive self-defence the accused may have contemplated that his action would lead to death or serious injury. Both of these defences cause a charge of murder to be reduced to manslaughter. Where the accused kills the victim by an assault he need only intend to hurt or annoy in order to render himself liable for manslaughter, if he intended serious injury the crime would be murder.

In the case of manslaughter by criminal negligence and manslaughter by a criminal and dangerous act, it is not required that the accused do any more than intend to do the act or acts leading to death. He need not contemplate death or serious injury but, as we shall see, the test in both cases, embraces a set of situations where it would

4   (1964) 1 Frewen 297.

5   213.

6   See the discussion by Radzinowicz & Turner, "The Mental Element in Crimes at Common Law" in MACL 195.

7   The special rules relating to intoxication, insanity, and automatism are considered in Vol 2 and briefly in this volume in ch 4.

be extremely unlikely that an ordinary person would not have foreseen that the victim would be subjected to the risk of some injury. The tendency, in recent years, is for the courts to modify these tests further in order to mitigate the rigour of the crime of manslaughter in circumstances where the accused need have had no inkling that he might, by acting as he did, cause harm to the victim. Even so the courts in England,[8] Australia,[9] Canada[10] and Ireland[11] have accepted constructive liability in the crime of manslaughter. The question of the extent of mental culpability in the crime of manslaughter was put thus by Lord Salmon:

> . . . In manslaughter there must always be a guilty mind. This is true of every crime except those of absolute liability. The guilty mind usually depends on the intention of the accused. Some crimes require what is called a specific intention, for example, murder, which is killing with intent to inflict grievous bodily harm. Other crimes need only what is called a basic intention, which is an intention to do the acts which constitute the crime. Manslaughter is such a crime.[12]

As manslaughter is not a crime of intent it is clearly not possible to attempt it.

Many instances of unlawful killing will give rise to an overlap between the various internal categories of the crime of manslaughter. For instance, in the Australian case of *Pemble*[13] the accused and the victim, who were boyfriend and girlfriend, had just broken off a relationship. The victim was sitting on a car outside a hotel when the accused approached carrying a sawn off point 22 rifle. The prosecution were in a position to prove that the rifle went off, the bullet entering the back of the victim's head, killing her. The accused was convicted of murder and appealed to the High Court of Australia. Two of the five judges were in favour of ordering a retrial but the remaining three ordered that a manslaughter verdict be substituted. Barwick CJ analysed the facts on the basis that the accused had committed a dangerous act which amounted to an attempted assault. McTiernan J proceeded on the basis that it was an unlawful and dangerous act to discharge a firearm in a public place. Windeyer J found that the facts were such as to prove gross negligence against the accused.

Some cases of death which cannot be analysed on the basis of one category of manslaughter can easily fit under another. For instance, in *Lamb*[14] the accused and the victim were engaged in play acting with a firearm. The victim knew that the accused intended him no harm, and as he was labouring under the same mistake as the accused, he expected none. Both thought that the hammer on a revolver fell on the bullet in the chamber on which it rests (which in this instance was empty). In fact it struck the next one; when the trigger was pulled the chamber rotated. This next chamber contained a bullet. The case was argued before the jury as one of manslaughter by an assault. No assault was committed as the victim did not apprehend any harm.[15] The accused's conviction was overturned by the Court of

---

8   *Newbury & Jones* [1977] AC 500; [1976] 2 All ER 365; [1976] 2 WLR 918, 62 Cr App R 291 HL.
9   *Holzer* [1968] VR 481 SC.
10   Under s 205 of the Code. See Stuart 209-16.
11   *The People (A-G) v Crosbie & Meehan* [1966] IR 490 CCA.
12   *Newbury & Jones* [1977] AC at 509; [1976] All ER at 369; [1976] WLR at 923, Cr App R at 298.
13   (1971) 124 CLR 107 HC.
14   [1967] 2 QB 981; [1967] 2 All ER 1282; [1967] 3 WLR 888, 51 Cr App R 417 CA.
15   See par 6.03-6.09.

Appeal which commented that the case could have been presented to the jury on the basis that the accused's mistake on the operation of the revolver was due to his own criminal negligence.

Alternative Verdict

3.03 At common law a verdict of one felony cannot be returned on a count charging another.[16] The crimes of murder and manslaughter were originally the single crime of homicide[17] which has led to a distinction from this principle. Notwithstanding that murder and manslaughter are both felonies, where murder is charged, the jury may return a verdict of manslaughter. The penalty for murder is mandatory penal servitude for life.[18] The maximum penalty for manslaughter is penal servitude for life.[19]

It is generally accepted that, at common law, a jury have an unfettered discretion to find the accused not guilty or to return a verdict on a lesser included offence. This power cannot be exercised by a jury who are in ignorance of it. The only statement in Irish law as to whether the jury must be informed of their power leans against that proposition. In *The State v McMullen*[20] the accused committed a robbery. The Civic Guards were called and one member pursued the accused who shot at and killed him. The trial judge refused to leave manslaughter to the jury on the ground that the killing of an officer apprehending a felon was constructive murder.[21] At the first trial the jury returned twice to ask if they could return a verdict of guilty of manslaughter and were told by the trial judge that they could not. Following the disagreement of that jury, at a later trial the accused was convicted. His appeal to the Court of Criminal Appeal was argued on the ground that the alternative verdict should have been left to the jury. This argument was dismissed by the Court:

> There is abundant authority . . . that where no defence of manslaughter appears on a murder case as it stands before the Court, the judge is entitled, even bound, to withdraw manslaughter from the jury and direct that their verdict must be guilty or not guilty of murder . . . Nevertheless we are asked to say that even where the judge has directed the jury, as is his province to do, that in law manslaughter is not open, and that they must find murder or acquit, still he must go on and tell them that though bound by their oaths to act according with his direction, they are entitled to ignore his direction and the law, and if they so wish, to bring in a verdict of manslaughter and require him to record it. We express no opinion as to the effect of a jury so acting, but it is abundantly clear that the Judge must, in a proper case, as this is, direct the jury that they cannot find manslaughter. . . .[22]

This ruling was given at a time when murder could be committed by reckless conduct and by the commission of a felony. Since the Criminal Justice Act, 1964

---

16   See generally Ryan & Magee 365-71.
17   Kaye, "The Early History of Murder and Manslaughter" (1967) 83 LQR, 365-95, 569-601. See also Dixon, "The Development of the Law of Homicide" (1935) 9 ALJ (Supplement) 64.
18   Criminal Justice Act, 1964, s 5.
19   Penal Servitude Act, 1891, s 1(2).
20   [1925] 2 IR 9 CCA.
21   This has been abolished by s 4 of the Criminal Justice Act, 1964. See par 3.36-3.37.
22   At 28.

murder can only occur where the accused acts purposively. Whether the accused acted with intent or was merely reckless or thoughtless, constitutes the difference between murder and manslaughter in the majority of trials. The test for murder is an exacting one.[23] The felony-murder rule applied with a rigidity which is no longer possible; the law now requires a subjective intent to kill or cause serious injury.[24] Where evidence exists, on the prosecution or defence cases, which would establish a defence, the onus is on the prosecution to disprove that evidence.[25] There is no reason, in principle, why such a rule should not apply to the question of intent and the existence of defences special to manslaughter. With the abolition of constructive murder the idea of a certain verdict on a murder charge in particular circumstances has been removed from this branch of the law. It is always within the province of the jury to consider whether or not the accused acted with the requisite intent.

Nonetheless, circumstances can arise where no issue capable of raising a defence amounting to manslaughter can occur. The accused may deny involvement in the crime and the victim may have died in the clearest circumstances raising the presumption that the accused, whoever he was, intended to kill or cause serious injury.[26] If there is no rebuttal of that presumption there is no issue to go to the jury which might reduce their verdict to manslaughter.[27] The sole issue would be whether the accused should be convicted of murder or acquitted. The trial judge can, in a proper case, direct that the only possible verdicts are murder or an acquittal[28] provided that view is legally correct.[29]

Where there is evidence to support a defence it is clearly part of the duty of the trial judge to put the defence case to the jury and instruct them as to its elements in law.[30] But if a defence issue is not raised, and there is no evidence to reasonably support a manslaughter verdict the trial judge need not put a non-existent defence to the jury. The Australian High Court has held that if, in these circumstances, the jury ask for a direction on manslaughter they must be informed of the alternative verdict but that the trial judge may add an expression of his own opinion that on no view of the evidence, which the jury might reasonably take, can such a verdict be returned.[31] Where the issue giving rise to the possibility of a manslaughter verdict is not raised by cross-examination or by evidence but is merely put to the jury in a

23 See ch 2.

24 For further discussion see par 3.34.

25 *The People (A-G) v Quinn* [1965] IR 366 CCA.

26 *Fazal* (1990) 91 Cr App R 256.

27 *Porritt* [1961] 3 All ER 463; [1961] 1 WLR 1372, 45 Cr App R 348 CCA; *Walker* [1974] 1 WLR 1090 at 1094; [1974] Crim LR 368 PC.

28 *Hamilton* [1961] Crim LR 405 CCA; *Ma Wai Fun* [1962] HKLR 61 CA.

29 *Kwaku Menshah* [1946] AC 83 PC; *Sharmpal Singh* [1962] AC 188; [1962] 2 WLR 238 PC; *Rumping* [1964] AC 814; [1962] 3 All ER 256; [1962] 3 WLR 763, 46 Cr App R 398 HL; *Penderson* (1979) 11 CR (3d) 20 Alta CA.

30 *The People (A-G) v Quinn*, fn 25; *Ward* (1989) 42 A Crim R 56 CCA NSW holding that defences must be put to the jury when available on the evidence and that this principle holds even though the defence do not wish a particular defence to be put provided that putting such a defence is necessary to ensure a fair trial.

31 *Beavan* (1954) 92 CLR 660 HC; *Mullins* (1961) 78 WN (NSW) 115 SC; *Holden* [1974] 2 NSWLR 548 CCA; *Gammage* (1969) 122 CLR 444 at 451 HC.

closing submission by counsel a similar situation applies; the judge may express his view on the matter but must not remove from the jury the power to find the alternative verdict of manslaughter.[32]

In *Tajber*[33] the accused believed that the victim had, prior to their marriage, raped his wife. He detained him at gunpoint with the intention of assaulting him but, when he tried to escape, shot him three times, the last time while he was on the ground, killing him. After a complex trial the jury asked the trial judge whether a verdict of manslaughter was open. They were told by the trial judge that they had a right to return this verdict. He did not make any further comment as to the propriety of such a verdict in the circumstances. This course was criticised by the Federal Court of Australia, Gallop J commenting:

> The trial judge may decline to accept the jury's verdict and ask them to reconsider it in the light of the conduct of the trial, his charge to the jury and any further direction he thinks it desirable to give. Such a course is appropriate where the circumstances of the case are such that the accused person should be found guilty of murder or should be acquitted and yet the jury improperly return a verdict of manslaughter where there is in fact no material on which such a verdict may properly be returned. But if, on reconsideration, they refuse to alter it their verdict of not guilty of murder but guilty of manslaughter must be accepted. . . . The trial judge should have directed the jury that, if they found all the elements of murder established, they had the power to return a verdict of manslaughter, but that they would fail in their duty or be false to their oaths were they to return such a verdict despite their findings and merely upon merciful or compassionate grounds.[34]

The accused may "go for broke" and insist on either a murder verdict or an acquittal. In such circumstances, where evidence exists which would justify a possible verdict of manslaughter, the trial judge should draw the attention of the jury to the relevant evidence and direct them accordingly.[35]

In summary the trial judge must instruct the jury that they may return a manslaughter verdict as an alternative to murder, where the evidence supports such a possible verdict or where the issue is raised by counsel. This duty does not prevent the judge expressing an accurate view to the effect that a manslaughter verdict cannot reasonably be returned. Where the evidence discloses no defence amounting to a reduction of a murder charge to manslaughter the judge need not instruct the jury as to the alternative verdict.[36] The ultimate test is whether the failure to inform the

---

32 *Gammage*, fn 31; *Anderson* [1965] NZLR 26 CA. See further Howard 75-76.

33 (1986) 23 A Crim R 189 FC.

34 At 199-200. Further see Neaves J at 205-6 and Spender J at 209.

35 *Parker* (1964) 111 CLR 665 at 681; [1963] Crim LR 569 HC; *Howe* (1980) 32 ALR 478 HC. Generally see *Fairbanks* [1986] 1 WLR 1202, 83 Cr App R 251 CA.

36 In *Fazal* (1990) 91 Cr App R 256 the Privy Council commented that it was right not to leave the alternative verdict to a jury where it was a wholly unnecessary and unrealistic confusion to a clear cut decision. The issue in that case was as to the complicity of the accused. The wounds to the victim were incapable of being inflicted accidentally. See also *Kearney* (1989) 88 Cr App R 380; [1988] Crim LR 580 CA. In *Wardrobe* (1987) 29 A Crim R 198 the Court of Criminal Appeal of Victoria commented that an issue should only be left to the jury if it is capable of being given effect to by a process which can fairly be described as reasoning. In *Lei & Wong* (1982) 25 A Crim R 32 the New South Wales Court of Criminal Appeal held that an issue as to manslaughter should have been left to the jury where the accused stated that he used a knife to strike out at the accused.

jury as to the alternative verdict of manslaughter renders the murder verdict unsafe.[37] The proper approach[38] is for the jury to consider the murder count first. If they acquit they may then go on to consider manslaughter.[39]

A corporation may be guilty of manslaughter.[40] A person attacking an obviously pregnant woman, with intent to harm her, is guilty of manslaughter, at least, if the child, being subsequently born alive, dies from injuries or disease caused by the attack.[41]

Assault Manslaughter

3.04 It is manslaughter for the accused to kill the victim by an assault where the accused intends to hurt or cause the victim more than trivial harm.

Of all the species of constructive manslaughter, assault manslaughter appears to be the one most often prosecuted.[42] If the accused intends to cause serious injury by his assault, murder will be committed if death results.[43] If would seem that, at the other end of the scale, all but the most trivial assaults, coming within the *de minimis* rule, will, if they cause death, be manslaughter.[44] In 1922 Kenny wrote:

37   *Elliott & Hitchins* (1983) 9 A Crim R 238 at 262/3 CCA NSW; *Chong & Toh* (1989) 40 A Crim R 22 Fed Ct.

38   In Australia the Appeal Court will set aside a verdict of a jury where it would be unsafe, or dangerous, to allow the verdict to stand, even though there is sufficient evidence to support the verdict as a matter of law. *Chamberlain (No. 2)* (1984) 153 CLR 521 HC; *Morris* (1987) 163 CLR 454 HC. For the Irish view see *The People (DPP) v Egan*, Supreme Court, unreported, 1990. Judges should not make rulings of fact where there is material on which a jury can decide an issue either way; *Stewart* (1988) 36 A Crim R 13 CCA Queensland.

39   *Saunders* [1988] AC 148; [1987] 2 All ER 973; [1987] 3 WLR 355, 85 Cr App R 334; [1987] Crim LR 781 HL.

40   *S&Y Investments v Commerical Union of Australia* (1986) 21 A Crim R 204 S Ct N Territory; *R v Coroner for East Kent, ex parte Spoon & Others* (1989) 88 Cr App R 10 DC. See Field & Jorg, "Corporate Liability and Manslaughter: Should we be going Dutch?" [1991] Crim LR 156.

41   *Prince* (1988) 44 CCC (3d) 510 Manitoba CA. The child must however be born alive; *Sullivan* (1988) 43 CCC (3d) 65 BC CA.

42   For examples of this type of manslaughter see the facts of *The People (A-G) v Quinn* [1965] IR 366 CCA; *The People (A-G) v Keatley* [1954] IR 12 at 15 CCA, Maguire CJ: ". . . it is clear that the applicant had no intention of killing the deceased. . . . The death was, accordingly, unintended both in fact and in law, and criminal responsibility only arises if it was caused by an unlawful act. The blow struck by the applicant was, at least, a contributing cause of death, and a conviction for manslaughter could be sustainable if that blow was unlawful". Willis in "Manslaughter by the Intentional Infliction of Some Harm: A Category that should be Closed" (1985) 9 Crim LJ 109 disputes the validity of assault manslaughter and the view in Howard 99 that it is straightforward and causes no difficulty.

43   Criminal Justice Act, 1964, s 4. See par 2.34-2.36.

44   Stephen in his *Digest* 182-83 (6th ed., 1904) gives the following illustrations of assault manslaughter: "(1) A knowing that B is suffering disease of the heart, and intending to kill B, gives B a slight push, and thereby kills B. A commits murder. (2) A in the last illustration pushes B unlawfully, but without knowledge of his state of health or intention to kill him or to do him grievous bodily harm. A commits manslaughter. If A laid his hand gently on B to attract his attention, and by so doing startled and killed him, A's act would be no offence at all. (3) A finding B asleep on straw lights the straw meaning to do B serious injury but not to kill him, B is burned to death. A commits murder. (4) A waylays B, intending to beat, but not intending to kill him or do him grievous bodily harm. A beats B and does kill him, this is manslaughter at least and may be murder if the beating were so violent

Where some trivial blow is struck, with the intention of producing mere momentary pain, and death unexpectedly results from it, then, if it is an unlawful blow, the striker will be guilty of manslaughter.[45]

In 1922 it was doubtful if the assault manslaughter rule had any independent existence from manslaughter committed by an unlawful act.[46] The majority of reported instances of manslaughter by an unlawful act were committed through an assault[47] but no statement of principle is discernible.[48]

Current Test

A modern example comes from the Supreme Court of Victoria. In *Holzer*[49] a companion of the accused picked a fight with a companion of the victim on the street. The accused thereupon punched the victim in the mouth, cutting the inside of his lip, causing him to fall and to strike his head on the road. He later died. The accused was asked in evidence as to what he was hoping to effect by the punch and said "I didn't hope to cause him any real serious harm but when I threw the punch at him I hit him in the mouth and it would have cut his lip or bruised his lip or something", and also stated "In my opinion it would just cut his lip to tell him to wake himself up". The case was argued before Smith J and a jury on the basis of assault manslaughter and criminal and dangerous act manslaughter. After reviewing the authorities the judge gave his view of assault manslaughter:

> Under the first of these doctrines the law, as I see it, is that a person is guilty of manslaughter if he commits the offence or if he commits the offence of battery on the deceased and death results directly from that offence and the beating or other application of force was done with the intention of inflicting on the deceased some physical harm not merely of a trivial or negligible character, or, it would seem with the intention of inflicting pain, without more injury or harm to the body than is involved in the infliction of pain which is not merely trivial or negligible.[50]

as to be likely, according to common knowledge, to cause death. (5) A strikes at B with a small stick, not intending either to kill or to do him grievous bodily harm. That blow kills B. A commits manslaughter". (footnotes omitted). Further see East 256: "He who voluntarily, knowingly and unlawfully intends hurt to the person of another, though he intended not death, yet if death ensue, is guilty of murder or manslaughter according to the circumstances". Stephen in his *History* III p 22 puts the matter thus: "It is manslaughter if the intention is to inflict bodily harm, not grievous . . .".

45   (1922) 115.

46   Archbold (1922) 879: "All struggles in anger whether by fighting, wrestling or in any other mode, are unlawful, and death occasioned by them is manslaughter at the least. *Canniff* (1840) 9 C&P 359." [173] ER 868.

47   See par 3.24.

48   The principle clearly emerges from the cases however. The textbook writers are in agreement: Smith & Hogan 350; Howard 99. The analysis in Russell 588-98 is made with a view to showing the necessity for a conscious mental element.

49   [1968] VR 481 SC.

50   At 482. See also the decision of the Australian High Court in *Mamote Kulang* (1964) 37 ALJR 416 where Windeyer J commented: ". . . at common law a man is guilty of manslaughter if he kills another by an unlawful blow, intended to hurt, although not intended to be fatal or to cause grievous bodily harm". Further see *Ryan* [1966] VR 553 SC; *Ward* [1972] WAR 36 CCA. In Canada under s 205 of the Code where death is caused by an unlawful act it is manslaughter; *Smithers* (1978) 40 CRNS 79 Sup Ct.

There seems no reason in principle why the doctrine should be confined to a battery. A psychic[51] assault is sufficient. So in *Conner*[52] the accused threw a piece of iron at a child with the object of frightening it but she struck and killed another of her children. In that case the transferred malice could only have been of a physical assault. In *Hayward*[53] the accused chased his wife threatening her. She died as a result of exhaustion and shock which caused an aggravation of her abnormal heart condition. The direction to the jury was that no violence need be visited upon the victim but that death caused by fright alone as a result of an illegal act sufficed for manslaughter. An assault can also be committed by recklessness.[54]

There appears to be no reported case expressly approving reckless assault as a basis for assault manslaughter. In that instance the assault would be unintentional and more appropriately dealt with under the heading of criminal and dangerous act manslaughter, or manslaughter by criminal negligence.

Criminal Negligence

3.05 It is manslaughter for the accused to kill the victim by an act or omission amounting to criminal negligence.[55] Criminal negligence is conceptually the same as negligence in the law of tort though it is more serious in nature.[56]

Nature

Manslaughter is alone among serious crimes capable of being committed by inadvertence. As such gross negligence manslaughter has been criticised[57] as imposing the stigma of criminality and consequent punishment upon a person who did not intend to kill and who was not even reckless[58] as to causing injury.[59] The kernel of the argument against imposing criminal liability based on negligence is that

---

51   See par 6.03-6.09.

52   (1835) 7 C&P 438, 173 ER 194.

53   (1908) 21 Cox 692. In *Towers* (1874) 12 Cox 530 the accused assaulted a girl who was nursing a baby which, on the girl screaming in fright, had convulsions and died. Williams instances this as an example of manslaughter by negligence; *TBCL* 2 (1st ed.) 238. See further *Curley* (1909) 2 Cr App R 109 CCA and Elliott, "Frightening a Person into Killing Himself [1974] Crim LR 15.

54   *K (a minor)* [1990] 1 All ER 331; (1990) 91 Cr App R 23 DC.

55   Gamble, "Manslaughter by Neglect (1977) 1 Crim LJ 247; 31 Aus LJ 630; O'Hearn, "Criminal Negligence: An Analysis in Depth" (1964) 7 CLQ 27; Colvin, "Recklessness & Criminal Negligence" (1982) 32 UTLJ 345; Williams *TBCL* 90; Radzinowicz & Turner, "The Mental Element of Crimes at Common Law" in MACL 195 reviewed at (1980) 58 Can Bar Rev 660; Fletcher, "The Theory of Criminal Negligence: A Comparative Analysis" (1971) 119 U Pa L Rev 401; Fruchtman, "Recklessness & The Limits of Mens Rea" (1958) 1987) 29 CLQ 315; Snelling, "Manslaughter by Negligent Act or Omission" MNAD (1958) 1 Aus LJ 630; Synota, "Mens Rea in Gross Negligence Manslaughter" [1983] Crim LR 7761; Briggs, "In Defence of Manslaughter" [1983] Crim LR 764.

56   For the entirely different standard adopted in New Zealand see *Yogasakaran* [1990] 1 NZLR 399; (1990) 14 Crim LJ 200 CA.

57   For example Williams, *TBCL*, ch 12.

58   The word is used in this work as meaning the unjustifiable taking of a serious foreseen risk; see par 2.36-2.37.

59   Particularly see Turner in MACL 195; Russell 588-98; Penal Methods Refom Committee of South Australia—Fourth Report (1980) par 18.

it involves the punishment of a negative state of mind; that is punishing the accused for what he failed to think of. Despite the requirement that the negligence which must be proved against the accused amounted to a much worse form of carelessness that in civil law, it is objected that as negligence is a negative state of mind such a test is meaningless; degrees of what is absent cannot exist.

The courts have, however, made it clear that liability for death based on carelessness will only be imposed in circumstances where the accused can fairly be said to have been morally culpable. It is submitted that the State punishes people for negligence because it is a state of mind. It involves a failure to take proper precautions for a task or failing to prevent a result through not exercising proper care. That may include neglecting to pay heed while doing something, or failing to prepare adequately for an undertaking, or failing to act in all the circumstances where a duty to act is clearly imposed. In any of these cases blame attaches to the accused because he either has not applied his mind to the task or has not taken such ordinary care as any responsible person would have felt compelled to take in the circumstances. The accused is held accountable because by the application of concentration the death of the victim could have been avoided.

Those who engage in hazardous tasks must take care. Those whose duties involve the care of the dependent are morally under an obligation to take reasonable steps to ensure the health of their charges. If in either case failure to take heed could be the cause of a serious injury a compelling reason exists that persons with this responsibility should apply themselves to their task. Where they fail to do so, in clear derogation of their responsibilities, they commit a wrong. It is arguable that this is merely the absence of care and is thus a neutral, or negative, state of mind. It is submitted that this is not so. In these circumstances the accused would have been placed in, or will himself have undertaken to be in, a situation where the exercise of attention was of considerable importance to others. To fail to use one's mind in these circumstances is, in itself, a state of mind, albeit one capable of being regarded as mere inattention. If that state of mind is morally blameworthy to a high degree it can properly be treated as criminal negligence.[60]

History

3.06 At common law the defence of killing by misadventure was early on limited by a requirement that the misfortune should not have been caused by the wanton or reckless conduct of the accused.[61] By the foundation of the State in 1922 it had become settled that the civil test of negligence was inappropriate for imposing criminal liability as manslaughter. Kenny characterised the degree of negligence required to found liability for manslaughter as "wicked negligence".[62] Archbold stated:

---

60 Those supporting such a view include Hart, "Negligence, Mens Rea and Criminal Responsibility" (in *Punishment and Responsibility,* 1968) and Pickard, "Culpable Mistakes and Rape: Relating Mens Rea to the Crime" (1980) University Toronto LJ 75.

61 Kaye, "The Early History of Murder and Manslaughter" (1967) 83 LQR at 593, who traces this rule to Brooke in the 17th c.

62 Kenny (1922) 122.

Where death results in consequence of a negligent act, it would seem that to create criminal responsibility the degree of negligence must be so gross as to amount to recklessness. Mere inadvertence, while it might create civil liability, would not suffice to create criminal liability.[63]

Manslaughter would not have been committed had the death not been capable of being avoided by full diligence.[64]

The balance of the authorities were in favour of an objective test of gross negligence; it was not necessary to prove that the accused was aware of the grave risk he was creating though his acts or omissions.

Development

3.07 It was no simple task to explain to a jury that carelessness in the context of gross negligence manslaughter required a higher degree of fault than in a civil case but did not require the prosecution to prove that the accused was aware of the risk he was creating. In 1925 the Court of Criminal Appeal in *Bateman*[65] attempted an elucidation of the jury charge:

> In explaining to juries the test which they should apply to determine whether the negligence, in the particular case, amounted to or did not amount to a crime, judges have used many epithets such as "culpable", "criminal", "gross", "wicked", "clear", "complete". But whatever epithet be used, and whether an epithet be used or not, in order to establish criminal liability the facts must be such that, in the opinion of the jury, the negligence of an accused went beyond a mere matter of compensation between subjects and showed such disregard for the life and safety of others as to amount to a crime against the State and conduct deserving of punishment.[66]

This test is unclear as to degree and imprecise as to definition. Criminal rules stated by reference to epithets designed to allow a jury convict on the basis that a case is a bad one tend to invite the exercise of prejudice. Williams instances[67] the case of *Pike*.[68] The accused was in the habit of consensually administering an anaesthetic to women in order to have sexual intercourse with them in that state. One died and Pike was convicted of manslaughter. If the factor of perverse sexuality

---

63   Archbold (1922) 890. For example in *Markuss* (1864) 4 F&F 356, 176 ER 598, Willes J is reported as stating ". . . every person who dealt with the health of others was dealing with their lives; and every person who so dealt was bound to use reasonable care and not to be grossly negligent. . . . It was not, however, every slip that a man might make that rendered him liable to a criminal investigation. It must be a substantial thing". In *Gylee* (1908) 1 Cr App R 242 it was held that honest negligence was sufficient for manslaughter if it was sufficiently gross.

64   *Dalloway* (1847) 3 Cox 273. Whether the death was required to have been a direct and immediate result of the accused personal neglect or default; *Pocock* (1851) 17 QB 34, 5 Cox 172, 117 ER 1194. The classic example of the application of these two principles at that time was of the man who lets a rock fall from a building onto the street below: if it was done in a quiet town in a place where no one was likely to pass it would be an accident, if done in a populous town, manslaughter, and if done without warning to the person beneath at a time when it was likely that persons would be passing, murder: Fost 262; 1 Hale 472, 475; 3 Co Inst 57; Archbold (1922) 890; Kenny (1922) 123; Stephen *History* III at 64.

65   [1925] All ER 45, 28 Cox 33, 19 Cr App R 8 CCA.

66   All ER at 48, Cox at 36, Cr App R at 11-12.

67   *TBCL* at 588.

68   [1961] Crim LR 114, 574.

had been removed from the case and the anaesthetic was administered as an amusement between friends the case would take on an entirely different complexion. Neither judges nor juries can be trusted with reflex to facts; legal rules, particularly in so emotive an area as criminal law, should be stated with precision.

The existing situation was little helped by the House of Lords decision in *Andrews*.[69] Lord Atkin, delivering the leading opinion, approved *Bateman* and continued:

> Simple lack of care such as will constitute civil liability is not enough: for purposes of the criminal law there are degrees of negligence: and a very high degree of negligence is required to be proved before the felony is established. Probably of all the epithets that can be applied "reckless" most nearly covers the case. It is difficult to visualise a case caused by reckless driving in the connotation of that term in ordinary speech which would not justify a conviction for manslaughter: but it is probably not all embracing, for "reckless" suggests an indifference to risk, whereas the accused may have appreciated the risk and intended to avoid it but shown a high degree of negligence in the means adopted to avoid the risk as would justify a conviction.[70]

In this context a clearer statement of the law was needed.

The Irish Test

3.08 The test applied in Irish law can be clearly stated. In *The State (A-G) v Dunleavy*[71] manslaughter was charged on the basis that the accused, a taxi driver, had killed the victim, a cyclist, by driving into him on a main road over 40 feet wide in an unlit car and whilst the victim was only seven feet from his own kerb side. It was clear that the accused had driven on the wrong side of the road. The jury were instructed by means of a paraphrase of Bateman's case in terms requiring that ". . . the negligence of the accused went beyond a mere matter of compensation between subjects and showed such a disregard for the lives and safety of others as to amount to a crime against the State and conduct deserving punishment . . .". The Court of Criminal Appeal held such a direction in cases of criminal negligence manslaughter to be inadequate. It lacked an elucidation of the differing degrees of negligence and failed to explain the nature of the negligence which had to be proved against the accused. The Court disapproved the use of the word "reckless" as sufficient, by itself, to explain the test for criminal negligence manslaughter; "reckless" could mean a subjective state of the accused taking a substantial and unjustifiable risk of death, or it could mean the heedless taking of such, or any, risk. Gavin Duffy J, for the Court, held that:

> . . . a more satisfactory way of indicating to a jury the high degree of negligence necessary to justify a conviction for manslaughter, is to relate it to the risk or likelihood of substantial personal injury resulting from it, rather than to attach any qualification to the word "negligence" or to the driver's disregard for the life or safety of others. . . . If the negligence proved is of a very high degree and of such a character that any reasonable driver, endowed with ordinary road sense, and in full possession of his

---

69   [1937] AC 576; [1937] 2 All ER 552, 26 Cr App R 34, 30 Cox 576 HL.
70   AC at 583, All ER at 556, Cox at 583, Cr App R at 47. See also *Bonnyman* (1942) 28 Cr App R 131 CCA.
71   [1948] IR 95 CCA.

faculties, would realise, if he thought at all, that by driving in the manner which occasioned the fatality he was, without lawful excuse, incurring, in a high degree, the risk of causing substantial personal injury to others, the crime of manslaughter seems clearly to be established.[72]

The Court continued by laying down the appropriate direction in terms of the points which the jury must have clearly explained to them:

(a) That negligence in this connection means failure to observe such a course of conduct as experience shows to be necessary if, in the circumstances, the risk of injury to others is to be avoided—failure to behave as a reasonable driver would.

(b) That they must be satisfied that negligence upon the part of the accused was responsible for the death in question.

(c) That there are different degrees of negligence, fraught with different legal consequences; that ordinary carelessness, while sufficient to justify a verdict for a plaintiff in an action for damages for personal injuries, or a conviction on prosecution in the District Court for carelessness or inconsiderate driving, falls far short of what is required in the case of manslaughter; and that the higher degree of negligence which would justify a conviction on prosecution in the District Court for dangerous driving is not necessarily sufficient.

(d) That before they can convict of manslaughter, which is a felony and a very serious crime, they must be satisfied that the fatal negligence was of a very high degree; and was such as to involve, in a high degree, the risk or likelihood of substantial personal injury to others.[73]

A General Test

3.09 No special rule as to causation is in operation; the law is the same in murder and manslaughter.[74] There are circumstances where the accused may have been acting in a grossly negligent fashion and yet may not have caused the death of the victim. It is useful to remind the jury that the accused is not on trial merely for criminal negligence but for causing death thereby. The Court thus recited the old rule stated in *Dalloway*.[75] A child ran out before a cart in circumstances where the driver had no chance to stop. It was a relevant fact that the accused was negligent in not holding the reins, only if by pulling them he could have stopped the horses and thus averted the accident.

Although *The People (A-G) v Dunleavy* was a motor manslaughter case there is no legal basis for the formulation of a special test of criminal negligence which is applicable only in circumstances of driving.[76] Manslaughter by criminal negligence

---

72   At 101, 102.

73   At 102. In New Zealand the test simply applies the civil standard of negligence; *Yogasakaran* [1990] 1 NZLR 399; (1990) 14 Crim LJ 200 CA.

74   The early cases of *Pocock* (1851) 17 QB 34, 5 Cox 172, 117 ER 1194; *Haines* (1847) 2 C&K 368, 175 ER 152, *Ledger* (1862) 2 F&F 857, 175 ER 1319; *Hilton* (1837) 2 Lew 214, 168 ER 1132, were decided prior to a recent formulation of causation rules for homicide.

75   (1847) 3 Cox 273.

76   In reality motor manslaughter cases are more difficult to prove than other cases of manslaughter by criminal negligence. It can be said that very few fatal accidents would happen if the law relating to road safety was obeyed. For an analysis see Spencer, "Motor Vehicles as Weapons of Offence" [1985] Crim LR 29.

can be committed in a wide variety of situations of which driving a motor car is only one. Each situation will formulate its own standard of care by reference to the nature of the task undertaken, the responsibility reposed in or undertaken by the accused, and the degree of skill required as a minimum standard in fulfilling that responsibility. These factors set the standard of care which a reasonable person must achieve in order not to be held guilty of negligence. Criminal negligence is judged by the degree of departure from that standard. Whilst different situations give rise to different standards the degree of departure therefrom must, in each case, be sufficiently gross as to amount to a crime. Thus criminal negligence applies a universal test of gross derogation from the ordinary standard of care to be expected in individual sets of circumstances.[77]

Test Objective

3.10 The test formulated in Dunleavy is objective.[78] Criminal negligence manslaughter occurs where the accused causes the death of the victim by failing to observe the ordinary and necessary care expected in the circumstances in which he was acting, to the degree that the prosecution can prove, beyond reasonable doubt, that he was negligent in a very high degree, thereby bringing about a very high degree of risk of substantial personal injury to others.[79] It is not necessary for the accused to be aware of the extent of his negligence nor even to know that he was negligent at all.

As a matter of practical reality few persons will be convicted in circumstances where they do not know, or suspect, they are taking a serious risk. The prosecution are relieved of the burden of proving that awareness. Nor need the prosecution prove that the accused was aware that his negligence created any degree of risk of substantial personal injury to others, though the test is formulated at the outer extreme of carelessness where few, if any, will be unaware of the nature of the risk they are creating. Were the prosecution required to prove awareness of risk this element of the crime would incorporate an element of subjective recklessness. This is a different concept.[80]

In some instances the accused may also be aware that he is running a risk and believe himself to be careful in so doing. He will be guilty of criminal negligence if, on an objective test, his mistake amounts to criminal negligence as defined by the Dunleavy formula.[81]

The actions of the accused must be voluntary. This means that he must intend

---

77   In *Jackson & Hodgetts* (1989) 44 A Crim R 320 CCA Queensland the standard was applied in extraordinary circumstances. The accused wished to rid a shopping centre of a street-person who used to loiter there by leaving a can of Coke, laced with meat preservative, where he might drink it. The Court warned that manslaughter was not an offence of strict liability and that criminal negligence must be proved.

78   The case is analysed and approved on that basis by the Supreme Court of Victoria in *Nydam* [1977] VR 430.

79   *Dunleavy* [1948] IR 95 CCA.

80   See par 2.34-2.36.

81   *Andrews* [1937] AC 576 at 581/583; [1937] 2 All ER 552 at 554/555, 30 Cox 576 at 582-3, 26 Cr App R 34 at 47-48 HL.

to do the act, or omit to do the act, which causes the death of the victim. So in a case where, for example, the accused kills the victim in a motor accident by falling asleep at the wheel of his car the actions of the accused in losing control of the car whilst asleep, cannot amount to criminal negligence. His conduct in driving whilst in an exhausted state, or failing to cease driving when he felt sleep overcoming him, can amount to criminal negligence.[82] Thus the only mental element required for criminal negligence manslaughter is an intent to do the act, causing death, or a failure to do the acts which would save the victim from death where the accused is under a special duty so to act.[83] The Supreme Court of Victoria, in approving *Dunleavy*, put the matter thus in *Nydam*:

> No doubt manslaughter does involve *mens rea*. But to use the language of Lord Salmon in *DPP v Newbury* [1976] 2 WLR 918 at 923 the necessary intent is no more than an intent to do the acts which constitute the crime. The problem is to formulate the requirement in terms which will enable the jury to determine whether the case is one of murder by recklessness or manslaughter by criminal negligence. The requisite *mens rea* in the latter crime does not involve a consciousness on the part of the accused of the likelihood of his act's causing death or serious bodily harm to the victim or other persons placed in similar relationship as the victim was to the accused. The requisite *mens rea* is, rather, an intent to do the act which, in fact, caused the death of the victim, but to do that act in circumstances where the doing of it involves a great falling short of the standard of care required of a reasonable man in the circumstances and a high degree of risk or likelihood of the occurrence of death or serious bodily harm if that standard of care was not observed, that is to say, such a falling short and such a risk as to warrant punishment under the criminal law.[84]

3.11 The accused is only to be judged as being criminally negligent by reference to a consideration of the situation as it prevailed at the time when the acts or omissions are called into question. A slight mistake can have appalling consequences. Terrible consequences do not make an action criminally negligent. In *Akerele*[85] a doctor made a mistake in the degree of dilution of a substance to be given in an injection and thereby killed ten children. The Privy Council held a direction stressing the consequences of that action to be wrong. The result of an act could not add to its criminal nature, negligence depending on the probable, not the actual, result. The question in issue, therefore, is not how much harm was caused by the accused but how much harm could have been foreseen by a reasonable man in the situation and the culpability involved in not foreseeing that harm, and the degree of risk of personal injury to others.

The only reported exception to the requirement that the act or omission of the accused be voluntary is *Lipman*.[86] The victim was killed by the accused while he was under the influence of the hallucinogenic drug LSD. He apparently believed

---

82 *Scarth* [1945] St R Qd 38 CCA. See further *Callaghan* (1952) 87 CLR 115 HC Aus; *Evgeniou* [1964] 37 ALJR; *Nydam*, fn 78; and *Newbury & Jones* [1977] AC 500; [1976] 2 All ER 365; [1976] 2 WLR 918, 62 Cr App R 291 HL.

83 See par 3.14-3.20.

84 Fn 78 at 444. Further see Howard 99-109, Gillies 504-6.

85 [1943] AC 255; [1943] 1 All ER 367 PC.

86 [1970] 1 QB 152; [1969] 3 All ER 410; [1969] 3 WLR 819, 53 Cr App R 600 CA.

that he was under attack by snakes and, in this state, stuffed a sheet into the victim's mouth. It is obvious that the voluntary act of taking dangerous drugs can be, in itself, a dangerous or reckless act.[87] The Court of Appeal upheld the conviction on the basis of a criminal and dangerous act.[88] It is difficult to justify this decision.[89]

The lower courts in Canada similarly apply an objective test of fault.[90] In England the courts have settled on a test of recklessness[91] in objective terms.[92]

The universal acceptance of some form of objective test accords with an analysis that inadvertence can amount to moral culpability. Further, the courts seem reluctant to dispense with an objective test as a final catch-all in homicide for fear of guilty persons obtaining a complete acquittal. An example is *Larkin*[93] where the accused claimed he had cut his wife's throat with a razor when, whilst he was waving it around in order to terrify another man, she fell against it and died. As well, the stringency of the test for intent in murder cases will result in extreme difficulties of proof. Where the circumstances giving rise to such acquittals involves the accused strangling, or stabbing, the victim and them claiming that he acted with a blank mind and not knowing what he was doing,[94] the existence of a test of objective fault in criminal negligence manslaughter may ensure a conviction.[95] On the foregoing analysis, where the accused consciously takes up a deadly weapon in a state of extreme anger, or places himself in proximity to the victim in that state, he consequently may be guilty of criminal negligence on the *Dunleavy* formulation. In practice, on murder charges, counsel for the defence often concedes manslaughter by criminal negligence making the task of the jury easier in deciding whether the accused had an intent to kill or cause serious injury to the victim.

Subjective Elements

3.12 In the South African case of *Mbombela*[96] the court held that no account could be taken of "the race, or the idiosyncrasy or the superstitions or the intelligence of the person accused". There can be occasions where factors such as age, mental

---

87   *Hardie* [1984] 3 All ER 848; [1985] 1 WLR 64, 80 Cr App R 157 CA.

88   See further par 3.23-3.33.

89   On the basis of an analysis of the defence of intoxication in terms of basic and ulterior intent; *Majewski* [1977] AC 443; [1976] 2 All ER 142; [1976] 2 WLR 623, 62 Cr App R 262; [1976] Crim LR 374 HL.

90   Apparently despite a clear ruling to the contrary in *O'Grady v Sparlang* [1960] SCR 804; see Stuart 183-203.

91   *Seymour* [1983] 2 AC 493; [1983] 2 All ER 1058; [1983] 3 WLR 349, 77 Cr App R 215; [1983] Crim LR 742 HL; *Kong Cheuk Kwan* (1985) 82 Cr App R 18; [1985] Crim LR 787 PC; *Goodfellow* (1986) 83 Cr App R 23; [1986] Crim LR 468 CA.

92   In accordance with the House of Lords decision in *Lawrence* [1982] AC 510; [1981] 1 All ER 974; [1981] 2 WLR 524, 73 Cr App R 1; [1981] RTR 217; [1981] Crim LR 409; further see Smith & Hogan 352-55. This apparently will allow those who have considered the risk they are running as not involving danger to others to escape.

93   [1943] KB 174; [1943] 1 All ER 217, 29 Cr App R 18 CCA.

94   The prosecution must prove the mental element beyond reasonable doubt, though the jury, in some circumstances, can be satisfied that the quoted description of a mental state was due to subsequent amnesia and not to involuntary action.

95   See *Pemble* (1971) 124 CLR 107.

96   Quoted by Burchell & Hunt, *South African Criminal Law and Procedure* (2nd ed., 1983) 150.

retardation or physical hardship in the accused could only be ignored by the court at a risk of doing an injustice. For example a child placed in charge of a machine cannot be expected to exercise the same degree of care as an adult.[97] In the law of tort a policy of making no allowance for physical or mental disabilities[98] is justifiable in terms of both a policy of ensuring a uniform standard of conduct in an ordered society and in not disappointing the legitimate expectation to compensation of those who have been injured by objectively negligent acts. No such justification exists in criminal law. The high standard of fault used as a test for criminal negligence is clearly a reflection of a desire to find moral culpability in the accused, albeit judged objectively. A handicap in the accused may remove all element of wrongdoing.

There is no clear solution yet arrived at; those under a disability are rarely placed where they might cause a substantial risk of serious bodily harm or death and, one presumes, less often prosecuted. A possible answer, should such a case arise,[99] is to adopt the elements of the test of provocation most generally accepted in the common law world, that is to say, judging the accused objectively but taking as a standard by which he should be judged the reasonable person endowed with the accused's fixed characteristics, such as age, sex, or handicap but excluding personal idiosyncrasies and transient factors such as drunkenness.[1]

In Particular Cases

3.13 The tendency of the common law has been for rulings in individual cases to ultimately give rise to a principle. When that principle has been stated the previous rulings are of limited use. The Court of Criminal Appeal in *Dunleavy*[2] has elucidated the test to be applied in determining criminal negligence. Although this was a case of motor manslaughter there is no doubt, as Lord Atkin observed in *Andrews*[3] that the "principle to be observed is that cases of manslaughter in driving motor-cars are but instances of the general rule applicable to all cases of homicide by negligence". The care to be exercised by motorists is that which, in the circumstances, a reasonable driver will have exercised.[4] Gross negligence can occur by reason of drunkenness,[5]

---

97 In *Lowe* (1850) 3 C&K 123, 175 ER 489, the accused placed a boy in charge of a steam engine used to raise miners from a pit. A defect, which any competent engineer could have rectified, caused a lift of four men to be overturned, one man being thrown back down the pit and killed. The engineer, and not the boy, was charged with manslaughter. The boy protested his ignorance of the machinery and the engineer had insisted that he operate the lift.

98 McMahon & Binchy 102-10.

99 A classic opportunity arose in *Stone & Dobinson* [1977] QB 354; [1977] 2 All ER 341; [1977] 2 WLR 169, 64 Cr App R 186; [1977] Crim LR 166 CA. Both the accused were of very low intelligence and education. The point was not argued before the Court of Appeal. See further par 3.18.

1 The law of provocation and the place of this test in Irish law is discussed more fully in ch 4.

2 *The People (A-G) v Dunleavy* [1948] IR 95 CCA.

3 [1937] AC 576 at 583; [1937] 2 All ER 552 at 556, 30 Cox 576 at 583, 26 Cr App R 34 at 47 HL.

4 *The People (A-G) v Dunleavy*, fn 2. This in turn depends on such ordinary but diverse matters as the weather, visibility and traffic. *Murray* [1852] 5 Cox 509 (Ir). See the analysis by the Court of Criminal Appeal of the facts of *The People (A-G) v McKeogh* (1960) 1 Frewen 208. The topic is further discussed under the heading Dangerous Driving Causing Death.

5 *Walker* (1824) 1 C&P 320, 171 ER 1213; *Jones* (1869) 11 Cox 544.

speed,[6] inattention,[7] racing,[8] or by removing a part from a vehicle.[9] These are but instances.[10] Motorists are now more often charged with the lesser offence of causing death by dangerous driving, which carries the very much lower and possibly inadequate sentence of five years' imprisonment.[11] It is arguable that manslaughter should be charged in many more motoring cases than it in fact is.[12] Similarly, criminal negligence has been found in cases involving ships,[13] trains,[14] in the keeping of explosives,[15] of mines,[16] in firing weapons,[17] in dealing with alcohol,[18] caring for vicious animals[19] and using dangerous drugs.[20]

Professions

3.14 The test of requiring the accused to exercise such ordinary care as a reasonable person doing the particular task, or having a particular duty, would exercise suffices except in the cases of members of recognised professions. In that instance it is, however, only a modification of the test generally applicable; a specialist "is bound and entitled to be judged in relation to the fact that he is a member of a recognised profession with special knowledge, duties and privileges".[21] As in the law of tort the

---

6   *Swindall & Osborne* (1846) 2 C&K 230, 175 ER 95; *Dalloway* (1847) 2 Cox 273.

7   *Grout* (1834) 6 C&P 629, 172 ER 1394.

8   *Mascin* (1834) 6 C&P 396, 172 ER 1292.

9   *Sullivan* (1836) 7 C&P 641, 173 ER 280.

10   The older cases cited above apply equally to motorised transport: *Dalloz* (1908) 1 Cr App R 258 CCA; *Baldessare* 22 Cr App R 70; (1930) 29 Cox 193 CCA.

11   See par 3.35-3.41.

12   Spencer, "Motor Vehicles as Weapons of Offence" [1985] Crim LR 29. In a short report in *Beresford* (1952) 36 Cr App R 1, Devlin J criticised the preferring of lesser charges where the evidence disclosed a more serious offence, such as manslaughter. For common design as applied to motor cases see *Baldessare*, fn 10. For the approach of the Australian courts to this problem see Howard 103-4.

13   *Kong Cheuk Kwan* (1985) 82 Cr App R 18; [1985] Crim LR 787 PC; *Allen & Clarke* (1835) 7 C&P 153, 173 ER 58; *Green* (1835) 7 C&P 155, 173 ER 69; *Taylor & West* (1840) 9 C&P 672, 173 ER 1005; *Williamson* (1844) 1 Cox 97.

14   *Trainer* (1864) 4 F&F 104, 176 ER 488; *Birchall* (1866) 4 F&F 1087, 176 ER 918; *Gray* (1866) 4 F&F 1098, 176 ER 922; *Hilton* (1837) 2 Lew 214, 168 ER 1132; *Lowe* (1850) 3 C&K 123, 175 ER 489 (elevator in mine); *Benge* (1865) 4 F&F 504, 176 ER 665; *Smith* (1869) 11 Cox 210; *Pittwood* (1902) 19 TLR 37.

15   *Bennett* (1858) Bell 1, 169 ER 1143 CCR.

16   *Hughes* (1857) D&B 248, 159 ER 996 CCA; *Haines* (1847) 2 C&K 368, 175 ER 152; *Lowe* (1853) 3 C&K 123, 175 ER 489.

17   *Burton* (1721) 1 St Tr 481; *Heaton* (1896) 60 JP 508; *Campbell* (1869) 11 Cox 323; *Jones* (1874) 12 Cox 628. Other decisions are based on a criminal and dangerous act; *Weston* (1879) 14 Cox 346; *Skeet* (1866) 4 F&F 931, 176 ER 854; *Salmon* (1880) 6 QBD 79 CCR; *Hutchinson* (1864) 9 Cox 555; *Lamb* [1967] 2 QB 981; [1967] 2 All ER 1282; [1967] 3 WLR 888, 51 Cr App R 417 CA; *Moloney* [1985] AC 905; [1985] 1 All ER 1025; [1985] 2 WLR 648, 81 Cr App R 93; [1985] Crim LR 378 HL.

18   *Martin* (1827) 3 C&P 211, 172 ER 391; *Packard* (1842) C&M 236, 174 ER 487.

19   *Dant* (1865) L&C 567, 10 Cox 102, 169 ER 1517 CCA.

20   *Dalby* [1982] 1 All ER 916; [1982] 1 WLR 425, 74 Cr App R 348 CA and see *Cato* [1976] 1 All ER 260, [1976] 1 WLR 110, 62 Cr App R 41 CA.

21   Howard 104. There seems to be no basis for the Privy Council stressing in *Akerele* [1943] AC 255 at 263; [1943] 1 All ER 367 at 371, that special care need be taken in prosecuting criminal liability

professional is required only to possess ordinary or usual skill and knowledge judged by contemporary standards[22] and, if specialising in a particular discipline within a profession, such level of skill and knowledge as is ordinary or usual in that discipline.[23] General and approved practice, adhered to by a substantial number of reputable qualified practitioners, may be followed without fear of a finding of negligence, unless it is obviously defective; but a departure from such a practice is not necessarily negligent unless it involves what no similarly qualified and specialist practitioner, using ordinary care, would have taken.[24] If an unqualified person holds himself out as a professional he will be judged by the standards of that profession, or such speciality within it, which he claims to profess.[25]

Homicide by Omission

3.15 Where the accused is under a legally imposed duty of care, an omission to act, causing the death of the victim, if made with intent to kill or cause serious injury, can be murder;[26] but if made by failing to observe the ordinary and necessary care expected in the circumstances, to the degree that the prosecution can prove beyond reasonable doubt negligence in a very high degree, thereby bringing about a very high degree of risk of substantial personal injury to others, that omission is manslaughter.[27]

In principle there is no reason why manslaughter by omission should be decided by a test differing from manslaughter by the commission of criminal negligence. In *Tutton*[28] the Ontario Court of Appeal took a different view, holding that an objective test of criminal negligence by a marked and substantial departure from the standards of a reasonable person was the correct test in cases of manslaughter by commission, but cases of omission required knowledge of a risk or wilful blindness.[29] It is often difficult to find a factual distinction between acts of omission and those of commission. The only legal distinction which the common law has drawn is in requiring a duty to act before liability is imposed in cases of omission.

in a professional man. The evidence is simply more difficult to assess as the jury must acquaint themselves with the skills and practices of learned professions.

22   *Daniels v Heskin* [1954] IR 73 SC.
23   *O'Donovan v Cork County Council* [1967] IR 173 SC.
24   *Dunne (an infant) v The National Maternity Hospital* [1989] ILRM 735 SC. Generally see McMahon & Binchy, ch 14.
25   *Brogan v Bennett* [1955] IR 119 SC.
26   Archbold (1922) 869-71. See further Dennis, "Manslaughter by Omission" (1980) 33 Cur L Prob 255; Gamble, "Manslaughter by Neglect" (1977) 1 Crim LJ 247; Hughes, "Criminal Omissions" (1957) 67 Yale LJ 590; Glazebrook, "Criminal Omissions: The Duty Requirement in Offences Against the Person" (1960) 76 LQR 386; Hogan, "Omission and the Duty Myth" Criminal Law Essays 85; Williams, "What Should the Code do about Omissions?" (1987) 7 LS 92; and see comments on *Miller* [1983] 2 AC 161; [1983] 1 All ER 978; [1983] 2 WLR 539, 77 Cr App R 17; [1983] Crim LR 466 HL in (1984) 22 Atlal Rev 281; see also (1980) 43 MLR 685 and [1980] Crim Lr 552.
27   *The People (A-G) v Dunleavy* [1948] IR 95 CCA; *Lowe* [1973] QB 702; [1973] 1 All ER 805; [1973] 2 WLR 481, 57 Cr App R 365 CCA. At common law a breach of duty causing a private injury and being an outrage on the moral duties of society was an indictable misdemeanour. This included omissions. Thus an omission in these circumstances was an unlawful act which, at common law, if death was thereby caused, amounted to manslaughter; Archbold (1922) 2-3.
28   (1985) 44 CR (3d) 193.   29 Criticised in Stuart 186-87.

Murder

Provided the requisite mental element is present murder can be perpetrated by an omission. For instance, by a parent deliberately failing to feed a child[30] or, a person failing to attend to the needs of a helpless[31] or ill[32] person in their care. So in *Gibbins and Proctor*[33] the daughter of Gibbins died by being starved to death while he was living apart from his wife with Proctor. The other children did not suffer the same fate and the household had a good income from the employment of Gibbins. Roche J, later approved by the Court of Criminal Appeal, directed the jury:

> . . . If you think that one of these prisoners wilfully and intentionally withheld food from that child so as to cause her to weaken and to cause her grievous bodily injury as the result of which she died it is not necessary for you to find that he or she intended to kill the child then and there. It is enough for you to find that he or she intended to set up such a state of facts by withholding food or anything else as would in the ordinary course of nature lead gradually, but surely, to her death.

In England controversy has been occasioned by the decision of medical persons, following the birth of a handicapped child, not to operate to save life[34] and in one case, allegedly, to order the administration of a drug to prevent the child seeking sustenance.[35] In certain circumstances a doctor is not obliged to take extraordinary measures to save life. It is beyond doubt that a positive act taken with a view to causing the death of a person, whether handicapped or not, is murder.[36]

Duty Requirement

3.16 No liability arises for manslaughter by omission unless the accused was under a duty to the victim to perform the act, the neglect of which caused death.[37] In the absence of such a duty a person is under no legal, as opposed to moral, obligation to act:

> If I saw a man, who is not under my charge, taking up a tumbler of poison, I should not become guilty of any crime by not stopping him. I am under no legal obligation to protect a stranger.[38]

---

30   *Bubb* (1851) 4 Cox 455; see also *Condé* (1868) 10 Cox 547; *Self* (1776) 1 Leach 137; 1 East PC 226; *MacDonald* (1904) QSR 151 SC; *Brooks* (1902) 5 CCC 372.

31   *Marriott* (1838) 8 C&P 425, 173 ER 559; *Pelham* (1846) 8 QB 959, 115 ER 1135.

32   *Squire* (1799); Russell 407.

33   (1919) 13 Cr App R 134 CCA.

34   *Re B (a minor)* [1981] 1 WLR 1421 CA.

35   *Arthur* (1981) see [1985] Crim LR 705 and Smith & Hogan 52.

36   See par 1.22.

37   *Friend* (1802) R&R 20, 168 ER 662; *Marriott* (1838) 8 C&P 425, 173 ER 559. See further Archbold (1922) 871-72, 898-95; Kenny (1922) 120-23.

38   Per Hawkins J in *Paine*, *The Times* 25 February 1880. Stephen in his *History* III 10 put the matter thus: "By the law of this country killing by omission is in no case criminal unless the thing omitted is one which it is a legal duty to do. Hence in order to ascertain what kinds of killings by omission are criminal, it is necessary, in the first place, to ascertain the duties which tend to the preservation of life; a duty to do dangerous acts in a careful manner and to employ reasonable knowledge, skill, care, and caution therein; a duty to take proper precautions in dealing with dangerous things; and a duty to do any act undertaken to be done, by contract or otherwise, the omission of which would

The harshness of this rule has sometimes led to omissions being construed as part of a series of acts set in train by the accused.[39] Where the courts cannot make such an analysis the omission of the accused must take place within the context of a legal duty to the victim.[40]

At common law parents have an automatic duty to take all reasonable steps within their power to preserve the lives of their children; all citizens are under a duty to assist the police in the due course of duty in preserving the peace or effecting an arrest;[41] the person in charge of a ship must assist persons endangered at sea;[42] those who have undertaken a responsibility towards the old or infirm must act to preserve their health and life;[43] those who do work which involves a risk to the lives or safety of others must act conscientiously.[44]

It is probable that the heads of duty at common law are not closed. As we shall see the courts have used the existing authorities to impose a duty to act outside these specific instances and extend liability to situations where the relationship of the victim and the accused is such as to indicate to any reasonable citizen a duty in the accused to proffer assistance. In that context Smith & Hogan are correct in extending the scope of the duty to those who mutually undertake hazardous activities of a lawful[45] or even unlawful[46] variety.[47] Some of these recognised instances now require further comment.

---

be dangerous to life". Further see *Digest* (4 ed., 1887) Article 212. It is difficult to see why liability should not be imposed on a person who fails to assist an imperilled victim when he could do so with no prejudice to himself. The Quebec Charter of Human Rights and Freedoms provides at clause 2: "Every human being whose life is in peril has a right to assistance. Every person must come to the aid of anyone whose life is in peril either personally or by calling aid, or by giving him the necessary and immediate physical assistance, unless it involves danger to himself or a third person, or unless he has some further valid reason"; Stuart 81-83. There is no parallel provision in the Constitution, indeed the State's duty to provide assistance is limited by the practicalities of its resources in Article 40.3.

39   For example *Fagan v The Commissioner of Metropolitan Police* [1969] 1 QB 439; [1968] 3 All ER 442; [1968] 3 WLR 1120, 52 Cr App R 700 DC. The House of Lords appeared to move towards imposing liability for failing to counteract a danger created by the accused; *Miller* [1983] 2 AC 161; [1983] 1 All ER 978; [1983] 2 WLR 539, 77 Cr App R 17; [1983] Crim LR 466 HL; *Commonwealth v Cali* [1923] 141 NE 510, Massachussetts SC, *Fernandez* (1966) 2 SA 259 AD.

40   The burden of proof is on the prosecution to prove such a duty; *Edwards* (1838) 8 C&P 611, 173 ER 641; *Barrett* (1846) 2 C&K 343, 175 ER 142.

41   Subject to being called upon and being reasonably able to do so; *Brown* (1841) C&M 314, 4 St TR (NS) 1369, 174 ER 522.

42   Subject to being able to do so without endangering his own vessel, crew and passengers; s 6 Maritime Conventions Act, 1911 which applies even in time of war and in respect of an enemy, saved by s 37(8) of Merchant Shipping (Safety Convention) Act, 1952.

43   *Stone & Dobinson* [1977] QB 354; [1977] 2 All ER 341; [1977] 2 WLR 169, 64 Cr App R 186, [1977] Crim LR 166 CA.

44   Russell 402-3, Williams *TBCL* 265.

45   Instancing mountaineering, at 50-1.

46   Instancing drug-taking citing *Dalby* [1982] 1 All ER 916; [1982] 1 WLR 425, 74 Cr App R 348 CA and see *The People v Beardsley* [1967] 113 NW 1128 SC Michigan.

47   The law of tort has similarly extended its scope to a generalised duty of care independent of a prior instance; McMahon & Binchy ch 6. There is no decision that a situation where the law of tort would impose a duty is sufficient for the purposes of the law of manslaughter. The test for criminal negligence is similar to that for negligence in the law of tort save that a much graver breach is required

Specific Instances

3.17 Parents, and those in the position of parents, must act reasonably to attend to the physical needs of the children in their care.[48] The duty to act extends beyond a natural blood relationship where the accused has placed himself or herself in a relationship equivalent to parenthood with the child. Thus it has been common for persons who have entered into a quasi-spousal relationship with a parent,[49] or who have themselves undertaken parental duties towards the child, to be considered as having a legal duty to foster the child's development.[50] Where a person lives with the parent of a child a voluntary assumption of legal responsibility is readily to be implied from the care the accused has in the past given to the child. In *Bubb*[51] the accused was the sister-in-law of the widowed father of the young victim. The accused was charged with murder by systematic neglect. On the issue whether the accused had a legal duty to care for the victim Williams J instructed the jury:

> It is quite clear that the circumstance of the prisoner being in the position of an aunt of the deceased child, or being resident in the same house with the child, was not sufficient to cast upon her the duty of providing sufficient food and raiment for it. But if the prisoner undertook the charge of attending to the child, and of taking that care of it which its tender age required, a duty then arose to perform those offices properly; and if the prisoner, being in the capacity, as it were, of servant or nurse and having the charge of attending and taking care of the child, was furnished with the means of doing so properly, then the duty arose which is charged in this indictment, of giving it sufficient food and raiment, and if the prisoner neglected to perform that duty, beyond all question she is criminally responsible.[52]

Where a parental duty exists it can be discharged through another person but acceptance of that other person's neglect is equivalent to personal neglect.

One spouse is under a duty to the other to come to the aid of that spouse where it is reasonably necessary to preserve life or health.[53]

Parental and spousal duty in this context means a duty to take such steps, as in the circumstances, an ordinary conscious parent or spouse would take.[54] An obvious

than that which would impose liability in tort. Probably a general duty of care is insufficient as the common law has always sought, as the following pages illustrate, a specific duty of the accused towards the victim.

48   *Connor* [1908] 2 QB 26, 98 LT 932, 21 Cox 628; *Cole v Pendleton* (1896) 60 JP 359; 3 Co Inst 50; 1 Hawk C 61, s 16; 1 Hale PC 433. Old authorities suggest that duty only begins at birth. This matter is further discussed in ch 5.

49   *Gibbins & Proctor* (1918) 13 Cr App R 134 CCA.

50   *Condé* (1868) 10 Cox 547; *McDonald* (1904) QSR 151 SC; *Brooks* (1902) 5 CCC 372.

51   (1851) 4 Cox 455.

52   At 459.

53   *Russell* [1933] VLR 59; [1933] ALR 76 SC.

54   It is submitted that *Shepherd* (1862) L&C 147, 169 ER 1340, 9 Cox 123 CCR would not be followed. Mere carelessness is insufficient; *Large* (1939) 27 Cr App R 65 CCA. In Canada the duties of spouses, parents and those with responsibilties is set out in s 197(1) of the Code which provides: "Everyone is under a legal duty (a) as a parent, foster parent, guardian or head of family to provide necessaries of life for a child under 16 years; (b) as a married person to provide necessaries of life to his spouse; and (c) to provide necessaries of life to a person under his charge if that person is (i) unable by reason of detention, illness, age, insanity or other cause, to withdraw himself from that charge, and (ii) is unable to provide himself with necessaries of life". See Stuart 72-83.

example of the fulfilment of such a duty is the provision of food and shelter. The general duty can cause liability to be incurred in more unusual situations. In *Russell*[55] a husband was convicted of manslaughter when he stood by and watched his wife and two children drown themselves in a public swimming pool.[56] Specific criminal offences also provide for an omission which causes injury to children.[57] Similarly, a person is criminally responsible who undertakes to provide necessaries for another incapable of doing so for themselves by reason of age, infirmity or confinement. Brett J put the matter thus in *Nicholls:*[58]

> . . . if a grown-up person chooses to undertake the charge of a human creature, helpless either from infancy, simplicity, lunacy or other infirmity, he is bound to execute that charge without (at all events) wicked negligence, and if a person who has chosen to take charge of a helpless creature lets it die by wicked negligence, that person is guilty of manslaughter.[59]

Examples

3.18 A typical example is provided by *Instan*[60] where the accused neglected her aged aunt with whom she lived, by failing, during her last illness, to feed, or attend to her, or provide, or procure medical or other assistance. Similarly in *Stone and Dobinson*[61] the victim was a relation of Stone who came to live as a lodger with this unmarried couple and died due to undernourishment. On becoming bed ridden she met her death after some weeks of neglect caused, at least partly, by the filthy conditions inducing toxaemia and by the effects of prolonged immobilisation. The efforts of the accused persons were slight and ineffectual.[62] The couple appealed their conviction to the Court of Appeal on the ground that they were under no legal duty to care for the victim:

> The suggestion is, that heartless though it may seem, this is one of the situations where the appellants were entitled to do nothing . . . This Court rejects that proposition. Whether Fanny was a lodger or not she was a blood relation of the appellant Stone; she was occupying a room in his house; the appellant Mrs Dobinson had undertaken the duty of trying to wash her, of taking such food to her as she required. There was ample evidence that each appellant was aware of the poor condition she was in by mid July . . . no effort was made to summon an ambulance or the social services or the police despite . . . entreaties. . . . A social worker used to visit Cyril [their child]. No

55   Fn 53.
56   The facts may well have been otherwise but these were the facts proved by the prosecution. See further *Russell & Russell* (1987) 85 Cr App R 388; [1987] Crim LR 494 CA; *Smith* [1908] QLR 13 SC; *Duffy* (1880) 6 VLR 430 SC; *Egan* (1897) 23 VLR 159 SC; *Clarke & Wilton* [1959] VR 645 SC.
57   Dealt with in ch 7.
58   (1874) 13 Cox CC 75.
59   At 76. See also *Marriott* (1838) 8 C&P 425, 173 ER 559; *Pelham* (1846) 8 QB 959, 115 ER 1135; *Kelly* (1923) 32 CLR 509 HC.
60   [1893] 1 QB 450; [1891-4] All ER 1213, 17 Cox 602 CCR.
61   [1977] QB 354; [1977] 2 All ER 341 [1977] 2 WLR 169, 64 Cr App R 186; [1977] Crim LR 166 CA.
62   Both were of low intelligence and development. One wonders whether the factors of Stone being partially deaf, almost totally blind, having no sense of smell and being of low intelligence and Dobinson being ineffectual and inadequate and both caring for a mentally handicapped child should have, in justice, required a modification of the objective negligence test by taking these personal factors into account. The point was not argued. See par 3.12.

word was spoken to him. All these were matters which the jury were entitled to take into account when considering whether the necessary assumption of the duty of care for Fanny had been proved.[63]

The identification by the Court of the factors of blood relationship, physical proximity, assistance being preferred, awareness, and opportunity to obtain assistance is novel. It could be used in expanding the parameters of legally recognised duties of care beyond those traditionally adopted.

In *Taktak*[64] the accused procured a prostitute for a party. He left her there and was later summoned to pick her up. She was unconscious due to heroin consumption. He took her by taxi to a place where he made ineffectual attempts to treat her. Some time later he made two attempts to call a doctor but the girl was dead when he eventually arrived. It was argued on appeal that no duty of care arose in these circumstances. Carruthers J[65] proposed a broader principle for finding a duty of care which accords with the *Stone and Dobinson* approach of having regard to the entire circumstances:

> . . . the evidence led by the Crown was capable of satisfying the jury beyond reasonable doubt that the appellant owed a duty of care in law to Miss Kirby. That duty flowed from his taking her unconscious body into his exclusive custody and control and thereby removing her from the potentiality of appropriate aid from others. The legal principles are, I think, conveniently stated in 40 Am Jur 2d, par 90 at 383: "Generally speaking, the affirmative legal duty which is the vital element of a homicide charge based upon failure to supply medical or surgical attention may exist, first, where a statute imposes a duty to care for another; the second, where one stands in a certain status or relationship to another; the third, where one has assumed a contractual duty to care for another; and fourth, where one has voluntarily assumed the care of another and has so secluded the helpless person as to prevent others from rendering aid".
>
> For authority to support the fourth category reference may be made to *Nicholls* (1874) 13 Cox CC 75; *Stone* [1977] QB 354; (1976) 64 Cr App R 186; *Jones v United States*, 308 F 2d 307 (1962) and *People v Beardsley*, 113 NW 1128 (1907).
>
> The complexity of modern society is such that the duty of care cannot be confined to specific categories of legal relationships such as husband and wife, parent and child; the duty will also arise where one person has voluntarily assumed the care of another who is helpless, through whatever cause and so secluded such person to prevent others from rendering aid.
>
> Thus, I find the following passage in 100 ALR 2d 488, par 4 to be apposite: "Duties dictated merely by good morals, or by human considerations, are not generally within the domain of the law, and therefore one who did not become a good Samaritan by providing medical care when a witness to the distress of a sick or injured person does not become criminally responsible should death come to such a person because of a lack of medical attention. Legal rights and duties, however, may arise out of those complex relations of human society which create correlative rights and duties the performance of which is so necessary to the good order and well-being of society that the state makes their observance obligatory".[66]

---

63   QB at 361, All ER at 345-6, WLR at 175, Cr App R at 191.

64   [1988] 34 A Crim R 334 CCA NSW.

65   Yeldham J doubted the existence of a duty of care in these circumstances and Loveday J agreed with the other two judges that no criminal negligence had been established, agreeing with the reasons of Yeldham J.

66   At 357-58.

In *Miller*[67] the House of Lords identified a new principle of criminal liability based on an omission which could be expanded to form the basis for a general principle of legal liability where a person fails to act when it would be reasonable to do so. The accused was a squatter who went to sleep in a house holding a lighted cigarette. When he awoke the mattress was smouldering but he did nothing to put it out but instead moved to an adjoining room and fell asleep there. The house caught fire and the accused was convicted of arson.[68] The House of Lords upheld a direction to the jury that the accused had a general duty to take action to put the fire out. Lord Diplock put the matter thus:

> I see no rational ground for excluding from conduct capable of giving rise to criminal liability conduct which consists of failing to take measures that lie within one's power to counteract a danger that one has oneself created, if at the time of such conduct one's state of mind is such as constitutes a necessary ingredient of the offence.[69]

Other Duties

3.19 Others, such as jailers, schoolmasters, heads of religious and medical establishments and hostels will have persons in their custody. Where such a person in their care becomes helpless or ill they are required to proffer assistance. So a doctor whose wife is a morphine addict must seek help and that duty to assist is not fulfilled by merely confining his drug addicted wife and not seeking outside help.[70] The authorities imposing an obligation on masters to assist their apprentices and servants are not completely outdated.[71] Apart from persons having charge of establishments a legal duty to preserve life and health is appropriate in the quite common modern case of domestic servants who come from abroad speaking little of any European language.[72]

3.20 It is not a defence, in this context, that medical attention was not obtained by reason of a conscientious objection to such intervention.[73] If, for example, a parent of a gravely ill child hopes for God's assistance there can clearly be no intent to kill

---

67 [1983] 2 AC 161; [1983] 1 All ER 978; [1983] 2 WLR 539, 77 Cr App R 17; [1983] Crim LR 466 HL.

68 Contrary to s 1(1) and (3) of the (United Kingdom) Criminal Damage Act, 1971.

69 AC at 176, All ER at 981, WLR at 543, Cr App R at 21.

70 *Bonnyman* (1942) 28 Cr App R 131 CCA.

71 A distinction is drawn between servants, for whom the master is not obliged to provide medical aid, but is obliged otherwise to provide care, and apprentices, for whom he is obliged to provide both; *Sellen v Norman* (1829) 4 C&P 80, 172 ER 616, this would now be regarded as outdated. See further *Russell* 406-8; *Smith* (1837) 8 C&P 153, 173 ER 438; *Smith* (1865) 30 4 LJNC 153, L&C 606, 169 ER 1533, 10 Cox 82 CCR; *Chattaway* (1922) 17 Cr App R 7.

72 Howard, at 109-19, has gone so far as to argue that criminal negligence manslaughter has subsumed this category.

73 A dissenting spouse might apply to court under s 11 of the Guardianship of Infants Act, 1964 or a health board, or other concerned person, might seek a court order under the Children's Act, 1990. In such cases the court would be bound by the paramountcy of the child's welfare; *F v The Eastern Health Board*, Supreme Court, unreported 16 April 1990.

or cause serious injury and thus no charge of murder. Such a hope is not a defence to a charge of manslaughter,[74] though difficult problems of causation can occur.[75]

Manslaughter by neglect also occurs through failure to perform duties in employment.[76] There have been convictions where a manager of a mine failed to ventilate it, causing an explosion,[77] where neglect caused a bucket on a conveyor to be thrown down a mine shaft[78] and where a lift operator left the elevator mechanism in the care of a boy who protested his incompetence and later could not prevent the cage from overturning the pulley and killing a man.[79]

Duties can arise by virtue of their being voluntarily assumed, they can be imposed by statute (for example under the Road Traffic Acts) or by contract. If the law develops so as to allow for a general principle it will probably be based on more stringent tests of proximity than in the law of tort.

The external and mental elements of the crime must not be mixed. In *Dunleavy*[80] the mental element is cast in the form of a high degree of carelessness which involves a high risk of death or serious injury to others. The existence of a duty to take care and the breach of that duty by neglect are external elements.[81]

In *Bourne*,[82] McNaughten J said, *obiter*, that there was a duty on a doctor to perform an abortion when the life of the mother was at risk, failure to do so would be manslaughter. This opinion is unlikely to be accepted in this jurisdiction particularly in the light of Article 40.3.3 of the Constitution.[83]

It is an offence contrary to s 26 of the Offences Against the Person Act, 1861 to deprive an apprentice or servant of the necessaries of life.[84] A similar offence is provided for by s 6 of the Conspiracy & Protection of Property Act, 1875.[85]

74   *Downes* (1875) 1 QBD 25, 13 Cox 111 CCR; the manslaughter charge was based on wilful neglect contrary to the Poor Law (Amendment) Act, 1868. In *Senior* (1899) 1 QB 283; [1895-96] All ER 11, 19 Cox 219 CCR on a similar prosecution Russell LCJ expressed the view that the prosecution at common law would have the same result but Wills J refused to decide the point. In the third prosecution of a member of this religious sect, at the time called "the Peculiar People". In *Morby* (1881) 8 QBD 571, 15 Cox 35 CCR, a conviction was quashed on causation principles. The corresponding provision is s 12 of the Children's Act, 1908.

75   *Cyrenne* (1981) 62 CCC (2d) 238, Ontario Dist Ct, it was not proved that a refusal to allow a blood transfusion caused death. See also *Tutton* (1985) 44 CR (3d) 193 CA Ont. In Canada necessaries are defined as those tending to preserve life including food, clothing, shelter and medical treatment and also (obiter) to necessary protection of a child from harm: Stuart 78-80.

76   It was formerly the case that the duty used to be set out in the indictment; *Barrett* (1846) 2 C&K 343, 175 ER 142; *Edwards* (1838) 8 C&P 611, 173 ER 641. This rule has now been superseded by the Criminal Procedure Act, 1924.

77   *Haines* (1847) 2 C&K 368, 175 ER 152. The negligence of others was held to be no defence.

78   *Hughes* (1857) D&B 248, 159 ER 996 CCA.

79   *Lowe* (1850) 3 C&K 123, 175 ER 489. Lord Campbell CJ: "I am clearly of opinion that a man may, by a neglect of duty, render himself liable to be convicted of manslaughter, or even of murder".

80   See par 3.08.

81   See further Russell 403: "Those who have undertaken work upon the proper performance of which other persons' safety or lives may depend, are under a legal duty to perform that work or to give due and adequate warning of the danger, if they do not perform it".

82   [1939] 1 KB 687 at 693; [1938] 3 All ER 615 at 618-9 CCA.

83   See ch 5.

84   S 26: "Whosoever, being legally liable, either as a master or a mistress, to provide for any apprentice or servant necessary food, clothing, or lodging, shall wilfully and without lawful excuse refuse or neglect to provide the same, or shall unlawfully and maliciously do or cause to be done any bodily

Contributory Negligence

3.21 Traditionally the contributory negligence of the victim has not been regarded as a defence to a charge of manslaughter by criminal negligence.[86] In *Swindall and Osborne*,[87] Pollock CB put the matter thus in summing up to the jury:

> The prisoners are charged with contributing to the death of the deceased by their negligence and improper conduct; and if they did so, it matters not whether he was deaf, or drunk, or negligent, or in part contributed to his own death; for in this consists a great distinction between civil and criminal proceedings. If two coaches run against each other, and the drivers of both are to blame, neither of them has any remedy for damages against the other. . . . But in the case of loss of life, the law takes a totally different view: for there each party is responsible for any blame which may ensue, however large the share may be; and so highly does the law value human life, that it admits of no justification whenever life has been lost, and the carelessness or negligence of any one person has contributed to the death of another person.[88]

At the foundation of the State contributory negligence in the law of tort constituted a complete defence to an action based on negligence.[89] It has only been since 1961 that contributory fault by a defendant merely reduces the damages he may recover in proportion to that fault.[90] Hostility to the notion that the slightest fault by the victim relieved the accused of responsibility for gross negligence was therefore to be expected. In *The People (A-G) v Gallagher*[91] the accused was tried on manslaughter and ultimately convicted of careless driving. He was apparently travelling at high speed on the wrong side of the road in consequence of being involved in some kind of a race with another driver. A motor cyclist who was towards the middle of the road was killed by the accused's car. The issue in the Court of Criminal Appeal was whether the trial judge should have told the jury that the accused's driving had to be the sole cause of death. The Court adopted a

harm to any such apprentice or servant, so that the life of such apprentice or servant shall be endangered, or the health of such apprentice or servant shall have been or shall be likely to be permanently injured, shall be guilty of a misdemeanour, and being convicted thereof, shall be liable to be kept in penal servitude for the term of five years". The sections are quoted, as are all other sections from the Offences Against the Person Act, 1861, in accordance with the amendments introduced by the Penal Servitude Acts of 1864 and 1891 and by the Statute Law Revision Act, 1908.

85   S 6: "Where a master, being legally liable to provide for his servant or apprentice necessary food, clothing, medical aid, or lodging, wilfully and without lawful excuse refuses or neglects to provide the same, whereby the health of the servant or apprentice is or is likely to be seriously or permanently injured, he shall on summary conviction be liable either to pay a penalty not exceeding fifty pounds, or to be imprisoned for a term not exceeding six months".

86   Archbold (1922) 891; Kenny (1922) 128.

87   (1846) 2 C&K 230, 175 ER 95. Further see *Dant* (1865) L&C 567, 10 Cox 102, 169 ER 1517 CCA; *Hutchinson* (1864) 9 Cox 555; *Longbottom* (1849) 3 Cox 439; *Walker* (1824) 1 C&P 320, 171 ER 1213. In *Birchall* (1866) 4 F&F 1087, 176 ER 918, Wills J ruled that a person could not be criminally responsible for negligence when he would not have been responsible in an action for damages: at this time contributory negligence was a complete defence to a negligence action. The authority was not followed in *Jones* (1870) 11 Cox 544 and *Kew & Jackson* (1872) 12 Cox 355.

88   C&K at 232-33, ER at 97.

89   McMahon & Binchy 349-51.

90   Civil Liability Act, 1961 s 34.

91   [1972] IR 365, 106 ILTR 61 CCA.

traditional substantial causation approach. On the issue of contribution by the victim to his own death Kenny J for the Court said:

> The fact that the negligence of the dead or injured person may have been one of the causes of death or serious bodily harm, in the sense that it contributed in some way to the accident, is not a matter which should be put to the jury as being a ground on which they are entitled to acquit the accused.[92]

Application

3.22 This approach accords with the position adopted generally in common law countries that if the actions of the accused substantially contributed to the victim's death he does not escape liability because the victim also made a substantial contribution to his own death.[93] No other approach is indicated by the authorities on manslaughter by contributory negligence.

If the accused is driving at 90 mph in a built up area at a time when other road users are likely to be about, and in turning a corner he kills a pedestrian who is not paying particular heed to the traffic, the fault of the victim does not relieve the accused of responsibility. To take a more extreme example; if two cars driven by B and C, and carrying passengers, are each driving towards one another at a grossly excessive speed and both, on coming to a blind corner, move onto the incorrect side of the road, thereby colliding and causing the death of the passengers, both B and C will be guilty of manslaughter by criminal negligence.[94]

Exceptionally, situations may arise in which the negligent acts by the victim may be such as to show that the death of the victim is not due to the criminal negligence of the accused.[95] For example, the accused may injure himself in a remote area and thereby precipitate an ill-equipped surgeon into an emergency operation. In other instances the victim may have set in motion a train of events which caused the accused to react in a manner, which, because of the conduct of the victim, was less than careful. In such a situation the accused may be perceived as being grossly negligent unless the victim's conduct in setting in motion the relevant events is considered. When that is taken into account and it is apparent that the accused may have done no less badly than any reasonable or ordinary person (or if he is a professional, any reasonable or ordinary professional) in trying to cope with the situation there is no criminal negligence. Such a finding does not depend on the contributory negligence of the victim but is due to the fact that the standard of care to be expected of an accused depends on the circumstances in which he finds himself. It is otherwise where the accused himself has created a situation, through his own criminal negligence, which causes the victim to act in a hasty or ill-considered manner.

The sole issue for the jury remains as to whether the accused was guilty of criminal negligence to the exacting test set out in *Dunleavy*.[96]

---

92   At 370.
93   Howard 32-33; Stuart 209-39.
94   For the test see par 3.08.
95   *Bunney* (1894) QLJR 80 SC.
96   [1948] IR 95 CCA.

Criminal and Dangerous Act Manslaughter

3.23 For the accused to kill the victim by intentionally doing an unlawful act, which was also objectively dangerous,[97] is manslaughter.[98]

"Unlawful" in this context is confined to criminal acts of an inherently dangerous kind,[99] excluding acts ordinarily lawful but made into criminal offences by reason of the negligent way they are performed.[1] Examples of the latter are the offences of dangerous and careless driving.[2] "Dangerous" in this context requires, at a minimum, that the act or acts in which the accused was engaged were likely to injure another person.[3] As in assault manslaughter and criminal negligence manslaughter the actions of the accused must be voluntary,[4] but there is no requirement of mental fault. Thus the accused may be quite inadvertent to the fact that he is about to cause death or serious injury.[5] In circumstances where the accused did not know what he was doing due to intoxication or drug taking, the fact that he put himself into such a state can amount to criminal negligence.[6]

Circumstances can exist where it is necessary to rely on the alternative doctrine of criminal and dangerous act manslaughter. If the accused were to point a loaded gun at the victim in the course of play-acting a finding of manslaughter by criminal negligence would be open to a jury were the victim to be accidentally killed. If A

---

97 *Coomer* (1989) 40 A Crim R 417 CCA NSW.

98 Literature on this topic includes Williams, "Unlawful Act Manslaughter" (1975) 1 Monash LR 234; Wells, "Perfectly Simple English Manslaughter" [1976] 39 MLR 474; Sullivan, "Constructive Manslaughter—A Renewed Vigour" (1976) 39 MLR 727; Willis, "Manslaughter by the Intentional Infliction of Some Harm: A Category that Should be Closed" (1985) 9 Crim LJ; Howard, "An Australian Letter: More Developments in the Law of Homicides" [1962] Crim LR 435; Snelling, "Manslaughter by Unlawful Act" (1956) 30 ALJ 382; Westling, "Manslaughter by Unlawful Act: The 'Constructive' Crime which Serves no Constructive Purpose" (1974) Sydney LR 211; Williams, "Constructive Manslaughter" [1957] Crim LR 293; Buxton, "By Any Unlawful Act" (1966) 82 LQR 174; Law Reform Commission of Victoria—Discussion Paper No. 13—Homicide (1988).

99 *The People (A-G) v Maher* (1936) 71 ILTR 60; *Jennings* [1990] Crim LR 588 CA.

1 *The People (A-G) v Dunleavy* [1948] IR 95 CCA, unless these also amount to criminal negligence, in which case the appropriate finding is of manslaughter under this category. See further *Andrews* [1937] AC 576; [1937] 2 All ER 552, 30 Cox 576, 26 Cr App R 34 HL; *Lowe* [1973] QB 702; [1973] 1 All ER 805; [1973] 2 WLR 481, 57 Cr App R 365 CA. In England the House of Lords has held that the offence of causing death by reckless driving is identical in its ingredients with manslaughter by recklessness (the equivalent in that jurisdiction of criminal negligence manslaughter); *Seymour* [1983] 2 AC 493; [1983] 2 All ER 1058; [1983] 3 WLR 349, 77 Cr App R 215, [1983] Crim LR 742 HL; see further Smith & Hogan 352-5. In *Callaghan* (1952) 87 CLR 115, the High Court of Australia decided there was no difference between the degree of negligence required for criminal negligence manslaughter and for causing death by negligent driving; for criticism see Howard 103-4.

2 *The People (A-G) v Dunleavy*, fn 1.

3 *The People (A-G) v Crosbie & Meehan* [1966] IR 490 CCA, per Kenny J at 495.

4 *Newbury v Jones* [1977] AC 500; [1976] 2 All ER 365; [1976] 2 WLR 918, 62 Cr App R 291 HL. See further par 3.02.

5 *The People (A-G) v Crosbie & Meehan*, fn 3 at 495.

6 *Lipman* [1970] 1 QB 152; [1969] 3 All ER 410; [1969] 3 WLR 819, 52 Cr App R 600 CA, decided on a different principle. The facts of this are set out in par 3.11. The case was not followed in Australia; *Haywood* [1971] VR 755 SC. An entirely different approach is taken to the issue of drunkenness and voluntary conduct in Australia; *O'Connor* (1980) 29 ALR 449 HC. See further ch 4 and Walker, "Voluntary Intoxication: The Australian Response to *Majewski's* Case" (1979) 3 Crim LJ 13.

sets out on a robbery with B and C who were using what he reasonably thought were imitation pistols, and if in the course of the robbery C handed him a gun and he accidentally shot the victim, A could not have been guilty of a sufficiently high degree of negligence for manslaughter by criminal negligence. On the other hand he would have killed by a criminal and dangerous act. The victim was assaulted and the danger would be inherent in the robbery which, in the context of the threat of violence and the possibility of response, gave rise to a higher risk of injury to another person. If this case were to proceed on the basis of negligence, then the only fact on which the prosecution could focus would be the failure by the accused to believe the story of B and C that the guns were false. The law behind this example requires further analysis.

Development

3.24 In 1922 the law on manslaughter was even more unsettled than it is now. To kill another by an act amounting to felony was thought to be murder.[7] To kill another by an unlawful act was thought to be manslaughter.[8] The scope of an unlawful act, for this purpose, was very wide. Kenny wrote:

> Thus a person commits manslaughter if he accidentally kills someone else by conduct which amounts to a misdemeanour (as by taking part in an unlawful assembly) or even to a petty offence punishable similarly (as where a motorist exceeds the appointed limit of speed). And this rule has usually been regarded as holding good whenever the unlawful act which produced the death amounted to even a mere civil tort.[9]

The facts of the cases on which the Courts acted to convict of manslaughter are a more certain guide than the tentative statements of principle found in the law books at the time.[10] With one possible exception, all of these cases seem to be of acts which were either dangerous crimes directed against the victim or were acts of a kind which endangered life. After a full analysis and review Turner expresses this view:

> . . . if examination is made of the cases referred to in the text books in support of the proposition that manslaughter is committed if death ensues in the course of the commission of any unlawful act, it will be found that the circumstances in most, if not all, were such that some unlawful physical harm was either intended or knowingly risked by the prisoner.[11]

3.25 Thus one finds cases where the unlawful act consisted of an assault by the

---

7   *Beard* [1920] AC 479; [1920] All ER 21, 14 Cr App R 159, 26 Cox 573 HL. See further par 3.34-3.36.
8   Archbold (1922) 888; Kenny (1922) 119-21.
9   120, citing *Sasun, The Times* 18 May 1920 to the effect that even where the fatal result was so improbable that it could not have been anticipated the accused was still guilty, and *McNaughten* (1881) 14 Cox 576 (Ir). Stephen wrote in the *History* III 16, ". . . the expression 'unlawful act' includes, I believe, all crimes, all torts, and all acts contrary to public policy or morality, or injurious to the public; and particularly all acts commonly known to be dangerous to life". In his *Digest* (4th ed., 1887) Stephen does not give any examples of unlawful acts which are not criminal and not dangerous; Articles 222, 223. One deduces from this that, in practice, by this stage acts, apart from crimes, were not prosecuted as manslaughter if they caused death.
10   Fn 8 and 9.
11   Russell 590.

accused on the victim[12] or where the accused took a severe risk with the victim's safety.[13] A case which could be seen as a possible exception to these categories was *Sullivan*.[14] The victim was loading a cart with potatoes when a workmate, in order to play a practical joke, removed a restraining stick and caused the cart to tilt a large number of sacks of potatoes back onto the victim who hit his head on the ground and died. However, this case can be seen as a deliberate endangerment or as an assault.[15]

The Modern Test

3.26 In 1883 Field J in *Franklin*[16] refused to accept that the commission of a tort sufficed as an unlawful act in manslaughter. Franklin had taken a box from the stall of a refreshment cellar on Brighton Pier and carelessly thrown it into the sea where it hit and killed a person who was swimming. The judge put the case to the jury on the ground of criminal negligence stating:

> . . . it seems to me . . . that the mere fact of a civil wrong committed by one person against another ought not to be used as an incident which is a necessary step in a criminal case. I have a great abhorrence of constructive crime.[17]

It would appear that in the early days of the State people were convicted of manslaughter when they caused a death by driving and incidentally committed the crime of driving without a licence. In 1936 that practice was ended by Judge Sealy who refused to leave such a case to the jury.[18] In 1966 the Court of Criminal Appeal[19] accepted the formulation of this aspect of manslaughter laid down by the English Court of Criminal Appeal in *Larkin*:[20]

12 *Wild* (1837) 2 Lewin 214, 168 ER 1132 (kicking to eject a trespasser); *Caton* (1874) 12 Cox 624 (fighting); *Bradshaw* (1872) 14 Cox 83 (assault in the course of a game); *Moore* (1898) 14 TLR 229 (assault in the course of a game); *Hopley* (1860) 2 F&F 202, 175 ER 1024 (over-severe chastisement); *Campbell* (1869) 11 Cox 323 (firing a gun at the victim "without thinking or knowing it was loaded"); *Macklin & Murphy* (1838) 2 Lewin 225, 168 ER 1136 (beating a constable in the course of a riot); *Wiggs* (1784) 1 Leach 378, 168 ER 291 (throwing a stake at the victim); *Errington* (1838) 2 Lewin 217, 168 ER 1133 (lighted coals thrown at the victim); *Howlett* (1836) 7 C&P 274, 173 ER 121 (hitting the victim on the head with a tin can); *Griffin* (1869) 11 Cox 402 (beating a two year old child with a strap); *Goffe* (1672) 1 Vent 216, 86 ER 146 (hitting the victim's head several times against a door post); *Conner* (1835) 7 C&P 438, 173 ER 194 (throwing a piece of iron at a child).

13 *Phillips* (1778) 2 Cowp 830, 98 ER 1385 (firing at a boat in order to disable it); *Fenton* (1830) 1 Lewin 179, 168 ER 1004 (throwing large stones down a mine shaft); *Cheeseman* (1836) 7 C&P 455, 173 ER 202 (beating and neglecting a consumptive niece); *Senior* [1899] 1 QB 283; [1895-96] All ER 11, 19 Cox 219 CCR (refusing to allow medical attention to a dangerously sick child); *Towers* (1874) 12 Cox 530 (assaulting a girl nursing an infant which died of shock); *Hayward* (1908) 21 Cox 692 (abusing a spouse, causing cardiac arrest).

14 (1836) 7 C&P 641, 173 ER 280.

15 See *McNaughten & Others* (1881) 14 Cox 576 (Ir).

16 (1883) 15 Cox 163, after consulting Matthew J. Since this case there has been no reported instance of the accused being convicted of manslaughter simply on the basis of an unlawful act which was not a crime. This was a ruling at first instance and may not have been generally accepted.

17 At 165.

18 *The People (A-G) v Maher* (1936) 71 ILTR 60.

19 *The People (A-G) v Crosbie & Meehan* [1966] IR 490 CCA at 495.

20 [1943] KB 174; [1943] 1 All ER 217, 29 Cr App R 18 CCA; later approved by the House of Lords in *Newbury & Jones* [1977] AC 500; [1976] 2 All ER 365; [1976] 2 WLR 918, 62 Cr App R 291 HL.

If a person is engaged in doing a lawful act, and in the course of doing that lawful act behaves so negligently as to cause the death of some other person, then it is for the jury to say, upon a consideration of the whole of the facts of the case, whether the negligence proved against the accused person amounts to manslaughter, and it is the duty of the presiding judge to tell them that it will not amount to manslaughter unless the negligence is of a very high degree: the expression most commonly used is unless it shows the accused to have been reckless as to the consequences of the act. That is where the act is lawful. Where the act which a person is engaged in performing is unlawful, then, if it is at the same time a dangerous act, that is an act which is likely to injure another person, and quite inadvertently he causes the death of that other person by that act, then he is guilty of manslaughter.[21]

The Limits of the Test

3.27 A similar formulation of the rule is to be found in Australia[22] and in Canada.[23] Two questions arise on this formulation:

(1) what is an unlawful act for these purposes; and

(2) what is a dangerous act.

There are no recorded instances since 1922 of anyone being prosecuted in the State for unlawful and dangerous act manslaughter merely on the basis of a civil wrong. The unlawful act must amount to a crime.[24] This is not a complete answer. Circumstances can exist where the accused commits a crime and a dangerous act and yet could not be convicted of manslaughter. *Howard*[25] instances dangerously driving a car without insurance, a chemist illegally (by not recording the prescription) prescribing a dangerous drug for a customer and a surgeon, struck off the roll of medical practitioners for sexual misconduct, performing a dangerous operation on a friend.

The Court of Criminal Appeal introduced a further limitation in *The People (A-G) v Dunleavy*.[26] The accused killed a cyclist when he was clearly driving in a negligent fashion; without lights on a road 40 feet wide but within 7 feet of the kerb on his wrong side. On any reasonable view this was dangerous driving.[27] Part of the appeal was concerned with the charge of the trial judge, which, the Court of Criminal Appeal stated, could have left the jury with the impression that if the accused committed the unlawful act of dangerous driving that manslaughter was thereby committed.[28] The Court commented directly on the unlawful and dangerous act doctrine:

21   KB (this passage does not appear), All ER 219, Cr App R 32.

22   *Pemble* (1971) 124 CLR 107 HC; *Andrews* (1979) 2 A Crim R 182 CCA NSW; *Turner* [1962] VR 30 SC. Further authorities are cited in Howard 109-17 and Gillies 508-9.

23   Under s 205(5) of the Code: "A person commits culpable homicide where he causes the death of a human being (a) by means of an unlawful act, (b) by criminal negligence . . .". To this has been usually added the requirement that the act be dangerous; Stuart 211.

24   *Lamb* [1967] 2 QB 981; [1967] 2 All ER 1282; [1967] 3 WLR 888, 51 Cr App R 417 CA; *Holzer* [1968] VR 481 SC.

25   109.

26   [1948] IR 95 CCA.

27   Then a crime under s 51 of the Road Traffic Act, 1933, now a crime under s 53 of the Road Traffic Act, 1961 as amended.

28   At 103: "His instructions, taken as a whole, may reasonably have left the jury under the impression

The creation by statute of such minor offences of careless or inconsiderate driving has rendered the doctrine of the unlawful act as a basis for the felony of manslaughter no longer serviceable in this connection.[29]

3.28 The problem resurfaced[30] in *The People (A-G) v Crosbie & Meehan*. The victim, a docker, was killed by a knife, in the course of a fight. The prosecution had difficulty proving how the knife, carried by Crosbie, was used and with what intent. Meehan carried a foot long spanner. The knife was purportedly brought into a meeting, in contemplation of being used in self-defence by being waved about. The Court of Criminal Appeal, through Kenny J, reaffirmed the criminal and dangerous act doctrine:

> A person who produces a knife with the intention of intimidating or frightening another and not for self-defence commits an assault and the act done is therefore unlawful. When a killing resulted from an unlawful act, the old law was that the unlawful quality of the act was sufficient to constitute the crime of manslaughter. The correct view, however, is that the act causing death must be unlawful and dangerous to constitute the offence of manslaughter. The dangerous quality of the act must however be judged by objective standards and it is irrelevant that the person did not think that the act was dangerous . . . the statement of the law in *Larkin* . . . is correct. . . .[31]

Factual Application

3.29 If the nature of the crime constituting the criminal act is to be limited to certain crimes it is not apparent where the limitation is to be drawn.[32] In England it appears settled that the act of the accused must be an unlawful act in itself and not a lawful act done with such a degree of negligence that it thereby becomes a crime.[33] This

that, if the conduct of the applicant amounted to no more than the unlawful act of dangerous driving within the meaning of s 51 of the Road Traffic Act, 1933, this was necessarily sufficient to justify a conviction for dangerous driving".

29 At 99. A motor vehicle is a lethal object if driven dangerously. One wonders why the unlawful and dangerous act doctrine should not apply on the roads and why the creation of new crimes should thereby render the doctrine obsolete in this regard.

30 [1966] IR 490. Earlier in *The People (A-G) v Mohangi* (1964) 1 Frewen 297 at 300, through Henchy J the Court of Criminal Appeal had reaffirmed the criminal and dangerous act doctrine. The victim died when the accused caught her around the throat after an alleged confession of infidelity: "The defence made at the trial was that [the victim] met her death accidentally in circumstances which would constitute murder or manslaughter. It was submitted that death was due to vagal inhibition which apparently is death due to stoppage of the heart as a result of stimulation of the vagal nerves in the neck, and which may be caused by a slight degree of pressure in certain cases. It is not necessary to consider the arguments for or against the acceptance of this theory as a reasonable possibility or probability. It is sufficient to say that this defence would not result in a verdict of guilty to both murder and manslaughter if the jury were satisfied that the act which caused death was, firstly, unlawful and secondly, dangerous in the sense that it was likely to injure the deceased girl". No forensic evidence as to death was available because the accused had substantially destroyed the body.

31 At 495 par 3.25.

32 Howard 109-17 suggest that the crimes must be dangerous ones. He therefore argues that the act of the accused is unlawful because it is dangerous. The danger requirement is set so high in the decided cases that this branch of manslaughter has been subsumed under the criminal negligence category. This view represents a development of the law in this area which is possible following a scrutiny of the cases cited in this paragraph.

33 *Andrews* [1937] AC 576 at 584-85; [1937] 2 All ER 552 at 556-57, 30 Cox 576 at 584, 26 Cr App

accords with the *Dunleavy* statement. A view of the parameters of the application of the criminal and dangerous act manslaughter doctrine can be had by an examination of some of the facts of the cases in which it has been applied.

Manslaughter has occurred through the criminal and dangerous act doctrine where the accused knocked out a woman and, thinking she was dead, dragged her into the sea;[34] where the accused waved a razor about and the victim "fell against it" killing herself;[35] where the accused injected the victim with large quantities of heroin;[36] where excessive force was used in sexual intercourse;[37] where the accused pushed a paving stone down on top of a train;[38] where the accused, on an LSD "trip", assaulted the victim believing she was a snake;[39] where the accused committed a burglary of the home of an 82 year old man;[40] where the accused threatened the victim with a gun;[41] where the accused held the victim as a shield in order to resist arrest by armed police officers;[42] where the accused burned down a house in order to be rehoused, his family being inside;[43] and, more anciently, where the accused chased his wife threatening her and she dropped dead of fright[44] and where the accused threw an iron bar at a child, thereby killing another.[45] Australian examples include the accused approaching his former girlfriend from behind and discharging a sawn off shotgun[46] and the accused hitting the victim and causing him to strike his head.[47]

3.30 It is possible to view these cases as examples of assault manslaughter or criminal negligence manslaughter. In *Lamb*[48] no criminal act was committed where the victim and the accused were play-acting and the accused pointed a loaded revolver at the victim. Neither of them realised that when he pulled the trigger the revolver of the gun would rotate away from the empty chamber and the firing pin would strike the bullet in the next chamber. In the absence of a criminal act the case could have been dealt with on the basis that using a lethal weapon as a toy, without being expert as to the manner in which it discharged live bullets, was a criminally negligent act.

There is no reason why the prosecution should not put its case on the basis of

R 34 at 50 HL, a formulation similar to that just quoted from Dunleavy. See also *Lowe* [1973] QB 702; [1973] 1 All ER 805; [1973] 2 WLR 481, 57 Cr App R 365 CA; *Larkin* [1943] KB 174; [1943] 1 All ER 217, 29 Cr App R 18 CCA (another purported case of a waving weapon causing an accidental death); Smith & Hogan 347-51.

34   *Church* [1966] 1 QB 59; [1965] 2 All ER 72, [1965] 2 WLR 1220, 49 Cr App R 206 CCA.
35   *Larkin*, fn 33.
36   *Cato* [1976] 1 All ER 260; [1976] 1 WLR 110, 62 Cr App R 41 CA.
37   *Sharmpal Singh* [1962] AC 188; [1962] 2 WLR 238 PC.
38   *Newbury & Jones* [1977] AC 500; [1976] 2 All ER 365; [1976] 2 WLR 918, 62 Cr App R 291 HL.
39   *Lipman* [1970] 1 QB 152; [1969] 3 All ER 410 [1969] 3 WLR 819, 53 Cr App R 600 CA.
40   *Watson* [1989] 2 All ER 865; [1989] 1 WLR 684, 89 Cr App R 211; [1989] Crim LR 733 CA.
41   *Reid* (1975) 62 Cr App R 109; [1976] Crim LR 570 CA.
42   *Pagett* (1983) 76 Cr App R 279; [1983] Crim LR 394 CA.
43   *Goodfellow* (1986) 83 Cr App R 23; [1986] Crim LR 468 CA.
44   *Hayward* (1908) 21 Cox 692.
45   *Conner* (1835) 7 C&P 438, 173 ER 194.
46   *Pemble* (1971) 124 CLR 127 HC.
47   *Holzer* [1968] VR 481 SC. For further examples see Howard 109-17; Gillies 503-12.
48   [1967] 2 QB 981; [1967] 2 All ER 1282; [1967] 3 WLR 888, 51 Cr App R 417 CA.

alternative headings. The circumstances under which manslaughter is committed are so varied that it is impossible to judge the gravity of offences in advance on the basis of the category under which the offence is committed.

The unlawful and dangerous act doctrine has also been used in abortion cases on the basis that an abortion is both a criminal act and a dangerous operation.[49] The rationale of danger to the woman on whom the operation is performed is, however, questionable.[50] A possible development in this area is to treat any act which is committed in the course of a felony as manslaughter.[51]

Danger and Awareness

3.31 The second requirement is that the criminal act of the accused should be dangerous. This requirement excludes the doing of a lawful act with a degree of negligence which renders it criminal.[52] Turner comments that the facts of all the cases, in which this doctrine applies, involve the accused either intending, or knowingly risking, physical harm to the victim.[53] It is clear, in this branch of manslaughter, that as in criminal negligence manslaughter, the accused need not intend harm or be aware that he is putting the victim in danger.[54] The facts of the cases quoted have in common the factor that a reasonable person, doing what the accused was alleged to have done, would have been aware that he was risking the safety of another person. The test in *Larkin*, approved in *Crosbie & Meehan*, puts the matter higher: "a dangerous act, that is an act which is likely to injure another person".[55]

The acts which put another person into a position of likely injury must have been done voluntarily by the accused.[56] Apart from that, there is no requirement for a mental element; the accused need not be aware of the danger which he creates.[57]

---

49   *Newton* [1958] Crim LR 469; [1958] 1 BMJ 1242. See also "Therapeutic Abortion" by JDS Harvard [1958] Crim LR 600.

50   As traditionally stated in *Buck & Buck* (1960) 44 Cr App R 213; *Creamer* [1966] 1 QB 72; [1965] 3 All ER 257; [1965] 3 WLR 583, 49 Cr App R 368 CCA. Williams makes the point that an abortion in unskilled hands is dangerous but the operation, if performed by competent medical people, is as safe as any other operation: *TBCL* 277. In *Salika* [1973] VR 272 the Supreme Court of Victoria reserved the question of whether these cases were good law in that jurisdiction.

51   See par 3.34. Further *The People (A-G) v Cadden* (1957) 91 ILTR 97 CCA. See the criticism of such an idea at par 3.34-3.35.

52   See par 3.27-3.28.

53   See par 3.33

54   *The People (A-G) v Crosbie & Meehan* [1966] IR 490 CCA; *Newbury & Jones* [1977] AC 500; [1976] 2 All ER 365; [1976] 2 WLR 918, 62 Cr App R 291 HL; *Creamer* [1966] 1 QB 72; [1965] 3 All ER 257; [1965] 3 WLR 583, 49 Cr App R 368 CCA: "A man is guilty of involuntary manslaughter when he intends an unlawful act and one likely to do harm to the person and death results which was neither foreseen nor intended". QB at 82, All ER at 262, WLR at 592, Cr App R at 378. Harm, in this context, means physical harm. The unlawful act must be such that all sober and reasonable men would realise was likely to cause some, albeit not serious, harm; *Dawson & Others* (1984) 81 Cr App T 150; [1988] Crim LR 383 CA.

55   Quoted par 3.25 at 495.

56   See par 3.02.

57   *Lipman* [1970] 1 QB 152; [1969] 3 WLR 819, 53 Cr App R 600 CA, [1969] 3 All ER 410, would tend to go further on the reasoning of the Court of Appeal. This decision has been widely disapproved of by commentators and it would appear to be wrong.

That absence of mental fault is balanced by a stringent test as to what constitutes a dangerous act. In England the law developed through the insistence of some judges on an awareness requirement. This was later dressed-up by the higher courts as an objective test of high risk. So in *Church*[58] where the accused knocked out a woman and, thinking she was dead, put her body in a river, the Court of Appeal put the formula:

> . . . a degree of *mens rea* has become recognised as essential. . . . An unlawful act causing the death of another cannot, simply because it is an unlawful act, render a manslaughter verdict inevitable. For such a verdict inexorably to follow, the unlawful act must be such as all sober and reasonable people would inevitably recognise, must subject the other person to, at least, the risk of some harm resulting therefrom, albeit not serious harm. . . .[59]

The test in Church was approved by the House of Lords in *Newbury & Jones*[60] but presented in a new light so as not to require that the accused be aware of the risk he created:

> The test is still an objective test. In judging whether the act was dangerous the test is not whether the accused recognised it was dangerous but would all sober and reasonable people recognise its danger.[61]

3.32 This test is more exacting than that formulated in the context of criminal negligence manslaughter by the Court of Criminal Appeal in *Crosbie & Meehan*[62] of an act "likely to injure another person". The abhorrence of constructive crime, expressed by Field J in *Franklin*,[63] has been developed by the Supreme Court of Victoria so as to require a degree of danger so high as to be almost equivalent to a realisation of risk by the accused.[64] Thus in *Holzer*,[65] Smith J formulated the law by requiring of the accused an intention to do the criminal act, the basis of the charge, and also abstracting from the authorities a requirement of a danger of really serious injury:

> . . . the circumstances must be such that a reasonable man in the accused's position, performing the very act which the accused performed would have realised that he was exposing another or others to an appreciable risk of really serious injury. The view which I have expressed, that realisation of the risk created does not have to be proved

58   [1966] 1 QB 59; [1965] 2 All ER 72; [1965] 2 WLR 1220, 49 Cr App R 206 CCA.

59   QB at 70, All ER at 76, WLR at 1226, Cr App R at 213. Similarly in a civil case, the point of which was to determine whether manslaughter was committed, Lord Denning MR formulated the test: "In manslaughter of every kind there must be a guilty mind. Without it the accused must be acquitted: see *Lamb* [1967] 2 QB 981. In the category of manslaughter relating to an unlawful act, the accused must do a dangerous act with the intention of frightening or harming someone, or with the realisation that it is likely to frighten or harm someone, and nevertheless he goes on and does it regardless of the consequences". *Grey v Barr* [1971] 2 QB 554 at 568; [1971] 2 All ER 949 at 956 [1971] 2 WLR 1339 at 1341 CA.

60   [1977] AC 500; [1976] 2 All ER 365; [1976] 2 WLR 918, 62 Cr App R 291 HL.

61   AC at 507, All ER at 367, WLR at 922, Cr App R at 296. See *Dawson*, fn 54.

62   [1966] IR 490 CCA, quoted at par 3.27.

63   (1883) 15 Cox 163, quoted at par 3.25.

64   Thus Sholl J has required that the accused realise the danger; *Longley* [1962] VR 137 at 142 SC commented on in [1962] Crim LR 435.

65   [1968] VR 481 SC.

against the accused, is a factor in persuading me that the degree of apparent danger must be that which I have attempted to define, and that it is not sufficient, as it was held in *Church* [1966] QB 59, [1965] 2 All ER 72 (CCA), to show there was a risk of some harm resulting, albeit not serious harm. I may add that although under the doctrine of manslaughter by unlawful dangerous act, *mens rea* is necessary, this requirement is satisfied by proof of an intention to commit the assault or other criminally unlawful act of which the accused has been guilty. In this regard I would refer to *R v Lamb* [1967] 2 QB 981, [1967] 2 All ER 1282 (CA).[66]

Comparison with Criminal Negligence

3.33 The requirement that the criminal act expose the victim "to an appreciable risk of really serious injury" is comparable to the test for criminal negligence in Irish law, involving, "in a high degree, the risk or likelihood of substantial personal injury to others".[67] This latter test was imposed on a policy basis by the Court of Criminal Appeal because of the gravity of manslaughter as a crime. If the *Holzer* test were to be adopted in Ireland the risk run by the accused, in both criminal and dangerous act manslaughter and in criminal negligence manslaughter would be, in practical application, equivalent. The difference is that in the former the accused committed a crime and exposed another to an appreciable risk of really serious injury, but in the latter the accused was very negligent and exposed another to a high degree of risk of substantial personal injury. It is possible to view these tests as appropriate on a policy basis: the absence of a criminal act in criminal negligence manslaughter is balanced by a more grievous act of carelessness, on the standards which ordinary members of the community are expected to achieve. There is an argument, therefore, to be made in Irish law for abandoning the *Larkin* test and adopting the *Holzer* test.[68]

No Requirement of Aim

3.34 Finally there has been some suggestion that the actions of the accused must be aimed at or directed at someone. The only authority for this is *Dalby*.[69] The accused and the victim were both drug addicts. The accused obtained a substitute drug on prescription but supplied a large quantity to the victim on his request. He then died of an overdose. It is a measure of the confusion in the law of manslaughter that yet another principle was abstracted from the cases by the Court of Appeal:

> In the judgment of this Court, the unlawful act of supplying drugs was not an act directed against the person [the victim] and the supply did not cause any direct injury to him. The kind of harm envisaged in all the cases of involuntary manslaughter was physical injury of some kind as an immediate and inevitable result of the unlawful act, e.g. a blow on the chin which knocks the victim against a wall causing a fractured skull

66 At 482.
67 *The People (A-G) v Dunleavy* [1948] IR 95 at 102 CCA.
68 In Canada the test of "unlawful" under s 205 of the Code has been interpreted by the Ontario Court of Appeal as an act "such that any reasonable person would inevitably realise must subject another person to the risk of some harm resulting therefrom, albeit not serious harm"; *Tennant* (1975) 31 CRNS 1, 23 CCC (2d) 80 CA Ont.
69 [1982] 1 All ER 916; [1982] 1 WLR 425, 74 Cr App R 348 CA. A possible revival of this principle occurred in *Bell* [1989] Crim LR 730 CA.

and death, or threatening with a loaded gun which accidentally fires, or dropping a large stone on a train (*DPP v Newbury*) or threatening another with an open razor and stumbling with death resulting (see *Larkin*). In the judgment of this Court, where the charge of manslaughter is based on an unlawful and dangerous act, it must be an act directed at the victim and likely to cause immediate injury, however slight.[70]

It is submitted that this judgment should not be followed. It confuses the tests for assault manslaughter and unlawful and dangerous act manslaughter. Both were once part of the manslaughter by unlawful act doctrine but have long been regarded by the authorities as distinct. The case has not been followed.[71] It was politely distinguished by the Court of Appeal, as a case on causation, in *Goodfellow*.[72] The accused was convicted on the English equivalent of criminal negligence manslaughter, reckless manslaughter, and also of criminal and dangerous act manslaughter. The accused's act seemed not to have been directed at or against anyone. There is no authority, apart from *Dalby*, that it should have been.

Manslaughter by a Felony

3.35 In 1964 the Criminal Justice Act abolished constructive murder.[73] Constructive murder occurred where, irrespective of whether the accused had contemplated killing or causing serious injury, death was occasioned at a time when he had an intention to commit any felony whatsoever, or where the accused had an intention to oppose by force any officer of justice on his way to, in, or returning from the execution of the duty of arresting, keeping in custody, or imprisoning any person whom he was lawfully entitled to arrest, keep in custody, or imprison, or the duty of keeping the peace or dispersing an unlawful assembly, provided that the offender had noticed that the person so killed was such an officer so employed. The expression "officer of justice" included both officers and private persons who had a legal right so to act.[74] For example, exploding a bomb in the hope of prisoners escaping, without any thought of death occurring to anyone, was murder.[75] The classic example was of the accused who shot at a chicken intending to steal it and instead killed the victim: the accused would be guilty of murder because stealing was a felony.[76] Stephen argued persuasively in his *History of English Criminal Law* that the supposed doctrine, founded on a *dictum* of *Coke* repeated by *Holt*, was supported by no authority.[77] Yet his view had little effect and the rule was applied,[78] Stephen including it in his

---

70   All ER at 919, WLR at 429, Cr App R at 352.
71   *Mitchell* [1983] QB 741; [1983] 2 All ER 427; [1983] 2 WLR 938, 76 Cr App R 293 CA.
72   (1986) 83 Cr App R 23; [1986] Crim LR 468 CA.
73   See par 2.18.
74   *The State v McMullen* [1925] 2 IR 9 CCA.
75   *Desmond, Barrett & Others* (1868), *The Times*, 28 April 1868; *Allen & Others* (1867) 17 LT (NS) 223.
76   Fost 258-59; Stephen, *Digest* (4th ed., 1887) 167 (6th ed., 1904) 185.
77   Stephen *Hist.* III 67-69.
78   Thus in *Barrett's* case, fn 75, Cockburn LCJ was reported as stating: "If a person seeking to commit a felony should in the prosecution of that purpose cause, although it might be unintentional, the death of another, that, by the law of England was murder. There were persons who thought and maintained that where death thus occurred, not being the immediate purpose of the person causing the death, it was a harsh law which made the act murder. But the Court and the jury were sitting

Digest.[79] In England the law was modified by practice so that death occurring in the course of an abortion was regarded as manslaughter only.[80]

In 1920 the House of Lords approved the doctrine, in the context of rape, apparently limiting it to a felony which involved violence.[81] The Royal Commission on Capital Punishment, 1949-1953,[82] reported that the practice in abortion cases was not to charge murder, in the absence of extreme circumstances indicating that the accused must have contemplated that death or grievous bodily harm might have resulted from the operation: in cases of unintentional killing a judge would always direct the jury to bring in a verdict of manslaughter unless the felony was one involving violence. In an Irish abortion case in 1940[83] the judge apparently allowed the jury to bring in a verdict of manslaughter but in *The People (A-G) v Cadden*[84] the Court of Criminal Appeal expressly reserved the point as to whether the felony murder rule was limited to violent crimes and upheld a murder conviction on an abortionist because, apparently, abortion involved the unlawful infliction of physical force, which was violence.[85]

In *The People (DPP) v Murray*[86] Walsh J commented, *obiter*, on the effect of the abolition of the felony murder rule by s 4 of the Criminal Justice Act, 1964:

> In effect, the section introduced a new definition of murder. One of the consequences of that change was that some homicides were transferred from the category of murder to that of manslaughter.[87]

3.36 That "change" has never been effected in practice. There has never been a case put to a jury solely on the basis of the accused being guilty of manslaughter because death occurred in the commission of a felony. The prosecuting authorities seem to have taken the view that in these circumstances the case would have to be made out either as assault manslaughter, criminal negligence manslaughter, or manslaughter by a criminal and dangerous act.

Legally, that view the prosecuting authorities appear to have taken is correct for three reasons. Firstly there was never a doctrine of manslaughter by commission of a felony. That rule, if it existed, was confined to murder, manslaughter having its own constructive doctrine which became in turn the assault manslaughter and criminal and dangerous act manslaughter rules. The felony murder rule was stated by the institutional writers to be an aspect of the pre-1964 doctrine of malice aforethought in murder. The malice for the felony was transferred to the death of the victim and thereby supplied sufficient malice into the elements of the crime.

there to administer law, not to make or mould it and the law was what he told them". Quoted in Stephen, *Digest* (4th ed., 1887) 167-68 (6th ed., 1904) 185-86.

79 Fn 76 and 78.
80 *Lumley* (1911) 22 Cox 635.
81 *Beard* [1920] AC 479; [1920] All ER 21, 14 Cr App R 159, 26 Cox 573 HL.
82 Cmnd 8932, par 72-90 and Appendix 7(b).
83 *The People (A-G) v Daly* (1940) referred to in *The People (A-G) v Cadden* (1957) 91 ILTR 97 CCA.
84 Fn 83.
85 The actual reasoning of the judgment is highly obscure. Apparently the argument of counsel for the prosecution to this effect was upheld. The Court expressed the view that the strict vigour of the felony murder rule remained unaltered in Ireland.
86 [1977] IR 360 SC.
87 At 377.

With the abolition of the doctrine of malice aforethought in the Criminal Justice Act, 1964 the felony murder rule ceased to exist. The felony manslaughter rule cannot now be invented. Secondly, as previously stated, Stephen showed convincingly that the felony murder rule had its origin in a mistake by Coke and was unsupported by the authorities cited by him.[88] Although the doctrine was acted upon widely in the last century this does not right a mistake. Thirdly, if it is to be applied the weight of authority in England[89] and Australia[90] requires the rule to be applied in such a way as to make it indistinguishable from manslaughter by a criminal and dangerous act. Howard[91] gives the modern statement of the rule as it now stands in Victoria and South Australia:

> The present law requires an act by D, violent or dangerous to the person of another and, except in the case of arson, an incidental felony not constituted by that act itself.

There seems little point in discussing further a doctrine that is not part of Irish law.

Causing Death by Dangerous Driving

3.37 The stringency of the test for criminal negligence manslaughter laid down by the Court of Criminal Appeal in *The People (A-G) v Dunleavy*[92] necessitated the creation of a new offence penalising the negligent driver who caused death to other road users.[93] This offence of dangerous driving has less exacting elements than manslaughter. That offence was created by s 53 of the Road Traffic Act, 1961 and amended by s 51 of the Road Traffic Act, 1968 and by s 3 of the Road Traffic (Amendment) Act, 1984 which provides:

> (1) A person shall not drive a vehicle in a public place in a manner (including speed) which having regard to all the circumstances of the case (including the condition of the vehicle, the nature, condition and use of the place and the amount of traffic which then actually is or might reasonably be expected to be therein) is dangerous to the public.
>
> (2) A person who contravenes subs (1)[94] of this section shall be guilty of an offence and

---

88 Fn 77 and 78.

89 Set out in the Report of the Royal Commission on Capital Punishment, fn 82. For a history of the rule see Howard 56-62.

90 Howard 56-62.

91 At 59. Further see Gillies 493-500.

92 [1948] IR 95 CCA.

93 Criminal negligence is discussed at par 3.08-3.10.

94 S 104 of the Road Traffic Act, 1961 as amended by the Schedule to the Road Traffic Act, 1968 provides that where a person is charged with an offence of dangerous driving, contrary to s 53, he is not to be convicted of an offence unless he was warned at the time of the offence, or within twenty four hours thereafter, that the question of prosecuting him for an offence of speeding, driving without reasonable consideration, careless driving, or dangerous driving was being considered, or within fourteen days he was served with a summons, or within fourteen days a notice in writing was served on him stating the time and place at which the offence was alleged to have been committed and stating briefly the act or acts alleged to constitute the offence and stating the intention to prosecute him. Such a notice must be served personally on that person, or, where a mechanically-propelled

(a) in case the contravention causes death or serious bodily harm to another person, he shall be liable on conviction on indictment to penal servitude for any term not exceeding five years or, at the discretion of the court, to a fine not exceeding three thousand pounds or to both such penal servitude and such fine, and

(b) in any other case, he shall be liable on summary conviction to a fine not exceeding one thousand pounds or, at the discretion of the court, to imprisonment for any term not exceeding six months or to both such fine and such imprisonment.[95]

(3) In a prosecution for an offence under this section, it shall not be a defence to prove that the speed at which the accused person was driving was not in excess of the ordinary, general built-up area or special speed limit applying in relation to the vehicle.

(4) Where, when a person is tried on indictment or summarily for an offence under this section, the jury, or, in the case of a summary trial, the District Court, is of opinion that he was not guilty of an offence under this section but was guilty of an offence under s 52 of this Act, the jury or court may find him guilty of an offence under s 52 of this Act and he may be sentenced accordingly.[96]

vehicle was involved, on the registered owner thereof. Failure to comply with the requirement is not a bar to a future prosecution, however, where the court is satisfied either that the accused contributed to the failure, that the name and address of the owner of the mechanically-propelled vehicle could not with reasonable diligence have been ascertained in time for a summons or a notice, or, where a mechanically-propelled vehicle was not part of the offence, the name and address of the accused could not have been discovered with reasonable diligence for the service of summons or notice. It is presumed that the requirement had been complied with and if, notwithstanding failure to warn, the accused was at all material times aware of the occurrence in respect of which the prosecution for such offence was brought, failure to comply is not a bar to conviction. This latter criterion is so wide as to render the warning requirement meaningless as it is highly unlikely that a serious incident could occur without an accused being perfectly aware of that.

95 Under s 26 and s 16 in the second Schedule to the Road Traffic Act, 1961 disqualification is mandatory where death or serious bodily harm results or the offence is the second offence where the first offence, or one of the earlier offences, occurred in any period of three years and involved a mechanically-propelled vehicle, in either case disqualification must be for not less than six months—1 year where death occurs. A conviction for dangerous driving carries a mandatory endorsement of particulars of the offence on the defendant's driving licence—only where death does not occur, s 36(1), 1961.

96 S 52 provides: "(1) A person shall not drive a vehicle in a public place without due care and attention, as amended by s 50, 1968. (2) A person who contravenes subs (1) of this section shall be guilty of an offence". Penalty: On summary conviction three hundred and fifty pounds fine and/or three months' imprisonment. S 106 of the Road Traffic Act, 1961 as amended by s 6 of the Road Traffic Act, 1968 and by s 3 of the Road Traffic (Amendment) Act, 1984 provides: "(1) Where injury is caused to a person or property in a public place and a vehicle is involved in the occurrence of the injury (whether the use of the vehicle was or was not the cause of the injury), the following provisions shall have effect: (a) if the vehicle is not stationary after the occurrence, the driver of the vehicle shall stop the vehicle; (b) the driver or other person in charge of the vehicle shall keep the vehicle at or near the place of the occurrence for a period which is reasonable in all the circumstances of the case and having regard to the provisions of this section; (c) the driver of the vehicle, or if he is killed or incapacitated, the person then in charge of the vehicle shall give on demand the appropriate information to a member of the Garda Síochána, or if no such member is present, to one person entitled under this section to demand such information; (d) if—(i) injury is caused to property other than that of the driver of the vehicle and for any reason he or, if he is killed or incapacitated, the person then in charge of the vehicle does not at the place of the occurrence give the appropriate information to a person entitled under this section to demand it, or (ii) injury is caused to a person other than the driver of the vehicle, the driver of the vehicle, or, if he is killed or incapacitated, the person then in charge of the vehicle shall, unless he has already given the appropriate information to a member of the Garda Síochána, report the occurrence as soon as possible to such a member, and, if necessary, shall go for that purpose to the nearest convenient Garda station and also give on

(5) A person liable to be charged with an offence under this section shall not, by reference to the same occurrence, be liable to be charged with an offence under s 35 of the Offences Against the Person Act, 1861.

(6) Where a member of the Garda Síochána is of opinion that a person has committed an offence under this section he may arrest the person without warrant.

It is a matter of prosecutorial discretion as to whether to charge an accused who kills a person in a traffic accident, with manslaughter, dangerous driving or dangerous driving causing death.[97] A decision as to which charge is appropriate should be taken, as in any other case, by considering whether the facts reasonably disclose material from which the elements of one or other offence may be proved.[98]

Procedure

S 53 creates one offence with a dual mode of prosecution.[99] Where a person is acquitted on indictment for dangerous driving causing death, he cannot be subsequently prosecuted summarily for dangerous driving.[1] In consequence, both charges cannot appear in the same indictment, though a charge of dangerous driving may appear as a summary count in an indictment for a different indictable offence.[2] A person acquitted of either offence cannot be subsequently charged with careless driving contrary to s 52. Careless driving is an alternative verdict under s 53 and an accused has already been at peril of conviction on that offence.[3]

demand the appropriate information to the member". Penalty: Summary conviction in a case in which injury is caused to a person, a fine not exceeding one thousand pounds and/or imprisonment for a term not exceeding six months; in a case of injury to property a fine not exceeding three hundred and fifty pounds and/or imprisonment for a term not exceeding three months. For disqualifications see s 27 of the Road Traffic Act, 1961.

97   In general the police ought not to prefer a lesser charge which the evidence, reasonably construed, might indicate. *In re Beresford* (1952) 36 Cr App R 1 Devlin J at 3 stated: "The police can never be criticised if the jury think it right to reduce the charge, or even if the judge thinks it proper to withdraw it from the jury, but they can be criticised if they usurp the function of the proper tribunal by determining in advance what ought to be a triable issue. Similar considerations apply to the two charges of dangerous driving and careless driving. There are, I believe, too many cases where the justices are prevented from dealing with dangerous driving as such because the police have preferred the lesser charge". Generally see Leigh, *Police Powers in England and Wales* (2nd ed., 1985) 18-27.

98   Archbold (1966) par 2818 prefers the view that charges of manslaughter arising from the driving of a motor vehicle should now only be preferred in the most serious cases where the offence approximates to murder and gives an example of where a policeman is knocked down by the reckless driving of a stolen car. No authority is cited to support this opinion. The remarkable lenity of courts in dealing with motoring offences where a serious risk has been created or where a permanent injury has resulted is noted by Spencer, "Motor Vehicles as Weapons of Offence" [1985] Crim LR 29. The fact that a person was driving a motor vehicle should not be, in any rational legal system, a ground for reducing liability where according to the fault criteria applicable to an offence he has committed a grave wrong and caused serious injury to a victim. Such an approach is not manifest in any other circumstances where a crime may be committed.

99   *A-G (Ward) v Thornton* [1964] IR 458 at 483 SC.

1   *A-G (Ó Maonaigh) v Fitzgerald* [1964] IR 458 at 484 SC.

2   *A-G (Ward) v Thornton*, fn 99.

3   *A-G (McElwain) v Power* [1964] IR 458 at 486. It is probably wise to have separate counts for both s 52 and 53. In *The People (A-G) v Clifford* (1962) 29 Ir Jur Rep 41 it was held in the Circuit Court that a jury was not entitled to consider a charge contrary to s 52 where the accused has been granted a direction to acquit under s 53. A guilty plea to s 52 need not be accepted, in the District Court

Notwithstanding that death or serious bodily harm was caused by the driving of the accused the DPP retains the discretion to proceed against him summarily for dangerous driving.[4] The accused has no right to be tried on indictment even if the dangerous driving did cause death or serious bodily injury, provided that latter element is not stated in the charge.[5]

Definition

3.38 Ó Briain J adhered to a standard jury charge describing dangerous driving as:

> . . . driving in a manner which a reasonably prudent man, having regard to all the circumstances, would clearly recognise as involving a direct and serious risk of harm to the public.[6]

The Alberta Court of Appeal has held that, in judging whether driving was dangerous, the entire pattern of driving should be taken into account and not each individual facet. This accords with the wording of s 53. The proper approach is to consider the sum of the driving pattern: a sum may be greater than its individual parts. The court propounded, as a simple and workable test, the response of the tribunal of fact to the question:

> Would the ordinary prudent by-stander, without expert knowledge or the benefit of hindsight, have perceived an obvious risk that lives or safety would be endangered by the defendant's driving or his impaired physical condition.[7]

Both of these definitions clearly indicate that dangerous driving is committed by negligence. It is not an error in a jury direction to say that driving in a manner dangerous to the public is equivalent to negligent driving provided that a correct direction is given as to the degree of negligence involved.[8] That degree of negligence is sufficiently characterised by the Ó Brian direction.

Requirement of Fault

3.39 Dangerous driving does not require the degree of negligence which is appropriate for manslaughter.[9] Mere carelessness, however, is insufficient.[10] To be convicted of dangerous driving causing death the accused does not have to intend

where the accused is also charged with dangerous driving causing death; *The State (McCann) v Wine* [1981] IR 134.

4   *The People (A-G) v Wall*, High Court unreported, 9 June 1969, Butler J.

5   *The State (O'Donoghue) v District Justice of Limerick City*, High Court unreported 17 April 1986 Lynch J.

6   Reported [1963] 97 ILT 215 and referring back to *The People (A-G) v Quinlan* (1962) 96 ILT 123. In contrast Neylon J used to explain to juries that "dangerous driving" was an ordinary expression which was best approached by, firstly, deciding what facts had been proved by the prosecution and then considering whether, if the jury had been witnesses to such driving, they would have regarded it as dangerous.

7   F (1989) 52 CCA (3d) 357, per McClung JA at 363 for the Court. For the test of the offence see par 3.38.

8   *Buttsworth* (1984) 8 Crim LJ 337 CCA Sydney.

9   *The People (A-G) v Dunleavy* [1948] IR 95 at 102 CCA.

10   Otherwise a criterion based on s 52 of the Act would be sufficient.

to so drive, or to be reckless as to the circumstance of danger he is creating.[11] The offence is objective but the prosecution must demonstrate that some fault of the driver caused the situation relied on by the prosecution as constituting the offence.[12]

This offence was created against the background of an objective test of criminal negligence for manslaughter.[13] As we have noted, it is a back-up for this offence in the context of motoring. Further, the English precedents, at the time the Road Traffic Act, 1961 was passed, indicate that in the equivalent legislation the use of the words "dangerous driving" implied an objective test.[14] The special nature of the offence, providing an option to the prosecution to proceed on indictment where the dangerous driving causes death or serious injury, does not import an additional mental element with regard to the element of harm.[15]

As in manslaughter by criminal negligence a fault element is required. That fault element can best be described as a failure by the accused to attend to his driving as a reasonably careful driver should. It is, perhaps, unhelpful to characterise that departure in terms of degrees of fault; the formulation by Ó Briain J involves the objective creation of danger judged by the standards of a reasonably prudent person.[16] As in manslaughter by criminal negligence, the test contemplates that a reasonable and careful person, in the circumstances proved against the accused, would foresee a risk of harm. It is irrelevant, because an objective test is used, that the accused did not himself foresee that harm.[17]

A jury will decide whether or not the accused was guilty of dangerous driving by applying their collective experience of road and vehicle conditions, and the possible hazards which various manoeuvres are known to create, and asking themselves whether, in all the circumstances of the case, a reasonably prudent person would have foreseen a direct and serious risk of harm to the public.

Nature of the Fault Element

3.40 This objective fault element requires that the accused be in the wrong in contributing to the situation alleged to constitute dangerous driving. Just as cases of criminal negligence manslaughter proceed by finding objective fault in the

---

11   *McBride* (1966) 115 CLR 44 HC; *Buttsworth* (1984) 8 Crim LJ 337 CCA Sydney.
12   *Gosney* [1971] 2 QB 674; [1971] 3 All ER 220; [1971] 3 WLR 343, 55 Cr App R 502; [1971] RTR 321 CA.
13   See par 3.10.
14   Archbold (1966) 2846–47; Russell 631; *Hill v Baxter* [1958] 1 QB 277; [1958] 1 All ER 193; [1958] 2 WLR 76, 42 Cr App R 51; [1959] Crim LR 27 DC. See also *Evans* [1963] 1 QB 412; [1962] 3 All ER 1086; [1962] 3 WLR 1457, 47 Cr App R 62 CCA.
15   In this context, it is submitted, that the offence is entirely different in its nature from the former offence of capital murder analysed by the Supreme Court in *The People (DPP) v Murray* [1977] IR 360; par 2.36–2.37.
16   The parallels with the *Dunleavy* formulation, and in particular par (d) thereof are obvious. In contrast the *Dunleavy* formulation requires negligence of a very high degree involving a high degree of risk or likelihood of substantial personal injury to others. In those circumstances a reasonably prudent man would normally foresee the risk of death or serious injury. In a formulation by Ó Briain J a reasonably prudent man would usually foresee a direct and serious risk of harm to the public; further see par 3.08–3.10.
17   Again the position in criminal negligence manslaughter is parallel; see par 3.10.

circumstances leading to death,[18] dangerous driving adopts a similar analysis but through the application of a lesser standard of culpability. In *Gosney*[19] clear circumstances of objective fault were proved by the prosecution. The accused was found driving her car in the wrong direction up a dual-carriageway against on-coming traffic. She sought to adduce evidence that this circumstance had been caused, not by her own inattention, but by a deceptive road layout which might reasonably have caused a competent and careful driver to be put in the same situation. The Court of Appeal ruled that the fault element in dangerous driving required a consideration of what had led to the objective circumstances of danger:

> In order to justify a conviction there must be, not only a situation which, viewed objectively, was dangerous, but there must also have been some "fault" on the part of the driver, causing that situation. Fault certainly does not necessarily involve deliberate misconduct or recklessness or intention to drive in a manner inconsistent with the proper standard of driving. Nor does fault necessarily involve moral blame. Thus there is fault if an inexperienced or a naturally poor driver, while straining every nerve to do the right thing, falls below the standard of a competent and careful driver. Fault involves failure; a falling below the care or skill of a competent and experienced driver, in relation to the manner of driving and to the relevant circumstances of the case. A fault in that sense, even though it might be slight, even though it be a momentary lapse, even though normally no danger would have arisen from it, is sufficient. The fault need not be the sole cause of the dangerous situation. It is enough if it is, looked at sensibly, a cause. Such fault will often be sufficiently proved as an inference from the very facts of the situation. But if the driver seeks to avoid that inference by proving some special fact, relevant to the question of fault in this sense, he may not be precluded from seeking so to do.[20]

Examples from decided cases can be deceptive. It is clear from the terms of the section that the jury must have regard to all the circumstances of the case. Notwithstanding that, an isolated factor which shows a sufficient degree of carelessness can be sufficient.

Objective signs, such as skid marks[21] or damage to a vehicle[22] should be treated with caution. It is not necessary for the prosecution to lead direct evidence as to what occurred where the facts proven are such as to show beyond reasonable doubt that the accused's manner of driving was dangerous. In such circumstances the facts must be so strong, in the absence of any explanation as to mechanical defect, illness or any other excuse that is given, as to give rise to an inference that the accused was guilty of dangerous driving.[23]

---

18 See par 3.12.

19 [1971] 2 QB 674; [1971] 3 All ER 220; [1971] 3 WLR 343, 55 Cr App R 502; [1971] RTR 321 CA.

20 QB at 680, All ER at 224, WLR at 347, Cr App R at 508, RTR at 325. This judgment was approved by the New Zealand Court of Appeal in *Jones* [1986], NZLR 1. The burden of proof is the same as in any criminal case. Once the defence has adduced evidence reasonably capable of negativing fault, it is for the prosecution to disprove such evidence beyond reasonable doubt; *Spurge* [1961] 2 QB 205; [1961] 2 All ER 688; [1961] 3 WLR 23, 45 Cr App R 191 CCA; *The People (A-G) v Quinn* [1965] IR 366 CCA quoted at par 4.01.

21 *Devane v Murphy* (1958) Ir Jur Rep 73.

22 *Lord v Ball* [1981] RTR 211.

23 Wilkinson's *Road Traffic Offences* (14th ed., 1989) 5.30. See *Rabjohns v Burgar* [1972] Crim LR 46;

Examples of Fault

3.41 The cases indicate that dangerous driving has been found where a driver towed another vehicle in such a manner that it snaked dangerously about the road;[24] where a driver was momentarily inattentive and failed to see traffic lights;[25] for driving at speed;[26] for overtaking where the driver mistakenly believed he was on a dual-carriageway;[27] for overtaking two lanes of traffic at speed against traffic approaching from the other direction;[28] for driving a motor cycle in a built-up area at 64 mph in heavy traffic and overtaking a vehicle which itself was overtaking;[29] for cutting in on another motorist and ignoring a signal not to do so;[30] for driving a lorry at more than twice the speed limit along a normally busy road; for overtaking without a signal on a bend and "charging at narrow bridges";[31] and for driving a motor cycle at 60 mph while not holding the handlebars for four seconds.[32] Dangerous driving has also been found in Canada,[33] where the accused was impaired by alcohol and failed to see a clearly visible cyclist,[34] where a vehicle which could not be properly controlled was driven at highway speeds[35] and in the context of general impairment and endangerment to the lives or safety of others.[36] It was also dangerous driving to travel at 100 kmh, not keeping a proper look-out, too close to the centre of the road and with a high blood alcohol level.[37]

[1971] RTR 234 DC; *Wright v Wenlock* [1972] Crim LR 49; [1971] RTR 228 DC; *Lodwick v Jones* [1983] RTR 273 DC.

24   *Anderson v Transport Board* [1964] NZLR 881.

25   *Parker* (1957) 41 Cr App R 134 CCA.

26   In *Tribe v Jones* (1961) 59 LGR 582; [1961] Crim LR 835, the driving was in a 30 mph zone along a damp road at speeds between 45 and 65 mph. The High Court refused to interfere with the acquittal due to the absence of traffic and good visibility, road surface and weather conditions. In *Johnstone v Hawkins* [1959] Crim LR 459, 854 the Divisional Court refused to quash an acquittal where the accused had driven at 85 mph along a main road past a road junction controlled by a slow sign but where the driver had a good view down a minor road 20 yards from it. The Court also said that passing a junction at that speed was *prima facie* evidence of dangerous driving. In *Bracegirdle v Oxley* [1947] KB 349; [1947] 1 All ER 126 the Court of Criminal Appeal held that dangerous driving could be perpetrated through speed alone.

27   *Johnson* [1960] Crim LR 430.

28   *Squire v Metropolitan Police Commissioner* [1957] Crim LR 817 DC.

29   *Baker v Williams* [1956] 54 LGR 197 DC.

30   *Marson v Thompson* [1955] Crim LR 319 DC.

31   *Bracegirdle v Oxley*, fn 26.

32   Noted on p 4 of the *Guardian*, 28 January 1966. Examples in this sentence in the text are mostly taken from Wilkinson's *Road Traffic Offences* (14th ed., 1989) 5.41.

33   The Criminal Code CS 249 provides: "Everyone commits an offence who operates (a) a motor vehicle on a street, road, highway or other public place in a manner that is dangerous to the public, having regard to all the circumstances, including the nature, and use of that place and the amount of traffic that at that time is or might reasonably be expected to be on that place".

34   *Colby* (1989) 52 CCC (3d) 321 Alberta CA.

35   *Thomas* (1990) 53 CCC (3d) 245 BC CA.

36   *F* (1989) 52 CCC (3d) 357 Alberta CA.

37   *Leaf-Millram* (1987) 30 A Crim R 68 CCA SA.

Emergency

3.42 A driver is only obliged to act as a reasonably prudent person.[38] Circumstances can occur where, considered in isolation, a particular example of driving may be seen as dangerous. Where there is evidence that the conduct of the driver was as a result of a sudden emergency (if a reasonable doubt exists as to whether that emergency occurred) then the question is whether the accused drove in a reasonably prudent manner in those circumstances. A driver suddenly confronted by an emergency must not be judged by hindsight.[39] If a driver has made a reasonable choice in the context of an emergency he cannot, it is submitted, be guilty of dangerous driving. A choice cannot be reasonable where a reasonably prudent driver would clearly recognise it as involving a direct and serious risk of harm to the public. Situations can arise where the driver has no time to make a choice. His decision, even if wrong, may not amount to fault. Where the emergency is caused by the accused the question is then whether he drove dangerously in bringing about that situation.

Condition of Vehicle

3.43 The condition of the vehicle driven may, in itself, be sufficient evidence of dangerous driving if it is such that a reasonably prudent man would clearly recognise that it involved a direct and serious risk of harm to the public. In *Robert Millar (Contractors) Ltd* and *Robert Millar*[40] the Court of Appeal upheld the conviction of a lorry driver who, knowing that a tyre was dangerously worn, drove his vehicle. The tyre burst and caused the lorry to swerve and kill the occupants of an oncoming car.

Circumstances can occur where a driver is unaware of the defect in his vehicle and yet has failed to act as a reasonably prudent person by, for example, neglecting it over a long period of time or failing to subject it to any standard periodic check. The accused is obliged to act, whatever his degree of mechanical knowledge, as a reasonably prudent person and must not depart from the standard of maintenance and inspection appropriate to that standard. If he does so in a manner where such a person would clearly recognise a direct and serious risk of harm to the public, he drives dangerously.[41] The danger caused by the vehicle is not limited to mechanical

---

38   See par 3.38.

39   *R v Bristol Crown Court, ex parte Jones* (1986) 83 Cr App R 109; [1986] RTR 259 DC.

40   [1970] 2 QB 54; [1970] 1 All ER 577; [1970] 2 WLR 541, 54 Cr App R 158; [1970] RTR 147 CA. See also *Lie Yiu Koong and Another* [1985] LRC (Crim) 604 HK CA.

41   This test can be expressed by asking what the driver ought to have known in the circumstances. The test is not what the jury now know, with the benefit of hindsight, but whether the defect should have been known to the accused and whether it was sufficiently serious in its capacity for affecting control of the vehicle as to make driving in those circumstances dangerous. Where the effect is known to the accused the question is as to the degree of risk that would be appreciated by a reasonably prudent person. This requires a driver to have a reasonable or ordinary appreciation of the consequences of mechanical defects, just as he is required to have a reasonable or ordinary level of driving skills. Where the accused has a better mechanical edcuation than the ordinary driver the test for dangerous driving will be applied by giving the ordinary driver that level of knowledge and asking whether, in those circumstances, he would have clearly recognised a direct and serious risk of harm to the public if the vehicle was driven. Danger can also be created by the manner of driving combined with the defect. The test in s 53 of the Act requires all the circumstances of the case to be taken into account. In *Haynes v Swain* [1975] RTR 40; [1974] Crim LR 483, the Divisional

defects but may arise, for example, due to insecure loading.[42] The jury are not entitled to assume the existence of a sudden emergency or unknown mechanical defect.[43] Once evidence of such a defect or emergency is adduced the jury should acquit if that explanation leaves a real doubt in their minds.[44]

Automatism

3.44 In common with the offence of manslaughter the offence of dangerous driving does not require a mental element but it is necessary for the actions of the accused to have been voluntary.[45] If the driver's defence is that, at the relevant time, he was in a state of automatism or, for example, that he had lost control due to an attack by a swarm of wasps he must adduce evidence to raise that issue.[46] Where such a defence becomes a live issue the prosecution need only show that the actions of the accused were directed by a mind that was conscious of what his body was doing.[47] Such a state of divergence between will and act will not excuse if the accused could have taken steps to avoid it. So a driver should stop and take rest when he feels sleep overtaking him.[48] In *Quick*,[49] Lawson LJ explained the rule thus:

> Court held that where a car had been serviced by a garage all that could be assumed was that the car had been serviced and nothing else. It is submitted that this opinion, in the context of careless driving, is of dubious validity as the question remains as to what a reasonably prudent person would consider such a service involved. In the context of careless driving Wilkinson, *op cit*, 5.34-5.40 states: "No reasonable, prudent and competent driver will knowingly drive a motor vehicle with a worn tyre, defective steering or defective brakes, and if a driver does so he is *ipso facto* departing from the standard of a prudent, reasonable and competent driver". In England the offence is now one of reckless driving, causing death and reckless driving contrary to s 1 and 2 of the Road Traffic Act, 1972. Further see Smith & Hogan 482-87; *Lawrence* [1982] AC 510, [1981] 1 All ER 974; [1981] 2 WLR 524, 73 Cr App R 1; [1981] RTR 217; [1981] Crim LR 409 HL.

42   *Crossman* [1986] RTR 49, 82 Cr App R 333; [1986] Crim LR 406 CA.

43   *Hougham v Martin* [1964] Crim LR 414 DC; Wilkinson, *op cit*, 5.30. *Jones v Chief Constable of Avon* [1986] RTR 259, 83 Cr App R 109 DC; *Simpson v Peat* [1952] 2 QB 24; [1952] 1 All ER 447; [1952] 1 WLR 469 DC.

44   *Spurge* [1961] 2 QB 205; [1961] 2 All ER 688; [1961] 3 WLR 23, 45 Cr App R 191 CCA.

45   See the discussion of *Scarth* [1945] St R Qd 38 at par 3.10.

46   *Hill v Baxter* [1958] 1 QB 277; [1958] 1 All ER 193; [1958] 2 WLR 76, 42 Cr App R 51, [1959] Crim LR 27 DC. In *Richards v Gardner* [1974] RTR 477; [1974] Crim LR 119 the Divisional Court held that in the absence of such evidence it is not proper to theorise that such an event may have occurred. In *Moses v Winder* [1981] RTR 37; [1980] Crim LR 232 the Divisional Court held that while medical evidence was not essential to prove automatism the defence could rarely succeed without it; and see *Stripp* (1978) 69 Cr App R 318 CA; Smith & Hogan 42-44. Where such evidence is adduced it must be disproved by the prosecution; *Budd* [1962] Crim LR 49 CCA. IR *Cook v Atchison* [1968] Crim LR 266 the Divisional Court held a defendant's evidence that he must have had a mild black-out because of his inability to brake on seeing red traffic lights was insufficient to raise automatism in the absence of medical evidence. Thus a person who has aggravated a condition of high blood pressure, bringing on a black-out, and causing his car to be driven dangerously if he aggravated his state by drinking. *Sibbles* (1959) Crim LR 660.

47   *Lawrence* [1982] AC 510, [1981] 1 All ER 974; [1981] 2 WLR 524, 73 Cr App R 1 HL, [1981] RTR at 217; [1981] Crim LR 409 HL. Lord Diplock refers to *Caldwell* [1982] AC 341; [1981] 1 All ER 961; [1981] 2 WLR 509, 73 Cr App R 13; [1981] Crim LR 392 HL and *Allan v Patterson* [1980] RTR 97.

48   *Kay v Butterworth* (1945) 110 JP 75; *Henderson v Jones* [1955] Crim LR 318 DC. Wilkinson, *op cit* 5.31 volunteers the opinion that a person cannot be convicted of reckless driving if he falls asleep unless it can be shown there is evidence that there was a risk of his falling asleep but he nevertheless

A self-induced incapacity will not excuse . . . nor will one which could have been reasonably foreseen as a result of either doing, or omitting to do something, as, for example, taking alcohol against medical advice after using certain prescribed drugs, or failing to have regular meals while taking insulin.[50]

The English cases indicate that the defence of automatism will only succeed if the driving was involuntary, in the sense of being wholly uncontrolled and uninitiated by any function of conscious will.[51] Evidence that the vehicle was, at times during a journey, controlled, in the sense that it swerved or braked at appropriate points, indicates that the accused was driving.[52] In these circumstances the defence of automatism is not open.

Evidence of Intoxication and Other Incidents

3.45 Often the prosecution will seek to bolster a case of dangerous driving by reference not only to the incident alleged,[53] but to the fact that the accused was not in a fit condition to drive and to bad driving prior to the accident. The State is entitled to rely on such evidence provided it occurs within a reasonable distance and time of the allegedly dangerous driving,[54] and its probative value is not outweighed by its prejudicial effect.

Controversy has arisen as to the extent to which evidence of the consumption of alcohol is admissible on a charge of dangerous driving.[55] In *The People (A-G) v Regan*[56] the accused killed a Garda at a checkpoint. The evidence was that another Garda then observed him and formed the opinion that he was unfit to drive a motor car because of the consumption of intoxicating liquor. The evidence showed that he had drunk seven pints of beer at a period within four hours of the accident. Griffin J for the Court of Criminal Appeal stated:

. . . the admission of evidence of intoxicating liquor consumed by a driver should not

---

persisted in continuing to drive. It is submitted that if a person falls asleep that fact, without explanation, speaks for itself.

49   [1973] QB 910; [1973] 3 All ER 347; [1973] 3 WLR 26, 57 Cr App R 722; [1973] Crim LR 434 CA.

50   QB at 922, All ER at 356, WLR at 35 Cr App R at 735. The court approved the following direction to a jury in *HM Advocate v Ritchie* [1926] SC (J) 45: "Automatism is a defence to a charge of dangerous driving provided that a person takes reasonable steps to prevent himself from acting involuntarily in a manner dangerous to the public. It must be caused by some factor which he could not reasonably foresee and not by a self-induced incapacity".

51   *Watmore v Jenkins* [1962] 2 QB 572; [1962] 2 All ER 868; [1962] 3 WLR 463 DC.

52   *Broome v Perkins* [1987] RTR 321, 85 Cr App R 321; [1987] Crim LR 271 DC. See the criticism of this case in Wilkinson, *op cit* 5.29. It is submitted that there is no validity to distinction between automatism brought on by diabetes and by taking too much insulin; Quick, fn 49.

53   In *Horrix v Malan* [1984] RTR 112 the Divisional Court held that a charge was not bad for duplicity in referring to two incidences of driving separated by a ten minute and two mile interval as the charge related to one continuous activity; and see *Jones* [1974] ICR 310, 59 Cr App R 120 [1974] Crim LR 663 CA.

54   *Hallett v Warren* (1929) 93 JP 225; *Taylor* (1927) 20 Cr App R 74.

55   *The People (A-G) v O'Neill* [1964] Ir Jur Rep CCA; *The People (A-G) v Moore* [1964] Ir Jur Rep 6 CCA.

56   [1975] IR 367 CCA.

be confined to cases where there is evidence that the driving of the driver was adversely affected by drink. Cases frequently arise in which there is no direct evidence to show how the accused driver was affected by drink; for example, as in *Moore's* Case [1964] Ir Jur Rep 6, drivers often leave the scene of the accident before there is any opportunity for consideration of the sobriety or otherwise of the driver. In the view of this Court, evidence of intoxicating drink consumed by a driver should be admitted not only where it tends to show that the driver was in fact adversely affected by drink but also, as stated in *McBride's* case [1962] 2 QB 167, where it tends to show that the amount of drink taken was such as would adversely affect a driver.[57]

The Court characterised the amount of drink that would adversely affect a driver as "significant". They approved the judgment of Davitt P in *Moore's* case:

> The tendency of alcohol to affect adversely a person's faculties generally, and, in particular, his judgement of time, speeds and distances, as well as his ability to exercise functions requiring skill in performance, is, we think, a matter of common knowledge. Where a person has during a period of time which is material, consumed, a significant quantity it will, therefore, tend to render his driving unsafe. The evidence that he has consumed such a quantity during such a period is therefore in our opinion of probative value on a charge of dangerous driving and therefore relevant and admissible in law … what is "significant quantity"? The effect of drink upon a person's faculties will depend upon his tolerance to alcohol, and this in turn may depend upon his physical and psychological constitution. It will be a matter which the trial Judge will have to decide in each case.[58]

Evidence that the accused drove when affected by drugs or, it is submitted, by severe physical or emotional trauma, is subject to the same principle.[59]

Driving

3.46 The "vehicle" that the accused must be driving is not limited to a mechanically propelled vehicle. A person riding a bicycle may be guilty of the offence.

The accused must be driving the vehicle at the time of the offence. In *McQuaid v Anderton*[60] Heilbron J indicated that the concept of "driving" must not be given so wide a meaning as to include activities which cannot be said to be driving a motor vehicle in any ordinary sense of that word. She stated:

> The . . . Act does not define the word "drive" and in its simplest meaning we think that it refers to a person using the driver's controls for the purpose of directing the movement of the vehicle. It matters not that the vehicle is not moving under its own

---

57   At 373.

58   *Moore's* case, fn 55 at 9. The trial judge is not obliged to hear the entire of the evidence in deciding admissibility; *The People (A-G) v Regan*, fn 56 at 374.

59   Wilkinson, *op cit*, 5.32. In England this kind of evidence where the accused had visited public houses before driving was admitted in *Richardson* [1960] Crim LR 135; in *Fisher* [1981] Crim LR 135 CA, it was admitted where he had spent practically the whole day in public houses prior to driving; in *McBride* [1962] 2 QB 167; [1961] 3 WLR 549; [1961] 3 All ER 6, 45 Cr App R 262 CCA, it was admitted where the accused had more than the prescribed blood-alcohol level. Where ability to drive is substantially impaired an accused would be guilty of reckless driving causing death if he then drives because he is choosing to drive and the manner of his driving may be such as to create an obvious serious risk of causing physical injury to some person who happened, or might happen, to be using the road or of doing substantial damage to property; *Griffiths* [1974] Crim LR 629.

60   [1981] 1 WLR 154; [1980] 3 All ER 540; [1980] RTR 371 DC.

power or driven by the force of gravity, or even that it is being pushed by other well-wishers. The essence of driving is the use of the driver's controls in order to direct the movement, however that movement is produced.[61]

Two or more persons can engage in a common design to drive a vehicle in a criminally negligent fashion.[62] A party who is not "driving" can aid and abet the offence of dangerous driving causing death.[63]

Apart from automatism an accused can plead any other relevant defence, for example, necessity.[64]

The principles of causation applicable to this offence[65] do not differ from those in homicide.[66] In *Lie Yiu-koong and Another*[67] the Hong Kong Court of Appeal held that a person who had not driven a vehicle was nonetheless guilty of the offence provided he had made a more than "de minimis" contribution to the dangerous manner in which the vehicle was loaded.

Consequence

3.47 The consequence proscribed by the Act is "death or serious bodily harm". The latter element is akin to the intent in murder which is "to kill or to cause serious injury".[68] The concepts of death[69] and serious injury[70] are discussed elsewhere in the text.

The offence must take place in a "public place". This is defined by s 3 of the 1961 Act as meaning:

> Any street, road, or other place to which the public have access with vehicles whether as of right or by permission and whether subject to or free of charge. . . .[71]

Furious Driving

3.48 An alternative offence is created by s 35 of the Offences Against the Person Act,. 1861 which provides:

---

61   All ER at 542, WLR at 157. In *Jones v Pratt* [1983] RTR 54 the Divisional Court held that a front seat passenger in a moving car who grabbed the steering wheel and pushed it, in order to avoid an animal on the road, could not properly be described as driving the car; further Wilkinson, *op cit*, 1.51–1.52.

62   *Baldessare* (1930) 22 Cr App R 70, 29 Cox 193 CCA.

63   Robert Millar, par 3.40.

64   *Conway* [1989] QB 290; [1988] 3 All ER 1025; [1988] 3 WLR 1238; (1988) Cr App R 343; [1989] RTR 85; [1989] Crim LR 74 CA; *Fry* (1977) 36 CCC (2d) 396.

65   See par 2.10 and par 3.21.

66   *The People (A-G) v Gallagher* [1972] IR 365, 106 ILTR 61 CCA. See par 3.21. In *Cornish* (1988) 33 A Crim R 91, the Court of Criminal Appeal of South Australia held that where the victim was not wearing a seat belt nonetheless the accused's action in crashing the car was a substantial cause of death and therefore sufficient.

67   [1985] LRC (Crim) 604.

68   Criminal Justice Act, 1964, s 4.

69   See par 1.17–1.18.

70   See par 2.34–2.35.

71   The relevant cases are cited and discussed in the context of ch 11.

Whosoever, having the charge of any carriage or vehicle, shall, by wanton or furious driving or racing, or other wilful misconduct or by wilful neglect, do or cause to be done any bodily harm to any person whatsoever, shall be guilty of a misdemeanour, and being convicted thereof shall be liable, at the discretion of the Court, to be imprisoned for any term not exceeding two years, with or without hard labour.

This offence serves a useful purpose only because there is no requirement that the accused be warned of an impending prosecution and because there is no requirement that it should occur in a public place.

The prosecution must prove a degree of lack of care which would amount to dangerous driving. "Wanton" indicates positive lack of care and "wilful" implies something of a negative nature.[72] The offence is structured similarly to dangerous driving causing death. The prosecution do not need to prove an intention to cause injury or bodily harm; the accused's driving must be voluntary and if it falls below the normal standard so that it could be described as "misconduct" and is thereby a substantial cause of bodily harm to any person the offence is made out.[73] The section can also be used where a motor vehicle is used to assault a person.[74] It is submitted that the offence of dangerous driving can also so be used.

The section applies to all carriages and vehicles, public or private, to bicycles and to motor bicycles.[75] If the accused is charged with an attempt the section, in common with all other offences of attempt, requires a specific intent.[76]

Draft Indictments

3.49 There follow the appropriate forms of indictment for the offences considered in this chapter:

MANSLAUGHTER

Statement of Offence
Manslaughter
Particulars of Offence
AB on the   at   unlawfully killed CD.

NORTHERN IRELAND

Statement of Offence
Manslaughter contrary to s 2(1) of the Criminal Law (Jurisdiction) Act, 1976.
Particulars of Offence
AB on   at   Northern Ireland, unlawfully killed CD.

---

72   Wilkinson, *op cit* 5.55.
73   *Cooke* [1971] Crim LR 44. See *Burdon* (1927) 20 Cr App R 80 where the Court of Criminal Appeal upheld a conviction under the section by reason of the amount of liquor taken and the manner of driving.
74   For assault see ch 6.
75   *Archbold* (1922) 954; *Parker* (1895) 59 JP 793.
76   *Mohan* [1976] QB 1; [1975] 2 All ER 193; [1975] 2 WLR 859; [1975] RTR 337, 60 Cr App R 272; [1975] Crim LR 283 CA.

DANGEROUS DRIVING CAUSING DEATH

Statement of Offence

Dangerous driving causing death contrary to s 53 of the Road Traffic Act, 1961 as amended by s 51 of the Road Traffic Act, 1968.

Particulars of Offence

AB on the   at   , a public place, drove a vehicle being a   in a manner (including speed) which having regard to all the circumstances of the case, including the condition of the vehicle, the nature, condition and use of the place and the amount of traffic which then actually was or might reasonably be expected then to be therein was dangerous to the public and thereby caused the death of (or serious bodily harm to) CD.

CHAPTER FOUR

Defences

4.01 This chapter considers in detail the specific defences to murder. These are provocation and excessive self-defence. For the sake of completeness a short outline of the other major defences is also sketched. A full treatment of these is reserved for Volume 2 as these are general to the criminal law.

Burden of Proof

The burden of proof is on the prosecution in respect of every fact which constitutes either a denial of the charge or a defence. This prosecution burden is discharged by disproving the existence of the material supporting the denial or defence beyond reasonable doubt. The only exception to this rule is insanity where the accused must clearly prove that he is insane.[1] An analysis of the correct approach was made by Walsh J in *The People (A-G) v Quinn*.[2] His remarks deal with self-defence but the principles enunciated constitute the correct approach to the defences which follow in this chapter:

> When the evidence in a case, whether it be the evidence offered by the prosecution or by the defence, discloses a possible defence of self-defence the onus remains throughout on the prosecution to establish that the accused is guilty of the offence charged. The onus is never upon the accused to raise a doubt in the minds of the jury. In such a case the burden rests on the prosecution to negative the possible defence of self-defence which has arisen and if, having considered the whole of the evidence, the jury is either convinced of the innocence of the prisoner or left in doubt whether or not he was acting in necessary self-defence they must acquit. Before the possible defence can be left to the jury as an issue there must be some evidence from which the jury would be entitled to find that issue in favour of the appellant. If the evidence for the prosecution does not disclose this possible defence then the necessary evidence will fall to be given by the defence. In such a case, however, where it falls to the defence to give the necessary evidence it must be made clear to the jury that there is a distinction, fine though it may appear, between adducing the evidence and the burden of proof and that there is no onus whatever upon the accused to establish any degree of doubt in their minds. In directing the jury on the question of the onus of proof it can only be misleading to a jury to refer to "establishing" the defence "in such a way as to raise a doubt". No defence has to be "established" in any case apart from insanity. In a case where there is evidence, whether it be disclosed in the prosecution case or in the defence case, which is sufficient to leave the issue of self-defence to the jury the only question the jury has to consider is whether they are satisfied beyond reasonable doubt that the accused killed the deceased (if it be a case of homicide) and whether the jury is satisfied beyond reasonable doubt that the prosecution has negatived the issue of self-defence. If the jury is not satisfied beyond reasonable doubt on both of these matters the accused must be acquitted.[3]

---

1   See par 4.45.
2   [1965] IR 366 CCA.
3   At 382–83, Ó Dálaigh CJ, Lavery, Kingsmill Moore & Teevan JJ agreeing.

Provocation

4.02 Where the accused, in killing the victim, acts under the influence of provocation[4] his crime will amount only to manslaughter, and not murder, notwithstanding that the accused intended to kill or cause serious injury.[5] The test in Irish law is subjective. The provocation under which the accused was acting must be such that having regard to the particular accused's character, temperament and circumstances, it causes him to temporarily lose control of himself to the extent that he ceased to be master of himself when he killed the victim.[6] The accused must use no more force than is reasonable having regard to the effect the provocation had on him.[7]

The test in Irish law is unique in the common law world. It is necessary to consider the test in greater detail and against the common law rules in other countries. This will show the circumstances which led to the rejection of those rules in this jurisdiction. The law requires revision. The test applied in practice is not binding but is merely a suggested solution by the Court of Criminal Appeal to the problems associated with this defence.[8]

Where there is evidence of provocation, the defence should be left to the jury whether or not it is specifically raised at the trial.[9]

Common Law Background

4.03 Kaye traces the first reported instance of provocation as a defence to murder

4   Ashworth, "The Doctrine of Provocation" (1976) 35 CLJ 272; Law Reform Commission of South Australia—4th report—"Substantive Criminal Law" (1977) 21-24; "Law Reform Commission of New Zealand Report on Culpable Homicide" (277); Criminal Law Revision Committee of England Working Paper on Offences Against the Person (1976) par 54; Brett, "The Physiology of Provocation" [1970] Crim LR 634; Wildman, "Is the Reasonable Man Obsolete" (1981) 14 Loyola of LAL Law Review 435; Archbold & Kait, "A Postscript to *R v Hill*: Wither Goest Provocation" (1987) 29 CLQ 172; Wells, "The Death Penalty for Provocation" [1978] Crim LR 662; Bennion, "Provocation The New Law" (1978) 41 MLR 722; Gold, "Provocation—Young Offender" (1978) 20 CL 306; Bayne, "Automatism and Provocation in Canadian Case Law" (1975) 31 CRNS 257; Berger, "Provocation and the Involuntary Act" (1967) 12 McGill LJ 202; O'Regan, "Indirect Provocation and Misdirected Retaliation" [1968] Crim LR 319; Ashworth, "Self-Induced Provocation and the Homicide Act" [1973] Crim LR 483; Snelling, "Manslaughter upon Chance Medeley" (1957) 31 ALJ 102; Orchard, "Provocation—The Subjective Element" [1977] NZLJ 77; Brown, "The Subjective Element in Provocation" (1959) 1 University of Malaya LR 288; Yeo, "Provocating the Ordinary 'Ethnic' Person: A Juror's Predicament" (1987) 11 Crim LJ 96; Howard, "What Colour is the Reasonable Man" [1961] Crim LR 41; Williams, "Provocation and the Reasonable Man" [1954] Crim LR 740; Brown, "The 'Ordinary' Man in Provocation: Anglo-Saxon Attitudes and 'Unreasonable Un-English Man'" (1964) 131 CLQ 203; Prevezer, "Criminal Homicides other than Murder" [1980] Crim LT 530; Wasik, "Cumulative Provocation and Domestic Killing" [1982] Crim LR 29; English, "Provocation and Attempted Murder" [1973] Crim LR 727.

5   *The People (DPP) v Mac Eoin* [1978] IR 27 CCA. Clearly, if the accused did not intend to kill or cause serious injury he cannot be guilty of murder; generally see ch 2.

6   *Mac Eoin*, fn 5 at 31, 34.

7   *Mac Eoin*, fn 5 at 34, 35. This test results from a misunderstanding of the law by the Court.

8   *Mac Eoin*, fn 5.

9   *Bullard* [1957] AC 635; [1961] 3 All ER 470; [1957] 3 WLR 656, 42 Cr App R 1 PC; *Ward* (1989) 42 A Crim R 56 CCA NSW.

to *Robinson's* case in 1576.[10] The accused and the victim were fighting, the victim fled, the accused went into his house, fetched a staff and pursued and killed the victim. The killing was manslaughter because it was done in a "continuing fury".

The concern of the law was, and remains, to distinguish between a cold blooded killing and an uncontrollable burst of violence. For the defence to succeed the accused must have killed the victim, not from any deliberate motive but whilst acting under a temporary suspension of reason.[11] As such the law is policy motivated as a concession to human infirmity. Anger is a commonplace emotion which can cause people to do what, in more temperate moments, they would otherwise avoid and which they later regret.

4.04 Prior to the Criminal Evidence Act, 1898 in England and the Criminal Justice (Evidence) Act, 1924 in Ireland, an accused person could not generally give evidence in his own defence. The jury were deprived of the advantage of hearing his testimony as to the personal effect of the provocation on his composure. It was imperative for the law to develop a test whereby the jury could consider the effect of provocation on a person whose actions could only be judged by what other people described him doing or saying.

Turner[12] considers that, in early English law, the method of dealing with the defence of provocation was for the jury to find facts as proved and for the judge to rule, as a matter of law, whether the defence was made out. When the jury function evolved to the role which it now has, of simply recording a verdict, a major change occurred. Judges began to direct juries that the accused was to be judged by the standard of the reasonable man in reacting to the provocative circumstances in issue. This test was first reported in 1869, as stated by Keating J in addressing a jury in *Welsh*:[13]

> There must exist such an amount of provocation as would be excited by the circumstances in the mind of a reasonable man, and so as to lead the jury to ascribe the act to the influence of that passion. . . . The law contemplates the case of a reasonable man, and requires that the provocation be such that such a man might naturally be induced, in the anger of the moment, to commit the act.[14]

Emergence of the Reasonable Man Test

4.05 It is likely that prior to 1869 the reasonableness of a person's conduct was merely a guide to the jury in considering the evidence, through the accounts of observers, as to how the accused behaved. By constant usage this guide came to be elevated to a rule of law.[15] Notwithstanding that the accused was later available to give evidence, the reasonable man test continued to govern the consideration of his reaction to provocation. The law was concerned with the effect of that provocation

10   Kaye, "The Early History of Murder and Manslaughter" (1967) 83 LQR 365-95, 569-601 at 589.
11   1 East PC 238; Foster 255; *Hayward* (1833) 6 C&P 157, 172 ER 118.
12   In *Russell* 526-29. See further the cases therein cited.
13   (1869) 11 Cox 336.
14   At 338.
15   Turner so argues: *Russell* 533-37, pointing out that in *Lynch* (1832) 5 C&P 324, 172 ER 995 Tenterden CJ invited a jury to take the accused's weak intellect into account.

on the accused only to the extent that it required him to have lost self-control. The actual effect of provocation having that result only sufficed in law to establish the defence if, in addition, a reasonable man would have reacted in the same way.[16] What a reasonable man was was never defined in criminal law.[17] Everyone, who was not insane, was subject to the same rule.[18]

In a series of restrictive rulings the English courts made it clear that such factors as mental deficiency,[19] pregnancy,[20] youth[21] and sensitivity about a handicap or special quality[22] could not be taken into account in assessing how a reasonable man would[23] have reacted. The zenith of the movement which ignored the characteristics of the person on trial and left the ultimate test of provocation to be decided by the reactions of a hypothetical ordinary or reasonable person, was reached in the decision of the House of Lords in *Bedder*.[24] Bedder was a sexually impotent boy of eighteen who had attempted to have intercourse with a prostitute in a courtyard off a public street. She jeered him for his failure and also, during a struggle in which she tried to release his grip on her, had slapped him in the face, punched him in the stomach and kicked or kneed him in the groin. He retaliated by stabbing her twice with a knife. The House of Lords refused to invest the hypothetical reasonable man with the characteristic of impotence: apparently it would have been wrong to recognise a physical characteristic which preyed on the accused's mind. The law had already arrived at a position where it had to discount an unusually excitable or pugnacious temperament and, by the standards applied at the time, it was considered by the Lords that a reasonable man would cease to be reasonable if deprived of his reason; that the normal man ceased to be normal when given abnormal characteristics.[25] A desire to keep those of murderous disposition in check by imposing a uniform standard of behaviour in society was the policy underlying the law.[26]

16   *Lesbini* [1914] 3 KB 1116, 24 Cox 516, 11 Cr App R 7 CCA; *Mancini* [1942] AC 1; [1941] 3 All ER 272, 28 Cr App R 65 HL; *Holmes* [1946] AC 588; [1946] 2 All ER 124 HL. The classic statement of the rule is by Devlin J in *Duffy* [1949] 1 All ER 932 CCA, criticised in Williams, *TBCL* 529-30.

17   *McCarthy* [1954] 2 QB 105; [1954] 2 All ER 262; [1954] 2 WLR 1044, 38 Cr App R 74 CCA.

18   *Ward* [1956] 1 QB 351; [1956] 1 All ER 565; [1956] 2 WLR 423, 40 Cr App R 1 CCA.

19   *Alexander* (1913) 9 Cr AR 139, 23 Cox 604 CCA; *Lesbini* [1914] 3 KB 1116, 24 Cox 516, 11 Cr App R 7 CCA. See also *Griffin* (1980) 23 SASR 264 SC.

20   *Smith* (1915) 11 Cr AR 81 CCA.

21   *Camplin* [1978] AC 705; [1978] 2 All ER 168; [1978] 2 WLR 679, 67 Cr App R 14 HL (this was the trial judge's ruling in this case).

22   *Bedder* [1954] 2 All ER 801; [1954] 1 WLR 1119, 38 Cr App R 133 HL. See also *Lukins* (1902) 19 WN (NSW) 90 where the New South Wales Supreme Court disapproved provocation having an effect through insane delusions and *Enright* [1961] VR 663 where the Supreme Court of Victoria discounted an obsession about being called a "bastard".

23   Williams argues that the test is how a reasonable man might have reached—*TBCL* 537; further see *Gillies* 313-14.

24   Fn 22.

25   The Supreme Court of Canada had adopted a similar position in *Wright* [1969] SCR 335. Further see *Parnerker* [1974] 449 SC affirming, (1973) 21 CRNS 129 SASK CA. The Canadian law is set out in s 215 of the Code; for an explanation see Stuart 452-55.

26   The argument of Avory J in *Lesbini*, fn 19 that if account were taken of character a good tempered man would be found guilty of murder and the bad tempered one of manslaughter, is repeated as a justification for the rule in the report of the Royal Commission on Capital Punishment 1949-1953 (Cmnd 8932) at par 142.

4.06 The test was not applied universally in common law jurisdictions. In Australia and in Papua New Guinea the law had to be applied to persons of non-European derivation and culture. The reasonable man rule was modified to take account of local conditions.[27] In Hong Kong the test varied to take into account the race of the accused.[28]

In New Zealand s 169 of the Crimes Act of 1961 provided the model for future developments of the provocation rule. The test read:

> (1) Culpable homicide that would otherwise be murder may be reduced to manslaughter if the person who caused the death did so under provocation.
>
> (2) Anything said or done may be provocation if:
> (a) In the circumstances of the case it was sufficient to deprive a person having the power of self-control of an ordinary person but otherwise having the characteristics of the offender, of the power of self-control; and
> (b) It did in fact deprive the offender of the power of self-control and thereby induced him to commit the act of homicide.
>
> (3) Whether there is any evidence of provocation is a question of law.
>
> (4) Whether, if there is evidence of provocation, the provocation was sufficient as aforesaid, and whether it did in fact deprive the offender of the power of self-control and thereby induced him to commit the act of homicide are questions of fact.

This test required that the objective element of the reasonable person have factored into it such significant and definite characteristics of the accused as made him different from an average person. To be taken into account the characteristic had to be of such a permanent nature as to be part of the individual's character and personality. Traits of unusual excitability, pugnaciousness or quick-temper were discounted. Further, there had to exist a connection between the special characteristic of the accused and the nature of the provocation.[29] It would not avail a person of one race to plead provocation as a result of being called by the derogatory epithet vulgarly applied to another race. Even if the provocation was sufficient to deprive such an ordinary person of the power of self-control the accused only had the benefit of the defence where he had in fact lost control of himself.

The Decision in Camplin

4.07 In the 1978 case of *Camplin*[30] the House of Lords used s 3 of the Homicide Act, 1957[31] to modify the test and bring it into line with the New Zealand model.

27 Morris & Howard, *Studies in Criminal Law* (Oxford, 1964) 93–99; Howard 82 and the cases therein cited; Glanville Williams, *TBCL*, and the cases therein cited; Brown, "The 'Ordinary Man' in Provocation" (1964) 13 ICLQ 103. Further see the citations at par 4.02.

28 *Ma Wai Fun* [1962] HKLR 61 CA.

29 *McGregor* [1962] NZLR 1069 CCA; *Romano* (1984) 14 A Crim R 168 CCA SA. For a full discussion of the common law test see Brookbanks, "Provocation—Defining the Limits of Characteristics" (1986) 10 Crim LJ 411.

30 [1978] AC 705; [1978] 2 All ER 168; [1978] 2 WLR 679, 67 Cr App R 14 HL (this was the trial judge's ruling in this case).

31 This provided: "Where on a charge of murder there is evidence on which the jury can find that the person charged was provoked (whether by things done or by things said or by both together) to lose his self-control, the question whether the provocation was enough to make a reasonable man

The accused was a fifteen year old boy who alleged that he had been forcibly buggered by the deceased who had then laughed at him. Applying the unmodified *Bedder*[32] ruling, the trial judge refused to instruct the jury to take into account the effect this conduct would have had on a reasonable person of fifteen. The House of Lords held that since s 3 of the Homicide Act, 1957 allowed words to constitute provocation[33] it would be illogical to discount the personal characteristics which caused those words to occasion a loss of self-control: it would be anomalous to accept that proposition as applying to words where physical characteristics were discounted. Further, they reasoned, age was not an abnormal characteristic but a normal stage of transition. The test as thus modified remained twofold; whether the accused had actually lost his self-control as a result of provocation and whether that provocation would have had a like effect on a reasonable person, but:

> The reasonable man referred to in the question is a person having the power of self-control to be expected of an ordinary person of the sex and age of the accused, but in other respects sharing such of the accused's characteristics as they think would affect the gravity of the provocation to him, and that the question is not merely whether such a person would in like circumstances be provoked to lose his self-control but also would react to the provocation as the accused did.[34]

4.08 Factors which could not be taken into account were exceptional excitability or pugnaciousness,[35] quick temper and drunkenness.[36] Factors which were mentioned by the Lords as coming within the modified test included race,[37] impotence,[38] physical defects,[39] age and the extremes thereof such as immaturity or senility[40] and pregnancy.[41] Following the New Zealand rulings, the English courts have required there to be a connection between such a special characteristic and the provocation in question before it can be taken into account.[42]

---

do as he did shall be left to be determined by the jury; and in determining that question the jury shall take into account everything both done and said according to the effect which, in their opinion, it would have on a reasonable man". See further Smith & Hogan 331-44. This test requires any evidence of loss of self control to be put to the jury who then consider it in the light of the objective test; *Doughty* (1986) 83 Cr App R 319; [1986] Crim LR 625 CA.

32 See par 4.05.   33 fn 31.

34 Lord Diplock, AC at 718, All ER at 175, WLR at 686, Cr App R at 21. For the nature of the test at the foundation of the State see Archbold (1922) 881-85; Kenny (1922) 116-18; Stephen *Digest* (4th ed., 1887) Articles 223, 224.

35 Lord Diplock at 717, Lord Simon at 725. (Subsequent references are to AC only.)

36 Lord Simon at 725 and see *Newell* (1980) 71 Cr App R 331; [1980] Crim LR 576 CA. The question of whether chronic alcoholism was a trait which could be taken into account under the test was left open by the court for future consideration.

37 Lord Diplock at 717, Lord Morris at 721.

38 Lord Diplock at 717, Lord Morris at 720.

39 Dwarfism, per Lord Morris at 720; hunchback, per Lord Simon at 724; a severe abscess on the cheek, per Lord Simon at 724.

40 Lord Morris at 721, Lord Simon at 724.

41 Lord Simon at 724.   42 *Newell*, fn 36.

This view of the law has been adopted in Australia[43] and, substantially, in Canada.[44]

The Irish Decision

4.09 Almost simultaneously[45] with the decision in *Camplin*[46] the Court of Criminal Appeal delivered its decision in *The People (DPP) v Mac Eoin*.[47] The issue before the court was whether an intent to kill or cause serious injury was consistent with provocation.[48] In ordering a retrial the court took the opportunity to make some remarks on the test to be applied by the jury in considering the defence of provocation.[49]

The accused and the deceased had a long standing relationship. The deceased used to stay with the accused in his flat and eventually went to live there. The deceased had a drink problem and, when drunk, behaved aggressively. On the day of his death both men had been drinking heavily, the accused in a series of pubs and the deceased on his own in the flat. The remaining facts are given by Kenny J:

> The accused made up a makeshift bed for himself (there was only one bed in the flat) and got into it. After some time the deceased came towards the bed shouting: "You are going" and "You are going now". When the accused sat up in the bed the deceased produced a hammer from behind his back and hit the accused on the head with it. The hammer fell on the floor and the two of them struggled for it. The accused got it and the deceased started to punch him. In evidence he said that he was terrified because the deceased looked dangerous: He then said:—"I simmered over and I completely lost control of myself". He hit the deceased on the head with the hammer and the deceased fell on the floor. The accused then stooped down and in a rage hit the deceased a number of blows (which he estimated from 3 to 6) with the hammer on the head and killed him.[50]

4.10 The Court was invited to declare its abandonment of so much of the test of provocation as required that a reasonable man would have lost control on being subjected to the same provocation as the accused. The Court declared that the objective aspect of the test for provocation should be abandoned. These remarks, whilst not necessary to the decision before the Court, have been used in practice in instructing juries since that time. It is possible that the Supreme Court or the Court of Criminal Appeal may wish to declare that these *obiter* remarks should not in the future be followed and opt instead for a modification of the common law rule along *Camplin* lines. This has not happened; a situation caused principally by the sparsity

43   *Dincer* [1983] 1 VR 460 SC; *Dutton* (1979) 21 SASR 356 SC; *Croft* (1981) 3 A Crim R 307 CCA NSW; *Bedelph* [1980] Tas SR 23 CCA; *Gillies* 311-13; Howard 77-89; Fairall & O'Connor 194-96.

44   *Hill* (1985) 51 CR (3d) 97 SC; Stuart 452-55.

45   The decision in *Camplin* was given on 6 April 1978, in *Mac Eoin*, clearly without knowledge of the decision in *Camplin*, on 17 April 1978.

46   Par 4.07.

47   [1978] IR 27 CCA.

48   See par 4.17-4.18.

49   These remarks were, strictly, *obiter*. In this text reference to the position in other common law countries is therefore also made.

50   At 29.

of appeals by the prosecution to the Supreme Court from the Central Criminal Court the absence of a right of appeal by the prosecution to the Court of Criminal Appeal and the practical reality that juries given the *Mac Eoin* direction rarely convict. This latter situation arises in part from the obscurity of language in the judgment.

4.11 The Court adopted the dissenting judgment of Murphy J in *Moffa*.[51] The factors excluded from the modified *Camplin* test[52] were not to be discounted, in particular hot-temper.[53] Subjectivity was to be preferred in the criminal law to objectivity.

The Court adopted as the test of provocation the remarks of Devlin J, in directing a jury, in *Duffy*.[54] This quotation from that charge should be read by removing the words in brackets which contain the objective element in the test:

> Provocation is some act or series of acts, done by the dead man to the accused which (would cause in any reasonable man, and) actually caused in the accused, a sudden and temporary loss of self-control, rendering the accused so subject to passion as to make him or her for the moment not master of his mind.[55]

After referring to the fact that this test had been criticised by Smith & Hogan,[56] by Turner[57] and by Williams[58] the Court declared:

> In the opinion of this Court the objective test in cases of provocation should be declared to be no longer part of our law.[59]

The rationale for the inclusion of an objective test is to exclude from the defence of provocation those who are drunk or are of an unusually excitable, bad tempered or pugnacious disposition.[60] This policy has been expressly rejected. As the decisions of juries are now based on an entirely subjective question their decisions have become difficult to appeal as they constitute findings of fact and not of law.[61]

---

51 (1977) 13 ALR 225 at 242 HC; see also *Johnson* (1976) 136 CLR 619 at 671 HC and *Webb* (1977) 16 SASR 309 SC.

52 See par 4.08.

53 [1978] IR 27 at 32: "Words which would have no effect on the abstract reasonable man may be profoundly provocative to one having knowledge of what people say about him (sic). A hot-tempered man may react violently to an insult which a phlegmatic one would ignore".

54 [1949] 1 All ER 932 CCA.

55 At 31-32.

56 *Criminal Law* (3rd ed., 1973) 213-15.

57 *Russell on Crime* (12th ed., 1964) ch 29.

58 "Provocation and the Reasonable Man" [1954] Crim LR 740.

59 At 34. It is not clear what power the court was exercising in making this declaration. They did not seem to be declaring the test unconstitutional. They simply thought it not to be a good law. If that was so change was a matter for the Oireachtas. The Court of Criminal Appeal has since struck down a rule of the common law as unconstitutional; *The People (DPP) v T* (1988) 3 Frewen, considered in [1989] DULJ and (1990) ILT.

60 *Walker* [1969] 1 All ER 767; [1969] 1 WLR 311, 53 Cr App R 195 CA; *Enright* [1961] VR 663, 669 SC: "[The ordinary man] is brought into the doctrine for the purpose of denying the benefit of it not to those who react unreasonably to provocation but only to those whose reactions so show a lack of self-control falling outside the ordinary or common range of human temperaments". Further see Howard 79-81; Smith & Hogan 339.

61 *The People (DPP) v Kelly (No. 2)* [1983] IR 1; [1983] ILRM 271 CCA, SC.

Proportionality

4.12 A separate test of proportionality, whereby the accused when provoked was required to retaliate only in corresponding measure to the provocation offered, never existed at common law.[62] That test was peculiar to the defence of self-defence whereby the accused was required, on an objective standard expanded to take into account the difficulties experienced by a person under attack, to retaliate only to the extent necessary to defend himself from attack.[63] References in judgments on provocation to proportion were no more than an attempt to assist juries to glean from all the circumstantial evidence as to whether the accused, in killing the victim, was truly acting from an uncontrollable passion or was using the insult or attack of the victim to take the opportunity to kill him. As a matter of common experience a trivial insult can cause anger or another strong emotion, but not to the extent of a person using a deadly weapon to kill. Were that to happen it would be a strong indication of either pre-meditation or the impulse to kill coming from a cause other than the provocation. A contrary rule requiring proportion between provocation and resentment as a matter of law, as opposed to a consideration to assist in the weighing of evidence, would have been contrary to the weight of authority.[64] In *Mancini*[65] Viscount Simon LC stated:

> It is of particular importance (a) to consider whether a sufficient interval has elapsed since the provocation to allow a reasonable man time to cool and (b) to take into account the instrument with which the homicide was effected, for to retort, in the

---

62   Russell 548-53.

63   Expressly retained in *The People (A-G) v Dwyer* [1972] IR 416, 108 ILTR 17 SC. See further par 4.29.

64   The authorities cited by Turner in Russell ch 29 are *Lynch* (1832) 5 C&P 242, 72 ER 995 (the victim and the accused had been drinking, exchanged words and then blows. On the police coming the accused went away and then returned and stabbed the victim with a bread or cheese knife. The accused was of weak intellect); *Thomas* (1837) 7 C&P 817, 173 ER 356 (Parke B instructed the jury in terms that: "If a person receives a blow and immediately avenges it with any instrument he may happen to have in his hand, then the offencer will only be manslaughter, provided that the blow is to be attributed to that passion of anger from that previous provocation . . ."); *Sherwood* (1844) 1 C&K 556, 174 ER 936 (the accused, having been struck with a sweeping brush and subjected to verbal abuse, cut his wife's throat. Pollock CB, while admitting the words alone (as the law then stood) could not be sufficient provocation, said that a blow which normally would not in itself be sufficient provocation might, if accompanied by words of abuse, be rendered so); *Smith* (1866) 4 F&F 1066, 176 ER 910 (an adulterous wife, on returning home to her husband, taunted him with her preference for her late lover, abused him and spat in his fact. He thereupon stabbed her in the throat. Byles J held that such an assault coupled with the surrounding abuse and taunts could form sufficient provocation if the cumulative effect was a serious assault); *Hopper* [1915] 2 KB 431; [1914-15] All ER 914, 11 Cr App R 136 CCA (there was a fist fight between the victim and the accused. The accused killed the victim with a rifle. There had been "much drinking"); *Larkin* [1943] KB 174; [1943] 1 All ER 217, 29 Cr App R 18 CCA (the accused threatened the victim and another with a knife. The victim, his wife, allegedly fell on it and cut her throat); *Maddy* (1671) 1 Vent 158, 86 ER 158, 86 ER 108 (the accused found his wife and the victim in adultery and picked up a stool and killed the victim: "And the Court were all of opinion that it was but manslaughter, the provocation being exceedingly great and found there was no precedent malice"); *Ayes* (1810) R&R 167, 168 ER 742 (blows were exchanged between the accused and the victim and on the victim being knocked to the ground the accused stamped on him violently two or three times). The common factor in these cases is an act of violence done under the influence of passion.

65   [1942] AC 1; [1941] 3 All ER 272, 28 Cr App 65 HL.

heat of passion induced by provocation, by a simple blow, is a very different thing from making use of a deadly instrument like a concealed dagger. In short, the mode of resentment must bear a reasonable relationship to the provocation if the offence is to be regarded as manslaughter.[66]

The Correct Test

4.13 In the context of a murder trial in which the issue of provocation is considered, the issues of time and mode of retort are no more than items of evidence. They assist in a consideration of whether the case being made by the accused that he was provoked is genuine. Unfortunately the statement of Viscount Simon was taken up and used by judges as a separate legal test.[67] Subsequently the Privy Council[68] and the Court of Appeal[69] have interpreted the "proportionality requirement" in the manner in which it originally applied. The way the accused reacted may assist the jury in deciding whether his actions were inspired by a loss of self-control or by an independent intent to kill or do serious injury apart from the provocation. The courts in Australia[70] and Canada[71] also take that view.

Loss of self-control is not necessarily absolute and may be a question of degree. An insult may inflame a person to the extent of replying with an angry blow or, if the provocation is extreme, a person may feel such extreme anger or emotion which causes him to use deadly force or a deadly weapon.[72] In *Mac Eoin* the Court of Criminal Appeal apparently revived[73] the proportionality test:

> If the accused raises the defence that he was provoked and establishes that and nothing more, we do not mean that the prosecution must prove beyond reasonable doubt that he was not provoked. The nature of the provocation may not justify the force used judged by the accused's state of mind. But the inquiry to be made by the judge first and then by the jury must centre not on the reasonable man but on the accused and his reaction to the conduct or words which are said to be provocative.
>
> When the defence of provocation is raised, we think that the trial judge at the close of the evidence should rule on whether there is any evidence of provocation which, having regard to the accused's temperament, character and circumstances, might have caused him to lose control of himself at the time of the wrongful act and whether the provocation bears a reasonable relation to the amount of force used by the accused.
>
> If there is evidence on which the jury could reach a decision favourable to the accused on this issue, the trial judge should allow the defence to be considered by the jury and should tell them that, before they find the accused guilty of murder, the prosecution

---

66   AC at 9, All ER at 277, Cr App R at 74.

67   Smith & Hogan 341-42; Russell 549 and the cases therein cited. In Australia see *Dacosta* (1968) 118 CLR 186 HC.

68   *Phillips* [1969] 2 AC 130; [1969] 2 WLR 581, 53 Cr App R 132 PC; *Edwards* [1973] AC 648; [1973] 1 All ER 152; [1972] 3 WLR 893, 57 Cr App R 157 PC.

69   *Brown* [1972] 2 QB 229; [1972] 2 All ER 1328; [1972] 3 WLR 11, 56 Cr App R 564 CA.

70   *Johnson* [1976] 136 CLR 619 HC; Howard 86. A similar view is taken in New Zealand; *Smith* [1989] 3 NZLR 405 CA.

71   *Squire* (1975) 26 CCC (2d) 219 Ont CA; Stuart 455.

72   *Phillips*, fn 68.

73   Neither *Phillips*, fn 68, nor *Brown*, fn 69, were cited to the Court or referred to in its judgment but the overruled Privy Council case of *Perera* [1953] AC 200; [1953] 2 WLR was ". . . A blow with a fist . . . will not excuse the use of a deadly weapon". *Mancini* [1942] AC 1; [1941] 3 All ER 272, 28 Cr App R 65 HL, is also cited in the judgment but not quoted.

must establish beyond reasonable doubt that the accused was not provoked to such an extent that, having regard to his temperament, character and circumstances, he lost control of himself at the time of the wrongful act. Then the jury should be told that they must consider whether the acts or words, or both, of provocation found by them to have occurred, when related to the accused, bear a reasonable relation to the amount of force he used. If the prosecution can prove beyond reasonable doubt that the force used was unreasonable and excessive having regard to the provocation, the defence of provocation fails.[74]

It is submitted that this passage is incomprehensible.

Objective or Subjective Test

4.14 The question arises as to whether an objective or subjective test of proportionality is to be applied. The only clear *ratio* of the remarks of the Court is its decisive rejection, in this branch of the law, of the objective test. Proportionality cannot therefore be used as a back-door reintroduction of objective standards. Further, the Court, although it uses the words "reasonable retaliation", twice also states that the nature of the provocation and the force used must be judged "by the accused's state of mind". After a recitation of all the relevant circumstances and any special characteristics that the accused possesses, which might cause an inflammation of his passion the test could therefore be stated to the jury thus: did the effect of all this trigger such a loss of self-control in the accused that he no longer was the master of his own mind and therefore could not stop himself from doing the acts which caused the victim's death?

That test is completely subjective. It recites the relevant facts. It invites the jury to consider the accused, not as a reasonable or ordinary man but as an individual having a separate and individual character. It calls attention to such special factors of that character as are in evidence and may have contributed to the loss of self-control, for example, a racial insult to a person of minority status. Finally it asks whether the effect of the provocation on the accused caused a loss of self-control to the degree that the accused was caused to kill and not merely to retaliate with insulting words or hurtful blows. It may be unreasonable in those circumstances for an ordinary man provoked by a slap to stab in response, it may not be unreasonable for a wife labouring under years of physical abuse to finally crack and reach for a bread knife.[75]

The three references to reasonable retaliation in the passage quoted above are, it is to be noted, qualified twice by the statement that such is to be judged "by the accused's state of mind" and " related to the accused". One wonders how a subjective test can incorporate an element based on reason which, on the classic definition of provocation, must be absent to excuse killing. The answer, in the absence of decided authority on a test unique in the common law world, would appear to be twofold.

4.15 Firstly, as declared in s 2 of the Criminal Law (Rape) Act, 1981, reasonableness is an instrument which a jury is entitled to use in assessing the credibility of a particular accused's version of events. This test is general to the criminal law, is not specific to the crime of rape. People are individuals; the test in *Mac Eoin* takes into

74   At 34, 35.
75   See particularly the fact of *R* (1981) 28 SASR 321 SC SA, discussed at par 4.25.

account all the characteristics which make up an individual. A violent upsurge of emotion is not an uncommon experience and is one which a jury are uniquely in a position to assess. The actions of the deceased in killing may be likely, or unlikely, depending on the provocation offered. In assessing the defence case, in order to determine whether a reasonable doubt exists, the jury can use the common experience of ordinary people as a useful comparison to the actions of the accused.

Secondly, the enquiry into provocation is solely as to the genuineness of an account of loss of self-control to a degree where death or serious injury was intended but where the accused could not avert, and is thus not to be blamed for, the formation and consummation of that intent.

The inquiry, therefore, is not whether there was a balance between what the victim did to the accused and what he did in retaliation. A true test involves a consideration of the degree of force of the emotion in the accused, his consequent lack of ability to control it and what the accused, in that state, does to the victim. In order to assess the pitch of the emotion and its dominance over the subsequent actions of the accused, the jury must look at his personality. To assess whether the accused killed the victim whilst driven by that state, they must return to the question of whether a person in that state could reasonably be expected to kill another person. The balance is between the emotion generated and the force used.[76] As a matter of reality juries will not be willing to acquit an accused where a death is claimed to result from an insubstantial provocation. In this way the community sets standards of behaviour for its members.

The test incorporated in s 210.3(1)(b) of the Model Penal Code explicitly allows the community to set standards of behaviour by incorporating a test of reasonable explanation or excuse from a subjective viewpoint:

> A criminal homicide constitutes manslaughter when homicide which would otherwise be murder is committed under the influence of extreme mental or emotional disturbance for which there is a reasonable explanation or excuse. The reasonableness of such explanation or excuse shall be determined from the viewpoint of a person in the actor's situation under the circumstances as he believes them to be.

The adoption of a subjective test calls into question the validity of the other guidelines to the defence at common law.[77]

Test Used in Common Law Countries

4.16 Under the Camplin test the question of proportionality was explained by Barwick CJ, for the Australian High Court, in *Johnson*:[78]

> The proportion of the fatal act to the provocation is part of the material on which the jury should consider whether the provocation offered the accused was such as would have caused an ordinary man, placed in all the circumstances in which the accused stood, to have lost his self-control to the point of doing an act of the kind and degree of that by which the accused killed the deceased. That proportion is not, in my opinion,

---

76 The New Zealand Law Reform Commission argue for a subjective test in their report on *Culpable Homicide* as do the South Australian Criminal Law and Penal Reform Methods Committee in their report—*The Substantive Criminal Law*, 21-24.

77 See par 4.19-4.27.

78 (1973) 136 CLR 619 HC.

a separate matter to be decided after it has been decided that an ordinary man would
have lost self-control in the circumstances by reason of provocation. The relationship
of the fatal act to the provocation is perhaps best expressed by saying that the
provocation must be such as would lead an ordinary man in the accused's circumstances
to so lose his self-control as to do an act of the kind and degree as the act by which
the accused killed the deceased.[79]

Under the test in *Mac Eoin* the trial judge retains the power, abolished in
England,[80] to withdraw the defence from the jury where no reasonable jury,
properly instructed, could reach the conclusion that the killing occurred as a result
of provocation. Having regard to the entirely subjective nature of the test it would
be rare for such a power to be exercised in this jurisdiction. The inquiry is as to the
state of mind of the accused which, unlike the legal question of the state of mind of
a reasonable or ordinary man, is a question of fact. There appears to be no record
of an appeal following a refusal by a trial judge to allow the jury to consider the
defence. Cases have occurred where the defence have not pursued provocation,
preferring to concentrate the attention of the jury on the issue as to whether the
accused intended to cause death or serious injury.

Where evidence of provocation exists the trial judge must instruct the jury on
that defence despite the fact that it is not relied upon by counsel for the accused.[81]

The Emotion Provoked

4.17 It is not settled whether the emotion generated by the provocation is limited
to anger. It is submitted it is not. Any emotion powerful enough to deprive an
accused person of self-control, to the degree that he cannot stop himself killing or
causing serious injury, is within the ambit of the law.[82] There is a limit, however,
to what can be accepted. King CJ in *R*,[83] a domestic killing case, observed:

> The loss of self-control which is essential, is not to be confused with the emotions of
> hatred, resentment, fear or revenge. If the appellant, when in control of her mind and
> will, decided to kill the deceased because these emotions or any of them had been
> produced in her by the enormity of the deceased's past behaviour and threatened future
> behaviour or because she considered that it was the only way in which she or her
> children could be protected from the deceased's molestations in the future, the crime
> would nevertheless be murder. The law of a well ordered and civilised society cannot
> countenance deliberate killing, even to the extent of treating it as extenuated, as a
> response to the conduct of another however abhorrent that conduct might be. Nor
> can society countenance killing a person as a means of averting some apprehended
> harm in the future. The law of course permits the use by a person of force, even to the
> extent of inflicting death, but that is necessary to defend that person against immediately

---

79   At 636. In New Zealand, a credible narrative is required before the defence is left to the jury: *Matoka*
     [1987] 1 NZLR 340 CA.
80   Homicide Act 1957, s 3; Smith & Hogan 331-34.
81   See par 3.03. *The People (A-G) v Commane* (1957) 1 Frewen 400, 404 CCA and see *Gilbert* (1977)
     66 Cr App R 237; [1978] Crim LR 216 CA; *Camplin* [1978] AC 705; [1978] 2 All ER 168; [1978]
     2 WLR 679, 67 Cr App R 14 HL; *Johnson* [1989] 2 All ER 839; [1989] 1 WLR 740, 89 Cr App R
     148; [1989] Crim LR 738 CA.
82   There appears to be no decision directly in point. The only fixed criterion is a loss of self-control
     to the point where homicidal impulses cannot be checked.
83   (1981) 28 SASR 321 SC SA.

threatened harm. But the law has always and must always set its face against killing by way of prevention of harm which is merely feared for the future. Other measures which are peaceful and lawful must be resorted to in order to deal with threats of future harm.[84]

If the accused is truly provoked to the extent of losing self-control it may be impossible to identify a particular emotion. Practice shows that the most common emotions causing homicidal impulses are anger and jealousy.[85] In *Van Den Hock*[86] it was accepted that loss of self-control due to fear and panic arising from a provocative incident required the defence to be left to the jury.

Intent

4.18 If the accused does not intend to kill or cause serious injury his homicide of the victim cannot be murder.[87] The argument that a killing under provocation does not amount to a voluntary act has never been accepted by any court in a common law jurisdiction. Hence killing under provocation is always manslaughter. If it were otherwise the accused would be entitled to be acquitted on a defence of automatism.

Situations can occur where what was done by the victim are either accepted by the defence as not constituting evidence of provocation[88] or are ruled by the trial judge not to come within the *Mac Eoin* test.[89] Instead the defence may rely on an absence of intent by the accused in killing the victim. The accused may give evidence that he had no knowledge he was killing the victim. In practice when a defence is framed in terms of evidence that his mind "went blank" the question for the jury is "did the accused intend to kill or cause serious injury to the deceased?" This does not constitute a reliance on the defence of provocation but is a case based on absence of intent. The defence may concede that the killing was manslaughter.[90] This may be because the actions of the accused were an intentional assault, or amounted to a criminal and dangerous act or that the accused was criminally negligent in putting himself into a situation where his emotions were aroused in the presence of a deadly weapon or an opportunity to kill.[91] As has been previously mentioned, the law of

84 At 324–5.
85 The most cogent analysis is to regard the acts of the accused as being an overwhelming upsurge of the death instinct. This is present together with the life instinct in all normal people. The strength of either may depend on character but either trait is developed through use; Fromm, *The Anatomy of Human Destructiveness* (London, 1974). In *Browne* [1973] NI 96 at 108, Lowry LCJ stated: "I would prefer to say that provocation is something unwarranted which is likely to make a reasonable person angry or indignant".
86 (1986) 23 A Crim R 98 CCA Vict.
87 Criminal Justice Act, 1964, s 4. See par 2.18.
88 The writer has, for example, acted in cases of domestic murder where the defence conceded that it was not provocation for a wife to say she was leaving her husband. In two cases, in particular, the defence conceded manslaughter and argued for a reduction to manslaughter from murder before the jury. The basis for such an argument was, in both cases, the evidence of the accused that prior to the killing his mind went blank and that he only recovered a consciousness of his actions after the victim's death. See further par 2.18.
89 [1978] IR 27 CCA. The writer has never seen such a case.
90 This would constitute a plea to the lesser offence.
91 See generally ch 3.

manslaughter casts a safety net in which society catches those guilty of culpable homicide who must otherwise be acquitted of murder because they lacked intent.

In 1946 the House of Lords appeared to state that an intention to kill or cause grievous bodily harm was inconsistent with the defence of provocation, save in the case where a spouse was discovered in the act of adultery.[92] This unfortunate and incorrect statement is no longer accepted.[93] It was repeated by the trial judge in *Mac Eoin* and was the actual point of appeal in that case. The Court of Criminal Appeal rejected that analysis:

> The dichotomy which the trial judge in this case put before the jury on three occasions between the existence of an intention to kill or cause serious injury and the effect of provocation does not exist . . . an intention to kill or cause serious injury is consistent with provocation and does not prevent this defence from reducing murder to manslaughter unless the prosecution prove that the accused was not provoked.[94]

In this context the objective test cuts both ways. In the common law world, where the *Camplin* adjusted objective test prevails,[95] the accused must have been shown to have lost self-control. A situation which would cause an ordinary or reasonable person to lose self-control is a necessary prerequisite of the accused showing actual loss of self-control. Whilst satisfaction of the objective test can be an indicator in favour of loss of self-control, in an individual accused, it is not decisive. An extremely phlegmatic person may not have reacted to even the most objectively severe provocation. In this jurisdiction the jury, in their deliberation on the subjective test, are entitled to consider how an ordinary person would have reacted to the situation facing the accused. Despite severe provocation the accused may have acted from a motive of anger or jealousy formed in cold blood and used an objectively provocative situation in order to murder the deceased. Although a reasonable or ordinary person may have been provoked, by the circumstances that are proven, the accused's character or temperament may have had little influence on a previously formed homicidal motive. Consequently the killing may have been a controlled action. In each instance the enquiry is as to whether a particular person lost command of his actions.

A history of abusive conduct by the victim can, however, lead separate but slight provocative acts to have a cumulative effect which genuinely causes a loss of self-control.[96]

Other Parameters

4.19 We now proceed to discuss the parameters placed by the common law on the defence of provocation and the status of those in Irish law.

Provocation by a Lawful Act

There is no separate requirement that the actions of the victim must have been

92   *Holmes* [1946] AC 588; [1946] 2 All ER 124 HL.
93   *Perera* [1953] AC 200; [1953] 2 WLR 238 PC; Howard 78-9.
94   [1978] IR 27 at 31.
95   See par 4.07-4.08.
96   See par 4.25-4.27.

unlawful to constitute provocation. Were it to be decided that there is such an additional requirement a breach of the peace, or the statutory offence of conduct which might lead to a breach of the peace,[97] would suffice. It is arguable that a reasonable man would not be provoked by a lawful act. Such a test has, however, no place in Irish law.[98] In England no such requirement is now made.[99] A rule to that effect may once have existed at common law[1] but has since been abandoned.[2] The rule that mere words could never amount to provocation has also been discarded.[3] The Supreme Court of South Australia has, by a majority, expressly rejected a requirement of unlawfulness, King CJ stating:

> It seems, however, that unlawfulness as a separate requirement has become obsolete. It is not mentioned in the classic formulation in *R v Duffy* [1949] 1 All ER 932 and has not been mentioned in modern cases decided in the High Court of Australia, the House of Lords or Privy Council. This is not surprising. In times, when the criteria of provocation were "expressed in terms directed to duels and personal quarrels among men who ordinarily bear arms or to violence produced by violence" (*Parker* (1963) 111 CLR 610 per Dixon CJ at 630) it was natural to include the unlawfulness of the conduct as one of the criteria. The modern cases, however, are not for the most part concerned with clashes between armed men, but with provocative conduct of a different type, very often consisting of matrimonial infidelity or wounding words or gestures, which conduct is frequently not unlawful. If the requirement of unlawfulness which was considered to be one of the criteria of provocation could be satisfied by a tendency of the conduct towards a breach of the peace, the requirement added nothing to what is required by the objective test as to self-control.[4]

4.20 The preamble to the Constitution puts forward the attainment of "true social order" as one of the four basic objectives of the fundamental law of the State. Situations can occur where an unlawful element should be sought in the victim's conduct before the accused is entitled to rely on provocation. For instance the victim may be a Garda who is lawfully arresting the accused, or a Prison Officer who is requiring him to observe prison rules, or another official of the State requiring a citizen to observe the law. Were a defence to an intentional killing to be allowed on the basis of the accused's subjective reaction to law enforcement, the purpose of the Constitution would be undermined. If the modified objective test in *Camplin* were applied, a reasonable person showing the accused's permanent characteristics could not, as a matter of law, be provoked by a lawful requirement made of him.

As we have moved to an entirely subjective test it is appropriate to express the

---

97 Dublin Metropolitan Police Act, 1842, s 14(13), applying to the Dublin Metropolitan District only.
98 See par 4.11.
99 Smith & Hogan 333; *Doughty* (1986) 83 Cr App R 319; [1986] Crim LR 625 CA (a baby crying).
1   Kenny (1922) 117 puts the defence as requiring "gross provocation"; Archbold (1922) 881 speaks of "considerable provocation". Such tests incorporate an unlawful element by the standard they set. Adultery, for example, the main exception to the requirement of a physical provocation, may only have sufficed where the parties were married; *Palmer* [1913] 2 KB 29, 23 Cox 277; *Greening* [1913] 3 KB 846, 25 Cox 269; *Alexander* (1913) 9 Cr App R 139, 23 Cox 604; but see *Larkin* [1943] KB 174; [1943] 1 All ER 217, 29 Cr App R 18 CCA; *Gauthier* (1943) 29 Cr App R 113; *Arden* [1975] VR 449 SC. For homosexual acts as provocation see *Fisher* (1837) 8 C&P 182, 173 ER 452.
2   There seems to be no modern case requiring unlawfulness as a separate element of the defence.
3   *Camplin* [1978] AC 705; [1978] 2 All ER 168; [1978] 2 WLR 679, 67 Cr App R 14 HL.
4   *R* (1981) 28 SASR 321 at 327 SC SA.

duty of citizens to obey the law in terms of a public policy removing the defence from those who claim to be provoked by a lawful requirement made of them by someone with legal authority so to do.[5] That situation should not be confused with the separate requirement that the victim's conduct be unlawful. The dissent of Zelling J in R^6 can be seen as expressing the public policy requirement of protection for those who enforce the law:

> There is no instance that I can find anywhere in the books of lawful acts constituting provocation and it would be a very serious thing if it were so, for example, a police office lawfully arresting an accused person could be killed and the accused plead provocation arising out of a completely lawful act . . . we would be taking away protection from persons in the community, such as the police, in an area where protection is completely necessary.[7]

An unlawful arrest may be resisted with reasonable force.[8] Even a reasonable man could be provoked by such a serious infringement of liberty as an unlawful arrest.[9] As provocation is a subjective condition for the accused to be provoked it is necessary that he know of the illegality.[10]

Provocation and Third Parties

4.21 Any citizen may come to the aid of any other who is being attacked.[11] Prior to *MacEoin*[12] it would have been necessary to have regard to the rules of common law in order to determine whether the accused was entitled to rely on the defence of provocation. Briefly,[13] it was recognised that provocation could occur by attacking the accused's friend,[14] by unlawfully imprisoning any citizen,[15] by adultery

5   At common law such a policy requirement is expressed. For instance in *Bourne* (1831) 5 C&P 120, 172 ER 903, Park J instructed a jury that if a victim was acting in defence of his brother against the accused's attack, the killing of the victim could not be under provocation. Similarly in *Willoughby* (1791) 1 East PC 288, the defence of provocation was refused to a soldier where a landlord was unlawfully ejecting him from a public house.

6   Fn 42.

7   At 331. Similarly the warning of Howard 87 that the law "would be self-contradictory if a lawful act could amount to provocation" is, correctly, more reconciliable with modern case law, as opposed to the Codes he quotes on the public policy bar in favour of law enforcement officials.

8   What constitutes reasonable force depends on the force offered and the seriousness of the evil to be averted: See par 4.29.

9   Stephen *Digest* (1887) Article 224, (1904) Article 245. This was doubted in *Palmer* [1971] AC 814; [1971] 1 All ER 1077; [1971] 2 WLR 831, 55 Cr App R 223 PC.

10   A different rule may have existed at common law allowing the accused to rely on a legal technicality of which he was not aware: *Allen* (1867) 17 LT (NS) 222; *Tooley* (1709) 2 Ld Raym 129, 92 ER 349; but see *Ford* (1817) R&R 329, 168 ER 828.

11   *The People (A-G) v Keatley* [1954] IR 12 CCA.

12   [1978] IR 27 CCA.

13   O'Regan, "Indirect Provocation and Mis-directed Retaliation" [1968] Crim LR 319.

14   *Mawgridge* (1706) Kel 119, 17 St Tr 57, 84 ER 1107.

15   *Tooley* (1709) 2 Ld Raym 129, 92 ER 349. Stephen's *Digest* (1887) Article 224 (c), (1904) Article 245 (c) states the rule thus: "An unlawful imprisonment is a provocation to the person imprisoned, but not to bystanders, though an unlawful imprisonment may amount to such a breach of the peace as to entitle a bystander to prevent it by the use of force sufficient for that purpose. An arrest by officers of justice, whose character as such is known, but who are acting under a warrant so irregular as to make the arrest illegal, is provocation to the person illegally arrested, but not to bystanders".

with the accused spouse or partner,[16] by an assault on the accused's daughter by her husband[17] and by the victim committing buggery on the accused's son.[18] The reasonable man test incorporates all the situations where the law considered a loss of self-control might be understandable.

As a subjective test is now operated in this jurisdiction, no rule of the common law restricts either the mode of provocation or the party to whom it is offered. The sole question is whether the person charged with the crime of murder was provoked. Acts of violence or degradation offered even to a stranger could be such as to cause a person to lose self-control to the extent of being unable to stop an impulse to kill or cause serious injury. Experience tends to indicate that the closer the relationship, in terms of either kinship or affection, the more gravely an offence to another person will be felt. On a subjective test these considerations will, no doubt, influence a jury: the decisive factor remains the reaction of the accused.

Provocation can also be offered by two or more persons acting together.[19] For example, a spouse may commit adultery with another.[20] A mistake may occur where, for example, the accused aims a deadly blow at his provoker but, by accident, kills another.[21] The Court of Criminal Appeal of Victoria in *Gardiner*[22] have decided that provocation need not emanate from the victim. The Court held that where a sudden and temporary loss of self-control continued to operate and a person in close proximity to the person provoking the accused was thereby killed, the defence was open. The facts of the case were that the accused entered his former lover's room. He was taunted by her with his lack of sexual prowess and informed that she and another person, who was sleeping in a nearby room, had enjoyed sex. The accused then entered this person's bedroom and found him asleep and naked. He killed him with a statue and then returned to his former lover's room and killed her.

Mistake

4.22 The elements of the defence of mistake are uncertain in Irish law. In Australia an honest but unreasonable mistake which negatives the mental element of crime is a defence.[23] Thus the accused may unreasonably believe a man to be a tree and shoot it for target practice. He cannot be guilty of murder on that state of mind, but he is unlikely to raise a reasonable doubt if the facts, as he contends that he saw them, are outlandish. Whether the accused has reasonable grounds for his belief is a matter of

---

16 *Parker* (1963) 111 CLR 610; [1963] Crim LR 569 HC and the cases cited at par 4.19, fn 1.

17 *Harrington* (1866) 10 Cox 370; and see *Terry* [1964] VR 248, 250-51 SC, where Pape J commented that he did not see any reason "why the doctrine should be confined to relatives, for the relationship between the person attacked and the accused must be a relevant factor when the question of whether an ordinary man would be likely to lose his self-control as a result of the provocative is being considered by the jury".

18 *Fisher* (1837) 8 C&P 182, 173 ER 452.

19 *Kenney* [1983] 2 VR 470 SC.

20 *Davies* [1975] QB 691; [1975] 1 All ER 890; [1975] 2 WLR 586, 60 Cr App R 253 CA *Twine* [1967] Crim LR 710.

21 *Brown* (1776) 1 Leach 148, 168 ER 117; *Gross* (1913) 23 Cox 455; *Porritt* [1961] 3 All ER 463; [1961] 1 WLR 1372, 45 Cr App R 348 CCA.

22 (1989) 42 A Crim R 279.

23 Howard 371-76. Further see par 4.38.

evidence in guiding the jury on a decision as to whether such belief was honestly held.[24] Irish law applying a subjective test of provocation is likely to follow these principles. Where the accused honestly, but mistakenly, believes that the victim was provoking him he should not be denied a defence because that mistake was unreasonable.[25] Equally, the lack of reasonableness in that belief may weigh against the accused in determining his honesty. It is submitted that the requirement of the common law that mistaken provocation be both honest and reasonable[26] is inconsistent with *Mac Eoin*.[27]

Drunkenness

4.23 Experience shows that the intoxicated are both more likely to take offence over a trivial insult and to make mistakes which a sober person would avoid. Where the accused becomes intoxicated to the degree that he cannot, or does not, intend to kill or cause serious injury[28] he is not guilty of murder.[29] At common law, evidence that the accused was drunk is admissible in order to assist in showing actual loss of self-control.[30] In applying the dual test operated in common law countries,[31] of actual loss of self control by the accused in circumstances where a reasonable or ordinary man would have reacted likewise, in 1954 the English Court of Criminal Appeal in *McCarthy*[32] stated authoritatively[33] that the reasonable man was never to be invested with the characteristic of drunkenness:

> We see no distinction between a person who by temperament is unusually excitable or pugnacious and one who is temporarily made excitable or pugnacious by self-induced intoxication. It may be that an excitable, pugnacious or intoxicated person may be more easily provoked than a man of quiet or phlegmatic disposition, but the former cannot rely upon his excitable state of mind if the violence used is beyond that which a reasonable, or as we may perhaps say, an average person would use to repel an act which can in law be regarded as provocation.[34]

---

24   *Pappajohn* (1980) 14 CR (3d) 243 SC; *Beckford* [1988] AC 130; [1987] 3 All ER 425; [1987] 3 WLR 611, 85 Cr App R 378 [1988] Crim LR 116 PC; Stuart 246-59; Smith & Hogan 85-90.

25   A defence of mistaken provocation may be pleaded: *Hansford* (1987) 86 CCC (3d) 74 Alberta CA.

26   *Brown* (1766) 1 Leach 148, 168 ER 177; *Letenock* (1917) 12 Cr App R 221 CCA; *Hall* (1928) 21 Cr App R 48, 28 Cox 567 CCA; *Croft* [1981] 1 NSWLR 126, 3 A Crim R 307 CCA; *Kenny* [1983] 2 VR 470 SC Vict.

27   [1978] IR 27 CCA.

28   The status of this rule is uncertain in Irish law: Law Reform Commission Report on Malicious Damage, par 31-36. On the defence of drunkenness see further par 4.43-4.44.

29   Criminal Justice Act, 1964, s 4.

30   *Webb* (1977) 16 SASR 309, 314 SC; *Croft* (1981) 3 A Crim R 307, 320 CCA NSW; *Tennant* (1975) 31 CRNS 1, 23 CCC (2d) 80 CA Ont; *Squire* (1977) 2 SCR 13, 29 CCC (2d) 497 reversing 31 CRNS 314 Ontario CA; *Olbey* [1980] 1 SCR 1008, 50 CCC (2d) 257 SC; *Barton* [1977] 1 NZLR 295 CA; *Thomas* (1837) 7 C&P 817, 173 ER 356; *Cooke* (1986) 39 SASR 225 SC; Gillies 310; Williams, *TBCL* 541; O'Connor & Fairall 194.

31   See par 4.07.

32   [1954] 2 QB 105; [1954] 2 All ER 262; [1954] 2 WLR 1044, 38 Cr App R 74 CCA.

33   Cases which appear to have taken account of drunkenness in the objective element are *Hopper* [1915] 2 KB 431, [1914-15] All ER 914, 11 Cr App R 136 CCA; *Letenock* (1917) 12 Cr App R 221 CCA. Their reasoning is however confused. See further Wiliams, *TBCL*, 541.

34   QB at 112, All ER at 265, WLR at 1048, Cr App R at 81.

Persons of hot-temper were expressly included within the wholly subjective test of provocation laid down by the Court of Criminal Appeal in *MacEoin*.[35] Obviously, the difference between hot-temper, or a trait of character which causes the accused to have reactions more violent to provocation than in the case of ordinary people, and drunkenness, is that the latter is wholly self-induced and is of short duration in its effect.[36]

There are strong policy reasons for excluding the effect of alcohol, drugs or other intoxicants from the jury's consideration of the defence of provocation. Firstly, the defence is a concession to human frailty. Except in the case of a chronic alcoholic, people have a choice of whether to drink and of how much they drink. Secondly, the criminal law treats intoxicated people as if they had not drunk or taken drugs at all, save in crimes where specific intent is required.[37] Thirdly, the preamble to the Constitution states as one of the four objectives of the fundamental law, the attainment of true social order. Discounting voluntary intoxication could assist in that aim by judging people as they ordinarily are and not as they have temporarily caused themselves to be. Finally, there is no authority for allowing drunkenness to govern the application of the defence of provocation. To the contrary Smith & Hogan argue that as a drunken mistake can relieve the accused of liability for murder[38] no lesser rule should be applied to a drunken mistake as to provocation.

Self-Induced Provocation

4.24 The accused is not entitled to exploit his own weakness, or that of the victim, in order to bring about a situation of explosive temper which he knows will result in a killing.[39] The situation is analogous to a person who drinks in order to get himself into a homicidal state; in that situation drunkenness is not a defence even though at the moment of killing the accused may be so intoxicated as to be incapable of acting with intent.[40] Similarly, the accused is not entitled to engineer a situation of conflict knowing that the victim will be on the receiving end of his violent temper.[41] Nor can the accused incite the victim to provoke him in order to hide behind the mask of the defence and deliberately kill.[42] The policy of the law remains a concession to human frailty; in contrast the deliberate exploitation of mental weakness is conscious and outside the scope of the concession.

Public policy also bars the defence where the provocative conduct of the victim

---

35 [1978] IR 27 CCA.

36 In *Newell* (1980) 71 Cr App R 331; (1980) Crim LR 576, the Court of Appeal reserved for future consideration whether chronic alcoholism, as opposed to mere intoxication, could be a trait of an ordinary person and thus be taken into account under the revised Camplin test.

37 See par 4.43-4.44, and particularly the contrary view taken by the Australian High Court.

38 At 343 citing *Wardrope* [1960] Crim LR 770 and see the examples given by Lord Denning in *Gallagher* [1963] AC 349; [1961] 3 All ER 299; [1961] 3 WLR 619, 45 Cr App R 316 HL.

39 Ashworth, "Self-induced Provocation and the Homicide Act" [1973] Crim LR 483.

40 *Gallagher* [1963] AC 349; [1961] 3 All ER 299; [1961] 3 WLR 619, 45 Cr App R 316 HL.

41 The only authority which approaches this situation on the facts, is *Mason* (1756), Fost 132, 168 ER 66 (after a fight in a tavern the accused left threatening to kill the victim. He returned with a sword and asked the victim to strike him with a stick. The accused then killed him with a sword).

42 *Newman* [1948] VLR 61, 66 SC.

is the predictable result of the criminal behaviour of the accused.[43] In *Edwards*[44] the accused called on the victim in order to blackmail him. According to the accused, the deceased responded by attacking him with a knife. Then the accused captured the knife and dispatched him. The Privy Council held the defence should have been left to the jury on the basis, it would appear, that the law required the accused to weather the normal reactions of a blackmailed person, but that the alleged knife attack went beyond that point. Lord Pearson stated:

> No authority has been cited with regard to what may be called "self-induced provocation". On principle it seems reasonable to say that (1) a blackmailer cannot rely on the predictable results of his own blackmailing conduct as provocation sufficient to reduce his killing of the victim from murder to manslaughter, and the predictable results may include a considerable degree of hostile reaction by the person sought to be blackmailed, for instance vituperative words or even some hostile action such as blows with a fist; (2) but if the hostile reaction by the person sought to be blackmailed goes to extreme lengths it might constitute sufficient provocation even for the blackmailer. (3) There would in many cases be a question of degree to be decided by the jury.[45]

Against this statement of the law it can also be argued that the removal of the defence from the accused because of his criminal conduct is to re-create a kind of constructive murder where otherwise it has been abolished. No reason is advanced as to why, apart from the fact that his experience might suggest a violent reaction, the accused is required to act with an even temper where the victim's reaction genuinely causes a loss of self-control. The only basis for the rule is public policy. This might be better served by applying the normal rule and reflecting the accused's wickedness in an appropriate sentence.

The Provocative Act and the Background

4.25 There is no defence to murder of killing under extenuating circumstances.[46] The defence of provocation requires an identifiable act or series of acts which causes the accused to lose self-control. Calculated killing cannot come within the defence, however understandable individual circumstances may make such conduct, as this lacks the element of loss of self-control on which the defence hinges. This requirement is understandable. Where the accused can plan his action he has sufficient mental control to decide not to kill; a consideration which does not apply where the accused is forced into a state of extreme emotion.[47] The matter was put thus by Lord Devlin in *Duffy*:[48]

---

43 As we have seen public policy appears also to bar the defence in cases of self-inflicted drunkenness, par 4.23; and where the victim's provocative conduct is the product of law enforcement, par 4.20.

44 [1973] AC 648; [1973] 1 All ER 152; [1973] 3 WLR 893, 57 Cr App R 157 PC.

45 AC at 658, All ER at 158, WLR at 901, Cr App R at 168. Followed in *Johnson* [1989] 2 All ER 839; [1989] 1 WLR 740, 89 Cr App R 148; [1989] Crim LR 738 where the Court of Appeal applying s 3 of the Homicide Act, 1957 held that whether or not there were elements in the conduct of the accused which justified the conclusion that he had started the trouble and induced others, including the deceased, to react towards him in a violent fashion, the defence of provocation should nonetheless be left to the jury.

46 Wasik, "Cumulative Provocation and Domestic Killing" [1982] Crim LR 29. Further see par 4.17.

47 Brett, "The Physiology of Provocation" [1970] Crim LR 634.

48 [1949] 1 All ER 932 CCA.

Circumstances which induce a desire for revenge are inconsistent with provocation, since the conscious formulation of a desire for revenge means that a person has had time to think, to reflect, and that would negative a sudden temporary loss of self-control, which is of the essence of provocation.[49]

A history of violent or abusive conduct leading to emotions which generate a decision by the accused to remove the source of that misery is not provocation.[50] However, a history of incidents which may have contributed to the eventual loss of self-control, or which explain the act or acts identified by the defence as constituting provocation, can be considered by the jury in deciding whether the accused actually lost self-control.[51]

4.26 It has sometimes been stated that the reaction of the accused to the provocation must be sudden.[52] It is submitted that this is not a rule of law but a guide to the jury in considering whether the killing was done on reflection or under the impulse of a violent emotion following on the failure of self-control.[53] So in *Jeffrey*,[54] Smith J stated:

> Where there has been a sustained course of cruelty which has built up to, and ultimately precipitated, an explosion of passion and loss of self-control, the whole chain of events, and not merely the concluding episode is relevant to the question of adequacy of provocation.[55]

Barry J held that although the reaction of the accused must contain an element of suddenness,[56] the breakdown of self-control may be gradual under the cumulative effect of an unalleviated pressure arising from a series of provocative incidents.[57]

The requirement of an identifiable incident or series of incidents and the test of sudden reaction has usually been applied in a liberal fashion.[58] In *R*[59] the victim and

49 At 932.

50 *Croft* [1981] 1 NSWLR 126, 140, 3 A Crim R 307 CCA; *R* (1981) 28 SASR 321 SC SA quoted at par 4.17; *Ibrams & Gregory* (1981) 74 Cr App R 154 at 160 CA.

51 *Hopkins* (1866) 10 Cox 229. Further cases are cited in *Wasik*, fn 84. See also *Hill* (1981) 3 A Crim R 397 CCA (3d) NSW; *Croft*, fn 88; *Daniels* (1983) 7 CCC (3d) 542 NWT CA; *Conway* (1985) 17 CCC 481 Ont CA. The background of a relationship can be relevant to show fear giving rise to a killing, even on a question of self-defence, thus evidence of a "battered wife syndrome" is admissible for the purpose of showing that the force used was reasonable; *Lavelle* (1990) 55 CC (3d) 97, 76 CR (3d) 329 SC.

52 Archbold (1922) 884; *Maddy* (1671) 1 Vent 158, 86 ER 108; *Mawgridge* (1706) Kel 119, 17 St Tr 57, 84 ER 1107; *Hayward* (1833) 6 C&P 157, 172 ER 1188; Fost 296.

53 1 East PC 238 speaks of actions which might "heat the blood to a proportional degree of resentment and keep it boiling to the moment of the act so that the party may rather be considered as having acted under a temporary suspension of reason than from any deliberate malicious motive". It is argued by Brett, fn 85, that a long gap may be evidence of heightened passion.

54 [1967] VR 467 SC.   55 At 484.

56 Citing *A-G for Ceylon v Perera* [1953] AC 200 at 206 PC.

57 Quoting from *Parker* (1963-64) 111 CLR 610 HC.

58 For example *Hall* (1928) 21 Cr App R 48, 28 Cox 567 CCA (gap of 15-20 minutes before knifing); *Parker* [1963-64] 111 CLR 610 HC (gap of 20 minutes before the accused followed the victim. The victim's final provocative act was, apparently, to run off with the victim's wife. The accused followed and knocked them both down with a car. The accused's wife moaned and this act led the accused to kill the victim with a knife. Both the accused's wife and the victim were at the time very badly hurt as a result of being run down with the car).

59 (1981) 28 SASR 321 SC SA.

the accused were married with five daughters. The victim, the husband, had committed incest with all the daughters, two of whom had left and two of whom had, shortly before, said they intended leaving. The morning before the killing the accused had purchased a rifle and ammunition. That day the victim raped one of his daughters and cut her with a knife. On the morning of the killing the victim confessed his incestuous behaviour to his wife. After the accused returned from work one of her daughters told her of another rape attempt. A row followed and the victim protested his repentance and expressed desires for a happy future. The accused sat by the bed smoking a cigarette as the victim slept. After a time she went outside and got an axe and killed her husband.

The decision of the trial judge to withdraw provocation from the jury was overturned by the Supreme Court of South Australia. The Court reasoned that the ferocity of the wife's attack was evidence from which provocation might be inferred[60] when seen against the backdrop of her family history. Such a situation, if it had led to a cold-blooded intention to kill was, the Court stated, murder, but in the instant case a view consistent with loss of self-control could be taken. A retrial was ordered with a warning that the evidence could be construed either in favour of or against the application of the defence. In contrast in *Thornton*[61] the accused had married the deceased, her husband, in 1987. He drank violently and on occasions had assaulted her. In May 1989 he committed a serious assault which resulted in his being prosecuted. The accused then left home and on her return the deceased tried to reform his drinking. On the evening of 14 June 1989, following a weekend troubled by serious domestic rows, the accused found the victim on a couch. He had begun drinking again and she tried to persuade him to come to bed. He refused and called her derogatory names and told her that he would kill her if she had been seeing other men. She went to the kitchen in order to calm down and to look for a blunt weapon to protect herself. She found a carving knife and sharpened it. The deceased again refused to come to bed and told the accused that he would kill her when she was asleep. The accused then claimed that she held the knife over the deceased's stomach while he was still lying on the couch and brought it slowly towards him thinking that he would ward it off. This did not happen and the victim was stabbed in the stomach and killed. It was argued before the Court of Appeal that the necessity for a sudden and temporary loss of self-control was no longer part of the defence of provocation. Bedlam LJ indicated that in cases of domestic violence, which culminated in the death of a partner, there was frequently evidence given of provocative acts committed by the deceased in the past. It was in that context that the jury had to consider the accused's reaction. In every such case, the question for the jury was whether or not the moment the fatal blow was struck the accused had been deprived for that moment of the self-control which previously he, or she, had been able to exercise. The appeal was therefore rejected.

---

60 The Court reiterated that loss of self-control need not be so described where evidence supports that inference; citing *Lee Chun Chuen* [1963] AC 220; [1963] 1 All ER 73; [1962] 3 WLR 1461 PC.
61 *The Independent*, 30 July 1991 CA.

Presence

4.27 The subjective test laid down by *Mac Eoin*[62] is, it is submitted, inconsistent with any requirement that the accused be actually present at the provocative incident.[63] Although presence at a provocative scene strengthens the tendency towards a loss of self-control, a sensitive person may react violently on being told of an incident. Presence as a requirement was taken to extreme lengths by the Supreme Court of Victoria in *Arden*.[64] It ruled that a protestation of rape by the de facto spouse of the accused could not be provocation where it led to the later killing of the rapist.

Crimes other than Murder

4.28 In the last century, prior to the Offences Against the Person Act, 1861, provocation could be raised as a defence to wounding with intent to murder[65] and wounding with intent to cause serious bodily harm.[66] This has not been the modern understanding of the defence in England[67] or in Canada,[68] provocation being confined to cases of murder.[69]

It is possible to argue that if an attempt to murder results from provocation this causes the accused to lose self-control so that the accused is, in fact, attempting manslaughter. Manslaughter cannot be committed intentionally and therefore cannot be attempted. Attempts necessarily involve an intent to commit the completed crime. Where the accused has a defence of provocation or excessive self-defence he must have intended to kill or cause serious injury. Where the accused could not have been convicted, because of provocation, of the substantive crime were the victim to have died it has been contended the substantive crime could not

---

62 [1978] IR 27 CCA.

63 The authority appears to be *Fisher* (1837) 8 C&P 182, 173 ER 452; *Ball* (1924) 18 Cr App R 149 CCA; *Terry* [1964] VR 248, 250-51 SC and see Lanham, "Provocation and the Requirement of Presence" (1989) 13 Crim LR 133 where it is argued that the better test is to require a reasonable belief than the actual presence of the victim at the time of provocation.

64 [1975] VR 449 and see *Guerin* [1967] 1 NSWR 255 CCA; *Quartly* (1986) 22 A Crim R 252 CCA NSW. In *Holmes* [1946] AC 588; [1946] 2 All ER 124 HL, Viscount Simon stated that where information as to an occurrence was given to the accused, if the occurrence itself as seen or experienced by the accused could be provocation, then his being informed of it could also be provocation.

65 *Thomas* (1837) 7 C&P 817, 173 ER 356. On this topic see English, "Provocation and Attempted Murder" [1973] Crim LR 727; Fairall, "Provocation, Attempted Murder and Wounding with Intent to Murder" (1983) 7 Crim LJ 44.

66 *Hagin* (1837) 8 C&P 167, 173 ER 445. Some of the decisions of this time are explicable by the mandatory death penalty where attempted murder involved poisoning or the infliction of actual bodily harm, a situation changed by the 1861 Act. Stephen *History* III 114-15.

67 *Cunningham* [1959] 1 QB 288; [1958] 3 All ER 711; [1959] 2 WLR 63, 43 Cr App R 79 CCA; *Bruzas* [1972] Crim LR 367; Peck, *The Times*, 5 December 1975.

68 *Campbell* (1977) 38 CCC (2d) 6 Ont CA.

69 The Queensland Code, s 269 and the Western Australian Code, s 246 allow provocation as a defence to non-fatal assaults.

70 Arguing from *Haughton v Smith* [1975] AC 476; [1973] 3 All ER 1109; [1974] 2 WLR 1, 58 Cr App R 198; [1974] Crim LR 305 HL. Further on attempts see par 2.41.

have been attempted.[70] Murder cannot be attempted in these circumstances.[71] In cases of shooting or wounding[72] with intent to murder decisions from Victoria[73] offer support for the proposition that the intent to commit murder can only be found by the jury where if the victim had died the accused would have committed murder. This test would not be fulfilled where the accused acted under provocation in what he did to the victim. Consequently, it is submitted the defence of provocation only applies when murder is charged.

As there is no offence of attempted manslaughter at common law there would be no lesser included offence were these decisions to be accepted by an Irish court.[74] The English Criminal Law Revision Committee has recommended the applicability of provocation to attempted murder,[75] subject to the necessary statutory modification.

Lawful Use of Force

4.29 Reasonable force may be used, where it is necessary, in order to defend oneself, or another,[76] against an attack, in order to defend one's property, in order to effect a lawful arrest or in order to prevent the commission of a grave crime.[77] The degree of force to be used is limited by the necessity of the occasion and the use of unnecessary force is an assault.[78] A person subjected to an attack is not obliged to measure his response with exactitude.[79] He may use reasonable force which, in this context, means the force which a reasonable person would consider necessary in the circumstances faced by the accused.[80] Small errors in the degree of responsive action

---

71   *Duvivier* (1982) 29 SASR 217, 5 A Crim R 89 SC SA; but see *Wells* (1981) 28 SASR 63 SC and the comment of the Federal Court of Australia at [1979] 1 Crim R 464 at 470. Further see the contradictory decisions in *Smith* [1964] NZLR 834 SC Christchurch and *Laga* [1969] NZLR 417 SC Auckland.

72   See par 2.40-2.42.

73   *Newman* [1948] VLR 61 SC; *Spartels* [1953] VLR 194 SC; but see *Falla* [1964] VR 78 SC; *Bozikis* [1981] VR 587 SC, and in the Australian Capital Territory *Helmhout* (1980) 1 A Crim R 103, 30 ACTR 1 SC ACT; Howard 139-45; Williams, *TBCL* (1st ed.) 500-1.

74   Ryan & Magee 365. Such considerations make it wise to add an alternative count to the indictment of wounding with intent to do grievous bodily harm. Howard 143 considers there is no power to bring in the alternative verdict to the statutory charge; Further see O'Connor & Fairall 199-200. At common law the attempt would be incorporated into the substantive offence.

75   14th Report Offences Against the Person, 1980 (Cmnd 7488).

76   *The People (A-G) v Keatley* [1954] IR 12 CCA.

77   See generally Kenny (1922) 103-4, 154-56; Archbold (1922) 879-81, 886-88, 933-34; Smith & Hogan (1st ed., 1965) 230-38. For a comprehensive modern statement see McKay [(1957] VR 560; [1957] ALR 648 SC.

78   *Russell on Crime* (10th ed., 1950) 763, quoted with approval in *The People (A-G) v Keatley* at 17, fn 5; *Penn* (1989) 44 A Crim R 131 CCA West Aus. Generally see Yeo, "Proportionality in Criminal Defences" (1988) 12 Crim LJ 211.

79   *Robinson* (1984) 4 NIJB 19, per MacDermott J. The dictum of Holmes J in *Brown v USA* (1921) 256 US at 343 is apposite: "Detached reflection cannot be demanded in the presence of an uplifted knife". See further *Zecevic* (1987) 71 ALR 641 HC.

80   The approach in the Supreme Court of Walsh J, Budd J concurring, in *The People (A-G) v Dwyer* [1972] IR 416 at 420, 108 ILTR 17, is to ask whether the accused believed on reasonable grounds that the force used was reasonably necessary for his protection. Butler J, Ó Dálaigh CJ concurring,

will therefore be discounted, for a measure of latitude is appropriate where a person may have little time to think or assess his response to a breach of the law.[81]

There is no obligation to await a blow.[82] Defensive action may be taken where an attack is reasonably anticipated and no course of action alternative to the use of force is reasonably open.[83] It follows that there is no rigid requirement that the accused retreat as far as possible or take all other steps open to him before resorting to force.[84] An immediate resort to violence, or a failure to take alternative courses of action, may be evidence indicating that force was not reasonably necessary or that the accused was acting from an improper motive.

The defence is, in common with all other defences in criminal law, limited to those who take action in good faith and do not, under the guise of the situation in question, act from motives of revenge or ill-will.[85] It is not self-defence to carry a knife intending to kill on a fight breaking out.[86] Where force is used in a situation where the law allows it and in a degree which is reasonable in the circumstances, it is a complete defence which entitles the accused to be acquitted.

Parents are entitled to use reasonable and moderate force to chastise their children and this entitlement extends to school teachers and those acting in the place of or on behalf of a parent.[87]

---

at 429 approaches the question on the basis of whether the force used was reasonably necessary. Both tests are objective and neither is likely to differ in the result they produce when put to a jury.

81   Thus in *Palmer* [1971] AC 814 at 832; [1971] 1 All ER 1077 at 1088, [1971] 2 WLR 831 at 844, 55 Cr App R 223 at 242 PC, Lord Morris stated: "If there has been an attack so that defence is reasonably necessary it will be recognised that a person defending himself cannot weigh to a nicety the exact measure of his necessary defensive action. If a jury thought that in a moment of unexpected anguish a person had done only what he honestly and instinctively thought was necessary that would be most potent evidence that only reasonable defensive action was taken". This statement was made in attempting to justify a rejection of the half-way defence in murder (see par 4.30): the evidence of the accused on the objective question is no better or worse than any other person. The accused must still behave reasonably despite being under attack. The fact that he thought his actions necessary is only a defence where a reasonable person would have behaved as he did.

82   Kenny (1922) 154. For an example see *Xiao Jing Wang* (1990) Crim LJ 200 NZ CA. The facts were that the accused and the victim were married. He had threatened to kill his wife but she killed him later while he was comatose from alcohol. Despite the fact that the accused had tied up the victim and tried to strangle and then smother him and then stabbed him several times the jury had accepted provocation. The New Zealand Court of Appeal, however, ruled that though self-defence could be raised where there was a pre-emptive strike, the existence of alternative causes of action would mean that a pre-emptive strike could not be reasonable in the circumstances.

83   *Lane* (1983) 8 A Crim R 182 CCA Vict. It is submitted that this is the correct formulation of the defence in distinction to authorities which impose a requirement that an attack be imminent; *Devlin v Armstrong* [1971] NI 13 at 33 CCA.

84   *Julien* [1969] 2 All ER 856, 858; [1969] 1 WLR 839, 842, 53 Cr App R 407, 411 CA; *McInnes* [1971] 3 All ER 295; [1971] 1 WLR 1600, 55 Cr App R 551 CA; *Morgan v Colman* (1981) 27 SASR 334 SC. A mistake induced by intoxication as to the degree of force necessary in self-defence is not operative: *Beckford* [1988] AC 130; [1987] 3 All ER 425; [1987] 3 WLR 611, 85 Cr App R 378; [1988] Crim LR 116 PC.

85   *The People (A-G) v Commane* (1975) 1 Frewen 400 CCA.

86   *The People (A-G) v O'Brien* (1969) 1 Frewen 343 CCA.

87   *Terry* [1955] VLR 114, 116-17 SC; *Hopley* (1860) 2 F&F 202 at 206, 175 ER 1024 at 1026; Smith & Hogan 386; Howard 145-46.

Excessive Self-Defence

4.30 Where a person subjected to a violent and felonious attack endeavours, by way of self-defence, to prevent the consummation of that attack by force, but, in doing so exercises more force than is necessary, but no more than he honestly believes to be necessary, and thereby kills, he is guilty of manslaughter and not murder.[88] It is probable that the rule is wider in its application and operates also where a person honestly believes himself to be in a situation where he may lawfully use force, even though, on an objective legal view, he is incorrect in that assessment. No authority directly supports this extension of the rule. This text argues for such an extension. If that argument is correct the rule as to self-defence may be simply stated: where the accused kills the victim intending to kill or cause serious injury but an issue as to self-defence is raised then—

(1) the accused is entitled to be acquitted where both objectively and subjectively, the situation was one where he was entitled to resort to the use of force and the amount of force used was no more than was reasonably necessary;

(2) the accused is guilty of murder where, on a subjective test, he had no honest belief that the situation was one where he was entitled to resort to the use of force, or where he had no honest belief that the amount of force he in fact used was more than was reasonably necessary;

(3) the accused is not guilty of murder but guilty of manslaughter where, tested objectively, the situation was one where he was not entitled to resort to the use of force, or where, tested objectively, the amount of force he in fact used was more than was reasonably necessary, but, in either case,[89] on a subjective test he honestly believed the situation was one where he was entitled to resort to force or that the amount of force he in fact used was more than was reasonably necessary;[90]

(4) where the accused is subjected to an attack he may also be provoked into an uncontrolled state where he kills, which may entitle him, apart from the above stated rules, to the defence of provocation.[91]

Development and Rationale

4.31 Early English decisions seem to allow the possibility of an accused,[92] when

---

88   *The People (A-G) v Dwyer* [1972] IR 417, 108 ILTR 17 SC; *The People (A-G) v Commane* [1975] 1 Frewen 400 CCA. This sentence follows the words of the certified point of law answered by the Supreme Court in *Dwyer* merely adding the words "and thereby kills". For a full review of developments in common law countries see Douglas, "The Demise of Excessive Self-Defence Manslaughter in Australia" (1988) 12 Crim LJ 28.

89   Conceivably the defence may apply where both situations are concurrent, that is to say there is a double mistake by the accused.

90   These rules are adapted from those suggested by Gillies 257.

91   *Palmer* [1971] AC 814; [1971] 1 All ER 1077; [1971] 2 WLR 831, 55 Cr App R 223 PC. For a detailed consideration of the defence see par 4.01-4.28.

92   Generally see Doran, "The Doctrine of Excessive Defence: Development Past Present and Potential" (1985) NILQ 314; Snelling, "Killing in Self-Defence" (1960) 34 Aus LJ 130; Morris & Howard, "Studies in Criminal Law" (1964) 127-31 Ch 4; Manson, "Excessive Force in the Supreme Court of Canada" 29 CR (3d) 364; O'Brien, "Excessive Self-Defence: A Need for Legislation" (1983) 25 CLQ 441; Editorial [1988] Crim LR 1; Howard, "An Australian Letter: Excessive Defence" [1964]

attacked and using unreasonable force and killing, being convicted of man-slaughter.[93] In modern law this principle was received in *McKay*.[94] A chicken farmer in Victoria, subjected to persistent thefts, shot and killed a thief in an attempt to arrest him. Lowe J held:

> If the occasion warrants action in self-defence or for the prevention of felony or the apprehension of the felon but the person taking action acts beyond the necessity of the occasion and kills the offender the crime is manslaughter—not murder.[95]

The principle was accepted by the High Court of Australia[96] on a basis, stated by Stephen J in *Viro* that:

> ... the moral culpability of a person who kills another in defending himself but who fails in a plea of self-defence only because the force which he believed to be necessary exceeded that which was reasonably necessary falls short of the moral culpability ordinarily associated with murder.[97]

Unfortunately, in *Viro*[98] the High Court attempted a clarification of the law which restated it on a basis which was so complex as to lead to the destruction of the rule notwithstanding the acknowledgement by the court of the justice of the underlying principle.[99] Mason J set forth the following propositions:

> 1(a) It is for the jury first to consider whether when the accused kills the deceased the accused reasonably believed that an unlawful attack which threatened him with death or serious bodily harm was being or was about to be made upon him.
> (b) By the expression "reasonably believed" is meant, not what a reasonable man would have believed but what the accused himself might reasonably believe in all the circumstances in which he found himself.
>
> 2. If the jury is satisfied beyond reasonable doubt that there was no reasonable belief by the accused of such an attack no question of self-defence arises.
>
> 3. If the jury is not satisfied beyond reasonable doubt that there was no such reasonable belief by the accused, it must then consider whether the force in fact used by the accused was reasonably proportionate to the danger he believed he faced.
>
> 4. If the jury is not satisfied beyond reasonable doubt that more force was used than was reasonably proportionate it should acquit.
>
> 5. If the jury is satisfied beyond reasonable doubt that more force was used, its verdict should be either manslaughter or murder, that depending upon the answer to the final question for the jury—did the accused believe that the force he used was reasonably proportionate to the danger which he faced?
>
> 6. If the jury is satisfied beyond reasonable doubt that the accused did not have such a

Crim LR 448; Howard, "Two Problems in Excessive Defence" [1968] 84 LQR 343; Smith, "Excessive Defence—A Rejection of Australian Initiative" [1972] Crim LR 524.

93   Morris & Howard, *Studies in Criminal Law* (1964) 127-31; Stephen *History* III 67; Howe (1958) 100 CR 448 HC.
94   [1957] VR 560; [1957] ALR 648 SC.
95   At 563.
96   *Viro* (1978) 141 CLR 88, 18 ALR 257 HC, rejecting *Palmer* [1971] AC 814; [1971] 1 All ER 1077; [1971] 2 WLR 831, 55 Cr App R 223 PC.
97   At 139 CLR.
98   Fn 96.
99   *Zecevic* (1987) 71 ALR 641 HC, see particularly the judgment of Mason CJ.

belief the verdict will be murder. If it is not satisfied beyond reasonable doubt that the accused did not have that belief the verdict will be manslaughter.[1]

4.32 Clearly, these propositions are incomprehensible to a jury. They could have been framed by judges in language more digestible to ordinary people. Directions were, however, given to juries by way of a direct quotation from the above. This caused confusion.[2] The Australian High Court, by a majority, in *Zecevic*[3] abandoned the defence in order to remove the difficulties caused by the *Viro* directions and in order to make self-defence in murder conform with both the general law and that accepted in the common law world.[4] So stated self-defence is a complete answer to a murder charge or fails completely, subject to the prosecution proving intent or an alternative defence, for example that of provocation, being open to the accused. That is not the law in Ireland.

4.33 In *The People (A-G) v Dwyer*[5] a fight commenced outside a chip shop brought on, in part, by abusive behaviour on the part of the accused to the parents of one of the two deceased. Dwyer gave evidence that he believed the victim, or his cohorts, to have some implement with which, he alleged, he had been hit on the head and claimed he was in fear for his life. At the trial it was beyond doubt that Dwyer had a knife and had stabbed and killed his victim, Philip Ney. There was a dearth of evidence to suggest that the actions of Dwyer were proportionate to the necessity of the occasion. The trial judge directed the jury in terms of the defence of self-defence requiring the force used in reply to be objectively proportionate to the necessity of the occasion. The subjective belief of Dwyer, if accepted by the jury to the extent of raising a reasonable doubt, was therefore irrelevant. The Supreme Court disagreed. Two judgements were delivered and the rationale of each differed.[6] Walsh J[7] reasoned that s 4 of the Criminal Justice Act, 1964 had changed the mental element for murder and had made the test for establishing this element entirely subjective. The belief of the accused was the determinative test as to intent. People who act honestly towards a lawful end, self-defence, cannot intend the criminal act of murder. An intentional assault is committed when the force used is not justified objectively and where death results that is manslaughter:[8]

> Our statutory provision makes it clear that the intention is personal and that it is not to be measured solely by objective standards. In my opinion, therefore, when the evidence in a case discloses a question of self-defence and where it is sought by the prosecution to show that the accused used excessive force, that is to say more than

1 CLR 146-7, ALR 303.

2 *McManus* (1985) 2 NSWLR 448 at 461-2 CCA; *Lawson & Forsythe* [1986] VR 515 at 547 SC.

3 Fm 99.

4 England had rejected the defence in *Palmer*, fn 35, and *McInnes* [1971] 3 All ER 295; [1971] 1 WLR 1600, 55 Cr App R 551 CA; Smith & Hogan 247-49. The Supreme Court of Canada had quashed provincial acceptance of the defence in *Faid* (1983) 33 CR (3d) 1 SC; Stuart 461.

5 [1972] IR 416, 108 ILTR 17 SC.

6 Fitzgerald J, at 425, concurred in the question put to the court being answered in the affirmative but did not give a judgment or give any reasons.

7 Budd J concurring.

8 See par 3.04.

would be regarded as objectively reasonable, the prosecution must establish that the accused knew that he was using more force than was reasonably necessary. Therefore, it follows that if the accused honestly believed that the force that he did use was necessary, then he is not guilty of murder. The onus, of course, if upon the prosecution to prove beyond reasonable doubt that he knew that the force was excessive or that he did not believe that it was necessary. If the prosecution does not do so, it has failed to establish the necessary malice. If, however, at the same time it does establish that the force used was more than was reasonably necessary it has established that the killing was unlawful as being without justification and not having been by misadventure.[9]

4.34 Butler J[10] accepted the proposition, stated in Howe, that a person whose plea of self-defence fails only by reason of the amount of force he used being objectively unreasonable lacks the full degree of culpability associated with murder. His analysis is similar to that of Walsh J save that it is based on the proposition that where the accused is attacked and uses disproportionate force, his intention in so acting is not primarily to kill or to cause serious injury, but to defend himself:

> A person is entitled to protect himself from unlawful attack. If in doing so he uses no more force than is reasonably necessary, he is acting lawfully and commits no crime even though he kills his assailant. If he uses more force than may objectively be considered necessary, his act is unlawful and, if he kills, the killing is unlawful. His intention, however, falls to be tested subjectively and it would appear logical to conclude that, if his intention in doing the unlawful act was primarily to defend himself, he should not be held to have the necessary intention to kill or cause serious injury. The result of this view would be that the killing, though unlawful, would be manslaughter only.[11]

The focus of the defence is the honest belief of the accused. It is this belief which reduces his intentional action in killing the victim from murder to manslaughter. No honest belief as to the use of force can be held where the victim has already been rendered immobile by a blow to the head when the force used to kill him is sought to be justified as being in self-defence.[12]

Reason for the Defence

4.35 There is no evidence that the defence has caused confusion or injustice in its operation. Moral culpability is, in common human understanding, scaled in gravity. Some intentional killings are less culpable than the guilt normally associated with the crime of murder. Yet, they are culpable due to the intention with which they occur or the avoidable nature of the human emotions giving rise to an impetus for an attack with deadly force. Similar considerations thus apply both to provocation and the half-way house defence.

The defence is capable of being simply stated and has been so stated by the Supreme Court. When put into accessible language it is easily understood.[13] The alternative of allowing persons who have killed in culpable circumstances to be

9   At 424.
10   Ó Dálaigh CJ concurring.
11   At 429. An alternative view is that the decision by the accused amounted to gross negligence, a view which would be open even under the English rules; *Foxford* [1974] NI 181.
12   *The People (A-G) v Commane* (1975) 1 Frewen 400 CCA.
13   See *McNamara* [1963] VR 32 SC.

acquitted, is a real danger were the defence to be abolished. The fear of leaving manslaughter as an easy option for a jury is belied by the serious consideration juries in fact give to these cases. Such an apprehension is, in any event, an expression of mistrust in the ability of ordinary people to fulfil the function which the Constitution has given them.[14]

A proper direction allows three verdicts in a murder trial where self-defence is properly open, of acquittal, murder or manslaughter. It would be unjust to remove the defence as a person honestly using excessive force to repel a deadly attack cannot be properly classified as a murderer. Were the common law position, of murder or acquittal, to be applied, juries would be tempted to acquit rather than perpetrating such an obvious injustice.

Scope of the Defence

4.36 There appears to be no reason of logic or policy why a defence which applies to an honest mistake as to the amount of force necessary in self-defence, should not apply equally where the accused honestly uses force in a situation in which, if his belief was correct, he would legally have been entitled to so act.[15] Where, for example, the accused kills a member of his family in his own home at night, believing, perhaps through a combination of fear of raiders due to a spate of violent burglaries[16] and bad light, that there was a dangerous intruder in the house, there is no reason in principle why his culpability should be considered by a different rule than that in *Dwyer*.[17] To result in a complete acquittal the defence of lawful use of force requires that, objectively and subjectively, a situation existed where force might be used and that the actual force used was limited to the necessity of the occasion.[18] Where, on either leg of the test, the accused acts illegally, on an objective test, but honestly believes either that there existed facts which entitled him to use force, or that the necessity existed to use the degree of force he actually used, he would lack culpability judged by his own state of mind. The law still accepts the objective test in regulating the use of force and the accused would therefore be guilty, but only because of that criterion. To apply the reasoning of Walsh J, in *Dwyer*, to the example given, the accused clearly intended to kill or cause serious injury but under the influence of a belief that such force was appropriate in the circumstances. Applying the reasoning of Butler J in *Dwyer*, to the example given, the intention of the accused was primarily to defend himself and his family and not to kill or cause serious injury. On the *Howe*[19] test the accused lacks the moral culpability ordinarily associated with murder.

It is possible to question the necessity for a conviction at all in these circumstances since the accused, on the basis of his own perceptions, is free of guilt. Objective

14   Article 38.
15   Those situations are briefly sketched at 4.29.
16   Such as occurred in remote rural areas in the early to mid 1980's. For an example of the possible consequences see the horrific facts leading to the death of the Willis brothers set out in the reports of *The People (DPP) v Quilligan & O'Reilly*, *Irish Times*, July 1989.
17   *The People (A-G) v Dwyer* [1972] IR 417, 108 ILTR 17 SC.
18   See par 4.29.
19   (1958) 100 CLR 448 HC.

standards continue to apply but may be particularly unfortunate in their operation where, as in murder, a mandatory life sentence must be imposed. Since the failure to make such inquiry as a reasonable person would or the failure to give to a situation the degree of attention and foresight which allows society to attain a "true social order"[20] is avoidable and therefore culpable, a conviction for unlawful killing appears appropriate.[21] Degrees of guilt vary by ability, experience and the state of emotion into which a situation may have precipitated a person. It is therefore arguable that the flexible sentence applicable to manslaughter is appropriate.

The half-way defence should apply where the accused unlawfully used force believing himself to be in a situation where it could legally have been used. Such a development has not been sanctioned by any decision at common law. In *Dwyer*, Walsh J warned:

> . . . I am confining myself strictly for the purposes of this case to the actual terms of the question and, in particular, to the reference to the person being "subjected to a violent and felonious attack" ... I do not wish to be taken to subscribe to all the dicta in *R v Howe* (1958) 100 CLR 448 as the dicta in that case appear to indicate a wider area than has been raised in the questions before this court. For example, at p 460 of the Australian Report Chief Justice Dixon speaks of "an attack of a violent and felonious nature, or at least of an unlawful nature, was made or threatened so that the person under attack or threat of attack reasonably feared for his life or the safety of his person from injury, violation or indecent or insulting usage. This would mean that an occasion has arisen entitling the person charged with murder to resort to force to repel force or apprehended force" . . . the present case is by its terms confined to the first type of attack mentioned in the passage quoted. I do not say that I would not follow the view of the learned judges of that court in an appropriate case and I express no view upon that. . . .[22]

4.37 In Australia the defence was, prior to its abolition, applied to self-defence against violent or sodomitical attack and to the prevention of theft or the arrest of the thief.[23] There is merit in allowing the defence to extend to honest mistakes as to situation, as well as to proportion, in that this results in a simplification of the law. This solution was supported by Deane J in his dissenting judgment in *Zecevic*:[24]

> The actual reasoning in the majority judgments in *Viro* supports the conclusion that the proper verdict in a case of homicide where self-defence fails as a complete defence by reason only of the fact that the accused's genuine belief that he was acting in reasonable self-defence was not reasonably held is manslaughter regardless of whether the absence of the element of recklessness is caused by the unreasonableness of the

---

20 Constitution, Preamble.

21 It is certainly well entrenched in the *Dwyer* judgments, fn 17.

22 At 424-25. In *Tikos (No. 2)* [1963] VR 306 at 313 the Supreme Court of Victoria limited the situation to one "which warranted the accused acting with intent to do some kind of grievous bodily harm at the least". Doran considers that if so the accused should be acquitted; (1985) 36 NILQ 314, 318. There is support for extending the application of the rule to cases of acute pain; *Lane* (1983) 8 A Crim R 182, 184 CCA Vict. Further see Gillies 260-1.

23 Howard 90. It is possible to read *Zecevic* [1987] 71 ALR 641 HC as a denial of the applicability of the defence where the accused unreasonably believed that an attack was going to be made on him. However the judgments of Wilson, Dawson and Tohey JJ proceeded to reject the defence in principle, but arguably these remarks are *obiter*.

24 Fn 23. This suggestion was not supported by Gaudron J who also dissented.

perception of an occasion of self-defence or the unreasonableness of the belief that the force used was not excessive. If that view be accepted, as I think it should be, much of the difficulty in the *Viro* formulation disappears as there is no longer any necessity to distinguish between the first and second stage requirements of reasonableness.[25]

It has already been argued that this view should be accepted in this jurisdiction. A rule thus reformulated is expressed by *Gillies*:[26]

> Where D kills a person in circumstances amounting to murder, but claims he or she acted in self-defence, (1) D is entitled to be exonerated where the decision to use force and the amount of force used was subjectively and objectively reasonable; (2) D is guilty of murder where he or she lacked an honest belief in the necessity to resort to force by way of self-defence, or where D lacked an honest belief that the quantum of force used was reasonable; (3) D's liability is reduced to manslaughter where D's conduct (that is both the decision to resort to force and the quantum implied) was subjectively reasonable, but (in respect of either D's decision to use force or the quantum implied) was objectively unreasonable.

The arguments in favour of extending the defence to attempted murder and the offences of wounding with intent to murder are set out under the treatment of this topic in the context of the defence of provocation and will not be repeated here.[27] Such a proposition has received support in the context of excessive self-defence.[28]

General Defences

We now proceed to sketch defences general to the criminal law.

Mistake of Fact

4.38 The relevance of mistake of fact as a defence can only be determined by first isolating and defining the elements of the offence. Where the element in respect of which a mistake is made is one of strict liability the offence only requires that the accused should do the act which comprises that element.[29] Hence mistake is not a defence in those circumstances. Where the mental element of an offence is negligence then a negligent mistake will not excuse.[30] Where the mental element of an offence is criminal negligence then a genuine mistake arrived at in a criminally negligent fashion will not excuse. Where the mental element of the offence consists of knowledge or intent, then the existence of a belief by the accused which, if it were true, would mean that his act were innocent, relieves him of liability.[31] Where the mental element of the offence consists of recklessness then wilful blindness as to the true facts will not absolve the accused of liability.[32] Wilful blindness has also been held to be equivalent to knowledge for offences of recklessness.[33]

25 At 657. See further *Halmhout* (1980) 1 A Crim R 103, 30 ACTR 1 SC ACT.
26 257.   27 See par 4.28.
28 *Bozikis* [1981] VR 587 SC. But see *Falla* [1964] VR 78 SC.
29 *Prince* (1875) LR 2 CCR 154; [1874-80] All ER 881, 13 Cox 138 CCR, discussed by Cross, "Centenary Reflections on Price's Case" (1975) 91 LQR 540.
30 *Foxford* [1974] NI 181.
31 Generally see Smith & Hogan 85-90, 207-9.
32 *He Kaw Te* [1985] 59 ALJR 620 HC.
33 Wilful blindness is a subjective element: Williams CLGP 159; *Sand* (1985) 19 A Crim R 170, 173

At common law it was generally accepted that for a mistake to constitute a defence it must have been reasonable.[34] Historically, it is possible to interpret this requirement as an evidential guide to the jury formulated at a time when the accused was not entitled to give evidence. More recently the requirement that a mistake negativing intention, knowledge or recklessness, be both honest and reasonable has been abandoned both in Canada[35] and in England.[36] Australian law developed in a more complex fashion. It allowed a denial of an essential element to be merely honest but required the positive assertion of a justification or excuse to be both honest and reasonable.[37] More recently it has been asserted that the latter defence of honest and reasonable mistake applies only to offences which involve some element of strict liability.[38]

In considering whether a particular mistaken belief asserted by the accused was genuinely held, the jury are entitled to have regard to the presence or absence of reasonable grounds for that belief.[39]

Duress

4.39 The elements of the defence of duress were explained by Murnaghan J in *The People (A-G) v Whelan*[40] as:

> . . . threats of immediate death or serious personal violence so great as to overbear the ordinary power of human resistance should be accepted as a justification for acts which would otherwise be criminal. The application of this general rule must be subject to certain limitations. The commission of murder is a crime so heinous that murder should not be committed even for the price of life and in such a case the strongest duress would not be any justification. We have not to determine what class of crime other than murder should be placed in the same category. . . . Where the excuse of duress is applicable it must further be clearly shown that the overpowering of the will was operative at the time the crime was committed, and, if there was reasonable opportunity for the will to reassert itself, no justification can be found in antecedent threats.[41]

It is unclear whether the phrase "the ordinary power of human resistance" applies an objective, subjective or modified test of the *Camplin* type.[42] In England the

CCA Vict: ". . . an offender whose suspicions are aroused that a substance is probably narcotic goods, but who refrains from making any enquiries for fear that he may learn the truth, is to be treated as knowing that the object was narcotic goods".

34 *Tolson* (1889) 23 QBD 168; [1886-90] All ER 26, 16 Cox 629 CCR; *Kenny* (1922) 65-69; Russell 71-86.

35 *Pappajohn* (1980) 14 CR (3d) 243 SC; Stuart 241-72.

36 *Williams* [1987] 3 All ER 411; [1983] 78 Cr App R 276; [1984] Crim LR 163 CA; *Beckford* [1988] AC 130; [1987] 3 All ER 425; [1987] 3 WLR 611, 85 Cr App R 378; [1988] Crim LR 116 PC. It has also been argued that where a genuine mistake is made as to the quantum of force used in self-defence the accused is thus relieved of liability; *O'Grady* [1987] QB 995; [1987] 3 All ER 420; [1987] 3 WLR 321, 85 Cr App R 315; [1987] Crim LR 706 CA.

37 *Fairall & O'Connor* 45-62.

38 Brett Waller and Walker 667 arguing from *He Kaw Te*, fn 70. This appears to the writer not to be a correct interpretation of this case.

39 This is discussed in the context of rape in ch 8.

40 [1934] IR 519 CCA. For a general review see further Yeo, *Compulsion in the Criminal Law*, (Sydney, 1990).

41 At 526; see similarly *Hurley & Murray* [1967] VR 526 at 543 per Smith J SC Vict.

42 As to which see par 4.07, 40.8. In England the test is the modified objective test; *Howe* [1987] AC

existence of a time lapse between the threat[43] and the criminal action, and the availability of an alternative course of action have been held, on an extraordinary set of facts, not to be fatal to the defence.[44]

4.40 The House of Lords have, in *Howe*,[45] reversed the previously stated position that accessories before the fact[46] and principals in the second degree[47] to murder, may plead the defence; it is now not available to any party to murder. In Canada it has been held that a person forced at gun point to drive two acquaintances to the scene of a robbery where a by-stander was then killed, could not be considered to have formed a genuine common intention with the perpetrators.[48] There is no authority in favour of this defence being open to a party to murder who participates in the act of killing. A possible solution to the applicability of the defence to murder, is to cause it to reduce the crime to manslaughter[49] on the basis that the accused in such circumstances lacks the moral culpability normally associated with murder. This comment is equally applicable to the defence of necessity.

The defence is unavailable to a person who voluntarily joined an association of violent criminals[50] or, it appears, recklessly joined an organisation which he should have realised was violent and liable to subject him to duress.[51] The English Court of Appeal, have, however, held that knowledge of the violent propensities of the organisation is essential before the accused can be deprived of the defence of duress.[52] This accords with the subjective approach to determining liability for an offence.[53]

417; [1987] 1 All ER 771; [1987] 2 WLR 568, 85 Cr App R 32; [1987] Crim LR 480 HL. A similar test is applied in South Australia; *Pazaloff* (1986) 130 LSJS 20 at 28. There seems no reason to apply a test different to the wholly subjective one adopted in *Mac Eoin* [1987] IR 27 CCA. On the defence generally see Smith & Hogan 200-4; O'Connor & Fairall 144-65; Stuart 393-405 (on s 17 of the Canadian Code).

43 Which may be to third parties, such as de facto spouse, *Hurley & Murray*, fn 41.

44 *Hudson* [1971] 2 QB 202; [1971] 2 All ER 244; [1971] 2 WLR 1047, 56 Cr App R 1 CA; see also *Hurley & Murray*, fn 41.

45 Fn 80. Followed in *Pang Shun-yee & Others* [1988] LRC (Crim) 235 HC Hong Kong. In *Gotts* [1991] 2 All ER 1 the Court of Appeal decided that the principle in *Howe* applied to bar a defence to attempted murder. The Court commented that as the sentence was at learge it could be tailored to meet the degree of culpability which the evidence disclosed.

46 *Kray* [1970] 1 QB 125; [1969] 3 All ER 941; [1969] 3 WLR 831, 53 Cr App R 569 CA.

47 *Lynch* [1975] AC 653; [1975] 1 All ER 913; [1975] 2 WLR 641, 61 Cr App R 6; [1975] Crim LR 707 HL; *Abbot* [1977] AC 755; [1976] 3 All ER 140; [1976] 3 WLR 462, 63 Cr App R 241; [1976] Crim LR 563 PC.

48 *Paquett* (1976) 30 CCC (2d) 417 SC; applied in *Curran* (1978) 38 CCC (2d) 151 Alberta CA. It was respectfully suggested that this is the correct approach and that a person forced at gun-point to drive someone to the scene of a murder has no purpose of killing or causing serious injury within the statutory definition of the mental element of that offence as defined by s 4 of the Criminal Justice Act, 1964. A similar consideration would apply to the question of common design if the tentative analysis in this work of that topic is accepted; see par 1.10-1.11.

49 A solution adopted in *McCafferty* [1974] 1 NSWLR 89 SC; over-ruled by *McConnell* [1977] 1 NSWLR 714 CCA. Further see the arguments of Morris & Howard, *Studies in Criminal Law* 141-44.

50 *Fitzpatrick* [1977] NI 20 CCA; *Sharp* [1987] QB 853; [1987] 3 All ER 103; [1987] 3 WLR 1, 85 Cr App R 207; [1987] Crim LR 566 CA.

51 *Calderwood & Moore* [1983] NI 361 CA. See further on this organisation, *The Shankill Butchers* (1989).

52 *Shepherd* (1987) 86 Cr App R 47; [1987] Crim LR 686 CA.

53 It is submitted that the subjective approach is correct: *Raroa* [1987] 2 NZLR 486 CA. Further see

The defence should not be inflexibly excluded as, by an analogy with the principles applicable to allowing a withdrawal from a common design,[54] it can be just to allow the defence of duress to a person who has done all within his power to leave an evil organisation. This latter test may not be met without the accused communicating with the police.[55]

Marital Coercion

4.41 At common law it was presumed that where a wife committed a crime in the presence of her husband she acted under his immediate coercion and was thus excused from punishment.[56] This defence did not apply to crimes of a heinous character or those which were dangerous in their consequences. In *The State (DPP) v Walsh and Connelly*[57] the Supreme Court held that the defence was inconsistent with the Constitution; it had thus been abolished since 1937.

Necessity

4.42 Necessity, subject to stringent safeguards, is a defence to a criminal charge.[58] Traditionally, it has been thought that allowing necessity as a defence would endanger social order.[59] Where the defence has been allowed to operate it has been carefully circumscribed.[60] In *Loughnan*[61] the defence of necessity was accepted by the Supreme Court of Victoria. The court favoured accepting the defence subject to limitations set out by Crockett J:

> (1) The harm to be justified must be committed under pressure either of physical forces or by some human agency so that "an urgent situation of imminent peril" has been created. (2) The accused must have acted with the intention of avoiding greater harm so as to have made possible "the preservation of at least an equal value". (3) There was open to the accused no alternative, other than that adopted by him, to avoid the greater harm or "to conserve the value".[62]

For example, the defence was made out where the accused broke the speed limit

---

Yeo, "The Threat Element in Duress" (1987) 11 Crim LJ 165.

54   *Becerra & Cooper* (1975) 62 Cr App R 212 CA; *Whitefield* (1984) 79 Cr App R 36; [1984] Crim LR 97 CA.

55   *Jensen* [1980] VR 194-201 SC.

56   Archbold (1922) 21-24.

57   [1981] IR 412 at 449 SC.

58   Generally see Smith & Hogan 222-29; O'Connor & Fairall 104-15; Stuart 432-49. Kenny (1922) 74-77 generally favoured the defence, subject to his statement at 75: "It is clear that no ground of defence can be accepted in any case (1) where the evil averted was a less evil than the offence committed to avert it, or (2) where the evil could have been averted by anything short of the commission of that offence, or (3) where more harm was done than was necessary for averting the evil".

59   *Southwark London BC v Williams* [1971] Ch 734; [1971] 2 All ER 175; [1971] 2 WLR 467 CA.

60   A defence of duress of circumstances is gaining growing acceptance in England; *Denton* (1987) 85 Cr App R 246; [1987] RTR 129 CA; *Conway* [1989] QB 290; [1988] 3 All ER 1025; [1988] 3 WLR 1238, 88 Cr App R 343; [1989] RTR 85; [1989] Crim LR 74 CA. See further, in the context of the civil action, *Howard v Shirlstar Container Transport Limited* [1990] 3 All ER 366 CA.

61   [1981] VR 443 SC Vict.

62   At 460. See further the conditions laid down by the Supreme Court of Canada in *Perka* (1984) 42 CR (3d) 113, 14 CCC(3d) 385, 386.

while driving his son to hospital. There was a real possibility of death and the speeding was not so gross as to operate as another danger.[63]

Two further limitations may be mentioned. Circumstances whereby murder would be an avoidance of greater harm may never, or perhaps can never, arise.[64] As with duress, necessity may never be a defence to that charge.[65] Although the Supreme Court of Canada have expressed a different view,[66] an accused should be disentitled to plead the defence by reason of the necessity arising in the course of a criminal activity which he has voluntarily undertaken.[67] It is submitted that the constitutional aim of obtaining "true social order"[68] cannot be achieved by allowing the defence of necessity to be pleaded by those who have brought about the circumstances requiring the necessity by their own criminal activities.

As circumstances can arise where it would be unjust not to allow a defence of necessity to an accused, and as justice is the fundamental principle upon which the legal system under the Constitution is based,[69] it is submitted that the defence is implied in Article 40.3.3, even if it is not recognised in the common law inherited on independence in 1922.

Intoxication

4.43 Reasons of policy and an adaptation of the fault principle in criminal law, have traditionally inspired the common law to exclude self-induced intoxication by alcohol and dangerous drugs as a defence.[70] Where the crime consists merely of the voluntary commission of the external elements of the offence, the fact that the accused was not acting consciously, due to intoxication is irrelevant.[71] For example, where the accused kills the victim by an unlawful and dangerous act, but believes, due to having taken LSD, that he is fighting a snake in the underworld, he is nonetheless guilty of manslaughter.[72] Where, however, the mental element of the

---

63 *White* [1987] 31 A Crim R 194 D Ct NSW.

64 The obvious example is a shipwreck; *Dudley & Stevens* (1884) 14 QBD 273; [1881-5] All ER 61, 15 Cox 624 CCR.

65 In *Dudley & Stevens*, fn 64, the eventual result was a conviction for murder. Morris & Howard, *Studies in Criminal Law*, 141-44 argue for reduction from murder to manslaughter in these crimes. In *U.S. v Holmes* (1842 Fed Cas No 15383) 26 Fed Cas 360, the result was manslaughter, apparently because the members of the crew saved each other in preference to the passengers in circumstances where there was no necessity to preserve the life of a crew member, because, for example, he was required to navigate the vessel. *Dudley & Stevens* was approved by the House of Lords in *Howe* [1987] AC 417; [1987] 1 All ER 771; [1987] 2 WLR 568, 85 Cr App R 32; [1987] Crim LR 480 HL.

66 *Perka*, fn 62.

67 It is submitted that the views expressed by MacDonald JA of the Nova Scotia CA in *Salvador* (1981) 59 CCC (2d) 591 are correct. S 3.02.2 of the Model Penal Code bars the defence of necessity in crimes where the mental element is recklessness or negligence and also where the accused has acted recklessly or negligently in bringing about the situation requiring the choice of harms or evils.

68 Constitution, Preamble.

69 *McGee v A-G* [1974] IR 284 at 318, 109 ILTR 29 per Walsh J, SC.

70 Archbold (1922) 19-21; *Kenny* (1922) 59-62; *Beard* (1920) AC 479; [1920] All ER 21, 14 Cr App R 159, 26 Cox 573 HL. Thus an intoxicated mistake is not a defence: *O'Grady* [1987] QB 995; [1987] 3 All ER 420; [1987] 3 WLR 321, 85 Cr App R 315; [1987] Crim LR 706 CA.

71 Generally see Smith & Hogan 209-22; O'Connor & Fairall 214-32; Stuart 363-83.

72 *Lipman* [1970] 1 QB 152; [1969] 3 All ER 410; [1969] 3 WLR 819, 53 Cr App R 600 CA. This decision has been heavily criticised. It is suggested respectfully that it is incorrect. Manslaughter must

crime requires that the accused intend a result, evidence of intoxication may be considered on the question of whether that intention may have been absent.[73] In the example given the accused had no intent to kill or cause serious injury. Although that situation was brought about by his taking drugs, he would not be guilty of murder. Intoxication cannot supply an element of an offence which is otherwise lacking.

A distinction between crimes of basic intent and specific intent was adopted by the House of Lords in *Majewski*.[74] Although the distinction is artificial[75] (for example drunken attempts to commit a crime of basic intent nevertheless require intent) the decision has been followed, by a majority, in the Supreme Court of Canada.[76] Essentially for reasons of policy, the accused is judged by his actions as if they were done when sober and the voluntary element of crime is replaced by the fault of drunkenness or by recklessness as to unforeseen consequences.[77]

4.44 The High Court of Australia has specifically rejected *Majewski* in *O'Connor*.[78] Two sets of reasons were advanced in favour of discarding the analysis of the House of Lords. Firstly the basic/specific intent distinction was considered to be incoherent and productive of absurd results (the intoxicated attempt example). Secondly, and significantly in the light of the discussion of recklessness in *The People (DPP) v Murray*,[79] drunkenness could not replace the mental element by making it the equivalent of recklessness; such an analysis would undercut the basic theory that recklessness requires indifference to foreseen consequences and, further, that the act of drunkenness was remote from the subsequent fault. The position that the High Court arrived at was to allow evidence of intoxication, howsoever caused, to be

be committed by a voluntary act, the action of Lipman was not conscious. Generally see ch 3. For further references see fn 10; *Hutchins* [1988] Crim LR 379 CA.

73 It is not necessary that the accused should have been incapable of forming the intent, but that he did not form the intent; Smith & Hogan 210; *Pordage* [1975] Crim LR 575 CA; *Sheehan* [1975] 2 All ER 960; [1975] 1 WLR 739, 60 Cr App R 508; [1975] Crim LR 339 CA; *Hart* [1986] 2 NZLR 408 CA.

74 [1977] AC 443; [1976] 2 All ER 142; [1976] 2 WLR 623, 62 Cr App R 262; [1976] Crim LR 374 HL.

75 Smith & Hogan at 213 set out the result of this categorisation on various offences, as does Stuart at 369-70. For discussion on possible solutions in this jurisdiction see the Law Reform Commission report on Malicious Damage (LRC 26-1988) par 31-6.

76 *Leary* (1977) 33 CCC (2d) 473; discussed by Stuart 363-83; for a review see *Parker* (1977) 19 CLQ 286; for the approach in New Zealand see *Tihi* [1990] 1 NZLR 340 CA.

77 Where the accused is intoxicated due to medical drugs a general foresight that the accused may commit crime may suffice; see the discussions by Smith & Hogan at 216-7, on *Bailey* [1983] 2 All ER 503; [1983] 1 WLR 760, 77 Cr App R 76; [1983] Crim LR 533 CA; *Hardie* [1984] 3 All ER 848; [1985] 1 WLR 64, 80 Cr App R 157 CA. Where the drugs are unknown to general experience a jury is entitled to expert evidence on their effects; *Skirving* [1985] QB 819; [1985] 2 All ER 705; [1985] 2 WLR 1001, 81 Cr App R 9; [1985] Crim LR 317 CA.

78 (1979-80) 29 ALR 449 HC. The Court stated that the evidence must be capable of raising a reasonable doubt as to intent or voluntariness at 466 per Barwick CJ. In Victoria a similar approach to the defence had long been established; *Keogh* [1964] VR 400 SC; for a discussion see Brett Waller & Walker 743-67. The reasoning was rejected in New Zealand—*Kamipeli* [1975] 2 NZLR 610 CA; and in South Africa—*Chretien* [1981] 1 SA 1097 SC.

79 [1977] IR 360 SC. See par 2.37.

admitted in order to show that the mental element of the crime was absent. This is similar to the English treatment of involuntary intoxication.[80]

In the crime of manslaughter the actions of the accused must have been voluntary.[81] His drunkenness or other involuntary actions may have been, in themselves, criminally negligent or, alternatively, could have been avoided but for criminal negligence.[82] Where drunkenness was self-induced the tendency has been to ignore it from insufficiently considered policy reasons.[83]

An intent aided by alcohol remains valid. So where the accused decides to kill but becomes totally drunk for the purpose of carrying out his decision, he cannot rely on his own self-induced lack of intent.[84] In theory[85] where the accused is driven insane by alcohol he will be judged by the insanity defence.[86]

In common with the defences of duress and necessity a possible solution to the applicability of this defence to murder is that it should cause the offence to be reduced to manslaughter. Again the basis of the argument is that a person who kills, whilst drunk, lacks the moral culpability normally associated with murder.[87] A drunken intent is, nevertheless, an intent.[88]

Insanity

4.45 Since 1800 persons who have successfully pleaded the defence of insanity have not achieved their freedom. Notwithstanding the fact that the verdict is, in substance if not in form, a finding that a person did not have the capacity to commit crime, the accused is held in the Central Mental Hospital[89] pending his recovery.[90] Scepticism by lawyers as to the insanity claimed by accused persons and their psychiatrists[91] coupled with a judicial attitude that deterrence was valid even in the face of mental illness caused the law on insanity to be restricted in its operation.[92]

---

80   See the discussion at Smith & Hogan 218. In Australia the element of negligence, if it is relevant, may be excluded by involuntary intoxication.

81   *Martin* (1983–1984) 51 ALR 540 HC.

82   See par 3.08.

83   *Lipman*, fn 11.

84   *A-G for Northern Ireland v Gallagher* [1963] AC 349; [1961] 3 All ER 299; [1961] 3 WLR 619, 45 Cr App R 316 HL.

85   Stuart at 365–66 regards this rule as a "dead letter" and points out that there is only one decision accepting it; *Davis* (1881) 14 Cox 563.

86   *Beard*, fn 70.

87   See pars 6.39–6.41.

88   *Sheehan*, fn 73, quoted and approved in *Kamipeli*, fn 78.

89   Criminal Lunatics Act, 1800, s 1; Lunacy (Ireland) Act, 1821, ss 16–18; Central Criminal Lunatic Asylum (Ireland) Act, 1845, s 8; Mental Treatment Act, 1961, s 39.

90   The Supreme Court have now decided that the decision as to whether to continue to hold someone in custody following a finding of insanity is one for the Executive and not for the Courts: *Gallagher v A-G*, Supreme Court unreported January 1991.

91   This scepticism may not be entirely misplaced; Carney, "Anachronism of our Criminal Insanity Laws" (13 January 1990) *Irish Times* indicates that in Michaelmas Term 1989 a verdict of guilty but insane was sought by the defence in four trials out of seven taking place before the Court and was achieved in three (quoting statistics compiled by Patrick Morrissey, Registrar of the Central Criminal Court). See further Mackey, "Fact and Fiction about the Insanity Defence" [1990] Crim LR 247.

92   For a full analysis see O'Hanlon, "Not Guilty Because of Insanity" (1968) IR Jur (ns) III 61.

The burden of proof is on the accused to clearly show that he was insane at the time when he committed the act.[93] Where the accused is suffering from an insane delusion,[94] but the delusion is not so complete as to render him insane, he is to be judged, apparently, according to the M'Naghten Rules of 1843.[95] Whereas it has been accepted in England[96] that the Rules are of general application in deciding insanity, in Ireland they have been limited to their stated purpose of defining the law with respect to insane delusions.[97] The result is an absence of a specific definition of insanity. The formula most usually adopted is that of *Stephen*:

> No act is a crime if the person who does it, at the time when it is done, is prevented, either by defective mental power or by any disease affecting his mind (a) from knowing the nature and quality of his act, or (b) from knowing that the act is wrong, or (c) from controlling his own conduct, unless the absence of the power of control has been produced by his own default.[98]

An irresistible impulse, unless it was one caused by the accused's own fault,[99] is accepted as part of the insanity plea. In *The People (A-G) v Hayes*,[1] Henchy J held:

> . . . certain serious mental diseases, such as paranoia or schizophrenia, in certain cases enable a man to understand the morality or immorality of his act or the legality or illegality of it, or the nature and quality of it, but nevertheless prevent him from exercising a free volition as to whether he should or should not do the act. In the present case the medical witnesses are unanimous in saying that the accused man was, in medical terms, insane at the time of the act. However, legal insanity does not necessarily coincide with what medical men would call insanity, but if it is open to the jury to say, as say they must, on the evidence, that this man understood the nature and quality of his act, and understood its wrongfulness, morally and legally, but that nevertheless he was debarred from refraining from assaulting his wife fatally because of a defect of reason, due to his mental illness, it seems to me that it would be unjust, in the circumstances of this case, not to allow the jury to consider the case on these grounds.[2]

The accused is required to be suffering from a disease of the mind or a mental defect. Consequently transient or natural mental states, such as anger or drunkenness, are not within the scope of the defence.[3] A person who is acting in an involuntary

---

93   *The People (DPP) v O'Mahony* [1985] IR 517, 522 SC.

94   For example, the accused may believe he was God and that the victim was Satan when he killed; *Landry* (1988) 48 CCC (3d) 552 Quebec CA.

95   *Doyle v Wicklow County Council* [1974] IR 55, 67. The Rules are set out in Archbold (1922) 15-17.

96   *Windle* [1952] 2 QB 826; [1952] 2 All ER 1, 36 Cr App R 85 CCA.

97   *Doyle v Wicklow County Council*, fn 95.

98   *Digest* (1894 ed.) Article 28. In *The People (A-G) v Coughlan* (28 June 1968) unreported, *The Irish Times*, Kenny J is reported to have put an issue of insanity to the jury on the broad proposition of whether the act was caused by a disease of the mind and given as examples these three incidents cited by Stephen.

99   See Goode, "On Subjectivity and Objectivity in Denial of Criminal Responsibility: Reflections on Reading Radford" (1987) 11 Crim LJ 131; *Radford* (1985) 20 A Crim R 388 CA SA.

1   Henchy J, 13 November 1967 Central Criminal Court unreported.

2   Accepted as a correct statement of the law by the Supreme Court in *Doyle v Wicklow County Council*, fn 34 at 71; *Charest* (1990) 57 CCC (3d) 312 CA Quebec.

3   Dickson, "A Legacy of Hadfield, McNaughton v MacLean" (1957-58) 31 ALJ 255 at 260: "The reason why it is required that the defect of reason should be 'from disease of the mind', in the classic

state cannot know the nature and quality of his act.[4] Where there is a conscious control by the mind over the body the question is whether or not the accused knew what he was doing was wrong.[5] "Wrong" in the context of the *Stephen* formulation means wrong according to the standards adopted by reasonable men.[6] It does not mean legally wrong.

4.46 Psychiatric evidence is not admissible save where the mental processes of the accused are outside the normal scope and experience of ordinary people and therefore require expert assistance.[7] The trial judge is entitled to comment adversely on the failure of the defence to allow a psychiatrist nominated by the State to examine an accused who is presented as being insane through psychiatric testimony led by the defence.[8]

Apart from being insane at the time when the offence was committed a person may be unfit to plead at his trial due to mental illness, defect or injury. The issue is whether the accused is able to understand the indictment, the effect and nature of a plea of guilty or not guilty, to challenge a juror to whom he might wish to object, to instruct counsel and follow and understand the details of the evidence.[9] Juries try this issue under a form of oath which casts the question as one of insanity.[10] On this issue the burden of proof is on the prosecution to establish on fitness beyond

phrase used by Sir Nicholas Tindal seems to me no more than to exclude drunkenness, conditions of intense passion and other transient states attributable either to the fault or to the nature of man. In the advice delivered by Sir Nicholas Tindal no doubt the words 'disease of the mind' were chosen because it was considered that they had the widest possible meaning. He would hardly have supposed it possible that the expression would be treated as one containing words of the law to be weighed like demands. I have taken it to include, as well as forms of physical or material change or deterioration, every recognisable disorder or derangement of the understanding whether or not its nature, in our present state of knowledge, is capable of explanation or determination."

4   *Sullivan* (1984) AC 156; [1983] 2 All ER 673; [1983] 3 WLR 123, 77 Cr App R 176 HL.

5   Smith & Hogan 192. In Canada because s 16 of the Code casts the defence in terms of "appreciating the nature and quality of the act or omission", the test is whether or not he was unable fully to appreciate not only the nature of the act, but the natural consequences that would flow from it, that is the mental capacity to foresee and measure the consequences of the act"; Stuart 335 quoting the Report of the Royal Commission on the Law of Insanity as a Defence in Criminal Cases (1956) at 13.

6   *Doyle v Wicklow County Council*, fn 95 at 70, following *Stapleton* (1952) 86 CLR 358 HC. This means "morally wrong"; *Landry* (1991) 62 CCC (3d) 117 SC; *Ratti* (1991) 62 CCC (3d) 105.

7   *Turner* [1975] QB 834; [1975] 1 All ER 70; [1975] 2 WLR 56, 60 Cr App R 80 CA. The Court of Appeal upheld the refusal of a trial judge to allow the accused in support of a defence of provocation on a murder charge to call a psychiatrist to prove that prior to the offence he had shown no signs of mental illness and had not required psychiatric treatment, that he had a deep emotional tie with the deceased which was likely to have caused an explosive outburst of rage after her confession of infidelity and that he had shown profound grief after the crime. The Court held his previous lack of psychiatric history irrelevant and the other factors to be matters within the ordinary scope of human experience upon which the jury did not need expert help; and see *Cameron* (1990) 50 A Crim R 397 CA WA. Medical evidence is not essential to prove insanity; where it is pleaded, the words and actions of the accused may suffice whether contemporary to the alleged offence and prior thereto and, it is submitted, words and actions subsequent to the date; *Dart* (1878) 14 Cox 143; *Rivett* (1950) 34 Cr App R 87.

8   *Malcolm* (1989) 50 CCC (3d) 172 Manitoba CA.

9   *Robertson* [1968] 3 All ER 557; [1968] 1 WLR 1767, 52 Cr App R 690 CA.

10 Juries Act, 1976, s 19(2).

reasonable doubt if they so plead, and on the defence if they so assert, on the balance of probability.[11] A person found unfit to plead is subject to detention in the same way as a person found insane at his trial.[12]

As will be seen from the foregoing sketch of the law this topic constitutes a further example of the abrogation of responsibility by the Oireachtas to reform, or in this case even to form, the law. The law lacks not only coherence but form.

Automatism

4.47 It is a fundamental requirement of criminal law that the accused perform the act or omission which constitutes the external element of the crime. It has always been a defence at common law that the action of the accused was involuntary.[13] Automatism is the defence of being unable to physically control one's actions notwithstanding that one's body appears to have committed the external element of the offence. A successful plea of automatism entitles the accused to a complete acquittal.[14] The burden of proof is on the prosecution to disprove the evidence supporting automatism once a proper foundation for that defence has been laid.[15] In *Rabey*[16] Ritchie J, on behalf of the majority of the Supreme Court of Canada, accepted this formulation as a definition of automatism:

> Automatism is a term used to describe unconscious, involuntary behaviour, the state of a person who, though capable of action, is not conscious of what he is doing. It means an unconscious involuntary act, where the mind does not go with what is being done.[17]

The defence is often difficult to distinguish from insanity.[18] This difficulty is compounded by the uncertain definition of insanity in Irish law.[19] The English courts have taken the view that as the M'Naghten Rules require that the accused be suffering from a disease of the mind, transient states caused by external factors are more properly described as automatism.[20] But a transitory abnormality or disorder

11   *Robertson*, fn 9. Generally see Ryan & Magee 269-71.

12   Criminal Lunatics Act, 1800, s 2; Lunacy (Ireland) Act, 1821, s 17; Central Criminal Lunatic Asylum (Ireland) Act, 1845, s 8; Mental Treatment Act, 1961, s 39.

13   1 Hale PC 434: "If there be an actual forcing of a man, as if A by force takes the arm of B and the weapon in his hand, and thereby stabs C whereof he dies, this is murder in A but B is not guilty". For an example see par 1.08.

14   *Charlson* [1955] 1 All ER 859; [1955] 1 WLR 317, 39 Cr App R 37 CCA.

15   The English courts have a restrictive view as to what evidence is sufficient holding that the word of the accused will rarely be sufficient; *Dervish* [1968] Crim LR 37 CA; *Cook v Atchison* [1968] Crim LR 266 DC; *Stripp* (1978) 69 Cr App R 318 CA; *Pullen* [1991] Crim LR 457 CA.

16   (1980) 15 CR (3d) 225 SC. See similarly *Radford* (1985) 20 A Crim R 388 CCA SA reviewed by Goode, "On Subjectivity and Objectivity in Denial of Criminal Responsibility: Reflections on Reading Radford" (1987) 11 Crim LJ 229.

17   At 232.

18   The Law Reform Commission of Tasmania in their report, "Insanity, Intoxication and Automatism" (LRC 61, 1989) recommend a radical solution to the problems associated with these defences of committing the accused into the hands of the civil authority for psychiatric assessment and if he was found to be ill and dangerous then confined, under civil law, to a secure mental hospital.

19   Par 4.45-4.46.

20   *Quick* [1973] QB 910; [1973] 3 All ER 347; [1973] 3 WLR 26, 57 Cr App R 722 CA; *Burgess, The Times*, 28 March 1991, CA.

caused by an internal factor, whether functional or organic, which manifested itself in violence and which might recur is considered in English law to be insanity.[21] Involuntary actions caused by internal factors are to be categorised within the classification of disease of the mind and are therefore to be treated as insanity.[22] In adopting that classification the courts have been motivated by a policy consideration that persons whose violent behaviour is likely to recur ought not to be discharged but should be forced to undergo treatment. In consequence where violent conduct is likely to be recurrent the defence have been confined to pleading insanity.[23] In *Rabey*[24] the accused became attached to a student in his university. On the day before he assaulted her he discovered a letter she had written to a friend expressing a sexual interest in another male student and referring in disparaging terms to the accused. The following day he took a rock from the geology laboratory and, apparently on meeting the victim by chance, struck her with the rock and began to choke her. A defence psychiatrist testified that during the assault the accused was in a complete dissociative state. The defence of automatism was successfully pleaded at the trial. On appeal Martin JA held that automatism was not open on the evidence reasoning:

> . . . the distinction to be drawn is between a malfunctioning of the mind arising from some cause that is primarily internal to the accused, having its source in his psychological or emotional make-up, or in some organic pathology, as opposed to a malfunctioning of the mind, which is the transient effect produced by some external factor such as, for example, concussion. Any malfunctioning of the mind or mental disorder having its source primarily in some subjective condition or weakness internal to the accused (whether fully understood or not) may be a "disease of the mind" if it prevents the accused from knowing what he is doing, but transient disturbances of consciousness due to certain specific external factors do not fall within the concept of disease of the mind. . . .[25]

In common with the defence of intoxication, automatism cannot be pleaded where the involuntary state of the accused was caused by his own fault in, for example, taking alcohol or drugs.[26] Automatism should be distinguished from a defence based on a plea that the accused did not act with intent. Intent is only relevant where the mental element of a crime requires that the accused act with the purpose of causing the external element. Automatism is more fundamental in its attack on the proof of the prosecution case. In murder the accused must intend to kill or to

---

21   *Burgess* [1991] 2 All ER 769 CA; *Bingham* [1991] Crim LR 433 CA.

22   *Kemp* [1957] 1 QB 399; [1956] 3 All ER 249; [1956] 3 WLR 724, 40 Cr App R 121. In contrast, see Charlson, fn 52. Involuntary conduct arising from psychomotor epilepsy is insanity: *Bratty v A-G for Northern Ireland* [1963] AC 386; [1961] 3 All ER 523; [1961] 3 WLR 965, 46 Cr App R 1 HL. See further the cases cited at par 3.41 and *Youseff* (1990) 50 A Crim R 1 CCA NSW.

23   See for example, *Kemp*, fn 59; *Bratty*, fn 59; *Rabey*, fn 54. Smith & Hogan argue in support of this reasoning at 188-89. The social overtones to these cases is discussed at Howard 319-22.

24   Fn 16.

25   37 CCC (2d) 461 at 477-78. The judge accepted sleep-walking as coming within the defence. The judgment was later approved by the Supreme Court of Canada, at 283. Martin J, for the majority, required automatism to identify an external factor and also required that the disorder of the mind must not relate to some subjective weakness of the accused. Criticised by Stuart 93-5.

26   *Lipman* [1970] 1 QB 152; [1969] 3 All ER 410; [1969] 3 WLR 819, 53 Cr App R 600 CA. Further see Smith & Hogan 40-1. See also par 4.43.

cause serious injury.[27] Where A runs down B in his motor car while attempting to escape the Gardaí, he kills B knowing of the risk his driving is causing to the public, but not intending to kill or to cause serious injury to anyone. If A kills B, in the same circumstances, but due to the fact that his car has just been invaded by a swarm of bees[28] and, due to the pain he is experiencing, lacks physical control over his body, he will not have acted in a voluntary fashion and therefore cannot be guilty even of dangerous driving.[29]

It is important to identify the acts alleged to constitute the crime. A person who is asleep while driving his car, when he kills another in a road accident, is not, if only the fact that he is asleep is taken into account, acting in a voluntary fashion. His failure to exercise care by stopping and taking rest may be an act of criminal negligence or recklessness.[30]

Infancy

4.48 Age is the primary factor in deciding whether infancy is a defence to a criminal charge. A person under the age of seven is conclusively presumed to lack discretion and is therefore not punishable in any criminal prosecution.[31] A child between the ages of seven and fourteen is presumed not to have reached the age of discretion. This presumption may be rebutted by strong and pregnant evidence of a mischievous discretion.[32] The capacity to commit crime is not measured by the age of the child but by strength of understanding and judgment.[33] The test for a mischievous discretion is whether the child knew what he was doing wrong, in the sense that it was gravely or seriously wrong.[34] In criminal proceedings against a person under fourteen the evidence of a mischievous discretion should be clear and strong beyond all doubt and contradiction before it may rebut the presumption.[35] This evidence

---

27   Ch 2.

28   The defence may be relevant to both. In *Hall* (1988) 36 A Crim R 368, the Court of Criminal Appeal of New South Wales held that medical evidence, which supported the accused being in a state of automatism at the time of the offence due to cerebral oedema could negate the element of voluntariness which is a necessary element of the offence of larceny, and that similarly it might raise a doubt as to intent.

29   Par 3.41. In *Broome v Perkins* [1987] RTR 321, 85 Cr App R 321; [1987] Crim LR 271 DC, a diabetic in a hypoglycaemic state was denied the defence on a charge of driving without due care and attention as he had braked and veered his car away from situations of accident whilst claiming to be unconscious of what he was doing.

30   *Scarth* [1945] St R Qd 38 CCA. Similarly a diabetic may be at fault in failing to take drugs which control his condition; *Bailey* [1983] 2 All ER 503; [1983] 1 WLR 760, 77 Cr App R 76; [1983] Crim LR 533 CA; *Hennessy* [1989] 2 All ER 9; [1989] 1 WLR 287; [1989] RTR 153, 89 Cr App R 10 CA.

31   1 Hale 28; 1 Hawk ch 1, s 1; 4 Bl Com 23; *Carter* [1774] 1 Cowp 220, 98 ER 1054. For a general discussion see Archbold (1922) 10-11; Kenny (1922) 49-51.

32   1 Hale 25, 27.

33   4 Bl Com 23. So a girl of thirteen has been executed for killing her mistress; 1 Hale 26; 4 Bl Com 23.

34   *Gorrie* (1918) 83 JP 136. In *JM v Runeckles* (1984) 79 Cr App R 255 DC the Divisional Court held that it was not necessary to prove that the child knew that what he had done was morally wrong but that he must know that it was seriously wrong in the sense of it not being merely naughty or mischievous.

35   Archbold (1922) 11; 4 Bl Com 23; 1 Hale 25, 27.

may be gathered from the nature of the act itself,[36] from the intelligence and understanding of the child,[37] and from the behaviour of the child immediately subsequent to the offence.[38]

In practice two questions should be left to the jury: firstly, whether the accused committed the offence; and secondly, whether at the time he had a guilty knowledge that he was doing wrong in the sense that it was gravely wrong and not merely naughty or mischievous.[39] The fact that the child did the acts constituting the elements of the offence is not, of itself, any evidence whatever of the guilty state of mind which is essential for conviction.[40]

Incapacity to commit crime due to infancy ends absolutely upon a person attaining the age of fourteen. The presumption of incapacity becomes stronger the further the accused is from the age of fourteen.[41] At that age they are presumed to be responsible for their actions and capable of distinguishing good from evil.[42] They are therefore subject to the same rule of construction as are others of more mature age.[43]

The law as to infancy has been reformed extensively in England.[44] It is difficult to justify a situation, springing from ancient precedent, which allows a seven year old child to be prosecuted on indictment with the full panoply of the law. A more rational consideration of the appropriate principles to be applied to children is long overdue.

Unconstitutionality

4.49 Article 15.5 of the Constitution forbids the Oireachtas to impose a retroactive penal sanction. Article 40, and the Preamble to the Constitution, require that society be ordered through the instrument of justice. An argument of unconstitutionality essentially raises the defence that despite the commission of the crime the accused cannot be found guilty because the crime does not exist. The Constitution is the fundamental law of the State and no offence which, in definition, or in practice, operates an injustice, is consistent with the fundamental law.[45] The High Court and Supreme Court are vested with exclusive authority to enquire into, and, if necessary, declare statutes passed since 1937 to be inconsistent with the Constitution.[46] The District Court and Circuit Court are entitled to carry out the same exercise with regard to laws prior to that date.[47] This provides the Circuit Criminal Court with

36   *JM v Runeckles*, fn 34.
37   In *JM v Runeckles*, fn 72, regard was had to the conduct of and to the handwriting of the child.
38   *Runeckles*, fn 72; *York* [1748] Fost 70, 168 ER 35; generally see Smith & Hogan 179-80; Howard 343-46; Stuart 314-16.
39   Archbold (1922) 11; Smith (1845) 1 Cox 260.
40   Archbold (1922) 11, citing *Kershaw* (1902) 18 TLR 357, 37 LJ Newsp 120.
41   *X v X* (1958) Cr App 1; [1958] Crim LR 805 DC.
42   *Smith* (1845) 1 Cox 260.
43   1 Hale 25, 1 Hawk ch 1; Archbold (1922) 12.
44   The Children & Young Persons Act, 1933, s 50 as amended by The Children & Young Persons Act, 1963, s 16.
45   *McGee v A-G* [1974] IR 284, 109 ILTR 29 SC.
46   Generally see Kelly 269-327 and Supplement 71-89.
47   Kelly 273.

a power of review over common law which has remained unexercised since the foundation of the State.

4.50 An appeal to the courts that a criminal provision is unconstitutional must cross a number of fundamental hurdles. Before it can be considered the accused must be directly affected by the constitutional point and all statutory and procedural questions must have been firstly disposed of.[48] Acts passed subsequent to the Constitution are presumed not to be in conflict with it.[49] An Act of the Oireachtas will not be declared unconstitutional if it is possible to reasonably construe it in a constitutional manner.[50] Finally, provisions of the Constitution cannot be picked at random from the text for the purpose of declaring any provision unconstitutional. Where there is a conflict between constitutional rights this must be resolved in favour of those rights more fundamental; the rights themselves may only be declared on a reading of the purpose and objective of the Constitution from its entire text.[51]

4.51 In *McGee v The Attorney General*[52] s 17 of the Criminal Law (Amendment) Act, 1935 was declared unconstitutional. This made it a criminal offence, punishable by six months' imprisonment, to sell contraceptives or import them into the State. In *Norris v The Attorney General*[53] the Supreme Court refused a declaration that ss 61 and 62 of the Offences Against the Person Act, 1861 and s 11 of the Criminal Law (Amendment) Act, 1885 were inconsistent with the Constitution. The Christian nature of the State was not infringed by a law which declared homosexual acts to be criminal offences. According to the court, the general thinking among theologians had not yet moved to the stage of considering these acts to be in accordance with natural law. In *King v A-G*[54] the plaintiff was found guilty of two offences of "loitering with intent" contrary to s 4 of the Vagrancy Act, 1824. He was also convicted of possession of house breaking implements with intent to steal. The proof of intent may be inferred from the acts and declarations of the accused assisted by the presumption that a person intends the natural and probable consequences of his acts or it may be expressly proved by the accused's own admission. The "intent" portion of the offence "loitering with intent" was proved by the prosecution establishing such intent from the circumstances of the known character of the accused. This meant, under the legislation, that, in distinction to the vast majority of offences in the criminal calendar, the prosecution were entitled to make reference to the accused's previous convictions for the purpose of proving his guilt. Consequently, where two persons, A and B, were seen by a Garda wandering around a deserted street in the middle of the night A, if he had just been released from serving a prison sentence, was more likely to be convicted than B, for precisely the

---

48   *Cahill v Sutton* [1980] IR 269 SC.
49   *The State (Sheerin) v Kennedy* [1966] IR 379 SC.
50   *East Donegal Co-Operative v A-G* [1970] IR 317 SC.
51   *Murray v Ireland* [1985] IR 532 SC.
52   Fn 45.
53   [1984] IR 36 HC, SC.
54   [1981] IR 233 SC.

same activity. This legislation was struck down by the High Court, and, on appeal, by the Supreme Court. The discrimination between persons with previous convictions and those without was held repugnant to the tenor of the Constitution. The vagueness of the definition of the offence violated an unspecified guarantee that the elements of an offence should be stated with clarity, so as thereby to be capable of standard proofs and a defence in which clearly defined elements were available for dispute.

Those cases may be examples of a principle of fundamental justice in criminal law which is rapidly changing the criminal law in Canada.[55]

The Constitution contains within it the possibility of further argument based on an implied requirement of fairness in criminal law. In particular, Canadian decisions provide a wealth of material for arguing that fundamental standards of justice must apply to the definitional, as well as the procedural elements of an offence. A strict requirement of a mental element imposing moral turpitude,[56] and corresponding to the elements of the offence[57] and fundamentally based on the attribute of guilt is already implicit in the Irish practice of criminal law though not yet explicit in court judgments.[58]

Consent

4.52 The defence of consent is considered in the context of assault in chapter 6 and in the context of rape in chapter 8.

Entrapment

4.53 The defence of entrapment[59] is rarely relevant to the offences considered in this volume. The defence is not made out where the police merely provide the accused with an opportunity to commit an offence in circumstances where there is a reasonable suspicion that he is already engaged in such conduct.[60] In Canada entrapment operates to stay proceedings where the police have gone further than providing an opportunity and instead employed tactics designed to induce someone into the commission of an offence.[61] The defence is recognised in the United States as a substantive defence where the criminal design originates with the officials of the government and they implant into the mind of an innocent person the disposition to commit an offence and induce its commission in order that they may prosecute.[62] In Australia entrapment involves inducing a person to commit a crime which

---

55   For example, see *Logan* (1990) 58 CCC (3d) 391 SC; *JTJ* (1990) 59 CCC (3d) 1 SC; *Rodney* (1990) 58 CCC (3d) 408 SC.

56   *DeSousa* (1990) 62 CCC (3d) 95 CA Ontario.

57   *Parish* (1990) 60 CCC (3d) CA New Brunswick.

58   See *Kirkness* (1990) 60 CCC (3d) 97 SC; *Logan* (1990) 58 CCC (3d) 391 SC; *Rodney* (1990) 58 CCC (3d) 408 SC; *JTJ* (1990) 59 CCC (3d) 1 SC; *Ellis-Don Ltd* (1990) 61 CCC (3d) 423 CA Ontario; *Dubois* (1990) 62 CCC (3d) 90 CA Quebec.

59   For a full review see Fisse, "Entrapment as a Defence" (1988) 12 Crim LJ 367.

60   *Voutsis* (1989) 47 CCC (3d) 451 Saskatchewan CA; *Mack* (1988) 44 CCC (3d) 513 SC.

61   *Voutsis*, fn 98; *Kenyon* (1990) 61 CCC (3d) 538 CA BC; *Meuckon* (1990) 67 CCC (3d) 193 CA BC.

62   *Sherman v US* (1958) 356 US 369; *US v Russell* (1973) 411 US 423.

otherwise he or she would not, or would have been unlikely to, commit. A distinction is drawn between entrapping the unwary innocent and the unwary criminal.[63]

In this jurisdiction the practice has been to allow the trial judge to exercise a discretion to exclude evidence on the illegality principle where the Gardaí have acted in a fundamentally unfair manner. The defence has not yet been successfully pleaded.[64]

63   *Sloane* (1990) 50 A Crim R 270 CCA NSW.
64   *Dental Board v O'Callaghan* [1969] IR 181.

CHAPTER FIVE

Offences Related to Childbirth

5.01 Traditionally the law of homicide is applicable only where the victim has been born and has achieved an existence independent of the mother.[1] At common law it was a misdemeanour to kill the unborn child in the womb after it had "quickened".[2] This stage was reached approximately sixteen or eighteen weeks after conception. Medical science at the time considered that vitality was then given to the foetus.[3] Usually what had occurred was that the mother was then first able to feel the child moving. This led to the misunderstanding that it had then become "alive" for the first time.[4]

On 7 September 1983 the 8th Amendment to the Constitution was enacted guaranteeing the right to life of the unborn with due regard to the equal right to life of the mother.[5] Article 40.3.3 now provides:

Admhaíonn an Stát ceart na mbeo gan breith chun a mbeatha agus, ag féachaint go cuí do chomhcheart na máthar chun a beatha, ráthaíonn sé gan cur isteach lena dhlíthe ar an gceart sin agus róthaíonn fós an ceart sin a chosaint is a shuíomh lena dhlíthe sa mhéid gur féidir é.[6]

The impetus for the change arose from an argument that in the absence of explicit protection of the right to life of the unborn, no fundamental law had proved capable of withstanding arguments in favour of legalised abortion.[7] It was feared that, as in other countries,[8] the human rights provisions of the Constitution could be

---

1   See par 1.18-1.20. There is a vast literature on the subject of abortion. The following may be found to be of use: Potts, Diggery & Peel, *Abortion* (1977); Glover, *Causing Death and Saving Lives* (1977); Williams, *The Sanctity of Life and the Criminal Law* (1958); Sarvis & Rodman, *The Abortion Controversy* (1973); Veitch & Tracey, "Abortion in the Common Law World" [1974] 22 AJ CL 652; Hart, "Abortion Law Reform: The English Experience" (1972) 8 Melbourne ULR 389; "The Role of the Law of Homicide in Fetal Destruction" [1971] 56 Iowa LR 658.

2   1 Hawk ch 31, s 16; 1 Hale PC 433; 3 Co Inst 50.

3   See the quotation from Dr Paris quoted in *Wycherley* (1838) 8 C&P 262, ER.

4   The early legislation on abortion made it a crime only after this point; *Scudder* (1928) 1 Mood 216, 168 ER 1246. In *Wycherley* [1838] 173 ER 486, 8 C&P 262, a jury of matrons was empanelled to decide whether a prisoner under sentence of death was quick with chlid. They were instructed that this mean "pregnant". In the 1861 Offences Against the Person Act the distinction was abandoned, probably as being in conflict with then current theories in medical sciences.

5   For citations on the right to life of the unborn see par 1.18-1.20. The Dáil debates on the Amendment are at 399 *Dáil Debates* 1353 and 341 *Dáil Debates* 2001.

6   "The State acknowledges the right to life of the unborn and, with due regard to the equal right to life of the mother, guarantees in its laws to respect and, as far as practicable, by its laws to defend and vindicate that right." For discussion as to when life begins see par 1.18.

7   McMahon & Binchy 606. This point is further developed by Binchy in ch 11 of *Abortion and the Law* (1983 ed. Flannery). The nature of the arguments for and against can be seen in all of the national newspapers in the two weeks leading up to the vote. Prior to that in *Finn v A-G* [1983] IR 155 SC an injunction was sought, and refused, to prevent the referendum from taking place.

8   As it was in the USA; *Roe v Wade* (1973) 410 US 113, and more recently in Canada; *Morgentaler &*

interpreted in order to allow a woman to decide in favour of abortion because it was medically preferable to a continuation of the pregnancy, or because the State had no valid interest in interfering with that choice. Those arguments are not now likely to succeed because of the Amendment.

Another possible interpretation of the Amendment was as a directive by the people to the Oireachtas to pass regulatory laws enforcing the right to life of the unborn child.[9] There has, however, been no reaction from this quarter. The subject has been left untouched. Aspects of the law are in a gravely unsettled state which legislation could easily clarify.

Prohibition

5.02 The law on abortion is contained in ss 58 and 59 of the Offences Against the Person Act, 1861 and s 10 of the Health (Family Planning) Act, 1979:

1861   S 58 Every woman, being with child, who, with intent to procure her own miscarriage shall unlawfully administer to herself any poison or other noxious thing, or shall unlawfully use any instrument or other means whatsoever with the like intent, and whosoever, with intent to procure the miscarriage of any woman, whether she be or be not with child, shall unlawfully administer to her or cause to be taken by her any poison or other noxious thing, or shall unlawfully use any instrument or other means whatsoever with the like intent, shall be guilty of felony, and on being convicted thereof shall be liable to be kept in penal servitude for life.[10]

S 59 Whosoever shall unlawfully supply or procure any poison or other noxious thing, or any instrument or thing whatsoever, knowing that the same is intended to be unlawfully used or employed with intent to procure the miscarriage of any woman, whether she be or be not with child, shall be guilty of a misdemeanour, and being convicted thereof shall be liable to be kept in penal servitude for any period not less than three years and not exceeding five years.[11]

1979   S 10 Nothing in this Act shall be construed as authorising—

(a) the procuring of an abortion,

(b) the doing of any other thing the doing of which is prohibited by s 58 or s 59 of the Offences Against the Person Act, 1861 (which sections prohibit the administration of drugs and the use of instruments to procure abortion or the supplying of drugs or instruments to procure abortion) or

(c) the sale, importation into the State, manufacture, advertising or display of abortifacients.

Others (1988) 37 CCC (3d) 449 SC.

9   *SPUC v Grogan* [1989] IR 753, 771 SC McCarthy J: "It is unfortunate that the Oireachtas has not enacted any legislation at all in respect of the constitutionally guaranteed right".

10   The sections are quoted, as are all other section from the Offences Against the Person Act, 1861, in accordance with the amendments introduced by the Penal Servitude Acts of 1864 and 1891 and by the Statute Law Revision Act, 1908. An offence under s 59 may also fall within s 58; *Turner* [1910] 4 Cr App R 203, 206 CCA.

11   The penalty is in accordance with s 1 of the Penal Servitude Act, 1891. An offence under s 58 may also fall within s 59, see fn 10. Material which advocates abortion is banned under s 16(1) of the Censorship of Publications Act, 1929 as amended by s 12(1) of the Health Family (Family Planning) Act, 1979.

5.03 S 59 was new law in 1861. Its purpose was to ensure that acts preparatory to the commission of an abortion were made criminal without reliance on the law of attempts or, as was previously the case, making liability depend on complicity in the principal offence under s 58.

If the woman herself is charged under s 58 she must be pregnant. If she is in error as to her pregnancy no crime is committed, provided she acts alone. Her actions will fall outside the definition of the crime and she will not be guilty of attempt: if she had succeeded in her endeavour no crime would have been committed.[12] In the case of any other person, it is not material whether the woman was pregnant or not. It has been held that a woman, mistakenly believing herself to be pregnant, may be convicted of conspiring with another to procure her own miscarriage[13] and with aiding and abetting[14] the offence.[15] Thus it is only in cases where the accused acts alone, and not in concert with another, that she must be pregnant to allow a crime to be committed.[16]

Noxious

5.04 "Poison or any other noxious thing" is a phrase common to both s 58 and s 59. In *Cramp*[17] the substance administered was oil of juniper which, in small quantities, was harmless. Field J expressed a view:

> The statute speaks first of poisons, secondly, of other things. If the thing administered is a recognised poison the offence may be committed though the quantity given is so small as to be incapable of doing harm. What was the thing administered in the present case? So much oil of juniper. Was this proved to be noxious? It was, consequently "a noxious thing".[18]

It is difficult to define what a "recognised poison" might be. Lord Coleridge CJ, in *Cramp*, defined poison as "that which when administered is injurious to health or life".[19] Substances derive their effect both from their nature and from their dosage and manner of administration.[20] The distinction drawn is not of assistance as poisons are present, in small quantities, in many useful and ordinarily available substances such as cosmetics and food.

To qualify as "noxious" the thing administered, supplied or procured must be

---

12 *Haughton v Smith* (1975) AC 476; [1973] 3 All ER 1109; [1974] 2 WLR 1, 58 Cr App R 198; [1974] Crim LR 305 HL. Further see par 2.41.

13 *Whitechurch* [1890] 24 QBD 420; [1886-90] All ER 1001, 16 Cox 743 CCR. Where a number of parties enter into an agreement to do an act that agreement is a criminal conspiracy if one of them would be guilty of an offence if the agreement is carried through; *Duguid* (1906) 21 Cox 200 CCR, further see Smith & Hogan 282-83, Russell 1471-76.

14 The punishment is the same as that for a principal offender. The procedure is as if the accused was the principal offender; Accessories and Abettors Act, 1861.

15 *Sockett* (1909) 72 JP 428, 1 Cr App R 101 CCA; the allegation of pregnancy was missing from the indictment but was found as a fact by the jury.

16 Criticised by Williams *CLGP* 637 and *TBCL* 366; defended by Hogan, "Victims as Parties to Crime" [1962] Crim LR 683, 690.

17 (1880) 5 QBD 307, 14 Cox 401 CCR.

18 309, 310, Stephen J expressed the same view as to things which "have acquired the name of poisons".

19 QBD at 308, Cox at 403.

20 Greaves expresses a different view; noted at Russell 603, fn 23.

harmful or mischievous either in quality or in the nature or quantity actually taken.[21] Where a substance has the effect of causing a miscarriage this, in itself, is evidence that it was noxious despite the prosecution being unable to lead any evidence as to its nature.[22] The substance taken must, objectively, be poisonous or noxious. It is not sufficient that the accused believed that the substance would cause an abortion:

> A mere guilty intention is not sufficient to constitute a crime. There must be an intent coupled with an overt act tending to the perpetration of the crime. The administration of a glass of pure water is no offence within the section.[23]

A failure to commit the crime, due to the manner in which the accused tried to commit it, is an indictable attempt.[24] The administration of a harmless substance does not amount to the offence,[25] unless taken in such a quantity, or, it is submitted, in such a manner as to be noxious.[26] Nor does it appear to be necessary to prove that the thing administered would have an effect on pregnancy, provided it is poisonous or noxious and was administered with intent to procure a miscarriage.[27] The South Australian Court of Appeal has held[28] that the reference to "other means", in corresponding legislation, refers to "something that is, in the common experience of mankind and in some reasonable degree, capable of producing the result". The Court rejected the contention that belief in efficacy brought an act within the definition of the crime.

Cause to be Taken

5.05 Under s 58 the accused must "administer to or cause to be taken by" the pregnant woman, the poison or noxious thing. To be an administering of a substance it is not necessary for there to be an actual delivery by the hand of the accused.[29] The phrase "cause to be taken" is wider and may include any act or omission by the accused which allows the thing in question to be taken by the pregnant woman.[30]

---

21 *Hennah* (1877) 13 Cox 547. A substance harmless or beneficial in small quantities (such as a sleeping tablet) is noxious if taken in sufficient quanitites to injure, aggrieve or annoy within the meaning of s 24 of the Offences Against the Person Act, 1861; *Marcus* [1981] 2 All ER 833; (1981) 1 WLR 774, 73 Cr App R 49 CA. The Court seemed to accept the definition in the Shorter Oxford English Dictionary of "injurious, hurtful, harmful, unwholesome". Three quarters of a sleeping tablet has been held not to be noxious; *Weatherall* [1968] Crim LR 115. In *Hill* (1985) 81 Cr App R 206; [1985] Crim LR 384 the Court of Appeal accepted that to be "noxious" it was not necessary that the substance be injurious to health provided it is objectionable or unwholesome. See *Hill* (1986) 83 Cr App R 386 HL.

22 *Hollis* (1873) 12 Cox 463 CCR.

23 Pollock CB in *Isaacs* (1862) ER 1371, L&C 220, 9 Cox 228 CCR.

24 *Brown* (1899) 63 JP 790; for a further discussion of the theory of Attempt see *Haughton v Smith* (1975) AC 476; [1973] 3 All ER 1109; [1974] 2 WLR 1, 58 Cr App R 198; [1974] Crim LR 305 HL and par 2.41.

25 *Perry* (1874) 2 Cox 233; *Hennah*, fn 21.

26 *Cramp*, fn 17. In Australia the meaning is confined to something likely to harm a pregnant woman; *Linder* [1938] SASR 412 CA and see *Barton* [1931] 25 QJ PR 81.

27 *Marlow* (1964) 49 Cr App R 49 CCA.

28 *Linder*, fn 26 at 415.

29 *Walford* (1899) 34 LJ Newsp 116 (noted in Russell 604) doubting *Cadman* (1852) 168 ER 1206, 1 Mood 114; *Gaylor* (1857) D&B 288, 7 Cox 253, 169 ER 1011 CCR.

30 *Harley* (1830) 172 ER 744, 4 C&P 369; *Wilson* (1857) 169 ER 945, D&B 127 CCR; *Farrow* (1857)

Procure

5.06 It follows from the wording of s 58 that a person may concurrently commit an offence under s 59.[31] "Procure" means to produce by endeavour;[32] in s 58 the word means bring about. In s 59 that word, in the context of "supply or procure", has been defined:

> ... as ... limited to the case of a person who, with the knowledge referred to in that section, obtains from the possession of some other person, the instrument or article the subject matter of the offence.[33]

It is, therefore, no offence to gather instruments or things for the purpose of carrying out an abortion provided they are already in the possession of the accused. This interpretation defeats the purpose of s 59 which is to criminalise acts preparatory to the carrying out of an abortion. It is contrary to the ordinary meaning of the section. In the ordinary use of language it is, no more nor less, a procuring of an article to remove it from a place where it has been put as is purchasing it or getting it from someone else.[34]

5.07 The Court of Criminal Appeal in *Hillman*[35] held, under s 59, that once the accused intends that an article or substance is to be used with intent to procure an abortion, it is irrelevant that the party to whom it was to be supplied had no such intention. Erle CJ reasoned:

> ... the statute is directed against the supplying or procuring of poison or noxious things for the purpose of procuring abortion with the intention that they shall be so employed and knowing that it is intended that they shall be so employed. The defendant knew what his own intention was, and that was, that the substance procured should be employed with intent to procure miscarriage.[36]

It is submitted that the decision is wrong. One cannot know something unless it is a reality. An accused cannot know that an instrument or thing is intended to be used for an abortion unless it is to be so used. The external element of the offence is clearly framed so as to require the person to whom the accused gives, or for whom the accused procures, the article, to actually have such an intention.

Intention

5.08 Under s 58 the accused must intend to procure her own miscarriage or, if a

169 ER 961, D&B 164 CCA; *Fretwell* (1862) 169 ER 1345, L&C 161 CCR. Procuring a poison under a threat of suicide but not desiring that it be taken, is not a "causing to be taken" within the section; for cases on the use of instruments see Taylor, *Medical Jurisprudence* (9th ed.) 141 (cited in Russell 604).

31   *Turner* [1910] 4 Cr App R 203, 206 CCA.

32   *A-G (SPUC) v Open Door Counselling Ltd* [1988] IR 593, 616 HC & SC.

33   Cooper J, for the majority, in *Scully* (1903) 23 NZLR 380, 384 CA; followed in *Mills* [1963] 1 QB 522; [1963] 1 All ER 202; [1963] 2 WLR 137, 47 Cr App R 49 CCA.

34   See the dissenting judgment of Denniston J in *Scully*, fn 33.

35   (1863) L&C 343, 169 ER 1424, 9 Cox 386 CCR, followed in *Scully*, fn 33.

36   At 387. Followed even though the person through whom the request as made was the agent of a policeman in *Titley* (1880) 14 Cox 502, Stephen J.

person other than the pregnant woman is alleged to be the offender, must intend to cause a miscarriage in another, whether she is actually pregnant or not. "Intent" in this context requires the accused to act with the purpose prohibited by the section of procuring a miscarriage.[37] The old cases[38] whereby intent was allowed to be proved from the accused having carried out previous operations, are no longer authoritative in the light of the revision of the similar fact evidence rule, by the House of Lords, in *Boardman*.[39]

Where an ectopic pregnancy occurs or where a hysterectomy has to be performed because, for example, of cancer, it is normal practice in this jurisdiction to proceed with the operation, despite the incidental destruction of the unborn life.[40] In a situation where a medical condition requires treatment, and that treatment involves, as an incident, the possible destruction of the foetus, the doctor does not intend to procure a miscarriage. His purpose is to operate in order to cure a pressing medical condition.

Prior to the Amendment the range of circumstances were recognised in accepted medical practice. The situations included ectopic pregnancy, cancer of the uterus, abdominal pregnancy with haemorrhage which could not be treated other than by the removal of the foetus, and severe eclampsia.[41] In all these cases the practice was directed to saving the life of the mother on whom the unborn child is completely dependent. The Amendment has not had the effect, it is submitted, of altering the law as the Oireachtas either acting on the authority of the Constitution or exercising their political power, have not changed the meaning in criminal law of intent. Despite the mother and child being expressed, in the text of Article 40.3.3, as having equal rights, the State has undertaken the duty of protecting that right only in so far as that is practicable. Where, due to dependence of the unborn child on its mother, its life is incidentally ended due to a medical procedure undertaken, in good faith, in order to preserve the life of the mother, the Constitution does not require that an accepted medical procedure should not be followed. Were the text to be otherwise construed the mother would first lose her life due to a medical condition, and the foetus would also perish, at around the same time, or very shortly afterwards.[42]

The Amendment is self-executing[43] and does not require legislation for its implementation. The text of the Amendment does not conflict with the prohibition set out in ss 58 and 59. The purpose of the Amendment, it is submitted, was to

---

37   For a discussion of intent see par 2.19.

38   E.g. *Bond* [1906] 2 KB 389, 21 Cox 252; *Palm* (1910) 4 Cr App R 253.

39   [1975] AC 421; [1974] 3 All ER 887; [1974] 3 WLR 673, 60 Cr App R 165; [1975] Crim LR 36 HL. For a further discussion see par 8.86.

40   Professor John Bonnar, personal communication. It is apparently misleading to speak of the destruction of unborn life in the case of an ectopic pregnancy as the condition is usually discovered due to the blockage causing a rupture and destroying the foetus. It may also be necessary to remove the foetus in the case of an abdominal pregnancy, because of severe haemorrhage which necessitates an operation. In the case of severe eclampsia it is accepted practice to cause an early delivery and then to treat the mother. In all these cases a failure to treat the mother would result in her death. Obviously, as the foetus is completely dependent on her it would not survive in those circumstances.

41   Professor John Bonnar, personal communication.

42   See the discussion on inconsistent decisions on intent at par 2.31.

43   *SPUC v Grogan* [1989] IR 753 SC.

protect that existing law from a charge of inconsistency on constitutional grounds. Where the purpose of an act is to bring about a situation, but the actor knows that another act or situation is a certain or near certain consequence of his action, he intends that consequence.[44] None of the instances recognised in the leading authorities which support that proposition consist of an act which is not, in itself, contrary to law. In consequence, the concept of oblique intention does not cause a doctor acting for the purpose described in the foregoing paragraph, to intend to procure a miscarriage.

Miscarriage

The Victorian language of the Offences Against the Person Act might be thought to cause difficulty in the use of the word "miscarriage". It could be argued that s 58 is not applicable, where a pregnancy is intentionally terminated by a caesarian section or where a child is deliberately killed in the womb and later removed by this procedure. The use of the caesarian procedure involved considerable danger at the time when the Act was drafted. The purpose of the section in outlawing the destruction of life in the womb is clear. A miscarriage need not necessarily occur solely through the birth canal. The word can simply be construed as meaning the cessation of the carrying of a child. Such an interpretation is now, in any event, required in order to interpret the section in accordance with the Constitution.[45]

There is nothing in the Constitution or the law to indicate that where a child has died naturally in the womb of natural causes, a doctor cannot operate to then empty the womb of its contents.

Necessity

5.09 It is possible that a situation might arise where the accused would seek to argue, in defence of a charge under s 58 or s 59, that his action was taken to save the life of the mother; that the defence of necessity[46] thereby defeats the prosecution case. In *Bourne*[47] a surgeon openly carried out an abortion on a girl of fourteen who was pregnant as a result of multiple rape. The accused claimed that a failure to carry out the procedure would have resulted in grave damage to the mental health of the girl. The United Kingdom Infant Life (Preservation) Act, 1929 had been passed to rectify the common law anomaly which gave no protection to children in the course of birth.[48] The Act incorporated a defence that the child had been killed "for the purpose only of preserving the life of the mother". At the trial (where the accused was acquitted by the jury) MacNaghten J held that this defence had always existed

---

44   See par 2.22.

45   *East Donegal Co-Operative v A-G* [1970] IR 317 SC.

46   See par 4.42 The defence does not apply to murder *Howe* [1987] AC 417; [1987] 1 All ER 771; [1987] 2 WLR 568, 85 Cr App R 32; [1987] Crim LR 480 HL. Further see Perkins, *Criminal Law* (3rd ed., New York 1982) 1065-1067.The defence has been applied in a manslaughter case; *US v Holmes* (1842) 26 Fed Cas No. 15383 (the accused was convicted but the defence of necessity to manslaughter is discussed in Baldurn J's charge to the jury.

47   [1939] 1 KB 687; [1938] 3 All ER 615 CCA.

48   See par 1.18. No parallel legislation has been passed here. The Act allowed for an alternative verdict of abortion and *vice versa*.

under s 58, being implied by the word "unlawful".[49] Williams disagrees; in 1861 abortion was not safe by the then current standards of medical practice and, in consequence, no exceptions were grafted on to the general prohibition.[50] The judge laid down a standard which was the basis of English law until the Abortion Act, 1967:[51]

> It permits the termination of pregnancy for the purpose of saving the life of the mother. As I have said, I think these words ought to be construed in a reasonable sense, and, if the doctor is of opinion on reasonable grounds and with adequate knowledge that the probable consequence of continuance of pregnancy will be to make the woman a physical or mental wreck, the jury are quite entitled to take the view that the doctor who, under these circumstances, and in that honest belief, operates, is operating for the purpose of preserving the life of the mother.[52]

5.10 Menhennitt J of the Supreme Court of Victoria drew heavily on the *Bourne* judgment in *Davidson*.[53] The case was decided on legislation parallel to s 58[54] but without the same close interrelationship as the two English statutes, each of which carried alternative verdicts of abortion and child destruction on a charge on the other offence. The focus of the judge's reasoning was, once more, the word "unlawful". He implied a requirement that the defence of necessity be absent to render abortion unlawful. In deciding when necessity could be established as a defence to abortion he ruled:

> . . . the accused must have honestly believed on reasonable grounds that the act done by him was necessary to preserve the woman from some serious danger. As to this element of danger, it appears to me in principle that it should not be confined to danger to life but should apply equally to danger to physical or mental health provided it is a serious danger not being merely the normal dangers of pregnancy and child birth. . . .
>
> Accordingly, to establish that the use of an instrument with intent to procure a miscarriage was unlawful, the Crown must establish either (a) that the accused did not honestly believe on reasonable grounds that the act done by him was necessary to preserve the woman from a serious danger to her life or her physical or mental health (not being merely the normal dangers of pregnancy and child birth) which the continuance of the pregnancy would entail; or (b) that the accused did not honestly believe on reasonable grounds that the act done by him was in the circumstances proportionate to the need to preserve the woman from a serious danger to her life or her physical or mental health (not being merely the normal dangers of pregnancy and childbirth), which the continuance of the pregnancy would entail.[55]

49   No authorities were cited to support this view. It is probable that such a defence had in fact been read into the 1861 Act. However, it had never before been used to justify an intervention which was not immediately necessary in order to save the life of the mother. In (1938) 2 MLR 126 Seabourne Davies relates that, in medical circles, the word "unlawful" in s 58 was assumed to imply an exception where the life or health of the mother was in danger.

50   *TBCL* 295.

51   For materials of the Act see fn 1.

52   KB at 693-94, All ER at 619. The test was further extended to include social pressures; Smith & Hogan 365-66.

53   [1969] VR 667 reviewed in Elliott, "An Australian Letter" [1969] Crim LR 511.

54   Crimes Act, 1958, s 69: "Whosoever . . . with intent to procure the miscarriage of any woman whether she is or is not with child unlawfully administers to her or causes to be taken by her any poison or other noxious thing, or unlawfully uses any instrument or other means with like intent shall be guilty of felony and shall be liable. . . ."

55   671-72. Followed in *Wald* [1971] 3 NSW DCR 25 and extended to take account of economic,

Unlawfulness, in the context of s 58, must primarily derive from the Constitution. A plea of necessity, therefore, must involve a countervailing constitutional right.[56] The only relevant right is the equal right to life of the mother. The exploration of what the true law is on this subject becomes circuitous, but the purpose of the Amendment in preserving the existing law and practice is, it is submitted, the best guide in the absence of legislation.

Ancillary Crimes

5.11 The territorial jurisdiction of the criminal law of the State does not ordinarily extend beyond its boundaries.[57] An offence committed abroad can only be prosecuted in Ireland if jurisdiction has been extended, in respect of that crime, to places other than the State.[58] That has not been done in the case of abortion.[59] Nor does it appear to be arguable that supplying persons with the means to reach a place where an abortion can be performed is an offence under s 59; the nature of what is done being beyond what the words in the section could reasonably mean.[60]

The advertising within the State of the service of abortion, available elsewhere, and the provision of assistance to those who wish to travel for such a purpose could amount to the common law offence of conspiracy to corrupt public morals by those who so act.[61] Thus far there have been no prosecutions. Hamilton P in *A-G (SPUC) v Open Door Counselling Limited*[62] stated:

> In a prosecution alleging a conspiracy to corrupt public morals, it would, however, be a matter for a jury to decide whether the activities of the defendants amounted to a conspiracy to corrupt public morals and whether in fact public morals were corrupted.[63]

Since December 1986 two companies, who had been referring women to abortion clinics in the United Kingdom for the purpose of further considering that option, have been subject to an order from the High Court, subsequently amended by the Supreme Court, restraining them:

> . . . from assisting pregnant woman within the jurisdiction to travel abroad to obtain abortion by referral to a clinic, by the making for them of travel arrangements, or by

social or medical grounds which could result in serious danger to the woman's physical or mental health, NSW Dist Ct.

56   *SPUC v Grogan* [1989] IR 753, 765, 769 SC.

57   See par 1.15-1.16.

58   *Board of Trade v Owen* [1957] AC 602; [1957] 1 All ER 411 HL; *Stonehouse* [1978] AC 55; [1977] 2 All ER 909; [1977] 3 WLR 143, 65 Cr App R 192, [1977] Crim LR 455 HL; generally see Smith & Hogan 268-69, 298-300.

59   *A-G (SPUC) v Open Door Counselling Ltd* [1988] IR 593, 609-11 HC & SC; generally see Findlay, "Criminal Liability for Complicity in Abortions Committed outside Ireland" (1980) XV (ns) Ir Jur 88; Williams, "Venue and the Ambit of Criminal Law" (1965) 81 LQR 276, 395, 518.

60   As constructed under the Ejusdem Generis rule: generally see Cross, *Statutory Interpretation* (2nd ed., 1987) 132-35.

61   *A-G (SPUC) v Open Door Counselling Ltd*, fn 59, 611-15.

62   Fn 59.

63   Fn 59, 614 relying on a dictum of Woolfe J in *A-G v Able* [1984] QB 795, 808; [1984] 1 All ER 277, 284; [1983] 3 WLR 845, 854, 78 Cr App R 197, 204, [1984] Crim LR 35.

informing them of the identity and location of and method of communication with a specified clinic or clinics or otherwise.[64]

Since December 1989 certain other persons, alleged to be responsible for a student handbook, have been subject to a Supreme Court injunction restraining them from publishing or distributing or assisting in the printing, publishing or distribution of any publication, produced under their aegis, providing information to persons (including pregnant women) of the identity and location of and method of communication with a specified clinic or clinics where abortions are performed.[65]

5.12 A person may be committed for contempt of court where, although not a party to a proceeding, he with full knowledge of an order and the acts required or restrained by it, nevertheless aids and abets in committing a breach of such order.[66] This wrong falls within the jurisdiction of the court to deal with contempt of its proceedings and obstruction of the course of justice.[67] A party who, knowing of an order of the court, wilfully causes its breach thereby obstructs the course of justice and is also liable for attachment for contempt.[68]

5.13 Article 38.5 of the Constitution guarantees trial by jury on a criminal charge. Where the contempt is either actually or constructively[69] in the face of the court that right inures to the benefit of the alleged offender. The distribution of functions between judge and jury differs from an ordinary criminal trial. In a criminal trial the jury retain the unfettered power to find the accused not guilty.[70] Criminal contempt trials are tried by a different procedure. The judge rules as a matter of law whether specified conduct amounts to contempt, the role of the jury is to decide facts.[71] We presume the procedure will be that the jury will be asked certain specified questions and, on answering them, the judge will decide, on the basis of the facts so found, whether a contempt has been committed.[72]

Where a person aids and abets another to commit a breach of a court order this form of contempt is arguably civil in nature though requiring proof of knowledge of the court order.[73] Where a person acts independently and interferes with the

---

64 *A-G (SPUC) v Open Door Counselling Ltd*, fn 59, 627.

65 *SPUC v Grogan* [1989] IR 753, 766, 769, 771.

66 *Moore v A-G* [1930] IR 471, 486-87 SC; *Times Newspapers Ltd v Attorney General, The Independent*, 23 April 1991. Generally see Keane, *Equity and the Law of Trusts in Ireland* (1988) 15.44. In *Attorney General v Times Newspapers Limited* [1991] 2 All ER 398 the House of Lords held that a person who knowingly impeded or interfered with the administration of justice by the court in an action between two other parties was guilty of contempt of court notwithstanding that he was neither named in any order of the court nor had assisted a person against whom an order was made to breach it.

67 Fn 66.

68 *Z Ltd v A* [1982] QB 558; [1982] 1 All ER 556; [1982] 2 WLR 288, [1982] 1 Lloyd's Rep 240 CA.

69 As in *A-G v Conneely* [1947] IR 213, 81 ILTR 82 HC and the *State (DPP) v Walsh and Conneely* [1981] IR 412 SC.

70 Devlin, *Trial by Jury* (1965) 87.

71 *Walsh & Conneely*, fn 69 at 438, 442.

72 No such trials have as yet taken place. The Supreme Court appeared to step back from jury trial for contempt in a two paragraph judgment approving a trial judge trying a hotly disputed contempt in a summary manner without a jury in *Re Kelly & Deighan* [1984] ILRM 424, 431.

73 *Z Ltd*, fn 68.

course of justice by wilfully defying, or acting so as to nullify the effect of a court order the wrong committed is the criminal offence of interference with the course of justice.[74] While the point has yet to be finally settled[75] it appears that those who deliberately help women to obtain abortions in the United Kingdom and elsewhere, are guilty of the offence of obstructing the course of justice and must be tried by a judge with a jury in the special manner previously outlined for contempt.

5.14 Where a mother is killed in the course of an unlawful abortion operation the courts have traditionally convicted the person performing it of manslaughter.[76] It is submitted that there is no legal basis for such a result other than one grounded on the accused being liable for criminal negligence[77] or on the basis that the accused committed a criminal act dangerously.[78]

The text of Article 40.3.3 and its nature as self-executing[79] renders it probable that any threat to destroy unborn life would be restrained by an injunction.[80]

Statistics

5.15 There have been no prosecutions under s 58 or s 59 within the last ten years. Within that time the statistics on the number of Irish women having abortions in England are worth quoting: 1968–64; 1969–122; 1970–261; 1971–577; 1972–974; 1973–1192; 1974–1406; 1975–1562; 1976–1802; 1977–3598; 1982–3650; 1983–3677; 1984–3946; 1985–3887; 1986–3918; 1987–3673; 1988–3893; 1989–3721.[81] The subject remains one producing deeply divided responses.[82]

---

74   There seems to be no decision directly in point. In *D* [1984] AC 778; [1984] 1 All ER 574, [1984] 2 WLR 112, 78 Cr App R 219; [1984] Crim LR 103 HL and CA, a breach of a Wards of Court order by a husband was treated as a criminal contempt. The husband consented to the order. The revival of jury trials for contempt was not approved by the Court of Appeal. Perkins com *op cit* 592, points out that criminal and civil contempt can, and do, overlap.

75   The definite opinion of Finlay P in *The State (Cummins) v McRann* [1977] IR 78 HC, that the doctrine of separation of powers required the courts to set their own procedures in both criminal and civil contempt, was not followed by the Supreme Court in *Walsh & Conneely*, fn 69; see McCormick, "Right to Jury Trial in Cases of Contempt" (1983) Oct Sept Gazette Inc LS of Irl.

76   *Buck* (1960) 44 Cr App R 213. In the Australian states which have retained the felony murder rule such a death would be murder; *Salika* [1973] VR 272 SC.

77   The older cases are outdated reasoning on the basis of a mental element in murder and manslaughter which is no longer current; *Whitmarsh* [1898] 62 JP 711; *Bottomley* [1903] 115 LT 88; *Lumley* (1911) 22 Cox 635.

78   For ciminal negligence see par 3.08 and for manslaughter by a criminal and dangerous act see par 3.23.

79   *A-G (SPUC) v Open Door Conselling Ltd*, fn 59, 605-7.

80   For the entirely different approach by the English courts see *C v S* [1988] QB 135 [1987] 1 All ER 1230; [1987] 2 WLR 1108 CA and the cases therein cited.

81   Compiled from statistics of the United Kingdom Office of Censuses and Surveys and published in the *Irish Times*, 5 January 1990 and 17 February 1990.

82   See Dublin Medical Social Research Board, *Termination of Pregnancy, England, Women from the Republic of Ireland* (sic) (1983, 1984); *Women Hurt by Abortion* (Cork, 1988); Burke, *Profile of First 202 Women to Attend Open Door* (Dublin, 1983).

Infanticide

5.16 At the foundation of the State there was no specific power to reduce a murder conviction to a lesser offence where a mother,[83] in distressed circumstances, killed her child shortly after birth.[84] Distress was often present, not just due to the natural factors of child birth, hormonal changes and the weight of the charge of a new life, but also due to the emphasis placed on the marital status of the parents.[85] Up to the Criminal Justice Act of 1964 a murder conviction carried the death sentence but, in these cases, that sentence was always commuted. The wretched mother was thus, in practice, considered differently from other persons convicted of murder.[86]

Reform

The United Kingdom parliament made an attempt to formalise this position with the Infanticide Act, 1922.[87] The Act failed in its purpose, principally, because it applied only to a "newly born child", a phrase given a restrictive interpretation.[88] It was replaced by the Infanticide Act, 1938 which is the model for the legislation in this jurisdiction. S 1 of the Infanticide Act, 1949 provides:

> (1) On the preliminary investigation by the District Court of a charge against a woman for the murder of her child, being a child under the age of twelve months, the Justice may if he thinks proper, alter the charge to one of infanticide and send her forward for trial on that charge.

> (2) Where upon the trial of a woman for the murder of her child, being a child under the age of twelve months, the jury are satisfied that she is guilty of infanticide, they shall return a verdict of infanticide.

> (3) A woman shall be guilty of felony namely infanticide if—
> (a) by any wilful act or omission she causes the death of her child being a child under the age of twelve months,
> (b) the circumstances are such that but for this section the act or omission would have amounted to murder.
> (c) at the time of the act or omission the balance of her mind was disturbed by reason of her not having fully recovered from the effect of giving birth to the child or by reason of the effect of lactation consequent upon the birth of the child—

> and may for that offence be tried and punished as for manslaughter.[89]

Apart from the power to reduce the offence of murder to infanticide given to the

---

83 Generally see Davies, "Child Killing in English Law" (1937) 1 MLR 203.

84 If there was no proof as to intention a manslaughter verdict might be returned, but this was an application of the ordinary law. See for example *The People (A-G) v Cleary* (1934) 1 Frewen 14 CCA.

85 See for example the facts of *Cleary*, fn 1 and also *The People (A-G) v Edwards* [1935] IR 500 and ch 7 of Deale, *Beyond Any Reasonable Doubt* (1971). The status of illegitimacy was abolished by the Status of Children Act, 1987.

86 Criminal Law Revision Committee, "Offences Against the Person Report", par 109 (Cmd 7844).

87 For an account see Davies, "Child Killing in English Law" (1937) 1 MLR 203.

88 *O'Donoghue* (1927) 20 Cr App R 132, 28 Cox 461 CCA; Hale, *The Times*, 22 July 1936.

89 Circuit Court jurisdiction; powers of arrest appropriate to felony. In *The People (A-G) v Mulligan* [1957] Ir Jur Rep 71 it was accepted that on a charge of murder the Court is entitled to accept a plea of guilty of infanticide where the child is under twelve months and the prosecution does not object to this course being taken.

District Court and the jury on a trial, the new offence may also be charged from the outset.[90] It may be clear, on an initial Garda investigation, that the circumstances of the killing fit within the Act. Then it is not appropriate to charge the accused with murder.

Elements

5.17 The inclusion of lactation as a disturbing factor on the balance of the mother's mind appears to have no foundation in scientific reality.[91]

The wording of the Act casts no persuasive burden on the accused. Infanticide, as a defence, must be considered by the jury where it has been raised, on the evidence, as an issue and the burden is on the prosecution to disprove beyond reasonable doubt the material which supports it.[92] The issue is whether the balance of the accused's "mind was disturbed by reason of her not having fully recovered from the effect of giving birth". The English Criminal Law Revision Committee[93] considered this wording to be too restrictive. In 1980 they recommended that it be changed to:

> Where a woman by any act or omission causes the death of her child, being a child under the age of 12 months, but at the time of the act or omission the balance of her mind was disturbed by reason of the effect of giving birth to that child or circumstances consequent upon that birth then, notwithstanding that the circumstances were such that but for this section the offence would have amounted to murder or manslaughter, she shall be guilty of an offence of infanticide.

In making that recommendation the committee were influenced by evidence from the Royal College of Psychiatrists that the effect of giving birth was joined as a factor in child killings by (1) the birth of the baby highlighting inadequate social environment such as housing; (2) the stress of a new burden on those in poverty; (3) psychological injury and stresses caused to the mother by family members where she was perceived as being unable to cope with the baby, and; (4) failure in bonding by the mother being sick and so unable to fully care for the baby.

It is submitted that the wording of the Act is broad enough to apply in these situations. The effect of giving birth cannot be exclusively restricted to physical exhaustion or hormonal changes. There is no warrant for treating the body in isolation from the mind. The main result of giving birth is that the mother has a child to care for. That does not occur in isolation from society but within whatever social pattern has been established. If stress from that situation results due to the presence of a baby that, it is submitted is part of the effect of giving birth. Where such stress causes a disturbance of the balance of the mother's mind and she kills her child, whilst in that state, she is guilty only of infanticide. Further, it is submitted,

90   Criminal Law Revision Committee, "Offences Against the Person Report", par 107.
91   The medical evidence to the Criminal Law Revision Committee, "Offences Against the Person Report", indicated that a syndrome known as "lactation insanity" was recognised in the early part of the century but the current view was that there was little or no evidence to support the existence of such an illness.
92   *The People (A-G) v Quinn* [1965] IR 366 CCA. See further par 4.01.
93   Offences Against the Person Report, par 106.

that the wording of the section supports this argument: the effect of giving birth is unlikely to be physically present for up to twelve months thereafter.

5.18 The requirement of a disturbance to the balance of the mind is not exacting. Although no guidance is to be had from authority it is appropriate to compare the test with that for insanity.[94] The defence of diminished responsibility, which does not apply in this jurisdiction,[95] under s 2 of the United Kingdom Homicide Act, 1957 requires ". . . such abnormality of the mind (whether arising from a condition of arrested or retarded development of mind or any inherent causes or induced by disease or injury) as substantially impaired his mental responsibility . . .".[96]

Where a mother gives birth to one child and, because of the effect of the birth of that child, kills another, the Act does not apply. Her liability for murder or manslaughter is to be tested on ordinary principles.

It is submitted that there is no reason why a mother cannot legally attempt to cause the death of her child whilst the balance of her mind was disturbed by reason of not being fully recovered from the effect of giving birth.[97]

Concealment of Birth

5.19 Where a mother was charged with the murder of her child a prosecution might fail due to a weakness in the evidence in the necessary proof of causation of death. Death in those circumstances occurred in private or the body of the infant could not be found.

Since 1623 a series of enactments[98] have made it a criminal offence for a mother to dispose of her child's dead body by secretly concealing it. The policy behind these statutes was to ensure that those mothers who were acquitted of murder were convicted of concealment.[99] The legislation currently in force extends to any person, including the mother, secretly concealing the dead body of a child.[1] S 60 of the Offences Against the Person Act, 1861 provides:

> If any woman shall be delivered of a child, every person who shall, by any secret disposition of the body of the said child, whether such child died before, at, or after its birth, endeavour to conceal the birth thereof, shall be guilty of a misdemeanour, and being convicted thereof shall be liable at the discretion of the court, to be imprisoned for any term not exceeding two years, with or without hard labour: provided, that if any person tried for the murder of any child shall be acquitted thereof, it shall be lawful for the jury by whose verdict such person shall be acquitted, to find,

---

94 See par 4.45-4.46.

95 *The People (DPP) v O'Mahony* [1985] IR 517 SC.

96 The Criminal Law Revision Committee, fn 91, par 101-102, considered that the special test for infanticide should be retained and not merged in diminished responsibility, on the basis that the test for that defence, was more onerous and exacting.

97 The Criminal Law Revision Committee, fn 1 par 113, disagree; but see *Smith* [1983] Crim LR 739.

98 21 Jac 1 Ch 27; 43 Geo 3 Ch 58; 9 Geo 4 Ch 31; 10 Geo 4 Ch 34.

99 See the text of 21 Jac 1 ch 27.

1 Archbold (1922) 919; Kenny (1922) 129-30. It is also a common law misdemeanour to dispose of a dead body with intent to prevent an inquest from being held; *Stephenson* (1884) 13 QBD 331, 15 Cox 679 CCR; Archbold (1922) 2, 141, 1345; Russell 1420-1421.

in case it shall so appear in evidence, that the child had recently been born, and that such person did, by some secret disposition of the dead body of such child, endeavour to conceal the birth thereof: and thereupon the court may pass such sentence as if such person had been convicted upon an indictment for the concealment of the birth.[2]

Child

5.20 The offence is only possible where a woman has first been delivered of "a child". The test for determining this is whether on being born the child was of sufficient maturity to have been capable of living. A live birth is not essential to the charge. The law was put by Erle J in *Berriman*:[3]

> . . . it is not necessary that it should have been born alive, but it must have reached a period when, but for some accidental circumstances, such as disease on the part of itself, or its mother, it might have been born alive. There was no law which compels a woman to proclaim her own want of chastity; and if she had miscarried at a time when the foetus was but a few months old, and therefore could have no chance of life, you should not convict her upon this charge. No specific limit can be assigned to the period when the chance of life begins; but it could, perhaps, be safely assumed that, under seven months, the great probability is that the child would not be born alive.[4]

This statement continues to represent the law though expert evidence may show that children under seven months have lived after birth.[5]

The child must be dead when it is secretly disposed of.[6] So in *Bell*,[7] a case dismissed before the Court for Crown Cases Reserved for Ireland, a girl was allegedly delivered of a baby in County Antrim and hid the live baby where it later died.[8]

It is submitted that it is not necessary for the child to be identified as the son or daughter of any particular person.[9]

Concealment

5.21 There must be a secret disposition of the body of the child. The mental element is an intention to conceal its birth, not, apparently, from a single individual, but from society in general.[10] Whether there is a secret disposition is a matter of inference,

---

2   Misdemeanour; this offence is an alternative verdict on a charge of murder.

3   (1854) 6 Cox 388.

4   At 392. See also *Holt* (1937) 2 J Cb L 69.

5   In *Colmer* (1864) 9 Cox 506, Martin B held that a foetus having the shape of a child but which was not bigger than a man's finger, was a child within the section. In *Hewitt & Smith* (1866) 4 F&F 1101, 176 ER 923 the question was left to the jury as an issue of fact.

6   *May* (1867) 10 Cox 448 CCA.

7   (1874) Ir Rep 8 CL 542. The case was dismissed on the basis that there was no evidence of the death of the child. The court mentioned that there was defective evidence as to whether the birth took place at all. Nobody saw the child. The only evidence as to birth being the witnessing of the accused going for a late night walk, blood on the floor of her room and the opinion of a doctor that the accused had given birth within the previous week.

8   While it is not possible that by concealing a live baby the charge will lie but if further steps of concealment are taken after it dies then see *Hughes* (1850) 4 Cox 447.

9   Contrary see *Williams* (1871) 11 Cox 684, and see *Bell*, fn 7, the prosecution chose to prosecute a woman for concealing the birth of her child. This was not proved. Neither was such an averment in the indictment necessary as children come into the world only by being born.

10   *Morris* (1848) 2 Cox 489, decided under 9 Geo 4 ch 31.

beyond reasonable doubt, from all the facts proved by the prosecution. Concealment may be secret though in the most public place, provided it is not much visited by the public.[11] It is thus a question of fact:[12]

> The concealment must be by a secret disposition of the body, and such a disposition could only be secret by placing it where it was not likely to be found. Secrecy was the essence of the offence.[13]

Any concealment, provided it is secret, comes within the section and it is irrelevant whether it was intended only to be temporary. In *Gogarty*,[14] the accused placed the body on a bed on which she was sitting and covered it with a quilt. The temporary nature of this disposal did not prevent the case being left to the jury.

5.22 To constitute a disposition there must be some effort made by the accused. Merely leaving the child, without doing more, in the place where it was born, is insufficient.[15] Evidence against concealment is to be had from the prior arrangements of the mother to be attended to at birth[16] or from her telling others of her pregnancy. This is not necessarily conclusive.[17]

There appear not to have been any prosecutions for this offence in recent times.[18]

Draft Indictments

5.23 There follow the appropriate forms of indictment for the offences considered in this chapter.

ABORTION

Statement of Offence

Causing a noxious thing to be taken to procure miscarriage, contrary to s 58 of the Offences Against the Person Act, 1861.

Particulars of Offence

AB on the   at   with intent to procure the miscarriage of a woman

---

11   *Brown* (1870) LR 1 CCA 244, 11 Cox 517.

12   *George* (1868) 11 Cox 41—placing the body in a box in a frequented room, not; *Nixon* (1866) 4 F&F 1040—body placed in street; *Clark* (1883) 15 Cox 171; *Rosenberg* (1906) 70 JP 264—body placed on bed covered with petticoat—accused also lay on the bed—not; *Farnham* (1845) 1 Cox 349—body wrapped in petticoat in bottom of box in the middle of some linen—left to jury; *Goode* (1853) 6 Cox 318—body in attic, not; *Waterage* (1846) 1 Cox 338—taking body to sister for burial, not; *Bate* (1871) 11 Cox 686—body taken away by two other persons, not; *Cook* (1870) 11 Cox 542—body in locked room—case left to jury; *Brown*, fn 11—body in field clsoe to wall in back of yard where it was not easy to see—case left to jury; *Clark* (1866) 4 F&F 1040 where Martin B held that it was a question of law whether the disposition could or could not be secret.

13   *Sleep* (1864) 9 Cox 559 at 561.

14   (1855) 7 Cox 107 (Ir). Further cases are cited at Archbold (1922) 920 and Russell 609-10.

15   *Wilkinson* (1829), Russell 610; *Turner* (1839) 8 C&P 755; *Durham* (1843) 1 Cox 56. Further cases are cited in Archbold (1922) 921 and Russell 610.

16   *Higley* (1830) 4 C&P 366, 172 ER 366; Russell 609.

17   *Douglas* (1836) 1 Mood 480, 7 C&P 644; Archbold (1922) 920; Russell 609.

18   A case of this kind, in the most extraordinary circumstances, occurred in 1985. See the Report on the Kerry Babies.

named CD, unlawfully caused to be taken by her (or administered to her or used an instrument or other means on her) a noxious thing.

Statement of Offence
Supplying an instrument knowing that such was to be used to procure miscarriage, contrary to s 59 of the Offences Against the Person Act, 1861.
Particulars of Offence
AB on the   at   unlawfully supplied (to) or procured (for) CD an instrument (or poison or noxious thing or things) knowing that same was intended to be used or employed with intent to procure the miscarriage of a woman named CD.[19]

INFANTICIDE

Statement of Offence
Infanticide, contrary to s 1 of the Infanticide Act, 1949.
Particulars of Offence
AB on the   at   unlawfully killed CD, a child, then being under the age of 12 months.

CONCEALMENT OF BIRTH

Statement of Offence
Endeavouring to conceal birth, contrary to s 60 of the Offences Against the Person Act, 1861.
Particulars of Offence
AB on the   at   endeavoured to conceal the birth of a child by secretly disposing of the dead body of the said child.

Addendum

In *A-G v X and Others*, Supreme Court, 5 March 1992, the Supreme Court held, by a majority, that abortion was lawful where it was established, as a matter of probability, that there was a real and substantial risk to the life, as distinct from the health, of the mother which could only be avoided by the termination of her pregnancy. In this case a fourteen year old girl had been molested by an older man and eventually made pregnant. On discovering this she threatened suicide and evidence was adduced, on an application by the Attorney General to prevent her from terminating her pregnancy, to the effect that her psychological state was such that there was a real risk of suicide. Three of the judges indicated that an injunction could be granted against a woman to prevent her travelling to another jurisdiction, for the purposes of obtaining an abortion, where that abortion would not be lawful in Ireland. Having regard to the difficulty of supervising and enforcing such an injunction the court has a discretion in the exercise of that power.

---

19   It may be unnecessary for a woman to exist or for anyone other than the accused to have such intent.
     See par 4.07.

CHAPTER SIX

Assault

6.01 The law of assault has traditionally distinguished between assault and battery.[1] The parameters of these two separate crimes are explained by *East:*[2]

> An assault is any attempt to offer with force and violence to do a corporal hurt to another, whether from malice or wantonness; as by striking at him, or even by holding up one's fist at him in a threatening or insulting manner, or with such other circumstances as denote at the time an intention, coupled with a present ability of using actual violence against his person; as by pointing a weapon at him within the reach of it. Where the injury is actually inflicted, it amounts to a battery, (which includes an assault;) and this, however small it may be; as by spitting in a man's face, or in any way touching him in anger without any lawful occasion. But if the occasion were merely accidental and undesigned, or if it were lawful . . .; it is no assault or battery in the law.
> . . .

In contrast the Queensland Code S 245 and the Western Australian Code S 222, drafted by Griffith to codify the common law,[3] provide:

> A person who strikes, touches, or moves, or otherwise applies force of any kind to, the person of another, either directly or indirectly, without his consent, or with his consent if the consent is obtained by fraud, or who by any bodily act or gesture attempts or threatens to apply force of any kind to the person of another without his consent, under such circumstances that the person making the attempt or threat has actually or apparently a present ability to effect his purpose, is said to assault that other person, and the act is called an assault.
>
> The term "applies force" includes the case of applying heat, light, electrical force, gas, odour, or any other substance or thing whatever if applied in such a degree as to cause injury or personal discomfort.

6.02 Even in legal language the word "battery" has fallen out of usage. Professor Williams has suggested that an assault, in the form of creating apprehension of violence to the victim, should be referred to as a "psychic assault".[4] That suggestion is followed in this work and the term "battery" is abandoned, save for historical references.[5]

The definition of assault is taken from the common law but the punishment is provided by statute, being a maximum of one year's imprisonment on indictment, or six months,[6] imprisonment and/or a fifty pound fine on summary conviction.[7]

---

1   Archbold (1922) 930-31, Kenny (1922) 151-54; McMahon & Binchy 402-6, Turner in *MACL* 344.
2   1 East PC 406; Stephen, *Digest* (5th ed.), 262.
3   Howard 122-25.   4   *TBCL* 173 et seq.
5   This is in accord with the practice of drawing indictments. An indictment does not have to refer specifically to an assault or battery, the former will include the latter unless they are distinguished by specific words; *Jones v Sherwood* [1942] 1 KB 127 DC and see *Kingston* (1884) 18 SALR 76 SC.
6   The right to opt for trial by indictment for common assault is vested solely in the prosecutor; *A-G (O'Connor) v O'Reilly*, High Court, unreported November 1976.
7   This offence is probably the most frequently prosecuted in the criminal calendar.

The elements of the offence are of great importance as a host of offences are built upon the proof of the commission of an assault. The structure of these offences divides them into basic assaults aggravated either by the harm thereby done,[8] the nature of the intent of the accused,[9] the status of the victim,[10] or the circumstances of commission.[11] There is no rationality to this disparate collection of offences either in the elements by which they are defined or in the range of sentences which they may attract.[12] Some offences are obsolete. Many more are cast in the language of a former age. The offences share the fact that they are built upon the base of the crime of assault. Assault is thus available as an alternative verdict[13] where the circumstances of aggravation or its accompanying mental state are not proven.[14]

An assault involves violence, either actual or apprehended. The offence is supplemented, by statute, to take account of the infliction of harm by other means, such as by poisoning.[15]

In general, a person cannot consent to acts of assault which will cause him actual bodily harm. The topic is further considered at par 8.16.

Psychic Assault

6.03 A psychic assault is committed where the accused intentionally or recklessly, by some physical act or gesture, causes the victim reasonably to apprehend immediate unlawful violence.[16] For example the accused may rush in a menacing fashion at the victim or raise a weapon to him. It was formerly thought that a psychic assault was merely an attempted assault.[17] While that view is correct in most cases, it is inaccurate in general. A psychic assault can be committed where an assault is impossible. So it is an assault to point an unloaded or imitation gun at the victim in the pretence of being about to fire it.[18] In essence the crime amounts to the creation in the victim of the apprehension of violence.[19] It is not possible to commit the crime by acting without the victim's knowledge, even in a manner which would have objectively

---

8   Offences Against the Person Act, 1861, ss 20, 47.

9   Offences Against the Person Act, 1861, ss 14, 21, 22, 30, 31, 33, 38, 39, 41, 62, Larceny Act, 1916, s 23, Criminal Law (Jurisdiction) Act, 1976, s 5.

10   Offences Against the Person Act, 1861, ss 36, 37, 38, 40, Customs Consolidation Act, 1876, s 193.

11   Offences Against the Person Act, 1861, ss 28, 29, 34, Night Poaching Act, 1828, s 2. Further see Indecent Assault and Sexual Assault, ch 8.

12   An aggravated assault under s 47 does not include rape and indecent assault as circumstances of aggravation.

13   Provided the crime includes in its definition the element of assault, which is not the case, for example, under ss 18 and 20 of the Offences Against the Person Act, 1861. See par 6.20.

14   Ryan & Magee 365-71.

15   See ch. 7.

16   *Mansfield Justices, ex parte Sharkey* [1985] 1 All ER 193; [1984] IRLR 496; *Logdon* [1976] Crim LR 121.

17   Hawk, ch 62, s 1; Archbold (1922) 930; Kenny (1922) 151. For a further discussion of fear as causation see par 2.15-2.17.

18   *Everangham* (1949) 66 WN (NSW) 122 CCA; *Logdon*, fn 16; *St. George* (1840) 9 C&P 483, 173 ER 921.

19   Russell 652-55.

caused him to fear violence had he perceived the actions of the accused.[20] Pointing a gun at the back of a person's head or holding a hatchet over him while he sleeps, are not assaults.

Apprehension

6.04 The element of apprehension may, similarly, be missing where the victim reasonably believes he is aware of facts which remove his apprehension. In *Lamb*[21] the apprehension normally experienced by a person when a loaded revolver is pointed at him was absent due to a mistaken belief, shared by the accused and the victim, that neither of the two bullets in the chamber would be discharged because they were not opposite the firing pin. A more extreme decision is the dismissal of an assault in *Ryan v Kuhl*.[22] The incident took place in neighbouring cubicles of a public toilet. The accused stuck a carving knife through a hole in the partition in order to stop an annoyance by the victim, who testified that this action and the sight of the knife had not frightened him since he knew that the accused could go no further in such an action while he remained safely inside.

The creation of the fear or apprehension of violence in the victim is an external element of the offence. As such it is considered, like any external element, by an objective evaluation. The reaction of the victim is not necessarily determinative. External facts are real and are treated objectively. The mental element of crime takes account of differences in human perception and can allow for subjective distortion of external facts. Consequently, unjustifiable fears by the timid and brave reactions by the valiant neither create nor negative the offence. The only valid test is the reaction of the ordinary or reasonable man. A courageous response to deadly violence, whereby a particular victim may not have feared violence is not an answer to the charge.[23] This external element is defined in terms of the victim reasonably apprehending or fearing violence. He need not feel fear provided that he reasonably anticipates violence from the circumstances proved.[24] Similarly, the requirement of immediacy in the definition is treated objectively and is subject to the requirement of reasonableness.

Immediacy

6.05 An expectation of violence can be immediate although the protagonist is in another room,[25] or is on the other side of a locked door apparently about to break it down.[26] In *Logdon*[27] it was satisfied by the accused opening a drawer and showing the victim a gun and declaring that he would hold her hostage. In *Smith v Chief*

---

20   *State v Barry* (1912) 45 Mont 598, 124 Pac 775 SC; *Pemble* (1971) 124 CLR 107 at 134, 139-41 HC.
21   [1967] 2 QB 981; [1967] 2 All ER 1282; [1967] 3 WLR 888, 51 Cr App R 417 CA. Counsel for the Crown conceded that this was not an assault.
22   [1979] VR 315 SC.
23   *Brady v Schatzel* [1911] St R Qd 206 SC; *McNamara* [1954] VR 137 SC.
24   *Horncastle* (1972) 8 CCC (2d) 282 NPCA.
25   *Lewis* [1970] Crim LR 647 CA.
26   *Beech* (1912) 7 Cr App R 197, 23 Cox 181 CCA.
27   [1976] Crim LR 121.

Superintendent Woking Police Station[28] by the accused peering in through a bedroom window at the victim in her night clothes. In *Stephens v Myers*[29] by a menacing advance by the defendant who stopped just outside striking distance. In *Vartzokas v Zaukur*[30] the victim was a hitch-hiker who had accepted a lift from the accused. On being asked for sexual favours the victim indicated that she wished to leave the car. The accused accelerated and then threatened to bring her to the house of "a mate" where he would "really fix you up". The passenger jumped and the accused was convicted of assault. An appeal was taken in relation to sentence only.

Arguably the requirement of immediacy is satisfied by any action on the part of the accused which objectively indicates that an assault is about to take place. It follows that where a threat is made, even in the most menacing fashion, of future violence an assault is not thereby committed. A contrary decision was reached in the New South Wales civil case of *Barton v Armstrong*.[31] The defendant telephoned the plaintiff and threatened violence. Taylor J rejected the contention that the apprehended harm was required to be perceived by its purported subject as being imminent. He held that the essence of the wrong was the creation of apprehension and that the fulfilment in violence need not be perceived as being immediate:

> Threats which put a reasonable person in fear of physical violence have always been abhorrent to the law as an interference with personal freedom and integrity, and the right of a person to be free from the fear of insult. If the threat produces the fear or apprehension of physical violence then I am of the opinion that the law is breached, although the victim does not know when the physical violence may be effected.[32]

6.06 Similarly in *Knight*[33] a series of violent threats were made, in the grossest terms, over the telephone to a magistrate. The accused was, unknown to the victim, some miles away. No communication was made that the threat would be carried out immediately. Consequently, the words could not amount to an assault:

> . . . the evidence in the present case went no further than to merely show that threats had been made to the various callers and serious threats they were. But as to there being any evidence that these threats were threats of immediate violence it is clear that they were not. They were mere threats which could have been executed at any time if at all.[34]

S 16 of the Offences Against the Person Act, 1861 creates the offence of threatening to kill or murder. This crime has little effect on the general law as it is restricted to threats uttered in writing.[35] This offence would not have been created if the common law of assault had been sufficient to deal with this situation.

---

28   (1983) 76 Cr App R 234; [1983] Crim LR 323 DC.
29   (1830) 4 C&P 349, 172 ER 785 (note, this is a civil case).
30   (1989) 44 A Crim R 243 SC S Aus. The decision at first instance is reported at (1988) 34 A Crim R 11.
31   (1969) 2 NSWR 451 CA.
32   At 603. See *Rozsa v Samuels* [1969] SASR 205 at 207 SC.
33   (1988) 35 A Crim R 314 CCA NSW.
34   Per Lee J at 317. See further par 6.07.
35   See par 2.39.

Words

6.07 Although it has been powerfully argued to the contrary,[36] the mere use of words cannot constitute an assault.[37] The law traditionally looked for some form of menacing gesture. Active menace can either be found or reasonably read into many situations where threatening words are used. Thus where I park my car and in opening the door touch it against the car of another person who then threatens to break my leg, this is not an assault. It becomes one when that other advances towards me or gestures as if to carry out his threat.

The mischief the law penalises is the creation of an apprehension of immediate violence in the mind of another. Clearly, words can assist in that wrong, or they can be superfluous. A gesture can be supplied, it is suggested, by the act of the accused moving into physical proximity to the victim.

Where the law moves away from the test of whether an ordinary person would have apprehended immediate violence,[38] it tends towards unreality. In *Byrne*[39] the British Columbia Court of Appeal held that there was no assault where the accused approached a theatre box office and, with a jacket over his arm, said at least four times in a short space of time "I've got a gun, give me all your money or I'll shoot".[40]

It was held to be an assault, in a civil case, for the victim to be threatened with having his neck broken by men who gathered around him and tucked up their sleeves. It is arguable on the facts of *Logdon*,[41] that menacing words spoken by a stranger in a dark city back street which engender fear can be an assault, by reason of what is said and the circumstances under which the words are uttered. If a further requirement of an act or gesture is insisted on, it can easily be found in the accused moving into proximity to the victim in order to convey his menacing message.

6.08 Just as circumstances can negative what would otherwise be an assault[42] so can words. The leading example is *Tubervell v Savage*.[43] The fact of the plaintiff taking hold of his sword and stating "If it were not assize time I would not take such language" negated the assault. Such a neutralisation by words clearly does not occur where the words are uttered after the victim has been put in apprehension. For example the accused may point a gun for a few seconds at a terrified victim and then laugh and say "it isn't loaded".

It can be an assault to threaten the victim with violence unless he does as

---

36 Williams, "Assault and Words" [1957] Crim LR 219. See further the discussion of the cases in par 6.06. Smith & Hogan 377 point out that the authority in favour of words not being assault by not being capable of constituting an assault is slight.

37 *Dullaghan v Hillen & King* [1957] Ir Jur Rep 10, at 143 Judge Fawsitt: ". . . mere words no matter how harsh, lying, insulting and provocative they may be, can never amount in law to assault". Further see Howard 125.

38 It is submitted that this is the correct approach; *Wilson* [1955] 1 All ER 744; [1955] 1 WLR 493, 39 Cr App R 12 CCA; *Ansell v Thomas* [1974] Crim LR 31 CA.

39 (1968) 3 CR NS 190, 63 WWR 385, 3 CCC 179 CA Br Col.

40 Criticised by Stuart 65-6. In contrast in *Read v Coker* (1883) 13 QB 850, 138 ER 1437, 1 WR 417, 1 CLR 746.

41 See par 6.06, fn 36.

42 *Ryan v Kuhl* [1979] VR 315 SC.

43 (1669) 1 Mod Rep, 3, 2 Keb 545, 84 ER 341. The alternative spelling is Tuberville.

requested. In such circumstances words do not cancel the apprehension of violence, which would otherwise exist, where either the force threatened is more than may lawfully be used[44] or where the accused has no right to make the demand in question.[45] In *Rozsa v Samuals*[46] the accused was a taxi driver who jumped a queue ahead of his colleagues. The victim remonstrated with the accused, to no effect, and then threatened him with a punch in the head. The accused responded by reaching into the dashboard of his taxi and producing a table knife saying "I will cut you to bits if you try it" and made a move out of his taxi which was frustrated by the victim slamming the door. The accused argued before the Supreme Court of South Australia claiming that what was done did not amount to an assault. Hogarth J ruled:

> . . . if a threat is made to apply force unless the person assailed complies with some unlawful demand . . . "Your money or your life" . . . it would be idle to say that there was not a threat to apply force to the person of another in circumstances in which the person making the threat had, or at least had caused the other to believe on reasonable grounds that he had, present ability to effect his purpose; and therefore an assault had been committed . . . The proper test to determine whether or not there was an assault is to ask, if [the victim] had attempted to strike the appellant in the manner which he threatened, would the appellant have been justified in defending himself by using the table knife? If he would have been justified in doing so, then he was entitled to make the conditional threat, and there was no assault.[47]

The mental element in the crime of assault is the realisation in the mind of the offender that his demeanour will produce the expectation of violence in the mind of another.[48] As such it may be committed by intention or recklessness.

Assault

6.10 An assault occurs where the accused, intentionally or recklessly, causes force to be applied to the body or clothing of the victim.

Violence

The force to be applied to the victim does not have to be violent. Kissing or touching another, who does not invite such conduct, expressly or by their behaviour, is an assault.[49] Traditionally the protection of the law, in tort and crime, has been against the least trespass to the person.[50] This is misleading. Life would be impossible if

---

44   *Rozsa v Samuals* [1969] SASR 205 at 207 SC. Smith & Hogan 357 express the view that a threat to kill in order to effect a lawful purpose would be lawful where the carrying out of such a threat would not; approved in *Cousins* [1982] QB 526; [1982] 2 All ER 115; [1982] 2 WLR 621, 74 Cr App R 363; [1982] Crim LR 444 CA.

45   *Police v Greaves* (1964) NZLR 295 CA; *Logdon* [1976] Crim LR 121.

46   Fn 44.

47   Drawing heavily on Williams, "Assault and Words" [1957] Crim LR 219, at 222-23 and the American cases therein cited: *State v Mayerfield* (1867) 61 NC 108; *Hairston v State* (1877) 54 Miss 689. Because of the lack of proportion the judge found that the actions of the taxi driver in waving the table knife constituted an assault.

48   Russell 652 citing Comyns' *Digest* (London, 1822) 275.

49   And may be an indecent assault; *Leeson* (1968) 52 Cr App R 185 CA. See further par 8.36.

50   *Power v Cook* (1869) IR 4 CL 247; *Dullaghan v Hillen* [1957] Ir Jur Rep 10.

every trifling contact with a stranger constituted a crime.[51] Every person is, by his living and moving about in society, taken to consent to such minimal contact as is necessary and usual to perform the tasks of everyday life.[52] It is not an assault to seek the attention of another by tapping his shoulder.[53] Alternatively, the law does not concern itself with trifles; the power to grant a discharge being retained by the Courts on a conviction for a criminal offence and expressly recognised in the context of assault by s 44 of the Offences Against the Person Act, 1861. Robert Goff LJ in *Collins v Wilcock*[54] put the boundary where social contact ends and an assault is committed in these terms:

> . . . most of the physical contacts of ordinary life are not actionable because they are impliedly consented to by all who move in society and so expose themselves to the risk of bodily contact. So nobody can complain of the jostling which is inevitable from his presence in, for example, a supermarket, an underground station or a busy street; nor can a person who attends a party complain if his hand is seized in friendship, or even if his back is (within reason) slapped. Although such cases are regarded as examples of implied consent, it is more common nowadays to treat them as falling within a general exception embracing all physical contact which is generally acceptable in the ordinary conduct of daily life.[55]

No Requirement of Anger

6.11 It was formerly common to explain the limitations of implied consent in terms of a requirement that an assault be angry, revengeful, rude or insolent.[56] While this language is appropriate in describing such acts as kicking a man, spitting at him[57] or throwing him out of his chair[58] it has led to unnecessary confusion[59] and has been abandoned.[60] The better test is to ask whether the actions of the accused were outside what can reasonably be expected in the circumstances of the social context in which it took place. This allows the jury to apply contemporary social standards. However, where the victim had, prior to the assault, expressly withdrawn consent to the ordinary contact of daily life, any touching of his person is an assault.[61] If that assault is trifling, it can be dealt with by the absolute discharge of the accused.

---

51 In general people are anxious, because of phylogenetically conditioned privacy instincts, to avoid all such contact.

52 McMahon & Binchy 403.

53 *Coward v Baddeley* (1859) 4 H&N 478, 157 ER 927; *Donnolly v Jackman* [1970] 1 All ER 987, [1970] 1 WLR 562, 54 Cr App R 229 DC; *Phillips* (1971) ALR 740 at 746.

54 [1984] 3 All ER 374; [1984] 1 WLR 1172, 79 Cr App R 229; [1984] Crim LR 481 CA.

55 All ER at 378, WLR at 1177, Cr App R at 234. Further see *Boughey* (1986) 60 ALJR 422, 161 CLR 10.

56 Russell 655.

57 Cotesworth (1704) 6 Mod 172, 87 ER 928.

58 *Hopper v Reeve* (1817) 7 Taunt 698, 129 ER 278.

59 Smith & Hogan 448-49.

60 *Faulkner v Talbot* [1981] 3 All ER 468; [1981] 1 WLR 1528, 74 Cr App R 1; [1981] Crim LR 705 DC.

61 See *Donnolly v Jackman* [1970] 1 All ER 987; [1970] 1 WLR 562, 54 Cr App R 229 DC. It is submitted this decision is incorrect.

The Victim

6.12 The victim, in this context, includes the clothes he is wearing. In *Day*[62] it was held to be an assault where a man's coat was slashed with a knife while it was on his back and in *Thomas*[63] where the hem of a girl's skirt was rubbed. In *Humphries v Connor*[64] it was not an assault to remove an orange lily from the clothes of a lady but this is best regarded as a policy decision.

The crime is committed even though the victim was unaware of what was done to him. The essence of the offence is not the creation of apprehension, as in psychic assault, but the unwarranted interference with the person of another.

Kinds of Force

6.13 Most usually an assault is committed by delivering a blow with a limb or by using a weapon of some kind. Some kind of force must be applied. The Queensland and Western Australian[65] codes contemplate that an assault can be committed by applying "heat, light, electrical force, gas, odour or any other substance or thing whatever", the only condition being that its degree has to be such "as to cause injury or personal discomfort".[66] There are no common law decisions directly in point. There is reason why the law should adapt in order to punish modern as well as traditional means of committing a wrong. Blackstone writes that "every man's person is sacred, and no other having a right to meddle with it, in any the slightest manner".[67] Throwing a canister of CS gas at a person or suddenly making a deafening noise on a telephone line is, it is submitted, as much an interference with his person as striking or pushing him.[68] Circumstances where electricity, light or odour are applied to a victim would almost necessarily involve either a touching, which would be an assault outside the context of ordinary social contact, or some other wrong such as false imprisonment[69] though it is not an assault to cause the victim to consume poison.[70] In that case there is no application of force, the secretive nature of the

62   (1845) 1 Cox 207.

63   (1985) 81 Cr App R 331; [1985] Crim LR 677 CA; the accused was acquitted of indecent assault.

64   (1867) 17 Ir CLR 1. This was a civil case and the defendant, a police constable, had his defence upheld that he removed the lily gently and quietly in accordance with his duty to take reasonable measures to keep the peace.

65   Quoted at par 6.01.

66   This latter concept conforms with United States tort law restricting battery tyo harmful or offensive conduct; Prosser & Keeton (5th ed.) 39: "A harmful or offensive contact with a person, resulting from an act intended to cause the plaintiff or third person to suffer such a contact, or apprehension that such a contact is iminent, is a battery"—quoting Second Restatement of Torts par 13. "The plaintiff is entitled to protection according to the usages of decent society, and offensive contacts or those which are contrary to all good manners, need not be tolerated. . . . The test is what would be offensive to an ordinary person not unduly sensitive as to personal dignity."

67   3 Bl Com 120. See par 6.10.

68   One could, however, direct electricity into a swimming pool or switch on the current into an appliance which the victim was repairing or examining. Shining a light in someone's eyes can be done as an interrogation aid, in which case the victim is imprisoned. Russell 652-53 tentatively accepts the extension of the Code as being part of the common law.

69   Howard 125 comments that the Code formulation is "probably not beyond the spirit of the law".

70   *Hanson* (1850) 2 C&K 912, 4 Cox 138; *Walkden* (1845) 1 Cox 282 but see *Button* (1838) 8 C&P 660. On this topic see further ch 7.

poisoning being such that the victim is tricked into taking it himself. Further, poison is not a force but is the cause of a biochemical reaction.[71]

Similarly, there is no application of force in abandoning a baby.[72] It is an assault to take a baby away by a trick[73] because this necessarily involves a touching. The specific problem of abandonment of children is provided for by the creation of a separate crime in s 27 of the Offences Against the Person Act, 1861:

> Whosoever shall unlawfully abandon or expose any child, being under the age of two years, whereby the life of such child shall be endangered, or the health of such child shall have been or shall be likely to be permanently injured, shall be guilty of a misdemeanour, and being convicted thereof shall be liable to be kept in penal servitude for the term of five years.[74]

Direct Act

6.14 The old law that an assault must be a direct act[75] seems to be abandoned. In *K (a minor)*[76] a schoolboy mischievously took a tube of acid down to the school toilets. Startled by footsteps he poured it into an electrical face and hand dryer, the nozzle of which was pointing upwards. When the footsteps receded he left the acid[77] but later claimed that he had intended to return and wash it out. Another schoolboy used the dryer and was permanently scarred. On a case stated to the High Court the act of K was held to be an assault notwithstanding the indirect manner in which the force was applied to the victim. Parker LJ stated:

> . . . in my judgment there can be no doubt that if a defendant places acid into a machine with the intent that it shall, when the next user switches the machine on, be ejected onto him and do him harm there is an assault when the harm is done. The position

---

71 In general. Kenny (1922) 153 explains ". . . it is essential to an assault that there should be a personal exertion of force by the assailant". Poisoning is considered at par 7.15-7.16.

72 *Renshaw* (1847) 2 Cox 285; *Boulden* (1957) 41 Cr App R 105 CCA. As to what constitutes abandonment see *Falkingham* (1870) LR 1 CCR 222, 11 Cox 475; *White* (1871) LR 1 CCR 311, 12 Cox 83.

73 *March* (1844) 1 C&K 496, 174 ER 909.

74 The Court of Crown Cases Reserved held that this offence had been committed where a mother placed a child in a hamper and sent it by rail to the father of the child where it arrived in less than an hour, the child later died from causes which were not attributable to this fact; *Falkingham*, fn 72. Abandonment, in this context, means leaving a child to its fate; *Boulden* (1957) 41 Cr App R 105 and see *Falkingham*; *White*, fn 72. It is submitted that the elements of this offence require voluntary abandonment of a child, being reckless as to whether the life of the child would be endangered, or its health permanently injured. The age of the child may be proved by the production of a birth certificate coupled with evidence of identity or other evidence showing when the child was born; see par 8.60. It is an "abandonment" for a father to fail to bring his child in from outside the house where its mother had left it; *White*, fn 72. It is an "exposure" for a father to needlessly compel his children to go with him on a long journey during a night of bad weather; *Williams* (1910) 26 TLR 290, 4 Cr App R 89. Where a mother left her child, at the age of ten days, at the bottom of a dry ditch where it was found soon after, Parke B ruled: ". . . it is said in some of the books that an exposure to the inclemency of the weather may amount to an assault, yet, if that be so at all, it can only be when the person suffers a hurt or injury of some kind or other from the exposure"; *Renshaw* (1847) 2 Cox 285.

75 For an account see Williams, *TBCL*, 179- 80.

76 [1990] 1 All ER 331, 91 Cr App R 23 DC.

77 Failing to avert a course of conduct he had wrongfully commenced. See par 3.14-3.20.

was correctly and simply stated by Stephen J in *R v Clarence* (1888) 22 QBD 23 at 45, [1886-90] All ER Rep 133 at 145, where he said: "If a man laid a trap for another into which he fell after an interval the man who laid it would during the interval be guilty of an attempt to assault, and of an actual assault as soon as the man fell in". This illustration was also referred to by Wills J in the same case in relation to s 20 of the 1861 Act. Wills J there also referred to *R v Martin* (1881) 8 QBD 54, [1881-5] All ER Rep 699, saying (at 36): "The prisoner in that case did what was certain to make people crush one another, perhaps to death, and the grievous bodily harm was as truly inflicted by him as if he had hurled a stone at somebody's head". In the same way a defendant who pours a dangerous substance into a machine just as truly assaults the next user of the machine as if he had himself switched the machine on. So too in my judgment would he be guilty of an assault if he was guilty of relevant recklessness.[78]

Illustrations of indirect assault prior to this decision included encouraging a dog to bite, riding over a person with a horse, driving one vehicle into another, pushing a drunken man into another,[79] causing a panic in a theatre after placing an iron bar across the doorway,[80] smacking a horse so that it throws its rider[81] and tossing a firework into a crowded place where it was thrown from person to person eventually striking the victim and putting out his eye.[82] The weight of authority therefore supports the decision in *K*.

Omissions

6.15 In *Fagan*[83] an accused accidentally (according to himself) drove his car onto a policeman's foot and left it there, for a time, before removing it, knowing the suffering he was causing. Though the Divisional Court, by a majority, analysed the crime in terms of a continuing series of acts involving deliberation, their reasoning does not change the fact that the accused was convicted for omitting to remove his car. Probably the correct analysis of the case is in terms of the mental element being a deliberate failure to rectify an intentional situation which, it has been suggested, was, when considered as a whole, a deliberate act.[84] It was held not to be an assault for a policeman, stationed at a door, to stand still, like a door or wall, to prevent a person entering by obstruction.[85] It would appear to follow that failing to remove oneself from the path of a cyclist is not an assault.[86]

Facts will seldom occur where force is applied to a victim by a mere omission. Normally the accused will move himself, or some part of himself (such as his foot), into position in anticipation of a collision. That is an assault.

---

78 At 333-34.

79 All from Russell 656.

80 Martin (1881) 8 QBD 54; [1881-85] All ER 669, 14 Cox 633 CCR, a case under s 20 of the Offences Against the Person Act, 1861; see par 6.20 for the different wording of this section.

81 *Dodwell v Burford* (1670) 1 Mod 24, 86 ER 703.

82 *Scott v Shepherd* (1773) 2 Wm Bl 892, 96 ER 525. Williams instances as a possible assault driving a passenger in a car into an obstruction or, as a psychic assault, pretending to do so. He is undoubtedly correct; *TBCL* 179.

83 [1969] 1 QB 439; [1968] 3 All ER 442; [1968] 3 WLR 1120, 52 Cr App R 700 DC.

84 Williams, *TBCL* 155-56; Stuart 72-4.

85 In general the law is against the proposition that an assault is capable of being committed by an omission; *Innes v Wylie* (1844) 1 C&K 257, 8 JP 280, 174 ER 800.

86 Kenny (1922) 152.

Mental Element

6.16 An assault may be committed by intention or recklessness.[87] Assault is part of a series of offences treated by the Offences Against the Person Act, 1861. Many of the other forms of assault are subject to a statutory requirement of malice, which means, in this context, a requirement that the accused act intentionally or recklessly.[88] The Court of Appeal in *Venna*[89] supported a coherent reading of these sections by interpreting them as requiring a common mental element for the basic offence of assault:

> In our view the element of *mens rea* in the offence of battery is satisfied by proof that the defendant intentionally or recklessly applied force to the person of another. If it were otherwise, the strained consequence would be that an offence of unlawful wounding contrary to s 20 of the Offences Against the Person Act, 1861 could be established by proof that the defendant wounded the victim either intentionally or recklessly, but if the victim's skin was not broken and the offence was therefore laid as an assault occasioning actual bodily harm contrary to s 47 of the 1861 Act, it would be necessary to prove that the physical force was intentionally applied.
>
> We see no reason in logic or in law why a person who recklessly applies physical force to the person of another should be outside the criminal law of assault. In many cases the dividing line between intention and recklessness is barely distinguishable.[90]

An application of force which occurs by accident is not an assault, as where a man's horse takes fright and charges into a person.[91] Negligence is not equivalent to recklessness.[92]

Assault Occasioning Actual Bodily Harm

6.17 S 47 of the Offences Against the Person Act, 1861 provides:

> Whosoever shall be convicted upon an indictment of any assault occasioning actual bodily harm shall be liable to be kept in penal servitude for the term of five years and whosoever shall be convicted upon an indictment for a common assault, shall be liable to be imprisoned for any term not exceeding one year, with or without hard labour.[93]

Harm

"Actual bodily harm" means any hurt or injury calculated to interfere with the health or comfort of the victim. It need not be an injury of a permanent character nor need

---

87 Russell 656; *Spratt* [1991] 2 All ER 210 CA. For Canadian decisions apparently contradicting the wording of the Code see Stuart 136.

88 *Cunningham* [1957] 2 QB 396; [1957] 2 All ER 412; [1957] 3 WLR 76, 41 Cr App R 155 CCA.

89 [1976] QB 421; [1975] 3 All ER 788; [1975] 3 WLR 737, 61 Cr App R 310 CA.

90 QB at 429, All ER at 793-4, WLR at 743, Cr App R at 314. See further *K (a minor)* [1990] 1 All ER 331, 91 Cr App R 23 DC. Recklessness in Irish law is discussed at par 2.37.

91 *Gibbons v Pepper* (1695) 2 Salk 638, 91 ER 538; *Stanley v Powell* [1891] 1 QB 86.

92 See ch 1.

93 Common assault an alternative verdict; *Oliver* (1860) 8 Cox 384; s 1 of the Penal Servitude Act, 1891 provided for the increase of all sentences of penal servitude of three years to five years. The sections quoted from the Offences Against the Person Act, 1861, as are all quotations from that Act in this work, in accordance with amendments introduced by the Penal Servitude Acts of 1864 and 1891 and by the Statute Law Revision Act, 1908. The penalty on summary conviction is twelve months' imprisonment and/or a £100 fine.

it amount to what would be considered to be grievous bodily harm.[94] It includes a tattoo,[95] a scar on the face,[96] and a blow on the head which renders the victim unconscious for a time.[97] No permanent or visible injury is required. Experience indicates that convictions are recorded under the section in respect of broken bones or teeth[98] and assaults which cause more than a trivial injury such as a bruise or a scratch.[99] In *Miller*[1] the accused was charged with raping his wife but found guilty on the second count of assault occasioning actual bodily harm. This occurred during the course of violent "persuasion" which brought on hysteria. The trial judge ruled:

> The bodily harm alleged is said to be the result of the defendant's actions, and they were, if the jury accepts the evidence, that he threw the wife down three times. There is evidence that afterwards she was in a hysterical and nervous condition . . . There was a time when shock was not regarded as bodily hurt, but the day has gone by when that could be said. It seems to me now that, if a person is caused hurt or injury resulting, not in any physical injury, but in an injury to the state of his mind for the time being, that is within the definition of "actual bodily harm".[2]

Arguably this ruling is incorrect. Being thrown to the ground three times would naturally occasion bodily harm in the form of painful bruising and stiffness. The section does however restrict its application to "bodily" harm. In the absence of physical injury, such as concussion, which may well have been present in the *Miller* case, it is submitted that nervousness or hysteria is not bodily harm. The presence of these symptoms may, however, be evidence of bodily suffering within the definition of the crime.

Mental Element

6.18 The aggravating factor of bodily harm takes the penalty for a simple assault, prosecuted on indictment, from one year to five years. The English courts have proceeded, until recently, on the basis that the only difference between the two species of assault provided for in s 47 is that the form carrying five times the penalty for simple assault, should cause actual bodily harm to the victim. In other words "occasioning" imports no mental element into the definition of the offence.[3]

---

94   Archbold (1922) 931, 940. The Court of Criminal Appeal definition in *Donovan* [1934] 2 KB 498; [1934] All ER 207, 30 Cox 187, 25 Cr App R 1, is that actual bodily harm includes any hurt or injury calculated to interfere with the health or comfort of the victim, provided it is something more than merely transient or trifling. And see *Miller* [1954] 2 QB 282, [1954] 2 All ER 529; [1954] 2 WLR 138, 38 Cr App R 1; *Percali* (1986) 42 SASR 46 SC; *Coulter* (1987) 62 ALJR 74.

95   *Burrell v Harmer* [1967] Crim LR 169 DC.

96   *K (a minor)* [1990] 1 All ER 331, 91 Cr App R 23 DC.

97   *The People (DPP) v Hamell*, unreported, Special Criminal Court, 9 October 1990. See *The Irish Times*, 10 October 1990. The accused was acquitted of wounding with intent to do grievous bodily harm, contrary to s 18, on the basis of lack of proof of intent, where he was proved to have struck a Garda with a stone a number of times with a purpose, as found by the Court, of escaping. He was convicted under s 47.

98   Personal observation.

99   Williams, *TBCL*, 187. In *Scatchard* (1987) 27 A Crim R 136 the Supreme Court of Western Australia held that catching someone in a headlock so that it hurt was not, of itself, an assault which "does to that other person bodily harm".

1   Fn 94.

2   [1954] QB at 292; [1954] 2 All ER at 534; [1954] 2 WLR at 145, 38 Cr App R at 10.

3   Smith & Hogan 396-97; Williams, *TBCL* 191; Gillies 445.

In *Roberts*[4] the victim was assaulted, by being grabbed at by the accused, while he ordered her to take off her clothes. She jumped and suffered concussion and grazing. The Court of Appeal rejected a contention that the accused must foresee that the actions of the victim will result in the harm suffered. The element of "occasioning actual bodily harm" was stated in terms of causation only:

> The test is: was it the natural result of what the alleged assailant said and did, in the sense that it was something that could reasonably have been foreseen as the consequence of what he was saying or doing? As it was put in one of the old cases it had got to be shown to be his act, and if of course the victim does something so "daft" . . . or so unexpected, not that this particular assailant did not actually foresee it but that no reasonable man could be expected to foresee it, then it is only in a very remote and unreal sense a consequence of his assault, it is really occasioned by a voluntary act on the part of the victim which could not reasonably be foreseen and which breaks the chain of causation between the assault or the harm or injury. . . .[5]

6.19 This formulation defines the offence as being one of intentional or reckless assault causing bodily harm which the accused need neither have intended nor foreseen. Where the accused assaults A by punching him in the chest, A may suffer slight bruising ordinarily insufficient to be described as actual bodily harm; the accused is guilty of an assault and may be sentenced to one year's imprisonment. Where the accused assaults B who is, unknown to the accused, suffering from high blood pressure, the blow may cause a medical condition necessitating hospitalisation. On the *Roberts* analysis the accused is guilty under s 47 and liable to five years' penal servitude. In *Spratt*[6] the Court of Appeal held that recklessness as to actual bodily harm was required under the section if the accused was to be found guilty. The Court further reviewed the situation in *Parmenter*[7] and upheld *Spratt* as being consistent with the authorities.[8]

Since the analysis of the former offence of capital murder by the Supreme Court in *The People (DPP) v Murray*[9] it is submitted that a requirement of a mental element, in the shape of either intention or recklessness, in respect of each external element of the offence, is to be preferred to the older line of authority culminating in *Roberts*. While this is presumed in respect of statutory offences[10] the words of a section can make it clear that a particular element requires no corresponding mental element. The words "assault occasioning actual bodily harm" could be viewed as equivalent

---

4 (1971) 56 Cr App R 95 CA.

5 At 102. See further Elliott, "Frightening a Person into Injuring Himself" [1974] Crim LR 15 and further par 2.15-2.17. For cases upholding this analysis see *Spratt* [1991] 2 All ER 210 CCA; *Savage* [1991] 2 All ER 220; [1990] Crim LR 709 CA.

6 *The Times*, 14 May 1990.

7 [1991] 2 All ER 225, 92 Cr App 68; [1991] Crim LR 41 CA. *The Times*, 20 July 1990.

8 As to this see the comment in [1990] Crim LR 710. *Spratt* was upheld in *Parmenter*, fn 7. A point of law was certified for the attention of the House of Lords and the Court remarked that: ". . . it seems scarcely credible that 129 years after the enactment of the Offences Against the Person Act, 1861, three appeals should come before this court within one week which reveal the law to be so impenetrable".

9 [1977] IR 360

10 Henchy J at 399.

to a mere requirement of causation.[11] Two factors are present which influenced the Supreme Court in *Murray*:[12] a difference in the external elements of the offence and a greatly enhanced penalty on the aggravating factor occurring. The contrary argument, that society is entitled to seek retribution in terms of the harm actually caused by the offence without reference to the purpose or foresight of its perpetrator is, it is submitted, overridden by these two elements.[13]

In *Parmenter*[14] the Court of Appeal decided that where a person is charged with assault occasioning actual bodily harm the offence is not made out if the accused acts without intending or appreciating the risk of the possibility of physical harm. In the case the jury's verdict on a charge of unlawfully and maliciously inflicting grievous bodily harm, contrary to s 20, had been given following a direction that the test of intent was objective and it was not, therefore, implicit in the verdict that the jury had found that the accused intended or recognised the risk of physical harm.[15]

Proof

It is submitted that proof of intent or recklessness as to bodily harm can be supplied by proof that the accused assaulted the victim intending or being aware that he would thereby interfere with the victim's health or comfort in a more than transient or trifling way. Such a mental element can be inferred from the circumstances proved by the prosecution, including the declarations of the accused, the nature of the attack, and the gravity of the injury to the victim.[16]

Wounding, Inflicting and Causing

6.20 S 20 and 18 of the Offences Against the Person Act, 1861 provide:

> 20 Whosoever shall unlawfully and maliciously wound or inflict any grievous bodily harm upon any other person, either with or without any weapon or instrument, shall be guilty of a misdemeanour, and being convicted thereof shall be liable to be kept in penal servitude for the term of five years.

> 18 Whosoever shall unlawfully and maliciously by any means whatsoever wound or cause any grievous bodily harm to any person, or shoot any person, or, by drawing a trigger or in any other manner attempt to discharge any kind of loaded arms at any

---

11 Walsh J proceeds with his analysis on the basis of discovering the true meaning of the intention of the Oireachtas. The High Court of Australia decided in *Coulter* (1980) 30 A Crim R 471 that the offence of assault occasioning actual bodily harm does not require an intent to cause that harm.

12 Henchy J at 395-96, Griffin J at 408-9, Kenny J at 421, Parke J agreeing at 424.

13 It can further be argued that in contrast to ss 18 and 20 of the Act the offence punished in s 47 is an assault and the words of aggravation are stated as a consequence, as opposed to an intent, as in s 18, or a type of injury as in s 20. The analysis in the text is supported, on consitutional grounds in *De Sousa* (1990) 62 CCC (3d) 95 CA Ontario, and on the grounds of construction in *Parish* (1990) 60 CCC (3d) 350 CA New Brunswick.

14 [1991] 2 All ER 225, 92 Cr App R CA.

15 See par 6.24. A point of law was certified for the attention of the House of Lords and the Court remarked that ". . . it seems scarcely credible that 129 years after the enactment of the Offences Against the Person Act, 1861, three appeals should come before this court within one week which reveal the law to be so impenetrable".

16 For recklessness see par 2.37. For proof of intent see ch 2. For the presumption that a person intends the natural and probable consequences of his action see par 2.20-2.28.

person, with intent in any of the cases aforesaid, to maim, disfigure, or disable any person, or to do some other grievous bodily harm to any person, or with intent to resist or prevent the lawful apprehension or detainer of any person, shall be guilty of felony, and being convicted thereof shall be liable to be kept in penal servitude for life.

Both of these sections are scheduled under the Criminal Law (Jurisdiction) Act, 1976 which means that these offences if committed in Northern Ireland will be offences contrary to s 2(1) of that Act.

A comparative analysis of the provisions of the 1861 Act is a futile exercise. Most were drawn from existing enactments[17] and placed together with no regard for structure or internal consistency.[18] S 20 does not require an assault but refers to wounding the victim or inflicting on him grievous bodily harm.

The authorities are now agreed that no assault is required for an "infliction".[19] Equally, s 18 does not require an assault but refers to wounding the victim or causing him grievous bodily harm with the ulterior intent mentioned in the section. The argument that an assault, or an assault occasioning actual bodily harm, was included in the, now repealed, section 19A of the Crimes Act (Victoria) 1858, which created the more serious offence of inflicting grievous bodily harm, was rejected by the Supreme Court of Victoria. Hence the jury were not empowered to enter a verdict on the lesser offence:[20]

> . . . We have come to the conclusion that although the word "inflicts" . . . does not have as wide a meaning as the word "causes" . . . the word "inflicts" does have a wider meaning than it would have if it were construed so that inflicting grievous bodily harm always involved assaulting the victim. . . . Grievous bodily harm may be inflicted . . . either where the accused has directly and violently "inflicted" it by assaulting the victim, or where the accused has "inflicted" it by doing something, intentionally, which, though it is not itself a direct application of force to the body of the victim, does directly result in force being applied violently to the body of the victim, so that he suffers grievous bodily harm. Hence, the lesser misdemeanours of assault occasioning actual bodily harm and common assault . . . are not necessarily included in the misdemeanour of inflicting grievous bodily harm. . . .[21]

Infliction

6.21 Examples of "infliction" under s 20 include causing a panic in a theatre by turning out the lights and placing an iron bar across the door, thus causing the patrons to crush one another;[22] frightening a woman so that she tried to climb out of a window, was restrained by her daughter, and then suffered a broken leg in a fall when the accused ordered that she be let go;[23] and chasing the victim so that he put his hand through a glass door.[24]

17   Stephen *History* III, 108-20.
18   Criminal Law Revision Committee, 14th Report Offences Against the Person (Cmnd 7844, 1980), par 149-251; Law Commission, Draft Criminal Code (No. 177, 1989).
19   *Salisbury* [1976] VR 452 SC Vict; *Wilson & Jenkins* [1984] AC 242; [1983] 2 All ER 448; [1983] 3 WLR 686 HL.
20   Ryan & Magee, 365-71.   21   At 641.
22   *Martin* (1881) 8 QBD 54; [1881-5] All ER 699, 14 Cox 633 CCR.
23   *Halliday* (1889) 61 LT 701; [1886-90] All ER 1028 CCR. Further see *Beech* (1912) 7 Cr App R 197, 23 Cox 181 CCA; *Lewis* [1970] Crim LR 647 CA.
24   *Cartledge v Allen* [1973] Crim LR 530.

The relaxation of the requirement that an assault must directly inflict violence on the victim, previously noted,[25] and the interpretation of "infliction" in *Salisbury*,[26] results in there being no practical difference between an offence under s 47 of assault occasioning actual bodily harm, and an offence under s 20. It is difficult to see the interpretation of *K (a minor)*[27] as being anything other than an infliction. Since an infliction is now construed as an assault the separate sections are super-fluous.[28]

S 20 uses the word "cause". This does not require an assault.[29] It is unfathomable as to how one causes grievous bodily harm to a person other than, to use the words in *Salisbury*, by a direct application of force to the body of the victim. Further "inflict" in ordinary language may mean no more than causing an unpleasant result.[30] *Smith & Hogan*[31] express the view:

> If force is applied, directly or indirectly by [the accused], harm is "inflicted". If harm is caused without the use of force, it is not inflicted but, if grievous, and intentionally caused, it may be the subject of an indictment under s 18.

Harm

6.22 The phase "grievous bodily harm" in ss 18 and 20 should, according to the House of Lords in *Smith*,[32] be given its ordinary and natural meaning of bodily harm of a really serious kind.[33] In *The People (A-G) v Messitt*[34] the Supreme Court approved that definition:

> Nor in the phrase "or do some other grievous bodily harm" is there anything to indicate bodily harm must be permanent. The only requirement is that it should be "grievous". . . I see no reason to seek a definition of "grievous" but if one should be sought then I think Lord Kilmuir's "really serious" in *Director of Public Prosecutions v Smith* [1961] AC 290, 334, is as simple and effective a definition as one could desire.[35]

25   See par 6.14.
26   Followed by the House of Lords in *Wilson & Jenkins* [1984] AC 242; [1983] 2 All ER 448; [1983] 3 WLR 686 HL.
27   [1990] 1 All ER 331, 91 Cr App R 23 DC, case stated, noted par 6.14.
28   Smith & Hogan 399 suggest that "force" is the common element to ss 47 and 20. Therefore *Clarence* (1888) 22 QBD 23; [1886-90] All ER 133, 16 Cox 511 CCR is distinguishable on the grounds that consensual intercourse giving the victim venereal disease does not involve force. The Courts in Australia have interpreted force in the context of rape, as being supplied by the simple act of sexual intercourse; Howard 151 and the authorities there cited.
29   *Austin* (1973) 58 Cr App R 163; [1973] Crim LR 778 CA; *Lambert* [1977] Crim LR 164.
30   The Shorter Oxford English Dictionary defines "inflict" as: "(a) To lay on as a stroke, blow or wound; to impose as something which must be suffered or endured; to cause to be born. (b) To impose something unwelcome".
31   399.
32   [1961] AC 290; [1960] 3 All ER 161; [1960] 3 WLR 546, 44 Cr App R 261 HL.
33   *Saunders* [1985] Crim LR 230 CA. In *Ashman* (1858) 1 F&F 88, 175 ER 638, Willes J instructed a jury that: "it is not necessary . . . [that grievous bodily harm] should be either permanent or dangerous: if it be such as seriously to interfere with comfort or health . . ."; *Cox* (1818) R&R 362, 168 ER 846 CCR; *Wood* (1830) 1 Mood 278, 4 C&P 381, 172 ER 749 CCR.
34   [1974] IR 406. And see *The People (A-G) v Goulding* [1964] Ir Jur Rep 54 where the Court of Criminal Appeal overruled a charge by a trial judge that grievous bodily harm meant an interference with the health or comfort of another and stated that the interference must be serious.
35   Ó Dálaigh CJ at 415, Walsh & Fitzgerald JJ agreeing.

6.23 The alternative external element describing harm in s 20 is a wound. This is also one of four possible external elements in s 18. It is insufficient to constitute a wound that the skin was broken only in the outer layer,[36] the injury must involve a breaking through the continuity of the whole skin, that is the inner and outer layers.[37] The injury need not be to the outer skin of the body provided it involves access through a bodily orifice as, for example, is the case with the mouth and rectum[38] so it is not a wound to injure the victim in the eye with a pellet fired from an air pistol, if the result is an internal rupture of the blood vessels.[39] The word wound, however, includes incised wounds, puncture wounds, lacerated wounds, contused wounds, and gunshot wounds.[40] It is usual in cases where a wounding is charged to have medical evidence available as to the nature of the injury.[41] It has been held in Australia that since penetration of the inner skin would cause free bleeding, evidence of such bleeding would be sufficient that a wound was inflicted.[42]

Mental Element, s 20

6.24 The mental element in s 20 is "maliciously". In this context the wounding or infliction of grievous bodily harm must be done by the accused intentionally or recklessly.[43] Logically, this implies that the accused either intended to wound or inflict grievous bodily harm, or took a substantial and unjustifiable risk that he might wound or inflict grievous bodily harm.[44] The English courts have, however, taken the view that an intention to cause fright or terror is equivalent to malice.[45] The facts of these cases in which this decision was reached are such that it was possible to infer foresight by the accused of serious harm to the victim.[46] The English courts have further decided that foresight of the particular kind of injury covered by s 20 is unnecessary once the accused foresaw physical harm to some other person. The leading decision is *Mowatt*.[47] The victim was robbed by a person who was in the company of the accused and who then ran away. The victim seized Mowatt and demanded to know his whereabouts. Mowatt knocked the victim down. Mowatt

---

36   *McLoughlin* (1838) 8 C&P 653, 173 ER.

37   *The People (A-G) v Messitt*, fn 34 at 412-13.

38   *C (a minor) v Eisenhower* [1984] QB 331; [1983] 3 All ER 230; [1983] 3 WLR 537; [1983] Crim LR 567 DC.

39   *Eisenhower*, fn 38 at 341.

40   *Shea* (1848) 3 Cox 141 (Ir).

41   Either by calling a doctor or admitting his report under s 21 of the Criminal Justice Act, 1984.

42   *Devine* (1982) 8 A Crim R 45 CCA Tas.

43   *Cunningham* [1957] 2 QB 396; [1957] 2 All ER 412; [1957] 3 WLR 76, 41 Cr App R 155 CCA.

44   For a discussion of intention see ch 2. For discussion of recklessness see par 2.37. As to the statement of alternative offences in mental states see rule 5 of the Indictment Rules under the Criminal Justice (Administration) Act, 1924, First Schedule.

45   *Halliday* (1889) 61 LT 701; [1886-90] All ER 1028 CCR. Further see *Beech* (1912) 7 Cr App R 197, 23 Cox 181 CCA; *Martin* (1881) 8 QBD 54; [1881-5] All ER 699, 14 Cox 633 CCR.

46   In *Martin*, fn 45, QBD at 57, the verdict of the jury was that the accused intended to cause terror. Professor Williams points out that this should be regarded as insufficient for a crime of maliciously inflicting harm; *TBCL* 195. However if Martin really only intended terror he need not have put an iron bar across the theatre door.

47   [1968] 1 QB 421; [1967] 3 All ER 47; [1967] 3 WLR 1192, 51 Cr App R 402 CA.

was seen by the police to sit astride the victim and rain a series of blows into his face, lift him up and throw him down on the ground, thereby wounding him and causing him serious harm. He was charged under s 18 but convicted of the lesser included offence under s 20. He appealed on the ground that the trial judge had failed to direct the jury on the meaning of "maliciously". The Court of Appeal dismissed the appeal.[48] On the mental element under s 20 they stated:

> In the offence under s 20, and in the alternative verdict which may be given on a charge under s 18—for neither of which is any specific intent required—the word "maliciously" does import on the part of the person who unlawfully inflicts the wound or other grievous bodily harm an awareness that his act may have the consequence of causing some physical harm to some other person. That is what is meant by "the particular kind of harm" in the citation from Professor Kenny's *Outlines of Criminal Law* [16th edition 1952, p 186]. It is quite unnecessary that the accused should have foreseen that his unlawful act might cause physical harm of the gravity described in the section, i.e. a wound or serious physical injury. It is enough that he should have foreseen that some physical harm to some person, albeit of a minor character might result.[49]

In contrast is the decision in *Savage*.[50] Bad feeling existed between two young ladies. One decided to throw the contents of a beer glass over the other. The glass slipped and caused a wound. The direction of the trial judge to the jury was clearly wrong: it was to the effect that if the accused let go of the glass unintentionally and this consequence of her unlawful assault caused a wound she would be liable for unlawful wounding under s 20. The Court of Appeal reversed the conviction, in effect holding that foresight of a wetting was insufficient for the charge to be made out. It follows that a wetting cannot constitute "some physical harm . . . albeit of a minor character".

It is possible to wonder what harm is sufficient. If that harm is to be identified, it is submitted, it can only be identified as it is stated in the section, that is, a wound or really serious harm. If the accused intends any lesser form of harm that coincidence of purposive action, or unjustified risk-taking, with an assault is clearly an assault occasioning actual bodily harm under s 47. As the legislature has specifically provided for such a situation with a distinct crime it is wrong to distort s 20 to make the offence thereby created equivalent to s 47. Further, it would be gravely inconsistent with basic principle to fail to require a mental element cast in the language of the section. Consequently, it is submitted, s 20 requires the voluntary infliction of a wound or grievous bodily harm, the accused intending such harm or being aware that such

---

48   The analysis of whether a direction should be given as to the meaning of malice is based on the then current notion that the foresight of an ordinary person is irrefutably attributed to the accused. For an analysis see par 2.25. As this is clearly wrong it is not reproduced here. It is submitted that the trial judge must instruct the jury on the meaning of intent and, if it is a live issue on the facts, recklessness.

49   QB at 426, All ER at 50, WLR at 1196, Cr App R at 406-7. It is a misdirection to indicate to the jury that the accused should have foreseen that his unlawful act might cause some physical harm, as the use of those words might indicate to the jury that the test was whether he ought to have foreseen the harm. The test is whether he actually foresaw that harm; *Parmenter* [1991] 2 All ER 225, 92 Cr App R 68; [1991] Crim LR 41 CA.

50   [1991] 2 All ER 220; [1990] Crim LR 709 CA.

harm may result and unjustifiably risking that occurrence.[51] By analogy with rape[52] as no one can be justified in risking a wound or grievous bodily harm to another person by means of an unlawful assault or infliction, there does not have to be a risk amounting to a probability present in the mind of the accused.

An analysis in the foregoing terms was accepted by the Court of Appeal in *Parmenter*.[53] The court held that the mental element under s 20 required that the accused intend to cause the particular kind of harm specified in the section or was reckless as to whether he did so: it was insufficient to merely establish that the accused had committed the assault which had caused the harm.

Mental Element, s 18

6.25 The mental element under s 18 is also expressed in terms of malice. The basic mental element is therefore equivalent to s 20[54] but also requires an ulterior intent. It is appropriate to echo the comment of Stephen[55] that the section is laboriously complex, creating 24 separate offences by means of 4 external acts coupled with 6 possible intents.[56] The scheme of the section presents itself thus:

1. Wounding
2. Causing grievous bodily harm[57]
3. Shooting at any person
4. Trying to fire loaded arms at any person

Done with any one of the following six intents:

1. An intent to maim
2. An intent to disfigure
3. An intent to disable
4. An intent to do some other grievous bodily harm
5. An intent to resist lawful apprehension
6. An intent to resist lawful detainer

Intent

Intention in this context is a concept of general application which has already been considered in the context of murder.[58] Intent must be proved as stated in the indictment. Where the accused is charged, for example, with an intent to do grievous bodily harm, and the jury find that his acts were done to resist his lawful apprehension he must be acquitted.[59] Intent may be coincident. Thus an accused may intend to prevent his lawful apprehension through causing grievous bodily harm and so may

---

51 Now see *Parmenter*, fn 49 and see par 6.19.
52 See ch 8.
53 [1991] 2 All ER 225, 92 Cr App R 68.
54 See par 6.24.   55 *History* III, 117.
56 As to the statement of these in the alternative see rule 5 of the Indictment Rules under the Criminal Justice (Administration) Act, 1924. A count is not bad for duplicity under this section, for speficying the intent in the alternative; *Naismith* [1961] 2 All ER 735; [1961] 1 WLR 952 C-MAC.
57 See par 6.22.
58 See par 2.19. In England intention has the same meaning in this context as in the law of murder; *Smith & Hogan*, 402.
59 *Duffin & Marshall* (1818) R&R 365, 168 ER 1031 CCR.

be convicted on a charge which contains his latter intent.[60] Intent is proved in the same way as on a murder charge.[61]

Situations can occur where a maiming, or grievous bodily harm, can occur due to the voluntary act of the accused, without his having such an intent. So in *Abraham*[62] the victim was a gamekeeper who had ordered the accused, a poacher, off land. The accused ran off but after having gone some 50 yards shot the victim. Parke B ruled that as the intention of the accused was to frighten the victim rather than to inflict an injury he could not be convicted.

It is submitted that the approach to intent under s 18 should be no different to that in murder. Where the accused has a purpose which he fulfils, knowing that the harm covered by the section is a highly probable or virtually certain consequence of his action, it may be inferred that he intended that harm.[63]

6.26 If the indictment is cast in form of an intent to cause, for example, grievous bodily harm to A but the accused misses and wounds B, he may be indicted for wounding B with intent to cause grievous bodily harm to A.[64] If the accused intends to cause grievous bodily harm to a person he believes to be A, but is in fact B, he may be convicted of wounding that person with intent to cause him grievous bodily harm.[65] It has been held that an intent to resist lawful apprehension is not negatived by the accused believing that it is unlawful.[66] It is submitted that this is incorrect. In such a case the purpose of the accused is to resist an unlawful arrest, and in terms of the mental element of crime he is entitled to be judged on the facts as he believed them to be.[67]

Harm

6.27 A maim is an injury to a part of a man's body which may render him less able for fighting.[68] A disfigurement is an external injury which may detract from the personal appearance of the victim.[69] To disable is to create a permanent disability, which is beyond a temporary injury.[70] This archaic phraseology was subjected to a modern analysis in *The People (A-G) v Messitt*,[71] Ó Dálaigh CJ for the Supreme Court stating:

60   *Gillow* (1825) 1 Mood CC 85, 168 ER 1195 CCR.
61   See ch 2. In *Wheeler* (1844) 1 Cox 106, Alderson B instructed the jury that striking a blow was not of itself sufficient to show an intent to do grievous bodily harm even though grievous bodily harm thereby resulted. It is submitted that this was incorrect. A person is presumed to intend the natural and probable consequences of his action and the question therefore is whether or not grievous bodily harm would result from the kind of blow struck by the accused and as to whether there is any evidence to suggest that this may not have been his purpose.
62   (1845) 1 Cox 208.
63   See par 2.22.
64   *Monger* [1973] Crim LR 301 CCR. Further see *Smith & Hogan* 402.
65   *Smith* (1855) Dear 559, 169 ER 845, 7 Cox 51 CCA; *Stopford* (1870) 11 Cox 643.
66   *Bentley* (1850) 4 Cox 406.
67   *Williams* [1987] 3 All ER 411; (1983) 78 Cr App R 276; [1984] Crim LR 163 CA.
68   1 Hawk ch 55, s 1; *Sullivan* (1841) C&M 209, 174 ER 475.
69   Archbold (1922) 940.
70   *Boyce* (1824) 1 Mood 29, 168 ER 1172.
71   [1974] IR 406 at 414.

The use of the words "or to do some other grievous bodily harm" after the words "maim, disfigure or disable" indicate if it were necessary to do so, that "maiming" and "disfiguring" and "disabling" are, severally, species of "grievous bodily harm". To maim is to do an injury to the body which causes loss of a limb or the use of it; here it seems to me permanency is an element. But "disable" and "disfigure" do not necessarily employ permanency; indeed modern surgical skills can go a great distance to undoing what heretofore would formerly have been "disablement" or "disfigurement".

Reform

6.28 The law penalising serious assaults is in a state of chaos. The Criminal Law Revision Committee[72] propose retaining the present law on common assault but replacing sections 47, 20 and 18 with offences of:

1. Intentionally causing serious injury (maximum of life imprisonment).

2. Recklessly causing serious injury (maximum of five years' imprisonment).

3. Intentionally or recklessly causing injury (maximum of three years' imprisonment).

While this scheme is not ideal and may pay insufficient attention to the varying degree of harm and blame which occur in assaults it is clearly better than what we presently have. Manslaughter may be committed by criminal negligence. The mental element of this crime does not require an awareness in the accused person that his action was likely to lead to death or serious injury.[73] An assault may only be committed by intention or recklessness.[74] It is anomalous for the law to be framed in such a way that an accused is guilty of manslaughter if the victim dies due to his criminal negligence but may be guilty of no offence if the victim is seriously injured and lives on. It is submitted that any reform of this law should make it an offence to cause injury by a criminally negligent act or omission.

Other Assaults with Intent

6.29 The complex character of the offences already considered is compounded by the existence of several other crimes comprising the infliction of harm with ultérior intent. Most, however, are of little practical importance, reflecting the social conditions in the mid-Victorian era. Ss 11, 12, 13, 14 and 15 of the 1861 Act punish acts done with intent to commit murder.[75] The offence of choking with intent, contrary to s 21, is considered under the heading of poison.[76] Offences concerned with the use of explosives with ulterior intent are considered in chapter 9.

Placing a Man Trap

6.30 S 31 of the Offences Against the Person Act, 1861 provides:

Whosoever shall set or place, or cause to be set or placed, any spring gun, man trap, or other engine calculated to destroy human life or inflict grievous bodily harm, with the intent that the same or whereby the same may destroy or inflict grievous bodily

72 14th Report Offences Against the Person (Cmnd 7844, 1980), par 149-251.
73 See par 3.10.   74 See par 6.16.
75 See par 2.38.   76 See par 7.15-7.16.

harm upon a trespasser or other person coming into contact therewith, shall be guilty of a misdemeanour, and being convicted thereof shall be liable to be kept in penal servitude for the term of five years; and whosoever shall knowingly and wilfully permit any such spring gun, man trap, or other engine which may have been set or placed in any place then being in or afterwards coming into his possession or occupation by some other person to continue so set or placed, shall be deemed to have set and placed such gun, trap, or engine with such intent as aforesaid: provided that nothing in this section contained shall extend to make it illegal to set or place any gin or trap such as may have been or may be usually set or placed with the intent of destroying vermin: provided also, that nothing in this section shall be deemed to make it unlawful to set or place or cause to be set or placed, or to be continued set or placed, from sunset to sunrise, any spring gun, man trap, or other engine which shall be set or placed, or caused or continued to be set or placed, in a dwelling house, for the protection thereof.[77]

The meaning and proof of intent has been previously considered.[78] It has been held that it is manslaughter to cause death by an engine set in contravention of this section.[79] This section, however, requires an intention to kill or inflict grievous bodily harm, and if death thus results it is murder, not manslaughter.[80] An alarm gun loaded with a live cartridge containing shot is an engine within the meaning of the section[81] as is a spring gun loaded with a live cartridge.[82] In *Munks*[83] the Court of Criminal Appeal held that an "engine" meant a mechanical contrivance and did not therefore apply to an arrangement of electric wires contrived to administer a possibly fatal shock to any intruder into the accused's house. Such a contrivance can be used to assault someone. Death resulting from the use of it would be manslaughter.[84]

With Intent to Commit Felony

6.31 S 38 of the Offences Against the Person Act, 1861 provides:

Whosoever shall assault any person with intent to commit felony . . . shall be guilty of a misdemeanour, and being convicted thereof shall be liable, at the discretion of the Court, to be imprisoned for any term not exceeding two years, with or without hard labour.[85]

---

77   Misdemeanour: three years' penal servitude or two years' imprisonment: indictable: Circuit Court jurisdiction.

78   See ch 2. Thus in *Bavastock* [1954] Crim LR 625 mistakenly putting a loaded cartridge into a spring gun set merely to frighten poachers was held not to be within the section. The Court also held that the section did not create absolute liability but put the burden of proof on the defence to establish that the accused had no intent or guilty knowledge. There seems no warrant for this latter analysis.

79   *Heaton* (1896) 60 JP 508.

80   Criminal Justice Act, 1964, s 4.

81   *Smith & York* (1902) 37 LJ (Newsp) 89; Archbold (1922) 952.

82   *Bavastock*, fn 78.

83   [1964] 1 QB 304; [1963] 3 All ER 757; [1963] 3 WLR 952, 48 Cr App R 56 CCA. Electricity is a noxious thing for the purposes of ss 23 and 24; Donald, *The Times*, 9 May 1955. The section does not apply to instruments set with intent to injure other than human beings such as dog-spears; *Jordin v Crump* (1841) 8 M&W 782, 151 ER 1256; *Wootton v Dawkins* (1857) 2 CB (NS) 412, 140 ER 477. I am indebted to a member of An Garda Síochána for the following example of an offence under the section: A man was tired of his car being continually taken, he wedged a dagger between the seat and the floor and on coming back and finding his car broken into there was blood on the seat.

84   *Pratt, The Times*, 9 October 1976.

85   Assault is an alternative verdict.

The elements of the offence consist of an assault with an intent to commit any felony. The intent is proved in the same way as in murder.[86] Most commonly the victim will be assaulted by the accused who has an intention of stealing something.[87] It is an offence contrary to s 62, to assault a person with intent to commit buggery.[88] It is also an offence, contrary to s 40, to assault a seaman with intent to hinder him.[89]

Robbery

For the sake of completeness mention must be made of the offences of robbery, and of assault with intent to rob, which of their nature involve the use or threat of force. S 23 of the Larceny Act, 1916 as inserted by s 5 of the Criminal Law (Jurisdiction) Act, 1976 provides:

> (1) A person is guilty of robbery if he steals, and immediately before or at the time of doing so, and in order to do so, he uses force on any person or puts or seeks to put any person in fear of being then and there subjected to force.

> (2) A person guilty of robbery or of an assault with intent to rob, shall be liable on conviction on indictment to imprisonment for life.[90]

Stealing is defined in s 1 of the Larceny Act, 1916 as fraudulently taking and carrying away, without the consent of the owner and without a claim of right made in good faith, anything capable of being stolen with intent, at the time of such taking, permanently to deprive the owner thereof.[91]

It is a matter for the jury to determine whether force was used or threatened against any person. The judge should direct the jury as to the necessity for this element and thereafter it is a matter for their common sense and knowledge of the world.[92] It has been held to be a use of force to nudge a person so that he momentarily loses his balance[93] and to wrench a bag from a shopper's hand.[94] An intent to rob, in this context, is proved in the same way as intent in the crime of murder.[95] Typically the accused may threaten the victim with a weapon, demanding money or push into a person on a street attempting, either himself or through accomplices, to rifle through the victim's bag or search their person. Under subs 1 the prosecution

---

86   Ch 2.

87   Larceny Act, 1916, s 2.   88   See par 8.51.

89   Whosoever shall unlawfully and with force hinder or prevent any seaman, keelman, or caster from working at or exercising his lawful trade, business, or occupation, or shall beat or use any violence to any such person with intent to hinder or prevent him from working at or exercising the same, shall, on conviction thereof before two Justices of the Peace, be liable to be imprisoned and kept to hard labour in the common gaol or house of correction for any term not exceeding three months; provided that no person who shall be punished for any such offence by reason of this section shall be punished for the same offence by virtue of any other law whatsoever.

90   Assault is clearly an alternative verdict. Felony; this offence is scheduled under s 2 of the Criminal Law (Jurisdiction) Act, 1976. If committed in Northern Ireland it therefore constitutes an offence contrary to s 2. For precedent indictment see chs 9 and 10.

91   See further *McCutcheon*, 22-40.

92   *Dawson & James* (1976) 64 Cr App R 170 CCA.

93   *Dawson & James*, fn 92.

94   *Clouden* [1987] Crim LR 56 CA. Further see *McCutcheon* 69-74. The corresponding section in England is s 8 of the Theft Act, 1968.

95   Ch 2.

must prove that something was stolen but under subs 2 they need only prove that the accused had an intent to rob the victim.

Assaults on Particular Victims

6.32 An assault may also be aggravated by the status of the victim. A number of statutes impose increased penalty for an assault where the person assaulted is a member of a law enforcement agency, or is engaged on a task which is sought to be protected by the imposition of an aggravated penalty. It is an offence to interfere with a clergyman,[96] to assault an officer assisting a vessel in distress,[97] to assault a Garda,[98] to interfere with a seaman,[99] to impede persons escaping from shipwrecks[1] and to shoot at a customs officer.[2]

96 Offences Against the Person Act, 1861, s 36: "Whosoever shall, by threats or force, obstruct or prevent, or endeavour to obstruct or prevent, any clergyman or other minister in or from celebrating divine service or otherwise officiating in any church, chapel, meeting house, or other place of divine worship, or in or from the performance of his duty in the lawful burial of the dead in any churchyard or any other burial place, or shall strike or offer any violence to, or shall, upon any civil process, or under the pretence of executing any civil process, arrest any clergyman or other minister who is engaged in, or to the knowledge of the offender is about to be engaged in, any of the rights or duties in this section aforesaid, or who to the knowledge of the offender shall be going to perform the same or returning from the performance thereof, shall be guilty of a misdemeanour and being convicted thereof shall be liable thereof, at the discretion of the court, to be imprisoned for any term not exceeding two years with or without hard labour". On the meaning of divine service see *Matthews v King* [1934] 1 KB 505, 30 Cox 27. The sections are quoted, as are all other sections from the Offences Against the Person Act, 1861, in accordance with the amendments introduced by the Penal Servitude Acts of 1864 and 1891 and by the Statute Law Revision Act, 1908.

97 Offences Against the Person Act, 1861, s 37: "Whosover shall assault and strike or wound any magistrate, officer, or other perons whatsoever lawfully authorised, in or on account of the exercise of his duty in or concerning the preservation of any vessel in distress, or of any vessel, goods, or effects wrecked, stranded, or cast on shore, or lying under water, shall be guilty of a misdemeanour, and being convicted thereof shall be liable to be kept in penal servitude for any term not exceeding seven years".

98 See par 6.34.

99 Offences Against the Person Act, 1861, s 40: "Whosoever shall unlawfully and with force hinder or prevent any seaman, keelman, or caster from working at or exercising his lawful trade, business or occupation, or shall beat or use any violence to any such person with intent to hinder or prevent him from working at or exercising the same, shall, on conviction thereof, before two Justices of the Peace, be liable to be imprisoned and kept to hard labour in the common gaol or house of correction for any term not exceeding three months: provided that no person who shall be punished for any such offence by reason of this section shall be punished for the same offence by virtue of any other law whatsoever".

1   Offences Against the Person Act, 1861, s 17: "Whosoever shall unlawfully and maliciously prevent or impede any person, being on board of or having quitted any ship or vessel which shall be in distress, or wrecked, stranded, or cast on shore, in his endeavour to save his life, or shall unlawfully and maliciously prevent or impede any person in his endeavour to save the life of any such person as in this section aforesaid, shall be guilty of felony, and being convicted thereof shall be liable to be kept in penal servitude for life". See also Merchant Shipping Act, 1906, ss 30, 36 and 43 as to leaving seamen behind.

2   Customs Consolidation Act, 1876, s 193: "If any person shall maliciously shoot at any vessel or boat belonging to his Majesty's navy, or in the service of the Revenue, or shall maliciously shoot at, maim, or wound any officer of the army, navy, marines, or coast guard, being duly employed in the prevention of smuggling, and on full pay, or any officer of customs or excise, or any person acting in his aid or assistance, or duly employed for the prevention of smuggling, in the execution

6.33 Where an offence is cast as a wrong done to a particular class of persons then for the accused to be guilty of that offence, he must be aware that the victim belongs to that particular class.[3] In *The People (DPP) v Murray*[4] three members of the Supreme Court expressly stated that in a prosecution for assaulting a police officer in the execution of his duty an awareness of the status for the victim was essential.[5] The mental element in this context requires recklessness: that the accused consciously disregarded a substantial and unjustifiable risk that the victim was of the status described in the offence.[6] The most important category of aggravated assault is the offence of assaulting a Garda.

Assault on Garda

6.34 Two separate enactments make it an offence to assault, resist or obstruct a Garda. The difference between them is that the later enactment is triable summarily only. S 38 of the Offences Against the Person Act, 1861 provides:

> Whosoever . . . shall assault, resist, or wilfully obstruct any Peace Officer, in the due execution of his duty, or any person acting in aid of such officer, or shall assault any person with intent to resist or prevent the lawful apprehension or detainer of himself or of any other person for any offence, shall be guilty of a misdemeanour, and being convicted thereof shall be liable, at the discretion of the court, to be imprisoned for any term not exceeding two years, with or without hard labour.[7]

The other offence, which covers precisely the same wrong, is created by s 12 of the Prevention of Crimes Act, 1871 as extended by the Prevention of Crimes Amendment Act, 1885, which by s 1 thereof if construed as one with the earlier Act:

1871   12 Where any person is convicted of an assault on any Constable when in the execution of his duty, such person shall be guilty of an offence against this Act, and shall, in the discretion of the Court, be liable to either pay a penalty not exceeding twenty pounds, and in default of payment to be imprisoned, with or without hard labour, for a term not exceeding six months; or to be imprisoned for any term not exceeding six months, or in case such person has been convicted of a similar assault within two years, nine months, with or without hard labour.

1885   2 The provisions of the twelfth section of the said recited Act shall apply to all cases of resisting or wilfully obstructing any constable or peace officer when in the execution of his duty. Provided that in cases to which the said Act is extended by this Act the person convicted shall not be liable to pay a greater penalty than five pounds,

of his office or duty, every person so offending, and every person aiding, abetting or assisting therein, shall, upon conviction, be adjudged guilty of felony, and shall be liable, at the discretion of the court, to penal servitude for any term not less than five years, or to be imprisoned for any term not exceeding three years".

3   See par 2.36.

4   [1977] IR 360.

5   Walsh J at 382, Henchy J at 398-99, Parke J agreeing with Henchy J at 424. Griffin J did not reach a conclusion on the cases at 411 and Kenny J at 420-21 did not consider the matter.

6   Henchy J at 403-5, Griffin J at 414, Kenny J at 421, Parke J agreeing with Henchy and Griffin JJ at 424. The headnote of this case is wrong in stating that knowledge of the status of the victim is required.

7   If the accused is charged with assaulting a Garda in the execution of his duty assault would be an alternative verdict if the accused was not aware that the victim was a Garda.

or in default of payment to be imprisoned, with or without hard labour, for a greater term than two months.[8]

Background to Offence

Members of An Garda Síochána operate within a common law scheme whereby they are obliged to keep the peace and to prevent and detect crime. The powers which they have are limited and arise from common law or statute. A duty to act does not necessarily imply a power. If any Garda action involves the infringement of the legal or constitutional rights of a citizen it must be justified as an exercise, in good faith, of some lawful authority.[9] An officer will be acting lawfully, and thus in the course of his duties, only if his actions are within the ambit of the power conferred by statute.[10] An officer can, however, do anything which an ordinary citizen might do with impunity.[11]

It can be argued that as the quoted sections require the officer to be acting "in the due execution of his duties" this implies that the act in question must have been done in fulfilment of an obligation.[12] This argument has been rejected in England[13] and, if correct, is limited in its scope. Our law lacks a coherent statement of the inter-relationship between Garda duties and powers, on the one hand, and the right of the citizen to resist, if necessary by force, an infringement of his rights.

It is submitted that the correct approach is to examine the Garda action in those terms (1) whether the Garda was acting to enforce the law, to keep the peace, or to detect crime; (2) whether there was an interference with any recognised legal or constitutional right of a citizen; (3) if there was such an interference it can only be justified by reference to a police power exercised, in good faith, within the ambit of that power laid down by statute, or by common law; (4) if the actions are not within the ambit of the exercise of such power they are unlawful and can thus not have been done in the due execution of duty.[14] It is outside the scope of this work to give a detailed exposition of police powers.[15] The obscurities of these powers, and the divergence of our law from that in the United Kingdom renders a short treatment necessary.

---

8   Misdemeanour, alternative verdict of assault charged with assault on a constable, twenty pounds fine or six months' imprisonment, nine months if a previous conviction within two years, for resisting or wilfully obstructing only the fine of £5, imprisonment and default; summary only; District Court has jurisdiction.

9   *Waterfield* [1964] 1 QB 164; [1963] 3 All ER 659; [1963] 3 WLR 946, 48 Cr App R 42 CCA; *Collins v Wilcock* [1984] 3 All ER 374; [1984] 1 WLR 1172, 79 Cr App R 229; [1984] Crim LR 481 CA.

10 *Pedro v Diss* [1981] 2 All ER 59, 72 Cr App R 193 DC.

11 *Malone v Metropolitan Police Commissioner* [1980] QB 49; [1979] 1 All ER 256; [1978] 3 WLR 936, 69 Cr App R 4; [1978] Crim LR 555 CA.

12 *Roxburgh* (1871) 12 Cox 8; *Betts v Steven* [1910] 1 KB 1; [1908-10] All ER 1245, 22 Cox 187 DC.

13 *Coffin* v Smith (1980) 71 Cr App R 221 DC.

14 In *Donnelly v Jackman* [1970] 1 All ER 987; [1970] 1 WLR 562, 54 Cr App R 229, the Divisional Court considers that a trivial interference, such as an unwelcome tap on the shoulder, did not amount to a sufficient wrong to bring the officer outside the course of his duties; *Pounder v Police* [1971] NZLR 1808 SC Auckland; *Bentley v Brudzinski* (1982) 75 Cr App R 217; [1982] Crim LR 825 DC; *Waterfield*, fn 7.

15 Ryan & Magee 84-176; Charleton, 23-43; Charleton, "The Powers of the Police" (1982) Gazette ICLSI 77-82, 101-5; Leigh, *Police Powers* (1st ed, 1935) ch 11.

Arrest

6.35 At common law a constable may arrest without warrant a person whom he finds committing a felony or on reasonably suspecting that a felony has been committed and of the person arrested being the perpetrator.[16] There is no power to arrest for misdemeanour after commission save where same has been given by statute.[17] Where the misdemeanour is committed in the presence of an officer he may arrest.[18] A police officer may also arrest[19] for breach of the peace, and on reasonably anticipating a breach takes such other steps as are necessary to prevent same.[20] The police may take reasonable steps to control the passage of traffic on the highway. An instruction given with the purpose of clearing such an obstruction is lawful.[21] A breach of the peace occurs where harm is done, or is likely to be done, to a person or to the property of a person, in his presence, or where a person is put in fear of being harmed through an assault, an affray, a riot, an unlawful assembly or other disturbance.[22] A constable may also arrest a person who has threatened to kill, beat or hurt another or to break the peace in his presence, provided that other complains to him at once.[23] The object of this power is not to prosecute but to bring the alleged wrongdoer before the District Court to be bound over to keep the peace.[24]

In addition many statutes give powers of arrest which can only be validly exercised within the conditions therein set out.[25] The most important, and it seems, generally exercised power of arrest and search is contained under ss 29 and 30 of the Offences Against the State Act, 1939:

---

16 Bullen & Leake (3rd ed., 1868) 795; *Dumbell v Roberts* [1944] 1 All ER 326 CA; Williams, "Arrest for Felony at Common Law" [1954] Crim LR 408.

17 *Griffin v Coleman* (1859) 4 H&N 265, 28 LJ Ex 134, 157 ER 840; *Kenlin v Gardiner* [1967] 2 QB 510; [1966] 3 All ER 931; [1967] 2 WLR 129 DC.

18 *Price v Seeley* (1843) 10 CL&F 28, 8 ER 651 HL; *Derecourt v Corbishley* (1855) 5 E&B 188, 119 ER 451; *North v Pullen* [1962] Crim LR 97 DC. See particularly the commentary in *North v Pullen* in the Crim LR which comments that common law arrest for misdemeanours is limited to breaches of the peace notwithstanding that the Divisional Court approved a statement in *Russell* which is ambiguous in that it suggests that there is a power of arrest for a misdemeanour committed in the presence of a police officer which does not amount to a breach of the peace. *Ryan & Magee* 97 confirms that there is no power of arrest at common law on suspicion of a misdemeanour other than in connection with a breach of the peace. This is the experience of the writer. To this it should be added that a police officer who does not witness a breach of the peace may arrest a wrong doer when called upon to do so by any person who did see the breach occur; *Timothy v Simpson* (1835) 1 CM&R 757. Further seen Williams, "Arrest for Breach of the Peace" [1954] Crim LR 588. The power to arrest for breach of the peace is also vested in a citizen.

19 *Howell* [1922] QB 416; [1981] 3 All ER 383; [1981] 3 WLR 501, 71 Cr App R 31 CA.

20 *Humphries v Connor* (1867) 17 Ir CLR 1; *Coyne v Tweedy* [1898] 2 IR 167; *O'Kelly v Harvey* (1879) 14 LR Ir 105; *Connors v Pearson* [1921] 2 IR 51.

21 *Broome* [1974] AC 587; [1974] 1 All ER 314; [1974] 2 WLR 58 HL; *Kavanagh v Hiscock* [1974] QB 600; [1974] 2 All ER 177; [1974] 2 WLR 421; [1974] Crim LR 255 DC.

22 *Howell*, fn 19. Williams, "Arrest for Breach of the Peace" [1954] Crim LR 578 at 579 considers that the definition of a breach of the peace must always envisage danger.

23 *Russell* 661, citing 2 Hale 88.

24 *Russell* 661.

25 A table of statutory powers of arrest is found at *Ryan and Magee* 525-33.

29 (1) Where a member of the Garda Síochána not below the rank of superintendent is satisfied that there is reasonable ground for believing that evidence of or relating to the commission or intended commission of an offence under this Act or the Criminal Law Act, 1976, or an offence which is for the time being a scheduled offence for the purposes of Part V of this Act, or evidence relating to the commission or intended commission of treason, is to be found in any building or part of a building or in any vehicle, vessel, aircraft or hovercraft or in any other place whatsoever, he may issue to a member of the Garda Síochána not below the rank of sergeant a search warrant under this section in relation to such place. (2) A search warrant under this section shall operate to authorise the member of the Garda Síochána named in the warrant, accompanied by any members of the Garda Síochána or the Defence Forces, to enter, within one week from the date of the warrant, and if necessary by the use of force, any building or part of a building or any vehicle, vessel, aircraft or hovercraft or any other place named in the warrant, and to search it and any person found there, and to seize anything found there or on such person. (3) A member of the Garda Síochána or the Defence Forces acting under the authority of a search warrant under this section may—(a) demand the name and address of any person found where the search takes place, and (b) arrest without warrant any such person who fails or refuses to give his name and address when demanded, or gives a name or address which is false or misleading or which the member with reasonable cause suspects to be false or misleading. (4) Any person who obstructs or attempts to obstruct any member of the Garda Síochána or the Defence Forces acting under the authority of a search warrant under this section or who fails or refuses to give his name and address when demanded, or gives a name or address which is false or misleading, shall be guilty of an offence and shall be liable—(a) on summary conviction, to a fine not exceeding £500 or to imprisonment for a term not exceeding 12 months, or to both, or (b) on conviction on indictment to imprisonment for a term not exceeding 5 years. (5) Any reference in subs (1) of this section to an offence includes a reference to attempting or conspiring to commit the offence.

30 (1) A member of the Garda Síochána (if he is not in uniform on production of his identification card if demanded) may without warrant stop, search, interrogate and arrest any person, or do any one or more of those things in respect of any person, whom he suspects of having committed or being about to commit or being or having been concerned in the commission of an offence under any section or sub-section of this Act or an offence which is for the time being a scheduled offence for the purposes of Part V of this Act or whom he suspects of carrying a document relating to the commission or intended commission of any such offence as aforesaid or whom he suspects of being in possession of information relating to the commission or intended commission of any such offence as aforesaid. (2) Any member of the Garda Síochána (if he is not in uniform on production of his identification card if demanded) may, for the purpose of the exercise of any of the powers conferred by the next preceding sub-section of this section, stop and search (if necessary by force) any vehicle or any ship, boat or other vessel which he suspects to contain a person whom he is empowered by the said sub-section to arrest without warrant. (3) Whenever a person is arrested under this section, he may be removed to and detained in custody in a Garda Síochána station, a prison, or some other convenient place for a period of twenty four hours from the time of his arrest and may, if an officer of the Garda Síochána not below the rank of Chief Superintendent so directs, be so detained for a further period of twenty-four hours. (4) A person detained under the next preceding sub-section of this section may, at any time during such detention, be charged before the District Court or a Special Criminal Court with an offence or be released by direction of an officer of the Garda Síochána, and shall, if not so charged or released, be released at the expiration of the detention authorised by the said sub-section. (5) A member of the

Garda Síochána may do all or any of the following things in respect of a person detained under this section, that is to say:—(a) demand of such person his name and address; (b) search such person or cause him to be searched; (d) photograph such person or cause him to be photographed; (e) take, or cause to be taken, the fingerprints of such person. (6) Every person who shall obstruct or impede the exercise in respect of him by a member of the Garda Síochána of any of the powers conferred by the next preceding sub-section of this section or shall fail or refuse to give his name and address or shall give, in response to any such demand, a name or an address which is false or misleading shall be guilty of an offence under this section and shall be liable on summary conviction thereof to imprisonment for a term not exceeding six months.

Under s 30 a person may be arrested for questioning both on suspicion of the commission of a scheduled offence and on suspicion of having information relating to a scheduled offence, whether same has been committed, or is intended. The section applies to all suspected criminals and not just to those who are suspected of being intent on undermining the institutions of the state.[26] Once arrested under this section a person may be questioned for any offence to which the scheduled offence is linked.[27] The lawfulness of the detention, or the extension of the detention, under s 30, is not dependent on the offence or the suspected offence which is the occasion for the detention, being the dominant concern of the members of the Garda Síochána when they may wish to question a detained person in respect of another offence. The arresting officer must be genuinely concerned with investigating a scheduled offence, albeit in the context of a more serious offence to which s 30 does not apply. The section cannot be used as a colourable device to arrest someone on a more serious charge. The classic example of a wrongful arrest is an arrest for malicious damage to a knife in order to investigate a murder where the knife suffered damage by contact with the skull of the victim. What cannot be done lawfully is to arrest a person by virtue of the powers given in s 30 of the Offences Against the State Act simply to make him available for the investigation of some other offence.[28] An arrest is lawful only if the accused is aware of the power under which he has been arrested.[29]

An arrest for felony, and most statutory powers of arrest, can only be made on reasonable suspicion of the accused's guilt. A power of arrest is also given to any person who finds another committing an indictable offence at night.[30] Reasonable suspicion does not require that the person arresting be certain of guilt but the arrest must be based on some information which will show that they acted reasonably.[31]

---

26   *The People (DPP) v Walsh* [1988] ILRM 137.

27   *The People (DPP) v Quilligan & O'Reilly (No. 2)* [1987] ILRM 606.

28   *The People (DPP) v Howley* [1989] ILRM 629 SC.

29   *The People (A-G) v McDermott* (1974) 2 Frewen 211; *The People (DPP) v Campbell & Others* (1983) 2 Frewen 131 CCA. The burden of proof is on the accused that he was not so aware.

30   The Prevention of Offences Act, 1851, s 11: "It shall be lawful for any person whatsoever to apprehend any person who shall be found committing any indictable offence in the night, and to convey or deliver him to some constable or other police officer, in order to his being conveyed, as soon as conveniently may be, before a justice of the peace, to be dealt with according to law". And by s 12: "If any person liable to be apprehended under the provisions of this Act shall assault or offer any violence to any person by law authorised to apprehend or detain him, or to any person acting in his aid or assistance, every such offender shall be guilty of a misdemeanour, and being convicted thereof shall be liable to be imprisoned . . . for any term not exceeding three years."

31   *Williams* [1954] Crim LR at 416.

In that context the Gardaí are entitled to have regard to matters outside the scope of admissible evidence[32] including ostensibly reliable hearsay.[33]

Reasonable force may be used to effect an arrest or to terminate violence subsequent to an arrest.[34] The reasonableness of the force used is to be judged by the nature of the resistance put up by the accused and, it is submitted, in extreme cases, by the nature of the offence arrested for or the evil which is sought to be prevented.[35]

Force may also be used in the suppression of an unlawful assembly but the degree of force used must always be moderate and proportionate to the circumstances of the case and the end to be attained.[36]

Testing and Questioning

6.36 In general a person may not be arrested for the purpose of questioning[37] but the time between arrest and charge may be used to question the suspect.[38] Where a person is arrested without a warrant by a Garda, on an offence which carries a possible maximum term of imprisonment of five years or more, he may be detained for the purpose of questioning if, on being taken to a Garda station, the member in charge considers there are reasonable grounds for believing that the detention is necessary for the proper investigation of the offence.[39] The normal period of detention of six hours may be extended by a superintendent for a further six hours.[40] The total period may be interrupted by illness or sleep. Where there is sufficient evidence to charge the accused he must be charged unless he is also detained on another offence.[41] The accused may be questioned, searched, swabbed or have skin or hair samples taken for firearms or explosives tests, have his property seized, and on the authority of a Superintendent, may be photographed and fingerprinted.[42] Strict regulations are to be observed in respect of this form of custody.[43] A person arrested under the Offences Against the State Act, 1939 may also be fingerprinted.[44]

---

32   *Hussein v Chong Fook Kam* [1970] AC 942; [1969] 3 All ER 1626; [1970] 2 WLR 441 PC.

33   *Lister v Perryman* (1870) LR 4 HL 521; *The People (DPP) v McCaffrey*, Court of Criminal Appeal, unreported 30 July 1984.

34   *Dowman v Ireland*, High Court, unreported, 5 July 1985, Barron J; *Reed v Wastie* [1972] Crim LR 221.

35   *Turner* [1962] VR 30 SC.

36   *Lynch v Fitzgerald (No. 2)* [1938] IR 382 SC.

37   *Dunne v Clinton* [1930] IR 366 CCA; *The People (DPP) v O'Loughlin* [1979] IR 85 CCA.

38   *The People (DPP) v Kelly* [1983] IR 1 CCA, SC.

39   Criminal Justice Act, 1987, s 4.

40   Criminal Justice Act, 1984, s 4(3).

41   Criminal Justice Act, 1984, s 4(5).

42   S 6(4) provides: "Any person who obstructs or attempts to obstruct any member of the Garda Síochána or any other person acting under the powers conferred by subs. (1) or who fails or refuses to give his name and address when demanded, or gives a name or address which is false or misleading, shall be guilty of an offence and shall be liable on summary conviction to a fine not exceeding one thousand pounds or to imprisonment for a term not exceeding twelve months or both".

43   Criminal Justice Act, 1984 (Treatment of Persons in Custody in Garda Síochána Stations) Regulations 1987 SI No. 119 of 1987.

44   Offences Against the State Act, 1939, s 30(5).

There is no power to require an arrested person to take part in an identification parade.[45] One who refuses is likely to obtain little judicial sympathy for identification by less formal methods.[46] Where the holding of an identification parade is reasonably possible evidence may be excluded of a less formal identification.[47]

A further power is given by s 52 of the Offences Against the State Act, 1939:

(1) Whenever a person is detained in custody under provisions in that behalf contained in Part IV of this Act, any member of the Garda Síochána may demand of such person, at any time while he is so detained, a full account of such person's movements and actions during any specified period and all information in his possession in relation to the commission or intended commission by another person of any offence under any section or sub-section of this Act or any scheduled offence.

(2) If any person, of whom any such account or information as is mentioned in the foregoing sub-section of this section is demanded under that sub-section by a member of the Garda Síochána fails or refuses to give to such member such account or any such information or gives to such member any account or information which is false or misleading, he shall be guilty of an offence.[48]

A prosecution resulting from this section was taken for the first time in *The People (DPP) v McGuinness and Others*.[49] Six persons had been arrested in proximity to the border in County Donegal in circumstances which might reasonably have given rise to a suspicion of involvement in a criminal offence, whether of subversive nature or not. They were arrested under s 30 for membership of an unlawful organisation and were held for questioning in a local Garda Station. Notwithstanding the fact that a demand was made in the terms of s 52 and the *Garda Guide* was produced to some of the accused in order to explain the penalty resulting from non-compliance, some of the accused refused to say anything. They were later convicted before the Special Criminal Court and sentenced to six months' imprisonment.

Search and Entering Premises

6.37 Reasonable force can be used in pursuance of a lawful power to enter premises. At common law a Garda may enter, without warrant, to prevent murder, where a felony has been committed and a suspect followed to a house, where a felony was about to be committed unless prevented and, to apprehend an offender running away from an affray[50] and to prevent an affray.[51] Even though an illegality is committed a deliberate and conscious breach of the accused's constitutional rights can be excused, and the evidence resulting therefrom consequently admitted, where a Garda acts to rescue a victim in peril and to prevent the imminent destruction of vital evidence.[52] In consequence of a valid arrest any evidence found on or in the possession of an arrestee, which is material evidence on the charge for which he is

45   *The People (A-G) v Martin* [1956] IR 22 CCA, per Lavery J at 28.
46   *The People (A-G) v Martin*, fn 45.
47   *The People (DPP) v O'Reilly* [1990] IR 415; [1991] ILRM 10 CCA.
48   Penalty 6 months' imprisonment.
49   Special Criminal Court, unreported, 27 June 1991.
50   *Swales v Cox* [1981] 1 All ER 1115.
51   See par 6.41.
52   *The People (A-G) v O'Brien* [1965] 142 at 170 SC. Generally see Charleton ch 3, 4.

arrested, or a charge in the contemplation of the arresting officer, or appears, on reasonable cause, to be stolen property or property in the unlawful possession of the arrestee, may be retained by the Gardaí use at the trial of the person arrested, or at the trial of any other person or persons on any criminal charge in which the property is to be used as evidence.[53] "Possession" in this context indicates articles within the immediate control of the arrested person.[54]

A search prior to arrest may take place only if consented to, or authorised by statute.[55] The search of a premises may only be made by search warrant, generally issued by a District Justice[56] who must himself reasonably suspect that articles, within the ambit of the statute, are to be found there[57] and persons found on the premises may be searched only if the statute authorising search contains that power and the face of the warrant specifies its exercise by the holder.[58] Where a search is being lawfully conducted pursuant to any power, a Garda who finds or comes into possession of anything which he believes to be evidence of any offence or suspected offence may seize it and retain it for use as evidence in any criminal proceedings or proceedings in relation to a breach of prison discipline.[59]

Scope of Offence

6.38 For the crimes under s 38 of the 1861 Act and s 12 of the 1871 Act to be committed a Garda officer must be assaulted, resisted, or wilfully obstructed. Assault has already been defined.[60] S 38 of the Offences Against the Person Act, 1861 is wider than the Prevention of Crimes Act, 1871, provisions. The Offences Against the Person Act is not confined to assaulting, resisting, or wilfully obstructing a peace officer. It extends also to any person acting in aid of such an officer and to any person

---

53 *Jennings v Quinn* [1968] IR 305 at 309; *Dillon v O'Brien & Davis* (1887) 20 LR Ir 300, 16 Cox 245 (Ir) SC.

54 *Chimel v California* (1969) 23 L Ed (2d) 685, 694.

55 See for example a power to stop and search vehicles reasonably suspected of conveying stolen property under the Dublin Metropolitan Police Act, 1842, s 29; a power to search for controlled drugs under s 23 of the Misuse of Drugs Act, 1977; and a power to stop and search vehicles under s 8 of the Criminal Law Act, 1976 on reasonable suspicion of offences having been, being, or about to be committed, that is to say: a scheduled offence under the Offences Against the State Act, 1939, offences under ss 2 and 3 of the Criminal Law (Jurisdiction) Act, 1976, murder, manslaughter and s 18 of the Offences Against the Person Act, 1861, offences under ss 23, 23A, and 23B of the Larceny Act, 1916, malicious damage by means of fire or an explosive substance, offences under the Firearms Act, 1925-1971 and under the Firearms and Offensive Weapons Act, 1990, s 12(1), escaping from lawful custody, offences of hi-jacking under s 11 of the Air Navigation and Transport Act, 1973 and s 10 of the Criminal Law (Jurisdiction) Act, 1976 and any offence under the Criminal Law Act, 1976.

56 However see s 29 of the Offences Against the State Act, 1939 and s 16 of the Crimes Act, 1871.

57 *Byrne v Grey* [1988] IR 31; *Berkeley v Edwards* [1988] IR 217. It is submitted that these two decisions are entirely inconsistent with each other and that *Byrne v Grey* is preferable and applicable to all statutes where a warrant is issued only on a District Justice entertaining a reasonable suspicion of the presence of illegal articles within the meaning of the statute authorising the issue of a warrant, being present on particular premises. See *The People (DPP) v Kenny* [1990] ILRM 569 SC.

58 *King* [1969] AC 304; [1968] 2 All ER 610; [1968] 3 WLR 391, 52 Cr App R 353 PC.

59 Criminal Law Act, 1976, s 9.

60 See par 6.10.

who is assaulted, the accused having the intention to resist or prevent the lawful apprehension or detainer of himself or any other person for any offence.

A "peace officer", in this context is not limited to a Garda. It extends to the sheriff and his officers in executing civil process[61] and to other officers charged with the duty of administering the processes of the court, including the service of civil summons[62] and the collection of taxes.[63] The crime of assaulting a person with intent to resist or prevent the lawful apprehension or detainer of the assailant or another is limited to those cases where any person, whether a Garda or a citizen is seeking to lawfully arrest for a criminal offence.[64] It is an indictable misdemeanour at common law to refuse to aid and assist a constable in the execution of his duty to preserve the peace.[65]

Assault, Resist, Obstruct

6.39 Apart from assault, accused must act with intent to resist or obstruct the peace officer.[66] Assault, in this context, has the same meaning as that already discussed in relation to the general law.[67]

"Resist", in this context, is an ordinary word which implies some use of force by the accused (whether amounting to or falling short of an assault) which necessitates the Garda, or person assisting him, to make some exertion of effort or application of force which would otherwise be unnecessary.[68] Examples would include the accused barring the door of his premises when told that Gardaí were about to enter on a search warrant, a person who being stopped by the Gardaí and informed that he is about to be searched under the Misuse of Drugs Acts tries to swallow a substance he is carrying rather than let officers inspect it;[69] or the person

---

61 The Sheriffs Act 1887, s 8(2) provides that where a Sheriff finds any resistance on the execution of a rite (which includes any legal process by s 38): ". . . he shall take with him the power of the county, and shall go in proper person to do execution, and may arrest the resistors and commit them to prison, and every such resister shall be guilty of a misdemeanour".

62 Russell 689.

63 Russell 689; *Clark* (1835) 3 A&E 287, 111 ER 422.

64 The main powers of a citizen to arrest are for felony and breach of the peace committed in his presence. The former is widely used, among others, by store detectives but can lawfully be exercised only where a felony has actually been committed and the citizen reasonably suspects that the accused is guilty of its commission. In civil cases out of such arrests the claim of justification most often fails due to a failure on the part of the store, employing the detective, to prove that the felony was committed. The most common felony in this context is that of larceny; Larceny Act, 1916, s 2.

65 *Brown* (1841) C&M 314, 4 St Tr (NS) 1369, 174 ER 522. The prosecution are required to prove that the Garda saw a breach of the peace committed; that there was a reasonable necessity for calling on the accused for his assistance; when duly called upon the accused, without any physical impossibility or lawful excuse refused to do so. It is not a defence that the aid of the accused would have been of no avail; Archbold (1922) 965.

66 *Rice v Connolly* [1966] 2 QB 414; [1966] 2 All ER 649; [1966] 3 WLR 17 DC; *Willmott v Atack* [1977] QB 498; [1976] 3 All ER 794; [1976] 3 WLR 753, 63 Cr App R 207 DC. There seems to be no reason in principle why a person cannot commit the crime by recklessness, being aware of a substantial and unjustifiable risk that his action will cause a resistance or obstruction to a Garda in the due execution of his duty. In practice, however, such a situation would be unlikely.

67 See par 6.10.

68 The Shorter Oxford English Dictionary defines "resist" as: "To withstand, strive against, oppose."

69 S 21(4) of the Misuse of Drugs Act, 1977 provides: "Any person who by act or omission impedes or obstructs a member of the Garda Síochána or a person duly authorised under this Act in the lawful

who is lawfully arrested impeding himself from being taken away or brought before the District Court by clinging on to whatever comes to hand.

6.40 The concept of wilful obstruction has been given a wide meaning. It is unlikely that an accused will accidentally resist or assault the police. An obstruction is more likely to occur by chance and thus the section is clarified by the addition of the word "wilful".

The words in the statute do not imply an assault but extend to acts done to interfere with Gardaí who, in the execution of their duty under statute or lawful orders, are seeking to arrest or to obtain evidence as to offences.[70] An obstruction has been defined as some action which makes it more difficult for the police to carry out their duties.[71]

It is submitted, however, that this view is simplistic. The analysis of police powers, whether it be in terms of assaulting, resisting or obstructing, proceeds on the same basis of an inquiry into the nature of the act done by the police, its effects on the rights of others, particularly the accused, and the presence or absence of a legal justification for that action.[72] An obstruction does not require an illegal act by the accused, independent of the offences set out above.[73] The imposition of duties and the conferment of powers cannot operate in isolation from the necessity of over-riding the rights of the individual to be free from interference. Where the Gardaí are permitted to lawfully make such interference the citizen is not entitled to behave as if the power or duty did not exist. A positive duty of co-operation, it would appear, is not imposed but the lawful exercise of a power implies a corresponding requirement that their exercise should not be impeded by the citizen.[74] It is not arguable that the Oireachtas, in conferring powers and imposing duties on the Gardaí, allows citizens, over whom those powers are exercised, to limit their effectiveness by acts of obstruction. It thus appears that an obstruction is some voluntary act[75] by the accused which impedes the performance of a duty by the Gardaí or interferes with the execution of their powers.

exercise of a power conferred by this Act shall be guilty of an offence, and if, in the case of a continuing offence, the impediment or obstruction is continued after conviction, he shall be guilty of a further offence". The penalty under s 27(6), inserted by s 6 of the Misuse of Drugs Act, 1984, is, on summary conviction, a fine not exceeding four hundred pounds or imprisonment for up to six months.

70   *Betts v Stevens* [1910] 1 KB 1; [1908-10] All ER 1245, 22 Cox 187 DC; *Bastable v Little* [1907] 1 KB 59; [1904-7] All ER 1147, 21 Cox 354 DC; Archbold (1922) 965. In Scotland the word obstruct has been construed as to require physical interference; Coutts, "Obstructing the Police" (1956) 19 MLR 411.

71   Per Lord Goddard CJ in *Hinchcliffe* v Sheldon [1955] 3 All ER 406 at 408; [1955] 1 WLR 1207 at 1209 DC. This is the definition cited in *The Garda Síochána Guide* (5th ed., 1981) 852.

72   See par 6.34.

73   *Dibble v Ingleton* [1972] 1 QB 480; [1972] 1 All ER 275; [1972] 2 WLR 163 DC.

74   A section which requires positive co-operation by the citizen is s 21(5) of the Misuse of Drugs Act, 1977 which provides: "Any person who conceals from a person lawfully exercising a power under s 24 of this Act any controlled drug, or with reasonable excuse fails to produce any book, record or other document which he has been duly required to produce under that section, shall be guilty of an offence".

75   In *Dibble v Ingleton*, fn 73, a divisional court held that omissions do not amount to an obstruction, hence the specific sections, such as s 21(5) making it an offence to omit to do something or, s 52 of

It is the duty of the Gardaí to enforce the law, to investigate the commission of crime and to keep the peace. Thus it is an obstruction to warn persons who are committing a criminal offence that they are about to be detected.[76] In *Green v Moore*[77] the accused was a probationer constable who, knowing that a police support group had arrived in the town in which he was stationed with a view to detecting over hours drinking in a local hotel, warned the landlord. He thereafter adhered to licensing hours. The Divisional Court held that it was an obstruction to give a warning in order that the commission of a crime should be suspended and equally an obstruction where the warning was given in order that the commission of a crime might be postponed until after the danger of detection had passed.

It appears that the duty to detect crime extends into situations where it is reasonable to suspect the commission of an offence. In *Hinchcliffe v Sheldon*[78] the obstruction consisted of the accused, the son of the public house owner, shouting a warning to his parents that the police were outside. The police arrived after licensing hours while the lights in the bar were still on and there followed a delay of eight minutes before they were admitted when no offence was detected. In *Westlie*[79] the British Columbia Court of Appeal held it to be an obstruction where plain clothes officers were patrolling the streets of Vancouver with a view to detecting petty crime and were frustrated by the accused walking with them and explaining that they were "undercover pigs" and "undercover fuzz".

The Gardaí, in the investigation of crime, are entitled to make enquiries. The citizen is not obliged to answer questions put to him or, in answering, to incriminate himself, s 52 of the Offences Against the State Act, 1939 and other minor powers excepted. It has been held to be an obstruction for a by-stander to advise a person not to answer questions being put by a police officer.[80] It is submitted that this decision is incorrect. Whilst the unquestioning application of a definition of "obstruction" as "making it more difficult for the police to carry out their duties" renders this situation an offence on its facts, it is submitted it cannot be an obstruction to point out to a citizen what his rights are in a given situation. This allows him the choice of exercise of those rights.[81] If the refusal to co-operate or answer questions is cast in offensive language this may amount to an offence within the Dublin

---

the Offences Against the State Act, 1939, making it an offence to fail to answer questions giving an account of movements between particular times.

76 *Betts v Stevens*, fn 70, where the accused was warning drivers exceeding the speed limit. In *Bastable v Little*, fn 70 a case of obstruction was not made out because it was not proved that a driver was exceeding the speed limit. This latter case was doubted in *Green v Moore* [1982] QB 1044; [1982] 1 All ER 428; [1982] 2 WLR 671, 74 Cr App R 250; [1982] Crim LR 233 DC.

77 Fn 76.

78 [1955] 3 All ER 406; [1955] 1 WLR 1207 DC.

79 (1971) 2 CCC (2d) 315.

80 *Steele v Kingsbeer* [1957] NZLR 552 SC Palmerston. Contrast *Dash v Police* [1970] NZLR 273 SC Christchurch and *Hogben v Chandler* [1940] VLR 285 SC; *Rice v Connolly*, fn 66.

81 This could be considered to be a corollary to the existence of the right in the first place; *State (Healy) v Donoghue* [1976] IR 325, 110 ILTR HC, SC.

Metropolitan District[82] but it is not otherwise an offence.[83] Where a police inquiry is answered by a false story an obstruction is committed.[84]

It is clearly an obstruction to fail to comply with a Garda direction to cease committing a criminal offence.[85] It is further an obstruction to do an act with the object of frustrating the exercise of a police power, such as concealing suspected stolen property, adulterating the breath prior to taking a "breathalyser" test[86] or to refusing to remain on the scene for that purpose.[87] In *Rice v Connolly*[88] Lord Parker CJ proposed that the jury should consider the offence in terms of three questions:

1. Was there any obstruction of a constable?

2. Was the constable acting lawfully in the execution of his duty?

3. Was the obstruction intended to obstruct the constable in the execution of his duty?

Assaults in Particular Circumstances

6.41 Assaults defined as being committed in particular circumstances are of little practical importance. As in the case of a wrong done to a particular class of person the accused must be reckless as to the existence of the circumstances to be guilty of his aggravated form of assault.[89] It is a felony to interfere with a person escaping from an endangered ship,[90] it is a felony to commit assault by means of an explosive.[91] Sexual assaults are considered in chapter 8. It is a felony to send explosives and other dangerous substances to persons with intent to harm them.[92] Finally it is a misdemeanour for a poacher to assault a game keeper.[93]

---

82   Dublin Police Act, 1842, s 14(13): "Every person who shall use any threatening, abusive or insulting words or behaviour, with the intent to provoke a breach of the peace, or whereby a breach of the peace may be occasioned [is guilty of an offence carrying a two pounds fine, Garda having the power to arrest where such is committed within the view of the Gardaí."

83   *Ricketts v Cox* (1981) 74 Cr App R 298; [1982] Crim LR 184 DC, criticised by Smith & Hogan 394.

84   *Matthews v Dwan* [1949] NZLR 1037 SC Auckland.

85   *Tynan v Balmer* [1967] 1 QB 91; [1966] 2 All ER 133; [1966] 2 WLR 1181 DC.

86   *Cunliffe* v Bleasdale [1972] Crim LR 567; *Neal v Evans* [1976] Crim LR 384 DC.

87   *Carey* [1970] AC 1072; [1969] 3 All ER 1662; [1966] 3 WLR 1169, 54 Cr App R 119 HL, or, in England, on being arrested for drunken driving, to refuse to give the keys of one's car to the police; *Stunt v Bolton* [1972] Crim LR 561. It appears the procedure in this country is to arrest the accused and to leave the car where it is. Generally see de Blácam, *Drunken Driving and the Law* 25-62.

88   [1966] 2 QB 414 at 419; [1966] 2 All ER 649 at 651; [1966] 3 WLR 17 at 21 DC.

89   See par 6.33.

90   Offences Against the Person Act, 1861, s 17: "Whosoever shall unlawfully and maliciously prevent or impede any person, being on board of or having quitted any ship or vessel which shall be in distress, or wrecked, stranded, or cast on shore, in his endeavour to save his life, or shall unlawfully and maliciously prevent or impede any person, in his endeavour to save the life of any such person as in this section first aforesaid, shall be guilty of felony, and being convicted thereof shall be liable to be kept in penal servitude for life."

91   Offences Against the Person Act, 1861, s 28. See ch 9.

92   Offences Against the Person Act, 1861, s 29. See ch 9.

93   The Night Poaching Act, 1828, s 2: "Where any person shall be found upon any land committing any such offence as is hereinbefore mentioned, it shall be lawful for the owner or occupier of such land, or for any person having a right or reputed right of free warren or chase thereon, or for the

Affray

6.42 An affray is a common law indictable misdemeanour, carrying a fine or imprisonment at the discretion of the court. The elements of affray and the penalty imposed on conviction have been the cause of such disquiet as to lead to the restatement and reform of the law in England.[94]

The essence of the offence is that the accused conducts himself in such a way as to cause the victim to be terrified.[95] An affray may be committed either by the accused fighting or openly making a show of force, so that a person of reasonably firm character might reasonably be expected to be thereby terrified. Coke said of the offence:

> An affray is a public offence to the terror of the King's subjects and is an English word and so called, because it affrighteth and maketh men afraid.[96]

Need Not be in Public

The sense in which Coke described the offence as "public" does not impart a requirement that the offence be committed in a public place. In *Button, Swain*,[97] the House of Lords accepted the ruling of McKenna J who, as trial judge, had identified the requirement that the offence be committed in public, as an error which had crept into the law. Notwithstanding the fact that this mistake had been elevated to a necessary ingredient of the offence for almost two hundred years[98] it was excised;

lord of the manor or reputed manor wherein such land may be situate, and also for any game keeper or servant of the persons herein mentioned, or any person assisting such game keeper or servant, to seize and apprehend such offender upon such land, or in case of pursuit being made, in any other place to which he may have escaped therefrom, and to deliver him, as soon as may be, into the custody of a peace officer, in order to his being conveyed before two justices of the peace; and in case such offender shall assault or offer any violence with any gun, cross-bow, fire-arms, bludgeon, stick, club, or any other offensive weapon whatsoever, towards any person hereby authorised to seize and apprehend him, he shall, whether it be his first, second, or any other offence, be guilty of a misdemeanour, and being convicted thereof shall be liable, at the discretion of the Court, to be transported beyond seas for seven years [penal servitude under the Penal Servitude Act, 1853] or to be imprisoned or kept to hard labour in the common gaol or house of correction for any term not exceeding two years; and in Scotland, whenever any such person shall so offend, he shall be liable to be punished in like manner". The prosecution must prove that the accused entered the land at night time, that he was armed with a weapon mentioned in the section; that he was on the land for the purpose of destroying game; that he was found on the land in the commission of the offence; that the person assaulted was a person protected by the section; and that an assault was committed. For further authority see Archbold (1922) 966-68; Russell 1046-1055.

94   Public Order Act, 1986.

95   The definitions in the standard texts vary widely and are to be seen in the light of the discussion of the cases which follow in this text. In particular the requirement that the victim be stricken with terror in public is an error and is no longer required. Thus Archbold (1922) 1227 "An affray is a public offence to the terror of the King's subjects. There may be an affray where no actual violence occurs, e.g. where a man arms himself with dangerous and unusual weapons in such a manner as will cause terror . . ."; Archbold (1966) 3594 "An affray is fighting of two or more persons to the terror of Her Majesty's subjects . . ."; Russell 263 "Affray, which is a misdemeanour at common law, is committed when to the terror of Her Majesty's subjects two or more persons in a public place either fight or offer or threaten to fight or display arms or weapons and comport themselves in such a way as to cause the people to anticipate an outbreak of violence".

96   3 Co Inst 157; 4 Bl Com 145; Archbold (1922) 337; 1 Hawk ch 63.

97   [1966] AC 591; [1965] 3 All ER 587; [1965] 3 WLR 1131, 50 Cr App R 36.

98   The error is identified as occurring in 4 Bl Com (1787) 145 and continuing in Archbold (1822) 337.

an erroneous view of the elements of a criminal offence could not be elevated by practice into a rule of law.

The definition in Coke distinguishes the offence from a private wrong. Ancient texts acknowledge the power of private persons and constables, to suppress an affray by parting, and keeping apart, or arresting the participants. A further power given to a constable is inconsistent with the requirement that the offence take place in public. Hawkins[99] states:

> And if an affray be in a house, the constable may break open the doors to preserve the peace; and if the affrayers fly to a house, he may follow them with fresh suit, he may break open the doors to take them.

The power to enter a house to suppress an affray would be unnecessary if it was essential to the commission of that offence that it take place in public. The error, nonetheless, was well established. In *O'Neill*,[1] Whiteside CJ, O'Brien J concurring, held that it was a necessary averment in an indictment for affray that it took place in public.[2] The error had also been accepted by the Court of Appeal in England prior to *Button, Swain*.[3]

If the offence takes place in public it is not necessary for the prosecution to prove that a by-stander was present or was reasonably likely to appear at the scene.[4] In *Taylor*[5] Lord Hailsham LC expressed the view that where an affray occurred in a private place that it would be surprising if the offence could be complete without the actual presence of onlookers to be frightened by the sight and sound of what was occurring.

Victim

6.43 It appears that the victim of an assault may also be the victim for the purpose of affray. In England the Court of Appeal have remarked on the possible absurdity of any contrary conclusion:

> G stands terrified, the sole spectator of the fighting and having nothing to do with either batch of contestants. At that point he is undoubtedly a by-stander and the offence of affray is complete. The fighting then becomes more wide-spread and G is himself attacked. If the arguments put forward by defending counsel in the present case are correct, the affray then ceases because there is no uninvolved spectator/by-stander. The attack on G then ceases and the situation becomes less serious but fighting

99   1 Hawk ch 63, s 16.

1   (1871) IR 6 CL 1 CCA.

2   At page 4: "Now what is the nature of the offence? It is a public offence, and, therefore, it must be alleged to have been committed in a public place. It is equally clear that the form of indictment which should have been followed describes it as an offence that had been committed in a public street or highway".

3   Fn 97; *Sharp* [1957] 1 QB 552; [1957] 1 All ER 577; [1957] 2 WLR 472, 41 Cr App R 86 CCA; *Morris* (1963) 47 Cr App R 202 CCA; *Clark* (1963) 47 Cr App R 203 CCA; *Mapstone* [1963] 3 All ER 930; [1964] 1 WLR 439; *Allan* [1965] 1 QB 130; [1963] 2 All ER 897; [1963] 3 WLR 667, 47 Cr App R 243 CCA; see also *Hunt & Swanton* (1845) 1 Cox 177 CCR.

4   Attorney General's reference (No. 3 of 1983) [1985] QB 242 [1985] 1 All ER 501 CA; [1985] 2 WLR 253, 80 Cr App R 150; [1985] Crim LR 207 CA; *Mapstone*, fn 97.

5   [1973] AC 964 at 987-88; [1973] 2 All ER 1108 at 1112-13; [1973] 3 WLR 140, 57 Cr App R 915 HL.

continues, does the offence of affray then start again? It seems to us clear that in any event the innocent victims of an affray may themselves fill the role of the so-called by-stander.[6]

The situation may thus be summarised: Whether the attack takes place in public or in private an accused who assaults a victim in such a manner that the victim, as a person of reasonably firm character, might reasonably be expected to be terrified, he is guilty of an affray; where two persons participate, by consent, in a fight, both will be guilty of an affray if the fight takes place in public in such a manner that a by-stander of reasonably firm character might reasonably be expected to be terrified, though the presence of such by-stander is not required; where that fight occurs in private that by-stander is required.[7]

Display of Force

6.44 An affray may also be committed by the accused displaying force. Hawkins[8] states:

> But granting that no bare words . . . carry in them so much terror as to amount to an affray; yet it seems certain, that in some cases there may be an affray where there is no actual violence; as where a man arms himself with dangerous and unusual weapons, in such a manner as will naturally cause a terror to the people, which is said to have been always an offence at common law. . . .

In *Meade*[9] the accused had quarrelled with his brother. He went to his house, and from the street, fired a revolver in the direction of his brother's bedroom. He was convicted on a count of going "armed in public without lawful occasion in . . . such a manner as to be a nuisance to and to alarm the public using the said street . . . ". Wills J instructed the jury that, irrespective of statute,[10] the accused was liable to punishment for making himself a public nuisance by firing a revolver in a public place with the result that the public was frightened or terrorised.[11]

Terror

The violence used or displayed must be such that a person of reasonably firm character might reasonably be expected to be terrified.[12] Lord Hailsham LC put the requirement thus:

> . . . it is essential to stress that the degree of violence required to constitute the offence of affray must be such as to be calculated to terrify a person of reasonably firm character.

6   Attorney General's Reference (No. 3 of 1983) [1985] QB 242; [1985] 1 All ER 501; [1985] 2 WLR 253, 80 Cr App R 150; [1985] Crim LR 207 CA. See also *Taylor* [1973] AC 964; [1973] 2 All ER 1108; [1973] 3 WLR 140, 57 Cr App R 915 HL.
7   Consent is not a defence to assault where actual bodily harm results; see par 8.16. The fight, could, however, take place by the clashing of knives or other weapons without hurt being caused to the participants.
8   1 Hawk ch 63, s 4.
9   (1903) 19 TLR 540.
10 2 Ed III ch 3 (not in force in Ireland).
11 The accused was found guilty and sentenced to two months' imprisonment.
12 *Taylor* [1973] AC 964 at 87-88; [1973] 2 All ER 1108 at 1112-13; [1973] 3 WLR 140, 57 Cr App R 915 HL.

This should not be watered down. Thus it is arguable that the phrase "might be frightened or intimidated" may be too weak. The violence must be such as to be *calculated* to terrify (that is, might reasonably be expected to terrify) not simply such as *might* terrify a person of the requisite degree of firmness.[13]

It has been commented that a fight with fists would not amount to an affray whereas the use of broken bottles or knuckle dusters and the drawing of blood might reasonably be expected to cause the terror required for an affray.[14] The Court of Appeal in England has commented that the offence should be reserved for serious cases which are not far short of a riot.[15]

Duplicity

6.45 An affray may continue over a period of time and over a wide area. An indictment is not bad for duplicity where it alleges that an affray took place on 31 August and 1 September "in divers streets".[16] An affray may be interrupted, for example by a coach journey from place to place;[17] the sentence may take into account the fact that one or more acts of violence occurred in the course of the offence.[18]

Sentences of up to seven years have been approved for the most serious offences.[19] The offence may also be aggravated by the location in which it occurs, such as a courtroom.[20] Although angry words[21] which do not amount to blows, cannot amount to an affray it appears that such persons may be bound to the peace.[22]

Assault Distinguished

Affray differs from assault in that it carries, as an essential element of the offence, an ingredient requiring that the circumstances be such that a by-stander of reasonably firm character might reasonably be expected to be terrified. A person charged with affray may raise the defence of self-defence.[23] Its utility occurs in circumstances where witnesses are unable to give details of individual assaults but are able to say that the fighting occurred due to the acts of certain persons.[24]

The wide role of judicial activism in defining the offence and the disparity between the sentence for affray and that for common assault and assault occasioning actual bodily harm make reform of the law an obvious priority.

13   *Taylor*, fn 12.
14   *Sharp*, per Lord Goddard CJ [1957] 1 QB at 559; [1957] 1 All ER at 579; [1957] 2 WLR at 475, 41 Cr App R at 91–92 CCA.
15   *Crimmas* [1976] Crim LR 693 CA.
16   *Woodrow* (1959) 43 Cr App R 105 CA.
17   *Jones* [1974] ICR 310, 59 Cr App R 120; [1974] Crim LR 663 CA.
18   *Coke* [1987] Crim LR 514 CA.
19   *Keys and Others* (1987) 84 Cr App R 204 CA; *Lutman* [1973] Crim LR 127.
20   1 Hawk ch 63, s 23.
21   1 Hale 456; 1 Hawk ch 63, s 2 and see *Woodrow*, fn 16.
22   Russell 265.
23   *Sharp and Johnson* [1957] 1 QB 552; [1957] 1 All ER 577; [1957] 2 WLR 472, 41 Cr App R 86 CCA.
24   *Button* [1966] AC 591; [1965] 3 All ER 587; [1965] 3 WLR 1131, 50 Cr App R 36; *Sharp* [1957] 1 QB 552, 559; [1957] 1 All ER 577, 579; [1957] 2 WLR 472, 475, 41 Cr App R 86, 91–92 CCA.

Defences to Assault

6.46 The defence of lawful use of force and consent are considered, briefly, in par 4.29 and par 8.16.

Draft Indictments

6.47 There follow the appropriate forms of indictment for the offences considered in this chapter.

COMMON ASSAULT

Statement of Offence
Common assault
Particulars of Offence
AB on the   at   assaulted CD.

ABANDONING A CHILD

Statement of Offence
Abandoning a child, contrary to s 27 of the Offences Against the Person Act, 1861.
Particulars of Offence
AB on the   at   unlawfully abandoned (or exposed) a child under the age of two years, whereby its life was endangered (or its health permanently injured or was likely to be permanently injured).

ASSAULT OCCASIONING ACTUAL BODILY HARM

Statement of Offence
Assault occasioning actual bodily harm contrary to s 47 of the Offences Against the Person Act, 1861.
Particulars of Offence
AB on the   at   assaulted CD thereby occasioning him actual bodily harm.

WOUNDING

Statement of Offence
Wounding, contrary to s 20 of the Offences Against the Person Act, 1861.
Particulars of Offence
AB on the   at   unlawfully and maliciously wounded CD.

INFLICTING GRIEVOUS BODILY HARM

Statement of Offence
Inflicting grievous bodily harm, contrary to s 20 of the Offences Against the Person Act, 1861.
Particulars of Offence
AB on the   at   unlawfully and maliciously inflicted grievous bodily harm upon CD.

ASSAULTS WITH INTENT

Statement of Offence

Wounding with intent, contrary to s 18 of the Offences Against the Person Act, 1861.

Particulars of Offence

AB on the   at   unlawfully and maliciously wounded CD with intent to do him grievous bodily harm, or to maim, disfigure or disable him, or to resist the lawful apprehension of the said AB.

Statement of Offence

Causing grievous bodily harm with intent, contrary to s 18 of the Offences Against the Person Act, 1861.

Particulars of Offence

AB on the   at   unlawfully and maliciously caused grievous bodily harm to CD with intent to do grievous bodily harm, or to maim, disfigure or disable him.

Statement of Offence

Attempting to shoot with intent, contrary to s 18 of the Offences Against the Person Act, 1861.

Particulars of Offence

AB on the   at   unlawfully and maliciously attempted to discharge a loaded pistol at CD with intent to do him grievous bodily harm or to maim, disfigure or disable him, or to resist the lawful apprehension of the said AB.

Statement of Offence

Assault with intent to commit felony, contrary to s 38 of the Offences Against the Person Act, 1861.

Particulars of Offence

AB on the   at   assaulted CD with intent to steal (or rob, or any felony) from the person of CD.

ROBBERY

Statement of Offence

Robbery contrary to s 23A of the Larceny Act, 1916 as inserted by s 5 of the Criminal Law (Jurisdiction) Act, 1976.

Particulars of Offence

AB on the   at   robbed CD of a sum of money in cash (or anything else capable of being stolen).

Statement of Offence

Assault with intent to rob, contrary to s 23A of the Larceny Act, 1916 as inserted by s 23 of the Criminal Law (Jurisdiction) Act, 1976.

Particulars of Offence

AB on the   at   assaulted CD with intent to rob her.

PLACING A MAN TRAP

Statement of Offence
Placing a man trap with intent to inflict grievous bodily harm contrary to s 31 of the Offences Against the Person Act, 1861.
Particulars of Offence
AB on the   at   caused to be placed a man trap, with the intent that the same might inflict grievous bodily harm upon a person coming in contact therewith.

ASSAULT ON A GARDA

Statement of Offence
Assault (or resist or obstruct) on a peace officer, contrary to s 38 of the Offences Against the Person Act, 1861.
Particulars of Offence
AB on the   at   assaulted (or resisted or obstructed) Garda CD, a peace officer, in the due execution of his duty.

Statement of Offence
Assault with intent to prevent lawful apprehension or detainer, contrary to s 38 of the Offences Against the Person Act, 1861.
Particulars of Offence
AB on the   at   assaulted CD with intent thereby to resist or prevent the lawful apprehension or detainer of himself (or of any other person).

ASSAULTS IN PARTICULAR CIRCUMSTANCES

Statement of Offence
Impeding saving of life, contrary to s 17 of the Offences Against the Person Act, 1861.
Particulars of Offence
AB on the   at   unlawfully and maliciously prevented or impeded CD in his endeavour to save the life of XY, who had quitted a ship in distress.

Statement of Offence
Assault on a gamekeeper, contrary to s 2 of the Night Poaching Act, 1828.
Particulars of Offence
AB on the   at   at 11 o'clock in the night-time, in the county of then being found unlawfully on certain land in the occupation of CD armed with a gun for the purpose of taking game, assaulted or offered violence with the said gun towards XY, a game keeper in the employment of the said CD, being a person authorised to seize and apprehend him, the said AB.

AFFRAY

Statement of Offence
Affray
Particulars of Offence
AB on the   at   unlawfully fought and made an affray.

Statement of Offence
Going armed so as to cause fear.
Particulars of Offence
AB on the   at   went armed in public without lawful occasion in such a manner as to alarm the public using the said place.
NOTE: This form of indictment is taken, as far as possible, from *Meade* (1903) 19 TLR 540.

IN NORTHERN IRELAND

Statement of Offence
Wounding contrary to s 2(1) of the Criminal Law (Jurisdiction) Act, 1976.
Particulars of Offence
AB on the   at   Northern Ireland, unlawfully and maliciously wounded CD.

Statement of Offence
Inflict grievous bodily harm, contrary to s 2(1) of the Criminal Law (Jurisdiction) Act, 1976.
Particulars of Offence
AB on the   at   Northern Ireland, unlawfully and maliciously inflicted grievous bodily harm upon CD.

For indecent assaults and other sexual offences see chapter 8.

CHAPTER SEVEN

Imprisonment, Poisoning and Other Offences

7.01 This chapter considers the various offences of false imprisonment and kidnapping, poisoning, cruelty to children and railway offences.

False Imprisonment

7.02 S 11 of the Criminal Law Act, 1976 provides:

(1) The offences of kidnapping and false imprisonment and an offence under s 10 of the Criminal Law (Jurisdiction) Act, 1976, shall be felonies.

(2) A person guilty of kidnapping or guilty of false imprisonment shall be liable on conviction on indictment to imprisonment for life.

Hawkins described false imprisonment as:

Every restraint of a man's liberty under the custody of another, either in a gaol, house, stocks, or in the street, whenever it is done without a proper authority.[1]

The offence of hijacking a motor vehicle contrary to s 10 of the Criminal Law (Jurisdiction) Act, 1976 is considered later in this volume.[2] The commission of that offence may concurrently, though not necessarily, involve false imprisonment, as where a person is forced at knife point to drive another to a particular place.

False imprisonment and kidnapping are separate crimes at common law.[3] The latter is, however, merely an aggravated form of the former. False imprisonment and kidnapping are both scheduled offences under the Criminal Law (Jurisdiction) Act, 1976. This means that where the offence is committed in Northern Ireland it constitutes an offence contrary to s 2 of that Act.[4]

Definition

7.03 False imprisonment occurs where the accused, intentionally, or recklessly,[5] unlawfully imposes, for any time,[6] a total restraint on the personal liberty of another,

---

1   1 PC, ch 9, s 1. For a modern discussion of the elements of this offence see the Criminal Law Revision Committee—*Offences Against the Person* (Cmnd 7844) par 225-251.

2   See par 10.27.

3   In *Brown* [1985] Crim LR 398 the Court of Appeal upheld concurrent sentences in respect of both crimes arising out of the one incident.

4   This section is quoted at par 9.12.

5   *Rahman* (1985) 81 Cr App R 349; [1985] Crim LR 596 CA.

6   Smith & Hogan 406-7, citing *Simpson v Hill* (1795) 1 Esp 431, 170 ER 409; *Sandon v Jervis* (1859) EB&E 942, 120 ER 760.

whether by constraining him or compelling him to go to a particular place,[7] or by confining him in a prison or police station or private place, or by detaining him against his will in a public place.[8] An assault is not an essential ingredient of the offence[9] though it commonly occurs in this context as does the threat of violence.

The essential element of the offence is the unlawful detention of the victim, or the unlawful restraint on his liberty.[10] The victim must be subjected to more than a mere obstruction; he must be confined.[11]

It is not necessary that the victim be aware that he was imprisoned.[12]

7.04 In *Rahman*[13] the English Court of Appeal defined the mental element of the offence as intention or recklessness:

> False imprisonment consists in the unlawful and intentional or reckless restraint of a victim's freedom of movement from a particular place.[14]

Circumstances where the accused will falsely imprison someone by an act or omission that is not purposive will occur rarely. An example would be of a security guard, under a duty to evacuate a place before finally securing it, who fails to make the proper checks, being aware that there is a high risk of someone being present in that place, but proceeding nonetheless to incarcerate them. In all of the cases coming before the Irish courts in recent years the facts proved by the prosecution were capable of no other interpretation than that the accused acted purposively. Consequently, while authority is unavailable, there is none to state that intent is the sole mental element required. Analogy with other offences against the person, such as assault and rape, indicate that in principle mental elements should be stated by reference to the alternative states of intention or recklessness.

Confinement

7.05 The offence is not dependent on the victim being imprisoned for a minimum time. The offence is committed even though the imprisonment is momentary.[15] It is clearly not a false imprisonment to detain someone momentarily in a social context for the purpose of attracting their attention.[16] It does not necessarily amount to an imprisonment that the victim was assaulted, but some violent incidents may involve

---

7   *Pocock v Moore* (1825) R&M 321, 171 ER 1035 CCR.

8   Russell 690, quoted with approval in *Dullaghan v Hillen* [1957] Ir Jur 10 at 15. Further see *MACL* 349.

9   The precedent indictment in Archbold (1922) 999 which specifies an assault contains this element as a superfluity; Russell 690; *Linsberg & Leies* (1905) 69 JP 107; *Hunter v Johnson* (1884) 13 QBD 225, 15 Cox 600.

10   *Dullaghan v Hillen*, fn 8 per Judge Fawsitt at 15.

11   Archbold (1922) 1000.

12   *Dullaghan v Hillen*, fn 8; *Murray v Minister for Defence* [1988] 2 All ER 521, [1988] 1 WLR 692. Although these are civil decisions Smith & Hogan 407 argue in favour of applying the same rule in imposing criminal liability.

13   (1985) 81 Cr App R 349; [1985] Crim LR 596 CA.

14   At 353. See also *Hutchins* [1988] Crim LR 379 CA.

15   *Simpson v Hill* (1795) 1 Esp 431, 170 ER 409; *Sandon v Jervis* (1859) EB&E 942, 120 ER 960; Smith & Hogan 406-7.

16   In this context see par 6.10.

the victim being dragged or held in a particular place. On principle, where the victim is confined by an assault an imprisonment occurs. In contrast a struggle or tussle which does not confine the victim is merely an assault. An assault is not an element of false imprisonment[17] but in practice that element is usually present.[18]

7.06 The victim must be confined within fixed boundaries. It is not a false imprisonment to block the victim's way so that he is required to retrace his steps or make a diversion.[19] There must be "a total restraint of the liberty of the person".[20] A discussion of the size of the place where the victim is confined is unnecessary and irrelevant in the context. People are usually confined to a small room or tied to a tree in a large forest.[21] In a civil context McMahon & Binchy comment:

> The extent of the confinement may vary: it can include confinement not only in a prison or barracks, but also in a house, or hotel, a car, a polling booth, a station, a boat, or a lavatory, for example.[22]

It has been held, in Texas, that it is an imprisonment to drive a car at speed knowing that a passenger wishes to alight.[23]

In *Kane v The Governor of Mountjoy Prison*[24] the applicant was kept under extremely close surveillance by Gardaí, in the expectation of the imminent arrival of a warrant for his extradition. By being aware of where Kane was the Gardaí would be in a position to arrest him on that warrant. He claimed that this surveillance activity amounted to a depravation of his personal liberty and consequently rendered his subsequent arrest unlawful. This contention was rejected by the Supreme Court, Finlay CJ stating:

> The essential feature of detention in this legal context is that the detainee is effectively prevented from going or being where he wants to go or be and instead is forced to remain or go where his jailer wishes him to remain or go.[25]

17 *Linsberg* (1905) 69 JP 107; *Hunter v Johnson* (1884) 13 QBD 225, 15 Cox 321. Williams states that false imprisonment can be committed only by force or the threat of force while kidnapping can alternatively be committed by fraud: "Can Babies be Kidnapped?" [1989] Crim LR 480. He cites the Canadian authority of *Metcalfe* (1983) 10 CCC (3d) 114 CA BC. If force or the threat of force is essential for false imprisonment it can never be committed by an omission. This opinion is contrary to authority; par 7.08. If force or the threat of force is a necessary ingredient in the case of commision then such can easily be found, for example, turning a key in a lock; see also *Hale* [1974] QB 819; *Linsberg* (1905) 69 JP 107; *Wekkard* [1978] 3 All ER 161; [1978] 1 WLR 921, 67 Cr App R 364 CA.

18 The precedent indictment in Archbold (1922) 999 included such an averment but this is unnecessary. See also 1 Hawk PC, ch 60, s 7.

19 *Bird v Jones* (1845) 7 QB 742, 115 ER 668; *Phillips v GNR* (1903) 4 NIJR 154.

20 Per Patteson J in *Bird v Jones*, fn 19 at 752, approved by O'Brien LCJ in *Phillips v GNR*, fn 19 at 155.

21 See the facts of *The People (DPP) v Prunty* [1986] ILRM 716 CCA. In *Cuchen & Meister v Home Office* [1958] 1 QB 496; [1958] 1 All ER 485, it was a false imprisonment to allow a person to leave an airport building.

22 At 410 (footnotes omitted); *Moore* (1990) 60 CCC (3d) 286 SC Prince Edward Island.

23 *McDaniel v State* (1942) 15 Tex Crim R 115; *Burton v Davies* [1953] QSR 26 SC Queensland.

24 [1988] ILRM 724.

25 At 735. In contrast to 22 March 1986 Evelyne Glenholmes was released by a District Justice because the documents supporting the warrant for her arrest were defective. The District Justice then issued an emergency warrant under s 49 of the Extradition Act, 1965 as he had been informed that a further arrest warrant had been issued in the United Kingdom which was then being forwarded to Ireland.

The victim will be imprisoned, notwithstanding that he had a means of escape, when he could not be reasonably expected to use it.[26] The accused will usually have imprisoned the victim in bringing him to the place of confinement.

Psychic Imprisonment

7.07 A false imprisonment may be psychic.[27] A confinement will only occur in this context where the victim has been dominated by the action of the accused and succumbs to that domination, thus losing his liberty.[28] A formal arrest is not required once it is made clear to the victim that he cannot leave and he submits to that direction.[29] There is no imprisonment where the victim runs away on being told that he is under arrest.[30] A request, which carries no compulsion, by a police officer that a person should accompany him to a station is not an imprisonment.[31] Going to a police station in consequence of a charge made against a person has been held to be an imprisonment.[32]

By Direction

7.08 It would be a false imprisonment for the accused to direct a Garda to arrest the accused.[33] No offence is committed where the accused merely informs a Garda, in good faith, of the nature of his suspicions. In such circumstances the accused will lack the mental element of the crime, genuinely believing that there is a lawful reason for exercising a power to restrain the victim's liberty.[34] A person cannot be liable where the arrest is made on the authority of a District Justice.[35] Where criminal proceedings are instituted maliciously and without reasonable and probable cause and in consequence of which a person suffers damage, the party responsible will be liable for the tort of malicious prosecution.[36]

Another District Justice ruled, on her being arrested a short time later, that "the release meant nothing in the events that followed" because while she was at large Miss Glenholmes had been kept under extremely tight surveillance; see the *Irish Times*, 24 March 1986. It is submitted that this decision was wrong and is clearly in conflict with *Kane's* case.

26   McMahon & Binchy 410; Salmond & Heuston 139 and the cases therein cited.

27   As may an assault see par 6.03-6.08.

28   *Phillips v GNR* (1903) 4 NIJR 154; *Alderson v Booth* [1969] 2 QB 216; [1969] 2 All ER 271; [1969] 2 WLR 1252, 53 CR App R 310 DC.

29   *Campbell v Tormey* [1969] 1 All ER 961; [1969] 1 WLR 189, 53 Cr App R 99.

30   *Russen v Lucas* (1824) 1 C&P 153, 171 ER 1141, Ry&M 26, 171 ER 930.

31   *Cant v Parsons* (1834) 6 C&P 504, 172 ER 1339.

32   *Peters v Stanway* (1835) 6 C&P 737, 172 ER 1442. Smith & Hogan 406 regard this decision as incorrect but point out that it was followed in *Conn v David Spencer Ltd* [1930] 1 DLR 805 SC BC.

33   *Gosden v Elphick & Bennett* (1849) 4 Exch 445, 154 ER 1297; *Austin v Dowling* (1870) LR 5 CP 534; *Grinham v Willey* (1859) 4 H&N 496, 154 ER 934.

34   See par 6.35.

35   *Lock v Ashton* (1848) 12 QB 871, 116 ER 1097; *Marrinan v Vibart* [1963] 1 QB 528; [1962] 3 All ER 380; [1962] 3 WLR 912 CA; similarly the accused's responsibility will cease on a magistrate authorising the detention or, for example, a doctor at an asylum deciding that it was justified in detaining the person; *Harnett v Bond* [1925] AC 669; [1925] All ER 110 HL.

36   Generally see McMahon & Binchy, 676-681; Salmond & Heuston, 461-72.

Omission

7.09 False imprisonment may be committed by an omission, as where a prisoner is detained after his acquittal or after the term of his imprisonment has expired.[37] Liability for an omission to release the victim will only arise where the accused was under a duty to act, arising either in contract,[38] or from a legal responsibility laid on him[39] to ensure the victim's release, or where the accused fails to counteract a danger which he himself has created.[40]

No liability for false imprisonment arises where the victim insists, in breach of contract, in being released from a place where his contract confines him earlier than the scheduled time.[41] So in *Burns v Johnston*[42] an employer extended the working hours by half an hour in circumstances where the factory gates were closed while work was in progress. One hundred and thirty employees were refused egress when they demanded to be let out half an hour early. It was held, on a case stated, that the employer was not bound to afford the employee facilities for breaking his contract and this ruling was affirmed on appeal.[43] An employee was entitled to leave early on applying, for adequate personal reasons, for a pass. None of the employees had so applied or given such reasons.

The defences to false imprisonment and kidnapping are considered below.

Restraint Made Unlawful

A detention which is initially lawful can become unlawful if, a term of imprisonment has expired or a prisoner subjected to remand has been acquitted.[44] Dicta in Irish law also suggest that a lawful imprisonment may become unlawful if a person detained in a Garda station is denied private access to his legal advisors[45] or where a prisoner is denied access to necessary medical attention,[46] to which he is entitled or detained in a place which is a health hazard,[47] or a person is moved for the purpose of harassing or isolating him from assistance or access to which he is entitled, or if he is subjected to serious ill-treatment while in custody.[48] All of these statements may be explained as being an identification of the circumstances under which judicial review will lie at the suit of a prisoner who is not detained strictly in accordance

37   *Mee v Cruikshank* (1902) 20 Cox 210.
38   *Herd v Weardale Steel Coal & Coke Co. Ltd* [1915] AC 67 HL. In the Court of Appeal Buckley & Hamilton LJJ considered that the remedy, in civil law, was in contract; [1913] 3 KB 771 CA.
39   As in the case of a governor of a prison; *Mee v Cruikshank*, fn 37.
40   *Miller* [1983] 2 AC 161; [1983] 1 All ER 978; [1983] 2 WLR 539, 77 Cr App R 17; [1983] Crim LR 466 HL; McMahon & Binchy 412.
41   *Herd v Weardale Steel & Coke Co. Ltd*, fn 38.
42   [1917] 2 IR 137, affirming [1916] 2 IR 444.
43   The analysis of the law of contract in that case does not conform with the modern approach to that subject.
44   *Mee v Cruikshank* (1902) 20 Cox 210.
45   *The State (Harrington) v Garvey*, High Court unreported, 14 December 1976 and see *The People (DPP) v Healy* [1990] ILRM 313 SC.
46   *Re The Emergency Powers Bill, 1976*; [1977] IR 159 at 173, 111 ILTR 29 at 32.
47   *Middleweek v Chief Constable of the Merseyside Police* [1990] 3 All ER 663 CA; *Weldon v Home* Office [1990] 3 All ER 672 CA; *R v Deputy Governor of Parkhurst Prison* [1990] 3 All ER 687 CA.
48   *The People (DPP) v Kelly (No. 2)* [1983] IR 1 at 21 CCA, SC.

with constitutional justice. In *Hague v Deputy Govenor of Parkhurst Prison*[49] the House of Lords decided against an interpretation of the tort of false imprisonment which would allow a breach of a prisoner's rights to render unlawful an otherwise lawful detention.[50] It was therefore impossible for a prisoner already lawfully detained to be subjected to a false imprisonment by being confined, for example, in a punishment cell in contravention of the prison rules or in the absence of circumstances requiring such restraint.[51] A prisoner may only be lawfully confined by those entitled so to do, that is the prison govenor and his officers, and a restraint by fellow prisoners, even within the confines of a prison, is unlawful.[52]

Kidnapping

7.10 It is a common law misdemeanour to steal and carry away or secrete a person against his will,[53] or if the victim is a boy under the age of fourteen[54] or a girl under sixteen years of age,[55] against the will of the parent or guardian of that child. The elements of the offence are so unclear, in Irish law, as a result of the Supreme Court's decision in *The People (A-G) v Edge*[56] that the offence is not charged. In practice the prosecution prefer to rely on the offence of false imprisonment.[57]

East defined the offence thus:

> The most aggravated species of false imprisonment is the stealing and carrying away, or secreting of some person, sometimes called kidnapping, which is an offence at common law.[58]

A kidnapping may be committed either by force or by fraud.[59]

In England the crime has been subject to analysis by the House of Lords in *D*.[60]

49 [1991] 3 All ER 733 HL.

50 Based in part on s 12(1) of the Prison Act, 1952 which reads: "A prisoner, whether sentenced to imprisonment or committed to prison on remand pending trial or otherwise, may be lawfully confined in any prison".

51 See the prior decision in *Weldon v Home Office*, fn 47; *R v Deputy Govemor of Parkhurst Prison*, fn 47; *Middleweek v Chief Constable of Merseyside Police*, fn 47.

52 *R v Deputy Governor of Parkhurst Prison*, fn 47 at 707, approved in *Hague v Deputy Govenor of Parkhurst Prison*, fn 49 at 744. A prison officer acting in bad faith by deliberately subjecting a prisoner to a restraint which he knows he has no authority to impose may also be personally liable to an action for false imprisonment as well as committing the tort of misfeasance in public office.

53 *The People (A-G) v Edge* [1943] IR 115, Murnaghan J at 128, Geoghegan J at 138, Black J at 160, Gavan Duffy J at 164.

54 Fn 53, Geoghegan J at 141, O'Byrne J at 145, Black J at 160, Gavan Duffy at 172.

55 Fn 53, O'Byrne J at 144, Black J at 162, Gavan Duffy J at 170.

56 Fn 53.

57 Thus in the case of *The People (DPP) v Prunty* [1985] ILRM 716 CCA, the victim William Summerville, who volunteered to go in place of his son, was taken at gunpoint from his home and tied for several days to a tree in the Wicklow mountains. The prosecution charged the accused with false imprisonment.

58 1 PC 429. In *Wellard* [1978] 3 All ER 161; [1978] 1 WLR 921, 67 Cr App R 364, the Court of Criminal Appeal held that the crime was complete when a person was deprived of his liberty and carried away from the place where he wished to be.

59 *Metcalfe* (1983) 10 CC (3d) 114 CA BC; see also Wellard, fn 58. This was a case where the victim acquiesced to go with the accused because he pretended to be a police officer.

60 [1984] AC 778; [1984] 1 All ER 449; [1984] 2 WLR 186, 79 Cr App R 313; [1984] Crim LR 558 HL and CA; cricitised by Williams, "Can Babies Be Kidnapped?" [1989] Crim LR 473.

Lord Brandon defined the parameters of the offence:

> ... six matters relating to the offence of kidnapping clearly emerge. Firstly, the nature of the offence is an attack on, and infringement of, the personal liberty of an individual. Secondly, the offence contains four ingredients as follows: (1) the taking or carrying away of one person by another, (2) by force or by fraud, (3) without the consent of the person so taken or carried away and (4) without lawful excuse. Thirdly, until the comparatively recent abolition by statute of the division of criminal offences into the two categories of felonies and misdemeanours ... the offence of kidnapping was categorised by the common law as a misdemeanour only. Fourth, despite that, kidnapping was always regarded, by reason of its nature, as a grave and (to use the language of an earlier age) heinous offence. Fifth, in earlier days the offence contained a further ingredient, namely that the taking or carrying away should be from a place within the jurisdiction to another place outside it; this further ingredient has, however, long been obsolete and forms no necessary part of the offence today. Sixth, the offence was in former days described not merely as taking or carrying away a person but further or alternatively as secreting him; this element of secretion has, however, also become obsolete, so that, although it may be present in a particular case, it adds nothing to the basic ingredient of taking or carrying away.[61]

It is submitted that the offence may be committed by either intention or recklessness.[62] In contrast to the position adopted by the Supreme Court in *Edge*,[63] the House of Lords in *D* held that the consent of the victim was the material element of the offence, notwithstanding that the victim was of a young age. Younger children were expected to lack the intelligence and understanding to consent. Whether the victim consented, at any age, was a matter for the jury. Lord Brandon expressed the view that he did not expect a jury to find at all frequently that a child under fourteen had sufficient understanding and intelligence to give its consent.[64] It appears implicit in the judgments in *Edge*[65] that a parent or parents could not be convicted of kidnapping their own child.

Excuse

7.11 In *D* the House of Lords held that a parent could be convicted of kidnapping its own child (which was what had occurred in that case). Lord Bridge limited the crime, as regards a parent, where the taking was done in contravention of the order of a court of competent jurisdiction restricting his or her parental rights. The majority decision placed parents in the same category as strangers requiring, simply, the absence of a lawful excuse. It has been held that a husband may be convicted of kidnapping his wife.[66] A belief by an attempted kidnapper that a friend required to be taken by force from the premises of a religious sect which, he thought, was placing her in moral and spiritual danger, was not a defence.[67] The Court of Appeal held that the law did not recognise as a lawful excuse the conduct of anyone kidnapping

---

61 AC at 800, All ER at 453, WLR at 192 Cr App R at 318.
62 *Rahman* (1985) 81 Cr App R 349; [1985] Crim LR 596 CA (a case of false imprisonment).
63 Fn 53.
64 AC at 806, All ER at 457, WLR at 197, Cr App R at 323.
65 Fn 53.
66 *Reid* [1973] QB 299; [1972] 2 All ER 1350; [1972] 3 WLR 395, 56 Cr App R 703 CA.
67 *Henman* [1987] Crim LR 333 CA.

another unless it could properly be said that there had arisen a necessity, recognised by the law as such, causing the would-be kidnapper to act in that way.

The law recognises that parents have to discipline their children. Those acting as guardians in place of the parent are in the same position. Reasonable and moderate punishment may be inflicted on a child.[68] This may include taking a child against his will from a particular place or punishing him by confining him to a place for a period of time. The question of what constitutes reasonable and moderate punishment will be decided according to contemporary standards as to the relationship between parents and children.[69]

It is lawful to arrest and detain someone, either as a Garda or as a citizen, within the scope of a recognised power of arrest either at common law, or under statute, exercised in good faith.[70]

Child Stealing

7.12 S 56 of the Offences Against the Person Act, 1861 provides:

> Whosoever shall unlawfully, either by force or fraud, lead or take away, or decoy or entice away or detain, any child under the age of fourteen years, with intent to deprive any parent, guardian, or other person having the lawful care or charge of such child, of the possession of such child, or with intent to steal any article upon or about the person of such child, to whomsoever such article may belong, and whosoever shall, with any such intent, receive or harbour any such child, knowing the same to have been, by force or fraud, led, taken, decoyed, enticed away, or detained as in this section before mentioned, shall be guilty of felony and being convicted thereof shall be liable to be kept in penal servitude for any term not exceeding seven years and, if a male under sixteen years of age, with or without whipping: Provided that no person who shall have claimed any right to the possession of such child, or shall be the mother or shall have claimed to be the father of an illegitimate child, shall be liable to be prosecuted by virtue hereof, on account of getting possession of such child, or taking such child out of the possession of any person having the lawful charge thereof.[71]

Age is proved in the same way as in cases of under-age sexual intercourse.[72] Intent will be proved by inference from all the circumstances.[73] The natural consequence of taking a child away will be to deprive the parent or guardian of the possession of that child. An intent to deprive the parent permanently of the possession of the child is not necessary.[74] An accused may be convicted under the section even though the child is no longer in his custody and there is no evidence to show where it has gone.[75] The acts of force or fraud may be committed or exercised upon the parent

68   *Terry* [1955] VLR 114 SC; *Hopley* (1860) 2 F&F 202, 175 ER 1024.

69   Detention for such a period or in such circumstances as to take it outside the realms of reasonable parental discipline is unlawful and this is for a jury to decide; *Rahman* (1985) 81 Cr App R 349; [1985] Crim LR 596 CA. Generally see Smith & Hogan 386; Howard 145-46.

70   See par 6.35.

71   The sections are quoted, as are all other sections from the Offences Against the Person Act, 1861, in accordance with the amendments introduced by the Penal Servitude Acts of 1864 and 1891 and by the Statute Law Revision Act, 1908.

72   See par 8.60.

73   For a full discussion, in the context of murder, see ch 2.

74   *Powell* (1915) 24 Cox 229, correcting *Jones* (1912) 22 Cox 212.

75   *Johnson* (1884) 15 Cox 481 CCR.

or guardian of the child, or on the child itself, or on any other person.[76] It was held in *Duguid*[77] that persons who entered into a conspiracy with the mother of a child under fourteen to take the child away from its lawful guardian were indictable despite the fact that the mother herself could not be convicted of an offence under the section or of a conspiracy to commit it.[78]

Abandonment

7.13 In contrast to the foregoing provisions in relation to false imprisonment, kidnapping and child stealing, it is an offence to force a seaman on shore and leave him behind, or otherwise leave him behind, outside the jurisdiction.[79] The master of the ship is also guilty of an offence unless the seaman is discharged before being left behind.[80] It is an offence to abandon a child.[81]

Interfering with Consciousness with Intent

7.14 The inapplicability of the law of assault to situations where the accused caused his victim to take poison or some other drug[82] led to the creation of offences to penalise those wrongs. The offence introduced, for the first time, by s 21 of the Offences Against the Person Act, 1861 provides:

> Whosoever shall, by any means whatsoever, attempt to choke, suffocate, or strangle any other person, or shall by any means calculated to choke, suffocate, or strangle, attempt to render any other person insensible, unconscious, or incapable of resistance, with intent in any of such cases thereby to enable himself or any other person to commit, or with intent in any of such cases thereby to assist any other person in committing any indictable offence, shall be guilty of felony, and being convicted thereof, shall be liable to be kept in penal servitude for life.[83]

The section is confined to attempts.[84] The attempt must be made with intent[85] to commit an indictable offence, which must be specified. In contrast s 22 of the Offences Against the Person Act, 1861 creates an offence similar to the foregoing in terms of its intent, and in terms of the harm sought to be caused to the victim. The harm is expressed in terms of the completed offence as well as in terms of an attempt:

> Whosoever shall unlawfully apply or administer to or cause to be taken by, or attempt to apply or administer to, or attempt to cause to be administered to or taken by, any person, any chloroform, laudanum, or other stupefying or overpowering drug, matter,

---

76 *Bellis* (1893) 17 Cox 660 CCR, this case overruled *Barrett* (1885) 15 Cox 658 where it was held that the force must be on the child itself.

77 (1906) 21 Cox 200 CCR.

78 Russell 694.

79 Merchant Shipping Act, 1906, s 43.

80 Merchant Shipping Act, 1906, s 36(1) and (3); further see Russell 694-95.

81 See par 6.13.

82 See par 6.13.

83 The sections are quoted, as are all other section from the Offences Against the Person Act, 1861, in accordance with the amendments introduced by the Penal Servitude Acts of 1864 and 1891 and by the Statute Law Revision Act, 1908.

84 For a short discussion of attempts see par 2.41.

85 Intent is discussed in par 2.41.

or thing, with intent in any of such cases thereby to enable himself or any other person to commit, or with intent in any of such cases thereby to assist any other person in committing any indictable offence, shall be guilty of felony, and being convicted thereof shall be liable to be kept in penal servitude for life.[86]

Proof of the nature of what was administered will normally be a matter for expert evidence. Where the effect of the victim taking the substance in question is to stupefy or overpower him, then an inference can be drawn as to its nature. In practice the ordinary evidence of intent will be that the victim was robbed or otherwise injured whilst under the influence of that substance.[87] S 3(3) of the Criminal Law Amendment Act, 1885 contains a special provision penalising the administration of substances in the context of procuring sexual intercourse.[88]

The Criminal Law Revision Committee[89] recommended the repeal of these sections and their replacement with offences of causing injury and the offence of administering any substance which in the circumstances is capable of interfering substantially with another's bodily functions. Ss 21 and 22 are of little practical importance.

Poisoning

7.15 Poison may be administered in the context of an assault; for example, where the accused jabs his victim with a venomous umbrella. More often poison is placed in food or drink that the victim may consume. No assault is thereby committed;[90] an offence outlawing such conduct is needed. The law on poisoning is contained in ss 23 to 25 of the Offences Against the Person Act, 1861:

> 23 Whosoever shall unlawfully and maliciously administer to or cause to be administered to or taken by any other person any poison or any other destructive or noxious thing, so as thereby to endanger the life of such person, or so as thereby to inflict upon such person any grievous bodily harm, shall be guilty of felony, and being convicted thereof shall be liable to be kept in penal servitude for any term not exceeding ten years.

> 24 Whosoever shall unlawfully and maliciously administer to or cause to be administered to or taken by any other person any poison or any other destructive or noxious thing, with intent to injure, aggrieve, or annoy such person, shall be guilty of a misdemeanour, and being convicted thereof shall be liable to be kept in penal servitude for the term of five years.

> 25 If, upon the trial of any person for any felony in the last but one preceding section mentioned, the jury shall not be satisfied that such person is guilty thereof, but shall be satisfied that he is guilty of any misdemeanour in the last preceding section mentioned, then and in every such case the jury may acquit the accused of such felony and find him guilty of such misdemeanour, and thereupon he shall be liable to be punished in the same manner as if convicted upon an indictment for such misdemeanour.

---

86   Re-enacting, with amendments, s 3 of the Prevention of Offences Act, 1851. Fn 83.
87   Archbold (1922) 945.
88   See par 8.24.
89   14th Report, Offences Against the Person (Cmnd 7844) par 205-14.
90   See par 6.13.

In this context "maliciously" requires proof that the accused (1) intended to do a particular kind of harm that in fact was done or (2) was reckless as to whether such harm should occur or not (the accused foreseeing that the particular kind of harm might be done but going on to take the risk of it) and is not limited to, nor does it require, any ill will towards the victim.[91]

Sections Disjunctive

S 23 is expressed in terms of the accused intentionally or recklessly causing poison to be taken and the victim's life thereby being endangered, or his thereby being caused grievous bodily harm. In *Tulley v Corrie*[92] it was held that if the substance was administered only with intent "to injure, aggrieve or annoy" (in other words the offence under s 24) but it in fact inflicted grievous bodily harm on the victim then this amounted to the offence under s 23. Since *The People (DPP) v Murray*[93] this analysis is no longer applicable. The accused must foresee the unlawful consequence, as defined by the section, in the sense that he must intend it or be reckless as to its occurrence.

Administration

Technical decisions as to what constitutes an administration are unnecessary in the context of the language of the section which broadens the scope of the external element to any act or omission of the accused which results in the substance being taken by the victim.[94] In *Dones*[95] the accused squirted a solution of ammonia on a man in the course of a fight.[96] The trial judge quashed the indictment on the grounds that this did not constitute an offence contrary to s 24, expressed in the indictment as "causing a noxious thing to be administered". It is submitted that where the accused acts with the result that the victim obtains the detriment of the substance then he has caused that substance to be taken by the victim. Such an interpretation conforms to the ordinary use of language.

Poison

Ss 58 and 59 of the Act also use the phrase "poison or other noxious thing". The discussion of that phrase in context of abortion is equally applicable.[97] The use of the word "destructive", it is submitted, covers such substances as drugs which cause physical or mental harm. The word is hardly necessary in the context of the wide definition given to the word "noxious".[98]

---

91   *Cunningham* [1957] 2 QB 396; [1957] 2 All ER 412; [1957] 3 WLR 76, 41 Cr App R 155 CCA. Intent is discussed in ch 2, recklessness in par 2.37.

92   (1867) 10 Cox 640; similarly *Cato* [1976] 1 All ER 260; [1976] 1 WLR 110, 62 Cr App R 41 CA.

93   [1977] IR 360 SC.

94   See par 5.05.

95   [1987] Crim LR 682.

96   It is arguable from the text of s 29 of the Act which penalises the use of acid that the use of the words in that section "or cast or throw out or upon or otherwise apply to any person, any corrosive fluid. . . ." implies an activity is covered by s 29 which is not covered by s 23 and 24. It is submitted, however, that to squirt a poison in someone's eye or on someone's skin, causes it to enter into the person's system and that it is thereby "taken by" that person.

97   See par 5.04.   98 See par 5.04.

A substance which is not harmful may become "noxious" when administered in a large quantity.[99] In *Cato*[1] the Court of Appeal refused to take account of the fact that the victim had an increased tolerance to drugs. The victim was a heroin addict and had a high tolerance to that drug. On a charge under s 23, the court held that heroin, so administered, was noxious because it was liable to cause injury in common use. The extraordinary characteristics of the victim were discounted as irrelevant to the section.

Mental Element

7.16 S 24 requires that the accused act with an intent to injure, aggrieve or annoy the victim. In deciding whether the person acted with an intent "to injure, aggrieve or annoy" regard must be had to the object of the accused and not merely the effect of the substance.[2] It is thus unlawful to cause a woman to take a substance given with the object of exciting her sexual passion[3] and to administer tablets to some boys with the object of disinhibiting them and thereby facilitating indulgence in unlawful homosexual activity.[4]

Smith & Hogan define the mental element in terms of whether or not the accused has a malevolent or benevolent purpose.[5] It is submitted that this is correct. In *Hill*[6] the Court of Appeal give this example:

> The accused may, in one case, administer the noxious thing with the intent that it would itself injure the person in question; but in another case he may have an ulterior motive as for example when he administers a sleeping pill to a woman with an intent to rape her when she is comatose. In either case he will, in our judgment, have an intent to injure the person in question, within the words in the section. By way of contrast, if a husband puts a sleeping draft in his wife's nightcap, without her knowledge, because he is worried that she has been sleeping badly and wishes to give her a decent night's sleep, he will commit no offence. So, in each case it is necessary to ask the question: Did the accused have the intention, in administering the noxious thing, to injure the person in question? And in each case it is necessary to look, not just at his intention as regards the immediate effect of the noxious thing upon that person, but at the whole object of the accused.[7]

The Criminal Law Revision Committee[8] recommended the repeal of s 23 in the context of the creation of a new offence of causing serious injury with intent to cause serious injury, or attempting to commit that offence, and causing serious injury recklessly; s 24 should be replaced by an offence of administering to another, without his consent and without lawful excuse, any substance which, in the circumstances

---

99   *Hennah* (1877) 13 Cox 547.

1   [1976] 1 All ER 260; [1976] 1 WLR 110, 62 Cr App R 41 CA.

2   *Hill* (1985) 81 Cr App R 206; [1985] Crim LR 384 CA partially reversed at (1986) Cr App R 386.

3   *Wilkins* (1861) L&C 89, 9 Cox 20.

4   *Hill*, fn 2.

5   404-05, doubting *Weatherall* [1968] Crim LR 115, where the object of putting a sleeping tablet in the victim's tea was to enable her handbag to be available for search for letters proving that she was committing adultery.

6   Fn 2.

7   Quoted from Smith & Hogan cases 371, Cr App R at 210.

8   14th report—Offences Against the Person (Cmnd 7844) par 184-91.

is capable, and which that person knows may be capable, of interfering substantially with the other's bodily functions.

Railway Offences

7.17 The law of assault extends to the person of the victim and his clothing.[9] Where a person assaults a vehicle in which someone is travelling, being aware of their presence, and being aware that it is highly likely that the person will thereby be injured, an intention to assault that person may be inferred.[10] Where a person knowingly takes a substantial and unjustifiable risk that his conduct will result in an injury to another an assault will be committed by recklessness.[11]

This analysis is modern. It was until recently believed that an assault could only be committed by a direct act.[12] In that context an attack on a vehicle in which a person was travelling might not have been regarded as an assault. Thus the sections of the Offences Against the Person Act, 1861 penalising various forms of assault[13] would have been regarded at that time as inapplicable where the assault was made to a vehicle in which the victim was travelling or where the harm was caused by indirect means. Mechanised transport was, at the time, provided by railways. A desire to protect passengers from indirect attacks on their safety led to the creation of statutory offences providing for this wrong. The danger of high speed transport led to the creation of offences of negligence in endangering passengers. This trend was continued by offences penalising those who drive dangerously on the roads.[14] With the growth of motorised transport on the roads the legislature did not extend the criminalisation of indirect attack on railways to motor cars. Instead it created the various offence of dangerous and careless driving.[15]

Ss 32 and 33 of the Offences Against the Person Act, 1861 provide:

> 32 Whosoever shall unlawfully and maliciously put or throw upon or across any railway, any wood, stone, or other matter or thing, or shall unlawfully and maliciously take up, remove, or displace any rail, sleeper, or other matter or thing belonging to any railway, or shall unlawfully and maliciously turn, move, or divert any points or other machinery belonging to any railway, or shall unlawfully and maliciously make or show, hide or remove, any signal or light upon or near to any railway, or shall unlawfully and maliciously do or cause to be done any other matter or thing, with intent, in any of the cases aforesaid, to endanger the safety of any person travelling or being upon such railway, shall be guilty of felony, and being convicted thereof shall be liable, at the discretion of the court, to be kept in penal servitude for life and if a male under the age of sixteen years with or without whipping.

> 33 Whosoever shall unlawfully and maliciously throw, or cause to fall or strike, at, against, into, or upon any engine, tender, carriage, or truck, used upon any railway, any wood, stone or other matter or thing, with intent to injure or endanger the safety

9   See par 6.12.
10   See par 2.19.
11   See par 6.14.
12   See par 6.14–6.16.
13   As to which see ch 6.
14   See par 3.45.
15   See par 3.35–3.44.

of any person being in or upon such engine, tender, carriage or truck, or in or upon any other engine, tender, carriage or truck of any train of which such first-mentioned engine, tender, carriage or truck shall form part, shall be guilty of felony and being convicted thereof shall be liable to be kept in penal servitude for life.

Both sections require that the act of the accused be done "maliciously". The word bears the same meaning as in ss 23 and 24 of the Act.[16] The external element of s 32 requires that the accused does, or causes to be done, anything which causes an interference with the mechanism or equipment of a railway. This extends, by the use of the words "do or cause to be done any other matter or thing" to influence with the engine or railway carriages themselves.[17]

Elements of the Offences

The external element of s 33 consists of striking any part of a railway rolling stock with any object. The intent required in the case of ss 32 and 33 is to injure or endanger the safety of any person using the railway. It has been held that if there is no person travelling on the truck at which the object is aimed then there is no evidence to support the indictment.[18] An acquittal under s 32, it has been decided, is no bar to a subsequent prosecution, on the same facts, for an offence against s 33.[19] This is a doubtful result; being in possible conflict with constitutionally guaranteed fairness of procedure.[20]

Neglect

7.18 Neglect is penalised by s 34 of the Act:

Whosoever, by any unlawful act, or by any wilful omission or neglect, shall endanger or cause to be endangered the safety of any person conveyed or being in or upon a railway, or shall aid or assist therein, shall be guilty of a misdemeanour, and being convicted thereof shall be liable, at the discretion of the court, to be imprisoned for any term not exceeding two years with or without hard labour.

"Wilful" in this context[21] means that the act was done deliberately and intentionally, not by accident or inadvertence, but so that the mind of the person who does the act goes with it.[22]

---

16   See par 7.15-7.16; and see *Upton* (1851) 5 Cox 298.

17   There is no direct authority.

18   *Sanderson* (1859) 1 F&F 37, 175 ER 615. It is submitted this is no longer correct under s 33, once there is some person in some part of the train. It is not necessary to prove an assault, as by thowing an object, once the accused intended to injure or endanger the safety of some person; Russell 651. It has been held, under s 34, that it was the offence to cut overhead wires to a signal box as: "It is not causing an accident which this offence contemplates but causing a source of danger" per Widgery CJ in *Pearce* [1967] 1 QB 130 at 155 CCA.

19   *Gilmore* (1882) 15 Cox 85.

20   *Ashe v Swenson* (1970) 397 US 436, 90 S Ct 1189, 25 L Ed (2d) 469; *US v Wilson* (1975) 420 US 332, 95 S Ct 1013, 43 L Ed (2d) 232; *Illinois v Somerville* (1973) 410 US 458, 93 S Ct 1066, 35 L Ed (2d) 425.

21   *Holroyd* (1841) 2 M&R 339, 174 ER 308; Smith & Hogan 122-24; *Sheppard* [1981] AC 394; [1980] 3 All ER 899; [1980] 3 WLR 960, 72 Cr App R 82 HL.

22   Per Lord Russell in *Senior* [1899] 1 QB 283; [1895-96] All ER 11, 19 Cox 219 CCR; Archbold (1922) 953; *Holroyd*, fn 21. In *Senior* the accused allowed his child to die knowing that she needed

In *Strange*[23] the accused was acquitted where he arrived at the gates of a level crossing and shouted twice for the gate man. Receiving no answer he opened the gates himself and crossed the line. A passing train collided with the cart and was damaged.[24]

Examples of offences within s 34 include throwing a stone at an engine or carriages[25] and failing, as an engine driver, to keep a good look out for signals.[26]

The Criminal Law Revision Committee[27] have recommended that s 34[28] be retained but that s 32 and 33 should be replaced by a new offence of a similar kind but extended, in its scope, beyond railways to road and air traffic. This offence would be punishable by a maximum penalty of seven years' imprisonment. The trend in legislation in the past century was towards covering specific identified situations with precisely worded offences which, because of that exactitude, are generally inapplicable elsewhere. The vast bulk of specific offences relating to endangering a victim or of harming a victim in particular situations could properly be reformed by replacing these specific offences with a general offence of endangering a victim with intent to cause serious bodily harm and endangering a person recklessly or in

medicine. He was a member of a religious sect but the court held that he had wilfully neglected the child in a manner likely to cause injury to its health. *Holroyd* was decided under s 15 of 3 and 4 Vict ch 97 (1840) (Lord Seymour's Act) which had a requirement of acting unlawfully and maliciously: "Whosoever shall unlawfully and maliciously put, place, cast or throw upon or across any railway any wood, stone, or other matter or thing, or shall unlawfully and maliciously take up, remove, or displace any rail, sleeper, or other matter or thing belonging to any railway, or shall unlawfully and maliciously turn, move, or divert any points or other machinery belonging to any railway, or shall unlawfully and maliciously make or show, hide, or remove, any signal or light upon or near to any railway, or shall unlawfully and maliciously do or cause to be done any other matter or thing, with intent, in any of the cases aforesaid, to obstruct, upset, overthrow, injure or destroy any engine, tender, carriage, or truck, using such railway, shall be guilty of felony, and being convicted thereof shall be liable [to penal servitude for life or two years' imprisonment . . ."]; *Roberts v Preston* (1860) 9 CB (ns) 208. In *Holroyd* the judge told the jury "wilfully" meant that they should consider the acts to have been done wilfully if the defendant intentionally placed the rubbish on the line knowing that it was a substance likely to produce an obstruction; if, for instance, he had done so in order to throw upon the company's officers the necessary trouble of removing the rubbish.

23 (1870) 11 Cox 608 (Ir).

24 The accused was also acquitted under s 36 of the Malicious Damage Act, 1861: "Whosoever, by any unlawful act, or by any wilful omission or neglect, shall obstruct or cause to be obstructed any engine or carriage using any railway, or shall aid or assist therein, shall be guilty of a misdemeanour, and being convicted thereof shall be liable, at the discretion of the Court, to be imprisoned for any term not exceeding two years . . .". See also *Pittwood* (1902) 19 TLR 37.

25 *Bowray* (1846) 10 Jur 211; Archbold (1922) 954.

26 Archbold (1922) 954. In *Monaghen and Granger* (1870) 11 Cox 608, two boys having let a cart slide down an embankment and allowed it to come to rest close to railway tracks, were convicted. The jury found that the accused did not even realise or consider that the cart would come close to the tracks as there was a hedge in the way. Nevertheless, Piggott B convicted them on the basis that "the natural consequence of starting a cart in the first place was that it ran through the hedge". This reasoning is not in conformity with the modern approach to offences; see ch 2.

27 14th Report—Offences Against the Person (Cmnd 7844) par 192-98.

28 S 34: "Whosoever, by any unlawful act, or by any wilful omission or neglect, shall endanger, or cause to be endangered, the safety of any person conveyed or being in or upon a railway, or shall aid or assist therein, shall be guilty of a misdemeanour, and being convicted thereof shall be liable, at the discretion of the Court, to be imprisoned for any term not exceeding two years with or without hard labour".

circumstances of gross negligence. The reform of the New Zealand criminal code is an apposite model.[29]

Malicious Damage

7.19 The Malicious Damage Act, 1861 creates offences which are concerned with damage to property or obstructing the use of railways. These offences include blowing down a bridge,[30] interfering with a railway with intent to obstruct or damage rolling stock[31] and obstructing rolling stock.[32] The offence of interfering with the railway contrary to s 35 of the Malicious Damage Act, 1861 is a scheduled offence under the Criminal Law (Jurisdiction) Act, 1976. This means that where the offence is committed in Northern Ireland it will constitute an offence contrary to s 2 of that Act.[33] S 35 of the Malicious Damage Act, 1861 provides:

> Whosoever shall unlawfully and maliciously put, place, cast, or throw upon or cross any railway, any wood, any stone or any other matter or thing, or shall unlawfully and maliciously take up, remove, or displace any rail, sleeper, or other matter or thing belonging to any railway, or shall unlawfully and maliciously turn, move, or divert any points or other machinery belonging to any railway, or shall unlawfully and maliciously make or show, hide or remove, any signal or light upon or near any railway, or shall unlawfully and maliciously do or cause to be done any other matter or thing with intent, in any of the cases aforesaid, to obstruct, upset, overthrow, injure or destroy any engine, tender, carriage, or truck using such railway, shall be guilty of felony and being convicted thereof shall be liable, at the discretion of the court, to be kept in penal servitude for life or to be imprisoned and if a male under the age of sixteen, with or without whipping.

It is an offence for an employee of a railway company to be drunk, offend against the bye-laws, rules or regulations of the company, or to do or attempt to do any act, wilfully, maliciously or negligently so that the life or limb of a person using the railway is injured or endangered.[34]

Cruelty to Children

7.20 Children are especially vulnerable members of society. Numerous statutory and indictable offences have been created to protect children.

It is an indictable misdemeanour to refuse or neglect to provide sufficient food or other necessaries for any person such as a child, apprentice or servant, unable to

---

29 See the discussion by France, "Reforming Criminal Law—New Zealand's 1989 Code" [1990] Crim LR 827.

30 Malicious Damage Act, 1861, s 33 (penal servitude for life or imprisonment for two years).

31 Malicious Damage Act, 1861, s 35 (penal servitude for life or two years' imprisonment).

32 Malicious Damage Act, 1861, s 36 (two years' imprisonment). Obstruction in this context includes altering a signal so that the train, in obeying it, slows down; *Hadfield* (1870) 11 Cox 574 and signalling a train to stop; *Hardy* (1871) LR 1 CLR 278.

33 The section is quoted at 9.12. For precedent indictments see chs 2, 3, 6, 9 and 10.

34 Railway Regulation Act, 1840, s 13 (two months' imprisonment or a ten pounds fine, under s 14 the case may be sent forward for trial where imprisonment for two years may be imposed). The Law Reform Commission have recommended the replacement of all these offences with a much simpler offence which would apply generally to causing damage to property; Report on Malicious Damage (LRC 26-1988) par 15.

provide for and take care of himself whom the accused is obliged, by duty or contract to provide for,[35] so as thereby seriously to injure health.[36] The duty of support does not occur unless the victim is either of an age or condition, or is so dominated by the parent or employer as to be unable to provide for himself.[37] Thus neglect of a servant who is able to go elsewhere is not an offence.[38] The duty extends to those infirm persons who are under the care or control of another.[39] This element of the crime includes persons who are severely mentally ill.[40] The external elements of the offence comprise a duty to provide necessaries, where the victim is unable to fend for himself, and resulting death or injury to his health by this neglect. Neglect includes a refusal to provide. It is insufficient to show that the victim had suffered to an extent less serious than would amount to an injury to health.[41] Death which occurs in consequence of such neglect will be manslaughter[42] or, if done with an intent to kill or cause serious injury, murder. A parent is obliged to provide medical attention for his child[43] as well as food, shelter and clothing.

7.21 It is an offence contrary to s 26 of the Offences Against the Person Act for a master under contract[44] to provide his apprentice or servant with food, clothing or lodging to wilfully,[45] and without lawful excuse refuse or neglect to provide those necessaries or to unlawfully and maliciously cause bodily harm to an apprentice or servant, in either case so that the life of the apprentice or servant is endangered or his health permanently injured.[46] It is an offence contrary to s 27 of the Offences Against the Person Act, to abandon or expose a child under two years of age.[47]

By Statute

7.22 The main offence of cruelty to children is contained in s 12 of the Children Act, 1908, as amended by s 4 of the Children Act, 1957:

12   (1) If any person over the age of seventeen years, who has the custody, charge or care of any child or young person, wilfully assaults, ill-treats, neglects, abandons, or exposes

---

35   The circumstances under which such a duty occur are the same as in the law of manslaughter and this topic is dicussed at par 3.14-3.20.

36   Russell 696; *Friend* (1802) R&R 20, 168 ER 662.

37   Russell 696.

38   *Smith* (1865) 30 4 LJNC 153, L&C 606, 169 ER 1533, 10 Cox 82 CCR.

39   *Instan* [1893] 1 QB 450; [1891-4] All ER 1213, 17 Cox 602 CCR; further see 3.14-3.20 and *Anon* (1851) 5 Cox 279.

40   Russell 703; *Pelham* (1846) 8 QB 959, 115 ER 1135; *Smith* (1826) 2 C&P 449, 172 ER 203. For ill-treatment or wilful neglect of a mental patient see s 253 Mental Treatment Act, 1945.

41   *Phillpot* (1853) Dears 179, 169 ER 686; *Cooper* (1849) 1 Den 459, 20 LJMC 219, 169 ER 836; *Hogan* (1851) 2 Den 277, 169 ER 504.

42   See par 3.14-3.20.

43   *Senior* [1899] 1 QB 283; [1895-96] All ER 511, 19 Cox 219 CCR, further discussed par 7.18. The duty extends to an apprentice; *Mabbett* (1851) 5 Cox 339; Russell 597.

44   Russell 697 citing the ruling of Barton J, Belfast Assizes (1901).

45   For the meaning of this word see par 7.18.

46   The penalty is penal servitude for five years or imprisonment for two years. On summary conviction twelve months' imprisonment and/or a £20 fine.

47   See par 6.13.

such child or young person or causes or procures such child or young person to be assaulted, ill-treated, neglected, abandoned, or exposed in a manner likely to cause such child or young person unnecessary suffering or injury to his health (including injury to or loss of sight or hearing, or limb, or organ of the body, and any mental derangement), that person shall be guilty of a misdemeanour [penalty—on indictment one hundred pound fine or two years' imprisonment, on summary conviction—twenty five pound fine or six months' imprisonment] . . . for the purposes of this section a parent or other person legally liable to maintain a child or young person shall be deemed to have neglected him in a manner likely to cause injury to his health if he fails to provide adequate food, clothing, medical aid, or lodging for the child or young person, or if, being unable otherwise to provide such food, clothing, medical aid, or lodging, he fails to take steps to procure the same to be provided under the Acts relating to the relief of the poor.

(2) A person may be convicted of an offence under this section either on indictment or by a Court of Summary Jurisdiction notwithstanding that actual suffering or injury to health, or the likelihood of such a suffering or injury to health, was obviated by the action of another person.

(3) A person may be convicted of an offence under this section either on indictment or by a Court of Summary Jurisdiction notwithstanding the death of the child or young person in respect of whom the offence is committed.

(4) Upon the trial of any person over the age of seventeen indicted for the manslaughter of a child or young person of whom he had the custody, charge, or care, it shall be lawful for the jury, if they are satisfied that the accused is guilty of an offence under this section in respect of such child or young person, to find the accused guilty of such offence.[48]

(5) If it is proved that a person convicted under this section was directly or indirectly interested in any sum of money accruable or payable in the event of the death of the child or young person, and had knowledge that such sum of money was accruing or becoming payable, then—(a) in the case of a conviction on indictment, the court may in its discretion either increase the amount of the fine under this section so that the fine does not exceed two hundred pounds; or, in lieu of awarding any other penalty under this section, sentence the person to penal servitude for any term not exceeding five years; and (b) in the case of a summary conviction, the court in determining the sentence to be awarded shall take into consideration the fact that the person was so interested and had such knowledge.

(6) A person shall be deemed to be directly or indirectly interested in a sum of money under this section if he has any share in or any benefit from the payment of that money, though he is not a person to whom it is legally payable.

(7) A copy of a policy of insurance, certified by an officer or agent of the insurance company granting the policy to be a true copy shall in any proceedings under this section be prima facie evidence that the child or young person therein stated to be insured has been in fact so insured, and that the person in whose favour the policy has been granted is the person to whom the money thereby insured is legally payable.
(a) An offence under this section is in this part of this Act referred to as an offence of cruelty.

---

48   This does not entitle the jury to convict the accused on any of the lesser offences in s 12. They can only convict them of such offences if that is the verdict which they think should be returned upon the facts although he was charged with manslaughter; *Tonks* [1916] 1 KB 443, 25 Cox 228, 11 Cr App R 284 CCA.

13   Where it is proved that the death of an infant under three years of age was caused by suffocation (not being suffocation caused by disease or the presence of any foreign body in the throat or air-passages of the infant) whilst the infant was in bed with some other person over sixteen years of age, and that other person was at the time of going to bed under the influence of drink, that other person shall be deemed to have neglected the infant in a manner likely to cause injury to its health within the meaning of this part of the Act.[49]

7.23 A "child" means a person under the age of fourteen years.[50] The expression "young person" means a person who is fourteen years or upwards and under the age of sixteen years.[51] The age of a person may be proved by the production of a birth certificate coupled with evidence identifying him as the person named in that certificate.[52] The court should make due enquiry as to the age of an offender. This is done by hearing evidence on oath, but an order of the court is not invalidated by any subsequent proof that the age of that person has been incorrectly stated by the court.[53] Where the child appears to the court to be under sixteen it is for the defence to prove that the child is older.[54]

"Wilfully" will have the same meaning as in s 34 of the Offences Against the Person Act, 1861.[55]

It must be proved that the accused is over the age of seventeen years and has the custody, charge or care of the victim, who is a child or young person.[56] The use of two different words to describe the physical act of possessing a child and the obligation to maintain or protect it, casts the section widely. Essentially it is a question of fact as to whether a given set of circumstances are covered by the section. The term "custody" is applicable to the parent, or legal guardian, of the child and to any person who is liable to maintain that child.[57] A parent or legal guardian of a child or young person is legally liable to maintain him. It is submitted that it may be fairly inferred that a child who is living with a person over the age of seventeen years is under the care or control of that person. For this purpose marital status is irrelevant.[58]

49   Under s 133(28) the spouse of an accused is a competent but not a compellable witness. It may be that the uncompellability has not survived the enactment of the Constitution; *The People (DPP) v JT* (1988) 3 Frewen CCA. A power of arrest is granted to a Garda where an offence is committed within the view of the Garda and where the name and residence of such person are unknown or cannot be ascertained, or where a person has committed, or a Garda has reason to believe has committed, the offence and he has reasonable grounds for believing that such person will abscond or if the name and address of such person are unknown to and cannot be ascertained by the Garda. The power of health boards and others to apply for Fit Persons Orders under s 20 and 24 of the Act is now subject to the Children Act, 1990.

50   Children Act, 1908, s 131.

51   Children Act, 1908, s 131.

52   Further see par 8.60.

53   Children Act, 1908, s 123; *The State (Kenny) v Ó hUadaigh* [1979] IR 1 HC.

54   Children Act, 1908, s 123.

55   See par 7.18.

56   Children Act, 1908, s 12.

57   The old decision of *Butler v Gregory* (1902) 18 TLR 370 to the effect that a putative father who has not been adjudged to be parent of a child is not a parent within the Act, is no longer maintainable, it is submitted, in the light of the Status of Children Act, 1987.

58   *Liverpool Society for the Prevention of Cruelty to Children v Jones* [1914] 3 KB 813, 111 LT 806, 24 Cox 434.

Where evidence is given that a person is a parent he is presumed to have custody of the child.[59] A parent cannot, by leaving his wife and children and living apart from them, divest himself of the custody of his child, so as to free himself from liability to a conviction for an offence under the Act.[60]

The effect of the wrong on the victim must be such as to be likely to cause the child or young person unnecessary suffering or injury to his health. Actual suffering need not be proved: the offence is cast in terms of that result being likely. The action of another person interrupting the chain of causation and rescuing the child is not a defence.[61] A deliberate omission to supply medical or surgical aid to a child is a clear example of the wrong prohibited by the section.[62] The suffering or injury must be something more than a slight fright.[63] It is unnecessary to prove directly that the wrong of the accused caused, or was likely to cause, unnecessary suffering. The jury may determine this question from the circumstances proved.[64] A medical practitioner should be called to prove the condition of the child.[65]

Ill-Treatment

7.24 In contrast to a stranger a parent has a duty to intervene to prevent another ill-treating their child.[66] The words "assaults, ill-treats, neglects, abandons, or exposes" are not necessarily mutually exclusive. Wording the indictment should, however, be done with care.[67] An assault, in this context, will have the same elements as at common law.[68]

Evidence of an assault is unnecessary in order to prove ill-treatment. Bullying and frightening will suffice, or any course of conduct calculated to cause unnecessary suffering or injury to health.[69] Neglect occurs where the person in charge of the child has failed to take reasonable care. This is defined as an omission to take such steps as a reasonable parent would take; such as are usually taken in the ordinary experience of mankind.[70] The question is one of fact to be decided in each case on the evidence.[71] Failure by a parent to make necessary resort to social welfare, for the purpose of maintaining the child is neglect.[72] It is no answer to the charge against

---

59   Children Act, 1908, s 38(2).

60   Archbold (1922) 996; *Cole v Pendleton* (1896) 60 JP 359; *Connor* [1908] 2 KB 26, 98 LT 932, 21 Cox 628.

61   Children Act, 1908, s 12(2).

62   *Senior* [1899] 1 QB 283; [1895-96] All ER 11, 19 Cox 219 CCR; *Oakey v Jackson* [1914] 1 KB 213, 110 LT 41, 23 Cox 734.

63   *Whibey* [1938] 3 All ER 777, 31 Cox 58; (1938) 26 Cr App R 184 CCA.

64   Archbold (1922) 997, citing *Brenton*, 111 Cent Cr Ct Sess Pap 309.

65   Archbold (1922) 997.

66   *Russell & Russell* (1987) 85 Cr App R 388; [1987] Crim LR 494 CA. But there must be proof of presence by the parent or assistance or circumstances from which such an inference may be drawn; *Lane & Lane* (1986) 82 Cr App R 5 CA. Further see par 3.16-3.20.

67   *Beard* (1987) 85 Cr App R 395.

68   See par 6.01-6.16.

69   Archbold (1922) 996-97.

70   *Senior* [1899] 1 QB 283; [1895-96] All ER 11, 19 Cox 219.

71   *Oakey v Jackson* [1914] 1 KB 216, 110 LT 41, 23 Cox 734.

72   Children Act, 1908, s 12(1). Quoted par 7.22.

one parent, who has failed to provide necessaries for his children, that could have had recourse to social welfare for the purpose of maintainir Inability to provide necessaries is a defence to the charge, subject to the duty the means through social welfare. Evidence of the possession by the accused of such resources as usually would not be exhausted by the date of neglect can establish that the accused possesses those means on the date of charge.[74]

"Abandonment" means leaving a child to its fate. In *Boulden*[75] the father of five young children, aged between one and nine, had a quarrel with his wife. She left the house in which they had all been living and travelled to her parents' home in Scotland. That evening the accused telephoned the headquarters of the National Society for the Prevention of Cruelty to Children telling them that his five children were alone in his house and asking for someone to be sent to look after them. He gave a false story when asked why he could not look after them himself. Shortly after, the police arrived and found the house in darkness with the children alone in it. There was little food available to them. The accused later followed his wife to Scotland. A conviction under the section was upheld by the Court of Criminal Appeal.[76] "Exposure" means placing a child at the mercy of the elements.[77]

Procedure

7.25 The unsworn evidence of any child of tender years may be given as an exception to the rule that all witnesses must be sworn.[78] Where a Justice is satisfied by the evidence of a registered medical practitioner that the attendance at court of the injured child would involve serious danger to its life or health, the Justice may take its deposition which is then admissible in evidence at the trial if reasonable notice is given in writing to the person against whom it was taken, and the person has had an opportunity of cross-examining the child.[79] The court may dispense with the attendance of the child at the trial if satisfied that such attendance is not essential to a just hearing of the case.[80] The wife or husband of a person charged with an offence under the Children Act, 1908 may be called as a witness for either the prosecution or defence without the consent of the person charged.[81]

Other Offences

7.26 It is also an offence under the Children Act, 1908 for a person having the custody, charge or care of a child or young person to allow the child to beg,[82] to allow a child to be in a room containing an open fire grate,[83] to allow a child or

---

73   *Cole v Pendleton* (1896) 60 JP 359.

74   *Jones* (1901) 19 Cox 678.

75   (1957) 41 Cr App R 105 CCA.

76   See also *Falkingham* (1870) 11 Cox 475; *White* (1871) LR 1 CCR 311, 12 Cox 83.

77   *Williams* (1910) 26 TLR 290, 4 Cr App R 89. Further see Archbold (1922) 871.

78   Generally see Law Reform Commission Report on Child Sexual Abuse par 7.01-7.35. Generally see *A-G v Lannigan* [1958] Ir Jur Rep 59; *A-G v O'Sullivan* [1930] IR 552 CCA. See further par 8.90.

79   Children Act, 1908, s 28.   80 Children Act, 1908, s 31.

81   Criminal Justice (Evidence) Act, 1924, Schedule and s 4(1).

82   S 14. Penalty £25 fine and/or six months' imprisonment.

83   S 15. Penalty £10 fine.

young person to reside in or frequent a brothel.[84] It is an offence for any person having the custody, charge or care of a girl under the age of seventeen years to cause or encourage the seduction or prostitution or unlawful carnal knowledge of that girl.[85] A person is deemed to have caused or encouraged the seduction or prostitution or unlawful carnal knowledge of a girl, who has been seduced, or who has become a prostitute, or who has been unlawfully carnally known, if the person knowingly allowed the girl to consort with, or enter or continue in the employment of, any prostitute or person of known immoral character.[86] Under s 18 the District Court may require a parent to enter into a recognisance to exercise due care and supervision. Other sexual offences against children are considered in chapter 8.

Draft Indictments

7.27 There follow the appropriate forms of indictment for the offences considered in this chapter.

FALSE IMPRISONMENT

Statement of Offence
False imprisonment contrary to s 2(1) of the Criminal Law (Jurisdiction) Act, 1976.
Particulars of Offence
 AB on the   at   Northern Ireland falsely imprisoned CD and detained him against his will.
Statement of Offence
False Imprisonment
Particulars of Offence
AB on the   at   falsely imprisoned CD and detained him against his will.

KIDNAPPING

Statement of Offence
Kidnapping
Particulars of Offence
AB on the   at   took and carried away CD, by force (or by fraud) without his consent (or without the consent of his parent or guardian if the victim is a boy under the age of fourteen or a girl under the age of sixteen years of age).

CHILD-STEALING

Statement of Offence
Child-stealing contrary to s 56 of the Offences Against the Person Act, 1861.
Particulars of Offence
AB on the   at   by force or fraud, took away, or decoyed, or enticed away (or detained) CD, a child of the age of ten years, with intent to deprive XY, the father of the said CD (guardian or other person having the lawful care or charge),

---

84   S. 16. Penalty £25 fine and/or six months' imprisonment.
85   S. 17. Penalty two years' imprisonment.
86   S 17(2).

of the possession of the said CD (or with intent to steal any article upon or about the person of such child).

INTERFERING WITH CONSCIOUSNESS WITH INTENT

Statement of Offence
Attempting to render a person insensible with intent to commit an indictable offence contrary to s 21 of the Offences Against the Person Act, 1861.
Particulars of Offence
AB on the   at   did attempt to render CD insensible with intent to enable himself (or any other person) to commit the indictable offence of robbery (or any other indictable offence).

POISONING

Statement of Offence
Causing poison to be taken, thereby inflicting grievous bodily harm (or thereby endangering life) contrary to s 23 of the Offences Against the Person Act, 1861.
Particulars of Offence
AB on the   at   unlawfully and maliciously caused poison (or any other destructive or noxious thing) to be taken, thereby inflicting on such person grievous bodily harm (or thereby endangering the life of such person).
Statement of Offence
Causing poison to be taken with intent to injure, aggrieve or annoy, contrary to s 24 of the Offences Against the Person Act, 1861.
Particulars of Offence
AB on the   at   unlawfully and maliciously caused poison (or any other destructive or noxious thing) to be taken by CD, with intent to injure, aggrieve or annoy the said CD.

RAILWAY OFFENCES

Statement of Offence
Endangering the safety of railway passengers contrary to s 32 of the Offences Against the Person Act, 1861.
Particulars of Offence
AB on the   at   maliciously threw or put upon or across the railway a stone (wood or other matter or thing) with intent to endanger the safety of persons travelling or being upon the said railway.

CRUELTY TO CHILDREN

Statement of Offence
Cruelty to children contrary to s 12(1) of the Children Act, 1908.
Particulars of Offence
AB being a person over the age of seventeen, having the custody or charge of CD, aged   years, on the   at   (or between the   and   ) assaulted, ill-treated or neglected the said CD (or caused or procured him to be assaulted, ill-treated or neglected) in a manner likely to cause him unnecessary suffering or injury to his health.

CHAPTER EIGHT

Sexual Offences

8.01 This chapter deals with sexual offences. The rules of evidence related to those offences are also considered in the final sections.

Rape

8.02 Rape was formerly defined at common law as the unlawful carnal knowledge of a woman without her consent by force, fear or fraud.[1]

Definition

8.03 This definition is now of limited usefulness and has been entirely replaced by a statutory definition contained in s 2 of the Criminal Law (Rape) Act, 1981:

> 2(1) A man commits rape if—
> (a) he has unlawful sexual intercourse with a woman who at the time of the intercourse does not consent to it, and
> (b) at the time he knows that she does not consent to the intercourse or he is reckless as to whether she does or does not consent to it, and references to rape in this act or any other enactment shall be construed accordingly.

> 2(2) It is hereby declared that if at a trial for a rape offence the jury has to consider whether a man believed that a woman was consenting to sexual intercourse, the presence or absence of reasonable grounds for such a belief is a matter to which the jury is to have regard, in conjunction with any other relevant matters, in considering whether he so believed.

The crime contains two elements: an objective circumstance whereby a man has sexual intercourse with a woman who does not consent to having sexual intercourse with him, coupled with either knowledge on the part of the man that the woman does not consent, or recklessness on his part as to whether she is or is not consenting.

Procedure

8.04 Rape is a felony and is punishable by penal servitude for life.[2] The Central Criminal Court has (subject to the right of the Director of Public Prosecutions to invoke the jurisdiction of the Special Criminal Court) sole jurisdiction in the trial of rape, aggravated sexual assault, burglary with intent to commit rape, and of attempts or conspiracies to commit those offences; and of the offences of aiding, abetting, counselling or procuring any of those offences and of incitement to rape

---

1   East PC 434; Archbold (1922) 1016; Archbold (1954) 1933, the offence is dealt with at 1 Hale 627 et seq.
2   Offences Against the Person Act, 1861, s 48: "Whosoever shall be convicted of the crime of rape shall be guilty of felony, and being convicted thereof shall be liable to be kept in penal servitude for life". The section is quoted as amended by the Penal Servitude Acts of 1864 and 1891 and by the Statute Law Revision Act, 1908.

or incitement to the offence of aggravated sexual assault.[3] A person indicted for rape may be convicted of an attempt to commit rape;[4] or of "s 4 rape" (unlawful penetration of a bodily orifice)[5] or of aggravated sexual assault, or of sexual assault; or of the statutory felony of unlawful sexual intercourse with a girl under 15 contrary to s 1 of the Criminal Law (Amendment) Act, 1935; or the statutory misdemeanour of having unlawful sexual intercourse with a girl under 17 pursuant to s 2 of that Act; or of procuring sexual intercourse by threats, intimidation, false pretences, false representations, or by alcohol, or other intoxicant, or drugs, contrary to s 3 of the Criminal Law (Amendment) Act, 1885, as amended by s 8 of the Criminal Law (Amendment) Act, 1935.[6]

The Central Criminal Court, the Special Criminal Court, and the District Court as the preliminary examination court, must try rape offences,[7] aggravated sexual assault, attempted aggravated sexual assault, aiding, abetting, counselling or procuring aggravated sexual assault, or attempted aggravated sexual assault, incitement to aggravated sexual assault or conspiracy to any of the foregoing, in the absence of the public save for officers of the court, persons directly concerned in the proceedings, representatives of the press and such other persons as the judge, the justice or the court may permit to remain.[8] The verdict or decision of the court and the sentence on the accused must, however, be announced in public.[9] Where an issue arises[10] as to what questions relating to the victim's previous sexual history may be asked of her (or in the case of aggravated sexual assault or "s 4 rape" of him), or what evidence may be adduced relating thereto,[11] the trial judge, the Special Criminal Court or the District Justice hearing depositions on preliminary examination, must exclude from the court everyone except officers of the court and persons directly concerned in the proceedings; a parent, relative or friend may remain with the victim and similarly with the accused, where he or she is less than 18 years of age.[12]

---

3   The Criminal Law (Rape) Act, 1981 (hereinafter referred to as the Rape Act, 1981) s 1, as amended by s 10 and s 12 of the Criminal Law (Rape) (Amendment) Act, 1990 (hereinafter referred to as the Rape Act, 1990). The 1990 Act was signed by the President on 12 December 1990.

4   Criminal Procedure Act, 1851, s 9. Quoted par 1.23.

5   Rape Act, 1990, s 8. See par 8.49.

6   Rape Act, 1990, s 8. These offences are all considered subsequently in this chapter.

7   S 1 of the Rape Act, 1981, as amended by s 12 of the Rape Act, 1990, defines a rape offence as: ". . . rape, attempted rape, burglary with intent to commit rape, aiding, abetting, counselling and procuring rape, attempted rape or burglary with intent to commit rape, and incitement to rape and . . . rape under s 4, attempted rape under s 4, aiding, abetting, counselling and procuring rape under s 4 or attempted rape under s 4 and incitement to rape under s 4".

8   Rape Act, 1981, s 6 as substituted by s 11 of the Rape Act, 1990.

9   Rape Act, 1981, s 6(4) as substituted by s 11 of the Rape Act, 1990.

10 This issue must arise in the course of the sexual assault offence which is defined by s 1 of the Rape Act, 1981 as amended by s 12 of the Rape Act, 1990, as: "A rape offence and any of the following, namely, aggravated sexual assault, attempted aggravated sexual assault, sexual assault, attempted sexual assault, aiding, abetting, counselling and procuring aggravated sexual assault, attempted aggravated sexual assault, sexual assault or attempted sexual assault, incitement to aggravated sexual assault, or sexual assault and conspiracy to commit any of the foregoing offences." For a definition of "rape offence" see fn 7.

11 Applications under s 3 of the Rape Act, 1981, as substituted by s 13 of the Rape Act, 1990, or s 4(2).

12 Applications under s 3 of the Rape Act, 1981, as substituted by s 13 of the Rape Act, 1990.

The complainant in a sexual assault offence[13] is entitled to anonymity, subject to the interests of justice requiring that he or she be named or otherwise identified for the purpose of ensuring that witnesses come forward who might not otherwise be available.[14] The accused in a rape offence[15] is entitled to anonymity subject to his right to apply to a judge of the High Court, before the commencement of the trial, or the trial judge, to waive it, and subject to the right of a co-accused to lift that anonymity, for the purpose of causing witnesses to come forward, and subject to the right of the Director of Public Prosecutions to apply to lift that anonymity in the public interest.[16] In this context the prohibition goes beyond the publication of a person's name and extends to the publication of any material likely to lead members of the public to identify the accused as the person charged. Anonymity of the accused ceases on conviction.[17]

S 11 of the Rape Act, 1990 provides that in any proceedings for a rape offence or the offence of aggravated sexual assault, or attempted aggravated sexual assault, or of aiding, abetting, counselling or procuring the offence of aggravated sexual assault or attempted aggravated sexual assault, or of incitement to the offence of aggravated sexual assault, or conspiracy to commit any of these offences, the judge, the justice or the court, as the case may be, must exclude from the court, during the hearing, all persons except officers of the court, persons directly concerned in the proceedings, *bona* fide representatives of the press and such other persons (if any) as the court exercises its discretion to admit. A parent, relative or friend of the victim may remain in court. This provision also applies where the accused is not of full age. The verdict, decision, and sentence must be announced in public.

External Circumstances

The mental element of rape is fulfilled by proof of intention or recklessness. The external element is now discussed. It consists of sexual intercourse with a woman who does not consent.[18] This simple definition requires further analysis. Under s 4 of the Rape Act, 1990 a new species of rape was created. This consists of a sexual assault which includes penetration of a bodily orifice in a manner defined by that section. This new and separate offence is considered later in this chapter.

Marriage

8.05 At common law sexual intercourse was unlawful, save where it occurred within marriage.[19] According to Hale a husband could not be guilty of the rape of

---

13   See fn 10.

14   S 7 Rape Act, 1981 as amended by s 16(2) of the Rape Act, 1990.

15   See fn 7.

16   Rape Act, 1981, s 8, as amended by s 14 of the Rape Act, 1990.

17   Rape Act, 1990, s 8(1)(b).

18   It is a question of fact for the jury as to whether a person is a woman; *Cogley* (1989) 41 A Crim R 198 Vict CCA; *McGuinness* (1988) 35 A Crim R 146 WA CCA (test of external genitalia applied). Generally see Bailey & Harris, "Sex Change in Criminal Law and Beyond" (1989) 13 Crim LJR 353.

19   "It would be natural, however, for the framers of a statute in days when the canon law would be more in their minds than today, to refer to any intercourse outside the bond of matrimony as

his wife, as her consent to matrimony implied consent to sexual intercourse.[20] The full breadth of this principle was doubted even at an early stage[21] and a court order[22] or separation agreement could retract the wife's consent to sexual intercourse.[23] At common law, notwithstanding the continuance of the marriage bond, a husband could be charged as a principal in the second degree[24] as aiding or abetting a rape by another on his own wife.

In *Kowalski*[25] the Court of Appeal held that the consent to sexual intercourse implied by marriage did not extend to an act of fellatio forced on the wife, by the husband, at knife-point. The Court held that it was irrelevant that the act was undertaken as a preliminary to sexual intercourse. It was not within the consent implied in marriage and therefore required a separate or particular consent. Consent to such an act in the past was irrelevant and there was no principle implying such a consent to all future occasions where such an act might be demanded. The husband was accordingly convicted of indecent assault. A husband who, in the past, attempted to force his wife to have sexual intercourse with him using more than "gentle violence" could be convicted of assault.[26]

As to whether a husband who commits sexual acts on his wife, without her consent, either as a preliminary to sexual intercourse, or for the purpose of gratification in themselves, can be guilty of an indecent assault is undecided on the authorities. It can be argued that if the acts are unusual, as they were in *Kowalski*, then they require consent even within marriage. If however, the indecencies are in the nature of the normal preliminaries to sexual intercourse, it is arguable that they come within the marital rape immunity.[27] There appears to be no authority for holding that acts of indecent assault by a husband on a wife, which are not preliminary to sexual intercourse, are covered by the marital rape exemption. It is submitted that such an immunity does not exist.

In *R*[28] the Court of Appeal abolished the marital exemption. For our purposes

'unlawful'; and for their successors when drafting consolidating acts simply to repeat the word without a close consideration of its necessity or precise meaning". Law Reform Commission Consultation Paper on Rape (1987) page 9; Donovan J in *Chapman* [1959] 1 QB 100 at 104; [1958] 3 All ER 143 at 144; [1958] 3 WLR 401 at 402, 42 Cr App R 257 at 26 CCA; *Jones* [1973] Crim LR 710. See Grey, "Sexual Law Reform Society Working Party Report" [1975] Crim LR 323 at 329.

20   1 Hale PC 629.

21   See Brooks, "Marital Consent in Rape" [1989] Crim LR 877. See the remarks of the judges in *Clarence* (1888) 22 QBD 23; [1886–90] All ER 133, 16 Cox 511 CCR; Archbold (1922) 1019.

22   *Clarke* [1949] 2 All ER 448, 33 Cr App R 216.

23   *Roberts* [1986] Crim LR 188 CA. The controversy continues in England: Cases of *C, J and R* [1991] 1 All ER 755, 759, 747.

24   1 Hale PC 630; *Eldershaw* (1828) 3 C&P 396, 172 ER 472; *Waite* [1892] 2 QB 600, 61 LJ (MC) 187, 17 Cox CC 554 CCR.

25   (1988) 86 Cr App R 339; [1988] Crim LR 124, *The Times*, 9 October 1987.

26   *McN v McN* [1936] IR 177 HC; *G v G* [1924] AC 349 HL.

27   *Caswell* [1984] Crim LR 111. The commentary to this case was approved in *Kowalski* by the Court of Appeal, fn 25. And see *R (W) v W*, High Court, Finlay P, 1 February 1980, unreported; *Miller* [1954] 2 QB 282; [1954] 2 All ER 529; [1954] 2 WLR 138, 38 Cr App R 1. In *Caldwell* [1976] WAR 204 CCA it was held that a man who forced his wife to have sexual intercourse with him had been rightly convicted of unlawfully and indecently assaulting her.

28   [1991] 2 All ER 257 CA.

the reasoning of the Court supports the view that there is no residual immunity for a husband to sexually assault his wife, whether as a preliminary to sexual intercourse or as an act of gratification or violence in itself. The Court held that since the rule that a husband could not be guilty of raping his wife if he forced her to have sexual intercourse against her will, was an anachronistic and offensive common law fiction which no longer represented the position of a wife in present-day society, it should no longer be applied. Instead, the Court applied the principle that a rapist remained a rapist subject to the criminal law notwithstanding his marriage to the victim.

8.06 Following the recommendation of the Law Reform Commission[29] the marital rape exemption was abolished by s 5 of the Rape Act, 1990:

> 5(1) Any rule of law by virtue of which a husband cannot be guilty of the rape of his wife is hereby abolished.

It is clear that as a husband can be found guilty of raping his wife, any indecent act preliminary to rape can also attract criminal liability as an indecent assault. The intention of the Oireachtas was, it is submitted, to put a husband in the same category as a non-spouse in respect of sexual attacks on a woman. In this context any argued immunity for indecent acts, whether preliminary to sexual intercourse or not, cannot have survived the legislation.

Proceedings against a man in respect of rape by him on his wife cannot be instituted except by, or with the consent of, the Director of Public Prosecutions.[30]

Boys under 14

8.07 At common law a boy under 14 was irrefutably[31] presumed to be incapable of sexual intercourse[32] and could thus not be a principal in the first degree to rape or assault with intent to rape. This rule was abolished by s 5 of the Rape Act, 1990:

> Any rule of law by virtue of which a male person is treated by reason of his age as being physically incapable of committing an offence of a sexual nature is hereby abolished.

A defence of mental incapacity, based on infancy, is unaffected by the change.[33]

Sexual Intercourse

8.08 S 48 of the Offences Against the Person Act, 1861 provides that rape is a felony and fixes the maximum penalty for that crime at penal servitude for life. "Carnal knowledge" is the old term used by the law for sexual intercourse. This is defined by s 63 of the 1861 Act thus:

> Whenever, upon the trial for any offence punishable under this Act, it may be necessary to prove carnal knowledge, it shall not be necessary to prove the actual emission of seed in order to constitute a carnal knowledge, but the carnal knowledge shall be deemed complete upon proof of penetration only.[34]

---

29   Report on Rape par 18.   30   Rape Act, 1990, s 5(2).

31   *Phillips* (1839) BC&P 736, 173 ER 695.

32   1 Hale PC 630. This term included anal penetration. A boy could aid and abet; *Eldershaw* (1828) 3 C&P 396, 172 ER 472.

33   See par 4.48.

34   This was a re-enactment of s 18 of the Offences Against the Person Act, 1828.

Intercourse must be *per vaginam*.[35] Following a protracted and thorough debate the Law Reform Commission[36] recommended that the crime of rape should be defined by statute so as to include non-consensual sexual penetration of the vagina, anus and mouth of a person by the penis of another person, or of the vagina or anus of a person by an inanimate object held or manipulated by another person and that, as such, the crime of rape should be gender neutral as to the sex of the victim and the accused.[37] The change was recommended to update the law; it was considered that the word "rape" was now commonly used to describe those acts and was also so used to describe non-consensual buggery in men. The view had been expressed to the Commission that rape was the only word acceptable to the victims of these crimes as a name for the offence which had been committed against them. The Commission made this recommendation by a majority. Effect was given to this reform in s 4 of the Rape Act, 1990 which creates a new and separate offence from the crime of rape. It is discussed later in the text.[38]

8.09 It is well settled that the degree of penetration of the penis into the vagina which the law requires is the slightest penetration.[39] The fact that the victim's hymen was not ruptured does not assist the accused.[40] Thus in *The People (A-G) v Dermody*[41] the Court of Criminal Appeal held there to be sufficient evidence of sexual intercourse where "the evidence of the Prosecutrix was that the male organ of her assailant went into her vagina 'a wee bit'". The Court stating that "in law if the male organ is proved to have entered the opening of the vagina this amounts to penetration even if there is no emission".

Whereas penetration is necessary for sexual intercourse the ordinary use of language makes it clear that sexual intercourse ceases only on withdrawal. Because the common law described the external element in terms of penetration there is authority from Australia that the offence is thereby concluded.[42] The New Zealand Court of Criminal Appeal in *Kaitamaki*[43] has held rape to be a continuing offence where the crime was defined by statute as "the act of a male person having sexual intercourse with a woman or girl . . . without her consent" and where it was further

---

35   *Gaston* (1981) 73 Cr App R 164 CA.

36   Set out in part in their Consultation Paper on Rape (1987) pages 30–31 and in their report on Rape (1988) at par 15. A seminar was also held on 29 January 1988 by the Commission.

37   Law Reform Commission Report on Rape par 14.

38   See par 8.49. And see Leng, "The Scope of Rape" [1985] Crim LR 416.

39   *Hughes* (1841) 9 C&P 752, 2 Mood CC 190, 173 ER 1038 CCR, approving *Russen* (1777) 1 East PC 438, 1 Hale PC 628, 9 C&P 753n CCR; *Lines* (1844) 1 C&K 393, 174 ER 861.

40   *Hughes*, fn 39. The presence or absence of the hymen is, in modern terms, of far less importance than in the older cases. The law, reflected in the verdict of juries, pays little heed to the "good fame" of the woman, in contrast to Blackstone's view expressed at 4 Bl Com 213. The use of tampons by girls has rendered forensic evidence of rupture to the hymen, or the absence of this feature, easily capable of another explanation. Evidence of a new rupture or tear is of course capable of being objective evidence of sexual intercourse where this fact is actively in issue.

41   [1956] IR 307 at 312 CCA. See also *Papadimitropoulos* (1957) 98 CLR 249 at 255 HC; *Salmon* [1969] SASR 76 at 81 SC.

42   *Salmon*, fn 41, and the dissenting judgment of Woodhouse J in *Kaitamaki* [1980] 1 NZLR 59 at 64–65 CCA.

43   Fn 42.

provided "sexual intercourse is complete upon penetration". The Court held that the definition merely described the minimum conduct necessary to constitute sexual intercourse but did not render all that happened subsequent to penetration to be other than sexual intercourse. This was a continuing act which ended only on withdrawal. In other words, the act of sexual intercourse was complete upon penetration, in that this defined the minimum conduct necessary, but continued thereafter by the accused failing to withdraw. An innocent act of a continuing nature can become criminal during its progress as a result of a change in the state of mind of the accused.[44] The New Zealand legislature is, it is to be noted, similar to that in this jurisdiction. The concept of sexual intercourse being a continuing act was upheld, on appeal, by the Privy Council.[45] It follows that consent to sexual intercourse may be withdrawn by a woman at any stage, even after penetration. It is of practical application in such an instance and in situations where a man first realises the absence of consent during intercourse or where a person assisting the rapist, for example by keeping a lookout, becomes aware, during the act, of the absence of consent.

Consent

8.10 It should not be overlooked that the absence of consent of the victim is part of the external element of rape. Consent is a state of mind but it is external to the accused and is therefore an objective question. It is only the attitude which the accused has towards consent that is part of the mental element which is therefore a subjective question. The two relevant questions concern whether the victim consented in fact and the degree of awareness of that fact by the accused if she did not.

Earlier authorities emphasised that rape occurs by force without the victim's consent.[46] While one of the traditional elements of force, fear or fraud may be present in the majority of cases[47] they remain only species of the objective question: "at the time of sexual intercourse did the woman consent to it?"[48]

The victim may not consent because of a variety of circumstances. A person's

---

44 *Fagan v The Commissioner of Metropolitan Police* [1969] 1 QB 439; [1968] 3 All ER 442; [1968] 3 WLR 1120, 52 Cr App R 700 DC.

45 [1985] AC 147; [1984] 2 All ER 435; [1984] 3 WLR 137, 79 Cr App R 251; [1984] Crim LR 564 PC. Smith & Hogan argue against the decision at page 433 citing Woodhouse J, fn 42. Note, however, the wording in the Rape Act, 1981, s 2: "Who at the time of the intercourse does not consent to it". If the Oireachtas had meant "time of penetration" they could have said so.

46 *Bradley* (1910) 4 Cr App R 225; *Archbold* (1954) par 1942. A similar opinion is expressed in *Bourke* [1915] VLR 289, 292-293 SC, contra ibid 295-296. See Koh, "Consent and Responsibility in Sexual Offences" [1968] Crim LR 81, 150.

47 Smith & Hogan emphasised the shift away from the requirement of force in the middle of the 19th century, a tendency ignored by modern text book writers until the Heilbron Report in 1975 (Cmnd 6352).

48 This is the test as formulated by the Heilbron Committee and incorporated in the 1976 UK legislation and in turn copied, with an insignificant change in wording, but not in meaning, into our 1981 Rape Act. Consent may be given by an act or by a course of conduct; *Wilkes & Briant* [1965] VR 475 SC. There is no onus on the accused to prove that the woman consented and such a direction by a trial judge is incorrect; *Boney* (1986) 10 Crim LRJ 419 NSW CCA.

consent to indecent acts is void if that person is below the age of fifteen[49] but there is no minimum age which, by law, renders consent to sexual intercourse void. Sexual intercourse with a girl under the age of seventeen is a crime[50] and her consent to that act is no defence.[51] Such an act is not, however, rape unless the girl does not consent.

The victim's capacity to understand what is happening to her can be at issue. A child and a mentally handicapped woman[52] may both lack that degree of understanding that is necessary to constitute real consent. While there is authority that consent procured by animal passion is sufficient[53] the question, at common law, appears to be whether the victim was capable of exercising judgment on the question of consent or of distinguishing right from wrong.[54] The Supreme Court of Victoria in *Morgan*,[55] a case where the victim suffered from mental handicap, held that the jury should be directed that:

> It must be proved that she had not sufficient knowledge or understanding to comprehend (a) that what is proposed to be done is the physical act of penetration of her body by the male organ or, if that is not proved, (b) that the act of penetration proposed is one of sexual connection as distinct from an act of a totally different character.[56]

Such a test can equally be applied to children, where rape or sexual assault are the crimes charged, as in their case what is also at issue is the existence of sufficient understanding to enable them to give true consent. The absence of such understanding may be obvious by reason of the very young age of the victim. In such cases the prosecution may not need to do more than prove the age of the child.[57] However, it has been held to be a misdirection to instruct the jury that a child cannot consent to sexual intercourse but in an appropriate case such a misdirection will not affect the verdict on appeal if no injustice has been done.[58]

8.11 At common law fraud as to the nature and quality of the act and as to the identity of the person, but not fraud as to the attributes of the person, will vitiate consent:

> [R]ape is carnal knowledge of a woman without her consent: carnal knowledge is the physical fact of penetration; it is the consent to that which is in question; such a consent demands a perception as to what is about to take place, as to the identity of the man

---

49 Criminal Law (Amendment) Act, 1935, s 14.
50 See par 8.59.
51 *A-G (Shaughnessy) v Ryan* [1960] IR 181 SC.
52 For the offence of having sexual intercourse with an idiot, an imbecile or a feeble minded woman contrary to s 4 of the Criminal Law (Amendment) Act, 1935, see below.
53 *Fletcher* (1859) Bell CC 63, 169 ER 1168; *Barratt* (1873) LR 2 CCR 81. For a contrary view see Palles CB in *Dee* (1884) 15 Cox CC 579 at 587, 14 LR Ir 468 at 479.
54 *Archbold* (1922) 1020; *Archbold* (1954) par 1943. It should be noted that in *Pressy* (1867) 10 Cox 635 the accused was convicted of rape even though the victim, although she did not resist, knew that the accused was doing wrong. The authorities are confused.
55 [1970] VR 337.
56 At 341, approved by Williams *TBCL* 571.
57 *Harling* [1938] 1 All ER 307 at 308, 26 Cr App R 127, 128 CCA.
58 *Howard* (1965) 3 All ER 684; [1966] 1 WLR 13, 50 Cr App R 56 CCA.

and the character of what he is doing. But once the consent is comprehending and actual the inducing causes cannot destroy its reality. . . .[59]

Examples of fraud include *Flattery*[60] a case of a pretended surgical operation, or *Williams*[61] a sham voice improvement operation; the basic principle survives that where the victim consents to sexual intercourse, under a mistaken belief as to its nature, consent is vitiated.

Two confusing and contradictory decisions as to what representations can change the nature of the act consented to come from Canada. In *Bolduc*[62] the Supreme Court held that a medical doctor was not guilty of indecent assault where a patient in a hospital had consented, at his request, to an indecent examination in order to give practical experience to a "Dr Bird" who was, in fact, bogus. Bird (who was not a doctor) himself did not touch the victim. The court held, by a majority, that the fraud as to the identity of "Dr Bird" did not vitiate the nature and quality of the act performed by Dr Bolduc for his benefit. In *Maurantonio*[63] a bogus doctor conducted indecent examinations and was convicted. The Ontario Court of Appeal in upholding the conviction, through Hartt J, reasoned that there had been a misrepresentation as to the nature and quality of the act in the context of all the circumstances.

In *Flattery* and in *Williams* the victim had no idea that the act performed on them was sexual intercourse; such is a mistake as to the nature of the act. While the victim in *Bolduc* consented to the physical manipulation of her body, she understood its purpose to be medical and not prurient. The quality of the act performed by Dr Bolduc was the complete opposite. Whether one regards his misrepresentation as an inducing cause or as a mistake as to the attributes of Dr Bird, it is quite clear that no medical examination took place. That, it is submitted, is a fraud as to the nature of the act; what would have been decent was rendered indecent.

8.12 S 4 of the Criminal Law (Amendment) Act, 1885 provides:

> Whereas doubts have been entertained whether a man who induces a married woman to permit him to have connexion with her by personating her husband is or is not guilty of rape, it is hereby enacted and declared that every such offender shall be deemed to be guilty of rape.[64]

---

59 Per Dixon CJ in *Papadimitropoulos* (1957) 98 CLR 249 at 261 HC.

60 (1877) 2 QBD 410, 13 Cox 388 CCR. See also *Harms* (1944) 81 CCC 4 Saskatchewan CA.

61 [1923] 1 KB 340; [1922] All ER 433, 27 Cox 350, 17 Cr App R 56 CCA; *Case* (1850) 1 Den 580 CCR.

62 [1967] SCR 677; [1967] 3 CCC 294, 63 DLR (2d) 82 SC.

63 [1968] 1 OR 145. See also *Makray* (1982) 70 CCC (2d) 479 OCA. For a discussion of these cases see J.A. Scutt, "Fraud and Consent in Rape: Comprehension of the Nature and Character of the Act and its Moral Implications" (1976) 18 CLQ 312. In *Wolley v Fitzgerald* [1969] Tas SR 65 Chambers J held, on a case stated, that for the defendant to enter a hospital, pretending to be a doctor through medically unqualified, and inducing the victim to submit to a chest examination, did not give rise to the defence of consent. Such consent was induced by the false representation that the defendant was a doctor and also that the victim falsely believed that the examination was of a medical nature.

64 For a discussion on the history of this provision and its nature see the judgment of Dixon CJ in *Papadimitropoulos*, fn 59.

This provision is clear. It does not however deal with the case of an unmarried sexual partner. Prior to this section it had been held in England that consent by the victim was real even though induced by the accused impersonating her husband.[65] This decision was not followed by the Irish Court for Crown Cases Reserved in *Dee*.[66] It is likely that an Irish court would hold that a mistake as to the identity of a sexual partner does vitiate consent to sexual intercourse. The choice of a partner, even outside marriage, is the predominant factor which determines whether the act of sexual intercourse takes place at all. It is submitted that a mistake as to the identity of that person is fundamental to the consent given.

8.13 The attributes of a proposed partner have never been held sufficiently fundamental to vitiate consent; blandishments and misrepresentations as to status do not alter the nature and quality of the act or the identity of the partner.[67] In *Papadimitropoulos*[68] the High Court of Australia quashed a conviction where the victim, a young migrant speaking no English, had sexual intercourse with the accused after being duped by him into believing that the notice of intention to marry which they had signed in a Melbourne registry office was, in fact, a marriage ceremony. The victim's mistake was not as to the nature and quality of sexual intercourse or the accused's identity but rather as to his status in relation to her which, the Court held, was not sufficiently fundamental to vitiate consent. Similarly it is not rape for sexual intercourse to take place in circumstances where someone fails to reveal an important attribute prior to sexual intercourse, for example, the fact of venereal disease.[69]

---

65   *Barrow* (1868) 11 Cox 191, LR 1 CCR 156 CCR.

66   (1884) 15 Cox 579, 14 LR IR 468. See also *Gallienne* [1964] NSWR 919; (1963) 81 WN (NSW) (Pt 1) 94 at 96 CCA. The Criminal Law Revision Committee, 15th Report on Sexual Offences (1984, Cmnd 9213) at par 2.102 recommended that consent obtained through pretending to be another person should be included as a fraud whcih would vitiate consent.

67   See Stephen J in *Clarence* (1888) 22 QBD 23 at 44; [1886-90] All ER 133 at 144, 16 Cox 511 at 527 CCR.

68   (1957) 98 CLR 249 HC.

69   *Clarence*, fn 67. As to whether communicating such a disease would amount to an assault, the authorities are confused. In *Sinclair* (1867) 13 Cox 28 Shee J, following Willes J in *Bennett* (1866) 4 F&F 1105, 176 ER 925 held that if the accused, knowing he had a contagious disease and that the victim would not have consented if she was aware of this fact, had sexual intercourse with the victim then her consent was vitiated and the accused was guilty of an assault. However, in *Hegarty v Shine* (1874) 14 Cox 145, Ir LR 4 CL 288 no action for assault was held to be against a man who communicated a venereal disease to a woman who had been living as his 'paramour' on the grounds (1) that mere concealment did not constitute such a ground as to vitiate consent and (2) "*ex turpi causa non oritur actio*". In *Clarence*, fn 67, the majority held that a man could not be charged with inflicting bodily harm when he communicated a venereal disease to his wife or, obiter, to any woman. In *Foster v Foster* [1921] P 438 the earlier decision of *Ciocci v Ciocci* (1853) 1 Sp 121, 164 ER 70 was considered and the court held that a successful attempt by a husband who knows that he is suffering from venereal disease to have connection, against her will with his wife, who knows that he is so suffering, may in some circumstances be legal cruelty although the disease is not in fact communicated. See Lynch, "Criminal Liability for Transmitting Disease" [1978] Crim LR 612. In view of the current AIDS epidemic *Greenwood* (1858) 7 Cox CC 404 is of interest. The accused was found guilty of manslaughter on charge of rape and murder of a girl under ten. The jury found that the accused had connexion and that the victim's death had resulted therefrom but could not agree

In cases of doubt the prosecution should always frame an alternative count under s 3 of the Criminal Law (Amendment) Act, 1885 (procuring sexual intercourse by threats, intimidation, false pretences or representations, or by administering alcohol or drugs).[70]

Consent will also be absent where the victim is asleep[71] or is otherwise unconscious,[72] for example, through having taken alcohol.[73] It again should be emphasised that this is an external fact and that the accused's perception of it, for example, as allegedly implying consent through a long term relationship, may amount to a defence if he is believed to the extent that the jury have a reasonable doubt.

8.14 If the victim yielded to the will of her attacker through fear of death, or through duress, it is rape.[74] Emphasis on duress is a reflection of the common law's insistence on force as an element of the crime. The modern tendency is to direct the jury that consent is to be given its ordinary meaning and that there is a difference between consent and submission.[75] This accords with good authority as well as with good sense, since the wording of the statute simply requires that consent be absent but does not enquire as to whether there was sufficient reason for that absence. The Law Reform Commission recommended that, to clarify matters, s 324 G of the Criminal Code of Western Australia should be implemented here:

> "Consent" means a consent freely and voluntarily given and, without in any way affecting or limiting the meaning otherwise attributable to those words, a consent is not freely and voluntarily given if it is obtained by force, threat, intimidation, deception or fraudulent means.
>
> A failure to offer physical resistance to a sexual assault does not of itself constitute consent to a sexual assault.[76]

to a murder verdict. Wightman J instructed them that they might ignore the doctrine of constructive malice if they though fit and they returned a manslaughter verdict.

70 As amended by s 8 of the Criminal Law (Amendment) Act, 1935. See par 8.26. A precedent indictment is given at the end of this chapter.

71 *Mayers* (1872) 12 Cox 311; *Young* (1878) 38 LT 540, 14 Cox 114 CCR.

72 *Camplin* (1845) 1 C&K 746, 1 Cox 220, 169 ER 163, 174 ER 1016, 1 Den 89 (drink given to a woman to excite her); *Lang* (1975) 62 Cr App R 50 CA (it is a misdirection to tell a jury that the accused was guilty of rape if he gave drink to the victim in the hope that she would consent).

73 *Camplin*, fn 72. *Young*, fn 71. As to the perception of the accused see *Page* (1846) 2 Cox 133.

74 1 Hawk ch 41, s 6; *Hallett* (1841) 9 C&P 748, 173 ER 1036; *Rudland* 4 F&F 495, 176 ER 661; *Archbold* (1922) 1019.

75 *Olugboja* [1982] QB 320; [1981] 3 All ER 443; [1981] 3 WLR 585, 73 Cr App R 344 CA. In that case the Court of Appeal said that the question is simply: "At the time of the sexual intercourse did the woman consent to it? It is not necessary for the prosecution to prove that what might otherwise appear to have been consent was in reality merely submission induced by force, fear or fraud, although one or more of these factors will no doubt be present in the majority of cases of rape".

76 At par 16 of the Report on Rape (1988). In contrast the Criminal Law Revision Committee proposed that a statutory provision should make it clear that where threats other than explicit or implicit threats of immediate violence were employed by a defendant the woman would be regarded as consenting—15th Report on Sexual Offences (1984, Cmnd 9213) par 2.26-2.29 and see the discussion by Temkin, *Rape and the Legal Process* (London, 1987) 66 et seq. In *Holman* [1970] WAR 2, at 6, Stephen CJ said: "A woman's consent to intercourse may be hesitant, reluctant, grudging or tearful, but if she consciously permits it (providing her permission is not obtained by force, threats, fear or fraud) it is not rape".

Such an enactment would considerably broaden the scope of the acts which would vitiate consent to sexual intercourse. The Oireachtas did not follow the recommendation of the Commission and instead enacted a provision, which is entirely declaratory, and is probably to assist judges in directing juries on this complex issue by quoting it. S 9 of the Rape Act, 1990 provides:

> It is hereby declared that in relation to an offence that consists of or includes the doing of an act to a person without the consent of that person any failure or omission by that person to offer resistance to the act does not of itself constitute consent to the act.

8.15 It is not completely settled as to what type or character of threat will vitiate consent. In England a jury was directed to acquit a constable of rape where he induced a girl to have sexual intercourse with him by threatening to report her for an offence;[77] but a man who masqueraded as a security officer and induced a girl to consent to sexual intercourse by threatening to tell her parents that he had seen her behaving indecently in public was convicted.[78] The following propositions based on first principles are suggested as being of assistance:

(1) It is for the jury to examine with particular care the factors which induced the victim to have sexual intercourse with the accused. Any factor of threat should be first isolated and the jury should establish whether the existence of that threat has been proved by the prosecution beyond reasonable doubt.

(2) If a threat was made to the victim then its nature is of vital importance in determining the effect which it had on the victim. The jury should not consider the effect of that threat in isolation but in the context of all the factors relevant to detracting from or adding weight to its apparent nature. The average or reasonable victim is not the standard. The question is whether the particular victim consented.

(3) It is not an answer to a charge of rape, or any other offence, to which consent is a defence, that the victim submitted as a result of the threat. Submission does not amount to consent. Consent involves following one's own will with respect to a decision. Submission is a surrender to the will of another. It consists of following that person's will as a result of coercion. A failure to offer resistance does not, of itself, turn submission into consent.

(4) The jury should ask themselves whether the victim had any real choice in the matter. They should bear in mind that the law does not oblige a woman to submit to violence or to some other form of degradation;[79] nor does the law oblige her, by refusing her consent to sexual intercourse, to pass such suffering or degradation onto another.[80]

---

77   *Kirby* (unreported), *The Times*, 19 December 1961 referred to in *Olugboja*, fn 75.

78   *Wellard* [1978] 3 All ER 161; [1978] 1 WLR 921, 67 Cr App R 364 at 368 CA.

79   Common experience indicates that persons in younger age groups or who are handicapped in some way may more readily fall victim to a threat.

80   The question here would be one of fact, clearly the more remote the person threatened is from the victim the less likely it is that she would thereby be influenced. In *Cook* [1986] 2 NZLR 93 the Court of Appeal held that the prosecution do not necessarily have to prove a positive dissent as this was only one way of proving the absence of consent. There was no consent where there was a submission due to the victim fearing harm to her unborn child when she was eight and a half months pregnant.

(5) It may help the jury to consider if the alternative to sexual intercourse, put forward or threatened by the accused, was a lesser evil than an unwanted act of sexual intercourse. On a commonsense basis this may assist in deciding whether the victim was exercising a choice in the matter or was submitting her will, as a result of the threat, to that of the accused.

(6) If the accused was a person of authority in society (for example, a Garda), or exercised authority over the particular victim (for example, a parent or school teacher) this factor may have added considerable weight to the coercion.

(7) In considering the circumstances of the case the jury should bring to bear on their deliberations their collective commonsense; this would involve their own experience, wisdom and knowledge of how people behave in the circumstances proved by the prosecution.

(8) The burden of proof is on the prosecution to prove the absence of the victim's consent beyond reasonable doubt.

(9) The law as to fraud is unaffected by s 9 of the Rape Act, 1990.

Consent to Harm

8.16 The victim cannot consent to an act which has the purpose of, or will, probably cause him or her bodily harm.[81] A person under fifteen,[82] by virtue of s 14 of the Criminal Law (Amendment) Act, 1935, cannot consent to an indecent assault. In these circumstances, any consent given by the victim will be treated as void and thus create the legal fiction of an assault. This may be a strict liability element as, traditionally, for the accused not to be aware that the victim is under fifteen is no defence.[83] The circumstances which vitiate consent to sexual intercourse will similarly vitiate consent to indecent assault. In England a person who is mentally defective cannot consent to indecent assault.[84] No such provision has been enacted in this jurisdiction. However, if the mental defect is so profound that the victim

---

81   *Coney* (1882) 8 QBD 534, 15 Cox CC 46 CCR (prize fighting); *Donovan* [1934] 2 KB 498; [1934] All ER 207, 30 Cox 187, 25 Cr App R 1 CCA (caning a seventeen year old girl for sexual gratification); *Attorney General's Reference* (No. 6 of 1980) [1981] QB 715; [1981] 2 All ER 1057; [1981] 3 WLR 125, 73 Cr App R 63 CA; *Erisman* [1988] LRC (Crim) 386 Hong Kong HC (there can be consent provided the accused does not intend harm); *Cey* (1989) 48 CCC (3d) 480 Saskatchewan CA (vioent and dangerous conduct is to be excluded from the scope of implied consent and even where there is expressed consent an assault cannot be consented to where actual bodily harm is intended; *Jobidou* (1988) 45 CCC (3d) 176 CA Ontario. An extraordinary case is also reported in *The Independent* from 11 to 14 December 1990; in *Sharp & Others* a ring of men of homosexual inclination engaged in consensual mutilation and admitted various forms of assault notwithstanding the consent of these actions. The accused were eventually sentenced on 20 December 1990 by Judge Rant to terms of around four years' imprisonment. In *Lergesner v Carroll* (1989) 49 A Crim R 51 the Queensland Court of Criminal Appeal held that the line was to be drawn where the force applied does grievous bodily harm or wounds, only in such circumstances is consent not a defence.

82   Children who do not understand the nature of the act cannot consent to an indecent assault. *Locke* (1872) LR 2 CCR 10, 42 LJ (MC) 5. See par 8.10.

83   In this regard it is to be noted that the Criminal Law (Amendment) Act, 1935 as well as fixing the age limit for consent to indecent assault also abolished the defence of reasonable belief that the girl was over fifteen years from s 6 and 7 of the Criminal Law Amendment Act, 1885. For a discussion on this question see par 8.62. For LRC recommendations see par 8.62, 7.

84   Sexual Offences Act, 1956, s 14(4) and 15(3).

could not consent to sexual intercourse, it is submitted that her consent to indecent assault will similarly be vitiated.[85]

We will now proceed to consider how the belief of the accused affects the proof of the charge. It is of importance to bear in mind that, in this regard, the accused does not have to give evidence, or even an explanation. The sole question is as to whether this belief, if any, that the victim was consenting, is such as to raise a reasonable doubt in the collective mind of the jury.

The Accused's State of Mind

8.17 Under s 2 of the Rape Act, 1981 the crime of rape may be committed either intentionally or recklessly. The accused will have committed rape intentionally where he penetrates, or continues to have sexual intercourse with, the victim without her consent; knowing that what he is doing is to penetrate her or to continue the sexual intercourse in the knowledge that she does not consent. The accused will have committed rape recklessly[86] where he penetrates, or continues to have sexual intercourse with, the victim without her consent being aware that there is a possibility that the victim has not consented, or is not consenting.

Recklessness in Rape

8.18 The Irish case on the concept of recklessness is *The People (DPP) v Murray*.[87] In discussing the question of recklessness generally Henchy J stated in the course of his judgment:

> The test of recklessness in this context is well stated in the Model Penal Code—s 2.02(2)(c)—drawn up by the American Law Institute:—"A person acts recklessly with respect to a material element of an offence when he consciously disregards a substantial and unjustifiable risk that the material element exists or will result from his conduct. The risk must be of such a nature and degree that, considering the nature and purpose of the actor's conduct and the circumstances known to him, its disregard involves culpability of high degree".

Griffin J postulated a similar test in referring to the specific facts of *Murray*:

> First, as to the appellant Marie Murray, the *mens rea* required is not that she *ought* to have known that the possibility existed that the captor was a Garda (for that would be an objective test), but that she must necessarily have known that this possibility existed. Before there can be recklessness on her part there must be advertence to this possibility . . . The state of a person's mind can only be gathered from the known facts and all the surrounding circumstances.

---

85 See par 8.75–8.77.

86 See Temkin, "The Limits of Reckless Rape" [1983] Crim LR 5. For the definition of the risk in this context see par 8.18, fn 83.

87 [1977] IR 360 SC, Henchy J at 403, Griffin J at 417. It is thought helpful to repeat, in this context, one of the quotations from *Murray* at par 2.37. Reference should also be made to that paragraph wherein it is argued that recklessness must involve the accused taking a substantial risk. Some useful comments on this topic are in Gardner, "Reckless and Inconsiderate Rape" [1991] Crim LR 172. For an example of a case applying reckless indifference see *Evans* (1988) 12 Crim LJ 108 SA CCA.

These comments are helpful provided they are seen and interpreted in the context of a rape case.

The definition contained in s 2 of the Rape Act, 1981 is a statutory expression of that definition formulated by the House of Lords in the English case of *Morgan*.[88] The essence of the type of recklessness expressed in that case does not differ from that in the *Murray* decision. Recklessness occurs where the accused must have adverted to the possibility that the victim was not consenting but no matter how unreasonable his belief that the victim was consenting it afforded him a complete defence provided it was genuinely held. Applying the Model Penal Code definition and the remarks of Griffin J to the problem of consent to sexual intercourse, it is clear that the accused has a responsibility towards the victim to cease in his attentions if he is aware that the victim may not be consenting, or at least to make an enquiry, and that if he continues with the act having this possibility in mind he will be guilty of a high degree of culpability. For that reason it is more correct in law to state that the accused is reckless on being aware of a possibility of the victim not consenting and that the prosecution need not prove any higher element of risk than that.[89] Such risk can never be justifiable. In circumstances of intimacy, it is submitted that any risk of non-consent is substantial because a simple enquiry can, if it is unfounded, dispel it.

Instructing the Jury

8.19 The Heilbron Committee considered that merely to instruct a jury that a belief, however unreasonable, that the woman was consenting, entitled the accused to an acquittal, might give a misleading emphasis to what was only one aspect of the law.[90] Subs 2 is therefore an invitation to the jury to be balanced in their view and not to

---

88 [1976] AC 182; [1975] 2 All ER 374; [1975] 2 WLR 913, 61 Cr App R 136 HL. A useful definition of recklessness was given by the Full Court of Victoria in *Daly* [1968] VR 257 at 258-59: ". . . the Crown must establish beyond reasonable doubt that the accused either was aware that the woman was not consenting or else realised she might not be and determined to have intercourse with her whether she was consenting or not". Approved in *Hemsley* (1988) 36 A Crim R 334 NSW CCA. The approach of the Supreme Court of Canada is not entirely subjective. Although it is accepted that the true test for rape is an honest belief in consent and that it does not have to be based on some reasonable ground the approach is to test the evidence first to see if there is "an air of reality about it"; *Laybourne & Others* [1988] LRC (Crim) 340. In *Saragozza* [1984] VR 187 at 189 the Full Court of the Supreme Court of Victoria stated: "Once it is accepted that it is an element of the crime of rape that the accused either was aware that the woman was not consenting, or else realised that she might not be and determined to have intercourse whether she was consenting or not, the conclusion is inescapable that a man who believes that a woman is consenting cannot be guilty of the offence; for the existence of this belief is inconsistent with the presence of the mental element of the crime. Logic then insists that the reasonableness of the belief bears only on whether the accused in fact held it".

89 This is also the view taken by Smith & Hogan 437 and by Gillies 466-67: "It means of course that D has *mens rea* where D penetrates V knowing that she possibly does not consent to this, as opposed to knowledge that she probably is not consenting to penetration. It would be inappropriate to require knowledge of the probability of non-consent. Quite simply, if D knows there is the slightest chance that V does not consent, he should not penetrate."

90 Cmnd 6352 (1975) par 81. Such an unusual circumstance as the accused failing to realise that the victim is not consenting may occur where he is drunk; *Egan & Others* (1985) 9 Crim LRJ 254 Adelaide CCA (note the Australian position on drunkenness differs as to the question of intent and this is noted at par 4.43-4.44).

overlook the fact, while remembering the subjective nature of the test, that we all share broadly similar perceptions of reality. The law postulates that a good test of the accused's state of mind will be a consideration of whether his alleged belief had any foundation in the objective reality of what occurred between him and the victim. It is, however, entirely possible if somewhat unlikely that the accused could be innocent despite the fact that his belief that the victim was consenting was unreasonable and based on circumstances which would not have induced or supported such a belief in a reasonable person.[91] In such a complex subject the model directions set out by the English Court of Appeal in *Satnam*[92] may assist:

> In summing-up a case of rape which involves the issue of consent, the judge should, in dealing with the state of mind of the defendant, first of all direct the jury that before they could convict of rape the Crown had to prove either that the defendant knew the woman did not want to have sexual intercourse, or was reckless as to whether she wanted to or not. If they were sure he knew she did not want to they should find him guilty of rape knowing there to be no consent. If they were not sure about that, then they would find him not guilty of such rape and should go on to consider reckless rape. If they thought he might genuinely have believed that she did not want to, even though he was mistaken in his belief, they would find him not guilty. In considering whether his belief was genuine, they should take into account all the relevant circumstances (which could at that point be summarised) and ask themselves whether, in the light of those circumstances, he had reasonable grounds for such a belief. If, after considering those circumstances, they were sure that he had no genuine belief that she wanted to, they would find him guilty. If they came to the conclusion that he could not care less whether she wanted to or not, but pressed on regardless, then he would have been reckless and could not have believed that she wanted to, and they would find him guilty of reckless rape. . . .[93]

To this statement of the law two caveats must be entered. Firstly, in considering the circumstances upon which the accused's belief was based, the jury should be reminded that they should bear in mind that it is his perception of those facts, and not that of a reasonable person, which is at issue in the case. Secondly, echoing Griffin J's words in *Murray*, a person "cannot care less" unless he, at some stage, adverted to the possibility that the victim might not be consenting. A man cannot be indifferent, or wilfully blind to a possibility which he has not considered.[94]

It has been held that self-induced intoxication is no defence to rape whether the issue was intention, consent or mistake as to the identity of the victim.[95]

Attempted Rape

8.20 Academic theory apart, it is obvious that a person can only have sexual

---

91   Recent English cases on reckless rape are *Satnam* (1983) 78 Cr App R 149; [1985] Crim LR 236 CA; *Breckenbridge* (1984) 79 Cr App R 244; [1984] Crim LR 174 CA.

92   Bristow J at p 154 (1983) 78 Cr App R.

93   The practice in England is to charge the accused with two counts in the indictment based on the one indident, the first count alleging knowledge and the second recklessness; *Bashir* (1982) 77 Cr App R 59; [1982] Crim LR 687 CA.

94   *Pigg* [1982] 2 All ER 591 at 599; [1982] 1 WLR 762 at 772, 74 Cr App R 352 at 362 CA. The English courts have more recently supported subjective recklessness, the leading authority being Satman, fn 92 and see S. White, "Three Points on *Pigg*" [1989] Crim LR 539.

95   *Fotheringham* (1989) 88 Cr App R 206 CA. Further see par 4.43-4.44.

intercourse with another if he acts purposively.[96] In order to attempt a crime a person must intend to commit the completed crime.[97] As the offence of rape carries the alternative mental states of knowledge and recklessness as to the non-consent of the victim it could be argued that an attempted rape is impossible where the accused is reckless as to whether the woman is consenting to the act of sexual intercourse.

In *Khan*[98] a girl accompanied some youths to a flat where some of them succeeded in raping her while the appellants attempted but failed. The Court of Appeal held that in the circumstances no question of attempting to achieve a reckless state of mind arose; the attempt related to the physical activity and the mental state of the accused was the same as in the completed crime. A man did not recklessly have sexual intercourse nor did he recklessly attempt it. Recklessness in rape and attempted rape arose not in relation to the physical act of the accused but only in relation to his state of mind when engaged in the activity of having or attempting to have sexual intercourse. The offence did not, therefore, require any different intention on the part of the accused from that of the full offence of rape. The analysis by the Court of the mental element in the offence of rape involved two elements:

(1) The intention of the offender to have sexual intercourse with a woman;

(2) The offence was committed if, but only if, the circumstances were that: (a) the woman did not consent; and (b) the defendant knew that she was not consenting or was reckless as to whether she consented.

Sentence

8.21 It has been held in England that, other than in wholly exceptional circumstances, rape calls for an immediate custodial sentence in order to mark the gravity of the offence, emphasise public disapproval, serve as a warning to others, punish the offender and protect women.[99] In *The People (DPP) v Edward Tiernan*,[1] the Supreme Court declined to issue guidelines for judges in sentencing persons convicted of rape. In the course of his judgment Finlay CJ stated:

> Whilst in every criminal case a judge must impose a sentence which, in his opinion, meets the particular circumstances of the case and of the accused person before him, it is not easy to imagine the circumstance which would justify departure from a substantial immediate custodial sentence for rape and I can only express the view that they would probably be wholly exceptional.[2]

Parties

8.22 Only a male person may commit the offence of rape as a principal. There is

---

96 Disregarding the unlikely circumstances that a person might act in an automatous state. Recklessness, in this context, is a concept not impossible of imagination but ridiculous in practice.

97 For a further discussion see ch 4.

98 [1990] Crim LR 519 CA.

99 *Roberts & Roberts* [1982] 1 All ER 609; [1982] 1 WLR 133, 74 Cr App R 242; [1982] Crim LR 320 CA.

1   [1988] IR 250; [1989] ILRM 149 SC. For guidelines on rape in England see *Billam* [1986] 1 All ER 985; [1986] 1 WLR 349, 82 Cr App R 347; [1986] Crim LR 347 CA.

2   [1988] IR 250 at 253. The High Court of Australia have indicated that a sentence should differ where the victim initially consented and then later withdraws her consent following penetration; *Ibbs* (1987) 27 A Crim R 465.

no rule of law which restricts secondary parties to the male sex. A female person who, with the knowledge or recklessness required for the particular sexual offence in question, encourages or assists a man to commit a sexual offence on another woman, or, depending on the offence on another man, may be found guilty of aiding and abetting.[3] A man may be acquitted of rape on the ground that he mistakenly believed that the woman was consenting, but a woman who encouraged or assisted him in the act may be convicted notwithstanding this acquittal.[4]

The principles relating to common design[5] general to the criminal law are also applicable in the case of rape. In an appropriate case the prosecution may argue a case before the jury on an alternative basis of either the accused persons acting in concert in pursuance of a common design or each accused being individually guilty of rape.[6]

Burglary, Assault, with Intent to Rape

8.23 S 23A of the Larceny Act, 1916, inserted by s 6 of the Criminal Law (Jurisdiction) Act, 1976 makes it an offence to enter a building, or part of a building, with intent to rape. The offence is punishable by fourteen years' imprisonment but if the person who commits the offence has with him a firearm or imitation firearm, any weapon of offence or any explosive, he is liable under s 23(b) to imprisonment for life for aggravated burglary.

It must be proved that the accused entered the building, or part thereof, which he was not entitled to enter, having at the time such knowledge or recklessness which, in law, made that entry unlawful.[7] It is also necessary to show that the accused had an intent to rape when he so entered. This is best proved by showing that he committed the crime alleged to have been intended by him.[8] The prosecution may also prove any other facts from which the intent may be inferred by the jury.[9]

It is a misdemeanour to assault any person with intent to commit a felony.[10] There must be evidence from which the jury can infer that the intention of the accused was to rape the victim.[11] If indicted for assault with intent the accused may be convicted of a common assault.[12] Assault is considered in chapter 6.

---

3   *Ram* (1893) 17 Cox 609.
4   *Cogan & Leak* [1976] 1 QB 217; [1975] 2 All ER 1059; [1975] 3 WLR 316, 61 Cr App R 217; [1975] Crim LR 584 CA.
5   See par 1.10–1.11.
6   *Merriman* [1973] AC 584; [1972] 3 All ER 42, [1972] 3 WLR 545, 56 Cr App R 766; [1972] Crim LR 784 HL.
7   *Collins* [1973] QB 100; [1972] 2 All ER 1105; [1972] 3 WLR 243, 56 Cr App R 554 CA.
8   *Locost* (1664) Kel(J) 30, 84 ER 1067.
9   *Brice* (1821) R&R 450, 168 ER 892.
10 Offences Against the Person Act, 1861, s 38. See Spencer, "Assault with Intent to Rape—Dead or Alive?" [1986] Crim LR 120. For a discussion on the law in relation to assault see ch 6 and par 8.36.
11 *Lloyds* (1836) 7 C&P 318.
12 *Wilson* [1955] 1 All ER 744; [1955] 1 WLR 493, 39 Cr App R 12 CCA.

Unlawfully Procuring, Administration with Intent

8.24 An offence which is akin to rape, but, in contrast, rarely used in prosecutions is to be found in s 3 of the Criminal Law Amendment Act, 1885, as amended by s 8 of the Criminal Law (Amendment) Act, 1935:

> Any person who—
> (1) by threats or intimidation procures or attempts to procure any woman or girl to have unlawful carnal connexion, either within or without the Queen's dominions; or
> (2) by false pretences or false representations procures any woman or girl, not being a common prostitute or of known immoral character, to have any unlawful carnal connexion, either within or without the Queen's dominions; or
> (3) applies, administers to, or causes to be taken by any woman or girl any alcoholic or other intoxicant or any drug, matter, or thing, with intent to stupefy or overpower so as thereby to enable any person to have unlawful carnal connexion with such woman or girl, shall be guilty of misdemeanour, and being convicted thereof shall be liable at the discretion of the court to be imprisoned for any term not exceeding two years, with or without hard labour. Provided that no person shall be convicted of an offence under this section upon the evidence of one witness only, unless such witness be corroborated[13] in some material particular by evidence implicating the accused.

A finding of guilty on this offence is an alternative verdict on a charge of rape.[14] The offences under subs 1 and 2 are complete only where there has been sexual intercourse, otherwise an attempt may be charged. The offence may be completed outside the jurisdiction when the procuring is done within the jurisdiction.[15]

Under subs 1 and 2 "to procure" means to produce by endeavour. There must be some real procuration either completed or attempted. This may be negatived by evidence which shows that the girl was not really procured because she acted of her own free will.[16] It is a defence to subs 2 that the victim was "a common prostitute or of known immoral character". It is unlikely that the victim will be protected by the rape shield provisions;[17] it is stretching language to call a fraud an assault and the Oireachtas could have extended the scope of the section if they saw fit. The offence is made out where the accused procured the victim to have sexual intercourse, or administers a drug, etc. for that purpose.[18]

Threats or Intimidation

The nature of the "threats or intimidation" covered in subs 1 is unclear. It has been suggested that as the offence is less serious than rape, threats or intimidation of lesser

---

13   The question of corroboration is considered at the end of this chapter.

14   Rape Act, 1990, s 8.

15   *Johnson* [1964] 2 QB 404; [1963] 3 All ER 577; [1963] 3 WLR 1031, 48 Cr App R 25; [1963] Crim LR 860 CCA; *Glazebrook* [1959] Crim LR 774.

16   *Christian* (1913) 23 Cox CC 541, 78 JP 112. *Attorney General's Reference* (No. 1 of 1975), [1975] QB 773, [1975] 2 All ER 684 at 686; [1975] 3 WLR 11, 61 Cr App R 118 CA: "To procure means to produce by endeavour. You procure a thing by setting out to see that it happens and taking the appropriate steps to produce that happening" per Lord Widgery CJ. See also *Beck* [1985] 1 All ER 571; [1985] 1 WLR 22, 80 Cr App R 355 CA; *A-G (SPUC) v Open Door Counselling Ltd* [1988] IR 593 HC & SC.

17   Rape Act, 1981, s 3, as amended by Rape Act, 1990, s 13. This is considered at par 8.82.

18   *Williams* (1898) 62 JP 310. These offences can also be committed by a boy of fourteen under the Rape Act, 1990, s 6.

gravity will suffice for this crime.[19] For the purpose of the law of torts, intimidation must include a threat to do something unlawful and has been defined by Heuston:

> The wrong of intimidation includes all those cases in which harm is inflicted by the use of unlawful threats whereby the lawful liberty of others to do as they please is interfered with.[20]

The question is whether the threats or intimidation procured the sexual intercourse. A person is quite entitled to procure sexual intercourse by blandishments and boasts. The essence of the wrong under subs 1 is of removing the element of choice from human relations and substituting compulsion in its place. If the girl would have had sexual intercourse in any event, there is no procuration. If she had sexual intercourse because the accused caused her to feel that she had no choice in the matter because the alternative consequences were so unpleasant, then that surely is the mischief which subs 1 is designed to prevent.[21]

Representations

8.25 The false representations and false pretences in subs 2 go beyond those which would vitiate consent in rape.[22] Thus it was an offence for a married man to seduce the victim by a promise of marriage[23] despite there being no mistake as to the nature of the act or the identity of the partner which would be required for rape. A pretence under the Larceny Act, 1916 is limited to facts in the present.[24] There is no reason why representations cannot be made as to the future in this context, for example, by a promise to marry. No doubt, the circumstances whereby the accused procured the victim to have sexual intercourse with him are required by this section to be of a grave nature in order to attract the sanction of the criminal law.

The offence under subs 3 can be committed by a man on his own behalf or by a man or woman on behalf of another man. The wrong consists in the administration of the intoxicant etc. with intent to stupefy the girl and thereby have sexual intercourse with her when she is in that condition. Thus the offence is complete when the intoxicant has been administered with the relevant intent.[25]

Other Offences

8.26 What follows is of little practical importance, there having been no prosecutions for any of these offences within the last ten years. The provisions are included for the sake of completeness. The statutory provisions are therefore set out and references to the relevant authorities are made in the footnotes. The Criminal Law

---

19 Smith & Hogan 439-40.
20 Salmond & Heuston 421.
21 There may be a parallel with the law of blackmail in that threats should be such as to influence a reasonably courageous person; Smith & Hogan 589. For a fuller discussion on the essence of a threat see par 8.14-8.15.
22 *Williams* [1923] 1 KB 340; [1922] All ER 433, 27 Cox CC 350, 17 Cr App R 56 CCA.
23 *Williams* (1898) 62 JP 310.
24 *Bryan* (1857) D&B 265, 7 Cox CC 312 CCR, 159 ER 1002; *Dent* [1955] 2 QB 590; [1955] 2 All ER 805; [1955] 3 WLR 297, 39 Cr App R 131 CCA. On this see McCutcheon par 146.
25 *Shillingford* [1968] 2 All ER 200; [1968] 1 WLR 566, 52 Cr App R 188; [1968] Crim LR 282 CA.

(Amendment) Act, 1885, s 2 as amended by s 2 of the Criminal Law (Amendment) Act, 1912 as amended by s 7 of the Criminal Law (Amendment) Act, 1935 provides:

> 2 Any person who—
> (1) procures or attempts to procure any girl or woman[26] . . .[27] not being a common prostitute,[28] or of known immoral character,[29] to have unlawful carnal connexion, either within or without the Queen's dominions, with any other person or persons;[30] or
> (2) procures or attempts to procure any woman or girl to become, either within or without the Queen's dominions, a common prostitute;[31] or
> (3) procures or attempts to procure any woman or girl to leave the United Kingdom, with intent that she may become an inmate of or frequent a brothel[32] elsewhere; or
> (4) procures or attempts to procure any woman or girl to leave her usual place of abode in the United Kingdom (such place not being a brothel), with intent that she may, for the purposes of prostitution, become an inmate of or frequent a brothel within or without the Queen's dominions,
> shall be guilty of a misdemeanour, and being convicted thereof shall be liable at the discretion of the Court to be imprisoned for any term not exceeding two years, with or without hard labour.
> Provided that no person shall be convicted of any offence under this section upon the evidence of one witness, unless such witness be corroborated in some material particular by evidence implicating the accused.[33]

8.27 The Criminal Law (Amendment) Act, 1885 as amended by s 9 of the Criminal Law (Amendment) Act, 1935 provides:

> 6 Any person who, being the owner or occupier of any premises, or having, or acting or assisting in, the management or control thereof[34]—
> induces or knowingly offers any girl of such age as is in this section mentioned to resort

---

26   For the offence of procuring see par 8.24 and the references cited at fn 15 thereof. A woman is a girl if aged under twenty one. But at eighteen a woman may be a girl; *Jones* (1911) 6 Cr App R 290, 23 Cox CC 48 CCA.

27   The words "under twenty one years of age" were removed by s 7 of the Criminal Law (Amendment) Act, 1935.

28   This provision renders the entire section constitutionally dubious. Why should a prostitute or a promiscuous girl be any less entitled to the protection of the law than a chaste woman? Prostitution occurs where a woman offers her body for purposes amounting to common lewdness for payment in return; *de Munck* [1918] 1 KB 635, 26 Cox 302 CCA; *Webb* [1964] 1 QB 357; [1963] 3 All ER 177; [1963] 3 WLR 638, 47 Cr App R 265 CCA.

29   Fn 28. There appears to be no differing definition.

30   The effect of this is that the accused canot legally procure the victim to have sexual intercourse with another, but he can do so on his own behalf.

31   Fn 28.

32   An inmate lives in a brothel, a person frequents a brothel when on an extended or a repeated visit; *Nakhla v The Queen* [1976] AC 1; [1975] 2 All ER 138; [1975] 2 WLR 750; [1976] Crim LR 81 PC. A brothel is a place resorted to by persons of both sexes for the purposes of prostitution; *Singleton v Ellison* [1895] 1 QB 607, 18 Cox 79 DC.

33   A spouse is a competent but not compellable witness for charges under this Act, s 20; *Sandes* 184; *A-G v Power* [1932] IR 610. Charged under s 4 of 1885 Act, convicted but retrial ordered as wife (willing witness, called by prosecution without consent of accused) was not a competent witness at common law (evidence material). But now see *The People (DPP) v JT*, 3 Frewen CCA, unreported 27 July 1988 and also Charleton, "The Victim in Irish Constitutional Law" (1990) 8 ILTSJ 140.

34   The words bear their ordinary meaning.

to or be in or upon such premises for the purpose of being unlawfully and carnally known by any man, whether such carnal knowledge is intended to be with any particular man or generally,

(1) shall, if such girl is under the age of fifteen[35] years,[36] be guilty of felony, and being convicted thereof shall be liable at the discretion of the Court to be kept in penal servitude for life, or for any term not less than five years, or to be imprisoned for any term not exceeding two years, with or without hard labour; and

(2) if such girl is of or above the age of fifteen[37] and under the age of seventeen[38] years, shall be guilty of a misdemeanour, and being convicted thereof shall be liable at the discretion of the Court to be imprisoned for any term not exceeding two years, with or without hard labour.[39]

7 Any person who—

with intent that any unmarried girl under the age of eighteen[40] years should be unlawfully and carnally known by any man, whether such carnal knowledge is intended to be with any particular man, or generally—

takes or causes to be taken,[41] such girl out of the possession and against the will of her father or mother,[42] or any other person having the lawful care or charge of her,

shall be guilty of a misdemeanour, and on being convicted thereof shall be liable at the discretion of the Court to be imprisoned for any term not exceeding two years, with or without hard labour.[43]

8 Any person who detains any woman or girl against her will—

(1) in or upon any premises with intent that she may be unlawfully and carnally known by any man, whether any particular man, or generally, or

(2) in any brothel,[44]

shall be guilty of a misdemeanour, and being convicted thereof shall be liable at the discretion of the Court to be imprisoned for any term not exceeding two years, with or without hard labour.

---

35 S 9 of the Criminal Law (Amendment) Act, 1935 substituted fifteen and seventeen for thirteen and sixteen respectively.

36 Age must be proved. The birth cert will be produced and the girl identified; *Rogers* (1914) 10 Cr App R 276, 24 Cox 465 CCA; but age may also be proved by any other legal means; Cox [1898] 1 QB 179, 18 Cox 672 CCR; age must, however, be proved with precision; *The People (A-G) v O'Connor* [1949] 15 Ir Jur Rep 25.

37 Fn 35.

38 Fn 35.

39 The defence under this section of having reasonable cause to believe the girl was above the relevant age was abolished by s 9(c) of the Criminal Law (Amendment) Act, 1935. This shows the clear legislative intent, in the absence of such a defence, to make this element of the crime one of strict liability. For a discussion of this see par 8.58–8.67. A spouse is a competent but not compellable witness for offences under this section, see fn 33.

40 Fn 36.

41 This need not be by force and it is immaterial that the girl consents; *Mankletow* (1853) Dears 159, 6 Cox 143, 169 ER 678 CCR; *Robins* (1844) 1 C&K 457, 87 ER 101; *Timmins* (1860) Bell 276, 169 ER 1260, 8 Cox 401 CCR; Archbold (1954) par 1922.

42 Fraud destroys consent; *Hopkins* (1842) C&Mar 254, 174 ER 495. Consent is a question of fact; *Calthrop v Axtel* (1686) 3 Mod 168; 1 East PC 457, 87 ER 101; *Primelt* (1858) 1 F&F 50, 175 ER 621.

43 The defence under this section of having reasonable cause to believe the girl was above the relevant age was abolished by the schedule to the Criminal Law (Amendment) Act, 1935. In the absence of such defence, age is probably a strict liability element. See fn 39.

44 For the legal definition of a brothel, see fn 32.

8.28 The section goes on to provide that detention can consist of keeping a person's clothes from them. The detainee is exempt from legal liability if she steals clothes in those circumstances. Under s 10 a search warrant may be issued by the District Court. The section further elucidates the concept of detention by providing that girls under sixteen are deemed to be detained by virtue of their age if they are on the premises or in the brothel for the purpose of sexual intercourse; if aged from sixteen to eighteen detention can be against the will of the girl or that of her father, mother or guardian but if she is above eighteen years of age it must be against her own will. False imprisonment is considered in chapter 7.

Further offences of abduction include those of the abduction or detention of an heiress against her will and with intent to marry or have sexual intercourse with her contrary to s 53 of the Offences Against the Person Act, 1861;[45] of abduction or detention by force of a woman of any age with intent to marry or have sexual intercourse;[46] and abduction of a girl under sixteen against the will of her father, mother or guardian.[47] This last crime differs from the others as the law is not concerned with the wishes of the girl herself but with those of her parents or guardian.[48]

Sexual Assault

8.29 The indecent assault of a man or a woman was a crime at common law. The penalty was fixed by s 52 of the Offences Against the Person Act, 1861, in respect of an assault on a woman, at two years' imprisonment. This section was repealed by the Criminal Law (Amendment) Act, 1935 which, by s 6, replaced this by a penalty of two years' imprisonment for a first offence or from three to five years' penal servitude, or two years' imprisonment for a subsequent offence. That section was again repealed by s 10 of the Rape Act, 1981 which replaced the penalty by one of ten years' imprisonment in respect of an indecent assault on a female. The penalty for indecent assault on a male person remained ten years' penal servitude since it was so enacted by s 62 of the Offences Against the Person Act, 1861.[49]

Reform

8.30 The Rape Act, 1990 renamed the offence of indecent assault sexual assault,

45   Or if she is under 21 years of age, against the will of her parents or guardian.

46   Offences Against the Person Act, 1861, s 54: "Whosoever shall, by force, take away or detain against her will any woman, of any age, with intent to marry or carnally know her, or to cause her to be married or carnally known by any other peson, shall be guilty of felony, and being convicted thereof shall be liable to be kept in penal servitude for any term not exceeding fourteen years".

47   Offences Against the Person Act, 1861, s 55: "Whosoever shall unlawfully take or cause to be taken any unmarried girl, being under the age of sixteen years, out of the possession or against the will of her father or mother, or any other person having the lawful care or charge of her, shall be guilty of a misdemeanour, and being convicted thereof shall be liable, at the discretion of the court, to be imprisoned for any term not exceeding two years, with or without hard labour".

48   On all of these charges the spouse is a competent but not compellable witness; Criminal Law (Amendment) Act, 1885, s 20. See fn 33. As to the immateriality of a girl's consent see *Mankletow*, fn 41, and for cases on the subject see *Jarvis* (1902) 20 Cox 249 and *Archbold* (1954) 1923.

49   The sections are quoted, as are all other sections from the Offences Against the Person Act, 1861, in accordance with the amendments introduced by the Penal Servitude Acts of 1864 and 1891 and by the Statute Law Revision Act, 1908.

provided for a penalty of five years' imprisonment, and created the new crime of aggravated sexual assault punishable by life imprisonment. Sexual assault is also the basis of the new crime of "S 4 Rape". The acts which constitute aggravated sexual assault and would, formerly, have been punishable as indecent assaults, would constitute the more extreme and degrading examples of indecent (or sexual) assault:

> 2(1) The offence of indecent assault upon any male person and the offence of indecent assault upon any female person shall be known as sexual assault.
>
> (2) A person guilty of sexual assault shall be liable on conviction on indictment to imprisonment for a term not exceeding five years.
>
> 3(1) In this Act "aggravated sexual assault" means a sexual assault that involves serious violence or the threat of serious violence or is such as to cause injury, humiliation or degradation of a grave nature to the person assaulted.
>
> (2) A person guilty of aggravated sexual assault shall be liable on conviction on indictment to imprisonment for life.
>
> (3) Aggravated sexual assault shall be a felony.[50]

8.31 Unlike rape, the offence can be committed by men on men and women on men and women on women.[51] The incapacity of boys under fourteen has been abolished in respect of this crime.[52] These offences may be found as alternative verdicts on indictment to counts of rape, unlawful sexual intercourse with a girl under fifteen or seventeen and a verdict of sexual assault may be found on a charge of aggravated sexual assault.[53] A verdict of aggravated sexual assault may not, however, be found on a charge of sexual assault.

Effect of Reform

8.32 S 2 does not create a new offence but renames the offences of indecent assault on a female and indecent assault on a male.[54] Where the offence occurs in the circumstances detailed in s 3 a new offence is committed.[55]

The elements of the offence of sexual assault are not defined in the Act but the use of the words in subs 2(1) "shall be known as sexual assault" make it clear that the common law of indecent assault must be applied to the new offences.[56]

---

50   For an alternative verdict of attempt see the Criminal Procedure Act, 1851, s 9; powers of arrest appropriate to a felony.

51   *Armstrong* (1885) 49 JP 745; In *Hare* the court said *obiter* that a woman might be guilty of an indecent assault on another woman, [1934] 1 KB 354; [1933] All ER 550, 24 Cr App R 108, 30 Cox CC 64 CCA; *Mason* (1968) 53 Cr App R 12, a circuit case in which Veale J after a consideration of the authorities held that: "There is not and there never has been any offence known to the law of a woman having sexual intercourse with a boy aged under 16". This case was subsequently over-ruled by *Faulkner v Talbot* [1981] 3 All ER 468; [1981] 1 WLR 1528, 74 Cr App R 1; [1981] Crim LR 705 DC, in which similar facts were deemed to be an offence under s 15 of the U.K. Sexual Offences Act, 1956. S 15 of the 1956 U.K. Act is similar to s 14 of the Criminal Law (Amendment) Act, 1935 in that it limits the defence of consent to victims over sixteen (fifteen in the case of s 14 of the 1935 Act). See Mackesy, "The Criminal Law and the Woman Seducer" [1956] Crim LR 446, 529, 798.

52   Rape Act, 1990, s 6.

53   Rape Act, 1990, s 8.

54   In Canada a new and separate offence of sexual assault was created by s. 246.1 of the Criminal Code.

55   *Courtie* [1984] AC 463; [1984] 1 All ER 740; [1984] 2 WLR 330, 78 Cr App R 292; [1984] Crim LR 366 HL. The offence contains a new element.

8.33 S 5 of the Rape Act, 1990 abolished the defence of marriage.[57] The authorities would appear to indicate that if there was ever a defence of marriage to a charge of indecent assault then it was dependent upon a subsequent act of sexual intercourse taking place. As a husband can now rape his wife it seems also clear that marriage will not be a defence to a charge of indecent assault.[58]

The law relating to complaints by the victim, the relevance of her character and the restrictions imposed by statute on evidence and questions relating to that topic, and to corroboration and statutory changes thereto, apply equally to charges of sexual assault and aggravated sexual assault as they do to rape. These are dealt with at the end of this chapter.

Definition

8.34 An indecent assault has been defined as an assault (including a psychic assault) accompanied with circumstances of indecency.[59] The 1922 Archbold said of indecent assault: prove an assault accompanied with circumstances of indecency on the part of the defendant.[60] In *Court*[61] the House of Lords held that on a charge of indecent assault the prosecution must prove:

(1) That the accused intentionally assaulted the victim.[62]

(2) That the assault, or the assault and the circumstances accompanying it, are capable of being considered by right-minded persons as indecent.

(3) That the accused intended to commit such an assault as is referred to in (2) above.

It is submitted that this is the correct definition of a sexual assault. In an aggravated

56   It would be difficult to argue that the use of the word sexual altered the element of indecency in the definition of the crime, or that the indecency had to specifically relate to the genitalia, instead of in generally indecent circumstances. This argument was first held, in Canada, to be correct; *Chase* (1984) 40 CR (3d) 282 NBCA; and was then overruled; *Taylor* (1985) 44 Cr (3d) 263 (Alberta CA) and *Cook* (1985) 46 CR (3d) 129 (British Columbia CA). The Supreme Court of Canada finally over-ruled the New Brunswick Court of Appeal in *Chase* 45 DLR (HH) 98 and the approved decisions in *Taylor* and *Cook*.

57   LRC Report on Rape (1988) par 18. See par 8.05-8.06.

58   *Caswell* [1984] Crim LR 111. The commentary to this case was approved in *Kowalski* (1988) 86 Cr App R 339; [1988] Crim LR 124 CA. See par 8.06.

59   *Beal v Kelley* [1951] 2 All ER 763, 35 Cr App R 128 DC; *Johnson* [1968] SASR 132 at 134 SC; *Salmon* [1969] SASR 76 at 78 SC; *Leeson* (1968) 52 Cr App R 185 CA.

60   Page 1033—this is the sole entry under the heading 'Evidence'.

61   [1989] AC 28 at 42; [1988] 2 All ER 221 at 232; [1983] 2 WLR 1071 at 1085, 87 Cr App R 144 at 157; [1988] Crim LR 537 HL. See Sullivan, "The Need for a Crime of Sexual Assault" [1989] Crim LR 331.The definition proposed by the House of Lords does not differ from that in force at the foundation of the State. The stated elements, incorporating an intentional assault, merely take account of the practicality of the situation that no reckless indecent assault could occur; a test of decency by the standards of right-minded persons applies a legal phraseology to the direction used by juries to judges in this country that it is for them to say whether the act proved by the prosecution was decent or not; the requirement that a mental element should exist both in respect of the assault and the indecent element fulfils the analysis of criminal law in *The People (DPP) v Murray* [1977] IR 360 SC (further discussed in ch 2).

62   This appears to be inconsistent with the development of the law of assault which now allows it to be committed by recklessness. Generally see ch 6.

sexual assault the circumstances of indecency will be as described in s 3(1).

As the crime is defined in terms of an intentional act any evidence explaining the accused's conduct, whether an admission by him or otherwise, is admissible to establish whether he intended to commit an indecent assault.[63]

8.35 The vast majority of the cases coming before the courts will fit easily into the above definition. Typically, the victim will be a woman subjected to the unwanted sexual attentions of a man, or men, who will intentionally inflict on her all manner of sexual practices short of, or differing in legal definition from, rape. In those circumstances there will be little difficulty in finding that someone assaulted and inflicted an indecency on the victim. At the trial the issues will typically be as to whether the victim consented, or as to whether the accused is correctly identified as her assailant.[64] For completeness there follows an academic treatment of the crime.

Assault

8.36 The facts must disclose an assault or a psychic assault. At common law an assault is defined as beating or wounding and as including every touching or laying hold (however trifling) of another person or clothes in an angry, revengeful, rude, insolent or hostile manner.[65] The requirement of hostility is inappropriate in cases of indecent assault as the accused may be "affectionate" in his attitude or the victim may be a person under fifteen, incapable of legally accepting his attentions.[66] A line of decisions,[67] requiring hostility is not now followed in England, in Australia,[68] or in Canada.[69]

---

63   *Court*, fn 61.

64   For a discussion on the course of a trial see ch 1.

65   1 Hawk, ch 62, s 2; Archbold (1922) 930. For a further discussion see ch 6. Consent can be a defence to assault except where harm is intended or caused. This topic is discussed at par 8.16.

66   Criminal Law (Amendment) Act, 1935, s 14.

67   *Burrows* [1952] 1 All ER 58, 35 Cr App R 180 CCA (a boy touching the accused on his invitation; the accused was acquitted, *inter alia*, because of the absence of hostility); *Rogers* [1953] 3 All ER 644; [1953] 1 WLR 1017, 37 Cr App R 137 DC (the accused led his daughter, the victim, upstairs with his hand around her shoulder so that the victim should masturbate him); *Williams v Gibbs* (1958) Crim LR 127 (the accused indecently touched some small girls while drying them); *Mason* (1968) 53 Cr App R 12; *Phillips* (1971) ALR 740; *B* (1954) 71 WN (NSW) 138 at 139 CCA; (1971) 45 ALJR 467 HC.

68   The Court of Appeal has now held in *McCormack* [1969] 2 QB 442; [1969] 3 All ER 371; [1969] 3 WLR 175, 53 Cr App R 514, that an indecent act done to a girl of fifteen, with her consent and without hostility, is an indecent assault and in *Faulkner v Talbot* [1981] 3 All ER 468; [1981] 1 WLR 1528, 74 Cr App R 1; [1981] Crim LR 705 DC, Lane LCJ said that an assault "need not be hostile or rude or aggressive, as some of the cases seem to indicate"; Smith & Hogan 448. The High Court of Australia in *Boughey* (1986) 60 ALJR 422, 161 CLR 10 held that there is no central proposition that the intentional application of force to the person of an unwilling victim cannot constitute battery at common law . . . unless it be accompanied or motivated by positive hostility or hostile intent by the assailant towards the victim (161 CLR 10 at 27). The dictum of Barwick CJ in *Phillips*, fn 67, that "The circumstances of the physical contact of one person with another which makes that contact indecent make it unnecessary upon a charge of indecent assault to establish some 'hostility' over or above the actual circumstances of the indecency and the contact of the two persons" (1971) 45 ALJR at 473, was quoted with approval in *Boughey* (161 CLR 10 at 261).

69   *Cadden* (1989) 48 CCC (3d) 122 CA BC.

A psychic assault is defined at common law as an attempt to commit a forcible crime against the person of another;[70] by this is meant any action on the part of the accused which puts the victim, a reasonable person, under fear or apprehension of an immediate assault by the accused.[71]

The distinction is of practical importance. In *Court*[72] the House of Lords held that if the facts consisted of indecent touching neither the indecent circumstances, nor the touching itself, need be known to the victim for the charge to be made out. If there was a psychic assault it is necessary, it is submitted, for the victim to be aware of both the circumstances of indecency and of the assault itself.[73] The latter requirement in the case of "no touch" or psychic assault was not specifically endorsed by the House of Lords. It is of the essence of the wrong, in assault, that the victim should be caused to apprehend an assault; for the victim to be caused by the accused merely to apprehend an ordinary assault is, it is submitted, merely a common assault.[74] On the other hand, the integrity of the victim's person[75] and the victim's right to privacy[76] demand a more stringent protection against actual touching,[77] and support a rule of wrong despite unawareness.

Invitation to Touch

8.37 It is neither an assault nor a psychic assault for the accused to invite the victim to touch, for example, the accused's genitalia.[78] The victim can, of course, refuse the invitation and if the victim is reasonably under the apprehension that on refusal he or she would be grabbed by the accused in indecent circumstances, there would then be an indecent assault.[79]

In *Cadden*[80] the Court of Appeal of British Columbia held that there had been a sexual assault where the accused was a school teacher who indicated to students to perform sexual acts on him while in the classroom. While holding that words alone could not amount to an assault and noting the requirement of the Code that there be an act or gesture by the accused which amounts to an attempt or threat to apply

70   Archbold (1922) 930. For a further discussion see ch 6. The requirement of an attempt is now discarded as incorrect.

71   See the cases cited in Archbold (1922); 1 Hawk, ch 62, s 1; *Barton v Armstrong* [1969] 2 NSWR 451 CA. For a further discussion of assault and battery see ch 6. An actual attempt is unnecessary.

72   [1989] AC 28; [1988] 2 All ER 221; [1988] 2 WLR 1071, 87 Cr App R 144; [1988] Crim LR 537 HL.

73   See [1987] QB 156; [1987] 1 All ER 120; [1986] 3 WLR 1029, 84 Cr App R 210; [1987] Crim LR 134 CA.

74   It has been so held in South Australia; *Johnson* [1968] SASR 132 at 134 SC (the accused was caning the victim while, unknown to the victim, masturbating).

75   Bodily integrity is a constitutionally protected right, *Ryan v A-G* [1965] IR 294 SC.

76   As to which see *Kennedy v Ireland* [1987] IR 587; [1988] ILRM 472 SC.

77   Blackstone wrote: "The law cannot draw the line between different degrees of violence, and therefore totally prohibits the first and lowest stage of it; every man's person being sacred, and no other having a right to meddle with it, in any the slightest manner". 3 Bl Com 120, cited by Goff LJ in *Collins v Wilcock* [1984] 3 All ER 374 at 378; [1984] 1 WLR 1172 at 1177, 79 Cr App R 229 at 234 CA.

78   *Burrows* [1952] 1 All ER 58, 35 Cr App R 180 CCA; *Rogers* [1953] 2 All ER 644 at 646; [1953] 1 WLR 1017 at 1019, 37 Cr App R 137 at 140 DC. See also par 8.38.

79   *Rolfe* (1952) 36 Cr App R 4 CCA.

80   (1989) 48 CCC (3d) 122 CA BC.

bodily force, it was held that as the accused had the students in a controlled space, had exposed himself to them and spoke to them telling them what he wanted done, his acts and gestures did not amount simply to an invitation but rather constituted a threat to invade the bodily integrity of the victims. Since such threats to apply force, coupled with the accused's present ability to effect that purpose, constituted an assault within the meaning of the Code, he had been properly convicted.

Age

8.38 Persons under fifteen cannot consent to an indecent assault. S 14 of the Criminal Law (Amendment) Act, 1935 provides:

> It shall not be a defence to a charge of indecent assault upon a person under the age of fifteen years to prove that such person consented to the act alleged to constitute such indecent assault.

Where the act does not amount to an assault s 14 is of no significance. Thus it has been held that it is not an indecent assault for the accused to invite a girl of nine to touch his person[81] and it will not become an indecent assault unless the accused, during the act, takes hold of the victim.[82] Nor is it an indecent assault for the accused to similarly invite a small boy;[83] in that case a charge of gross indecency between male persons could be laid contrary to s 11 of the Criminal Law (Amendment) Act, 1885, provided the victim accepts the accused's invitation.[84] A charge of attempt could also be laid where the victim does not so accept.

The age of consent to sexual intercourse by a girl is seventeen, but there is no age of consent for a boy. Indecency between males will, however, always constitute a crime under s 11 of the Criminal Law (Amendment) Act, 1885. The position of small boys, lacking in discretion, and of girls, is covered by s 14 of the Criminal Law (Amendment) Act, 1935, which applies equally to both sexes. The consequence of this is that small boys and girls, under the age of fifteen, accepting the invitation of the accused to commit indecent acts with them will not render the accused criminally liable, unless the accused also takes active steps to touch the victim. In England this situation has been rectified by statute.[85] It is submitted that this Act only applies

81   *Fairclough v Whipp* [1951] 2 All ER 834, 35 Cr App R 138 DC.
82   This would be an assault by the accused on the victim and as the acts are clearly indecent the charge would be made out provided it could be proved that the accused intended to commit such an assault; *Faulkner v Talbot* [1981] 3 All ER 468; [1981] 1 WLR 1528, 74 Cr App R 1; [1981] Crim LR 705 DC (the act of sexual intercourse does not incorporate previous indecent acts: thus a woman does not have a defence to a charge of indecent assault on a boy under sixteen, where those acts were preliminary to the intercourse); *Court* [1989] AC 28; [1988] 2 All ER 221; [1988] 2 WLR 1071, 87 Cr App R 144; [1988] Crim LR 537 HL.
83   *Burrows* [1952] 1 All ER 58, 35 Cr App R 180 CCA.
84   See par 8.52–8.54.
85   The Indecency with Children Act, 1960, s 1(1) provides: "Any person who commits an act of gross indecency with or towards a child under the age of fourteen, or who incites a child under that age to such an act with him or another, shall be liable on conviction on indictment to imprisonment for a term not exceeding two years, or on summary conviction to imprisonment for a term not exceeding six months, or to a fine not exceeding two thousand pounds or to both". In England the possibility of such a technical acquittal is provided by: "Any person who commits an act of gross indecency with or towards a child under the age of fourteen, or who incites a child under that age to such an at with him or another, shall be liable on conviction on indictment. . . ."

where the touching is all one way and the accused does not, during the sexual acts, touch the victim in return. This, in practice, is a highly unlikely circumstance. It has also been argued that an assault may be committed if the impact is occasioned by the movement of the victim himself against some stationary matter provided that the accused has intentionally caused that impact.[86]

Child Abuse Reform

8.39 The Law Reform Commission in their report on Child Sexual Abuse[87] have recommended the creation of the new offence of "child sexual abuse" or "sexual exploitation", to replace the present offence of "indecent assault with consent". The offence should be defined as:[88]

(1) Intentional touching of the body of a child for the purpose of the sexual arousal or sexual gratification of the child or the person;

(2) intentional masturbation in the presence of a child;

(3) intentional exposure of the sexual organs of a person or any other sexual act intentionally performed in the presence of a child for the purpose of sexual arousal or gratification of the older person or as an expression of aggression, threat or intimidation towards the child; and

(4) sexual exploitation, which includes permitting, encouraging or requiring a child to solicit for or to engage in prostitution or other sexual act as referred to above with the accused or any other person, persons, animal or thing or engaging in the recording (on video tape, film, audio tape, or other temporary or permanent material), posing, modelling or performing of any act involving the exhibition of a child's body for the purpose of sexual gratification of an audience or for the purpose of any other sexual act referred to in sub-paragraphs (1) and (2) above.

8.40 This new offence should, it is proposed, include sexual intercourse and anal penile penetration. Only sexual activity engaged in for the sexual gratification of the accused or another, or as an expression of aggression, threat or intimidation should constitute an offence. In any prosecution for the offence, the onus should be on the accused to establish that he had no improper motive. The offence should be prosecutable summarily or on indictment at the election of the DPP. While the penalty for the offence would to some extent depend on its nature, the Commission suggest a maximum penalty of five to seven years' imprisonment.[89]

The Law Reform Commission also recommended that the present law under which the crime of indecent assault with consent can only be committed with children under the age of 15 should be extended so as to provide that the new offence can be committed by a "person in authority"[90] with a person of 15 or 16 years. This

---

86   Macksey, "The Criminal Law and the Woman Seducer" [1956] Crim LR 453, 542.

87   LRC 32-1990 in particular ch 4. For a full review of the literature see Geddis, Taylor & Heneghan, "Child Sexual Abuse" [1990] NZLJ 371 et seq.

88   The definition proposed by the Western Australian Task Force in its 1987 Report. LRC 32-1990 at par 1.10.

89   LRC 32-1990 par 4.19.

90   A "person in authority" is defined as "a parent, step-parent, grandparent, uncle or aunt, any guardian or person *in loco parentis* or any person responsible, even temporarily, for the education, supervision or welfare of a person below the age of 17". LRC 32- 1990 par 4.11.

recommendation is aimed particularly at the sexual abuse of young persons of this age by their parents or step-parents.[91] The Commission had no doubt that it should also be an offence in the case of boys between the ages of 15 and 17 where the perpetrator is such a person.[92]

Circumstances of Indecency

8.41 The circumstances which accompany the assault or battery must be objectively indecent. It is for the jury to decide whether what occurred was so offensive to contemporary standards of modesty and privacy as to be indecent.[93] Ordinarily this will not cause difficulty, as where the accused kisses the victim against her will and suggests sexual intercourse,[94] or where the accused, after exposing his penis to a boy who refused a request that he fondle it, grabbed the boy and pulled him towards himself.[95] In England it has been held that it was not an indecent assault for the accused, who was taking pornographic pictures of a number of boys, to touch them in a non-sexual way to indicate the next pose.[96] This decision is inconsistent with the definition of indecent assault; the touching does not, of itself, have to be indecent.[97]

8.42 In *Court*[98] the House of Lords identified three categories of conduct in indecent assault cases:

91 LRC 32-1990 par 4.20. For a review and outline of the evidential provisions see (1990) Gazette ILSI 381.

92 LRC 32-1990 par 4.32. For a further discussion of the relevance of age to consent see par 8.10-8.13.

93 *Court* [1989] AC 28 at 35; [1988] 2 All ER 221 at 229; [1988] 2 WLR 1071 at 1081, 87 Cr App R 144 at 154; [1988] Crim LR 537 HL: "The judge in assisting the jury in his summing up as to the meaning of an indecent assault adopted, *inter alia*, a definition used by Professor Glanville Williams in his *Text Book of Criminal Law* (2nd ed 1983), p 231: "'Indecent' may be defined as 'overtly sexual'". This is a convenient shorthand expression, since most, but not necessarily all, indecent assaults will be clearly of a sexual nature, although they, as in this case, may have only sexual undertones. A simpler way of putting the matter to the jury is to ask them to decide whether "right-minded persons would consider the conduct indecent or not". Lord Ackner in *Court*. Lord Griffiths put it another way: "By indecency is meant conduct that right-thinking people will consider an affront to the sexual modesty of a woman". [1989] AC 28 at 35; [1988] 2 All ER 221 at 223; [1988] 2 WLR 1073, 87 Cr App R 144 at 147 HL. See Williams, "What is an Indecent Assault?" [1987] NLJ 870. A similar test is put forward in Gillies 475.

94 *Leeson* (1968) 52 Cr App R 185 CA.

95 *Beal v Kelley* [1951] 2 All ER 763, 35 Cr App R 128 DC, which approved the definition from Archbold. However, this case was distinguished by Lord Ackner in *Court*: "In such a case (*Beal*) and in many others cited to us, the assault in itself was not indecent. It was the combination of the assault with circumstances of indecency, that established the constituents of the offence. In the instant case (spanking of a 12 year old girl), it is the assault itself—its true nature—an assault for sexual gratification, which was capable of amounting to an indencent assault". [1989] AC 28 at 43; [1988] 2 All ER 221 at 230; [1988] 2 WLR 1071 at 1083, 87 Cr App R 144 at 155 HL.

96 *Sutton* [1977] 3 All ER 476; [1977] 1 WLR 1086; [1977] Crim LR 569 CA.

97 *Leeson*, fn 94—the kiss in this case was, it is submitted, not in itself indecent, it was the suggestion that accompanied it, coupled with the kiss.

98 Fn 93 *Court* was followed by the Court of Criminal Appeal of New South Wales in *Harkin* (1989) A Crim R 296 which approved the test of indecent as being contrary to the ordinary standards of morality of respectable people. The Court held that an indecent assault must have a sexual connotation which may derive directly from the body area of the victim or the assailant and that the intentional touching of a girl's breast was sufficient but where an assault did not unequivocally

(1) An assault in circumstances incapable of being regarded as indecent. The secret motives of the accused in doing an objectively decent act will not change that act into an indecent one, as where the accused tried to remove a shoe from a girl's foot because it gave him a kind of perverted sexual gratification.[99]

(2) An assault in circumstances which are inherently indecent. In this category Lord Ackner[1] gives the following example:

> The defendant removes against her will, a woman's clothing. Such a case, to my mind, raises no problem. Those very facts, devoid of any explanation, would give rise to the irresistible inference that the defendant intended to assault his victim in a manner which right-minded persons would clearly think was indecent. Whether he did so for his own personal sexual gratification or because, being a misogynist or for some other reason, he wished to embarrass or humiliate his victim, seems to me to be irrelevant. He has failed, *ex-hypothesi*, to show any lawful justification for his indecent conduct.

(3) An assault in circumstances which are capable of being regarded as either decent or indecent.

8.43 In order to decide whether or not right-minded persons might think that a particular assault was indecent, Lord Ackner listed the following factors as being clearly relevant:[2]

> . . . the relationship of the defendant to his victim—were they relatives, friends or virtually complete strangers? How had the defendant come to embark on this conduct and why was he behaving in this way?
> Aided by such material, a jury would be helped to determine the quality of the act, the true nature of the assault and to answer the vital question—were they sure that the defendant not only intended to commit an assault upon the girl, but an assault which was indecent—was such an inference irresistible?

An intimate medical examination is, however, objectively indecent, and it is only the motivation of the doctor that makes it a decent act between the parties, if done for a proper motive.[3] Apart from this there can be no assault, provided no harm is done, where the victim consents.[4]

---

offer a sexual connotation it must be accompanied by some intention to obtain sexual gratification. For a contrasting analysis see *J* (1990) 58 CCC (3d) 167 CA Newfoundland.

99   *George* [1956] Crim LR 52, similarly, touching the hem of a girl's skirt is not, without more, objectively indecent; *Thomas* (1985) 81 Cr App R 331; [1985] Crim LR 677 CA or the preliminaries of normal sexual conduct such as taking a hand; *Kilbourne* [1972] 3 All ER 545; [1972] 1 WLR 1365, 56 Cr App R 828; [1972] Crim LR 637 CA.

1   [1989] AC 28 at 42; [1988] 2 All ER 221 at 230; [1988] 2 WLR 1071 at 1082, 87 Cr App R 144 at 155 HL. As the offence is intention based and thus entirely subjective it would be possible for a genuine belief that an attack was being carried out in the circumstances of decency to provide a defence. Such a belief would, of necessity, remove the accused's view of the situation far from the light in which an ordinary person would perceive it. In such circumstances he is unlikely to be acquitted. S 2 of the Rape Act, 1981 is entirely declaratory of the law in the sense that the jury is entitled to have regard to the perception of a reasonable or ordinary person in deciding whether or not the accused's belief was genuinely held in such circumstances. It is submitted that such an instance is highly unlikely to arise in practice.

2 .   Fn 95.

3   *Armstrong* (1885) 49 JP 745; *Court*, fn 95. See further par 8.11.

4   See par 8.16.

Aggravating Circumstances

8.44 The addition of new elements to the offence of indecent or sexual assault to make it aggravated sexual assault together with the increased penalty create a new offence.[5]

It will be an objective fact as to whether the aggravating circumstances mentioned in s 3 of the Rape Act, 1990 are present. Where the jury find that the accused inflicted serious violence or threatened serious violence on the victim, the aggravating circumstances will be made out. A further way in which aggravation can occur under s 3 is where the indecent assault causes serious injury, humiliation or degradation of a grave nature to the victim. This definition is wider and less specific than actual or threatened serious violence. It is difficult therefore to explain to a jury, in circumstances where those easily definable elements do not exist, as to how they should differentiate a sexual assault from an aggravated sexual assault.

Jury Direction

It is submitted that a proper direction should first explain what a sexual assault is (that is, an indecent assault) and should go on to mention the specific factors of serious violence or the threat thereof, which causes such an assault to become an aggravated sexual assault. The jury should be told that if those factors are not present the accused may still be found guilty of an aggravated sexual assault if they are satisfied beyond reasonable doubt that there is an injury to the victim which was of a grave or serious nature or where the victim was humiliated or degraded to a grave or serious degree by the actions of the accused. An injury in this context means a bodily injury; the context differentiates it from the psychic wrongs of humiliation and degradation. In deciding whether any of these elements were present they should have regard to the wrong actually suffered by the victim in the objective circumstances, bearing in mind that the purpose of this enquiry is to find whether the accused is guilty of a much more serious offence than sexual assault. They should also be told that on a charge of aggravated sexual assault they may find the accused to be guilty merely of a sexual assault.

It is an objective circumstance as to whether injury, humiliation or degradation of a grave nature was caused to the person assaulted. In this regard the standards prevalent among the community should be taken into account in accessing whether or not this additional external factor is present. In dealing with this question, it is submitted, the judge need merely instruct the jury that they should find as a matter of fact whether what was done by the accused to the victim caused an injury, humiliation or degradation of a grave nature. If the answer to that question is positive they should then go on to consider whether the accused intended such an assault, as opposed to a mere sexual assault.

---

5   *Courtie* [1984] AC 463; [1984] 1 All ER 740; [1984] 2 WLR 330, 78 Cr App R 292; [1984] Crim LR 366 HL; *The People (DPP) v Murray* [1977] IR 360 SC; further see ch 2. For jurisdiction see par 8.04.

Mental Element

8.45 Prior to the decision of the House of Lords in *Court*[6] it was held[7] that where the accused intentionally assaulted the victim with knowledge of the indecent circumstances or being reckless as to the existence of them, then the essential ingredients of the charge[8] were made out.

8.46 Lord Ackner for the majority in that case introduced a mental element[9] and supports his analysis:

> It cannot, in my judgment, have been the intention of Parliament, that an assault can, by a mere mistake or mischance, be converted into an indecent assault, with all the opprobrium which a conviction for such an offence carries.[10]

He went on to define this mental element thus:

> I, therefore, conclude that on a charge of indecent assault the prosecution must not only prove that the accused intentionally assaulted the victim, but that in so doing he intended to commit an indecent assault, i.e., an assault which right-minded persons would think was indecent. Accordingly, any evidence which tends to explain the reason for the defendant's conduct, be it his own admission or otherwise, would be relevant to establish whether or not he intended to commit, not only an assault, but an indecent one.[11]

8.47 It follows that a chaste motive on the part of the accused could turn an assault capable of being an indecent assault into a common assault. This was illustrated in the case of *Pratt*.[12] The accused had threatened two young boys and ordered them to undress and shine their torches on each other's private parts. The Assistant Recorder had admitted evidence from the defendant that his sole motive was to search for cannabis which he thought the boys had taken from him the previous afternoon. Contrary to the decision of the Court of Appeal,[13] the House of Lords

6 [1989] AC 27 AT 44; [1988] 2 All ER 221; [1988] 2 WLR 1071, 87 Cr App R 144; [1988] Crim LR 537 HL.

7 By the Court of Appeal in *Court* [1987] QB 156; [1987] 1 All ER 120; [1986] 3 WLR 1029, 84 Cr App R 210; [1987] Crim LR 134 CA.

8 In *Court* [1989] AC 28 at 42; [1988] 2 All ER 221 at 230; [1988] 2 WLR 1071 at 1083, 87 Cr App R 144 at 155; [1988] Crim LR 537 HL, under s 14(1) of the Sexual Offences Act, 1956 (U.K.). The Irish equivalent being s 2 of the Rape Act, 1990 for sexual assault or s 3 of the same Act for aggravated sexual assault.

9 He based his reasoning, *inter alia*, on L. Reid in *Sweet v Parsley* [1970] AC 132; [1969] 1 All ER 347; [1969] 2 WLR 470, 53 Cr App R 221 HL. This approach was specifically approved by the Irish Supreme Court in *The People (DPP) v Murray* [1977] IR 360. Indeed the same quotation from Lord Reid's judgment, used by Lord Ackner in *Court* [1989] AC 28 at 44; [1988] 2 All ER 221 at 228; [1988] 2 WLR 1071 at 1080, 87 Cr App R 144 at 153; [1988] Crim LR 537 HL, was held by Henchy J in *The People (DPP) v Murray* [1977] IR 360 at 399: ". . . whenever a section is silent as to *mens rea* there is a presumption that, in order to give effect to the will of Parliament, we must read in words appropriate to require *mens rea*".

10 [1989] AC 28 at 43; [1988] 2 All ER 221 at 228; [1988] 2 WLR 1071 at 1080, 87 Cr App R 144 at 153 HL.

11 [1989] AC 28 at 45; [1988] 2 All ER 221 at 231; [1988] 2 WLR 1071 at 1084, 87 Cr App R 144 at 156 HL.

12 [1984] Crim LR 41.

13 *Court* [1987] QB 156 at 163; [1987] 1 All ER 120 at 125; [1986] 3 WLR 1029 at 1035, 84 Cr App R 210 at 216; [1987] Crim LR 134 CA.

held that this case had been correctly decided. Sexual gratification experienced by the accused in the course of a medical, or other examination, conducted for proper reasons in circumstances of indecency, does not render that examination indecent.[14]

8.48 There is no intention apparent on the part of the Oireachtas to make the elements of the offence, which distinguish a sexual assault from an aggravated sexual assault, ones of strict liability.[15] Those circumstances of aggravation provide for a doubling of the potential penalty from five years' to life imprisonment. The offence itself is more than regulatory and is clearly criminal in character. It follows that for the charge of aggravated sexual assault to be made out the accused must have intended an assault of this nature which means the aggravating circumstances and the absence of the victim's consent to them. Most of the circumstances of aggravation will cause little difficulty as regards this mental element.

If the accused himself perpetrates any of those aggravating acts it is difficult to imagine situations in which he did not intend them. Of their nature they are purposeful actions. As was stated at the outset such cases will only in the rarest circumstances cause the kinds of difficulty set out in the preceding pages.

Section 4 Rape

8.49 The previous reform of the law which commended itself to the Oireachtas[16] involved the classification of unlawful acts of penetration of the victim's body within the crime of aggravated sexual assault. A concern for the correct labelling of offences, in accordance with the modern use of speech,[17] has led the Oireachtas to make a fundamental reform in the Rape Act, 1990.

Instead, however, of including offences of unlawful penetration of the victim's body within the definition of rape, the Oireachtas chose to create a new offence, which could shortly be described as a form of rape, but which in fact is a form of sexual assault, as previously discussed. S 4 of the Rape Act, 1990 provides:

> (1) In this Act "rape under section 4" means a sexual assault that includes:
> (a) penetration (however slight) of the anus or mouth by the penis, or
> (b) penetration (however slight) of the vagina by any object held or manipulated by another person.
> (2) A person guilty of rape under Section 4 shall be liable on conviction of indictment to imprisonment for life.
> (3) Rape under s 4 shall be a felony.

The offence is neutral with respect to the sex of the victim with regard to par

---

14 [1989] AC 28; [1988] 2 All ER 221 at 230; [1988] 2 WLR 1071 at 1083, 87 Cr App R 144 at 155 HL. Lord Ackner used the example of an unnecessary intimate medical examination being carried out by a doctor for either sexual gratification or some chaste motive such as research, which would be of no benefit to the patient. He avoided any contradiction by categorising this as an inherently indecent assault with the only issue being one of consent. The doctor's motivation could be reflected in the sentence.

15 *The People (DPP) v Murray* [1977] IR 360 SC.

16 Expressed in the Criminal Law (Rape) (Amendment) Bill, 1988.

17 This was the argument generally expressed at the Law Reform Commission Seminar by the proponents of this change.

(a). A male person may assault any other person by the means therein described. The offence as described in par (b) may, obviously, be perpetrated only on a female victim but the principal may be either a man or a woman. No rule of law restricts the secondary parties to the male sex.[18] A man or woman may aid, abet, counsel or procure any such offence.

The elements of the offence simply incorporate those of a sexual assault, that is an indecent assault, in aggravating circumstances which objectively include one or other of the actions prohibited by this section. Our previous discussion of sexual assault, and of sexual assault in circumstances of aggravation, do not, therefore, require repetition as the elements are precisely the same apart from the different prohibited action described in the new offence under s 4. These can be easily identified. The degree of penetration need only be slight.[19]

A person indicted for this offence may be convicted of aggravated sexual assault or sexual assault as an alternative verdict.[20]

Buggery

8.50 Buggery[21] is a felony of common law,[22] the penalty for which was fixed by s 61 of the Offences Against the Person Act, 1861:

> 61 Whosoever shall be convicted of the abominable crime of buggery, committed either with mankind or with any animal, shall be liable to be kept in penal servitude for life.[23]

> 62 Whosoever shall attempt to commit the said abominable crime, or shall be guilty of any assault with intent to commit the same, or of any indecent assault upon any male person, shall be guilty of a misdemeanour, and on being convicted thereof shall be liable to be kept in penal servitude for any term not exceeding ten years.

The latter is more correctly known as bestiality.[24] Consent is irrelevant in the case of either bestiality or buggery committed on human beings, as the law now stands.[25]

Definition

8.51 Buggery is defined at common law as the penetration, by the penis, of the

---

18 See par 8.22.

19 See par 8.09.

20 Rape Act, 1990, s 8(3).

21 Ó Síocháin, *Criminal Law of Ireland* (1987) 143 describes it as "the most abominable of all crimes". Why, one wonders? Sodomy is defined in the Shorter Oxford Dictionary as "an unnatural form of sexual intercourse, especially that of one male with another". It derives from the name of the early city beside the Dead Sea, Sodom, the destruction of which is recorded in the Bible (Gen XVIII-XIX).

22 The offence was first made punishable in the common law courts by 25 Henry 8, ch 6 (now repealed).

23 The sections are quoted, as are all other sections from the Offences Against the Person Act, 1861, in accordance with the amendments introduced by the Penal Servitude Acts of 1864 and 1891 and by the Statute Law Revision Act, 1908.

24 A domestic fowl is an animal for these purposes; *Brown* (1889) 24 QBD 357, 16 Cox 715 CCR.

25 *Bourne* (bestiality forced by a man on his wife), fn 29. For a discussion of the law in relation to homosexual offences see *Norris*, fn 23.

anus[26] of a man or woman[27] (whether that man is the husband of the victim or not)[28] or of intercourse (*per anum* or *per vaginam*) by a man or woman with an animal of either sex.[29] The latter is more specifically known as bestiality. Consent is irrelevant.

Where the complainant consented to the act the accomplice warning must be given to the jury as to the danger of a conviction on an accomplice's evidence in the absence of corroboration.[30] The consent of the parties is not a defence to the charge. Both parties are equally guilty.[31] The need for a warning in the absence of corroboration in a sexual case, is at the discretion of the trial judge.[32] Males under fourteen are legally capable of committing the offence.[33] The offence is committed on penetration, however slight,[34] and if penetration has not been achieved an attempt may be charged[35] or returned as an alternative verdict on indictment.[36]

It seems probable that the constitutional right to marital privacy would render a prosecution for buggery against a married couple an infringement of Article 40.3.[37] The evidence for such a prosecution is, however, unlikely to be forthcoming.

Where the prosecution is for an assault with intent to commit buggery the proofs are of an assault or psychic assault, with such an intent which can be proved either directly, or by inference from all the relevant surrounding circumstances.[38]

---

26 *Jacobs* (1817) R&R 331, 168 ER 830 CCR; *Norris v A-G* [1984] IR 36 at 41 HC, SC. In s 18 of the Offences Against the Person Act, 1828, buggery is listed among the crimes for which it it not necessary to prove "emision of seed", the offence being complete on proof of penetration only. Buggery was not included in s 63 of the 1861 Act which replaced this. Generally on the definition see 1 Hale 669; 1 Hawk ch 4; 1 East PC 480.

27 *Wiseman* (1718) Fortes Rep 91, 92 ER 774; *Jellyman* (1838) 8 C&P 604, 173 ER 637.

28 *Jellyman*, fn 27.

29 *Bourne* (1952) 36 Cr App R 125 CCA; *Packer* [1932] VLR 225 SC; 1 Hale 669; 1 Hawk ch 4; 1 East PC 480.

30 *Jellyman*, fn 27.

31 Archbold (1922) 1047; *The People v Bond* (1955) 136 Cal App (2d), 282 P (2d) 44; Stephen *Digest* (9th ed, 1950) Art 221. It follows that both a man and a woman, in cases on consent, may be a principal and the person penetrated is not usually an accessory; *Wiseman*, fn 27; *Jellyman*, fn 27; 3 Co Inst 59.

32 Rape Act, 1990, s 7 quoted in par 8.79–8.80. It has been judicially stated that corroboration is particularly required in cases of this kind, where the victim is an accomplice, *Tate* [1908] 2 KB 680, 77 LJ (KB) 1043; (1968) 21 Cox 693 CCA; *A-G v O'Sullivan* [1930] IR 552 CCA; *A-G v Duffy* [1931] IR 144 CCA; a warning should also be given to the jury as to the dangers of acting on the evidence of young boys in these cases; *Cratchley* (1913) 9 Cr App R 232 CCA; *Southern* (1930) 22 Cr App R 6, 142 LT 383, 29 Cox 621. As to the admissibility of fresh complaints in such a case see *Chesney v Newsholme* [1908] Prob 301 (admissible).

33 Rape Act, 1990, s 6, quoted par 8.07. Hale however states that a boy or girl under 14 cannot be guilty because of a lack of discretion; 1 Hale PC 670, 3 Co Inst 59, 1 East PC 480. For the defence of infancy see par 4.48.

34 *Reckspear* (1832) 1 Mood 342, 168 ER 1296. For bestiality see *Cozins* (1834) 6 C&P 351.

35 *Brown* (1889) 24 QBD 357, 16 Cox 715 CCR.

36 Criminal Procedure Act, 1851, s 9, quoted par 1.23. The Canadian courts have held there to be sufficient evidence of an attempt where the accused suggested buggery to the victim in a stable, spread a blanket on the floor and took down his trousers; *Delip Singh* (1918) 26 BCR 390. See also *Lankford* [1959] Crim LR 209 CCA.

37 *McGee v A-G* [1974] IR 284 at 313, 322, 109 ILTR 29 SC.

38 See ch 2. For assault see ch 6.

There have been no prosecutions that we can find in recent years where such acts were committed in private between consenting adults.[39]

Where the charge is of assault with intent to commit buggery such an intent must be proved[40] but not necessarily with the person assaulted.[41]

Gross Indecency

8.52 Ss 61 and 62 of the Offences Against the Person Act, 1861 made it a criminal offence to commit buggery and for persons to commit sexual assaults on men. It did not cover consensual homosexual acts between male persons which were not either buggery or attempted buggery. S 11 of the Criminal Law Amendment Act, 1885 was enacted to deal with this situation:

> Any male person who, in public or private, commits, or is a party to the commission of, or procures or attempts to procure the commission by any male person of, any act of gross indecency with another male person, shall be guilty of a misdemeanour, and being convicted thereof shall be liable at the discretion of the Court to be imprisoned for any term not exceeding two years, with or without hard labour.

Definition

8.53 The use of the term gross indecency clearly implies some act going beyond mere indecency, although there is no authority directly in point.[42] In *Hunt*[43] it was held that physical contact is not needed between the men. It suffices that two men put themselves in a position where it can be said that a grossly indecent exhibition is going on.[44] Whether there is gross indecency is a question of fact and it would be helpful for the judge to contrast acts of mere indecency and to leave it to the jury to decide if the indecency was gross.[45] For example, it has been held to be indecent for a man to spank a girl to give himself sexual pleasure[46] and it has been held to be grossly indecent for men to masturbate in sight of one another.[47]

---

39   For the approach of the English Courts to sentencing a person convicted of buggery with a boy see *Willis* [1975] 1 All ER 620; [1975] 1 WLR 292, 60 Cr App R 146; [1975] Crim LR 177; *White, The Independent*, 19 February 1990. For sentencing guidelines in the case of non-consensual buggery see *Wall* (1989) 11 Cr App R (S) 111. For observations on sentencing in cases of bestiality see *Higson, The Times*, 21 January 1984; *Williams* [1974] Crim LR 588.

40   For a discussion of intent see ch 2.   41   Russell 864.

42   In *Whitehouse* (1955) QWN 76 CCA a direction of a trial judge to the effect that both "indecency" and "gross" were ordinary English words which he would not define was upheld. Philip J indicated that the intention of the legislature in using the word "gross" had been to indicate that slight cases of indecency were not covered. In *Pinard & Maltais* (1983) 5 CCC (3d) 460 the Quebec Court of Appeal indicated: "whether an act is or is not an act of gross indecency depends upon the nature of the act, the circumstances and the time and place . . ."; in *Quesnel* (1979) 51 CCC (2d) 270, 280 the Ontario Court of Appeal indicated: ". . . the offence of gross indecency . . . may be defined as a marked departure from decent conduct expected of the average Canadian in the circumstances that existed".

43   [1950] 2 All ER 291, 34 Cr App R 135 CCA.

44   *Hunt*, fn 43 and see *Norris v A-G* [1984] IR 36 at 72 HC, SC (Henchy J).

45   In this regard see the remarks of McWilliam J in *Norris v A-G* [1984] IR 35 at 48 and McCarthy J at 101 HC, SC.

46   *Court* [1989] AC 28; [1988] 2 All ER 221; [1988] 2 WLR 1071, 87 Cr App R 144; [1988] Crim LR 537 HL.

47   *Preece & Howells* [1977] 1 QB 370; [1976] 2 All ER 690; [1976] 2 WLR 745, 63 Cr App R 28; [1976]

Elements

8.54 The act must be committed "with another male" and consequently the parties must be co-operating.[48] It follows that the accused must have been acting in concert with another man. Mere presence at an act of gross indecency between other men is insufficient. The crime does not include an act of gross indecency committed in the presence of, or directed at another man.[49] If the first accused and the second accused are charged together, the first accused may be convicted and the second accused acquitted.[50] If sufficiently proximate acts of persuasion or preparation occur they will amount to an attempt.[51] If the accused does not try to persuade the victim but grabs at him indecently this will be an indecent assault.[52]

An accused can be guilty of procuring another on his own behalf.[53] The offence can be appropriately charged where the accused, without any threat, asks the victim to handle him. If the victim consents the accused will not be guilty of an indecent assault provided the victim does the touching, but the accused will be guilty of procuring or attempting to procure gross indecency.[54] Procuring means producing a result by endeavour.[55] The accused can incite another to procure the act even though the accused does not have a particular person in mind.[56] A fresh complaint is admissible to prove the consistency of the victim's version of events in such a case[57] and the observations made concerning corroboration in sexual cases, willing parties being accomplices, and the observations concerning the dangers relating to the evidence of young boys and accomplices, apply with equal force here.

Although the accused must act in concert with another man, where two men are

---

Crim LR 392 HL; *Hornby* [1946] 2 All ER 487, 32 Cr App R 1 CCA.

48   *Preece & Howells* [1977] 1 QB 370; [1976] 2 All ER 690; [1976] 2 WLR 745, 63 Cr App R 28; [1976] Crim LR 392 HL; *Hornby* [1946] 2 All ER 487, 32 Cr App R 1 CCA.

49   *Hall* [1964] 1 QB 273; [1963] 2 All ER 1075; [1963] 3 WLR 482, 47 Cr App R 253 CCA. Lord Parker LCJ held that "the word 'with' in s 13 of the Sexual Offences Act, 1956, does not mean 'with consent of' but has the somewhat looser meaning of merely 'against' or 'directed towards'". This decision was not followed in *Preece and Howells*, fn 48, the Court of Appeal stating: "We think the complete offence requires the participation, the co-operation, of two men. . . . To construe the section so that the complete offence could be committed even though the other man did not consent could lead to the embarrassment of, and injustice to, innocent men". The wording of s 13 of the 1956 Act (U.K.) is identical to that in s 11 of the Act of 1885.

50   *Pearce* [1951] 1 All ER 493; (1952) 35 Cr App R 17 CCA; *Jones* [1896] 1 QB 4, 18 Cox CC 207 CCR.

51   *Cope* (1921) 16 Cr App R 77 (letter arranging to meet in a particular place at a particular time; sufficiently proximate); *Woods* (1930) 22 Cr App R (letter inviting the victim to come to another city and take up a job and have a sexual relationship, the accused masquerading in the letter as a woman; insufficiently proximate).

52   *Pearce*, fn 50.

53   In England this is no longer an offence as s 4(3) of the Sexual Offences Act, 1967 provides that it shall not be an offence under s 13 of the 1956 Act for a man to procure the commission with himself of an act of gross indecency by another man where that act, by reason of s 1 of the 1967 Act, is not an offence (i.e. a consensual act done in private by parties over 21 years of age).

54   *Burrows* [1952] 1 All ER 58, 35 Cr App R 180 CCA. See par 8.37.

55   See par 5.06.

56   *Bentley* [1923] 1 KB 403 CCA.

57   *Chesney v Newsholme* [1908] Prob 301.

charged together and the necessary standard of proof is achieved only against one, that accused may be convicted and the other acquitted.[58]

Homosexual Offences and Human Rights

8.55 In *Norris v A-G*[59] the High Court and the Supreme Court, by a 3:2 majority, found that s 61 and 62 of the Offences Against the Person Act, 1861 and s 11 of the Criminal Law Amendment Act, 1885 were not inconsistent with the Constitution. O'Higgins CJ, in giving the majority judgment, rejected contentions on the part of the plaintiff that to make criminal homosexual acts between men, which were not similarly treated if committed by women, amounted to invidious discrimination, that the plaintiff's right to privacy was subjected to an unwarranted interference not justified by the public good and that the prohibition on homosexual acts inhibited his right to the freedom of expression in and association enjoyed by heterosexuals. The Court held that the legislature was entitled to have regard to the social problems caused by male homosexuality in making it alone the subject of criminal offences and that the Christian and democratic nature of the State entitled it to make criminal acts regarded by the Christian churches as morally wrong and whereby social problems might be caused in the spread of disease and the disintegration and discouragement of marriage.

In the case of *Dudgeon v United Kingdom*[60] the European Court of Human Rights declared inconsistent with Article 8 of the European Convention on Human Rights similar provisions in the Law of Northern Ireland.[61] The *Dudgeon* decision did not bind the Supreme Court.[62] The State is obliged to respect the Convention in its domestic laws, but the Convention is not part of those domestic laws. Not surprisingly, Mr Norris appealed to the European Court of Human Rights and succeeded.

Reform

8.56 The Law Reform Commission has made recommendations to reform the law in relation to homosexual acts in general conformity with the need to comply with the Strasburg judgments and to protect public decency, the young and the mentally ill. The scope of these recommendations was already set out by Henchy J in the *Norris* case:

> . . . it will be necessary for such legislation to hedge in such immunity from criminal sanctions as it may think fit to confer (on acts of a homosexual nature in private between consenting adults) with appropriate definitions of adulthood, consent and privacy and with such exceptions relating to prostitution, immoral exploitation, publicity, drug

58 *Jones & Bowerbank* [1896] 1 QB 4; *Pearce*, fn 50; *Preece & Howells*, fn 47. It has been held in England that if the dispute in the trial is as to observation of both men it is inconsistent for one to be convicted and the other acquitted; *Batter, The Times*, 16 March 1990, where one accused denies the charge evidence of his guilty plea should be excluded at the trial of the other; *Mattison* [1990] Crim LR 117.

59 [1984] IR 35 HC, SC.   60 (1981) 4 EHRR 149.

61 Contained in the United Kingdom Sexual Offences Act, 1956, s 12 and 13.

62 *In re Ó Laighléis* [1960] IR 93.

abuse, commercialisation, family relationships and such other matters or areas of exception as the Oireachtas may justifiably consider necessary for the preservation of public order and decency.[63]

In its report on child sexual abuse[64] the Law Reform Commission recommends[65] that ss 61 and 62 of the Offences Against the Person Act, 1861 and s 11 of the Criminal Law (Amendment) Act, 1885 which render criminal acts of buggery and gross indecency between male persons be repealed and that there should be the same protection against both homosexual and heterosexual exploitation of the young. It follows from this recommendation that the "child sexual abuse" offence[66] which the Commission have recommended should be created to replace the present offence of "indecent assault with consent"[67] which should apply equally in the case of homosexual activity.

8.57 However, the Commission, which had recommended elsewhere in its report that vaginal sexual intercourse with girls between the ages of 15 and 17 should cease to be an offence, with certain exceptions, pointed to the difficulties of providing a "mirror" offence in the case of homosexuals. This would have as a consequence the legalising of consensual buggery of persons between the ages of 15 and 17 except where the other participant was a person in authority or was more than five years older than the person concerned.

Having considered the medical problems which could result from such a proposal, the commission recommended that anal penile penetration of boys and girls between the ages of 15 and 17 should continue to be an offence.

Pending the implementation of these recommendations the law remains as stated. If a person is convicted by our courts he must exhaust all domestic remedies available before appealing to the European Court of Human Rights.

Sexual Intercourse Unlawful by Reason of Age

8.58 Age is a factor in many sexual offences. It is a crime to have unlawful sexual intercourse with a girl under the age of seventeen.[68] The law fixes fifteen as the age at which a person may consent to indecent acts falling short of intercourse.[69] Eighteen is the age when a girl may be taken from her home without the consent

63 [1984] IR 35 Henchy J at 79, quoted with approval by McCarthy J at 104.

64 LRC 32 – 1990.

65 Fn 21 at par 4.29. The Incitement to Racial Hatred Act, 1990, makes it an offence to incite hatred by reason of a person's sexual orientation.

66 See below.

67 LRC 32 – 1990, par 4.31.

68 Criminal Law (Amendment) Act, 1935, s 1 and 2 (felony if under fifteen, penal servitude for life or imprisonment for two years; misdemeanour if from fifteen to seventeen, five years' penal servitude or two years imprisonment for a first offence, ten years' penal servitude or two years' imprisonment for subsequent offences). The only lawful justification being marriage, see below.

69 Criminal Law (Amendment) Act, 1935, s 14 (the penalty is that for sexual assault, five years' imprisonment or, for aggravated sexual assault which is a felony life imprisonment). The act can also amount to gross indecency between males. Sentencing guidelines in cases of unlawful sexual intercourse with girls under sixteen were given by the Court of Appeal in *Taylor & Others* (1977) 64 Cr App R 182 at 185.

of her parents or guardian.[70] A person may lawfully allow his premises to be used for sexual intercourse only if the girl is over seventeen.[71] A parent or guardian of a girl under twenty-one who causes or encourages or favours her seduction or prostitution may be deprived of her guardianship.[72] Twenty-one is the age at which an heiress may be abducted, even with her own consent, but without the consent of her parent or guardian.[73]

Unlawful Sexual Intercourse

8.59 The Criminal Law (Amendment) Act, 1935 provides by s 1 and 2:[74]

> 1(1) Any person who unlawfully and carnally knows any girl under the age of 15 years shall be guilty of a felony, and shall be liable on conviction thereof to penal servitude for life or for any term not less than 3 years or to imprisonment for any term not exceeding two years.
>
> (2) Any person who attempts to have unlawful carnal knowledge of any girl under the age of 15 years shall be guilty of misdemeanour, and shall be liable, in the case of a first conviction of such misdemeanour, to penal servitude for any term not exceeding five years nor less than three years or to imprisonment for any term not exceeding two years or, in the case of a second or any subsequent conviction of such misdemeanour, to penal servitude for any term not exceeding ten years nor less than three years or to imprisonment to any term not exceeding two years.
>
> 2(1) Any person who unlawfully and carnally knows any girl who is of or over the age of 15 years and under the age of 17 years shall be guilty of a misdemeanour and shall be liable, in the case of a first conviction of such misdemeanour, to penal servitude for any term not exceeding five years nor less than three years or to imprisonment for any term not exceeding two years or, in the case of a second or any subsequent conviction of such misdemeanour, to any term of penal servitude not exceeding ten years nor less than three years or to imprisonment for any term not exceeding two years.
>
> (2) Any person who attempts to have unlawful carnal knowledge of any girl who is of or over the age of 15 years and under the age of 17 years shall be guilty of a misdemeanour, and shall be liable, in the case of a first conviction of such misdemeanour, to imprisonment for any term not exceeding two years or, in the case of a second or any subsequent conviction of such misdemeanour, to penal servitude for any term not exceeding five years nor less than three years or to imprisonment for any term not exceeding two years.
>
> 3 No prosecution for an offence which is declared by this section to be a misdemeanour shall be commenced more than twelve months after the date on which such offence is alleged to have been committed.

If the accused is indicted for rape, or for an offence under s 1 he may be convicted,

---

70   Criminal Law (Amendment) Act, 1885, s 7 (misdemeanour, two years' imprisonment), see par 8.27.

71   Criminal Law (Amendment) Act, 1885, s 6, as amended by s 9 of the Criminal Law (Amendment) Act, 1935 (felony under fifteen, penal servitude for life or two years' imprisonment; misdemeanour if under seventeen, two years' imprisonment), see par 8.27.

72   Criminal Law Amendment Act, 1885, s 12.

73   Offences Against the Person Act, 1861, s 53 (felony, penal servitude for fourteen years or imprisonment for two years).

74   The Law Reform Commission in their report on child sexual abuse (LRC 32 – 1990) recommended that to maintain consistency of definition, the expression "carnal knowledge" and similar words in this Act should be replaced by the expression "sexual intercourse" as defined in s 1(2) of the Rape Act, 1981.

by way of alternative verdict, of an offence under s 3 of the Criminal Law Amendment Act, 1885, any other offence under s 1 or s 2 of the Act or of sexual assault or aggravated sexual assault.[75]

8.60 The age of the girl must be proved to have been under 17 or 15 years (whichever age applies) at the time of the offence. This may be done by producing a duly certified copy of the birth certificate, coupled with evidence of identity[76] or by the appropriate evidence from persons who knew the girl.[77] The evidence of age must be precise.[78] Direct evidence of age can be taken from someone who was present at the girl's birth.[79] In *The People (DPP) v JT*[80] the Court of Criminal Appeal held that the incompetence of a spouse at common law had not survived the enactment of the Constitution in respect of incest charges and that the public interest required that such a witness be compellable. By analogous reasoning a mother may be called as being the person in the best position to prove age.

Sexual intercourse is proved in the same way as in a rape case and the act is complete on penetration.[81] Consent is immaterial.[82] Where it is absent the act will also be rape[83] but this does not preclude a conviction for unlawful sexual intercourse.[84]

A girl who consents to the act is an accomplice and the jury should be warned of the dangers of convicting on her evidence.[85]

8.61 Prior to the enactment of s 7 of the Rape Act, 1990, this offence was one where the jury were warned of the dangers of convicting on the uncorroborated testimony of the victim in the absence of corroboration.[86] This warning is now at

75   Criminal Law (Amendment) Act, 1935, s 2; Rape Act, 1990, s 8. This large list of alternative verdicts surely requires that the accused be put on notice of the possibility of his being convicted of an offence for which he is not charged; *The State (Healy) v Donoghue* [1976] IR 325, 110 ILTR HC, SC. Arguably since the introduction of legal aid a person will obtain such information, in any event, from his legal representatives.

76   Under the Births and Deaths Registration Act, 1836; *Weaver* (1873) LR 2 CCR 85, 12 Cox 527 CCA; *Rogers* (1914) 10 Cr App R 276, 24 Cox 465 CCA (identity evidence is required as well as birth certificate).

77   The age may be proved by any legal means; *Cox* (1898) 1 QB 178, 18 Cox 672 CCR.

78   *The People (A-G) v O'Connor* [1949] 15 Ir Jur Rep 25. In *Cox* [1898] 1 QB 179 the age of a child victim was held to have been proved from three witnesses on a less technical basis. It is submitted that, as a matter of commonsense, in some circumstances, even in the absence of precise proof the age of a person may be gathered from their appearance. If there is a question of any doubt, however, the jury must give the accused the benefit of that doubt and acquit.

79   In *Nicholls* (1874) 13 Cox CC 75 evidence of the girl's mother was held admissible although it was subsequently shown that her recollection may not have been completely accurate.

80   3 Frewen CCA, unreported 27 July 1988. See Charleton, "The Victim in Irish Constitutional Law" (1990) 8 ILTSJ 140.

81   See par 8.08-8.09.

82   *A-G (Shaughnessy) v Ryan* [1960] IR 181 SC.

83   *Ratcliffe* (1882) QBD 74, 15 Cox 127 CCR; *Harling* [1938] 1 All ER 307, 26 Cr App R 127 CCA.

84   *Neale* (1844) 169 ER 140, 1 Den 36; Criminal Procedure Act, 1851, s 12.

85   It is probable that the corroboration requirement for an accomplice would only be required where the girl has sufficient understanding to make her act a voluntary one.

86   *Graham* (1910) 4 Cr App R 218; *Brown* (1910) 6 Cr App R 24; *Pitts* (1912) 8 Cr App R 126; *Dossi* (1918) 13 Cr App R 158.

the discretion of the trial judge.[87] As in a rape case, complaints by the victim voluntarily made at the first reasonable opportunity are admissible for the purpose of showing the consistency of her evidence.[88] Where the victim is a child and gives evidence other than on oath the accused cannot be convicted in the absence of corroboration.[89]

The age at which either sex can contract a valid marriage is 16,[90] though a foreign marriage can be valid under age.[91] If the accused believes himself to be married to the victim, the prosecution are not required to prove that such a marriage was not contracted between the accused and the victim.[92] None of the standard texts make the absence of a marriage between the accused and the victim a matter which the prosecution must prove.

Age

8.62 As age is one of the essential elements of these offences, in the sense that the acts are not normally otherwise criminal, the question arises whether ignorance by the accused as to the age of the girl, or his belief that she is over the requisite age constitute a defence. The answer appears to be no. The answer might well, however, be yes if a constitutional challenge were mounted. None of these statutory offences now incorporate an express defence of mistake on reasonable grounds. That was not always the case. The historical position is as follows:

1. The offence of taking a girl under sixteen out of the possession of her parents or guardian never incorporated the statutory defence of mistake as to her age.[93] The offence of taking a girl of eighteen out of the possession of her parents or guardian incorporated a statutory defence of belief supported by reasonable cause that the girl was over eighteen.[94] This defence was expressly repealed in 1935.[95]

---

87   See par 8.79–8.80.

88   See par 8.81.

89   Children Act, 1908, s 30, as amended by the Criminal Justice (Administration) Act, 1914, s 28(2). The Law Reform Commission in its report on child sexual abuse recommends that this section should be repealed and replaced by a provision enabling the court to hear the evidence of children under the age of 14 without requiring them to give evidence on oath or affirm where the court is satisfied that the children are competent to give evidence in accordance with the criteria already proposed in par 5.18 (i.e. the test of competency of children should be the capacity of the child to give an intelligible account of events which he or she has observed); LRC 32 – 1990 par 5.36.

90   S 1(1) of the Marriages Act, 1972. An exemption from this age restriction can be applied for before the marriage, to the High Court for "serious reasons" when it "is in the interests of the parties to the intended marriage". S 1(2) and s 1(3) of the 1972 Act. First time marriages by those under 21 require the consent of a guardian (or if there is no guardian, the High Court). S 19(1) of the Marriages (Ireland) Act, 1844 as amended by s 7 of the 1972 Act. See Shatter, *Family Law*, 79 and 98.

91   *Alhaji Mohamed v Knott (wife of 13)* [1969] 1 QB 1; [1968] 2 All ER 563; [1968] 2 WLR 1446; [1968] Crim LR 341.

92   None of the standard texts mention such a requirement and the proof of a special exemption from a general law is one solely within the competence of a defendant.

93   Offences Against the Person Act, 1861, s 55; *Prince* (1875) LR 2 CCR 154; [1874–80] All ER 881, 13 Cox CC 138 CCR.

94   Criminal Law Amendment Act, 1885, s 7.

95   Criminal Law (Amendment) Act, 1935, Schedule of Repeals.

2. The offence of abducting an heiress under twenty-one never incorporated a statutory defence of mistake as to her age.[96]

3. For a parent to cause, encourage or favour the seduction or prostitution of a girl under twenty-one is not usually a criminal offence. In 1885 the High Court[97] was given power to remove such a girl from the custody of her parents or guardian if she was under sixteen and in 1935 that age[98] was raised to twenty-one years.

4. In 1935 the Oireachtas fixed fifteen years as the age when "a person" could consent to, what otherwise, in the absence of consent, would be an indecent assault.[99] The offence of indecent assault never incorporated a statutory or common law defence of mistake as to age.

5. The Criminal Law Amendment Act, 1885 made it an offence for the owner or occupier or controller of premises to allow those premises to be used for the purpose of sexual intercourse with a girl under sixteen,[1] if the girl was under thirteen the offence was a felony and if under sixteen the offence was a misdemeanour. The statute incorporated the defence of reasonable cause to believe that the girl was over sixteen years of age. In 1935 the age for the misdemeanour was raised to seventeen years and the age for the felony was raised to fifteen years and the statutory defence was abolished.[2]

6. At common law it was rape to have sexual intercourse with a girl who lacked sufficient understanding to consent, whether by reason of illness or age.[3] In 1828 the Offences Against the Person Act, s 17, made it a felony to have sexual intercourse with a girl under ten years and a misdemeanour where the girl was under twelve years. This scheme was continued in s 50 and 51 of the Offences Against the Person Act, 1861. Neither of these statutes incorporated defences of mistake as to age. In 1885 a series of child prostitution scandals[4] led to the Criminal Law Amendment Act of that year, which by s 4 made it a felony, punishable by penal servitude for life or two years' imprisonment, to have sexual intercourse with a girl under thirteen years and by s 5 a misdemeanour punishable by two years' imprisonment, to have sexual intercourse with a girl under sixteen years. It was a statutory defence to the misdemeanour charge that the accused had reasonable cause to believe the girl to be sixteen years or more. The Criminal Law (Amendment) Act, 1935 repealed both these sections.[5]

7. The Law Reform Commission in their report on child sexual abuse[6] recommended that it should continue to be an offence, save in certain circumstances, for any male to have sexual intercourse with a girl under the age of 17 years.[7] In the

96 Offences Against the Person Act, 1861, s 53.
97 Criminal Law Amendment Act, 1885, s 12.
98 Criminal Law (Amendment) Act, 1935, s 10.
99 Criminal Law (Amendment) Act, 1935, s 14.
1 Criminal Law Amendment Act, 1885, s 6.
2 Criminal Law (Amendment) Act, 1935, s 9.
3 See par 8.75.
4 Honoré, *Sex Law* (London, 1978), p 82.
5 In the Schedule of Enactments Repealed. However, the clause at the end of s 4 concerning impersonation of the husband was not repealed. See par 8.12.
6 LRC 32 – 1990.
7 LRC 32 – 1990, par 4.07.

case of a girl between the ages of 15 and 17, sexual intercourse should be a criminal offence only where the male participant is "a person in authority" or at least five years older than the girl in question.[8] The maximum penalty for an offence of unlawful sexual intercourse with a girl between the ages of 13 and 17 should be seven years' imprisonment. This represents an increase from five years' penal servitude where the girl is aged between 15 and 17 and a reduction from penal servitude for life where the girl is aged between 13 and 15.[9] A person who has sexual intercourse with a girl under the age of 13 years should be liable to penal servitude for life. Accordingly, the relevant age of the girl in this context should be lowered from 15 to 13.[10] The Commission also recommended that there should be no change in the present law that where a person is charged with having sexual intercourse or sexual activity falling short of intercourse with a girl under a specified age, the girl is not subject to any criminal liability.[11] S 30 of the Children Act, 1908, as amended by s 28(2) of the Criminal Justice (Administration) Act, 1914 enables a child "of tender years" (the age is not defined by the statute) who does not, in the opinion of the court, understand the nature of an oath, to give evidence not upon oath if, in the opinion of the court, the child has sufficient intelligence to justify the reception of the evidence and understands the duty of speaking the truth. The test is not a question of age but is a question of the intelligence and actual mental capacity of the child witness and its sense and reason of the danger and impiety of falsehood.[12]

Mental Element

8.63 In 1875 the celebrated case of *Prince*[13] was decided. The accused was charged with abducting a girl of under sixteen years from her parents' possession.[14] The girl was thirteen but looked over sixteen and had told the accused that she was eighteen. The jury found that the accused believed, on reasonable grounds, that the girl was over sixteen. The Court for Crown Cases Reserved held that such a belief was no defence; the statute did not imply a mental element that the accused knew the age of the girl. As the words "knowingly" or "indecently" were absent, the act of taking a girl against the will of her parents was morally wrong and only a mistake as to the existence of her parents' consent was material. Finally, the Court reasoned, the statute was one of a series designed to protect young girls and their parents and to ensure that men having sexual intercourse with girls under the age of consent did so at their peril.

---

8   LRC 32 – 1990, par 4.12.
9   LRC 32 – 1990, par 4.10.
10 LRC 32 – 1990, par 4.09.
11 LRC 32 – 1990, par 4.23. The same should apply to any offence of anal penetration committed by a person in authority or by a person five years older than the boy in question or other sexual activity with boys under a specified age.
12 *The People (A-G) v O'Sullivan* [1930] IR 552, 64 ILTR 181 CCA. The Law Reform Commision have proposed in their Report on Child Sexual Abuse (LRC 32 – 1990) that the test of competence of children to give evidence should be the capacity of the child to give an intelligible account of events which he or she has observed; generally see ch 9 of the Report.
13 (1875) LR 2 CCR 154; [1874-80] All ER 881, 13 Cox CC 138 CCR.
14 Contrary to s 55 of the Offences Against the Person Act, 1861.

8.64 The intention of the Oireachtas in 1935 could not be clearer. With knowledge of the decision in Prince, and its application in practice to all sexual offences where age was a factor,[15] the Oireachtas abolished all the statutory defences based on mistake. In practice these offences have always been treated as if age were a strict liability element and, in terms of strict statutory construction this is correct.[16] In the later case of *Tolson*,[17] on a charge of bigamy, the Court for Crown Cases Reserved held that mistake as to a material element in an offence did excuse the accused, provided that mistake was reasonable.[18] The modern tendency in England,[19] Australia[20] and Canada[21] is to judge the accused in terms of his subjective culpability so that even unreasonably but genuinely held mistakes will excuse. It is stating no more than the obvious that a jury is assisted in judging the genuineness of the accused's mistake by asking whether there were any reasonable grounds on which to base it.

8.65 The question of whether a mistake in Irish law must be reasonable to absolve the accused of liability has yet to be decided by the higher courts. The use of a subjective standard in murder cases for reducing the verdict to one of manslaughter in cases of provocation,[22] objectively excessive but subjectively proportionate self-defence[23] and the subjective nature of the concept[24] lead us to the conclusion that the accused's mistake need not be reasonable. Where a question of mistake is raised by the accused it has been our invariable experience in the Circuit Court and Central Criminal Court that the jury are instructed to judge that mistake on subjective and not on objective grounds.

Such experience is irrelevant in the context of an offence where, on the authority of *Prince*,[25] a mistake as to age is immaterial. It could be argued that the decision should not be followed. The English courts were quick to distinguish it in the *Tolson* bigamy case of 1889.[26] There is probably no other crime tried on indictment where an essential element of the offence is one of strict liability. Such a position runs

---

15 Smith & Hogan 454. This principle is also applied in Australia; *Peters* [1956] VLR 743 SC.

16 In California it has been held that a mistake or ignorance to age is an answer to such charges unless there is a contrary rule in the Statute; *The People v Hernandez* (1964) 393 P (2d) 673, 30 Cal Rep 361 SC. In *Peters*, fn 15, the Supreme Court of Victoria upheld the *Prince* interpretation.

17 [1889] 23 QBD 168; [1886-90] All ER 26, 16 Cox 629 CCR.

18 Following the dissenting judgment of Brett J in *Prince* (1875) LR 2 CCR 154; [1874-80] All ER 881, 13 Cox CC 138 CCR: "That a mistake of facts on reasonable grounds, to the extent that, if the facts were as believed, the acts of the prisoner would make him guilty of no criminal offence at all, is an excuse, and that such excuse is implied in every criminal charge and every criminal enactment in England". [1874-80] All ER 881 at 895; [1875] LR 2 CCR 154 at 162, 13 Cox 138 at 156 CCR.

19 *DPP v Morgan* [1976] AC 182; [1975] 2 All ER 374; [1975] 2 WLR 913, 61 Cr App R 136 HL; *Westminster City Council v Croyalgrange Limited* [1986] 2 All ER 353; [1986] 1 WLR 674, 83 Cr App R 155; [1986] Crim LR 693 HL; *Williams* [1987] 3 All ER 411; (1983) 78 Cr App R 276; [1984] Crim LR 163 CA.

20 *McEwan* [1979] 2 NSWLR 926 CCA; *Saragozza* [1984] VR 187 SC.

21 *Pappajohn* (1980) 14 CR (3d) 243 SC.

22 *The People (DPP) v Mac Eoin* [1978] IR 27 CCA.

23 *The People v Dwyer* [1972] IR 416 SC.

24 See ch 2.

25 Fn 13.   26 Fn 17.

308   *Offences Against the Person*

contrary to the judgments of the Supreme Court in *The People (DPP) v Murray*.[27] The history of the Criminal Law (Amendment) Act, 1935 would appear to show an express intention to preserve strict liability in sexual offences cases relating to age, where it already existed, and to introduce it where it did not.

8.66 The remarks in *Prince* that age was immaterial in a sexual offence case because the act of abducting a young girl against the will of her parents was morally wrong would not now meet with universal acceptance. The implication that other offences related to sexual intercourse are to be similarly construed as strict in liability, because of the moral wrong involved, places an entire category of offences outside the standard analysis of criminal law adopted by the Supreme Court in *Murray*. It does not follow that where the belief of the accused, if correct, would involve him in a legally innocent act, a moral judgment on that act will suffice for an unlawful mental element. The fact that the law forms part of a code designed to protect young girls is, however, of legal importance as the excuse of a belief that the girl was of the age of consent is almost impossible to disprove beyond reasonable doubt. That argument cannot be made with regard to the essential element of consent in other sexual offences. In most cases the victim will not actively misrepresent that she consents whereas misrepresentation can be the situation in age offences; whether that misrepresentation is spoken or is implied by a particular appearance.

It is a matter of politics whether the Oireachtas wish to continue to make intercourse between very young people an offence; there may be moral and health reasons for doing so. It is difficult, however, to justify a conviction where the accused genuinely believed in a state of affairs which would render him blameless of any legal wrong. Prosecutions are extremely rare and would seem only to be taken where the accused is much older than the victim. A solution to the problem of mistake might be to require that it be reasonable. The Supreme Court of Ontario has held that similar provisions of the Canadian Criminal Code violate the fundamental justice provision in s 7 of the Constitutional Charter in the absence of an implied defence of mistake; they have, however, insisted that such a mistake be both honest and reasonable.[28]

Reform

8.67 The Law Reform Commission in its Report on Child Sexual Abuse[29] recommends[30] that in the case of offences where age is a factor, there should be a

27 [1977] IR 360, Walsh J at 383 was at pains to point out the policy reasons which necessitated strict liability with regard to the element of age in these offences; further see ch 2. In *Chard v Wallis & Another* (1988) 36 A Crim R 147 on a charge of procuring a boy under 18 for homosexual purposes the New South Wales Supreme Court refused to apply *Prince* commenting that there was something repugnant in the notion that a person could be guilty of a serious criminal offence merely by accident. See further ch 2.

28 *Roche* [1985] 46 CR (3d) 130; *Metro News Limited* (1986) 53 CR (3d) 289 (the charge of distributing obscene material). The court held that the prosecution was not required to prove the mental element but that the accused had to prove his honest and reasonable mistake on the balance of probabilities.

29 LRC 32 – 1990.

30 Par 4.13 to 4.15 of LRC 32 – 1990.

defence available to the accused that he genuinely believed at the time of the act on reasonable grounds that the girl had attained the age of consent or an age attracting a less serious penalty.[31] On the question of whether the approach to such a defence should be subjective or objective, the Law Reform Commission recommend that a similar approach to that taken by the legislature in the Rape Act, 1981, dealing with the issue of consent[32] should be adopted. This would mean that the accused would be entitled to be acquitted if he genuinely believed that the person concerned had reached the relevant age, but in arriving at a conclusion as to whether he did so believe, the court would be entitled to take into account the presence or absence of reasonable grounds on which such a belief could be based.[33] S 2 of the Rape Act does no more than declare the general law as to the manner in which a jury are entitled to approach their function of finding facts.[34]

Incest

8.68 Incest was an offence only in the church courts until 1908 when it was made an ordinary crime.[35] Marriages are forbidden within a wide range of relationships[36] but sexual intercourse is restricted within a much narrower range. The Punishment of Incest Act, 1908, as amended by s 12 of the Criminal Law (Amendment) Act, 1935 provides:

> 1(1) Any male person who has carnal knowledge of a female person, who is to his knowledge his grand-daughter, daughter, sister, or mother, shall be guilty of a misdemeanour, and upon conviction thereof shall be liable, at the discretion of the court, to be kept in penal servitude for any term not less than three years, and not exceeding seven years, or to be imprisoned for any time not exceeding two years with or without hard labour: provided that if, on an indictment for any such offence, it is alleged in the indictment and proved that the female person is under the age of fifteen years, the same punishment may be imposed as may be imposed under s 1 of the Criminal Law (Amendment) Act, 1935[37] (which deals with the defilement of girls under fifteen years of age).
>
> (2) It is immaterial that the carnal knowledge was had with the consent of the female person.
>
> (3) If any male person attempts to commit any such offence as aforesaid, he shall be

31 Par 4.14 of LRC 32 – 1990.

32 See par 8.03, 8.19.

33 Par 4.15 of LRC 32 – 1990.

34 See ch 1.

35 Honoré, *Sexual Law* (London, 1978), p 79; Bailey, "Incest: A Case Study in Law Reform Creation" [1979] Crim LR 708. The Law Reform Commission in their report on Child Sexual Abuse recommended no change in the law relating to incest (LRC 32 – 1990 par 4.33). However, the changes which the Commission recommended with regard to the expression "carnal knowledge" in the Crinminal Law (Amendment) Act, 1935, would apply with equal force to the Punishment of Incest Act, 1908. See Bailey, "Reforming the Law of Incest" [1979] Crim LR 749 and see Wolfram, "Eugenics and the Punishment of Incest Act, 1908" [1983] Crim LR 308.

36 Set our in Shatter, *Family Law* at p 80. The sentencing guidelines in incest cases are considered by the Court of Appeal in *Meggs, The Times,* 22 February 1989 and in *Attorney General's Reference (No. 1 of 1989)* [1989] 3 All ER 571; *Attorney General's Reference (No. 4 of 1989)* [1990] Crim LR 439.

37 S 1 of the Criminal Law (Amendment) Act, 1935, felony, penal servitude for life or imprisonment for two years; par 8.58-8.67.

guilty of a misdemeanour, and upon conviction thereof shall be liable at the discretion of the court to be imprisoned for any time not exceeding two years with or without hard labour.

(4) On the conviction before any court of any male person of an offence under this section, or of an attempt to commit the same, against any female under twenty one years of age, it shall be in the power of the court to divest the offender of all authority over such female, and, if the offender is the guardian of such female, to remove the offender from such guardianship, and in any such case to appoint any person or persons to be the guardian or guardians of such female during her minority or any less period: provided that the High Court may at any time vary or rescind the order by the appointment of any other person as such guardian, or in any other respect.

2 Any female person of or above the age of seventeen years, who with consent permits her grandfather, father, brother, or son to have carnal knowledge of her (knowing him to be her grandfather, father, brother, or son, as the case may be) shall be guilty of a misdemeanour, and upon conviction thereof shall be liable, at the discretion of the court, to be kept in penal servitude for any term not less than three years and not exceeding seven years, or to be imprisoned with or without hard labour for any term not exceeding two years.

3 In this Act the expressions "brother" and "sister", respectively, include half-brother and half-sister and the provisions of this Act shall apply whether the relationship between the person charged with an offence under this Act and the person with whom the offence is alleged to have been committed, is or is not traced through lawful wedlock.

By s 5 all proceedings for incest are to be held in camera: there is no discretion in this as there is in other cases involving indecent acts.[38] Proceedings for incest are to be commenced only by the Director of Public Prosecutions or with the consent of the Attorney-General.[39] A verdict of guilty of incest is an alternative verdict on an indictment for rape.[40]

Consent

8.69 As appears from s 1(2) consent is no defence to a charge of incest. If a woman is over the age of seventeen years and consents to incest, she will be guilty of an offence under s 2. If a girl under seventeen consents to incest this will not make her liable for any offence.[41] If, however, there is evidence to go to the jury that the woman consented, the jury must be cautioned that if they find her to have consented then she becomes an accomplice and the judge must warn the jury of the dangers of convicting on her uncorroborated testimony.[42] In law permission does not constitute consent[43] and whether there is consent is a question of fact for the jury.

---

38 See par 8.04.   39 S 6.

40 S 4(3). It was the case prior to the Criminal Law (Amendment) Act, 1935 that unlawful carnal knowledge of an underaged girl was an alternative verdict to a charge of incest. The 1935 Act did not incorporate this provision when it replaced the 1885 Act. Attempt is also an alternative verdict under s 9 of the Criminal Procedure Act, 1851.

41 *Whitehouse* [1977] QB 868; [1977] 3 All ER 737; [1977] 2 WLR 925, 65 Cr App R 33 CA.

42 *Stone* (1910) 6 Cr App R 89; *Davies v DPP* [1954] AC 378; [1954] 1 All ER 507; [1954] 2 WLR 343, 38 Cr App R 11; [1954] Crim LR 324 HL. As to the form of such a warning in an accomplice case see *The People (DPP) v McGinley* [1987] IR 340 at 343 CCA.

43 *Dimes* (1911) 7 Cr App R 43, 76 JP 47 CCA; *Olugboja* [1982] QB 320; [1981] 3 All ER 443; [1981] 3 WLR 585, 73 Cr App R 344 CA; *Burles* [1947] VLR 392 SC and see "Consent and Responsibility

Sexual Intercourse

8.70 Carnal knowledge has the same meaning as in rape and unlawful sexual intercourse.[44] Sexual acts short of carnal knowledge are not unlawful unless with a girl under fifteen years[45] or where those acts amount to a sexual assault[46] or are sufficiently proximate to amount to an attempt to commit incest.

Relationship

8.71 The relationship of the parties may be proved by an admission[47] or by a certificate of birth[48] coupled with identification of the child and her father by someone who knew them at the time of her birth. Although the presumption of legitimacy of children born to married parents is not followed in this jurisdiction it is submitted that the jury are entitled to infer parenthood from such evidence as marriage between her parents and the child being treated as a child of the family.[49] At common law a spouse was neither a competent nor a compellable witness for the prosecution. In *The People (DPP) v JT*[50] the Court of Criminal Appeal declared this rule inconsistent with the Constitution as being an unjust fetter on the duty of the State to vindicate the integrity of the family.

It is clear from s 3 that the Act applies equally to marital and non-marital children[51] but incest cannot be committed, in the absence of a blood relationship, with an adopted child.[52]

Mental Element

8.72 The mental element in the offence comprises, both under s 1 and s 2, an intent to have sexual intercourse and knowledge of the relationship between the parties.[53]

in Sexual Cases" [1968] Crim LR 81, s 8 of the Rape Act, 1988 is simply declaratory of the legal position on consent; see par 8.10–8.15.

44   See par 8.08–8.09.

45   Criminal Law (Amendment) Act, 1935, s 14.

46   See par 8.29–8.49.

47   *Jones* (1933) 24 Cr App R 55, 149 LT 143, 77 SJ 236, 29 Cox 637. In *Hemmings* [1939] 1 All ER 417 it was held insufficient evidence that a man had spoken of the daughter of a woman to whom he was now married, who had previously been married to another person, as his daughter. Atkinson J giving the judgment of the Court of Criminal Appeal held that mere evidence that the accused had intercourse with the mother of the victim during the currency of her previous marriage would have been insufficient. It is submitted that the latter part of this decision, based on the presumption of legitimacy, would not be followed in this jurisdiction where the test is merely a question of fact.

48   A public record is an exception to the rule against hearsay. As to the strict application of the rule against hearsay see *The People (DPP) v Prunty* [1986] ILRM 716 CCA.

49   There is no authority directly in point but these would be matters of circumstantial evidence from which the jury would be entitled to draw such a conclusion. If the accused raised the issue, however, the prosecution would have to disprove any suggestion he made as to non-paternity beyond reasonable doubt.

50   3 Frewen CCA, unreported 27 July 1988; Charleton, "The Victim in Irish Constitutional Law" (1990) 8 ILTSJ 140.

51   *Winch* [1974] Crim LR 487 CA.

52   The English Criminal Law Revision Committee in their 15th Report on Sexual Offences (Cmnd 9213), pars 8.15 to 8.36 recommended the extension of the crime to these relationships.

53   There is no decision that recklessness is sufficient.

Intent to have sexual intercourse can hardly be an issue but knowledge of the blood relationship can be of practical importance. So the accused may show that the girl was born two months after his marriage and that he is not the father.[54] A belief by the accused that his wife's daughter is the child of an adulterer is a defence.[55]

8.73 Because the state of the accused's mind is central to the offence, statements by him to others as to the paternity of his child do not infringe the hearsay rule but are admissible within the category of admission evidence.

In *Carmichael*[56] it was held that the accused was entitled to give evidence (1) that he had been told by his first wife, the victim's mother, that the victim had been begotten by another man and that he believed that statement to be true, (2) that he had told his second wife that he was not the father of the victim and (3) explaining statements made on certain occasions acknowledging the victim to be his daughter.

Duplicity

8.74 It is usual in incest cases to have a statement from a victim in a book of evidence alleging several acts of intercourse without giving specific days when they occurred. It is wrong simply to charge such crimes in one count as an indictment will then be bad for duplicity.[57] The proper course is to charge the first count as occurring between two stated dates and the second and subsequent counts as occurring between these same dates but on an occasion other than those mentioned in counts 1, 2 etc. The accused is entitled to information describing the offence with particularity, either by reference to a date, or if that is not possible by reference to other distinguishing features. In this jurisdiction these may be given in the indictment or in the book of evidence.[58]

Mental Handicap

8.75 Just as a woman may be unable to give consent to sexual intercourse because she is asleep, or otherwise unconscious, or is too young to understand the nature of the act, so consent may be absent due to mental handicap.[59] The uncertain nature

---

54   Anon, *The Times*, 20 January 1919.

55   *Bailie-Smyth* (1977) 64 Cr App R 76 CA. In this instance the defence was that the accused thought that the person in bed with him was his wife and not his daughter.

56   [1940] 1 KB 630; [1940] 2 All ER 165, 27 Cr App R 183, 56 TLR 517, 84 SJ 551, 31 Cox 409 CCA.

57   *Thompson* [1914] 2 KB 99.

58   In *S* (1990) 45 A Crim R 221 the High Court of Australia held that it was wrong for the trial judge to indicate that a jury could convict if they were satisfied that on at least one occasion an unlawful sexual penetration took place. In these circumstances the accused was prejudiced by being precluded from raising specific defences, such as an alibi, and the inability to later invoke a defence of autrefois acquit/convict. It was held that where an indictment alleges a number of acts of intercourse between specific dates it may be appropriate, if there is ambiguity, for the trial judge to order that particulars be given and identifying the offences charged, if not by reference to time then to other distinguishing features.

59   For a discussion see par 8.10. In England the test is whether someone is mentally defective. This occurs if the woman suffers from a severe impairment of intelligence and social functioning by comparison with persons of normal development. This test was introduced by s 45 of the Sexual

of the applicable test in this area renders it unsatisfactory to leave the protection of mentally handicapped women from sexual exploitation to the law of rape. It is of considerable importance to protect persons suffering from such a disability. Experience indicates that in typical circumstances a girl is spotted and induced into sexual intercourse, or other acts, by a male who has no interest in her as a person and who has no intention of offering her any attempt at a long-term relationship or marriage. The essence of the wrong done is that, unlike an ordinary girl, the handicapped one cannot see clearly the intentions of the predatory male, is too weak-willed to struggle against physical inclination and is not the personality equal of the male in any struggle for friendship and commitment. Exploitation in these circumstances can lead to unrealistic expectations and hurt beyond the range of disappointment in a relationship between equals.

8.76 The protection which the law now provides is in s 4 of the Criminal Law (Amendment) Act, 1935:

> (1) Any person who, in circumstances which do not amount to rape, unlawfully and carnally knows or attempts to have unlawful carnal knowledge of any woman or girl who is an idiot, or an imbecile, or is feeble-minded, shall, if the circumstances prove that such person knew at the time of such knowledge or attempt that the woman or girl was then an idiot, or an imbecile, or feeble-minded (as the case may be), be guilty of a misdemeanour and shall be liable on conviction thereof to imprisonment for any term not exceeding two years.
>
> (2) No prosecution for an offence which is declared by this section to be a misdemeanour shall be commenced more than twelve months after the date on which such offence is alleged to have been committed.[60]

The proofs involve the prosecution choosing and then proving the relevant category of mental handicap.[61] The language of the statute is outdated and insulting.

Offences Act, 1945 (as substituted by s 127(b) of the Mental Health Act, 1959 and amended by s 65(1) of the Mental Health (Amendment) Act, 1982). For an example see *Hall* (1987) 86 Cr App R 159 CA.

60 S 254 of the Mental Treatment Act, 1945 provides for an aggravated punishment where: "(a) a person who has been convicted on indictment of a misdemeanour under s 4 of the Criminal Law (Amendment) Act, 1935, and (b) the judge is satisfied that at the time when the misdemeanour was committed — (i) such person had the care or charge of the woman or girl in relation to whom the misdemeanour was committed, or (ii) such person was carrying on a mental institution and such woman or girl was a patient therein, or (iii) such peson was employed as an officer or servant in a mental institution or an institution for the detention of persons of unsound mind and such woman or girl was a patient or prisoner therein, the said s 4 shall have effect as if it provided that such person shall be liable on such conviction to penal servitude for any term not exceeding 5 years nor less than 3 years or to imprisonment for any term not exceeding 2 years."

61 The categories are not defined in Irish law. For a discussion of the possible definitions see Charleton, "Protecting the Mentally Subnormal Against Sexual Exploitation" [1984] DULJ 165. The Mental Deficiency Act, 1913, which did not extend to Ireland defined these categories as: "Idiots: persons who are so deeply defective in mind from birth or from an early age as to be unable to guard themselves against common physical dangers; Imbeciles: persons in whose case there exists from birth or from an early age mental defectiveness not amounting to idiocy yet so pronounced that they are incapable of managing themselves or their affairs, or in the case of children, of being thought to do so; Feeble-minded persons: persons in whose case there exists from birth or from an early age mental defectiveness not amounting to imbeciles, yet so pronounced that they require care, supervision and control for their own protection or for the protection of others, or, in the case of

Modern medical practice has not retained this categorisation but proceeds on a classification of mental handicap as mild, moderate, severe and profound. This is based on universally recognised intelligence quotient criteria.[62] Continuing use of such offensive terms in a statute is not conducive to the reporting of offences. The categories are not mutually exclusive. If the accused can raise a doubt to the effect that the victim, described for example as feeble-minded, is, in fact an imbecile he will be acquitted. It is also difficult to distort modern medical terminology into the categorisation provided by the Act.[63]

The circumstances of the intercourse must not amount to rape. It follows that the girl must consent to the act of sexual intercourse. If it cannot be proved beyond reasonable doubt that she consented then the accused must be acquitted. Such proof is difficult, if not impossible, in the context of the prosecution alleging a mental handicap. Her handicap may be so severe that she cannot consent in law. The wording of this statute involves the ludicrous situation where the commission of one crime is a defence on the charge of another. In such circumstances it can prejudice the accused that the charges be tried together.[64]

The mental element of the crime requires that the accused knew, at the time of the intercourse, of the particular mental handicap of the victim. Recklessness is, on the wording of the statute, insufficient.[65] In limiting the offence to carnal knowledge only acts of vaginal sexual intercourse are within the scope of the crime.

S 254 of the Mental Treatment Act, 1945 provides:

> Where—
> (a) a person has been convicted on indictment of a misdemeanour under s 4 of the Criminal Law (Amendment) Act, 1934 (No. 6 of 1935) and
> (b) the judge is satisfied that at the time when such misdemeanour was committed—(i) such person had the care or charge of the woman or girl in relation to whom the misdemeanour was committed,
> or
> (ii) such person was carrying on a mental institution and such woman or girl was a patient therein,

children, that they by reason of such defectiveness appear to be permanently incapable of receiving proper benefit from the instruction in ordinary schools."

62   Mild mental handicap is defined as IQ range 50-70; moderate mental handicap is defined as IQ range 35-49; severe mental handicap is defined as IQ range 20-34; profound mental handicap is defined as IQ range below 20.

63   A psychologist will normally give a report based on the definitions in which he or she has been trained and the court will then decide on the basis of that evidence and what they have heard from the victim and her parents or guardians, whether she properly fits within one of the statutory categories.

64   Such a ruling was made in the case of *The People (DPP) v MW* reported in [1984] DULJ 165. This case took place ten years later than the date stated in the short report. The Criminal Justice (Administration) Act, 1924, s 6(3) provides: "Where before trial or at any stage of a trial the court is of opinion that the accused may be prejudiced or embarrassed in the defence by reason of being charged with more than one offence in the same indictment or that for any other reason it is desirable to direct that he be tried separately for any one or more offences charged in the indictment, the court may order a separate trial of any count or counts in the indictment".

65   Knowledge is required. No specific decision attributes a particular kind of knowledge, whether constructive or otherwise, to the section. In the absence of authority it is submitted that the word should be given the same definition as in the case of receiving stolen property; *Berber v Levey* [1944] IR 405 CCA; *Hallon v Fleming* [1981] IR 489 SC.

(iii) such person was employed as an officer or servant in a mental institution or an institution for the detention of persons of unsound mind and such woman or girl was a patient or prisoner therein, the said s 4 shall have effect as if it provided that such person should be liable on conviction to penal servitude for any term not exceeding five years nor less than three years or to imprisonment for any term not exceeding two years.

In a typical case the principal evidence against the accused is that of the victim. If she can satisfy the judge that she is capable of giving sworn evidence, in that she understands the nature and consequences of an oath, this constitutes evidence that she does not fit within the categories of mental handicap defined by the section. No special provision allows the giving of evidence on oath.[66] It follows that in the absence of sufficient intelligence to take the oath, an accused must be acquitted where the evidence against him is that of the victim. The writer has never seen a case where the crime was capable of being proved solely by independent testimony.[67] An objection as to the swearing must be taken prior to the oath being administered.[68] The enquiry as to competence must take place in the presence of the jury whether the witness is a child or a mentally handicapped person.[69]

There is no requirement that there be corroboration before the jury can return a verdict of guilty.[70]

Reform

8.77 The Law Reform Commission have recommended[71] that s 4 should be replaced by an offence of having unlawful sexual intercourse with another person who was at the time of the offence mentally handicapped, or suffering from mental illness which in either case was of such a nature or degree that the person was incapable of guarding himself or herself against exploitation. It is proposed to make it an offence to commit acts of anal penetration or engage in other exploitative sexual activity with persons suffering from mental handicap or mental illness. These offences would be neutral as to the sex of victim and accused. The offences would be strengthened by a presumption that the accused knew of the handicap of the victim. An offence would not be committed where both parties were suffering from handicap. Higher penalties would continue to be provided in respect of persons who commit the offences while in charge of, or employed in, mental institutions, or

---

66 S 30 of the Children Act, 1908, as amended by s 28(2) of the Criminal Justice (Administration) Act, 1914, enables a child of "tender years" who does not, in the opinion of the court, understand the nature of an oath, to give evidence not upon oath, if, in the opinion of the court, the child has a sufficient intelligence to justify the reception of the evidence and understands the duty of speaking the truth. See *The People (A-G) v O'Sullivan* [1930] IR 552, 64 ILTR 181 CCA.

67 On the problems of the oath, see the report of the case of *The People (DPP) v JS* [1984] DULJ 165. Note that this case occurred ten years later than the date stated in the short report.

68 *The People (A-G) v O'Sullivan* [1930] IR 552 CCA.

69 *The People (A-G) v Keating* [1953] IR 200 CCA. Any requirement that the trial judge must enquire into the competence of the victim to give evidence on oath may be expressly waived by the accused; *The People (A-G) v Lannigan* [1958] Ir Jur Rep 59.

70 Sandes 110 states the opposite but he cites no authority. The better view is that the position as to corroboration is that outlined at the end of this chapter.

71 Report on Sexual Offences against the Mentally Handicapped (LRC 33-1990). For a review see (1990) Gazette 1 LSI 383.

where the accused had the care or charge of the victim. It is also proposed to alter the requirement of an oath or affirmation by extending it to persons capable of giving an intelligible account of events which he or she has observed.

The legal regime designed to protect the mentally subnormal against sexual exploitation is totally inadequate and has urgently required reform for over a decade.

Evidential Rules Relating to Sexual Offence Trials

8.78 We now consider some evidential rules which are inherent in the trial of sexual offences. This does not constitute an exhaustive treatment but a sketch for completeness' sake and as an aid to grasping this difficult area of policy.

Corroboration

8.79 In cases[72] of rape,[73] unlawful carnal knowledge,[74] indecent assault[75] (now called sexual assault and aggravated sexual assault), abortion[76] and other sexual offences against both males and females,[77] a conviction can be secured on the evidence of the victim alone. It was however a rule of practice, elevated to a rule of law in those cases,[78] to warn the jury "in unmistakable terms",[77] that it is dangerous to convict on the uncorroborated testimony of the prosecutrix,[80] and that a jury should weigh her evidence with great care.

As in accomplice cases[81] the degree and gravity of the warning would vary with the degree and gravity of the risk involved in accepting the evidence which required

---

72   See Williams, "Corroboration—Sexual Cases" [1962] Crim LR 662; Clarke, "Corroboration in Sexual Cases" [1980] Crim LR 362; Dennis, "Corroboration Requirements Reconsidered" [1984] Crim LR 316; Carter, "Corroboration Requirements Reconsidered: Two Comments" [1985] Crim LR 143; Oughton, "The Distressing Nature of Corroboration" [1984] Crim LR 265. On the subject of corroboration see generally Bronitt, "*Baskerville* Revisited—The Definition of Corroboration Reconsidered" [1991] Crim LR 30.

73   *The People (DPP) v Mulvey* [1987] IR 502 CCA. On the origin of the requirement of a warning see Geis, "Revisiting Lord Hale, Misogyny, Witchcraft and Rape" (1986) 10 Crim LJ 319; Lanham, "Hale, Misogyny and Rape" (1983) 7 Crim LR 148.

74   *The People (A-G) v Williams* [1940] IR 195 SC.

75   *The People (A-G) v Cradden* [1955] IR 130 CCA.

76   This is less clear. The point is simply mentioned by Sullivan CJ in his judgment in *Williams*, fn 74, at p 202, but in most abortion cases the main prosecution witness will also be an accomplice as was the case in *The People (A-G) v Levison* [1932] IR 158 CCA.

77   *The People (A-G) v O'Sullivan* [1930] IR 552 SC (sodomy); *The People (A-G) v Duffy* [1931] IR 144 CCA (gross indecency), the boys being willing and therefore accomplices; *Robertson* (1990) 47 A Crim R 412 CCA Queensland.

78   *The People (A-G) v Williams*, fn 74.

79   Per Maguire CJ in *The People (A-G) v Cradden* [1955] IR 130 at 141 CCA.

80   Meredith J in *Williams*, fn 74, disagreed with the use of the words "is dangerous"; he would have preferred the trial judge to point out that the conviction depended on one witness alone and to elucidate all matters affecting her credibility and leave it to the jury to determine the dangers of acting on her testimony; *Williams*, fn 74, at p 205-206. This direction is better followed now the law has been reformed.

81   *The People (A-G) v Linehan* [1929] IR 19; (1928) 63 ILTR 30; *The People (DPP) v McGinley* [1987] IR 340 CCA. A model direction in accomplice cases (from Judge Dominic Lynch) appears at p 343 of this Report. A sample of the old form of warning in sexual cases (from Roe J) is to be found in *The People (A-G) v Mulvey*, fn 73 at 507-509.

corroboration.[82] Where an adequate warning had been given the jury were also to be directed that they were entitled to act on the evidence of the witness, in those supposedly dangerous circumstances, if they were satisfied beyond all reasonable doubt that it was truthful.[83] Even in cases where there was clearly corroboration the warning had, nonetheless, to be given, in case the jury found that such evidence did not constitute corroboration of the witnesses' evidence.

It is a question of law for the judge to rule on what could constitute corroboration and for the jury to decide, in fact, if that evidence was corroboration.[84] Where a warning had not been given a conviction could be overturned on appeal despite the fact that there was ample corroboration of the witness's testimony.[85]

The Law Reform Commission recommended[86] the abolition of the mandatory warning rule and this was effected by s 7 of the Rape Act, 1990:

> (1) Subject to any enactment relating to the corroboration of evidence in criminal proceedings, where at the trial on indictment of a person charged with an offence of a sexual nature evidence is given by the person in relation to whom the offence is alleged to have been committed and, by reason only of the nature of the charge, there would, but for this section, be a requirement that the jury be given a warning about the danger of convicting the person on the uncorroborated evidence of that other person, it shall be for the judge to decide in his discretion, having regard to all the evidence given, whether the jury should be given the warning; and accordingly any rule of law or practice by virtue of which there is such a requirement as aforesaid is hereby abolished.
>
> (2) If a judge decides in his discretion to give such a warning as aforesaid it shall not be necessary to use any particular form of words to do so.

The following observations may be of assistance in relation to this question:

1. This section abolished only the mandatory warning in sexual cases. It does not abolish the need for such warning where the victim may have consented and therefore may be an accomplice. Thus where the victim is a willing participant in incest, homosexual acts, under-age sexual intercourse or where the victim is under

---

82   *The People (A-G) v Cradden*, fn 75; *The People (A-G) v Williams*, fn 74.

83   *Williams*, fn 74 at 204. For a fuller discussion on the law and its historical background see The Law Reform Commission Consultation Paper on Rape (1987) and the materials cited therein and see also O'Connor, "The Mandatory Warning Requirement in Respect of Complaints in Sexual Cases in Irish Law" (1985) 20 Ir Jur (ns) 43.

84   *Farid* (1945) 30 Cr App R 168; *McInnes* (1990) 90 Cr App R 99 CA.

85   *Tigg* [1963] 1 All ER 490; [1963] 1 WLR 305, 47 Cr App R 94 CCA. In *The People (DPP) v Scanlon*, unreported CCA 1 March 1985, a new trial was ordered on the ground, *inter alia*, that the trial judge's charge to the jury only dealt with the general law of corroboration and did not identify and isolate the only evidence tending to incriminate the accused.

86   The Law Reform Commission in their consultation paper on Rape 1987 quoted from the California Supreme Court in *The People v Rincon-Pineda*, 14 Cal (3d) 864, 538 P (2d) 247, 123 Cal Rptr 119 (1975) on the issue of the cautionary instruction thus: "There may well have been merit to Hale's assertion that a prosecution for rape was an ideal instrument of malice, since it forced an accused, on trial for his life, to stand alone before a jury inflamed by passion and to attempt to answer a carefully contrived story without benefit of counsel, witnesses, or even a presumption of innocence" at p 68.

15 and cannot legally, but does in fact, consent to a sexual assault or an aggravated sexual assault[87] the accomplice warning must still be given.[88]

2. A charge under s 2 (procuring sexual intercourse) or s 3 (obtaining sexual intercourse by threat, false pretences or drugs, etc.) of the Criminal Law (Amendment) Act, 1885[89] must be corroborated. The jury are not entitled to convict in the absence of corroboration in those cases.[90]

3. Corroboration is required of an element in the crime which is other than a sexual element. The law remains unchanged in such a case where corroboration was so required. Thus where a child's evidence is unsworn (under s 30 of the Children Act, 1908, as amended by s 28(2) of the Criminal Justice (Administration) Act, 1914) corroboration is required if the accused is to be convicted on this evidence. Similarly in treason and perjury corroboration is still required.[91]

4. Similarly there are probably other circumstances, which do not arise from the sexual nature of the case, where a jury should be warned of the danger of acting on the uncorroborated testimony of a witness. These circumstances include the sworn testimony of children.[92] There is also authority that a witness of bad character similarly requires the warning. Lord Hailsham has also suggested that the categories of suspect witness, requiring a warning, are not closed and that it is wise to give a similar warning about any prosecution witness where that witness could reasonably be suggested as having some purpose in giving false testimony.[93] Similarly, in visual identification cases, the *Casey* warning should be given.[94] In *L*[95] the High Court of

---

87   Consent by a girl under 15 is not a defence to these charges; s 14 of the Criminal Law (Amendment) Act, 1935, see par 8.38.

88   For the form of the warning see *The People (DPP) v McGinley* [1987] IR 340 at 343 CCA.

89   As amended by s 8 of the Criminal Law (Amendment) Act, 1935, see par 8.26 for s 2 and 8.24–8.25 for s 3.

90   Sandes (London 1951) at p 134–135 also lists, as requiring corroboration at law other offences under the Criminal Law (Amendment) Act, 1885 and 1935. This appears to be a mistake.

91   Treason (s 1 Treason Act, 1939), Perjury (*Muscot* (1714) 10 Mod 192, 88 ER 689); claimants to the property of deceased persons (*Rawlinson v Scholes*, 79 LT 350); personation at elections (Prevention of Electoral Abuses Act, 1923 as amended by Electoral Act, 1963 and Prevention of Electoral Abuses Act, 1982). Unlike the equivalent English statutory provision, s 146(5) of the Representation of the People Act, 1949, there is no requirement of corroboration in the Irish statute. However, it is submitted that it would be required in order to obtain a conviction. Speeding (Road Traffic Act, 1961 s 47 as amended by Road Traffic Act, 1968 s 26). See R.R. Pierse, *Road Traffic Law in the Republic of Ireland* (Dublin, 1989), 144–46.

92   *Hester* [1973] AC 296; [1972] 3 All ER 1056; [1972] 3 WLR 910, 57 Cr App R 212 HL; *DPP v Kilbourne* [1973] AC 729; [1973] 1 All ER 440; [1973] 2 WLR 254, 57 Cr App R 381; [1973] Crim LR 235 HL.

93   *Kilbourne* [1973] AC 729 at 740; [1973] 1 All ER 440 at 447; [1973] 2 WLR 254 at 262; (1972) 57 Cr App R 381, 393–394 HL. In *Spencer & Smails* [1987] AC 128; [1986] 2 All ER 928; [1986] 3 WLR 348, 83 Cr App R 277 HL it was held that where the witness was not in the accepted category requiring a warning but by reason of his peculiar mental condition and criminal connection fulfilled analogous criteria, the trial judge must warn that it was dangerous to convict on uncorroborated testimony, or give a warning to that effect.

94   *The People (A-G) v Casey (No. 2)* [1963] IR 38, 1 Frewen 521. In *The People (DPP) v Prunty* [1986] ILRM 716 CCA a similar warning was given in a case of a voice identification over a telephone. An identification parade should be held in all identification cases unless there is good reason to do otherwise; *The People (DPP) v O'Reilly* [1990] IR 415; [1991] ILRM 10 CCA, if the accused refuses to participate less formal means will suffice; *The People (DPP) v Martin* [1956] IR 22 CCA.

95   (1989) 43 A Crim R 463 HC.

Australia considered a case where the accused was convicted in 1988 of committing sexual offences with an under-aged girl twenty years previously in the 1960's. A warning was discretionary under the legislation. The Court held that by virtue of the lapse of time between the alleged offences and the trial the accused had been weakened in his means of testing the allegations; whereas contemporaneous questioning might distinguish fantasy from reality a long delay could harden fantasy, or semi-fantasy, into conviction. In such circumstances a warning was held to be essential.

In all such cases, having considered the warning, the jury is entitled to act on the testimony of the witness if satisfied beyond all reasonable doubt of its truth. Equally, the fact of there being corroboration, does not oblige the jury to convict.

5. It is probable that the higher courts will not overturn a conviction where the trial judge, in the exercise of his discretion, has not given a warning of the dangers of convicting in the absence of corroboration in a sexual offence case, where corroboration was in fact present.

6. The Law Reform Commission expressed these views on the discretionary warning in sexual cases:

> It can be expected that in a case where the warning is obviously most appropriate—e.g., where the parties already knew each other, the alleged rape took place in private and there were no marks on the alleged victim—judges will continue to warn juries of the danger of convicting where there is no evidence which supports or confirms the complainant's version of events.
>
> We had rejected in our Consultation Paper any prohibition on the giving of such a warning as being an unjustifiable interference with the exercise of the judicial function and adhere to that view. It has been suggested, however, that where the trial judge considers that a warning is necessary, he should be expressly prohibited from couching it in language suggesting that the evidence of complainants in cases of sexual assault should be treated with reserve. We do not think that this is either necessary or desirable. In particular cases, as a matter both of common sense and fairness to the accused, it may be perfectly reasonable for the trial judge to remind the jury that it was part of the defendant's case that the complaint was invented. In an appropriate case, where the evidence rested solely on the complainant's own version and this was the defence put forward, it would be clearly necessary for the trial judge to refer to the nature of that defence in his charge.[96]

It is to be noted that formerly a warning was considered particularly necessary in cases where the issue was consent.[97] Where the issue was identity such a warning

96 Report on Rape at par 30-31. A completely opposite view of legislative reform was taken by the Court of Criminal Appeal in Victoria in *Williams* (1987) 26 A Crim R 193 where the Court held that since the mandatory warning had been abolished the law no longer regarded complainants in sexual cases as an unreliable class of witnesses and that it was wrong for the judge to convey that to a jury. The Court indicated that if the judge looked for confirmatory or supporting evidence he should not do so in such a way as to indicate that he was directing the jury as to the law or giving them a warning which the law in its wisdom has found to be desirable. He should instead comment on the facts of an individual case and distinguish evidence which supports the testimony of the victim and evidence which may support the finding of the accused's guilt.

97 Archbold (1954) par 1949; *Graham* (1910) 4 Cr App R 218; *Lovell* (1923) 17 Cr App R 163; *Salman* (1924) 18 Cr App R 50 CCA. In G (1987) 24 A Crim R 370 the Supreme Court of South Australia indicated that since the mandatory warning had been abolished by the Evidence Amendment Act (No. 2), 1984 it is no longer a requirement of law or practice amounting to law, that the judge give a warning as to the need for corroboration of the evidence of the alleged victim. It is no longer a

was, under the former law, rarely necessary.[98]

The legislative reform places complainants in sexual cases in the same category as complainants in other crimes save that it was expressly provided that a warning may be given. Such a warning is not usually given in respect of other categories of complainants. It is submitted that the old form of warning should rarely now be used. An example is given in *Henry*:[99]

> . . . experience has shown that in these courts girls and women do sometimes tell an entirely false story which is very easy to fabricate, but extremely difficult to refute. Such stories are fabricated for all sorts of reasons . . . and sometimes for no reason at all.[1] It is submitted that the legislative change would be nullified were such a warning to be given. Instead a warning in terms of the fact that an allegation of a sexual assault may be fabricated for a hidden motive just as any other allegation may similarly be fabricated and that experience has indicated that such allegations have occurred in the past, that for these reasons the jury should scrutinise the evidence of the alleged victim with particular care (for reasons which arising on the evidence, the judge may state) and that they should bear this consideration in mind when deciding whether or not the prosecution have discharged the burden of proving their case beyond reasonable doubt. Such burden may be discharged, apart from the evidence of the alleged victim and the possibility that it may be given for a hidden motive, if there is evidence implicating the accused in the commission of the offence and thus supporting the evidence of that witness in the material particular. Despite the absence of such evidence the jury may still convict if they are satisfied beyond reasonable doubt of the truth and accuracy of the evidence of the alleged victim bearing in mind the possibility adumbrated.[2]

As the change in law is procedural there is no common law presumption against retrospection and the trial judge has a discretion to warn whether or not the offence took place prior to 12 December 1990.[3]

In *The People (DPP) v Reid*[4] Keane J summarised the law as to corroboration thus:

> It has never been a necessary precondition in our law to a conviction for rape or indecent assault that the testimony of the complainant be corroborated. A jury is free to convict a defendant in the absence of such evidence, where it is satisfied that the case against him has been proved beyond reasonable doubt. Wigmore remarked that, at common law, the evidence of the complainant is sufficient of itself to support a conviction in all offences "against the chastity of women". (S2061, P451). However, prior to the enactment of the Criminal Law (Rape) (Amendment) Act, 1990 . . . the law was that in all such cases the trial judge must warn the jury that it might be dangerous to convict upon the complainant's uncorroborated evidence. Such a warning was necessary, even where evidence was tendered as corroborating the

ground of appeal that the judge does not do so . . . and it is inappropriate to direct the jury in every case that it is unsafe to convict on the uncorroborated testimony of a complainant in a sexual case: there is nothing attending to the evidence of a complainant which, as such, necessarily renders it unsafe to convict on the uncorroborated testimony of that witness. Parliament, the Court indicated should be taken as saying the courts have gone too far in placing the uncorroborated testimony of a complainant in a sexual case in the same category as the evidence of an accomplice in offences generally; *Bizumic* (1986) 23 A Crim R 163 CCA Vict.

98   *Chance* [1988] QB 932; [1988] 3 All ER 225 CA.
99   (1968) 53 Cr App R 150; [1969] Crim LR 142.
1   At 153.
2   At 156-57.
3   *R* (1990) 47 A Crim R 426 HC. The 1990 Act was signed by the President on 12 December 1990.
4   Court of Criminal Appeal, unreported, 20 February 1991.

complainant's account, since it might be that the jury would not accept the evidence: *Attorney General v Cradden* [1955] IR 130.

It is also clear that the warning need not be stated in any particular form. The law was thus stated by Sullivan CJ in *The People (Attorney General) v Williams* [1940] IR 195: "I wish to make it clear that . . . I do not decide that the warning must be expressed in any particular terms. As was said in *Attorney General v Lenihan* the degree and gravity of the warning should vary according to the particular circumstances of the case. But in all cases in which there is not corroboration of the girl's evidence, the attention of the jury should be directed to that fact, and they should be told that they should weigh her evidence with great care before they decide to convict. In many cases, no further warning may be necessary; that is a matter to be determined in the first instance by the trial judge. Where an adequate warning has been given the jury should be told that they are entitled to act on the girl's evidence if they are satisfied beyond all reasonable doubt that it is truthful". Again, Maguire CJ giving the judgment of this court in *Cradden's* case, said that he wished: "to emphasise that the degree and gravity of the warning called for may vary with the degree and gravity of the risk involved in accepting the evidence which requires corroboration. It would be for the trial judge in each case to measure the strength of the warning having regard, in cases such as this, to what Hale . . . calls 'concurring circumstances which give greater probability to the evidence of the prosecutrix'."

These clearly established legal principles have been recently reaffirmed by the Supreme Court: see the judgment of O'Flaherty J in *The People (DPP) v Egan* [1990] ILRM 780 at p 788-789.

The nature of evidence in corroboration was explained by Lord Reading CJ in *R v Baskerville* [1916] 2 KB 658 as follows: "We hold that evidence in corroboration must be independent testimony which affects the accused by connecting or tending to connect him with the crime. In other words, it must be evidence which implicates him, that is, which confirms in some material particular not only the evidence that the crime has been committed, but also that the prisoner committed it".[5]

It is submitted that the correct form of warning, following the reform of the law, should follow the judgment of Meredith J in *The People (A-G) v Williams*.[6] An intimation that there is a particular danger in convicting merely because the case concerns a sexual crime is incorrect. That factor may influence the jury towards applying to a consideration of the facts of the case their knowledge of the nature of human passions which are particularly strong in sexual matters. The old view that a rape allegation is one which is easily made and difficult to disprove is inconsistent with the modern development of the burden of proof being on the prosecution to prove their case beyond reasonable doubt. If the trial judge wishes to mention a factor of danger he should do so in terms which do not dogmatically indicate that a danger is present in all cases where a woman, or a male victim, alleges a sexual offence against the accused. A danger may be present in such circumstances and may arise due to the fact that one person is alleging a crime against another who chooses to deny it. Where there are particular circumstances which might indicate the existence of motives of revenge or other motives which may induce a person to falsely accuse another, the trial judge should isolate these and commend them to the particular attention of the jury. It is submitted that the legislative reform enacted by s 7 of the Rape Act, 1990 would be nullified were trial judges to unthinkingly repeat

5   At 10-12 of the judgment.
6   Fn 74. The warning need not follow any particular definite form under the previous law; *The People (DPP) v Reid*, Court of Criminal Appeal, unreported, 20 February 1991.

the old form of warning based, as we believe it was, on a mistaken view of the nature of women's fantasies and motivations, a statistically unproven belief that most or many rape allegations were fabricated and which was formulated at a time when the criminal law had not yet definitively reached the position of requiring the prosecution to prove their case beyond reasonable doubt.

Similar considerations apply where the main witness for the prosecution is a child or is perceived to be of lesser status than an adult victim. In those instances it is the duty of the trial judge to isolate factors arising from the nature of the case which might indicate a particular danger of false accusation.

Under the former law a warning had to be given notwithstanding the obvious existence of corroboration. That is clearly no longer the position. Corroboration can support a prosecution case where a sexual offence is alleged, as in any other. It is submitted that the identification of corroboration, even apart from a warning that there may be a danger of convicting on the evidence of one witness in its absence, is an important task which should be fulfilled by the trial judge. This is so even if the trial judge decides that no particular warning is necessary beyond the usual exhortation to the jury to exercise particular care in considering their verdict, and in only returning a verdict of guilty if they are satisfied that all the elements of the case have been proved by the prosecution beyond reasonable doubt.

Nature of Corroboration

8.80 What constitutes corroboration must depend on the facts and circumstance of each case, on the defence set up by the accused, and on the nature of the question to be determined by the jury.[7] What is sought is evidence supporting the testimony of the victim that the crime was committed or that the accused was responsible, as may be appropriate depending on the facts of the case.[8] Thus if the defence is an alibi, evidence placing the accused with the victim at the time of the crime is corroborative.[9] Evidence from the victim of the use of articles during the crime

---

7   *The People (A-G) v Levison* [1932] IR 158, 165 CCA. For example in *The People (A-G) v Troy* (1950) ILTR 193, the Court of Criminal Appeal held that medical evidence that a boy had been interfered with did not corroborate the boy's evidence against the accused. Clearly it only corroborated the boy's testimony in relation to the interference but not in relation to the implication against the accused and of the accused. On corroboration generally see O'Connor, "The Mandatory Warning Requirement in Respect of Complaints in Sexual Cases in Irish Law" (1985) 20 Ir Jur (ns) 43; *Baskerville* [1916] 2 KB 658, 12 Cr App R 81; *The People (A-G) v Phelan* (1950) 1 Frewen 98 CCA; *Kerim* (1987) 28 A Crim R 439 Qd CCA. A helpful analysis is made in *McKeon* (1990) 31 A Crim R 357 by the Court of Criminal Appeal of Queensland through Connolly J at 358/9: "What is called for, as the Court laid down in *Baskerville*, is independent testimony which affects the accused by connecting or tending to connect him with the crime, evidence which implicates him, that is, which confirms in some material particular not only the evidence that the crime has been committed but also that the prisoner committed it". Commenting on corroboration in incest the judge indicated: "Independent evidence, whether confessional or otherwise which tends to show sexual desire for the victim and some measure of gratification of that desire, supports the case for the prosecution because it is consistent with the allegation made by the victim, it makes unlawful and unnatural behaviour credible and it serves to allay the natural concern of the jury that the victim's allegation is a fabrication".

8   *The People (A-G) v Phelan* (1950) 1 Frewen 98 CCA. *Baskerville*, fn 7, was confirmed in *Goss & Goss* (1990) 90 Cr App R 400 CA.

9   *The People (A-G) v McGrath*, unreported, quoted in *The People (A-G) v Kearns* (1946) ILTR 45. Thus

which the victim could only have known about had the crime been committed, and of later finding those articles in the accused's possession, corroborates the victim's testimony.[10]

In cases where the issue is consent, forensic evidence is usually led by the prosecution to establish bruising or other injuries on or in the victim's body or of torn or destroyed clothing consistent with a sexual assault. Such evidence can, of course, corroborate the victim's testimony of an attack with a sexual purpose, as opposed to a consensual act. It is commonplace for the accused to allege that such injuries occurred during "rough sex". A jury is entitled to regard the victim's distressed condition as corroborating her testimony that the sexual intercourse with the accused was non-consensual. This, however, constitutes very little corroboration and the jury should be cautious in relying on it.[11] The accused may argue that such evidence is equally consistent with regret after sexual intercourse. Such disputes are for the jury to resolve.

Silence cannot be corroboration[12] but lies told by the accused may be.[13] Evidence that the victim, at the first reasonable opportunity, made a complaint consistent with her testimony is not, in any circumstances, corroboration of that testimony but is merely evidence of the consistency of such allegations.[14]

The Complaint

8.81 In cases of rape, sexual assault, unlawful sexual intercourse,[15] buggery and gross indecency,[16] incest[17] and, it has been stated, all sexual offences whether consent is an issue or not,[18] the fact that the victim made an early complaint of the accused's conduct and the terms of that complaint,[19] are admissible in evidence. The practice in this country has been for the witness to the complaint to give evidence of what the victim said or the effect of what was said. These statements do not corroborate

in *Ensor* (1989) 89 Cr App R 139 CA the finding of a whip in the accused's house constituted corroboration of the victim's account as to lack of consent and being terrified of a whip where the accused alleged that she must have imagined the existence of this article.

10   *The People (A-G) v O'Sullivan* [1930] IR 552, 557-58, 64 ILTR 181 CCA.
11   *The People (DPP) v Mulvey* [1987] IR 502 CCA.
12   *The People (A-G) v Quinn* [1955] IR 366 CCA; *Lander* (1989) 46 A Crim R 238 CCA SA.
13   *Lucas* [1981] QB 720; [1981] 2 All ER 1008; [1981] 3 WLR 120, 73 Cr App R 159 CCA; *Credland v Knowler* (1951) 35 Cr App R 48 DC. According to the Court of Appeal in *Lucas* there were four criteria: (1) the lie had to be deliberate; (2) it has to relate to a material issue; (3) the motive for the lie had to be a realisation of guilt and fear of the truth, it is appropriate to warn the jury that people sometimes lied from other motives such as an attempt to bolster up a just cause or out of shame or a wish to conceal bad behaviour; (4) the statement had to be clearly shown to be a lie by evidence other than that which required to be corroborated, for example, by admission or by evidence from an independent witness; see also *Hemsley* (1988) 36 A Crim R 334 NSW CCA; *Kerim* (1987) 28 A Crim R 439 Qd CCA; *Hart* [1986] 2 NZLR 408 CA; *Galea* (1989) 46 A Crim R 158 CCA WA; *H* (1990) 49 A Crim R 396 CCA NSW.
14   *Osborne* [1905] 1 KB 551 CCR; *Lillyman* [1896] 2 QB 167 CCR.
15   *Osborne* [1905] 1 KB 551, 558-91 CCR.
16   *Wannell* (1922) 17 Cr App R 53; *Camelleri* [1922] 2 KB 122 CCA.
17   *The People (DPP) v JT* (1988) 3 Frewen CCA.
18   *Phipson*, 9.82; *Lovell* (1923) 17 Cr App R 163; *Evans* (1924) 18 Cr App R 123 CCA; *Osborne*, fn 14; *Lillyman* [1896] 2 QB 167 CCR.
19   *Lillyman*, fn 18.

the victim's testimony,[20] and the trial judge must so instruct the jury.[21] They are admitted to show the consistency of the victim's complaint and evidence and, where consent is in issue, that the victim's earlier conduct in making the complaint was inconsistent with consent.[22] Such evidence is usually given by a witness as well as by the victim but may be given by the victim alone when no supporting evidence is given.[23] Where the victim does not give evidence her complaint cannot be received through the evidence of another party.[24]

Such complaint must be made at the first opportunity which was reasonably afforded and cannot have been elicited by leading, inducing or intimidating questions.[25] The rule was put by Ridley J thus:

> . . . the mere fact that the statement is made in answer to a question in such cases is not of itself sufficient to make it admissible as a complaint. Questions of a suggestive or leading character will, indeed, have that effect, and will render it inadmissible; but a question such as this, put by the mother or other person, "What is the matter?" or "Why are you crying?" will not do so . . . in each case the decision on the character of the question put, as well as other circumstances, such as the relationship of the questioner and the complainant, must be left to the discretion of the presiding judge. If the circumstances indicate that, but for the questioning, there probably would have been no voluntary complaint, the answer is inadmissible. If the question merely anticipates a statement which the complainant was about to make, it is not rendered inadmissible by the fact that the questioner happens to speak first.[26]

The admissibility of such a complaint is a question for the trial judge,[27] and in each case he must decide whether the questions put to the victim, and her relationship with the questioner and the other circumstances render the complaint involuntary and not admissible.[28] All the circumstances must be taken into account. In *Freeman*[29] a complaint was admitted though elicited by the question "Have you been raped or something?" The circumstance suggesting the admission of this evidence was that the victim had already indicated a sufficient degree of distress for this to be regarded as merely accelerating, as opposed to suggesting, the complaint.[30]

20   *Wallwork* (1958) 42 Cr App R 153 CCA; *Redpath* (1962) 41 Cr App R 319 CCA; *Nazif* [1987] 2 NZLR 122 CA.

21   *Osborne*, fn 15; *Lillyman*, fn 18; *Coulthread* (1933) 24 Cr App R 14.

22   *Osborne*, fn 15; *Lillyman*, fn 18; *Redpath*, fn 20.

23   *Lee* (1911) 7 Cr App R 31.

24   *Wallwork*, fn 20; *Allingham* (1989) 42 A Crim R 175 CCA Qd. For a discussion see Barrington, "The Rape Law Reform Process in New Zealand" (1984) 8 Crim LJ 307 at 321.

25   *Osborne*, fn 15.

26   *Osborne*, fn 15 at 556 CCR. *Cross on Evidence* (7th ed., 1990) 284 interprets the requirement thus: "There are thus three conditions, although each is interpreted liberally: that the statement be spontaneous; that it be contemporaneous; and that it amount to a complaint".

27   *Cummings* [1948] 1 All ER 551 CCA; *Lillyman*, fn 18.

28   *Rush* (1896) 60 JP 777 (complaint made after a day to the victim's mother; rejected); *Norcott* [1917] 1 KB 347 (the victim crying and refusing to speak but on being pressed complained; admitted); *Wilbourne* (1917) 12 Cr App R 279 (complaint invited by the victim's sister and repeated to her mother; admitted).

29   [1980] VR 1 SC.

30   Cross suggests at 285: "The ultimate consideration should be simply whether the purpose of enhancing the witness's credibility by showing consistency between complaint and testimony will be achieved by admitting the earlier statement".

Whether the complaint was made at the first reasonable opportunity is to be considered in the context of the availability of a responsible person to whom the victim would care to confide, the time that elapsed since the crime[31] and, it is submitted, the individual response of the victim to trauma.[32]

The rules relating to complaints had their historical origin in the need for hue and cry in rape cases.[33] More recently they have provided a balance to the prosecution against the warning of the trial judge on the dangers of convicting on the victim's testimony, in sexual offence cases. As to whether this balance has now been upset by leaving that warning to the trial judge's discretion, time alone will tell.

The Character of the Victim

8.82 At common law evidence could be given by the accused that the victim was a woman of notoriously bad character for want of chastity or common decency or that she was a common prostitute[34] and as to her sexual history with the accused.[35] The victim could also be cross-examined on these matters; as her answers concerning her sexual history with the accused went to the issue, he could lead evidence on this,[36] but as her answers on her sexual history with men other than the accused went only to her credit, her answers on this point were final.[37] This was perceived as unfair to the victim as having the effect of putting her through an unnecessary experience of considerable trauma[38] the result of which might be to place the complainant herself on trial. Moreover the notion that a woman who has consented to sexual intercourse with a number of men in the past is likely thereby to have consented with the accused[39] does not have the same currency in modern times. S 3 of the Rape Act, 1981, as amended by s 13 of the Rape Act, 1990, provides:

31   *Kiddle* (1898) 19 Cox 77 (the victim, a child, came home and went out again and on returning home later complained; admitted); *Ingrey* (1900) 64 JP 106 (complaint made by letter three days later; rejected); *Rush* (1896) 60 JP 777 (complaint made the next day; rejected); *Pataney* (1907) 71 JP 101 (complaint made on the afternoon of similar acts three weeks before; rejected); *Hedges* (1909) 3 Cr App R 262 (complaint eight days later and after an earlier opportunity; admitted); *Corkin* (1989) 40 A Crim R 162 SAus CCA (a complaint made three months after the last of a series of incidents extending over years; rejected). In *Sant* [1989] 1 NZLR 502 the High Court indicated that in principle the circumstances as to the first opportunity would vary according to the type of person in whose company the complainant was, and the closeness in time to her first seeing a person to whom she was likely to make a complaint.

32   *Freeman*, fn 29.

33   1 Hale 633; 1 Hawk ch 41.

34   *Barker* (1829) 3 C&P 588, 172 ER 558; *Riley* (1887) 18 QB 481 CCR. The rules applied to rape (*Riley*), assault with intent to rape (*Clarke*, (1817) 2 Stark NP 241, 171 ER 633), indecent assault (*Holmes* (1871) LR 1 CCR 334, 12 Cox CC 137 CCR) and unlawful sexual intercourse; generally see Archbold (1954) par 1946.

35   *Riley*, fn 34; *Hodgson* (1812) Russ and Ry 211, 168 ER 765; *Clarke*, fn 34; *Barker*, fn 34; *Martin* (1834) 6 C&P 562, 172 ER 1364.

36   *Riley*, fn 35; *Martin*, fn 34; *Turner* [1944] 1 QB 463.

37   *Holmes*, fn 34; *Cockcroft* (1870) 11 Cox 410.

38   Law Reform Commission LRC Consulatation Paper on Rape (1987) p 19, Report on Rape par 22-28.

39   1 Hale PC 628, 629, 4 Bl Com 213. For a modern view, Report of the Advisory Group on the Law of Rape (1975), (Cmnd 6352) par 110-131.

(1) If at a trial any person is for the time being charged with a sexual assault offence[40] to which he pleads not guilty, then, except with the leave of the judge, no evidence shall be adduced and no question shall be asked in cross-examination at the trial, by or on behalf of any accused person at the trial, about any sexual experience (other than that to which the charge relates) of a complainant with any person; and in relation to a sexual offence tried summarily pursuant to s 12—(a) subs (2)(a) shall have effect as if the words "in the absence of the jury" were omitted,

(b) subs (2)(b) shall have effect as if for the references to the jury there were substituted references to the court, and

(c) this section (other than this paragraph) and subs (3) and (4) of s 7 shall have effect as if for the references to the judge there were substituted references to the court.

(2)(a) The judge shall not give leave in pursuance of subs (1) for any evidence or question except on an application made to him, in the absence of the jury, by or on behalf of an accused person.

(b) The judge shall give leave if, and only if, he is satisfied that it would be unfair to the accused person to refuse to allow the evidence to be adduced or the question to be asked, that is to say, if he is satisfied that, on the assumption that if the evidence or question was not allowed the jury might reasonably be satisfied beyond reasonable doubt that the accused person is guilty, the effect of allowing the evidence or question might reasonably be that they would not be so satisfied.

(3) If, notwithstanding that the judge has given leave in accordance with this section for any evidence to be adduced or question to be asked in cross-examination, it appears to the judge that any question asked or proposed to be asked (whether in the course of so adducing evidence or of cross-examination) in reliance on the leave which he has given is not or may not be such as may properly be asked in accordance with that leave, he may direct that the question shall not be asked or, if asked, that it shall not be answered except in accordance with his leave given on a fresh application under this section.

(4) Nothing in this section authorises evidence to be adduced or a question to be asked which cannot be adduced or asked apart from this question.

8.83 The same provisions apply to a trial in the Special Criminal Court to a preliminary examination in the District Court[41] and to the Children's Court.[42] In *The People (DPP) v McDonagh & Cawley*[43] Finlay CJ commented:

> Upon the true construction of this section it would appear necessary for the judge, in the absence of the jury, to hear all the necessary material which will permit him to reach a conclusion either with regard to questioning or with regard to the tendering of evidence concerning sexual experience of a complainant with persons other than the accused, and that it is a matter for his discretion in what form that information would be put before him, whether by way of sworn testimony or by way of a proof of evidence. It is obviously desirable where it is practicable for a ruling to be made at

40   A sexual assault offence is defined by s 1 of the 1981 Act, as amended by s 12 of the 1990 Act as rape, attempted rape, burglary with intent to commit rape, aiding, abetting, counselling and procuring rape, attemped rape or burglary with intent to commit rape, and incitement to rape; aggravated sexual assault, attempted aggravated sexual assault, sexual assault, attempted sexual assault, aiding, abetting, counselling and procuring aggravated sexual assault, incitement to aggravated sexual assault or sexual assault; and conspiracy to commit any of the foregoing offences.

41   S 4 of the 1981 Act. These applications must be in camera; s 6 of the 1981 Act as substituted by s 11 of the 1990 Act, s 6(3) which gives the right for the victim and the accused (if under 18) to have a parent, relative or friend in court.

42   S 5 of the 1981 Act.

43   CCA, unreported, 24 July 1990.

an early stage in the trial on any such application. It may not, however, always be possible to rule it on one occasion only, and there is nothing inconsistent with the provisions in the section in a further or different application at a later stage in the trial or with the renewal of an application or the postponement of a decision on it. The grounds on which the learned trial judge shall exercise his discretion are very clearly set out at section 3(2)(b), and solely consists of the question as to whether he is satisfied that if the evidence or question was not allowed, the jury might reasonably be satisfied beyond a reasonable doubt that the accused person is guilty, whereas, the effect of allowing the evidence or question might reasonably be that they would not be so satisfied.[44]

In England[45] applications under this section are treated by first asking whether the question or the evidence passes the test of relevancy at common law.[46] If the question is so relevant it is only then that the issue of unfairness to the accused in excluding the question or evidence arises. There is no issue as to whether the question or evidence would be fair to the victim.[47] This is not a matter of discretion but of logic. If the judge comes to the conclusion that he is satisfied that it would be unfair to exclude the evidence, then the evidence has to be admitted and the questions have to be allowed.[48]

8.84 The Court of Appeal has expressed the view that the purpose of the English equivalent to s 3 is to protect complainants from cross-examination as to credit alone. Cross-examination on the issue can be contradicted by the defence by testimony of their own whereas cross-examination as to credit is generally final.[49] Consequently, the sexual experience of the victim outside of marriage with men other than the accused, would rarely be admitted save where there was evidence of sexual promiscuity so strong or so close in time to the events in issue as to blur the gap between questions of credit and matters in issue in the trial. The view of the Court was that the course of the trial would determine the issues in the case and therefore the correct ruling that should be made under the section, questions and evidence

---

44　At 11-12. Note the similar analysis of May J in *Lawrence* [1977] Crim LR 492: ". . . in my judgment before a judge is satisfied or may be said to be satisfied that to refuse to allow a particular question or series of questions in cross-examination would be unfair to a defendant, he must take the view that it is more likely than not that the particular question or line of cross-examination, if allowed, might reasonably lead the jury, properly directed in the summing-up, to take a different view of the complainant's evidence from that which they might take if the question or series of questions were or were not allowed". The judge further distinguished between cross-examination as to the trustworthiness of the complainant's evidence and that designed to leave a tacit comment "well there you are, members of the jury, that is the sort of girl she is". The latter was not permissible under the section. The effect of the amendment introduced by s 13 of the Rape Act, 1990 is to amend the section so that leave must be asked if any sexual experience even with the accused man himself, is to be mentioned in evidence, where it is other than the occasion under question in the trial.

45　See Adler, "The Relevance of Sexual History Evidence in Rape" [1985] Crim LR 769; Elliott, "Rape Complainants' Sexual Experience with Third Parties" [1984] Crim LR 4.

46　*Viola* [1982] 3 All ER 73; [1982] 1 WLR 1138, 75 Cr App R 125; [1982] Crim LR 515 CA; *Ellis* [1990] Crim LR 717; *Riley* [1991] Crim LR 460 CA.

47　*Mills* (1979) 68 Cr App R 327 at 329; [1979] Crim LR 4560 CA.

48　*Viola* [1982] 3 All ER 73 at 77; [1982] 1 WLR 1138 at 1142, 75 Cr App R 125 at 130; [1982] Crim LR 515 CA.

49　The exceptions are bias or partiality, a witness's previous convictions, the witness's general reputation for untruthfulness and medical evidence affecting the reliability of a witness's evidence.

which go to the issue of consent being likely to be admitted.[50] For example, the fact that the victim was the mother of a child could not, of itself, be relevant.[51]

An issue might arise that the accused mistook the victim as consenting, being influenced by his prior knowledge of her promiscuity.[52] If the defence is that sexual intercourse took place in exchange for money evidence that the complainant was a prostitute may be relevant.[53] It follows that prosecution evidence as to the previous good character of the complainant should rarely be admitted, the purpose of the legislation being to exclude the complainant's sexual history from the consideration of the jury save where it becomes relevant to an issue at the trial.[54] Strikingly similar conduct by the complainant on another occasion, not necessarily close in time to the alleged rape, may lead to a judge allowing an application to cross-examine as to that occasion[55] and a previous false allegation of rape may be relevant as indicating a propensity, not to promiscuous behaviour, but to make false allegations and therefore may be relevant.[56] A limited question as to when the complainant last had sexual intercourse was admitted in *Fenlon & Others*[57] where swabs proved positive for the presence of semen and the question of whether intercourse had taken place with the accused was an issue at the trial.

The 1981 Act applied s 3 only to sexual experiences by the victim with persons other than the accused.[58] Under the 1990 amendment it also applied to prior sexual experience with the accused. As a matter of principle it can be stated that where that prior sexual experience with the accused is introduced simply to besmirch the character of the victim it should be excluded but where it is introduced to show that the victim was more likely to have consented to sexual intercourse, or that the accused mistook her as so consenting, it should be admitted.

8.85 Questions and evidence as to the victim's possible partiality, her previous convictions, her general reputation for untruthfulness and medical evidence affecting

50   *Viola*, fn 46 and fn 48; *Brown* (1989) 89 Cr App R 97 CA.

51   *Gervais* (1990) 58 CCC (3d) 141 CA Quebec.

52   *Barton* (1987) 85 Cr App R 5; [1987] Crim LR 399 CA; *Hinds & Butler* [1979] Crim LR 111. In *Barton*, O'Connor indicated that there was a difference between believing that a woman was consenting to intercourse and believing that a woman would consent if advances were made to her.

53   *Krausz* (1973) 57 Cr App R 466 CA. *The People (DPP) v McDonagh & Cawley*, fn 43.

54   *Allingham* (1989) 42 A Crim R 175 CCA Qd. In *Funderbunk* (1990) 90 Cr App R 466 the Court of Appeal held that where the victim alleged that she was a virgin and relied on this evidence to prove lack of consent that the issue had thereby become relevant and the defence should have been allowed to question her on this and, if met with a denial, to call disputed evidence. The issue had become one central to the issue of credit but was also sufficiently closely related to the subject matter of the indictment for justice to require investigation for the basis of such a challenge. In *Redguard* [1991] Crim LR 213 it was held that where the complainant alleged that she would not have allowed anyone other than her boyfriend to stay at her flat, let alone have a sexual relationship with her, that it was unfair to refuse to allow a cross-examination about a consensual sexual encounter with another man who stayed the night at her flat some two weeks after the alleged rape; and see *Lawrence* [1977] Crim LR 492.

55   Report of the Advisory Group on the Law of Rape, op. cit. par 2.66

56   *Cox* (1987) 84 Cr App R 132 CA.

57   (1980) 71 Cr App R 307 CA.

58   Sexual experience need not be physical but could, for example, relate to a conversation as a prelude to intercourse; *White* (1989) 46 A Crim R 251 CCA NSW.

the reliability of her evidence are outside the scope of s 3. Where any of these matters also arise from past sexual experience it is submitted that they should more usually be admitted whether as a question or as evidence, they being exceptions to the finality of questions as to credit.[59] They are therefore matters which the law of evidence, prior to the enactment of s 3, regarded as being of particular importance. In *Cox*[60] it was held that the defence should not have been prevented from cross-examining the victim as to whether, on a previous occasion she had sexual intercourse with another man and had falsely accused him of rape.

Similar Fact

8.86 The prosecution are not permitted to lead evidence of the accused having committed offences on other occasions, apart from those charged in the indictment, or to use evidence on one count in the indictment to corroborate or prove another, merely to blacken the accused's character and thereby render a conviction more likely. It is permissible to lead evidence of offences on other occasions if the manner in which, or the circumstances under which, those offences were committed is logically probative of the case being made by the prosecution or to rebut a defence otherwise open to the accused.[61] Human nature tends towards a natural, but often illogical, leap to a conclusion of guilt in relation to an offence from the mere fact that the accused had been involved in reprehensible conduct in the past. The prejudicial effect of such evidence needs, therefore, to be outweighed by its probative value. What is required is a stronger degree of probative force than that which would, on the application of the usual rules of evidence, cause a fact to be admitted simply because of its relevance.[62] It is the degree of similarity, or the probative nature of the previous relevant circumstances, which determines the capacity of the evidence to prove guilt; the bare possibility of collaboration between witnesses is not sufficient to call for its exclusion.[63]

The general principle was stated by the Supreme Court of Canada by McLachlin J for the majority thus:

> The analysis of whether the evidence in question is admissible must begin with the recognition of the general exclusionary rule against evidence going merely to disposition . . . evidence which is adduced solely to show that the accused is the sort of person likely to have committed an offence is, as a rule, inadmissible. Whether the evidence in question constitutes an exception to this general rule depends on whether

---

59   *Phibson* (London, 1982) 33.83-33.88; *The People (DPP) v McGinley* [1987] IR 340 CCA.

60   (1987) 84 Cr App R 132 CA.

61   *Makin v A-G for New South Wales* [1894] AC 57; [1891-4] All ER 24, 17 Cox 704 PC.

62   In *Boardman* [1975] AC 421; [1974] 3 All ER 887; [1974] 3 WLR 673, 60 Cr App R 165; [1975] Crim LR 36 HL Lords Wilberforce, Salmon and Morris used the phrase "strikingly similar". Lord Salmon referred to a similarity so unique or striking that commonsense would make it inexplicable on the basis of coincidence. Later in *Rance* [1975] 62 Cr App R 118; [1976] Crim LR 311 the Court of Appeal indicated that too much importance was being attached to this phrase and stated that the essential requirement was that the evidence of similar conduct should be "positively probative" in that it assisted the jury in their determination on some ground other than the defendant's bad character or disposition to commit the sort of crime charged. Similarly see *Scarrott* [1978] QB 1016; (1977) 65 Cr App R 125; *R* (1989) 46 A Crim R 512 CCA Tasmania.

63   *Hoch* (1988) 32 A Crim R 443 Qd CCA.

the probative value of the proposed evidence outweighs its prejudicial effect. In a case such as the present where the similar fact evidence sought to be adduced is prosecution evidence of a morally repugnant act committed by the accused, the potential prejudice is great and the probative value of the evidence must be high indeed to permit its reception. The judge must consider such factors as the degree of distinctiveness or uniqueness between the similar fact evidence and the offences alleged against the accused, as well as the connection, if any, of the evidence to issues other than propensity, to the end of determining whether, in the context of the case before him, the probative value of the evidence outweighs its potential prejudice and justifies its reception.[64]

Evidence that the accused has committed a crime on a different occasion can be admitted not as similar fact evidence but in order to prove something that is logically probative such as the fact that the accused had learned butchery in prison and that the body of the victim had been dismembered with professional skill.[65]

8.87 Essentially, in considering whether to admit the evidence the judge is looking for some factor connecting the previous behaviour with the offence charged which goes beyond a matter of mere coincidence or chance and which by its existence renders more likely the fact sought to be proved by the prosecution.[66]

In general evidence of a particular disposition, such as the fact that the accused is a homosexual, is not of sufficiently probative force to admit this as a fact proving the prosecution's case.[67] The similarity relied on by the prosecution may relate to the commission of the offence or the manner in which the accused sought his victims or any other factor, it is submitted, which is logically probative[68] by being sufficiently distinctive.

It is submitted that the fact that the accused, as the father of children, has committed sexual acts with his children other than the victim in the offence at trial, is evidence, of itself, of an extraordinary disposition which tends to support the

64 *B* (1990) 55 CCC (3d) SC. The facts of this case involved a charge of the accused having committed sexual acts with his daughter at a young age. Evidence was admitted from a woman who ten years ago had lived with the accused when her mother had a sexual relationship with him. The similarity which apparently moved the court to admit the evidence was the fact that the relationship had started out, in each case, as a father/daughter type relationship prior to the girl being seduced. Similarly see *Butler* (1987) 84 Cr App R 12 CA. The authorities are summarised thus: "1. Evidence of similar facts may be admissible in evidence, whether or not they tend to show the commission of other offences. This evidence may be admitted: (a) if it tends to show that the accused has committed the particular crime of which he is charged, (b) to support the identification of the accused as the man who committed a particular crime and, in appropriate cases, in order to rebut a defence of alibi, or (c) to negative a defence of accident or innocent conduct. 2. Admissibility is a question of law for the judge to decide. He must, in the analysis of the proffered evidence, be satisfied that: (a) the nature and quality of the similar facts show a striking similarly or what Scarman LJ in *Scarrott*, fn 62, describes as being of "positive probative value", and (c) the evidence of a similar act goes well beyond a propensity to act in a particular fashion. 3. Notwithstanding an established admissibilty in law the judge in the exercise of discretion may refuse to admit the evidence if its prejudicial effect outweighs its probative value".

65 *Kirwan* [1943] IR 279 CCA.

66 *Shore* (1989) 89 Cr App R 32 CA; *Wilmot* (1989) 89 Cr App R 341 CA; *Butler* (1987) 84 Cr App R 12 CA.

67 *Bartlett* [1959] Crim LR 285.

68 *Scarrott*, fn 65, disapproving *Novac* (1976) 65 Cr App R 107 CCA. But see *P* [1991] Crim LR 291 CCA.

prosecution case.[69] In *P*[70] a father was tried in respect of various counts of incest and rape against two of his daughters. The appeal came to the House of Lords on the point as to whether the evidence of one girl, against the accused, was admissible in respect of a charge where the other was the victim. The evidence of both girls described a prolonged course of conduct in relation to each of them where force was used. General domination of the girls, with threats against them unless they observed silence, and a domination of the wife which inhibited her intervention, was a characteristic of the case. The accused seemed to have an obsession for keeping the girls for himself. When the elder left the home the younger took on her role. Evidence had been led that the accused was involved in paying for abortions for both of the girls. Lord Mackay indicated that those circumstances taken together gave strong probative force to the evidence of each of the girls in relation to the incidents involving the other, and was sufficient to make it just to admit that evidence, notwithstanding its prejudicial effect. When a question of the admissibility of this kind of evidence arose the judge should first decide whether there was material on which the jury would be entitled to conclude that the evidence of one victim about what occurred was so related to the evidence given by another victim, that the evidence of the first victim provided strong enough support for the evidence of the second to make it just to admit it notwithstanding the prejudicial effect of admitting the evidence. Lord Mackay indicated that such a relationship or connection might take many forms and while "striking similarity" in the manner in which the crime was committed, consisting of unusual characteristics in its execution, might be one of these, it was by no means confined to such circumstances. Relationships in time and circumstances other than those might well be important relationships. Where the identity of the perpetrator was in issue something like a signature or other feature would be necessary. To transpose that requirement to other situations where the question was whether a crime had been committed, rather than who was the person who committed it, was to impose an unnecessary and improper restriction on the application of the principle. On the facts of the incident case, there was a sufficient relationship between the circumstances spoken of by the two daughters for their evidence mutually to support each other and to be therefore admissible in law.

Sexual disposition may become more probative where a defence of innocent association with a victim is put forward.[71]

---

69   To the contrary see *P* [1991] Crim LR 291 CA. It is submitted that the decision of the Court of Appeal in this case is wrong and it was later overruled by the House of Lords in *P* [1991] 3 All ER 337, reported in *The Independent*, 28 June 1991. Further see *Brooks* (1991) 92 Cr App R 36. The Court decided that the disposition of the accused, spending most of the day in bed and requiring to be waited on, and his rigorous discipline to his family and the mother's reported acquiescence were not strikingly similar. The difficulty with the Court's judgment is that it failed to have regard to all of the factors advanced on a global basis and discounted them individually without having regard to their probative effect when considered together. Leave to appeal to the House of Lords was granted but the case was overruled by their decision in *P* prior to the hearing.

70   Fn 69.

71   *King* [1967] 2 QB 338; [1967] 1 All ER 379; [1967] 2 WLR 612, 51 Cr App R 46; *Lewis* (1979) 68 Cr App R 310, 47 CCC (2d) 24.

Protecting the Victim

8.88 The Law Reform Commission in their report on Child Sexual Abuse[72] have made far reaching proposals for the reform of the law of evidence to make it easier for children to have access to the courts as witnesses in criminal prosecutions. The Commission proposes that the ordinary depositions, taken in the District Court, should be video-recorded and that the prosecution should be permitted to present this as evidence. They further propose the early interview of the child by an appropriate examiner and that a recording of this interview should be played as evidence in chief; the child would only be made available for cross-examination.[73] The Commission proposes that the court of trial should have the power to appoint, for special reasons, a child examiner through whom all questions would be asked.[74] The Commission also recommends that s 30 of the Children Act, 1908 should be repealed and replaced by a provision enabling the Court to hear the evidence of children without requiring them to give evidence on oath or affirm where the Court is satisfied that the children are competent to given evidence in accordance with the criteria identified by the Commission.[75] See the Criminal Evidence Bill, 1992, Part III.

At the time of writing it is not insisted, where children are witnesses that barristers be robed or wear the strange wigs required by the Rules of Court; screens have been used to shield the witness from the glare of the suspected offender;[76] informality of speech has been allowed and anatomically correct dolls have been used to allow children to assist their description of the sexual acts by miming with these dolls the offences perpetrated against them.[77]

Behaviour of Abused Children

8.89 The Law Reform Commission have recommended[78] that expert evidence should be admissible as to competence and as to children's typical behaviour and emotional reactions to sexual abuse.[79] Such evidence may be admissible at common law in an appropriate case. The New Zealand Court of Appeal laid down the conditions for the admissibility of such evidence thus:

> . . . before a psychologist or other similarly qualified person can be allowed to give evidence that a particular child has exhibited traits displayed by sexually abused children generally, it must be demonstrated in an unmistakable and compelling way and by reference to scientific material that the relevant characteristics are signs of child abuse. Always assuming that the psychologist in the present case was properly qualified to give evidence in this field . . . it was not properly established in the evidence that, in terms of the above dicta, children subject to sexual abuse demonstrate certain characteristics or act in peculiar ways which are so clear and unmistakable that they can be said to be concomitants of sexual abuse . . . or that expert evidence in this field was able to indicate

---

72   LRC 32-90.   73   See par 7.12-par 7.20.
74   See par 7.21-par 7.26. For a review see (1990) 84 Gazette ILSI 381.
75   See par 8.61.
76   Judge Kevin O'Higgins, personal communication.
77   *The People (DPP) v JT* (1988) 3 Frewen CCA.
78   Report on Child Sexual Abuse (LRC 32 – 1990).
79   Report par 6.04.

with a sufficient degree of compulsion, features which establish that the evidence of the complainant undertook and the reactions of other children from her own experience or have recourse to specialist literature to confirm her opinion.[80]

In *Manahan*[81] the Alberta Court of Appeal held that a clinical psychologist who was an expert in child sexual abuse could testify that in her opinion the complainant had not been coached and had not made up the incidents which she described.[82] In *C*[83] the British Columbia Court of Appeal admitted the evidence of a sexual abuse therapist on the basis that the behaviour of sexually abused children did not fall within the knowledge and experience of the jury who would therefore benefit from such an opinion.[84] The accused had been charged with sexual offences against his step-sons. There was no complaint until the victim had been removed from his home following his physical assault by the accused. Subsequently, the association continued. The expert testified as to the *indicia* of sexual abuse and these were related to the two victims. Her evidence explained the failure of the children to complain and the consistency with abuse of a subsequent continued association, why a child may tell an outsider, as opposed to a family member, and that the requirement of explaining the history of the abuse causes more memories to be sparked off as the involuntary forgetting self-protective mechanism was overcome. The Court indicated that where credibility was an issue an expert might be helpful to the jury who could draw an adverse inference against complainants for failing to disclose sexual abuse and delaying a complaint for several years. This was relevant, also, to the failure to complain to the boys' mother and the subsequent association. That evidence tended to show that the inferences which might well be drawn on the basis of commonsense and common experience should not be drawn as a matter of course in child sexual abuse cases. Such evidence required a careful charge by the judge as to the dangers of utilising this evidence and its proper role in the assessment of the facts.[85]

The Oath

8.90 S 30 of the Children Act, 1908 as amended by s 28(2) of the Criminal Justice

---

80 Accused [1989] 1 NZLR 714, 710-11 CA; *B* [1987] 1 NZLR 362 CA.

81 (1990) 61 CCC (3d) 139.

82 Conviction reversed on other grounds. 83 (1990) 57 CCC (3d).

84 Applying *Beland* (1987) 36 CCC (3d) 481 SC.

85 The actual warning by the trial judge is reproduced at 531 and is as follows: "The problem with her evidence, and I think it is a very significant problem, is that these symptoms that she describes can have other causes apart from sexual abuse. The symptoms are consonant with physical abuse and, of course, we know that there was some of that and that is not something that the accused is charged with. The evidence must also be reviewed with reservations because, obviously, some of the problems developed while the boys lived with Mr and Mrs C but a lot of the problems probably originated long before that. So, when you look at her evidence, I think you are going to have to weigh it very carefully. It is worthwhile evidence and I think evidence that you need to consider, but you need to consider it with reservation and great caution. She also, as I say, indicated that it is not uncommon for people who have been sexually abused and perhaps even physically abused to have these memory lapses and so on and that things do come back. So that explains, perhaps, why there are some inconsistencies in the evidence of the boys. Whether it is a satisfactory explanation and explains all the inconsistencies, I think is something that you will have to resolve and I think a lot of it is commonsense". Further see *Lavelle* (1990) 55 CCC (3d) 97, 76 CR (3d) 329 SC.

(Administration) Act, 1914 enables a child of "tender years" who does not, in the opinion of the court, understand the nature of the oath to give evidence not upon oath if, in the opinion of the court, the child has sufficient intelligence to justify the reception of the evidence and understands the duty of speaking the truth.[86] The Law Reform Commission have recommended that this section should be repealed and replaced by a provision enabling the court to hear the evidence of children under the age of 14, without requiring them give evidence on oath or affirm, where the court is satisfied that the children are competent to give evidence. These criteria would depend on competence. The court would make the ultimate decision based on the capacity of the child to give an intelligible account of events which he or she has observed.[87]

Draft Indictments

8.91 There follow the appropriate forms of indictment for the offences considered in this chapter.

RAPE

Statement of Offence
Rape contrary to s 2 of the Criminal Law (Rape) Act, 1981.[88]
Particulars of Offence
 AB, a male person, on   at   had unlawful sexual intercourse with CD, a woman, who did not consent to it, and at the time knew that CD did not consent to the intercourse or was reckless as to whether she did or did not consent to it.[89]

BURGLARY

Statement of Offence
Burglary contrary to s 23A of the Larceny Act, 1916, as inserted by s 6 of the Criminal Law (Jurisdiction) Act, 1976.
Particulars of Offence
AB, on   at   entered as a trespasser with intent to rape CD there.

UNLAWFUL PROCURING

Statement of Offence
Unlawfully procuring sexual intercourse contrary to s 3 of the Criminal Law Amendment Act, 1885, as amended by s 8 of the Criminal Law (Amendment) Act, 1935.
Particulars of Offence
AB, on the   at   by threats or intimidation (procured) attempted to

---

86　For an analysis see *The People (A-G) v O'Sullivan* [1930] IR 552, 64 ILTR 181 CCA.

87　Report on Child Sexual Abuse (LRC 32 – 1990) par 5.01-5.35.

88　The offence of rape was, in effect, created anew by this section. Later enactments did not alter the definition of the offence and references to them are superfluous; Criminal Procedure Act, 1924, Schedule, Rule 4(3).

89　In England, to assist the judge on sentence, rape with knowledge that the victim did not consent, and reckless rape should be charged in two separate counts; *Bashir* (1982) 77 Cr App R 59; [1982] Crim LR 687 CA. The stating of these in one count is in fact allowed by the Criminal Justice (Administration) Act, 1924, Schedule, Rule 5(1).

procure CD, a female person, to have unlawful carnal connexion with him (or with EF).

Statement of Offence

Unlawfully procuring sexual intercourse contrary to s 3 of the Criminal Law Amendment Act, 1885, as amended by s 8 of the Criminal Law (Amendment) Act, 1935.

Particulars of Offence

AB, on the　　　at　　　by false pretences or false representations procured CD, a female person, to have unlawful carnal connexion with him (or with EF).

Note: For administering a drug use the form contained in the Act.

SEXUAL ASSAULT

Statement of Offence

Sexual assault contrary to s 2 of the Criminal Law (Rape) (Amendment) Act, 1990.[90]

Particulars of Offence

AB, a male person,[91] on　　　at　　　, sexually assaulted CD, a female person (or a male person as the case may be).

AGGRAVATED SEXUAL ASSAULT

Statement of Offence

Aggravated sexual assault contrary to s 3 of the Criminal Law (Rape) (Amendment) Act, 1990.[92]

Particulars of Offence

AB, a male person, on　　　at　　　, sexually assaulted CD, a male person, in circumstances which involved serious violence (or the threat of serious violence or was such as to cause injury, humiliation or degradation of a grave nature) to CD.

Statement of Offence

Aggravated sexual assault contrary to s 3 of the Criminal Law (Rape) (Amendment) Act, 1990.

Particulars of Offence

AB, a male person, on　　　at　　　, sexually assaulted CD, a female person, in circumstances which involved serious violence (or the threat of serious violence or was such as to cause injury, humiliation or degradation of a grave nature) to CD.

S 4 RAPE

Statement of Offence

Rape, contrary to s 4 of the Criminal Law (Rape)(Amendment) Act, 1990.

Particulars of Offence

AB, a male person, on　　　at　　　, sexually assaulted CD, a female person,

---

90　Although the Act appears not to create a new offence it is possible that the words sexual assault might be given a different meaning to indecent assault.

91　The two offences of assault on the male and those on the female now run together, whereas formerly they were separate under s 52 and s 62 of the Offences Against the Person Act, 1861 and having different penalties; as they were created separately by the common law, it is probable that it is necessary to differentiate the victim and the accused by reference to sex.

92　This section creates a new offence by introducing new elements. It also provides for a different penalty from sexual assault.

in circumstances which included the penetration of the vagina of CD by an object held or manipulated by AB (by another person).

Statement of Offence
Rape, contrary to s 4 of the Criminal Law (Rape)(Amendment) Act, 1990.
Particulars of Offence
AB, a male person, on   at   , sexually assaulted CD, a male person, in circumstances which included the penetration of the anus of CD with his penis.

BUGGERY

Statement of Offence
Buggery
Particulars of Offence
AB, on   in   , committed buggery with a cow.

GROSS INDECENCY

Statement of Offence
Gross indecency contrary to s 11 of the Criminal Law Amendment Act, 1885.
Particulars of Offence
AB, a male person, on   at   , committed an act of gross indecency with CD, a male person.

UNDER AGE

Statement of Offence
Unlawful sexual intercourse contrary to s 1(1) of the Criminal Law (Amendment) Act, 1935.
Particulars of Offence
AB, a male person, on   at   , had unlawful carnal knowledge of CD, a girl under the age of fifteen years.
Note: For attempts prosecute contrary to s 1(2) of the Act.
Statement of Offence
Unlawful sexual intercourse contrary to s 2(1) of the Criminal Law (Amendment) Act, 1935.
Particulars of Offence
AB, a male person, on   at   , had unlawful carnal knowledge of CD, a girl over the age of fifteen years and under the age of seventeen years.
Note: For attempts charge contrary to s 2(2) of the Act.

INCEST

Statement of Offence
Incest, contrary to s 1 of the Punishment of Incest Act, 1908.
Particulars of Offence
AB, a male person, on the   at   , had unlawful carnal knowledge of CD, who is and was to his knowledge, his daughter.
Note: Where the victim is not under fifteen.
Statement of Offence
Incest, contrary to s 1 of the Punishment of Incest Act, 1908, as amended by s 12 of the Criminal Law (Amendment) Act, 1935.

Particulars of Offence

AB, being a male person, on the   at   had unlawful carnal knowledge of CD, who is and was to his knowledge, his daughter, and was at the time aged fourteen years. *Note:* To be used where the victim is under fifteen.

CARNAL KNOWLEDGE

Statement of Offence

Unlawful carnal knowledge of a girl contrary to s 1 of the Criminal Law (Amendment) Act, 1935.

Particulars of Offence

AB on   at   , had unlawful carnal knowledge of CD, a girl who was at the time aged fourteen years.

Statement of Offence

Procuring unlawful carnal connexion by threat, contrary to s 3 of the Criminal Law (Amendment) Act, 1885, as amended by s 8 of the Criminal Law Act, 1935.

Particulars of Offence

AB, on   at   procured CD to have unlawful carnal connexion with EF by threatening the said CD that if she failed so to do he would report her to the Gardaí as a shoplifter.

MENTAL HANDICAP

Statement of Offence

Unlawful carnal knowledge contrary to s 4 of the Criminal Law (Amendment) Act, 1935.

Particulars of Offence

AB, a male person, on the   at   , in circumstances which did not amount to rape, had unlawful carnal knowledge of CD who was then, to his knowledge, feeble-minded (an idiot, an imbecile).

CHAPTER NINE

Explosives

9.01 Explosives and firearms are frequently used for the purpose of inflicting injury to the person. It is convenient to deal with offences in relation to both explosives and firearms in this section of the work, which is completed by a note on possession. This chapter considers offences in relation to explosives, chapter 10 considers offences in relation to firearms and chapter 11 considers offensive weapons and ends with the note on possession.[1]

Legislation

9.02 The possession, use, manufacture and transport of explosives requires close control. This is affected by the Explosives Act, 1875 which is described in its long title as "An Act to amend the Law with respect to manufacturing, keeping, selling, carrying, and importing Gunpowder, Nitro- glycerine, and other explosive substances". The explosives offences most often prosecuted on indictment are to be found in the Explosive Substances Act, 1883 which has been extensively amended by s 4 of the Criminal Law (Jurisdiction) Act, 1976, which in addition, by s 2, creates the offence of doing an act in Northern Ireland, which if done in the State would constitute an offence scheduled under the Act.[2] That schedule includes offences under ss 2, 3 and 4 of the Explosive Substances Act, 1883. Further s 2 of the 1976 Act creates offences of participation in, and of being an accessory after the fact to the scheduled offences. Under s 19 of that Act the accused has a choice of jurisdictions as between Ireland and Northern Ireland and must have this option put to him prior to trial. These provisions and their regulations,[3] together with ss 12, 28, 29, 30, 64 and 65 of the Offences Against the Person Act, 1861 constitute the code of explosives offences. S 7(1) of the Explosive Substances Act, 1883, as amended by s 3 of the Prosecution of Offences Act, 1974, provides:

> If any person is charged before a justice with any crime under this Act, no further proceeding shall be taken against such person without the consent of the Director of Public Prosecutions, except as the justice may think necessary by remand, or otherwise, to secure the safe custody of such person.

9.03 In 1972 an attempt was made to amend and consolidate the law relating to explosives in the Dangerous Substances Act, 1972. This Act provided, under s 1(2),

---

1   The section is quoted at par 9.12. The precedent indictments are to be found at the end of this chapter.

2   Quoted par 9.17. For a discussion see *The People (DPP) v Campbell & Others* (1983) 2 Frewen 136 CCA.

3   These regulations include the Explosives (Potassium Nitrate and Sodium Nitrate) Order, 1986, SI 273 of 1986, the Explosives (Ammonium Nitrate and Sodium Chlorate) Order, 1972, SI 191 of 1972; the Explosives (Nitro-Benzene) Order, 1972, SI 233 of 1972: all made under s 104 of the Explosives Act, 1875.

that: "This Act shall come into operation on such day as the Minister[4] may by order appoint". No such ministerial order was made until 1979. In that year the Dangerous Substances (Amendment) Act, 1979 was passed which replaced s 1(2) of the 1972 Act with the following: "This Act shall come into operation on such day or days as the Minister may by order or orders appoint therefor either generally or with reference to any particular purpose or provision and different days may be so fixed for different purposes and different provisions".

The 1979 Act also gave the Minister the power to set up an Advisory Council to consider and advise him "on any matters arising on or in relation to the execution of the Dangerous Substances Act, 1972" which he might refer to them.

9.04 By means of the Dangerous Substances Act, 1972 (Commencement) Order, 1979,[5] the Minister, under the powers conferred on him by the amended s 1(2), brought the 1972 Act, apart from the provisions relating to explosives, into force. The reasons for leaving dormant the provisions of the 1972 Act which refer to explosive substances were given by the Minister[6] during the Dáil debate on the second stage of the Dangerous Substances (Amendment) Bill, 1979:[7]

> The 1972 Act consolidated and amended the law relating to explosives and petroleum and provided enabling powers in relation to other dangerous substances. The purpose of the Act was to regulate the industrial as distinct from the criminal use of these substances. My intention is to bring certain provisions of the Act into operation and at the same time to make comprehensive regulations relating to the areas of law affected. The Act provided for the repeal of controls under old statutes, and among these were certain parts of the Explosives Act, 1875. Because of a development in the meantime, which I shall presently explain, repeal of these provisions now would leave a serious gap in our laws for dealing with the criminal uses of certain substances, which, if freed from control, would tend to be used as explosives even though they were not considered to be explosives in 1972.
>
> In the latter part of 1972, after the legislation of that year had been passed, orders were made by the Government under the Explosives Act, 1875, prescribing ammonium nitrate, sodium chlorate and nitro-benzene to be explosives for the purposes of that Act.[8] Two of these substances were at the time in common use as weed killers or fertilisers, but it was established that they were also being used as ingredients in the manufacture of explosives. The needs of public order dictated that they should be controlled and, on the initiative of the Minister for Justice, the Government introduced the controls which they considered to be necessary. The position today is that the need for these controls remains.
>
> As I have indicated, the substances in question are not "explosives" within the terms of the Dangerous Substances Act, 1972; therefore they would cease to be controlled if that Act were brought into operation as drafted. Hence the need to leave the legal position with respect to explosives as it is for the time being, while bringing other provisions of the 1972 Act into operation. It is my intention to bring the Act into operation minus Part II, which relates to explosives, and also to arrange that the relevant provisions of the Explosives Act, 1875, shall remain in force.[9] Powers in relation to

---

4   Minister for Labour.   5 SI 297 of 1979 dated 28 September 1979.
6   Mr G. Fitzgerald, Minister for Labour.
7   *Dáil Debates*, Vol 315, p 2678-79.   8 Fn 2.
9   SI 297 of 1979 listed those parts of the 1972 Act not being brought into operation: the provisions relating to explosives: (a) Part II; (b) s 7(1) and schedule in so far as they refer to Towns Improvement

explosives will continue in force under the existing legislation and will remain with the Minister for Justice.[10]

The 1972 Act is used to control the storage and carriage of petroleum[11] and other dangerous substances,[12] such as those listed in the European agreement concerning the international carriage of dangerous goods by road.[13] It is extraordinary that the Oireachtas cannot implement a modern consolidating piece of legislation to replace those now considered in the text.

Definition

9.05 The Explosives Act, 1875, the Explosives Substances Act, 1883 and the Dangerous Substances Act, 1972 (not yet in force) each contain separate definitions of what constitutes an explosive:

1875   s 3   This Act shall apply to gunpowder and other explosives as defined by this section. The term "explosive" in this Act—(1) Means gunpowder, nitro-glycerine, dynamite, gun-cotton, blasting powders, fulminate of mercury or other metals, coloured fires, and every other substance, whether similar to those above mentioned or not, used or manufactured with a view to produce a practical effect by explosion or a pyrotechnic effect, and (2) includes fog-signals, fireworks, fuses, rockets, percussion caps, detonators, cartridges, ammunition of all descriptions, and every other adaptation or preparation of an explosive as above defined.
     s 104   Her Majesty may, by Order in Council, declare that any substance which appears to Her Majesty to be specially dangerous to life or property by reason either of its explosive properties, or any process in the manufacture thereof being liable to explosion, shall be deemed to be an explosive within the meaning of this Act, and the provisions of this Act (subject to such exceptions, limitations and restrictions as may be specified in the Order) shall accordingly extend to such substance in like manner as if it were included in the term explosive in this Act.

1883   s 9(1)   In this Act, unless the context otherwise requires,—the expression "explosive substance" shall be deemed to include any materials for making any explosive substance; also any apparatus, machine, implement, or materials used, or intended to be used, or adapted for causing, or aiding in causing, any explosion in or with any explosive substance; also any part of any such apparatus, machine or implement.

1972   s 9(1)   In this Act, "explosive" means a substance of a kind used to produce a practical effect by explosion or a pyrotechnic effect or anything of which that substance is an integral part. (2) For the purpose of this Act, the Minister may by order define the composition, quality and character of any explosive, and may classify explosives.

By s 8(1) of the Explosive Substances Act, 1883 ss 73-75 and s 89 and 96 of the Explosives Act, 1875 are incorporated into that Act. This makes the situation less confused than it appears. The term explosive is common to all three definitions. In

---

(Ireland) Act, 1854, Explosives Act, 1875, Customs and Inland Revenue Act, 1883, Local Government (Ireland) Act, 1898, Revenue Act, 1909; (c) s 7(2); (d) any other provision applicable to explosives within s 9(1) of the Act.

10   Fn 2.

11   Part III.

12   Part IV.

13   "ADR Agreement" done at Geneva on 30 September 1957; see SI 267 of 1986, which revoked the previous lists contained in SI 236 of 1980.

addition, the unsatisfactory definition in the 1883 Act is not to be read alone but in the light of the 1875 Act which expands and clarifies the meaning of the word "explosive".[14] The 1883 Act retains the search and forfeiture powers of the 1875 Act. As these apply only in respect of explosives a common definition is clearly implied into both Acts.[15] A situation where one was entitled to search for an explosive (defined in one particular way) but the possession of that substance was not a criminal offence because of a different definition applying was clearly not enacted by the legislature. The 1972 Act retains the substance of the earlier definitions, defining an explosive as something which produces "a practical effect by explosion or a pyrotechnic effect or anything of which that substance is an integral part". It has been decided that a petrol bomb,[16] a shotgun[17] and a pistol[18] are explosive substances.

Scope

9.06 The definition goes beyond materials which themselves explode. S 3 of the 1875 Act refers to "every other substance . . . used or manufactured with a view to produce . . ." and s 9 of the 1883 Act includes "any apparatus, machine, implement, or materials used, or intended to be used, or adapted for causing, or aiding in causing, any explosion". This embraces not only the chemical constituents of a bomb in their separated form, but also such items as milk churns or pieces of steel tubing intended to be used as receptacles for explosive chemicals or as makeshift mortar launchers. It is arguable that written directions as to the use or manner of triggering a bomb come within the words, used in s 9, "materials used . . . in causing, any explosion". No decision of which the writer is aware has gone that far. It is to be noted that the matters described in the definition are material objects whereas "directions" would constitute an intellectual component not intended to be outlawed by the Act.

Components

9.07 Items such as dynamite, nitro-glycerine and detonating fuses can reasonably be supposed to have an express function of exploding, or aiding in causing an explosion. Often, however, the question of the nature of a substance is one of the purpose to which it will be put; the constituent elements of bombs may often be industrial, domestic or agricultural substances or articles. A criminal purpose can change the nature of these articles into explosives. The proof of such a purpose is a matter of expert evidence as to the nature, potential and actual use in other instances of the substance or article and of necessary inference in all the circumstances.

The wide nature of the definition is exemplified by *Charles*.[19] Six defendants were indicted for conspiracy to cause an explosion and possession of an explosive

14 *Wheatley* [1979] 1 All ER 954; [1979] 1 WLR 144; [1978] 68 Cr App R 287 CA.
15 *Wheatley*, fn 14.
16 *Bouch* [1983] QB 246; [1982] 3 All ER 918; [1982] 3 WLR 673, 76 Cr App R 11 CA; *Elliott* (1984) 81 Cr App R 115; [1985] Crim LR 310 CA.
17 *Downey* [1971] NI 224 CCA.
18 *Fegan* [1972] NI 80 CCA.
19 (1892) 17 Cox 499.

substance in suspicious circumstances. The explosive substances described in the indictment were "a lead bolt", "a fuse", "a brass bolt and screw" and "brass-casting". None of these items, save for the fuse, could of itself explode. The prosecution proved a plan to manufacture a bomb, by sketches and directions for manufacturing it in the possession of the prisoners, of which these items were to be a part once explosive chemicals became available. Hawkins J rejected the contention that the Act only covered (1) the explosive substance itself or materials for its manufacture or (2) the machinery for causing the explosion or a part of it which is adapted for causing or aiding in causing it.

Nature of

9.08 In *Bouch*,[20] the English Court of Appeal approved a description of an explosive contained in the 1886 *Encyclopaedia Britannica*:

> Explosion may for our purpose be defined as the sudden or extremely rapid conversion of a solid or liquid body of small bulk into gas or vapour, occupying very many times the volume of the original substance, and, in addition, highly expanded by the heat generated during the transformation. This sudden or very rapid expansion of volume is attended by an exhibition of force, more or less violent according to the constitution or the original substance and the circumstances of explosion. Any substance capable of undergoing such a change upon the application of heat, or other disturbing cause, is called explosive.

The 15th edition (1983) of that work states:

> An explosive is any substance or device that can be made to produce a volume of rapidly expanding gas in an extremely brief period. There are three fundamental types: mechanical, nuclear and chemical.[21]

The expression "pyrotechnic effect" has not been judicially analysed and, practically, is of lesser importance. *The Shorter Oxford English Dictionary* gives the following among the meanings for pyrotechnic:

> (1) Of or pertaining to the use of fire in chemistry, metallurgy or gunnery—1731.
> (2) Of or pertaining to fireworks or the act of making them; of the nature of a firework—1825.

There is no entry in the 1885 or 1983 *Encyclopaedia Britannica* in respect of "pyrotechnic" save for a further reference under "Napalm" to "Pyrotechnic Gel" in the 1983 edition.

A ministerial power to define a substance as an explosive is contained in s 104 of the Explosives Act, 1875.[22] Potassium nitrate and sodium nitrate have been declared to be explosives under the 1875 Act.[23] It is hard to think of a substance which is used

---

20   [1983] QB 246; [1982] 3 All ER 918; [1982] 3 WLR 673, 76 Cr App R 11 CA; *Elliott* (1984) 81 Cr App R 115; [1985] Crim LR 310 CA.

21   Vol 21 at p 275: "Explosion: a violent expansion or bursting that is accompanied by noise and is caused by a sudden release of energy from a very rapid chemical reaction, from a nuclear reaction, or from an escape of gases or vapours under pressure (as in a steam boiler)".

22   See par 9.03 – par 9.04.

23   The Explosives (Potassium Nitrate and Sodium Nitrate) Order, 1986, SI 273 of 1986; The Explosives

in bombs and not known to a ballistics expert, or of a substance which cannot be exploded by an expert in test and demonstrated to be an explosive. A ministerial regulation defining a substance as an explosive must, in any event, be reasonable[24] and thus, in this context, capable of being sustained by expert testimony.

Control of Explosives

9.09 The powers of arrest and search, which apply to offences contrary to ss 2, 3 and 4 of the Act, are noted below.[25] The legislature has retained, through s 8(1) of the 1883 Act, the powers contained in ss 73, 74, 75, 89 and 96 of the Explosives Act, 1875. Under s 73 a power to enter and search and take samples is given to constables, government inspectors and local authority officers on a District Court warrant, or in the case of endangerment of life, on the warrant of a Garda Superintendent or government inspector, on reasonable cause for believing the commission of any explosives offence or contravention of the 1875 Act. Obstruction carries a £50 fine. The Secretary of State must be immediately informed in writing of such searches. S 74 gives powers of forfeiture to the District Court and allows constables and government inspectors to take steps to seize explosives or diminish the danger from explosives pending forfeiture proceedings. S 75 gives powers to inspect jetties, boats and other places to ensure that the provisions of the 1875 Act are not being infringed. S 89 gives power to fine in lieu of forfeiture and s 96 deals with the disposal of forfeited explosives and the funds to which fines must be paid.

Enquiry

9.10 Under s 6 of the Explosives Substances Act, 1883 the Director of Public Prosecutions[26] has the power, on believing on reasonable grounds that a crime contrary to the Act has been committed, to order an enquiry by a District Justice who may bind witnesses to appear before him and answer in the same way as in the District Court. No privilege against self-incrimination protects a witness from answering. His answers cannot be used against him in any future proceedings, civil or criminal. The witness may also be prosecuted for perjury. There is no record of this power having been used in Ireland in recent times.

The Dangerous Substances Act, 1972 should its provisions relating to explosives ever be brought into force,[27] would completely change the law regarding the prohibitions on explosives.

(Ammonium Nitrate and Sodium Chlorate) Order, 1972, SI 191 of 1972; The Explosives (Nitro-Benzene) Order, 1972, SI 233 of 1972. Further see par 9.03 – par 9.04.

24 It cannot fly in the face of fundamental reason or common sense; *Cassidy v Minister for Industry and Commerce* [1978] IR 297 SC; *State (Creedon) v Criminal Injuries Compensation Tribunal* [1982] IR 51 SC.

25 Par 9.12, fn 47; par 9.14, fn 47; par 9.17, fn 68.

26 As amended by the Prosecution of Offences Act, 1974, s 3.

27 See par 9.03-9.04.

1972 Act

9.11   The Dangerous Substances Act, 1972 bans the importation,[28] keeping,[29] sale,[30] purchase[31] and manufacture[32] of explosives subject to a licence granted by the Minister for Labour permitting such activity. On the issue of a certificate by an officer of the Garda Síochána, the purchase and keeping of explosives is permitted within the terms of that certificate.[33] The general ban does not extend to ammunition but this, due to its explosive nature, is prohibited by the 1883 Act as an explosive, and its manufacture is bound except under licence.[34] Special exemption from these provisions is given to aircraft and ships.[35] It is an offence, punishable summarily by a fine not exceeding £100 and/or six months' imprisonment, to contravene the provisions of the Act.[36] It is an offence, subject to the same penalty, to have possession or control of any explosive which is not clearly marked by its correct name and the word "explosive".[37] Forfeiture may follow a conviction.[38]

Extensive powers of search are granted by the 1972 Act. Briefly the provisions of the Act are policed by ministerial inspectors. These inspectors may enter, inspect and examine any premises at any time of the day or night, provided the inspector, on reasonable cause, believes the premises are being used for the manufacture, storage, packing or sale of any substance to which the Act applies.[39] He may take a Garda with him if he reasonably apprehends serious obstruction.[40] If he has reasonable cause to believe that an offence under the Act is being committed, he may obtain a warrant from the District Court to enter by force, but this requirement of a warrant may be dispensed with where it appears to him or her to be an emergency, in that delay would be likely to endanger life.[41] This may occur in practice in the majority of criminal, and especially subversive, cases.

The powers are wide beyond what seems to be necessary for merely inspecting legitimate manufacturing plants and other similar installations.[42] An inspector, on

---

28   S 10. Regulations for the grant and issue of licences can be made under s 36. The proof of the existence of such a licence would be on the accused; *Minister for Industry and Commerce v Steele* [1952] IR 304 SC, *The People (A-G) v Shribman and Samuels* [1946] IR 431 CCA.

29   S 11.

30   S 12.   31   S 12.

32   S 15.   33   S 13 and 11(1)(d).

34   S 14 and 15.   35   S 37.

36   S 47 and 52.   37   S 16.

38   S 56.

39   S 40. A reasonable belief is one founded on some grounds which, if subsequently challenged, will show that in exercising a power granted by statute or common law, the inspector or Garda acted reasonably; see generally *Glanville Williams* [1954] Crim LR 408 at 416. The ground of suspicion can be hearsay information or other material not generally admissible in a court; *Hussein v Chong Fook Kam* [1970] AC 492; [1969] 3 All ER 1626; [1970] 2 WLR 441 PC.

40   S 40(1)(b).

41   S 40(1)(c).

42   The Act does not express a limit itself to a supervisory role over legitimate installations. The only relevant power which contains limiting words, by way of a reference to a licensed premises, is that to take samples on suspicion that a substance may cause injury to employees: s 42(1). The inspector may, where he suspects an offence under the Act, seize any substance. For a similar controversy in relation to the use of s 30 of the Offences Against the State Act, 1939 against "non-subversives" see *The People (DPP) v Quilligan & O'Reilly* [1986] IR 495; [1987] ILRM 606.

suspecting the commission of an offence under the Act, may take possession of any substance and its container.[43] Further it is an offence for a person, found with an explosive in his possession or under his control, not to give an inspector or a Garda all the information he has as to how he came by the explosive.[44]

Criminal offences of a far more serious character are created by the 1883 Act but their nature is such as to necessarily involve the offender in the concurrent commission of offences under the 1972 Act and the extensive powers under that Act may assist in investigating the more serious explosive offences which follow.[45]

Section 2

9.12 S 2 of the Explosive Substances Act, 1883, as substituted by s 4 of the Criminal Law (Jurisdiction) Act, 1976[46] provides:

> A person who in the State or (being an Irish citizen) outside the State unlawfully and maliciously causes by an explosive substance an explosion of a nature likely to endanger life, or cause serious injury to property, shall, whether any injury to person or property is actually caused or not, be guilty of an offence and, on conviction on indictment, shall be liable to imprisonment for life.[47]

The elements of this offence require that it be proved that an explosion has been caused by an explosive substance,[48] that this explosion was of a nature likely to endanger life or cause serious injury to property (the terms of the section do not require actual endangerment or injury), that the explosion was caused in Ireland, or

---

43   S 44.

44   S 11(4). These answers may be used in court. A similar power under s 40(1)(g) provides that persons on the premises where a substance to which the Act applies are found or persons employed there within two months must answer all questions touching an examination or enquiry; the answers are not admissible against such persons.

45   A power granted in respect of a lesser offence may be used to investigate a more serious crime provided that there is a bona fide investigation which covers both crimes; *The People (DPP) v Quilligan & O'Reilly*, fn 42 and see *The People (DPP) v Walsh* [1986] IR 722.

46   The change introduced by this Act was to add an extraterritorial element.

47   Felony by virtue of s 20(8)(a) of the Criminal Law (Jurisdiction) Act, 1976 (note: as are s 2 and 3 of the Explosive Substances Act, 1883 and s 23, 23A and 23B of the Larceny Act, 1916); no powers of arrest are provided by this Act but the offence is scheduled under the Offences Against the State Act, 1939 and thus the powers of search under s 29 (search warrant issued by a Garda Superintendent reasonably believing that evidence of a scheduled offence, committed or intended, it to be found in the place) and the powers of arrest under s 30 (exercisable by any Garda suspecting an offence, the carrying of a document or the possession of information relating to an offence, committed or intended) can be exercised. Further powers of search are contained in s 8 of the Act, and further powers of search (overlapping) are contained in s 7 and 8 of the Criminal Law Act, 1976. Participation in the offence renders the accused liable as a principal both under the Accessories and Abettors Act, 1861 and s 5 of the 1883 Act. Proceedings under s 2 and 3 of the Act may be taken in any place in the State and the offences are then treated as if committed there; s 20(1) Criminal Law (Jurisdiction) Act, 1976. The consent of the DPP is needed to those proceedings; s 7 OF THE 1883 Act and s 3 of the Prosecution of Offences Act, 1974. The offences under s 2, 3 and 4 are scheduled under the Criminal Law (Jurisdiction) Act, 1976, which by s 2 makes it an offence for any person to commit those acts in Northern Ireland.

48   See par 9.05-9.09 for a definition.

if outside the State, that the accused was a citizen of Ireland[49] and that the accused acted unlawfully and maliciously. The word unlawfully in the section merely exculpates those who might, within the law, cause a serious explosion,[50] as, for example, under licence granted under the Explosives Act, 1875 or who otherwise have a defence.

Mental Element

9.13 Maliciously, in this statutory context, requires proof that the accused (1) intended to do a particular kind of harm that in fact was done or (2) was reckless as to whether such harm should occur or not (the accused foreseeing that the particular kind of harm might be done but going on to take the risk of it) and is not limited to, nor does it require, any ill will towards the victim.[51] This section has been traditionally interpreted to merely require that the accused intended to cause an explosion and, that on an objective view, the explosion was of the nature contemplated by the section.[52]

It is submitted that it is impossible to read the words "causes by an explosive substance an explosion of a nature likely to endanger life, or cause serious injury to property" so as to import the necessary subjective element into the intent and imply an objective element into the nature of the occurrence resulting from it. The tendency in Ireland is away from strict liability in respect of the elements of an offence towards requiring a mental element to correspond to the external elements.[53] This analysis seems appropriate here since the intent to cause the explosion cannot be divorced from its nature. It was surely not the intention of the legislature to penalise a person who explodes a "banger" for the unforeseen consequence of, for example, a huge explosion thereby occurring because of a gas leak in the vicinity. It follows that the accused must intend such a serious explosion or be reckless as to its occurrence.

The accused may be liable as the actor or as a participant in a common design or otherwise as a party to the offence, either at common law, or as provided for by s 5 of the Act.

Section 3

9.14 S 3 of the Explosives Substances Act, 1883, as substituted by s 4 of the Criminal Law (Jurisdiction) Act, 1976 provides:

---

49 The usual method of proof of citizenship involves the proof of a birth certificate in respect of the accused and evidence from the Department of Foreign Affairs that the accused has not renounced his Irish citizenship. It is also wise to prove that the particular location was situated in Northern Ireland as, in border areas, this is not a fact which the court will readily take judicial notice of; *The People (A-G) v McGeough*, CCA Unreported 19 November 1969.

50 Exshaw, "Some Illustrations of the Application and Meaning of 'Unlawful' in Criminal Law" [1959] Crim LR 503.

51 *Cunningham* [1957] 2 QB 396; [1957] 2 All ER 412; [1957] 3 WLR 76, 41 Cr App R 155 CA.

52 *Charles* (1892) 17 Cox 499.

53 The traditional view is expressed in the 43rd edition of Archbold, 19.362 this would seem to be inconsistent with *The People (DPP) v Murray* [1977] IR 360 SC. For a further discussion see ch 2.

A person who in the State or (being an Irish citizen) outside the State unlawfully and maliciously—

(a) does any act with intent to cause, or conspires to cause, by an explosive substance an explosion of a nature likely to endanger life, or cause serious injury to property, whether in the State or elsewhere, or

(b) makes or has in his possession or under his control an explosive substance with intent by means thereof to endanger life, or cause serious injury to property, whether in the State or elsewhere, or to enable any other person so to do,

shall, whether any explosion does or does not take place, and whether any injury to person or property is actually caused or not, be guilty of an offence and, on conviction on indictment, shall be liable to imprisonment for a term not exceeding twenty years, and the explosive substance shall be forfeited.[54]

Like the offence under s 2, extra-territorial jurisdiction is granted provided the accused is an Irish citizen[55] at the time of the offence. Unlike s 2 no explosion need have been caused. The restrictive definition of the crime of attempt caused the legislature in the instance of this Act to shy away from that concept and instead include in the wording of s 3 many acts which would traditionally be regarded not as attempts but as merely preparatory.[56] Thus in subs (a) the words "does any act with intent to cause" captures any act by the accused the purpose of which is ultimately to cause an explosion likely to endanger life or cause serious injury to property.

Intent

9.15 The proof of intent is, in the absence of an admission, a matter of necessary inference from the surrounding circumstances. Consequently the act or acts proved by the prosecution must point beyond reasonable doubt towards the inference that the accused's purpose in doing or participating in those acts was to cause an explosion contemplated by the section. Intent in the context of this section means that it is the purpose of the accused to cause that explosion. In deciding whether that intention exists the tribunal of fact is entitled to look at the accused's knowledge as to the consequences of his action and the objective probability as to what would, in fact, occur as a result of those acts. It can be inferred that the accused intended such an explosion if, to the accused's knowledge, it is a virtually certain consequence of those actions.[57] In practice this will cause little difficulty as the nature of involvement with explosives is, in practice, purposive.

It is to be noted that under subs (a) an intent to enable any other person to cause

---

54 Felony by s 20(8) of the Criminal Law (Jurisdiction) Act, 1976; the offence carries the same powers of arrest and search as offences under s 2 and can be participated in in the same way. The material in par 9.12, fn 47 is equally applicable to this section.

55 For the usual method of proof see par 9.12, fn 49.

56 An attempt may be defined as some act or acts by the accused, done with intent to commit the crime, the attempt of which the accused is charged with, which are more than merely preparatory of, but are proximate to, its commission or which point unequivocally in themselves towards the commission of the crime by the accused; for further discussion see par 2.32, 2.40-2.41.

57 Adopting the analysis of the House of Lords as to intent in *Moloney* [1985] AC 905; [1985] 1 All ER 1025; [1985] 2 WLR 648, 81 Cr App R 93; [1985] Crim LR 378 and *Hancock* [1986] 1 All ER 641; [1985] 3 WLR 1014; [1986] Crim LR 186. A fuller discussion of intent occurs in the context of murder in ch 2.

an explosion is not included as it is under subs (b). Where two people agree to cause such an explosion a conspiracy occurs. An agreement to do an unlawful act or to do a lawful act by unlawful means suffices as a definition, for our purposes; the offence being complete where agreement is reached between the conspirators.[58] The existence of such a conspiracy is, as in intent and in the absence of an admission by the accused, a matter of necessary inference from facts proved by the prosecution. In this context an agreement means a conscious understanding of a common design. The conspirators need not know each other or act simultaneously once they are actively part of a wider criminal enterprise knowing of its ultimate aim or criminal method.[59]

Under subs (b) it is an offence to make, possess or control an explosive substance with intent. The intent here required is that of endangering life or causing serious injury to property or of enabling any other person to endanger life or cause serious injury to property. As in subs (a) intent in this context is purposive and the remarks made and authorities cited previously are equally applicable.

External Elements

9.16 To "make" requires the accused to cause an explosive substance to exist where none was previously.[60] This is not difficult in the context of the wide definition of explosive substance.[61] If the accused takes a beer keg and cuts out a portion of the top with the purpose of making a "barrel bomb", that act of modification causes the keg to become an explosive substance. Such an act of itself is insufficient to prove guilt and the prosecution must prove the criminal intent as defined by the section. A note on possession follows the discussion of firearms and offensive weapons in chapter 11.

"Control" in this context requires the accused to actually have the explosive substance with him. Two or more persons can have control of a bomb whilst acting in pursuance of a common design[62] which involves the bomb being under their control. By way of distinction if the accused knows that the second accused will by a particular time have left a bomb for him in a particular place, once that is done, he will have possession of the bomb.[63] It is not until he goes and picks it up that the bomb is under his control. Every act of having a bomb under one's control will incorporate possession but not *vice versa*.[64] Further, the first accused can have control of a bomb and the second accused can have possession of it. Both concepts differ from ownership though the fact of ownership may be relevant in establishing

---

58   Per Cussen J in *Orton* [1922] VLR 469, 473 SC. The matter is further discussed at par 2.38.

59   *US v Bruno* (1939) 105 F (2d) 921 Circ CA, 2nd Circ, similarly *Blumenthal v US* (1947) 332 US 539. An extreme case is *Direct Sales v US* (1943) 319 US 703. The law as to conspiracy is fully discussed in vol 2; see also par 2.38.

60   The Shorter Oxford English Dictionary defines "make" as: "To produce by combination of parts, or by giving a certain form to a portion of matter; to construct, frame, fashion, bring into existence".

61   See par 9.05–9.08.

62   Control at par 10.22.

63   For a discussion see ch 11.

64   *Searl v Randolf* [1972] Crim LR 779 DC; *Peaston* (1978) 69 Cr App R 203; [1979] Crim LR 183 CA.

possession.[65] In the example the bomb left by the first accused for the second accused may be partly composed of a beer keg either stolen from B or supplied by B knowing that the offence of this type might be committed. The disparity in the range of possible circumstances prevents any necessary inference being drawn from the fact of ownership of itself.

The possession, control, or making of the explosive substance must be with the intent[66] of endangering life or causing serious injury to property. The section makes clear in respect of subs (a) and (b) that it does not affect liability if an explosion fails to take place, or if it does that no life or property was injured. Under subs (a) the explosion must be likely to endanger life or cause serious injury to property and, it is submitted, the accused must so intend.[67] Under subs (b) the nature of the explosion is irrelevant once the accused has the intent to make, possess or control the explosive so as to endanger life or cause serious injury to property. In practice however this difference is one of semantics only.

Suspicious Possession

9.17 The requirement of an intent to cause an explosion of a nature likely to endanger life or cause serious injury to property, as in s 2 and 3, is absent from s 4 of the Explosive Substances Act, 1883 which reads:

> (1) Any person who makes or knowingly has in his possession or under his control any explosive substance, under such circumstances as to give rise to a reasonable suspicion that he is not making it or does have it in his possession or under his control for a lawful object, shall, unless he can show that he made it or had it in his possession or under his control for a lawful object, be guilty of felony and, on conviction, shall be liable to penal servitude for a term not exceeding fourteen years, or to imprisonment for a term not exceeding two years with or without hard labour, and the explosive substance shall be forfeited.[68]
>
> (2) In any proceeding against any person for a crime under this section, such person and his wife, or husband, as the case may be, may, if such person thinks fit, be called, sworn, examined, and cross-examined as an ordinary witness in the case.

The concepts of making, having possession of an explosive, or having an explosive under one's control are common to s 4 and s 3(b) and the previous discussion is therefore not repeated.[69] An extraterritorial element is missing from s 4 in distinction from ss 2 and 3. However, under s 2 of the Criminal Law (Jurisdiction) Act, 1976 it

---

65   The concepts are used disjunctively and it seems incorrect to read them together as requiring and meaning only physical possession. That approach was however adopted by the Australian High Court in *Williams v Douglas* (1949) 78 CLR 521 that in that case the words were conjunctive "in his possession or control".

66   *Burton v Cooper* [1947] SASR 286 SC: "proof of ownership does not necessarily connote possession by the owner. A chattel may pass out of the custody of its owner. He will not necessarily retain possession. Where it is established that a particular person is the owner that may be an element, and it can be an important element in determining the present physical association of person and object. In some circumstances it will be sufficiently linked with proximity to indicate possession" per Mayo J at 293 citing *R v O'Meally* (No. 2) [1935] VLR 30 SC.

67   See par 9.15.

68   See par 9.12, fn 47. For a definition of "suspicion" and "inference" see par 10.31.

69   See par 9.16.

is an offence to possess explosives under these circumstances.[70] Irrespective of whether the accused is an Irish citizen or not, any offence committed under s 2, 3 and 4 of the Explosive Substances Act, 1883 in Northern Ireland constitutes an offence contrary to s 2 of the 1976 Act. That section states:

> 2(1) Where a person does in Northern Ireland an act that, if done in the State, would constitute an offence specified in the Schedule, he shall be guilty of an offence and he shall be liable on conviction on indictment to the penalty to which he would have been liable if he had done the act in the State.[71]

Reversed Proof

9.18 The provision of s 4(2) allowing an accused or the spouse of an accused to give evidence was, in 1883, an exception to the rule that an accused could not give evidence on his own behalf.[72] The provision exists to allow the accused to discharge the burden which the section places on him of proving a lawful object. That onus does not arise until the prosecution have proved possession in circumstances that make it suspicious. The scheme of the section was explained by Lord MacDermott LCJ in *Fegan*[73] thus:

> This provision illustrates a means of meeting a legislative problem recently considered by the House of Lords in *R v Warner* [1969] 2 AC 256; in relation to a charge of possessing drugs—the problem of how to curb a grave evil which postulates a guilty mind or mental element on the part of offenders, when proof of that guilty mind or mental element is likely to be a matter of inherent difficulty. S 4(1) of the Act of 1883 may be said to proceed by way of compromise. It does not make it an offence to possess explosive substances for an unlawful purpose, nor does it create an absolute offence by prohibiting the mere possession of explosive substances. Instead, its two limbs provide for a dual enquiry—(1) Was the person charged knowingly in possession under such circumstances as to give rise to a reasonable suspicion that his possession was not for a lawful object? and (2) If the answer to (1) is in the affirmative, has the person charged shown that his possession was for a lawful object? If the answer to (1) is in the affirmative and the answer to (2) in the negative a conviction follows; otherwise there must be an acquittal. The first limb allows for a conviction on reasonable *suspicion*. The second allows what may be very much a subjective defence, with the accused and his or her spouse permitted by s 4(2) (as an exception to the then existing law) to give evidence on oath as ordinary witnesses.

Probably the section may more properly be described as having three proofs. (1) Proof that the accused was knowingly in possession of an explosive substance,[74] (2) that such possession was in circumstances giving rise to a reasonable suspicion that the accused did not have it in his possession for a lawful object and (3) the absence of proof by the accused, on the balance of probabilities, that his possession was for

---

70 See par 9.02.

71 The remaining sub-sections deal with the liabilities of parties and inchoate aspects of the offence. The workings of the section are debated by the Court of Criminal Appeal in *The People (DPP) v Campbell & Others* (1983) 2 Frewen 131.

72 In England an accused and the spouse of an accused were granted the right to give evidence in s 1 of the Criminal Evidence Act, 1898, which did not extend to Ireland. Saorstát Éireann followed suit and passed an almost identical act in the Criminal Justice (Evidence) Act, 1924.

73 [1972] NI 80 at 82 CCA.

74 Knowingly in this context means awareness that it is an explosive.

a lawful object. The prosecution may use proof of the first element to infer the second:

> What he had in his possession may be gelignite, dynamite or gunpowder, but if he had it in his possession under such circumstances as to give rise to suspicion that he had it for something other than a lawful object, it is only a short step then for the jury, taking into account all the circumstances, to decide that he knew quite well that it was an explosive substance and that he had it in his possession for an unlawful purpose.[75]

Knowing possession is what is specified in s 4 in contrast to s 2 and 3. S 2 requires malice (intent or recklessness) and s 3 requires intent as the mental element of the crime. Knowledge that the object or substance is an explosive is therefore essential in order to satisfy the requirements of the individual sections.[76] It is legally impossible to have malice under s 2 or intent under s 3 without knowledge that the object is an explosive. In distinction under s 4 as the accused may be in possession of an object, not knowing it is a bomb, in objectively suspicious circumstances. He will commit no offence in the absence of proof that he knew what the object was. The word "knowingly" is therefore essential to the validity of a charge under s 4.[77]

In English law it is well settled that where a statute places a burden of proof on an accused in a criminal trial it may be discharged by evidence on the balance of probabilities.[78] If the accused is found in possession of a bomb under suspicious circumstances he must give evidence. If that evidence, consistent with innocence, could reasonably be true he would be entitled in ordinary course of a criminal trial to an acquittal.[79] But in cases such as s 4 the settled line of authority obliges him to go beyond that proof and show that his explanation, consistent with innocence, is likely to be true.[80] This is referred to as the persuasive burden of proof. Consequently a person may be convicted of a criminal charge despite the existence of a reasonable doubt as to his guilt. Where the law places a requirement on an accused of proving his innocence as a probability a situation may occur where a reasonable bystander would doubt the guilty of the accused. Despite this, on a traditional analysis, he must be convicted. Guilt is manufactured on a basis that is no more than legally mechanistic.[81] In Canada conviction by this means has been subject to constitutional reform.[82] In England the Law Reform Commission have recommended that where

---

75 Per Lord Goddard LCJ in *Hallam* [1957] 1 QB 569 at 573; [1957] 1 All ER 665 at 666, [1957] 2 WLR 521 at 523, 41 Cr App R 111 at 115 CCA.

76 It can be argued that possession consists of a legally sufficient degree of control, knowledge that the accused has that control and knowledge of recklessness as to the illicit nature of the object possessed; see ch 11.

77 *Stewart* (1959) 44 Cr App R 29 CCA; the proviso can be applied; *McVitie* [1960] 2 QB 483; [1960] 2 All ER 498; [1960] 3 WLR 99, 44 Cr App R 201 CCA.

78 *Carr-Briant* [1943] KB 607; [1943] 2 All ER 156, 29 Cr App R 76 CCA. This rule applies to all criminal statutes which place an evidential burden on the accused; *Jayesena v R* [1970] AC 618, [1970] 1 All ER 219; [1970] 2 WLR 448 PC.

79 *The People (A-G) v Oglesby* [1966] IR 162 CCA.

80 Fn 79.

81 The rule has been subjected to sustained academic criticism; see for example Williams, "The Evidential Burden—Some Common Misapprehensions" (1977) 127 NLJ 156 and "Evidential Burdens on the Defence" (1977) 127 NLJ 182.

82 *Oakes*, 26 DLR (4th) 200 SC.

a burden of proof is cast on an accused that it should be evidential only; that is the duty to give or adduce evidence which a properly instructed jury would be entitled to hold raised a reasonable doubt as to guilt.[83]

Proposed Solution

9.19 Under s 15 of the Misuse of Drugs Act, 1977 an accused will be presumed to have controlled drugs in his possession for the purpose of supplying them to another if the circumstances, including particularly the quantity of the drug in the accused's possession, make such an inference reasonable. The accused must then satisfy the court that his possession was not for such a purpose. This section, similarly, on a traditional analysis, requires the accused to prove, on the balance of probabilities, that his purpose in possessing the drug was not to supply it to another. In trials under this section Judge Moriarty has subjected the section to an analysis which avoids the potential injustice of a conviction where a reasonable doubt as to guilt exists. He informs the jury that the presumption arises only where the quantity of drugs in the possession of the accused, and/or the circumstances under which the drugs were found in his possession, are such as to reasonably raise an inference that they were possessed for the purpose of supplying them to another. If reliance is placed by the prosecution on the quantity alone the jury are instructed that it must be the kind of quantity which it is reasonable to infer a drug supplier would have. He tells the jury though the presumption will assist them in their deliberations that they should not convict the accused unless, on a consideration of the whole of the evidence, including the explanation given by the accused, they are satisfied beyond reasonable doubt that the drugs were possessed for the purpose of supplying them to another. In effect the accused must give evidence and so subject himself to cross-examination, but he need do no more to be acquitted than raise a reasonable doubt.

It is submitted that this valuable analysis should be applied to all cases where a persuasive burden of proof is cast on the accused. The real object of such sections is to require the accused, against whom a case has been made, on the prosecution evidence with the assistance of a presumption, to enter the witness box and subject himself to the scrutiny of cross- examination. A statutory presumption or inference should not be used to manufacture the guilt of an accused person where he has given evidence and the jury consider that such evidence has raised a reasonable doubt as to his guilt. In such circumstances, it is submitted, the only correct direction to the jury is that used by Judge Moriarty. Reliance on the persuasive burden to convict persons where there exists a reasonable doubt as to their innocence is constitutionally suspect.[84] The Quebec Court of Appeal has held, on constitutional grounds, that an accused is required merely to adduce evidence which raises a reasonable doubt or which might reasonably be true, in order to rebut a presumption.[85]

---

83   Criminal Law Revisions Committee 11th Report—Evidence (General), (Cmnd 4991) par 140 and the cases therein cited. A possible statutory draft compromise would be to provide that the accused must give evidence once a prima facie case has been established against him but that thereafter he had only to raise a reasonable doubt as to his lawful purpose.

84   In *Brauer* (1989) 45 Crim R 109 the Supreme Court of Queensland were content to tinker with the reversed onus, Thomas J holding that the evidence required to discharge an evidential burden may be lessened where an adversary is in a better position to know and prove essential facts.

85   *Dubois* (1990) 62 CCC (3d) 90 CA Quebec; Ellis, *Don Ltd* (1990) 61 CCC (3d) 423) CA Ontario.

Lawful Object

9.20 In *Fegan*[86] it was accepted that self-defence was a lawful object within the meaning of s 4. The accused and his wife were in possession of a pistol and ammunition. Since marrying outside their respective Christian denominations they had been subjected to severe harassment and the threat of violence from racists. Consequently they wished to defend themselves. The limits on the extent of the defence were stated thus by Lord MacDermott LCJ:[87]

> Possession of a firearm for the purpose of protecting the possessor or his wife or family from acts of violence, *may* be possession for a lawful object. But the lawfulness of such a purpose cannot be founded on a mere fancy, or on some aggressive motive. The threatened danger must be reasonably and genuinely anticipated, must appear reasonably imminent, and must be of a nature that could not reasonably be met by more specific means.

The fact that the possession of explosives is unlawful in itself[88] does not render the purpose for which it is held unlawful.[89] Where the threat, which makes the object of the possession lawful, passes the accused will not be able to make out a defence under the section as there will then be nothing on which to plead a lawful object.[90] A lawful object is not confined to an object within the jurisdiction, or in accordance with Irish law, but can be aimed at a foreign state once it is proved that the object is lawful within the law of that jurisdiction.[91]

Other Explosives Offences

9.21 Further explosives offences are contained in the Offences Against the Person Act, 1861, but as these are rarely used the sections will simply be quoted:

> 12 Whosoever, by the explosion of gunpowder or other explosive substance, shall destroy or damage any building with intent to commit murder, shall be guilty of felony, and being convicted thereof shall be liable to be kept in penal servitude for life.[92]
>
> 28 Whosoever shall unlawfully and maliciously, by the explosion of gunpowder or other explosive substance, burn, maim, disfigure, disable, or do any grievous bodily harm to any person, shall be guilty of felony, and being convicted thereof shall be liable, at the discretion of the court, to be kept in penal servitude for life or to be imprisoned and, if a male under the age of sixteen years, with or without whipping.[93]

---

86 [1972] NI 80 CCA. As to the limitations imposed on similar sections of the Firearms Act (NI) 1969 see *Porte* [1973] NI 198.

87 *Fegan* [1972] NI 80 at 8788 CCA.

88 Under the Dangerous Substances Act, 1972 or the legislation now in force; see par 9.02-9.03.

89 Attorney General's Reference (No. 2 of 1983) [1984] AC 456; [1984] QB 456; [1984] 1 All ER 988; [1984] 2 WLR 465, 78 Cr App R 183; [1984] Crim LR 289 CA.

90 Fn 89.

91 *Berry* [1985] AC 246; [1984] 3 All ER 1008; [1984] 3 WLR 1274, 80 Cr App R 98; [1985] Crim LR 102 HL.

92 The sections are quoted, as are all other sections from the Offences Against the Person Act, 1861, in accordance with the amendments introduced by the Penal Servitude Acts of 1864 and 1891 and by the Statute Law Revision Act, 1908.

93 Where an intent to disable is alleged the prosecution do not have to prove the intent was to disable permanently; *James* (1980) 70 Cr App R 215 CA.

29 Whosoever shall unlawfully and maliciously cause any gunpowder or other explosive substance to explode, or send or deliver to or cause to be taken or received by any person any explosive substance or any other dangerous or noxious thing, or put or lay at any place, or cast or throw at or upon or otherwise apply to any person, any corrosive fluid or any destructive or explosive substance, with intent in any of the cases aforesaid to burn, maim, disfigure, or disable any person, or to do some grievous bodily harm to any person, shall, whether any bodily injury be effected or not, be guilty of felony, and being convicted thereof shall be liable, at the discretion of the court, to be kept in penal servitude for life or to be imprisoned and, if a male under the age of sixteen years, with or without whipping.

30 Whosoever shall unlawfully and maliciously place or throw in, into, upon, against, or near any building, ship or vessel any gunpowder or other explosive substance, with intent to do any bodily injury to any person, shall, whether or not any explosion take place, and whether or not any bodily injury be effected, be guilty of felony, and being convicted thereof shall be liable, at the discretion of the court, to be kept in penal servitude for any term not exceeding fourteen years and, if a male under the age of sixteen years, with or without whipping.

64 Whosoever shall knowingly have in his possession, or make or manufacture, any gunpowder, explosive substance, or any dangerous or noxious thing, or any machine, engine, instrument, or thing, with intent by means thereof to commit, or for the purpose of enabling any other person to commit, any of the felonies in this act mentioned, shall be guilty of misdemeanour, and being convicted thereof shall be liable, at the discretion of the court, to be imprisoned for any term not exceeding two years, with or without hard labour and, if a male under the age of sixteen years, with or without whipping.[94]

9.22 It is a felony, punishable by imprisonment for two years or penal servitude for life, contrary to s 9 of the Malicious Damage Act, 1861 "unlawfully and maliciously, by explosion to destroy, throw down, or damage the whole or any part of any dwelling house, any person being therein, or any building whereby the life of any person shall be endangered". It is further a felony, punishable by up to fourteen years' penal servitude contrary to s 10 of the Malicious Damage Act, 1861 to "unlawfully and maliciously place or throw in, into, upon, under, against, or near any building any gunpowder or other explosive substance with intent to destroy or damage any building, or any engine, machinery, working tools, fixtures, goods or chattels, whether or not any explosion take place, and whether or not any damage be caused".

Draft Indictments

9.23 There follow the appropriate forms of indictment for the offences considered in this chapter.

CAUSING AN EXPLOSION

Statement of Offence

Causing an explosion, contrary to s 2 of the Explosive Substances Act, 1883 as substituted by s 4 of the Criminal Law (Jurisdiction) Act, 1976.

94   Under s 65 a District Justice on reasonable cause being given on oath that an explosive, dangerous or noxious substance is being made, kept or carried for the purpose of committing any felony in the act, may issue a warrant for searching any place in which the same is suspected.

Particulars of Offence

AB on the (being an Irish citizen)[95] at (in outside the State)[96] unlawfully and maliciously, by an explosive substance, caused an explosion of a nature likely to endanger life or cause serious injury to property.[97]

POSSESSION OF AN EXPLOSIVE SUBSTANCE

Statement of Offence

Possession of an explosive substance with intent, contrary to s 3 of the Explosive Substances Act, 1883 as substituted by s 4 of the Criminal Law (Jurisdiction) Act, 1976.

Particulars of Offence

AB on the (being an Irish citizen)[98] at (in outside the State)[99] unlawfully and maliciously had in his possession an explosive substance, to wit with intent by means thereof to endanger life or cause serious injury to property or to enable any other person so to do.[1]

SUSPICIOUS POSSESSION

Statement of Offence

Possession of an explosive substance in suspicious circumstances contrary to s 4 of the Explosive Substances Act, 1883.

Particulars of Offence

AB on the had in his possession an explosive substance, to wit under such circumstances as to give rise to a reasonable suspicion that he did not have it in his possession for a lawful object.

IN NORTHERN IRELAND

Statement of Offence

Possession of an explosive substance, with intent, contrary to s 2(1) of the Criminal Law (Jurisdiction) Act, 1976.

Particulars of Offence

AB on the at Northern Ireland, unlawfully and maliciously had in his possession an explosive substance, to wit with intent by means thereof to endanger life or cause serious injury to property or to enable any other person so to do.

Note: For other offences see the schedule to the Act and s 2 thereof.

---

95 To be inserted if the accused did this act outside the State but was an Irish citizen. If the act was done outside the State and in Northern Ireland, but AB was not an Irish citizen the indictment should be under s 2 of the Criminal Law (Jurisdiction) Act, 1976.

96 Fn 95.

97 Stated in the alternative under rule 5 of the Criminal Procedure Act, 1924 permitting this as an exception to the rule that an indictment is bad for duplicity.

98 Fn 95.

99 Fn 95.

1 Fn 97.

CHAPTER TEN

Firearms

10.01 The essential law regulating the use and possession of firearms is contained in five Acts of the Oireachtas: The Firearms Acts, 1925, 1964 and 1971, the Firearms & Offensive Weapons Act, 1990 which came into force on 1 January 1991[1] and, of lesser importance for our purposes, the Firearms (Proofing) Act, 1968.[2] The definition of a firearm changed on 1 January 1991. We consider it useful to set out both definitions in the text to take account of offences prior to that date. The definitional changes introduced are, however, of little importance in the context of the interpretation already given in this text to the existing definitions.

These Acts repealed and replaced the earlier United Kingdom statute, the Firearms Act, 1920. The present United Kingdom legislation is complex; firearms are divided into three categories; firearms, shotguns or air weapons. Each have special and distinct provisions.

Scheme

10.02 The scheme of our legislation imposes an absolute prohibition on the possession, use or carrying of firearms and ammunition[3] subject to a range of exceptions[4] on the holding of a firearms certificate or a certificate[5] authorising the possession of a firearms silencer.[6] Serious offences are created by the legislation of possession of a firearm or ammunition with intent to endanger life or cause serious injury to property;[7] possession of a firearm or imitation firearm whilst taking a vehicle without the consent of the owner;[8] using or producing a firearm or imitation firearm to resist arrest or to aid escape;[9] possession of a firearm or ammunition in

---

1   Which was passed on 12 June 1990. Part 2 of the Act which amends the definition of firearms commenced, by Ministerial order, on 1 January 1991.

2   Which came into operation on 16 April 1969 by virtue of the Firearms (Proofing) Act, 1968 (Commencement) Order, 1969. SI 64 of 1969.

3   S 2 of the 1925 Act as amended and substituted in part by s 3 of the 1971 Act.

4   S 2(3), (4) and (5) of the 1925 Act as amended and inserted by s 15 of the 1964 Act, s 16(4) as amended by s 5 of the 1990 Act, s 8 of the 1968 Act, s 3(c) of the 1971 Act, s 6 of the 1990 Act.

5   S 2 to s 8 (incl) of the 1925 Act as amended and substituted in part by s 9, 10, 11, 12, 13 and 16 of the 1964 Act and s 3 of the 1971 Act. Under s 24 of the 1964 Act the onus of proving an exception is on the accused.

6   S 7 of the 1925 Act.

7   S 15 of the 1925 Act as amended by s 4 of the 1971 Act, s 21(4) of the Criminal Law (Jurisdiction) Act, 1976 and s 14(1) of the Criminal Justice Act, 1984.

8   S 26 of the 1964 Act as amended by s 21(6)(b) of the Criminal Law (Jurisdiction) Act, 1976 and s 14(2) of the Criminal Justice Act, 1984.

9   S 27 of the 1964 Act as amended by s 21(6)(c) of the Criminal Law (Jurisdiction) Act, 1976 and s 14(3) of the Criminal Justice Act, 1984.

suspicious circumstances;[10] having a firearm or imitation firearm with intent to commit an indictable offence or to prevent or resist arrest;[11] and reckless discharge of a firearm.[12] Certain other offences of lesser importance are also considered.

The following offences are scheduled offences under the Criminal Law (Jurisdiction) Act, 1976:

Possessing a firearm or ammunition with intent to endanger life or cause serious injury to property contrary to s 15 of the Firearms Act, 1964, as amended;

Possession of a firearm while taking a vehicle without authority contrary to s 26 of the Firearms Act, 1964, as amended;

Use of a firearm to resist or aid escape contrary to s 27 of the Firearms Act, 1964, as amended;

Possession of a firearm or ammunition in suspicious circumstances contrary to s 27A of the Firearms Act, 1964, as amended;

Carrying a firearm with criminal intent contrary to s 27B of the Firearms Act, 1964, as amended.

This means that where such an offence is committed in Northern Ireland it constitutes an offence contrary to s 2(1) of that Act.[13]

Definition

10.03 The Acts make mention of three categories of weapon: firearm, sporting firearm and prohibited weapon. This latter category was not subject to amendment on the coming into force of the 1990 Act.

Prohibited Weapon

10.04 The Firearms Act, 1925 provides in s 1:

> In this Act—the expression "prohibited weapon" means and includes any weapon of whatever description designed for the discharge of any noxious liquid, noxious gas, or other noxious thing, and also any ammunition (whether for any such weapon as aforesaid or for any other weapon) which contains or is designed or adapted to contain any noxious liquid, noxious gas, or other noxious thing;

S 14 of the 1925 Act provided that it was an offence for a person, without the authority of the Minister for Defence, to manufacture, sell, purchase, hire, let, use, carry, possess or have in custody or control or knowingly have on the premises a prohibited weapon. This section was repealed by s 28 of the 1964 Act but s 2(1) of the 1964 Act brought prohibited weapons under the provisions applicable to firearms, simplifying the scheme of the legislation.[14] Devices which stun or disable

---

10 S 27A of the 1964 Act as inserted by s 8 of the Criminal Law (Jurisdiction) Act, 1976 and amended by s 14(4) of the Criminal Justice Act, 1984.

11 S 27B of the 1964 Act as inserted by s 9 of the Criminal Law (Jurisdiction) Act, 1976 and amended by s 14(5) of the Criminal Justice Act, 1984. The latter Act increased the penalty in all the foregoing cases (fn 5-9) but this should not be construed as having retrospective effect; *Deery* [1977] NI 164 CCA.

12 S 8 Firearms & Offensive Weapons Act, 1990.

13 This section is quoted at par 9.12. For precedent indictments see the end of this chapter.

14 Contrast the definition in the United Kingdom legislation contained in s 5 of the Firearms Act, 1968 as amended by the Firearms (Amendment) Act, 1988.

by discharging electricity through electrodes[15] or weapons which discharge incapacitating gas or liquid are firearms[16] because they are offensive weapons. If such a device operates through explosion, for example of compressed air or chemicals they will be outlawed by s 2, 3 and 4 of the Explosives Substances Act, 1883.[17]

Firearm

10.05 The definition of firearm is clarified by considering the definition prior to 1 January 1991. The amendment to the definition of a firearm contained in s 4 of the Firearms & Offensive Weapons Act, 1990 came into force on that date. The prior definition is best approached by setting out the various provisions which effect that task:[18]

> In this Act

1925   1(1) The word "firearm" means a lethal firearm or other lethal weapon of any description from which any shot, bullet, or other missile can be discharged;

1964   1(1) In the Principal Act and this Act, "firearm" shall include an airgun (which expression includes an air rifle or an air pistol) and any other weapon incorporating a barrel from which metal or other slugs can be discharged and a prohibited weapon.

1971   1(2) and, save where the context otherwise requires, includes a component part of a firearm.

1925   26(1) Nothing in this Act relating to firearms shall apply to any antique firearm which is sold, bought, carried, or possessed as a curiosity or ornament.[19]

Apart from the special category of prohibited weapon, it is clear that a firearm is a weapon which discharges shot, bullets, or missiles, by any means, including air, or is a barrelled weapon from which metal or other slugs may be discharged, the effect of such can be, in any such case, to cause death. It is not required that a prohibited weapon, in contrast, have lethal effect. The corresponding United Kingdom legislation requires that firearms have a barrel.[20] In the Irish legislation it appears to be correct to read the 1964 Act as adding a new category of weapon (barrelled weapons from which metal or other slugs may be discharged) onto an existing

---

15   Manufactured for commercial sale on the continent of Europe. Electric sticks are used to control cattle.

16   For example the types of anti-personnel canisters of gas (usually ammonia) carried by persons as a protection against mugging. Noxious in this context will have the same meaning as under the Offences Against the Person Act, 1861; *Cramp* (1880) 5 QBD 307, 14 Cox 401 CCR. For a full discussion see ch 5 and ch 7.

17   See par 9.05.

18   S 1(3) of the 1964 Act, s 7(3) of the 1971 Act. The 1968 Act does not so provide but provides at s 1 that the 1925 Act is the Principal Act and adopts the definition of firearms from that Act as amended and provides at s 14(2) that the 1925, 1964 and that Act may be cited together as the Firearms Acts, 1925-1990. As all the Acts amend one another, have overlapping provisions and deal with the same subject matter they should all be construed as one act.

19   See par 10.08. Under s 6 of the 1990 Act a superintendent of a district may grant an authorisation to entitle a person to have a disabled firearm in his possession where he is satisfied that the person has a good reason for wishing to keep it and may be permitted to do so without danger to the public safety or the peace.

20   S 57, Firearms Act, 1968 UK. The history of the definition of a firearm in the UK is traced in *Freeman* [1970] 2 All ER 413; [1970] 1 WLR 788, 54 Cr App R 251 CA.

definition, expanded to include airguns.[21] The intention of using the words "or other lethal weapon" in addition to firearm would include weapons which are not firearms but which could discharge missiles. The word "discharge" indicates an expulsion from the weapon.[22] That expression would not exclude the use of a funnel or chute in substitution for a barrel. The definition contained in s 4 of the 1990 Act[23] specifically includes within the definition of a firearm, a crossbow and any type of stun gun or other weapon for causing any shock or other disablement to a person by means of electricity or any other kind of energy emission.

Objective Test

10.06 The question of whether a weapon is or is not a firearm is an objective one. It is irrelevant that a particular object was not manufactured for use as a firearm but, for example, as a signal pistol.[24] Moreover the amendment introduced by s 3 of the 1971 Act captures component parts of firearms.[25] S 4 of the 1990 Act extends the range of that definition to certain telescopic sights and to silencers.[26] Where a firearm is incapable of discharging shots without being modified, the fact that it can be modified will include it in the definition of a component part of a firearm.[27] A weapon which has its firing mechanism removed still remains a firearm or a component part of a firearm.[28] The question of whether if the accused perceived the weapon as being something other than a firearm it will afford him a defence is discussed under the heading 'Possession' in chapter 11.

Lethal

10.07 A firearm must be lethal.[29] Prohibited weapons do not have to be lethal. In *Thorpe*[30] the United Kingdom Court of Appeal rejected a submission that the word "lethal" should be construed as requiring proof that the weapon was capable of causing injuries of a more than trivial nature and of a kind which it might reasonably be expected could lead to death. The Court considered itself bound by the earlier

21 S 2(1) of the 1964 Act. The 1920 Act read as s 12(1): "In this Act, unless the context otherwise requires—The expression 'firearm' means any lethal firearm or other weapon of any description from which any shot, bullet or other missile can be discharged, or any part thereof. . . ."

22 The Shorter Oxford English Dictionary defines discharge as: "2. The act of discharging a weapon or missile; firing off a firearm; letting fly an arrow, etc.".

23 See par 10.09.

24 *Read v Donovan* [1947] KB 326; [1947] 1 All ER 37, DC. Decided under s 32(1) of the Firearms Act, 1937 which defined "firearm" as: ". . . any lethal barrelled weapon of any description from which any shot, bullet or other missile can be discharged . . .".

25 See *Clarke* [1986] 1 All ER 846; [1986] 1 WLR 209, 82 Cr App R 308; [1986] Crim LR 334 CA.

26 See par 10.09.

27 *Caffetera v Wilson* [1936] 3 All ER 149, followed in *Freeman*.

28 *Clarke*, fn 25, applying *Pannell* [1983] 76 Cr App R 53; [1982] Crim LR 752 CA, and overruling *Jobling* [1981] Crim LR 625. These cases are on modifications to machine guns to attempt to take them out of the category of prohibited weapon under the then UK legislation, the 1968 Act, and render them merely firearms. The principle remains as stated.

29 The Shorter Oxford English Dictionary defines "lethal" as: "1. That may or will cause death; deadly, mortal. Now esp. of a dose of poison: sufficient to cause death. 1613".

30 [1987] 2 All ER 108; [1987] 1 WLR 383, 85 Cr App R 107; [1987] Crim LR 493 CA.

authority of *Moore v Gooderhan*[31] and the purposive interpretation given to the legislation in that case by Lord Parker CJ:

> . . . I think that [the justices] were fully entitled to give to the word "lethal" the sense that the injury must be of a kind which may cause death. That is the ordinary meaning of the word, but it is to be observed that in this connection one is not considering whether a firearm is designed or intended to cause injury from which death results, but rather whether it is a weapon which, however misused, may cause injury from which death may result. S 19 is designed to prevent, amongst other things, a weapon getting into the hands of a very small child who may misuse it by firing it point blank, and point blank, say, at an eye or an ear, or some particularly vulnerable part; and if it is capable of causing more than trifling or trivial injury when misused, then it is a weapon which is capable of causing injury from which death may result . . . I find it quite impossible on that finding to say that this was not a weapon which, when misused, was capable of causing injury from which death might result.[32]

Antique

10.08 The limited exception in the case of antique firearms depends on their objectively coming within that category and on the person dealing in, carrying or possessing them as objects of curiosity or ornaments. A person keeping an ancient flintlock musket in order to kill game or frighten would-be intruders would have possession of a firearm notwithstanding its age. In England it has been held that an honest and reasonable belief that a weapon was an antique affords no defence.[33] Whether such a weapon is, in fact, an antique is a question of fact and degree and the courts in England have refused to specify a particular age at which an article can properly be so described.[34] The stricture of this definition has caused the Oireachtas to insert a new exception allowing persons to hold a firearm lacking a necessary component part. This exception is contained in s 6(1) of the 1990 Act:[35]

6(1)   The Superintendent of the Garda Síochána of a district may grant an authorisation in writing to a person resident in the district, not being a person disentitled under the Firearms Acts, 1925-1990, to hold a firearm certificate, to have in his possession, without a firearm certificate, a firearm where he is satisfied that the firearm would not be a firearm but for s 4(1)(f) and that the person has a good reason for wishing to keep it and may be permitted to do so without danger to the public safety or the peace.

(2)   The superintendent of the district where the holder of an authorisation under this

---

31   [1960] 3 All ER 575; [1960] 1 WLR 1308 DC.

32   [1960] 3 All ER 575 at 576-77; [1960] 1 WLR 1308 at 1310-11. A lethal barrelled weapon may be so damaged or altered, whether by accident or design, or by the removal of so many components that it ceases to be a lethal weapon but in these circumstances the accused may still have possession of a component part of a firearm; *Clarke* [1986] 1 All ER 846; [1985] 1 WLR 209, 82 Cr App R 308; [1986] Crim LR 334 CA.

33   *Howells* [1977] QB 614; [1977] 3 All ER 417; [1977] 2 WLR 716, 65 Cr App R 86; [1977] Crim LR 354 CA.

34   *Richards v Curwen* [1977] 3 All ER 426; [1977] 1 WLR 747, 65 Cr App R 95; [1977] Crim LR 356 DC. The over 100 years old test was rejected by the Divisional Court in that case. In *Bennett v Brown* (1980) 71 Cr App R 109 the Divisional Court again rejected a test of over 100 years old and doubted that a firearm available for service in either World Wars in this century could be an antique.

35   In force since 1 January 1991.

section resides, may, at any time, attach to the authorisation any conditions, whether as regards safe custody or otherwise, which he considers necessary and may at any time revoke the authorisation.

The provision emphasises again that a firearm including a necessary component remains a firearm under the Acts.

Altered Definition

10.09 On the coming into force of Part II of the 1990 Act the definition of a "firearm" discussed above has been repealed. The current definition is contained in s 4 of the 1990 Act:

4(1)   In the Firearms Acts, 1925 to 1990, "firearm" means:
(a) a lethal firearm or other lethal weapon of any description from which any shot, bullet or other missile can be discharged;
(b) an air gun (which expression includes an air rifle and an air pistol) or any other weapon incorporating a barrel from which metal or other slugs can be discharged;
(c) a crossbow;
(d) any type of stun gun or other weapon for causing any shock or other disablement to a person by means of electricity or any other kind of energy emission;
(e) a prohibited weapon as defined in s 1(1) of the Firearms Act, 1925;
(f) any article which would be a firearm under any of the foregoing paragraphs but for the fact that, owing to the lack of a necessary component part or parts, or to any other defect or condition, it is incapable of discharging a shot, bullet or other missile or of causing a shock or other disablement (as the case may be);
(g) save where the context otherwise requires, any component part of any article referred to in any of the foregoing paragraphs and, for the purposes of this definition, the following articles shall be deemed to be such component parts as aforesaid:
(i) telescope sights with a light beam, or telescope sights, with an electronic light amplification device or an infra-red device, designed to be fitted to a firearm specified in paragraph (a), (b), (c) or (e), and
(ii) a silencer designed to be fitted to a firearm specified in paragraph (a), (b) or (e).

This definition differs from the prior definition by making it clear that a crossbow is subject to the control of the Firearms Acts, 1925 to 1990 and by including, as a component part of a firearm, both telescopic sights of the kind defined in s 4(1)(g) and silencers designed to be fitted to firearms. The inclusion of a "stun gun" is a welcome clarification but was unnecessary as the weapon described in s 4(1)(d) would have come, in any event, under the definition of "a prohibited weapon".[36]

Ammunition

10.10 The definition of ammunition is untouched by the 1990 Act. The provisions of the Acts in relation to ammunition are largely self-explanatory:

1925   1 The word "ammunition" (except where used in relation to a prohibited weapon) means ammunition for a firearm but also includes grenades, bombs, and other similar missiles whether the same are or are not capable of being used with a firearm, and also includes any ingredient or component part of any such ammunition or missile;

2 The provisions of this Act relating to ammunition shall be in addition to and not in derogation of any enactment relating to the keeping and sale of explosives.

36   See par 10.03.

Almost all ammunition will also be an explosive within the meaning of the Explosive Substances Act, 1883.[37] Ammunition generally works by exploding and expelling a missile or missiles and air and gas guns fire by causing compressed air or gas to explode with similar effect. The only exception would be those firearms which operate by non-explosive mechanical means, for example, crossbows. If an explosion is integral to the operation of either the firearm, or the ammunition which can be used in that firearm, the Explosive Substances Act, 1883 will also apply in addition to the Firearms Acts.

Imitation Firearm

Imitation firearms do not fire missiles. They are used to cause fear. The offences in respect of imitation firearms are more specific and limited than those in respect of firearms.[38] The definition is contained in s 25 of the 1964 Firearms Act:

> In this section and the next two sections "imitation firearm" means anything which is not a firearm but has the appearance of being a firearm.

In *Morris and King*[39] the imitation consisted of two pipes bound with tape and covered at the butt end with material. The Court of Appeal held that the relevant time in judging whether a thing is an imitation firearm is when the offence is alleged to have been committed and:

> In considering whether or not the thing looked like a firearm at that time, the jury are entitled to have regard to the evidence of any witnesses who actually saw the thing at that time, together with their own observation of the thing itself, if they have seen it. . . .[40]

The equivalent United Kingdom section excludes things which look like "any weapon of whatever description designed or adapted for the discharge of any noxious liquid, gas or other thing"; there is no such exclusion in the Irish legislation.

Basic Prohibition

10.11 The basic offence under the Firearms Acts is of possession of a firearm or ammunition without holding a firearm certificate. S 2 of the 1925 Act, as amended by s 3 of the 1971 Act provides:

---

37   The main ammunition offences are contrary to s 2 and s 15 (as amended by s 4 of the 1971 Act, s 21(4) of the Criminal Law (Jurisdiction) Act, 1976 and s 14(1) of the Criminal Justice Act, 1984) of the 1925 Act and s 27A (as inserted by s 8 of the Criminal Law (Jurisdiction) Act, 1976 and amended by s 14(4) of the Criminal Justice Act, 1984) of the 1964 Act.

38   The offences are contrary to s 26 (as amended by s 21(6)(b) of the Criminal Law (Jurisdiction) Act, 1976 and s 14(2) of the Criminal Justice Act, 1984) and s 27(1) (as amended by s 21(6)(c) of the Criminal Law (Jurisdiction) Act, 1976 and s 14(3) of the Criminal Justice Act, 1984) and s 27B (as inserted by s 9 of the Criminal Law (Jurisdiction) Act, 1976 and amended by s 14(5) of the Criminal Justice Act, 1984) of the 1964 Act.

39   (1984) 79 Cr App R 104; [1984] Crim LR 422 CA; see also *Debrelli* [1964] Crim LR CCA. S 57(4) of the Firearms Act, 1968 UK defines imitation firearm as: "any thing which has the appearance of being a firearm . . . whether or not it is capable of discharging any shot, bullet or other missile. ...."

40   (1984) 79 Cr App R 104 at 107. And see *Sloan* (1974) 19 CCC (2d) 190.

1925   2(1) Subject to the exceptions from this section hereinafter mentioned, it shall not be lawful for any person after the commencement of this Act to have in his possession, use or carry any firearm or ammunition save in so far as such possession, use, or carriage is authorised by a firearm certificate granted under this Act and for the time being in force.

(2) Save in any of the cases hereinafter excepted from this section, every person who after the commencement of this Act has in his possession, uses, or carries any firearm without holding a firearm certificate therefor or otherwise than as authorised by such certificate, or purchases, uses, has in his possession, or carries any ammunition without holding a firearm certificate therefor or in quantities in excess of those authorised by such certificate, or fails to comply with any condition subject to which a firearm certificate was granted to him, shall be guilty of an offence under this section.[41]

1964   24(2) Where, in a prosecution for an offence under the Principal Act, possession, use or carriage of a firearm or ammunition by a person is proved, it shall not be necessary to prove that the person was not entitled to have in his possession, use or carry a firearm or ammunition.

10.12 The activities prohibited by the section are the possession, use or carrying of a firearm without a firearm certificate or outside the limitations the certificate may impose[42] and the purchase, use, possession, production of, or carrying of ammunition without a firearm certificate or in quantities in excess of those allowed by that certificate.[43] A purchase can be made, for example, by mail order; all the other activities are encapsulated in the concept of possession.[44]

The maximum penalty provided by the section is, on summary conviction, a fine of £200 and/or one year's imprisonment, and on indictment a fine of £500 and/or five years' imprisonment.[45] Where however the firearm is a sporting firearm and the accused is not in the position where he did not hold a firearm certificate in respect of that weapon which has been revoked, he may be prosecuted summarily and fined a maximum of £50, for a first offence, and thereafter may be penalised by imprisonment for up to three months in addition to that fine.[46] A sporting firearm is a shotgun with a barrel not less than 24" in length or an unrifled airgun, or a rifled firearm of a calibre not exceeding .22".[47]

Any kind of firearm may be declared, by ministerial order, to be especially

---

41   Not categorised as a felony or misdemeanour; under s 25 of the 1925 Act trial is indictable or summary at the option of the prosecution; arrest under s 22(3) of the 1925 Act on name and address being demanded by a Garda and refused or suspicion of falsehood, the power being exercisable by first asking for a firearm certificate; further power to stop, search and arrest and seize firearms or ammunition under s 22(4) of the 1925 Act on the belief of a Garda as to the possession, use, or carrying of a firearm or ammunition; scheduled under the Offences Against the State Act, 1939 and if the powers of search under s 29, as substituted by s 5 of the Criminal Law Act, 1976, and arrest under s 30 can be exercised. Overlapping powers of search are contained in s 7 and 8 of the Criminal Law Act, 1976. Offences contrary to s 15 of the 1925 Act, 26, 27, 27A and 27B of the 1964 Act are scheduled for extra territorial jurisdiction under s 2 of the Criminal Law (Jurisdiction) Act, 1976.

42   S 3(4) of the 1925 Act as substituted by s 16(b) of the 1964 Act (amount of ammunition) and s 12 of 1964 (limited use of a shotgun).

43   S 3(4) of the 1925 Act as substituted by s 16(b) of the 1964 Act.

44   See ch 11.

45   S 2A(b) of the 1925 Act as substituted by s 3 of the 1971 Act.

46   S 2A(a) of the 1925 Act as substituted by s 3 of the 1971 Act.

47   S 2B of the 1925 Act as substituted by s 3 of the 1971 Act.

dangerous and if so declared such firearm cannot be a sporting firearm notwithstanding that they otherwise fit the foregoing description. In 1972 the Minister declared all pistols and revolvers to be especially dangerous.[48] This distinction as between firearms and sporting firearms operates as to penalty only[49] and solely in respect of offences under s 2 of the 1925 Act. It is immaterial for all other purposes.

Exceptions

10.13 The exceptions to the general prohibition in s 2 of the 1925 Act are numerous. The burden of proving such an exception is on the accused.[50] Exceptions from s 2 are in the case of permit holders (firearm),[51] Army and Gardaí members acting in the course of duty (firearm and ammunition),[52] persons engaged ordinarily in the carriage or warehousing of goods for reward and their employees (firearm and ammunition),[53] possession as part of the equipment of a ship (firearm and ammunition),[54] gillies (firearm and ammunition),[55] slaughtering of animals by a humane killer (firearm and ammunition),[56] registered firearms dealers and their employees in the ordinary course of business (firearm and ammunition),[57] auctioneers and their employees authorised under s 13 of the 1964 Act acting in the ordinary course of business (firearm and ammunition),[58] members of an authorised rifle or gun club engaged in competition or practice at a range or authorised place (firearm and ammunition),[59] persons operating and using authorised fun fair rifle ranges where the firearm is not a shotgun and does not exceed .23″ in calibre (firearm and ammunition),[60] persons authorised to conduct theatre or cinema rehearsals, performances or productions and those under them (firearm and ammunition),[61] the starting of athletic races by an authorised person (firearm and blank ammunition),[62] authorised persons taking part in a ceremony (firearm and blank ammunition

---

48 Firearms (Dangerous Weapons) Order, SI 251 of 1972.
49 *The State (Gleeson) v District Justice Connellan* [1988] IR 559 SC.
50 S 24 of the 1964 Act which provides: "(1) Where, in a prosecution for an offence under the Principal Act, the existence or non-existence of a firearm certificate, a licence under s 17 of the Principal Act, an authorisation under s 2 of the Principal Act, a permit under s 3 of this Act or an authorisation under s 13 of this Act is material, it shall not be necessary to prove that the certificate, licence, authorisation or permit does not exist". Where burden of proof is on an accused such is discharged, traditionally, on the balance of probabilities: *Carr-Briant* [1943] KB 607; [1943] 2 All ER 156, 29 Cr App R 76 CCA. For a further discussion see par 9.18-9.19.
51 S 2(3)(a) of the 1925 Act (under s 7 of the 1925 Act bringing ships' firearms or ammunition ashore for repair (and s 3 of the 1964 Act) shooting game whilst temporarily prohibited).
52 S 2(3)(b) of the 1925 Act.
53 S 2(3)(d) and s 2(4)(b) of the 1925 Act as inserted by s 15 of the Act of 1964.
54 S 2(3)(e) of the 1925 Act, but these cannot be brought ashore without a permit under s 7.
55 S 2(3)(f) of the 1925 Act.
56 S 2(3)(g) of the 1925 Act as amended by s 15(a) of the 1964 Act.
57 S 2(3)(c) and s 2(4)(a) of the 1925 Act as inserted by s 15 of the 1964 Act.
58 S 2(4)(c) of the 1925 Act as inserted by s 15 of the 1964 Act.
59 S 2(4)(d) of the 1925 Act as inserted by s 15 of the 1964 Act.
60 S 2(4)(e) of the 1925 Act as inserted by s 15 of the 1964 Act.
61 S 2(4)(f) of the 1925 Act as inserted by s 15 of the 1964 Act.
62 S 2(4)(g) of the 1925 Act as inserted by s 15 of the 1964 Act.

supplied by the Minister for Defence),[63] persons carrying out duties in proofing firearms in the Institute for Industrial Research and Standards (firearm and ammunition),[64] authorised persons (component part of a firearm),[65] and under s 66(2) of the Postal and Telecommunications Services Act, 1983 employees of An Post carrying a packet in the course of their duties.

10.14 Authorisations in respect of such exemptions are granted by a Garda superintendent,[66] on a consideration of the public safety. He may impose conditions, a breach of which will carry, on summary conviction, a maximum penalty of a £50 fine and/or six months' imprisonment and on conviction on indictment a maximum penalty of a £100 fine and/or two years' imprisonment.[67] S 25 of the 1925 Act applies this penalty to all offences under the Act for which a penalty is not otherwise stated, and also gives the Court a power of forfeiture under s 23(1).

Firearm Certificate

10.15 The most important exception is that in respect of persons holding a firearm certificate. The Minister has a limited power to grant a firearm certificate to persons not ordinarily resident in the State.[68] Otherwise the task of granting firearm certificates and fixing conditions as to the amount of ammunition that may be possessed or carried at any one time[69] or, if the firearm is a shotgun, limiting the use of the gun to killing animals or birds other than game and only on specified lands,[70] falls to a Superintendent of An Garda Síochána. An authorised Sergeant may renew, but not refuse to renew, a firearm certificate.[71]

Firearm certificates last for one year up to 31 July,[72] Ministers' certificates last for one calendar year.[73] Persons who are not entitled to hold a certificate in respect of a firearm or ammunition are those under sixteen years of age,[74] of intemperate habits or unsound mind,[75] under sentence of imprisonment or penal servitude or whose sentence has expired within five years and was in respect of a crime in which a firearm or an imitation firearm was used or threatened, under sentence for a crime

---

63   S 2(4)(h) of the 1925 Act as inserted by s 15 of the 1964 Act.
64   S 2(4)(i) of the 1925 Act as inserted by s 8 of the Firearms Proofing Act, 1968.
65   S 2(4)(j) of the 1925 Act as inserted by s 3 of the 1971 Act.
66   S 2(5) of the 1925 Act as inserted by s 15 of the 1964 Act and amended by s 3(d) of the 1971 Act.
67   S 25 of the 1925 Act. Special conditions as to responsibility apply to officers of rifle and gun clubs; s 2(5)(c) of the 1925 Act as inserted by s 15 of the 1964 Act.
68   S 3(2) of the 1925 Act.
69   S 3(4) of the 1925 Act as substituted by s 16 of the 1964 Act.
70   S 12 of the 1964 Act; s 3(5) of the 1925 Act was repealed by s 28 of the 1964 Act. The conditions are set out in the special form prescribed by the Firearms Regulations, 1976, SI 239 of 1976. The firearm must have a number or identification mark which must be put on the certificate; ibid Form II and s 3(6) of the 1925 Act.
71   S 9(3) of the 1964 Act.
72   S 3(3) of the 1925 Act, s 9(2) of the 1964 Act.
73   S 10 of the 1964 Act.
74   S 8(1)(a) of the 1925 Act as amended by s 17 of the 1964 Act.
75   S 8(1)(b) and (c) of the 1925 Act.

involving assault or who have received a sentence of at least three months for a crime involving an assault which has not expired five years previously.[76] Other disentitled persons are those under police supervision[77] or who are bound to a recognisance not to have a firearm.[78] The Superintendent may only grant a firearm certificate if satisfied that the applicant has a genuine reason to require a firearm, will not endanger the public safety or peace thereby and is not disentitled.[79] The Superintendent may revoke a firearm certificate for those same reasons or where the firearm is being used outside the limits set by the certificate.[80] In making such a revocation it may be necessary to give the holder of the firearm certificate a chance to make representations. This is particularly so if the superintendent is taking into account more than one incident of acting, or taking into account his own view of the character of the holder.[81]

Imports & Exports

10.16 The exportation, consignment[82] and importation[83] of firearms and ammunition is prohibited except to holders of a firearm certificate.[84] A further exception is granted to exports and consignments by the Defence Forces[85] and imports under the authority of the Minister for Defence for the Garda Síochána or the Defence Forces.[86] Written authorisation by a superintendent is otherwise required for export or consignment.[87] A licence from the Minister is otherwise required for importation.[88]

S 5 of the 1990 Act prohibits a person from selling, transferring or otherwise disposing of a firearm or ammunition to a person or body in a country which is proscribed for the purposes of that section without the authorisation of the superintendent of the district who must be satisfied that the transaction is authorised by the competent authorities of that country.[89] This prohibition does not apply to crossbows and stun guns and telescopic sights for cross bows.

---

76 S 8(1)(d) and (e) of the 1925 Act as substituted by s 17 of the 1964 Act.
77 S 8(1)(f) of the 1925 Act.
78 S 8(1)(g) of the 1925 Act.
79 S 4 of the 1925 Act.
80 S 5 of the 1925 Act. In deciding to grant or revoke a firearm certificate the Superintendent is not bound by the Rules of Evidence, nor is a court considering an appeal from that decision (in this jurisdiction by way of judicial review): *Kavanagh v Chief Constable of Devon and Cornwall* [1974] QB 624; [1974] 2 All ER 697; [1974] 2 WLR 762 CA. For procedures dealing with the weapon see s 6 of the 1925 Act as substituted by s 8 of the 1964 Act.
81 *Hourigan v Kelly*, High Court, unreported 26 April 1991, Egan J.
82 S 16 of the 1925 Act as amended by s 20 of the 1964 Act.
83 S 17 of the 1925 Act as amended by s 21 of, and repealed in part by s 28 of the 1964 Act. Customs officers have the same powers as in ordinary contraband cases; s 18 of the 1925 Act.
84 S 16(4) of the 1925 Act as amended by s 20 of the 1964 Act (export and consignment); s 21(1) of the 1964 Act (import).
85 S 16(5) of the 1925 Act.
86 S 17(8) of the 1925 Act.
87 S 16(1) of the 1925 Act.
88 S 17 of the 1925 Act as amended by s 21 of, and repealed in part by s 28 of the 1964 Act.
89 Note the exception in s 16(4) which is specifically upheld by this section.

Dealers

10.17 Persons who deal in firearms must be registered.[90] They may be removed from the register if they cease to carry on, or have a place of business, as a firearms dealer, in the State, constitute a danger to the public safety or peace, have been convicted under the Firearms Acts[91] or have failed to comply with a condition[92] of registration.[93] Firearms dealers must keep a register of all transactions; recording them within twenty four hours[94] and notifying a sale to the superintendent by registered post within forty eight hours.[95] No one may sell a firearm or ammunition to anyone other than the holder of a firearm certificate or an accepted person but all such sales must be notified by registered post to the superintendent within forty eight hours.[96]

Auctioneers authorised by the superintendent may sell guns and ammunition.[97] Apart from auctioneers only registered firearms dealers may, by way of trade or business, sell, repair, test, prove, expose for sale, have in possession for sale, repair, test or proof any firearm or ammunition.[98] This prohibition does not apply to the Institute for Industrial Research and Standards.[99] "Sell", in this context, is defined as including "letting on hire, giving and lending".[1] Purchase, in this context, includes "hiring, receiving and borrowing" and cognate words are accordingly construed.[2]

Garda Powers

10.18 Any Garda may, at any reasonable time, enter and inspect the premises of a firearms dealer.[3] Gardaí may also enter, at any reasonable time, premises used for the manufacture, sale, repair, test or proof of firearms; the premises of any person engaged in the carrying of goods for reward; the premises of any person engaged in warehousing goods for reward, any pier, quay, wharf, jetty, dock or dock premises; or any ship, boat, railway wagon, motor, lorry, cart, or other vessel or vehicle used for the conveyance of goods.[4] While in such place a Garda may inspect firearms and ammunition and, on reasonably suspecting them to contain firearms or ammunition,

---

90   S 9 of the 1925 Act as amended by s 18 of the 1964 Act; registration lasts for one year and the Minister allows registration dependent on the character of the applicant, the number and the public safety and peace. The procedures and forms are in the Firearms Regulations, 1976 SI 239 of 1976.

91   S 11(2).

92   Under s 9(8) and (9) of the 1925 Act as substituted by s 6(1) of the 1971 Act.

93   S 11(2A) of the 1925 Act as inserted by s 6(3) of the 1971 Act.

94   S 12 of the 1925 Act.

95   S 10(3)(b) of the 1925 Act.

96   S 10(2) and (3) of the 1925 Act as amended by s 19 of the 1964 Act and s 5 of the 1971 Act, for repairs and part replacement; s 10(4) of the 1925 Act substituted by s 19 of the 1964 Act and s 5 of the 1971 Act.

97   S 13 of the 1964 Act.

98   S 10 of the 1925 Act as amended by s 19 of the 1964 Act.

99   S 7 of the 1968 Act.

1   S 10(6)(b) of the 1925 Act as amended by s 19(c) of the 1964 Act.

2   Ibid.

3   Under s 13 of the 1925 Act obstruction carries a fine of £10 on summary conviction.

4   S 21 of the 1925 Act as amended by s 22 of the 1964 Act and s 9 of the 1968 Act.

may open any case, box or package.[5] He may seize the firearms or ammunition on reasonable suspicion of an illegal importation, exportation or consignment or the absence of a requisite proof mark for a firearm.[6] Persons having custody or control of the firearms or ammunition must co- operate with the Garda inspection and must also produce relevant documents and give the name and address of any consignor, consignee or owner of firearms or ammunition found.[7]

A Garda observing or believing a person to be in possession of, or using, or carrying a firearm or ammunition may demand a firearm certificate.[8] If none is produced or the person fails to satisfy the Garda that an exemption applies, the Garda may ask for a name and address, which if refused, or given so as to cause the Garda to suspect it to be false and misleading, the Garda may thereupon arrest that person.[9] In addition to such powers a Garda may stop, search and arrest any person whom he suspects[10] to be in possession of, or to be using or carrying a firearm in contravention of the Acts.[11] Such a person may be searched without being arrested and any firearm or ammunition found may be seized without the person being arrested. A Superintendent on reasonably suspecting that an offence under the Acts has been, is, or is about to be committed, may issue a search order in writing authorising the Gardaí to enter, if need be by force, and search premises.[12] Persons found on the premises must give their names and addresses. They may be arrested on reasonable suspicion of committing an offence under the Acts. If the premises are those of a firearms dealer, his business books and papers may be seized.

10.19 These powers are useful. All offences under the Firearms Act are scheduled under the Offences Against the State Act, 1939 and it is easier to arrest under s 30 and search under s 29 as substituted by s 5 of the Criminal Law Act 1976. Further, all offences under the Firearms Acts are incorporated into the Criminal Law Act, 1976 for the purposes of s 8 and 9 thereof which give very extensive powers of stopping, searching and seizure.[13] Further assistance is given to the Gardaí by s 15 of the Criminal Justice Act, 1984:

> (1) Where a member of the Garda Síochána—(a) finds a person in possession of any firearm or ammunition,
> (b) has reasonable grounds for believing that the person is in possession of the firearm or ammunition in contravention of the criminal law, and
> (c) informs that person of his belief, he may require that person to give him any

---

5   Ibid.
6   Ibid., s 4 of the 1968 Act, requiring a proof mark is brought into operation by ministerial order; no such order has been made. However the Firearms (Shotguns) (Proofing Methods, Marks and Fees) Regulations, 1969, SI 65 of 1969, provides detailed regulations for the proofing and marking of shotguns by the Institute for Industrial Research and Standards under s 12 of the 1968 Act.
7   Ibid. The penalty for non-cooperation is, on summary conviction a £10 fine for a first offence and a £20 fine thereafter.
8   S 22(1) of the 1925 Act.
9   S 22(3) of the 1925 Act.
10   Suspicions and beliefs in this context must be reasonably held.
11   S 22(4) of the 1925 Act.
12   S 24 of the 1925 Act as amended by s 23 of the 1964 Act.
13   S 8 as amended by s 17 of the 1990 Act.

information which is in his possession, or which he can obtain by taking reasonable steps, as to how he came by the firearm or ammunition and as to any previous dealings with it, whether by himself or by any other person.

(2) If that person fails or refuses, without reasonable excuse, to give the information or gives information that he knows to be false or misleading, he shall be guilty of an offence and shall be liable on summary conviction to a fine not exceeding £1,000 or to imprisonment for a term not exceeding twelve months or to both.

(3) Subs (2) shall not have effect unless the accused when required to give the information was told in ordinary language by the member of the Garda Síochána what the effect of his failure or refusal might be.

(4) Any information given by a person in compliance with a requirement under subs (1) shall not be admissible in evidence against that person or his spouse in any proceedings, civil or criminal, other than proceedings for an offence under subs (2).

Suppression of Firearms

10.20 Under s 4(1) of the Firearms Act, 1964 the Minister has power, if satisfied that it is necessary to do so in the interest of public safety, to make an order requiring every person in a specified area to hand over to the Gardaí for a period of up to one month, any firearm or ammunition of a particular class or classes on or before a date specified. Weapons not surrendered may, under s 4(4) be seized by the Gardaí after that date. To date only one such order was made, specifying as the area of application the entire State and specifying pistols, revolvers and rifled firearms over .22" calibre and ammunition therefor as weapons of the class to be surrendered.[14]

Possession with Intent

10.21 The most serious of the firearms offences is created by s 15 of the 1925 Act as amended by s 21(4) of the Criminal Law (Jurisdiction) Act, 1976 and s 14(1) of the Criminal Justice Act, 1984:

> Any person who, after the passing of this Act has in his possession or under his control any firearm or ammunition—
> (a) with intent to endanger life or cause serious injury to property, or
> (b) with intent to enable any other person by means of such firearm or ammunition to endanger life or cause serious injury to property, shall, whether any injury to person or property has or has not been caused thereby, be guilty of felony, and on conviction thereof shall be liable to suffer imprisonment for life and the firearm or ammunition aforesaid shall be forfeited.[15]

---

14 The Firearms (Temporary Custody) Order, 1972, SI 187 of 1972.

15 Arrest under s 22(3) of the 1925 Act on name and address being demanded by a Garda and refused or suspicion of falsehood, the power being exercisable by first asking for a firearm certificate; further power to stop, arrest and search and seize firearms or ammunition under s 22(4) of the 1925 Act on the belief of a Garda as to the possession, use, or carrying of a firearm or ammunition; scheduled under the Offences Against the State Act, 1939 and if the powers of search under s 29, as substituted by s 5 of the Criminal Law Act, 1976, and arrest under s 30 can be exercised. Overlapping powers of search are contained in s 7 and 8 of the Criminal Law Act, 1976. Offences contrary to s 15 of the 1925 Act, 26, 27, 27A and 27B of the 1964 Act are scheduled for extra territorial jurisdiction under s 2 of the Criminal Law (Jurisdiction) Act, 1976. In England, where suicide is not a crime, it has been held that an intent to endanger life must refer to the life of another, but suicide is still an offence in this jurisdiction; *Norton* [1977] Crim LR 478.

The Firearms Act, 1971 provides at s 4:

> For the removal of doubt it is hereby declared that in section 15 of the Principal Act references to life and property include references to life and property outside the area of application of the laws enacted by the Oireachtas.[16]

Possession is briefly considered in chapter 11.

Control

10.22 The phrase "has . . . under his control" will have the effect of requiring the accused to actually have the gun or ammunition in such circumstances as it can be fairly said that he is controlling it.[17] If a co-accused has the gun in his possession it is difficult to argue that the accused can be said, in such circumstances, to be controlling the firearm. There is, however, no decision that the doctrine of common design does not apply in such circumstances. It is, however, submitted that the use of the word control implies that the control of the weapon must be personal to the accused and immediately subject to any decision he may make as to its use, without the necessity for intervention or obedience by a third party.

The phrase "has . . . under his control" is also used in s 27A(1) of the 1964 Act.[18] Like the phase "has with him" in s 26(1) and 27B of the 1964 Act[19] it donates a more personal form of possession. Both phrases are embraced by the concept of possession but not *vice versa*. The Acts use a number of phrases: s 2 of the 1925 Act "possession, use or carry" and "purchase"; s 27A of the 1964 Act "in his possession or under his control"; s 26 and s 27B of the 1964 Act "has with him"; and s 27 of the 1964 Act "use or produce". Greater degrees of contact are required as one moves from the concept of possession to that of having a weapon with one or having a weapon under one's control.[20] "Possession" is a legal concept. "Having with" requires close possession so that the weapon is immediately available.[21] "Under control" can hardly demand any more stringent standard than that the weapon be controlled by the accused. It is so controlled if the accused is carrying it or it is within his grab area so that he can at all times control it.

Mental Element

10.23 Intent, in this context, means that the purpose of the accused in having the firearm or ammunition. A jury may infer such an intent, even though it may not be desired, where (a) the result is a virtually certain consequence of what the accused

---

16   Such a conclusion has been reached at common law in England under the equivalent UK provision, s 16 of the Firearms Act, 1968; *El Hakkaoui* [1975] 2 All ER 146; [1975] 1 WLR 396, 60 Cr App R 281; [1975] Crim LR 229 CA.

17   There is no specific authority as to what constitutes "control". See however the discussion in *Murphy* [1971] NI 193 CCA; further see *Hinde* [1977] RTR 328.

18   As inserted by s 8 of the Criminal Law (Jurisdiction) Act, 1976.

19   As inserted by s 9 of the Criminal Law (Jurisdiction) Act, 1976.

20   *Murphy* [1971] NI 193 CCA. Whether the kind of possession that the accused has of the weapon can be said to be under the accused's control or that the accused has it with him is a question of fact and degree; *Kelt* [1977] 3 All ER 1099; [1977] 1 WLR 1365, 65 Cr App R 74; [1977] Crim LR 556 CA.

21   See par 10.25.

has done and (b) the accused knows of that virtually certain consequence.[22] As with s 3 of the Explosive Substances Act, 1883, such intent may be proved, in the absence of an admission, by necessary inference beyond reasonable doubt from all the surrounding circumstances. The use of a weapon can allow such an inference.

The intent required is not to kill but to endanger life or cause serious injury to property. That intent need not be fulfilled by the accused succeeding in his purpose. In *Bentham and Others*[23] the accused took part in a robbery on 25 April, and while making their escape fired shots into a police car. The police raided their cottage on 8 June. Instead of resisting the accused hid themselves. Five guns were found, four of them loaded. The accused were charged with possession with intent to endanger life at the cottage between the two dates. It was argued that for the offence to be made out, the accused must be shown to have had a present and unconditional intention to endanger life and, as a matter of fact, their behaviour during the police raid in hiding themselves, and immersing some of the guns in water, was inconsistent with that intent. The Court of Appeal disagreed:

> We cannot accept that the only intent which falls within the section is an intent immediately and unconditionally to endanger life. The intent with which a man wounds another or detonates an explosive is an intent which accompanies the act, but possession is not an act done at a particular moment; it is a continuing state of things and in our view the intent to endanger life is something which may last as long as the possession lasts. It cannot therefore be limited to an intent to endanger life immediately. Nor do we see any reason why it should be limited to an unconditional intent. It would indeed in most cases be impossible to establish an unconditional intent to endanger life until the moment before a firearm was fired. The mischief at which the section is aimed must be that of a person possessing a firearm ready for use, if and when the occasion arises, in a manner which endangers life.[24]

An intent to endanger life is not present if the accused's intent is to scare off people in self-defence by the use of that firearm.[25]

Intent to Commit an Indictable Offence

10.24 A second offence of possession with intent is created by s 27B of the Firearms Act, 1964 as inserted by s 9 of the Criminal Law (Jurisdiction)Act, 1976 and amended by s 14(5) of the Criminal Justice Act, 1984:[26]

> (1) A person who has with him a firearm or an imitation firearm with intent to commit an indictable offence, or to resist or prevent the arrest of himself or another, in either case while he has the firearm or imitation firearm with him, shall be guilty of an offence and shall be liable on conviction on indictment to imprisonment for a term not exceeding fourteen years.

22 See ch 2 and par 9.05.

23 [1972] 3 All ER 271 CA. See also *Edgecombe* [1963] Crim LR 574 CCA.

24 Ibid. [1973] 1 QB 357 at 362-63; [1972] 3 All ER 271 at 275-76; [1972] 3 WLR 398 at 403, 56 Cr App R 618 at 625.

25 *Georgiades* (1989) 89 Cr App R 206 at 210 CA.

26 S 16 of the Firearms Act (United Kingdom), 1968, reads: "It is an offence for a person to have in his possession any firearm or ammunition with intent by means thereof to endanger life, . . . or to enable another person by means thereof to endanger life, . . . whether any injury . . . has been caused or not." (As amended by Schedule Part I of the Criminal Damage Act, 1971).

(2) In proceedings for an offence under this section proof that the accused had a firearm or imitation firearm with him and intended to commit an indictable offence or to resist or prevent arrest is evidence that he intended to have it with him while doing so.[27]

Has with Him

10.25 The phrase "has with him" is also to be found in the Firearms Act (Northern Ireland), 1969 And in the Firearms Act (United Kingdom), 1968, s 18(1) of which reads "It is an offence for a person to have with him a firearm or imitation firearm with intent to commit an indictable offence. . . ." This phrase was interpreted by Lord MacDermott for the Northern Ireland Court of Criminal Appeal thus:

> The firearm has to be "with" the offender. That is not to say that if the trespasser puts his weapon down for a moment and so that he can resume it at once, he is not within the section. A burglar who lays his gun on the top of the safe he is opening could hardly escape the section by doing so. But that is very different from the form of possession depending on a more remote control which is enough to satisfy the other enactments mentioned. For example, a burglar drives to the scene of his crime and leaves his car with his pistol inside it on the road opposite the house he breaks into. When arrested he will have a good answer to a charge under s 18(1), but none to a charge under s 1 of having in his possession a firearm without a firearm certificate. Under s 18 the offender must really be armed to his knowledge and must enter or be within the premises as an armed man.[28]

A similar conclusion was reached by the English Court of Appeal in *Kelt*[29] where the accused was arrested in his kitchen where the police also found a holdall containing a "robber's kit" which included a sawn-off shotgun.

The Court held that two phrases would not have been used in the Firearm Act if one meaning had been intended. A similar construction must be put on the use of the three phrases in the Irish legislation of "possession", "having with" and "control". The court concluded that "having with" was thus different from "in possession". The distinction was one of fact and degree:

> We have come to the conclusion that it is necessary when summing up a case in which an offence under s 18 is alleged, for the judge to make it clear to the jury that possession is not enough, that the law requires the evidence to go a stage further and to establish that the accused had it with him. Of course the classic case of having a gun with you is if you are carrying it. But, even if you are not carrying it, you may yet have it with you, if it is immediately available to you. But if all that can be shown is possession in

---

27 Not expressed to be a felony or misdemeanour; fourteen years' imprisonment provided for by s 14(5) of the Criminal Justice Act, 1984; indictable trial only; arrest under s 22(3) of the 1925 Act on name and address being demanded by a Garda and refused or suspicion of falsehood, the power being exercisable by first asking for a firearm certificate; further power to stop, search and arrest and seize firearms or ammunition under s 22(4) of the 1925 Act on the belief of a Garda as to the possession, use, or carrying of a firearm or ammunition; scheduled under the Offences Against the State Act, 1939 and if the powers of search under s 29, as substituted by s 5 of the Criminal Law Act, 1976, and arrest under s 30 can be exercised. Overlapping powers of search are contained in s 7 and 8 of the Criminal Law Act, 1976. Offences contrary to s 15 of the 1925 Act, 26, 27, 27A and 27B of the 1964 Act are scheduled for extra territorial jurisdiction under s 2 of the Criminal Law (Jurisdiction) Act, 1976.

28 *Murphy* [1971] NI 193 at 202 CCA.

29 [1977] 3 All ER 1099; [1977] 1 WLR 1365, 65 Cr App R 74; [1977] Crim LR 556 CA.

the sense that it is in your house or in a shed or somewhere where you have ultimate control, that is not enough.[30]

Intent

10.26 Intent will have the same interpretation as in s 15 of the 1925 Act.[31] The intent in this case is "to commit an indictable offence or to resist or prevent the arrest of another". The prosecution must specify which indictable offence they allege that the accused intended or, if there is doubt, specify alternatives.[32] The specific intent is proved, in the absence of an admission, by necessary inference, beyond all reasonable doubt, from the surrounding circumstances.[33]

A situation which has often arisen in practice is of a set of facts where accused A and accused B are seen in a car in the vicinity of a bank that is about to open or close. On being stopped and searched[34] they are found to have a revolver and a set of stocking masks. Clearly it may be inferred, unless there is an alternative explanation available, that they intend to rob the bank.

Possession is a continuing state of affairs. It is not necessary for the offence to be committed that an intent be formed before, or on, taking possession. If that were so the phrase "takes possession with intent" would have been used in the section.[35] Subs 2 of s 27B merely overcomes the possibility of an argument that accused A and accused B in the example may have intended to leave the revolver behind in the car and enter the bank disguised with masks. Fanciful possibilities do not have to be disproved by the prosecution as doubts based on them cannot be reasonable.[36] The section states the obvious and thereby shuts off a possible mistaken acquittal on a technicality.[37]

Having a Firearm whilst Unlawfully Taking a Motor Vehicle

10.27 S 26 of the 1964 Act, as amended by s 21(6)(b) of the Criminal Law (Jurisdiction) Act, 1976 and s 14(2) of the Criminal Justice Act, 1984 provides:

> (1) A person who contravenes subs (1) of s 112 of the Road Traffic Act, 1961, and who at the time of such contravention has with him a firearm or an imitation firearm shall

---

30 [1977] 3 All ER 1099 at 1103G; [1977] 1 WLR 1365 at 1370E, 65 Cr App R 74 at 78.

31 See par 10.21-10.23.

32 By analogy with the law as to burglary; Archbold (1966) 1819; *Pearson* (1910) 4 Cr App R 40.

33 See ch 2 and par 9.15.

34 S 7 and 8 of the Criminal Law Act, 1976 are the simplest powers to use in this context (Appendix 1).

35 *Houghton* [1982] Crim LR 112 CA, rejecting an analogy with the prosecution of the Prevention of Crimes Act (United Kingdom), 1953 and the leading authority thereunder, *Ohlson v Hylton* [1975] 2 All ER 490; [1975] 1 WLR 724; [1975] Crim LR 292 DC. In *Houghton* [1922] Crim LR 112 the Court of Appeal refused to follow the decision in *Ohlson v Hylton* in the context of an offence of having a firearm with intent to commit an indictable offence contrary to s 18(1) of the Firearms Act, 1968, as this Act was not limited to the carrying of firearms but was concerned with their use.

36 *Miller v Minister for Pensions* [1974] 2 All ER 372 CA.

37 The section does not raise a presumption requiring the accused to prove the negative on the balance of probability. If the accused can raise a doubt as to any element, including that stated in subsection 2, he is entitled to be acquitted. This matter is further discussed at par 9.19.

be guilty of an offence and shall be liable on conviction on indictment to imprisonment for a term not exceeding fourteen years.

(2) Where a person is charged with an offence under this section, it shall be a good defence to the charge for him to show that he had the firearm or imitation firearm to which the charge relates with him for a lawful purpose when he did the act alleged to constitute the offence under subs (1) of the said s 112.[38]

"Has with him" carries the same meaning as in section 23B above, denoting a more personal form of possession.[39] The words "use", "carry", or "produce" are not used in this section as they are elsewhere in the Act. It is thus clear that the offence is technical in nature. It is not required that the firearm be of any assistance to the accused in taking the vehicle or even that he show or produce the firearm to someone. The section merely requires that he have a firearm with him. S 112 of the Road Traffic Act, 1961 as amended by s 65 of the Road Traffic Act, 1968 and s 3(7) of the Road Traffic (Amendment) Act, 1984 provides:

(1)(a) A person shall not use or take possession of a mechanically propelled vehicle without the consent of the owner thereof or other lawful authority.

(b) Where possession of a vehicle has been taken in contravention of this subsection, a person who knows of the taking shall not allow himself to be carried in or on it without the consent of the owner thereof or other lawful authority.

(2) A person who contravenes subsection (1) of this section shall be guilty of an offence and shall be liable—

(a) on summary conviction, to a fine not exceeding £1,000 or, at the discretion of the court, to imprisonment for a term not exceeding 12 months, or to both such fine and such imprisonment;

(b) on conviction on indictment, to a fine not exceeding £2,000 or, at the discretion of the court, to imprisonment for a term not exceeding five years or to both such fine and such imprisonment.

(3) A person shall not use or take possession of a pedal cycle without the consent of the owner thereof or other lawful authority.

(4) A person who contravenes subs (3) of this section shall be guilty of an offence.

(5) Where a person is charged with an offence under this section, it shall be a good defence to the charge for him to show that, when he did the act alleged to constitute the offence, he believed, and had reasonable grounds for believing, that he had lawful authority for doing that act.

(6) Where a member of the Garda Síochána has reasonable grounds for believing that a person is committing or has committed an offence under this section, he may arrest the person without warrant.

(7) Where, when a person is tried on indictment or summarily for the larceny of a

---

38 Not expressed to be a felony or misdemeanour; fourteen years' imprisonment provided for by s 14(2) of the Criminal Justice Act, 1984; indictable trial only; arrest under s 22(3) of the 1925 Act on name and address being demanded by a Garda and refused or suspicion of falsehood, the power being exercisable by first asking for a firearm certificate; further power to stop, search and arrest and seize firearms or ammunition under s 22(4) of the 1925 Act on the belief of a Garda as to the possession, use, or carrying of a firearm or ammunition; scheduled under the Offences Against the State Act, 1939 and if the powers of search under s 29, as substituted by s 5 of the Criminal Law Act, 1976, and arrest under s 30 can be exercised. Overlapping powers of search are contained in s 7 and 8 of the Criminal Law Act, 1976. Offences contrary to s 15 of the 1925 Act, 26, 27, 27A and 27B of the 1964 Act are scheduled for extra territorial jurisdiction under s 2 of the Criminal Law (Jurisdiction) Act, 1976.

39 See par 10.25. "Armed" means physically carrying guns or knowing they were immediately available; *Jones* (1987) 85 Cr App R 285 CA.

vehicle, the jury, or, in the case of a summary trial, the District Court, is of opinion that he was not guilty of the larceny of the vehicle but was guilty of an offence under this section in relation to the vehicle, the jury or court may find him guilty of that offence and he may be sentenced accordingly.[40]

Hijacking

S 26 of the 1964 Act has become less used because of the passing of s 10 of the Criminal Law (Jurisdiction) Act, 1976 which provides:

> (1) A person who unlawfully, by force or threat thereof, or by any other form of intimidation, seizes or exercises control of or otherwise interferes with the control of, or compels or induces some other person to use for an unlawful purpose, any vehicle (whether mechanically propelled or not) or any ship or hovercraft shall be guilty of an offence and shall be liable on conviction on indictment to imprisonment for a term not exceeding fifteen years.
> (2) In the application of s 2 to this section, it shall be presumed, until the contrary is shown, that a purpose that is unlawful in the State is unlawful in Northern Ireland.
> (3) In this section—"Hovercraft" means a vehicle that is designed to be supported when in motion wholly or partly by air expelled from the vehicle to form a cushion of which the boundaries include the ground, water or other surface beneath the vehicle; "ship" includes any boat or other vessel; "vehicle" includes a railway train or any other railway vehicle.

This offence is a scheduled offence under the Criminal Law (Jurisdiction) Act, 1976. Where the offence is committed in Northern Ireland it constitutes an offence contrary to s 2(1) of that Act.[41]

Aiding Escape by Firearms

10.28 S 27 of the Firearms Act, 1964 as amended by s 21(6)(c) of the Criminal Law (Jurisdiction) Act, 1976 and s 14(3) of the Criminal Justice Act, 1984 provides:

> (1) A person shall not use or produce a firearm or an imitation firearm
> (a) for the purpose of or while resisting the arrest of such person or of another person by a member of the Garda Síochána, or
> (b) for the purpose of aiding or in the course of the escape or rescue of such person or of another person from the custody of the Garda Síochána or of the person in the charge of a prison, remand institution, St. Patrick's Institution or an institution where criminal lunatics within the meaning of the Criminal Justice Act, 1960), are detained.
> (2) A person who contravenes subs (1) of this section shall be guilty of an offence and shall be liable on conviction on indictment to imprisonment for life.[42]

40 Use means use a conveyance; *Stokes* [1982] Crim LR 695. Pushing a vehicle around a corner does not constitute use, nor does a mere intention to use constitute use; *Marchant* (1985) 80 Cr App R 361 CA. By s 3(1) of the Road Traffic Act, 1961 "use" includes park and cognate words are construed accordingly, "park" means keeping or leaving a vehicle stationary. Consent obtained by intimidation is void; *Hodgon* [1962] Crim LR 563 CCA. If consent is given but the use that the vehicle is put to goes beyond the consent then that use is unlawful; *McKnight v Davies* [1974] RTR 4; [1974] Crim LR 62 DC; *Peart* [1970] 2 QB 672; [1970] 2 All ER 823; [1970] 3 WLR 63, 54 Cr App R 374 CA.
41 The section is quoted at par 9.12. For precedent see chs 2, 3, 6, 7, 9 and 10.
42 Not specified as a felony or misdemeanour; life imprisonment provided for by s 14(3) of the Criminal Justice Act, 1984; indictable trial only; arrest under s 22(3) of the 1925 Act on name and address being demanded by a Garda and refused or suspicion or falsehood, the power being exercisable by

"Use or produce" in this context envisages the accused discharging a firearm or showing or brandishing a firearm or imitation firearm for one of the purposes of the section.[43] It is an offence at common law for a prisoner to escape from lawful custody[44] or for a gaoler negligently, or intentionally, to allow his prisoner to escape.[45] These offences require proof that the custody was lawful by virtue of a proper arrest, a warrant, remand or other lawful cause.[46] Similarly the offence of rescuing a prisoner requires that the prisoner be in lawful custody.[47]

In statute law the offence of being a person unlawfully at large, contrary to s 6 of the Criminal Justice Act, 1960, depends on the prosecution proving detention under a lawful sentence, the accused being released on a temporary release order and a breach of a condition of that release. The offence of aiding an escape from lawful custody, contrary to s 6(1) of the Criminal Law Act, 1976, expressly requires proof that the custody escaped from was lawful.[48] The offence of smuggling a banned article into prison, contrary to s 6(2) of the same Act, does not demand proof that any person, for whom the article may have been intended, was in prison lawfully. The offence of escaping lawful custody in Northern Ireland, contrary to s 3 of the Criminal Law (Jurisdiction) Act, 1976 requires proof of conviction and sentence or remand in lawful custody on an offence scheduled under the Act.[49] Thus offences at common law, and under statute law, of escaping or aiding an escape require proof that the detention sought to be broken was lawful.

Lawful Custody

10.29 The Oireachtas could have made it an element of an offence under s 27 of the Firearms Act, 1964 that the person to be rescued was in lawful custody by specifying "lawful arrest" or "lawful custody".[50] Such words do not require to be

first asking for a firearm certificate; further power to stop, search and arrest and seize firearms or ammunition under s 22(4) of the 1925 Act on the belief of a Garda as to the possession, use, or carrying of a firearm or ammunition; scheduled under the Offences Against the State Act, 1939 and if the powers of search under s 29, as substitued by s 5 of the Criminal Law Act, 1976, and arrest under s 30 can be exercised. Overlapping powers of search are contained in s 7 and 8 of the Criminal Law Act, 1976. Offences contrary to s 15 of the 1925 Act, 26, 27, 27A and 27B of the 1964 Act are scheduled for extra territorial jurisdiction under s 2 of the Criminal Law (Jurisdiction) Act, 1976.

43 It would seem that the use of a firearm or imitation firearm is not confined to discharging it (not used in the Acts) and the only way an imitation firearm can be used, as such, is to frighten an adversary. Such a situation is also covered by the words in the section "produce"; this is merely unnecessary overlap. Discharging a firearm in a public place is an offence contrary to s 10(2) of the Summary Jurisdiction (Ireland) Act, 1851, and wantonly discharging a firearm is an offence contrary to s 14 of the Dublin Metropolitan Police Act, 1842.

44 *Allan* (1841) C&M 295, 174 ER 513; 2 Hawk ch 19; 1 Hale 590, 2 Chit Cr L 159; Archbold (1922) 1168; 1 Hale 570, 600; Stephen *Digest of Criminal Law* (6th ed.) 115.

45 Russell 324.

46 Archbold (1966) 3421.

47 1 Co Inst 160; 1 Hale 606, 601, 2 Hawk ch 21; 2 Chit CR L 182; Stephen *Digest of Criminal Law* (6th ed.) 116; Archbold (1922) 1177.

48 The offence of failing to appear in accordance with the recognisance granting bail, contrary to s 13 of the Criminal Justice Act, 1984, requires proof of that recognisance.

49 *The People (DPP) v Campbell & Others* (1983) 2 Frewen 131 CCA.

50 Words which are unambiguously absent from a statute should not be read into it: *The People (DPP) v Quilligan & O'Reilly* (No. 1) [1986] IR 495; [1987] ILRM 606 SC.

read into the section for the purpose of giving it a constitutional construction.[51] Any arrest or detention is a restraint on liberty[52] and must be justified by reference to the lawful exercise of some power given to the person seeking to exercise it.[53]

A citizen is entitled to use reasonable measures of self-help, including force, to resist an unlawful action.[54] Where such self help goes beyond what is reasonable an assault is committed at common law.[55] There is, it is submitted, nothing unconstitutional in the Oireachtas requiring a person, who suspects he is unlawfully detained or is being unlawfully arrested to submit to a process which will cause his ultimate release on appearance before the courts where, if the detainee requires it, such arrest or detention must be justified.[56] Some common law countries have required that there be a proportion between the use of force in arrest and the nature or the harm sought to be prevented thereby.[57] It is reasonable to prevent the State using unrestrained force, in the face of opposition, to prevent a trifling harm or in an arrest for a minor offence. Equally, it is reasonable to limit the nature of the force a citizen may use against the agents of the State acting in effecting an illegal arrest or enforcing a detention which may be subsequently found to have been unlawful. What s 27 prohibits is the accused using or producing a firearm or imitation firearm to resist arrest by a Garda or to aid an escape from State custody. It is submitted that the prosecution are not required to prove that such arrest or custody was lawful.

Suspicious Possession

10.30 S 27A of the Firearms Act, 1964 as substituted by s 8 of the Criminal Law (Jurisdiction) Act, 1976 and amended by s 14(4) of the Criminal Justice Act, 1984 provides:

> (1) A person who has a firearm or ammunition in his possession or under his control in such circumstances as to give rise to a reasonable inference that he has not got it in his possession or under his control for a lawful purpose shall, unless he has it in his possession or under his control for a lawful purpose, be guilty of an offence and shall be liable on conviction on indictment to imprisonment for a term not exceeding ten years.
>
> (2) In the application of s 2 of the Criminal Law (Jurisdiction) Act, 1976, to this section, it shall be presumed, unless the contrary is shown, that a purpose that is unlawful in the State is unlawful in Northern Ireland.[58]

51 It is assumed that the Oireachtas did not intend to violate the Constitution; it is only if there is no other construction reasonably open that a statute will be construed as being inconsistent with it; *McDonald v Bord na gCon* [1965] IR 217 SC; *The People (A-G) v Conmey* [1975] IR 341 SC.

52 Guaranteed by Article 40.4.1 of the Constitution: "No citizen shall be deprived of his personal liberty save in accordance with law". As to what acts will constitute an infringement of personal liberty see ch 7.

53 *Collins v Wilcock* [1984] 3 All ER 374; [1984] 1 WLR 1172, 79 Cr App R 229; [1984] Crim LR 481 CA.

54 See par 4.29.

55 *The People (A-G) v Dwyer* [1972] IR 416 SC.

56 *Dunne v Clinton* [1930] IR 366 and unreported SC.

57 *Turner* [1962] VR 30 SC.

58 Not expressed to be a felony or misdemeanour; ten years' imprisonment provided for by s 14(4) of the Criminal Justice Act, 1984; indictable trial only; arrest under s 22(3) of the 1925 Act on name

The phrase "under his control" will have the same meaning as in s 15 of the 1925 Act and reference should thus be made to paragraph 10.25.

The section is based on s 4 of the Explosive Substances Act, 1883. There are four differences in the wording.

Elements

10.31 Firstly, s 4 of the Explosive Substances Act, 1883 requires that the accused have knowing possession of the explosive, whereas s 27A is silent. Possession does not occur without knowledge.[59] In this context the prosecution will be required to prove that the accused knew that he had the firearm. In the absence of such proof there is no possession.[60] If the accused does not know that the object is a firearm, it is submitted, he will not have possession of that object; nor can an inference of an unlawful purpose be drawn in those circumstances.

Secondly, s 4 of the 1883 Act refers to "circumstances giving rise to a reasonable suspicion" whereas s 27A refers to "circumstances giving rise to a reasonable inference". Suspicion has been referred to as:

> A state of conjecture or surmise where proof is lacking: "I suspect but I cannot prove". Suspicion arises at or near the starting point of an investigation of which the obtaining of prima facie proof is the end. When such proof has been obtained, the police case is complete, it is ready for trial and passes onto its next stage. . . .[61]

Inference has been referred to as:

> A reasonable conclusion drawn as a matter of strict logical deduction from known or assumed facts.[62]

This distinction will cause no difficulty in practice; an inference being a fact thought to exist from the existence of other facts and a suspicion being a state of mind whereby proven facts cause a belief that another fact or fact exists. What is common to both tests is of greater importance, being the fact inferred or suspected, which is that the accused has possession or control for an unlawful object.[63] That inference or suspicion can be drawn from the fact of unlawful possession; the unlawful possession of guns or bombs naturally giving rise, because of their nature,

---

and address being demanded by a Garda and refused or suspicion of falsehood, the power being exercisable by first asking for a firearm certificate; further power to stop, search and arrest and seize firearms or ammunition under s 22(4) of the 1925 Act on the belief of a Garda as to the possession, use, or carrying of a firearm or ammunition; scheduled under the Offences Against the State Act, 1939 and if the powers of search under s 29, as substituted by s 5 of the Criminal Law Act, 1976, and arrest under s 30 can be exercised. Overlapping powers of search are contained in s 7 and 8 of the Criminal Law Act, 1976. Offences contrary to s 15 of the 1925 Act, 26, 27, 27A and 27B of the 1964 Act are scheduled for extra territorial jurisdiction under s 2 of the Criminal Law (Jurisdiction) Act, 1976.

59   *Minister for Posts and Telegraphs v Campbell* [1966] IR 69 HC.
60   See the discussion in ch 11.
61   Lord Diplock in *Holgate-Mohammed v Duke* [1984] AC 437 at 443 HL quoting from Hussein v Chong Fook Kam [1970] AC 942 at 948; [1969] 3 All ER 1626; [1970] 2 WLR 441 PC.
62   Per Street CJ in *Gumett v Macquarie Co. Pty* (1953) 72 WN (NSW) 261 SC NSW.
63   S 4 of the 1883 Act used the word "object" instead of "purpose".

to a belief that the purpose of the accused was likely to be unlawful.[64] It is sufficient to intend such use, if necessary, either offensively or defensively.[65] Where the accused carried a knife and told the police that he carried it for his self-defence, the Divisional Court held that it was proper to draw an inference that for the purpose of defending himself, he would, if necessary, use the knife to cause injury.

10.32 Thirdly, under s 4 of the Explosive Substances Act, 1883, the accused is guilty "unless he can show that he made it or had it in his possession or under his control for a lawful object". S 27A states merely "unless he had it in his possession or under his control for a lawful purpose". The 1883 Act places a burden of proof on the accused which arises once suspicious possession is proved by the prosecution. This, traditionally, must be discharged by the accused on the balance of probabilities.[66] No such requirement is made under s 27A. Where the burden of proof is on the accused any case made by him which is less than what appears to the court to be probably true, requires that he be found guilty.[67] Thus it may be that a reasonable doubt can exist as to the accused's guilt, but he must still be found guilty. S 27A does not perpetuate this injustice, merely requiring that there be evidence, either on the prosecution or defence case, from which a reasonable doubt may be held by the tribunal of fact.

Fourthly, s 27A(2) provides that where a person is being prosecuted in Ireland for the commission of an offence in Northern Ireland, the prosecution need not show that the purpose inferred was contrary to the law of Northern Ireland. Once that purpose is contrary to the law of the State, it is for the accused to prove on the balance of probabilities[68] that his purpose was lawful in Northern Ireland. Where the accused is being prosecuted for an offence under s 27A inside the borders of the State, it has been held under s 4 of the Explosive Substances Act, 1883 that the lawful object may refer to what may lawfully be done in another State. The House of Lords have, pragmatically, placed the burden of proving the lawfulness of that object according to the law of the "target" State on the accused.[69] The general principle is that the accused need only adduce sufficient evidence of a defence and it is for the prosecution to disprove it beyond reasonable doubt.[70] The House of Lords ruling that the accused must prove foreign law showing his object to be lawful was made in the context of a burden of proof of lawfulness on the balance of probabilities being placed on the accused, which, as we have seen, is not applicable to s 27A.

---

64 *Hallam* [1957] 1 QB 569 at 573; [1957] 1 All ER 665 at 666; [1957] 2 WLR 521 at 523, 41 Cr App R 111 at 115 CCA.

65 *Patterson v Block, The Times,* 21 June 1984, DC.

66 *Fegan* [1972] NI 80 CCA.

67 See par 9.18-9.19. See particularly the reference to the analysis of Judge Moriarty of the presumption under s 15 of the Misuse of Drugs Act, 1977.

68 *Carr-Briant* [1943] KB 607; [1943] 2 All ER 156, 29 Cr App R 76 CCA. This rule applies to all criminal statutes placing a burden of proof on the accused; *Jayesena v R* [1970] AC 618, [1970] 1 All ER 219; [1970] 2 WLR 448 PC. But see 9.18-9.19.

69 *Berry* [1985] AC 246; [1984] 3 All ER 1008; [1984] 3 WLR 1274, 80 Cr App R 98; [1985] Crim LR 102 HL.

70 *The People (A-G) v Quinn* [1965] IR 366 CCA.

Lawful Purpose

The fact that the firearm or ammunition is held without the appropriate certificate does not render the purpose for which it is held, for that reason alone, unlawful.[71] Self-defence is a lawful object under the section. The danger must be reasonably and genuinely anticipated, be reasonably imminent, be of a nature that could only be met by the possession of the weapon and the cause for such apprehension must exist at the time of the possession.[72] Whether a purpose held by the accused is lawful will depend on the nature of that purpose, his reasons for having it, the existence or non-existence of other ways of effecting the purpose, and whether the excuse is reasonable.

An example occurred in *The People (DPP) v Kelso, Doherty and McGowan*.[73] The three accused were constables in the RUC but came across the border in order to avail of the more liberal public house licensing laws in this jurisdiction. Each was carrying a loaded hand-gun which was regulation issue to constables. They were acquitted by the Special Criminal Court on the basis that as they had proved that they had an honest and reasonable belief that their lives might be in danger and therefore required to be protected by these guns, they had a lawful purpose within the meaning of the section. There was another way of effecting the purpose of protecting themselves; staying at home unarmed and buying more expensive alcoholic drink there; this was not considered by the court.

Other Firearms Offences

10.33 Ss 14, 18 and 19 of the Offences Against the Person Act, 1861, create other firearms offences, which because of their lesser importance, need only be quoted here:

> 14 Whosoever shall . . . shoot at any person, or shall, by drawing a trigger or in any other manner, attempt to discharge any kind of loaded arms at any person . . ., with intent, in any of the cases aforesaid, to commit murder, shall, whether any bodily injury be effected or not, be guilty of felony; and being convicted thereof shall be liable to be kept in penal servitude for life.[74]

> 18 Whosoever shall . . . shoot at any person, or, by drawing a trigger or in any other manner, attempt to discharge any kind of loaded arms at any person, with intent, in any of the cases aforesaid, to maim, disfigure, or disable any person, or to do some other grievous bodily harm to any person, or with intent to resist or prevent the lawful apprehension or detainer of any person, shall be guilty of felony to be kept in penal servitude for life.[75]

> 19 Any gun, pistol, or other arms which shall be loaded in the barrel with gunpowder

71 *Attorney General's Reference* (No. 2 of 1983) [1984] AC 456; [1984] QB 456; [1984] 1 All ER 988 CA; [1984] 2 WLR 465, 78 Cr App R 183; [1984] Crim LR 289 CA.

72 *Fegan* [1972] NI 80 CCA; see also *Porte* [1973] NI 198 CCA as to what is a reasonable excuse. As to what is a reasonable excuse for carrying a loaded shotgun see *Taylor v Mucklow* [1973] Crim LR 750 DC.

73 [1984] ILRM 329 SCC.

74 The sections are quoted, as are all other sections from the Offences Against the Person Act, 1861, in accordance with the amendments introduced by the Penal Servitude Acts of 1864 and 1891 and by the Statute Law Revision Act, 1908.

75 For a further discussion see ch 6.

or any other explosive substance, and ball, shot, slug, or other destructive material, shall be deemed to be loaded arms within the meaning of this Act, although the attempt to discharge the same may fail from want of proper priming or from any other cause.

10.34 Offences also exist of being armed whilst smuggling goods contrary to s 189 of the Customs Consolidation Act, 1876 for which the penalty is three years' imprisonment; being found by night with an offensive weapon (which under s 25 of the Firearms Act, 1964 includes a firearm, whether loaded or not, or an imitation firearm) with intent to commit a burglary contrary to s 28 of the Larceny Act, 1916 for which the penalty is five years' penal servitude on a first offence and ten years thereafter; and burglary aggravated by reason of the possession of a firearm or imitation firearm contrary to s 23B of the Larceny Act, 1916 as inserted by s 7 of the Criminal Law (Jurisdiction) Act, 1976[76] for which the penalty is imprisonment for life under s 8 of the Criminal Law Act, 1976. It is also an offence to discharge a firearm in a public place, contrary to s 10(2) of the Summary Jurisdiction (Ireland) Act, 1851 for which the penalty is a fine not exceeding fifty pence and it is further an offence contrary to s 14 of the Dublin Metropolitan Police Act, 1842 to wantonly discharge a firearm for which the penalty is a fine of two pounds.

Reckless Use

10.35 S 8 of the Firearms & Offensive Weapons Act, 1990 provides at s 8:

A person who discharges a firearm being reckless as to whether any person will be injured or not, shall be guilty of an offence, whether any such injury is caused or not, and shall be liable:
(a) on summary conviction to a fine not exceed one thousand pounds or to imprisonment for a term not exceed twelve months or to both, or
(b) on conviction on indictment, to a fine or to imprisonment for a term not exceeding five years or to both.

Recklessness, in this context, will have the same meaning as that discussed in the context of the law of rape,[77] that is to say the unjustifiable taking of a substantial risk, where the accused is aware of that risk. Recklessness in this context is specifically limited to injury to a person.

Draft Indictments

10.36 There follow the appropriate forms of indictment for the offences considered in this chapter.

POSSESSION WITHOUT A FIREARM CERTIFICATE

Statement of Offence
Unlawful possession (or use or carrying) of a firearm (or ammunition) contrary to s 2 of the Firearms Act, 1925 as amended by s 3 of the Firearms Act, 1971 and s 4 of the Firearms & Offensive Weapons Act, 1990.
Particulars of Offence
AB on the   had in his possession (or unlawfully used or carried) a firearm

76   As amended by the Larceny Act, 1990.
77   See further ch 2 and ch 8.

(or ammunition) being a   such possession (or use or carrying) not being authorised by a firearm certificate granted under the Firearms Acts, 1925-1990 and for the time being in force.

POSSESSION WITH INTENT

Statement of Offence
Possession (or control) of a firearm (or ammunition) with intent, contrary to s 15 of the Firearms Act, 1925 as amended by s 4 of the Firearms Act, 1971 and s 21(4) of the Criminal Law (Jurisdiction) Act, 1976 and s 14(1) of the Criminal Justice Act, 1984, and s 4 of the Firearms & Offensive Weapons Act, 1990.
Particulars of Offence
AB on the   at   had in his possession (or under his control) a firearm (or ammunition) being a   with intent by means thereof to endanger life or cause serious injury to property or to enable any other person so to do.[78]

HAVING A FIREARM (OR IMITATION FIREARM) WITH INTENT

Statement of Offence
Having a firearm (or imitation firearm) with intent contrary to s 27(b) of the Firearms Act, 1964 as inserted by s 9 of the Criminal Law (Jurisdiction) Act, 1976 and amended by s 14(5) of the Criminal Justice Act, 1984, and by s 4 of the Firearms & Offensive Weapons Act, 1990.
Particulars of Offence
AB on the   at   had with him a firearm (or imitation firearm) with intent to commit the indictable offence of   (or resist or prevent the arrest of himself, or of CD).

HAVING A FIREARM WHILE TAKING A VEHICLE

Statement of Offence
Having a firearm (or imitation firearm) whilst committing an offence under s 112 of the Road Traffic Act, 1961, as amended, contrary to s 26 of the Firearms Act, 1964 as amended by s 21(6)(b) of the Criminal Law (Jurisdiction) Act, 1976 and s 14(2) of the Criminal Justice Act, 1984, and by s 4 of the Firearms & Offensive Weapons Act, 1990.
Particulars of Offence
AB on the   at   contravened s 112 of the Road Traffic Act, 1961, as amended, and had with him a firearm (or imitation firearm).

USING A FIREARM TO RESIST ARREST

Statement of Offence
Using (or producing) a firearm (or imitation firearm) to resist arrest contrary to s 27 of the Firearms Act, 1964 as amended by s 21(6)(b) of the Criminal Law (Jurisdiction) Act, 1976 and s 14(3) of the Criminal Justice Act, 1984, and by s 4 of the Firearms & Offensive Weapons Act, 1990.

---

78   Stated in the alternative under rule 5 of the Criminal Procedure Act, 1924 permitting this as an exception to the rule against duplicity.

Particulars of Offence

AB on the   at   used (or produced) a firearm (or imitation firearm) for the purpose of resisting his arrest by Garda CD.

Note: (for other alternatives see the text above).

SUSPICIOUS POSSESSION

Statement of Offence

Possession (or control) of a firearm (or ammunition) giving rise to an inference of an unlawful purpose contrary to s 27A of the Firearms Act, 1964 as substituted by s 8 of the Criminal Law (Jurisdiction) Act, 1976 and amended by s 14(4) of the Criminal Justice Act, 1984, and by s 4 of the Firearms & Offensive Weapons Act, 1990.

Particulars of Offence

AB on the   at   had in his possession (or under his control) a firearm (or ammunition) being a   in such circumstances as to give rise to a reasonable inference that he did not have it in his possession (or under his control) for a lawful purpose.

IN NORTHERN IRELAND

Statement of Offence

Producing a firearm in the course of escape, contrary to s 2(1) of the Criminal Law (Jurisdiction) Act, 1976.

Particulars of Offence

AB on the   at   Northern Ireland, produced a firearm in the course of an escape from CD the person in charge of (specify person, etc.).

Note: For alternatives see s 2(1) of the Schedule to the Criminal Law (Jurisdiction) Act, 1972.

Statement of Offence

Possession of a firearm with intent to endanger life contrary to s 2(1) of the Criminal Law (Jurisdiction) Act, 1976.

Particulars of Offence

AB on the   at   Northern Ireland, had in his possession a firearm with intent to endanger life.

Note: For alternatives see s 2(1) of the Schedule to the Criminal Law (Jurisdiction) Act, 1976.[79]

RECKLESS DISCHARGE

Statement of Offence

Reckless discharge of a firearm contrary to s 8 and s 4 of the Firearms & Offensive Weapons Act, 1990.

Particulars of Offence

AB on the   at   discharged a firearm being reckless as to whether any person would thereby be injured or not.

79   This is the form of indictment used in the trial of G.M. Sloan in the Special Criminal Court in April 1989.

CHAPTER ELEVEN

Offensive Weapons

11.01 This chapter considers the law on offensive weapons and, in the context of possession based offences considered in this work, provides a sketch of the law on possession.

Offensive Weapons

11.02 While explosives and firearms can obviously be used for deadly purposes other weapons can be turned to the same use. Prior to the Firearms & Offensive Weapons Act, 1990[1] there was no regulation of[2] the possession of dangerous weapons in public.[3] The 1990 legislation seeks "to control the availability and possession of offensive weapons and other articles",[4] considered to be of a dangerous or threatening nature by the creation of six new offences designed for that purpose.

The first four of these offences defines the element of possession in terms of the offence occurring when the accused "has with him"[5] the illicit article in question. This phrase is taken from s 27B of the Firearms Act, 1964, as inserted by s 9 of the Criminal Law (Jurisdiction) Act, 1976 and denotes a more personal form of possession.[6] The mental element which accompanies this external element is an intention to have such an article. This requires the accused to know that the article is with him.[7]

Having a Knife

11.03 S 9 of the Act provides:

(1) Subject to subs (2) and (3), where a person has with him in any public place any knife or any other article which has a blade or which is sharply pointed, he shall be guilty of an offence.[8]

(2) It shall be a defence for a person charged with an offence under subs (1) to prove

---

1   The Act came into force on 12 June 1990.

2   Apart from s 4 of the Vagrancy Act, 1824, as extended by s 15 of the Prevention of Crimes Act, 1871.

3   The corresponding English legislation is the Prevention of Crime Act, 1953, as amended by the Public Order Act, 1986, s 40(2) schedule 2 and the Restriction of Offensive Weapons Acts, 1959 and 1961.

4   Long title of the Act.

5   Ss 9(1), 9(4), 9(5), 10(1).

6   The discussion at 10.25 is equally applicable here. The mental element of possession is discussed below.

7   *Cugullere* [1961] 2 All ER 343; [1961] 1 WLR 858, 45 Cr App R 108 CCA.

8   Summary offence for which the penalty is a fine not exceeding £1,000 and/or twelve months' imprisonment; s 9(7)(a). See also *Edmonds* [1963] 2 QB 142; [1963] 1 All ER 828; [1963] 2 WLR 715, 47 Cr App R 114 CCA. For a discussion of the possession element see par 11.10-11.15.

that he had good reason or lawful authority for having the article with him in a public place.

(3) Without prejudice to the generality of subs (2), it shall be a defence for a person charged with an offence under subs (1) to prove that he had the article with him for use at work or for a recreational purpose.

(8) In this section "public place" includes any highway and any other premises or place to which at the material time the public have or are permitted to have access, whether on payment or otherwise, and includes any club premises and any train, vessel or vehicle used for the carriage of persons for reward.

S 9(1) is carefully drafted in order to include objects other than knives.[9] Objects which have a blade, but which are not knives, such as razors, swords, blades for shaving, hatchets, saws and scissors are included. "Sharply pointed" articles would include skewers, foils, slivers of glass, spears, arrows and the pointed bolts used in cross-bows.

All these articles are capable of a peaceful use. Under s 9(3) where the accused has such an article with him for the purpose of work or recreation it is justified. The offence does not occur, where, for example, a person is carrying a boning knife to his work in an abattoir. Apart from that defence a person may have "good reason or lawful authority for having the article with him in a public place". The phrase "lawful authority" has been construed narrowly as referring to those who have public duty to carry such an article, such as a soldier armed with a bayonet or combat knife.[10] The exception clearly also applies to a Garda who has taken possession of such an article following a search.[11]

Good Reason

The general defence is that the accused has "good reason" for having the article. The phrase used in s 9(4) to create, *inter alia*, a defence to having a flick-knife is "reasonable excuse". Such is a narrower test than that stated in s 9(2). Apart from work or recreation there may be many good reasons for carrying the wide range of objects included in s 9(1). An article may be required to effect a repair, or to be repaired or sharpened for lawful use, or to be sold or hired for a peaceful purpose.[12] Articles included in s 9(1) may often be included within the definitions of the more serious offences occurring in subsections (4) and (5). A uniform approach to construing these sections should be adopted. The purpose of the Act is to control the availability and possession of dangerous weapons. The authorities as to what constitutes a "reasonable excuse" under subs 4 clearly outlaw the carrying of

---

9   The ejusdem generis rule does not apply because there is no enumeration of things followed by general words but instead a statement of different categories of article. Generally see Cross, *Statutory Interpretation* (2nd ed., 1987) 132-35.

10   *Bryan v Mott* (1975) 62 Cr App R 71; [1986] Crim LR 64 DC, where it was held that a purpose of committing suicide is not a reasonable excuse even though honestly put forward; *Spanner* [1973] Crim LR 704, where the Court of Appeal held that security guards at dance halls were not entitled to carry a truncheon "as a deterrent" or "as part of the uniform". See also "Forgetting to Remove a Knife", *Bell v Atwell* [1987] 32 A Crim R 181 SC NSW and see par 11.08.

11   Under s 16 of this Act. See par 11.09.

12   But see s 12 quoted par 11.12.

dangerous articles for self-defence outside circumstances of imminent peril.[13] The definition of articles covered by s 9(1) is necessarily wider than in the other subsections. The defence clause must be more extensive in order to exclude the peaceful use of such articles. There is no warrant for interpreting the defence of "good reason" for having an article, under s 10(2), beyond peaceful uses; this would authorise the carrying of deadly weapons for self-defence. Such a construction would entirely defeat the object of the legislation; providing an extensive defence of self-help, by the use of violence, in a context where the Oireachtas have placed the duty of maintaining order, by force if need be, elsewhere.[14] It is submitted, therefore, that where an article is carried for self-defence it is not excepted from the general prohibition in s 9(1) save where there is imminent peril and no opportunity to seek assistance from the Gardaí.

11.04 Where the prosecution have proved that the accused had an article outlawed by s 9(1) in his possession in a public place he must give evidence to show that he had "good reason or lawful authority" for such possession. On a traditional analysis this requires him to fulfil the persuasive burden; to prove, on the balance of probabilities, the existence of that defence. It is submitted that the accused need only raise a reasonable doubt. To convict him, because he has not proved his innocence, on the balance of probabilities would incur a situation where persons could be convicted of a crime despite the existence of a reasonable doubt as to their guilt. This topic is discussed in the context of s 4 of the Explosive Substances Act, 1883.[15]

Public Place

11.05 Whether a place is a "public place" is a question of fact. If the public are permitted to have access to a place, but do not exercise it, it is nonetheless a public place.[16] Where the public exercise access to a place as a matter of fact, whether they are entirely welcome or not, it is a "public place".[17] Where an owner of a premises or place takes reasonable steps, such as the erection of notices, or the erection of some physical obstruction, to exclude the public, the place is not public.[18] The

---

13   See par 11.08.

14   It is submitted that the construction argued for is consistent with the object of "true social order" postulated in the Preamble to the Constitution as the Oireachtas have designated the executive function of maintaining order, by force if need be, to the Gardaí and the Defence Forces; generally see Forde, *Constitutional Law of Ireland* (1987) 134-36.

15   See par 9.17-9.19.

16   S 9(8). By way of contrast a definition is provided in the Road Traffic Act, 1961: "Any street, road or other place to which the public have access whether as of right or by permission and whether subject to or free of charge"; and in s 8 of the Licensing Act, 1902: "For the purpose of s 12 of the Licensing Act, 1872 and of ss 1 and 2 of this Act, the expression 'public place' shall include any place to which the public have access whether on payment or otherwise".

17   *Knox v Anderton* [1983] 76 Cr App R 156; [1983] Crim LR 114 DC. In *Powell* (1963) Crim LR 511 hospital grounds where visitors and friends of patients were allowed to enter was held to be a public place despite the restriction of access.

18   *Waters* (1963) 47 Cr App R 149; [1963] Crim LR 437 CCA; *Sandy v Martin* [1974] Crim LR 258 in which the Divisional Court held that there was no evidence for holding that a car park of a pub was open to the public an hour after licensing hours. In *Elkins v Cartlidge* [1947] 1 All ER 829 the Divisional Court held that the car park of an inn to which the public were invited, and in which

burden of proof is on the prosecution to establish that the place is public.[19] In general, a substantial portion of the public must have access to such a place.[20] Where that access is restricted to a particular class of persons the place is not public.[21]

The express terms of s 9(8) includes "club premises". These words express a legislative purpose[22] that where persons are permitted access to premises only on joining a club, or being accompanied by a member of a club, or some like restriction, the place is nonetheless a public place.

The inclusion of "any train, vessel or vehicle used for the carriage of persons for reward" extends the definition into public and private means of transport, the only criterion being that there is a charge for such a service.[23] Where a weapon is produced in a private place the circumstances may be such that it is reasonable for the jury to infer that it was brought by the accused through a public place prior to his entry.[24]

Having a Flick-knife or Other Weapon

11.06 A more serious offence is created by s 9(4):

> (4) Where a person, without lawful authority or reasonable excuse, (the onus of proving which shall lie on him), has with him in any public place—
> (a) any flick-knife, or
> (b) any other article whatsoever made or adapted for use for causing injury to or incapacitating a person,[25] he shall be guilty of an offence.

they parked their cars, was a public place. In *Knox v Anderton*, fn 17, the upper landings of a block of flats belonging to a local authority were not protected by doors or barriers or notices restricting entry and hence were a public place; *Wellard* (1884) 14 QBD 63, 15 Cox 559 CCR; Archbold (1966) 3835.

19   *A-G (McLoughlin) v Rhatigan* (1965) 100 ILTR 37 HC. Note that Davitt P appeared to adopt a different test in stating: "To prove that a place is a public place within the meaning of the Act the prosecution must prove that the public have a right of access thereto." (This was a case of drunken driving under the Road Traffic Act, 1961).

20   *Montgomery v Loney* [1959] NI 171 CA; *Edwards & Roberts* (1978) 67 Cr App R 228; [1978] Crim LR 564 CA. The Court of Appeal held that where a sufficiently substantial portion of the public to constitute "the public" were invited onto a place it thereby became a "road or other public place". The best proof is that the public were actually using the place; *Pugh v Knipe* [1972] Crim LR 247. A field where point-to-point races are being held is a public place; *Collinson* (1931) 23 Cr App R 49 CCA.

21   *Waters*, fn 18.

22   Which is not used in s 3(1) of the Road Traffic Act, 1961, or in s 8 of the Licensing Act, 1902, or in corresponding English definitions contained in s 1(4) of the Street Offences Act, 1959 and s 1(4) of the Prevention of Crime Act, 1953. See the approach of the Court of Criminal Appeal in *Collinson* (1931) 23 Cr App R 49 at 50.

23   For decisions on the meaning of what constitutes a street or public place under s 1(4) of the Street Offences Act, 1959 in England see Smith & Hogan, 466-67. For decisions as to what constitutes a public place under s 1(4) of the Prevention of Crime Act, 1953 in England which provides: "'Public Place' includes any highway and any other premises or place to which at the material time the public have or are permitted to have access whether on payment or otherwise"; or in s 9(1) of the Public Order Act, 1936 or s 16 of the Public Order Act, 1986. See Smith & Hogan, 426.

24   *Mehmed* [1963] Crim LR 780.

25   The definition is wider than the English Prevention of Crime Act, 1953 as amended by the Public Order Act, 1986, by including the element "incapacitating a person" contained in s 10 of the Theft Act, 1968, and the words "for use" are followed by "by him or by some other person". It is submitted

(9) In this section "flick-knife" means a knife—

(a) which has a blade which opens when hand pressure is applied to a button, spring, lever or other device in or attached to the handle, or

(b) which has a blade which is released from the handle or sheath by the force of gravity or the application of centrifugal force and when released is locked in an open position by means of a button, spring, lever or other device.[26]

This offence has in common with the offence under s 9(1) the elements of requiring a personal form of possession in that the accused must have the article "with him", the offence must be committed in a public place and a burden of proof is cast on the accused once these elements are proved against him. The discussion of these elements in s 9(1) is equally applicable here.[27]

The specific definition of "flick-knife" will cause little difficulty. The proof that an article is a flick-knife does not depend on expert evidence but may usually be proved, if the weapon is unavailable, by an account as to how it was seen working, or if the weapon is available, by a demonstration of its mechanism to the jury or District Justice.

Other articles must be demonstrated as having been made or adapted for use for causing injury to or incapacitating a person. Whether a particular article fits within that definition is a question of fact. Articles made for causing injury will include, for example, a firearm,[28] a dagger, a piece of chain fixed to a handle,[29] a cosh, or a knuckle-duster.[30] Articles made for incapacitating a person would include sprays which cause temporary blindness, or the loss of any other sense, CS gas, handcuffs and items which are manufactured in order to induce sleep. If an article is not made for that purpose but is merely intended to be so used then the accused should be charged under s 9(5). A machete and a catapult have been held, in England, not to be articles made or adapted for causing injury to the person.[31]

11.07 An inoffensive article may be adapted for causing injury. A nail may be pushed through a plank, a bottle or a glass may be broken so as to become dangerous, or a leg may be wrenched from a chair to make a club.[32] Ordinary articles may also be

---

that these words are unnecessary as that broadened definition is within the scope of the words used in the Irish Act which contains no limiting words which might exclude that definition.

26   Penalty; on summary conviction a fine not exceeding £1,000 and/or imprisonment not exceeding twelve months; on conviction on indictment to a fine, which is not limited, or to imprisonment for a term not exceeding five years or to both; s 9(7). For a discussion of the possession element par 11.14-11.22. The mental element of possession is discussed at par 11.18.

27   See par 11.02-11.05.

28   Probably only service rifles, revolvers and sporting firearms adapted for criminal purposes, such as by having the barrel sawn off, are included. Other firearms which were used for shooting game would not fall within the definition. All firearms are, in any event, subject to extensive control as ch 10 demonstrates.

29   All taken from Russell 646.

30   Smith & Hogan, 423 citing *Cosams*, 168 ER 274, 1 Leach 342: ". . . bludgeons, properly so-called, clubs and anything that is not in common use for any other purpose but a weapon are clearly offensive weapons within the meaning of the legislation", referring to the Smuggling Acts.

31   *Southwell v Chadwick* (1987) 85 Cr App R 235 CA.

32   Smith & Hogan, 423 gives the examples of razor blades inserted in a potato or cap peak, a bottle broken for the purpose of causing injury and a chair-leg studded with nails.

adapted for causing incapacity. So a bottle of washing-up liquid may be emptied and filled with ammonia so that it can be squirted in a person's face and cause temporary blindness,[33] surgical tape may be prepared so as to make a convenient gag and a drink may be "laced" with drugs. "Adapted" means, in this context, altered so as to become suitable for use for causing injury to or incapacitating a person.[34] This word, it is submitted, implies a conscious decision by the accused to alter an article for such a purpose. An accidentally broken bottle is a product of nature and not of human ingenuity.[35] Where the accused has an article which is neither made nor adapted, by him or anyone else, for the purpose of causing incapacity or injury to a person, but he intends to use it for that purpose he will commit an offence under s 9(5) or, where the article is pointed or has a blade, under s 9(1).

Excuse

11.08 Where the prosecution have proved that the accused has such an article with him in a public place the burden of proving a defence of "lawful authority or reasonable excuse" rests on the accused.[36] "Lawful authority" will have the same meaning as in s 9(1). The existence of a "reasonable excuse", it has been held, under the corresponding English legislation,[37] depends on whether a reasonable man would think it excusable to carry the flick-knife or other article. It is not enough that the accused's intentions were lawful.[38]

---

33 *Formosa* [1991] 1 All ER 131 CA the Court of Appeal held that a washing-up liquid bottle filled with hydrochloric acid was not a prohibited weapon within the meaning of s 5 of the English Firearms Act, 1968. The legislation makes it an offence to have ". . . any weapon of whatever description designed or adapted for the discharge of any noxious liquid . . .". The Court held that "adapted" was a word which must take its meaning from its context which, in this instance, had to mean that the object was altered so as to make it fit for the use in question: ". . . was the empty washing-up liquid bottle altered when it was filled with hydrochloric acid? The answer in our view is clearly No. There was no physical alteration to the bottle. The bottle remained the same. The addition of the acid did not change the bottle in any way. It follows that the bottle with the acid was not a weapon "designed or adapted" for the discharge of acid within the meaning of the section". (At 133-34). On the contrary, s 9(4) does not refer to "weapon" but refers to "any other article whatsoever made or adapted for use for causing injury". It is submitted that the word "adapted" does not require an alteration to the physical object so that the object alters in its composition apart from what was put into or onto it. It is difficult to see a qualitative difference between a nail through a chair leg and acid inside a bottle. The Shorter Oxford English Dictionary defines "adapted" as "fitted, fit, altered so as to fit". Other common meanings indicate that the article as adapted is now capable of use or has been made suitable for a purpose; *Raynor v US* (1966) 89 F (2d) 469, 471 Circ AC, 7th Circ. It has been held that a machete and a catapult are not made or adapted for causing injury to the person; *Southwell v Chadwick* (1987) 85 Cr App R 235 CA.

34 Smith & Hogan, 423 citing *Davison v Birmingham Industrial Co-Operative Society* (1920) 90 LJ KB 206; *Flower Freight v Hammond* [1963] 1 QB 275; [1962] 3 All ER 950; [1962] 3 WLR 1331 DC; *Hermann v Metropolitan Leather Co. Ltd* [1942] Ch 248; [1942] 1 All ER 249; *Maddox v Storer* [1963] 1 QB 451; [1962] 1 All ER 831; [1962] 2 WLR 958 DC.

35 Smith & Hogan, 423 consider that the article must be altered with intent to make it into, or use it as an article for causing injury or incapacity, citing *Maddox v Storer*, fn 33.

36 The extent of the burden is discussed at par 11.04, referring to par 9.17-9.19.

37 S 1(4) of the Prevention of Crime Act, 1963 as amended by the Public Order Act, 1986.

38 *Bryan v Mott* (1975) 62 Cr App R 71; [1976] Crim LR 64 DC. The Court held that in deciding whether there was a reasonable excuse one has to ask oneself whether a reasonable man would think it excusable to carry the offensive weapon in order to have it available for the purpose claimed.

What is abundantly clear is that this Act was never intended to sanction the permanent or constant carriage of an offensive weapon merely because of some constant enduring supposed or actual threat or danger to the carrier. People who are under that kind of continuing threat must protect themselves by other means notably by enlisting the protection of the police and in order that it may be a reasonable excuse to say "I carried this for my own defence" the threat for which this defence is required must be an imminent particular threat affecting the particular circumstances in which the weapon was carried.[39]

It follows that an excuse of self-defence is not sufficient unless the accused can show an imminent particular threat affecting the particular circumstances in which the weapon was carried;[40] a person under constant threat may not resort to deadly weapons but must seek assistance from the Gardaí.[41] It has been held in the United Kingdom that there was no reasonable excuse for carrying a knuckle-duster and truncheon against possible attempts to rob the accused of the wages he collected for his employees.[42] Nor was it reasonable for a taxi-man to carry a weighted rubber cosh for a defence against violent passengers,[43] for the accused to possess a milk bottle for the purpose of suicide,[44] or for security guards at a dance hall to carry a truncheon in order to deter trouble.[45] Carrying a catapult and a machete can be reasonable if they are to be used for the purpose of killing grey squirrels in order to feed wild birds being kept under licence.[46]

39   Per Widgery CJ in *Evans v Hughes* [1972] 3 All ER 412 at 415; [1972] 1 WLR 1452 at 1455, 56 Cr App R 813 at 817; [1972] Crim LR 558 DC.

40   *Evans v Hughes* [1972] 3 All ER 412 at 415; [1972] 1 WLR 1452, 56 Cr App R 813; [1972] Crim LR 558 DC; *Pittard v Mahoney* [1977] Crim LR 169 DC; *Evans v Wright* (1964) Crim LR 466 DC. In *Peacock* [1973] Crim LR 639 the Court of Appeal held that it was not reasonable for a person to carry a knife in fear of being attacked by a skinhead. The court was of the opinion that it would be very rare for someone who is not under immediate fear of attack to be able to rely on the carrying of a weapon for self-defence. In *Bradley v Moss* [1974] Crim LR 430 the Divisional Court held that there was too large a gap between a prior attack and the accused being in possession of a studded glove. In *Ball v Atwell* (1987) 32 A Crim R 181 the Supreme Court of New South Wales held that using a knife in the course of work (clearly a lawful purpose) but then forgetting to remove it would not alter the initial purpose for thich the knife was carried. Forgetting is not a "reasonable excuse"; *McCallan* (1988) 87 Cr App R 372 CA. It can be a reasonable excuse for carrying a machete and a catapult that they are to be used for killing grey squirrels in order to feed wild birds kept under licence; *Southwell v Chadwick* (1987) 85 Cr App R 235 CA.

41   See the discussion above and further see the discussion under s 4 of the Explosive Substances Act, 1883 at par 9.17-9.19 and the discussion of s 27A of the Firearms Act, 1964 as substituted by s 8 of the Criminal Law (Jurisdiction) Act, 1976 at 10.32. It should be noted that in *Hudson* [1971] 2 QB 202; [1971] 2 All ER 244; [1971] 2 WLR 1047, 56 Cr App R 1, the Court of Appeal accepted duress as a defence to a charge of perjury where the accused could have put herself under the protection of the Court or could have resorted to the police. It may be that there are situations where police protection would be ineffective and that therefore a person may have a "reasonable excuse" for resorting to weapons of violence. These situations will be rare but the requirement of a constitutional construction does not impose a requirement that a court ignore the factual reality of a situation.

42   *Evans v Wright*, fn 40. The Divisional Court held that this explanation was unreasonable as he had last collected wages some days prior but had left the weapons in his car. It may have been otherwise if he had been in the course of, or had just returned from collecting wages.

43   *Grieve v MacLeod* [1967] SLT 70; [1967] Crim LR 424.

44   *Bryan v Mott*, fn 39.

45   *Spanner* [1973] Crim LR 704. The court held that weapons should not be carried as a matter of routine or as part of a uniform.

46   *Southwell v Chadwick* (1987) 85 Cr App R 235 CA.

Having a Weapon with Intent

11.09 S 9(5) of the Act provides:

(5) Where a person has with him in any public place any article intended by him unlawfully to cause injury to, incapacitate or intimidate any person either in a particular eventuality or otherwise, he shall be guilty of an offence.[47]

(6) In a prosecution for an offence under subsection (5), it shall not be necessary for the prosecution to allege or prove that the intent to cause injury, incapacitate or intimidate was intent to cause injury to, incapacitate or intimidate a particular person; and if, having regard to all the circumstances (including the type of the article alleged to have been intended to cause injury incapacitate, or intimidate, the time of the day or night, and the place) the court (or the jury as the case may be) thinks it reasonable to do so, it may regard possession of the article as sufficient evidence of intent in the absence of any adequate explanation by the accused.

The elements of the offence again depend on the accused having the article with him in a public place and the discussion under s 9(1) is equally applicable here.[48] Any article may come within the scope of the offence provided the accused has the article with him for the purpose of injuring, incapacitating, or intimidating a person.[49] Heuston defines "intimidation" as ". . . the use of unlawful threats whereby the lawful liberty of others to do as they please is interfered with".[50] "Intent" in this context will mean "purpose".[51] That purpose of the accused may be inferred from all the surrounding circumstances, including the nature of the article and the time and the place where the accused has it with him. It is a question of fact[52] and may be proved by reference to all the surrounding circumstances, by what the accused actually did with the article[53] or by admission.[54]

In England it has been held that as the long title of the Prevention of Crimes Act, 1953 expresses a purpose of prohibiting "the carrying of offensive weapons in public

---

47   Penalty: on summary conviction a fine not exceeding £1,000 and/or imprisonment not exceeding twelve months; on conviction on indictment of a fine, which is not limited, or to imprisonment for a term not exceeding five years or to both; s 9(7).

48   See par 11.02.

49   Injury and incapacity are discussed at par 10.38.

50   *Salmond & Heuston*, 421 citing *Pete's Towing Services Ltd v N Industrial Union* [1970] NZLR 32 at 41 SC Auckland.

51   See par 2.19.

52   *Williamson* (1977) 67 Cr App R 35; [1978] Crim LR 229.

53   *Woodward v Koessler* [1958] 3 All ER 557; [1958] 1 WLR 1255 DC.

54   Smith & Hogan, 423 note that as the articles which have held to have been carried with an intent to cause injury under s 1(4) of the Prevention of Crime Act, 1953 as amended by the Public Order Act, 1986; a sheath knife, *Woodward v Koessler*, fn 53; a shot-gun, *Gipson* [1963] Crim LR 281 CCA; *Hodgson* [1957] NI 1; [1958] Crim LR 379 CCA; a razor, a sandbag, *Petrie* [1961] 1 All ER 466; [1961] 1 WLR 358, 45 Cr App R 72 CCA; *Gibson v Wales* [1983] 1 All ER 869; [1983] 1 WLR 393; a pick-axe handle, *Cugullere* [1961] 2 All ER 343; [1961] 1 WLR 858, 45 Cr App R 108 CCA; a stone, *Harrison v Thornton* [1966] Crim LR 388 DC; and a drum of pepper, *Parkins* (1980) 120 JP 250. They also refer to a stilletto heel as a dangerous weapon. The extended definition in the Irish legislation which includes an intent to incapacitate or intimidate would include the articles discussed under that heading in par 10.38 and also articles which are incapable of causing injury or incapacity but which, of their nature are intimidating, which might include, for example, articles alleged by the accused to carry contagious disease.

places". Where an article is initially carried for a lawful purpose, but is then used with intent to cause injury, the offence is not made out.[55] It is submitted that this analysis is inapplicable to the 1990 Act as its purpose is to control the availability and possession of those weapons and not, as the English legislation expresses it, to outlaw the "carrying" of those weapons. A person may have an article with him for a lawful purpose[56] and yet when an event occurs will form an intent to use the article in the manner outlawed by the section. In those circumstances it is difficult to see how the legislation can be construed to include an intent formed a considerable time prior to an incident but to exclude an intent formed only seconds or minutes prior. The use of the words "have with him" does not imply that the criminal intent must be formed prior to the accused exercising control over the weapon.[57] A continuous external element of a crime may be completed by the mental element at any time when it continues.

A person may defend himself with a dangerous weapon if the necessity of self-defence makes such use reasonable.[58]

Being an Armed Trespasser

11.10 A further offence is created by s 10(1) of the Act:

> (1) Where a person is on any premises as defined in subs (2) as a trespasser, he shall be guilty of an offence if he has with him—
> (a) any knife or other article to which s 9(1) applies, or
> (b) any weapon of offence (as defined in subs (2)).
>
> (2) In this section—"premises" means any building, or any part of a building and any land ancillary to a building;
> "weapon of offence" means any article made or adapted for use for causing injury to or incapacitating a person, or intended by the person having it with him for such use.[59]

The possession element is the same as that discussed in respect of s 9.[60] This section only applies where the accused is in or on a building or any land ancillary

---

55 *Ohlson v Hylton* [1975] 2 All ER 490; [1975] 1 WLR 724; [1975] Crim LR 292 DC: "To support a conviction under the Act the prosecution must show that the defendant was carrying or otherwise equipped with the weapon, and had the intent to use it offensively before any occasion for its actual use had arisen". For further authorities see Smith & Hogan, 424-25. Thus, for example, in *Jura* [1954] 1 QB 503; [1954] 1 All ER 696, [1954] 2 WLR 516, 38 Cr App R 53 CCA, the accused had obtained an air rifle at a shooting gallery for the purpose of firing at a target, but on losing his temper shot a lady who was with him. The Court of Criminal Appeal held that as he had a reasonable excuse for possession of the air rifle the unlawful use did not bring it within the section. The Court also expressed the opinion that offences of immediate intent are within the exclusive ambit of the Offences Against the Person Act, 1861. For a contrary decision on reasonable excuse see *Powell* [1963] Crim LR 511 and *Woodward v Koessler*, fn 53. Further see Archbold 19.439.

56 For the purpose of carpentry, as in *Ohlson v Hylton*, fn 55.

57 In *Houghton* [1982] Crim LR 112, the Court of Appeal decided that the offence of having a firearm with intent to commit an indictable offence, contrary to s 18(1) of the Firearms Act, 1968, did not require such an intent to be formed prior to the firearm being used.

58 See par 4.29.

59 Penalty: on summary conviction a fine not exceeding £1,000 and/or imprisonment not exceeding twelve months; on conviction on indictment to a fine, which is not limited, or to imprisonment not exceeding five years or to both; s 10(3).

60 See par 11.02. The mental element of possession is discussed below.

to a building.[61] A person who trespasses on a farm, while in possession of a weapon of offence, would not be within the definition of the offence while he was going through open fields, but would commit the offence where he enters a farm building or yard, or the yard or garden surrounding the farmer's house.[62]

"Weapon of offence" is a composite definition incorporating the elements of subs 9(4) and (5).[63] The accused does not have to enter the premises as a trespasser.[64] The accused must know that he is on the premises as a trespasser, or be reckless as to that fact.[65] A trespass occurs where the accused enters on or remains on the premises of another without the express or implied permission of the occupier.[66] An express invitation can be given by the occupier of a building or a member of that person's household.[67] The limits of implied permission to enter onto property are set by the customs and standards of society. It is not a trespass to go to the front door of another's house on a legitimate errand. It is otherwise if the implied permission has been expressly withdrawn[68] or where the accused enters for a purpose, or whilst on another's premises, forms a purpose inconsistent with the terms of the implied permission. So while it is lawful for a postman to go onto property for the purpose of placing something in a letter-box or a person distributing leaflets to go onto property for the purpose of placing something in a letter-box it is a trespass if either intends to commit a crime. In *The People (DPP) v McMahon*[69] the Supreme

---

61 Whether something is a building is a commonsense question of fact; *Brutus v Cozens* [1972] 2 All ER 1297. It need not be a completed structure. Further see the discussion as to what a building is in *Mason v Leavy* [1952] IR 40 HC.

62 The word "ancillary" means something subordinate or secondary; Stroud, *Judicial Dictionary*, 124. In *Killeen v Baron Talbot de Malahide* [1951] Ir Jur 19 Judge Shannon held that the terms "ancillary and subsidiary" must be interpreted having regard to the facts of each case and that "ancillary" means ministering in an active way while the words "ancillary and subsidiary" require the giving or doing of something actively benefiting the house and were not satisfied by proof that the land was aesthetically advantageous to the building. In the light of this uncertainty a definition should have been provided in the Act.

63 See par 11.06, 11.09.

64 Under s 23A of the Larceny Act, 1916, as inserted by s 6 of the Criminal Law (Jurisdiction) Act, 1976, the offence of burglary is defined: "(1) A person is guilty of burglary if, (a) he enters any building or part of a building as a trespasser and with intent to commit any such offence as is mentioned in subsection (2); or (b) having entered any building or part of a building as a trespasser, he steals or attempts to steal anything in the building or that part of it, or inflicts or attempts to inflict on any person therein any grievous bodily harm. (2) The offences referred to in subsection (1)(a) are offences of stealing anything in the building or part of a building in question, of inflicting on any person therein any grievous bodily harm or raping any woman therein and of doing unlawful damage to the building or anything therein. (3) References in subsection (1) and (2) to a building shall apply also to an inhabited vehicle or vessel, and shall apply to any such vehicle or vessel at times when the person having a habitation in it is not there as well as at times when he is there. (4) A person guilty of burglary shall be liable on conviction on indictment to imprisonment for a term not exceeding fourteen years". Further see McCutcheon, 74-84.

65 *Collins* [1973] QB 100; [1972] 2 All ER 1105; [1972] 3 WLR 243, 56 Cr App R 554 CA. Recklessness is discussed at par 2.36-2.37.

66 McMahon & Binchy, 428; Salmond & Heuston, 421 citing *Pete's Towing Services Ltd v N Industrial Union* [1970] NZLR 32 at 41 SC Auckland.

67 *Collins*, fn 65. A false pretence will vitiate permission; *Finnucane* (1837) C&D 1.

68 *The People (DPP) v Gaffney* [1986] ILRM 657 HC.

69 [1987] ILRM 87. And see *Purtill v Athlone UDC* [1968] IR 205 at 210, per Walsh J; *Jones & Smith* [1976] 3 All ER 54; [1976] 1 WLR 672, 63 Cr App R 47 CA; *Barker* (1983) 57 ALJR 426.

Court held that a party of Gardaí were trespassers when they entered a public house for the purpose of investigating suspected offences under the Gaming & Lotteries Act, 1956. The general invitation by a person running a licensed premises did not extend to Gardaí investigating crime; by reason of that purpose they were outside the implied invitation of the owner.[70]

Proof of the accused's knowing, or being reckless, that he was a trespasser is usually a matter of inference from the surrounding circumstances. Relevant factors include the place where he was found or seen, particularly whether such was outside the normal area where an implied invitation would exist and whether any obstacles were overcome or signs ignored to reach that position, the time when he was found, his clothing, his demeanour and his behaviour. It is submitted that where the accused is found in circumstances where normally an implied permission would exist that proof of a purpose outside the scope of the invitation is assisted by his having with him a weapon of offence to which the section applies,[71] and of his having no reasonable explanation for such behaviour.

Producing a Weapon

11.11 S 11 of the Act provides:

> Where a person, while committing or appearing to be about to commit an offence, or in the course of a dispute or fight, produces in a manner likely unlawfully to intimidate another person any article capable of inflicting serious injury, he shall be guilty of an offence. . . .[72]

The circumstances under which the offence may occur are extremely broad. Once the accused is committing an offence no limitation is placed in terms of category; extending it to the entire criminal calendar. The section also applies where the accused appears "to be about to commit an offence". As this is an external element it must be construed reasonably. The offence is therefore only committed where a reasonable man, perceiving what the accused is proved by the prosecution to have been doing, would conclude that he is about to commit an offence.

The offence is further broadened by the application of the section to a situation where the accused is in the course of "a dispute or fight".[73] The accused must produce[74] an article capable of inflicting serious injury. Experience shows that articles such as stones and sticks have been used to kill. Provided an article is reasonably capable of inflicting a serious injury[75] the offence occurs where the

---

70   At 89-91.

71   For a discussion on the articles to which s 9(1) applies see par 11.03; for a discussion of weapons of offence, which is an amalgamation of the definitions contained in s 9(4) and (1); see par 11.03-11.09.

72   Penalty: on summary conviction a fine of up to £1,000 and/or imprisonment not exceeding twelve months; on conviction on indictment to a fine, which is not limited or to imprisonment for a term not exceeding five years or to both; s 11.

73   The word "fight" implies an exchange of blows. The word "dispute" is defined by the Shorter Oxford English Dictionary as: "the act of arguing against, controversy, debate . . . a heated contention, a quarrel".

74   In the context "produce" would require the weapon to be shown or exhibited through the senses to another person. There is nothing in the section which would limit the production to a person involved in the immediate quarrel.

75   For a discussion of the meaning of "serious injury" see par 2.34-2.35.

accused produces it in a manner which is likely unlawfully to intimidate[76] another person. It is lawful to produce a weapon, in the course of a dispute, if such action is reasonably necessary for the purposes of self-defence.[77]

Dealing in Weapons

11.12 S 12 of the Act provides:

> (1) Any person who—
> (a) manufactures, sells or hires, or offers or exposes for sale or hire,[78] or by way of business repairs or modifies, or
> (b) has in his possession for the purpose of sale or hire or for the purpose of repair or modification by way of business, or
> (c) puts on display, or lends or gives to any other person, a weapon to which this section applies shall be guilty of an offence.
>
> (2) Where an offence under subs (1) is committed by a body corporate and is proved to have been so committed with the consent or connivance of or to be attributable to any neglect on the part of a director, manager, secretary or other officer of the body corporate, the director, manager, secretary or other officer or any person purporting to act in such capacity shall also be guilty of an offence.
>
> (3) A person guilty of an offence under this section shall be liable-
> (a) on summary conviction, to a fine not exceeding one thousand pounds or to imprisonment for a term not exceeding twelve months or to both, or
> (b) on conviction on indictment, to a fine or to imprisonment for a term not exceeding five years or to both.
>
> (4) The Minister may by order direct that this section shall apply to any description of weapon specified in the order except any firearm subject to the Firearms Acts, 1925 to 1990.
>
> (5) The Minister may by order amend or revoke an order made under this section.
>
> (6) The importation of a weapon to which this section applies is hereby prohibited.
>
> (7) Every order made under this section shall be laid before each House of the Oireachtas as soon as may be after it is made and, if a resolution annulling the order is passed by either such House within the next 21 days on which that House has sat after the order is laid before it, the order shall be annulled accordingly, but without prejudice to the validity of anything previously done thereunder.

The section does not apply until the Minister makes an order applying it to particular stated weapons. To date no orders are in force. A possible area of concern, apart from the weapons within s 9, 10 and 11, are those used in martial arts. Where a person is convicted under the Act, the weapon which forms the external element of the offence may be forfeited.[79]

---

76 See par 11.09.

77 See par 4.29.

78 These last twelve words are necessary because of the decision in *Fisher v Bell* [1961] 1 QB 394; [1960] 3 All ER 731; [1960] 3 WLR 919 DC.

79 This order does not take effect until appeal procedures are exhausted either by expiry of time for appeal or by a final decision; s 13.

Garda Powers

11.13 A Garda may arrest any person who is, or whom he reasonably suspects to be, in the act of committing any offence under s 9, 10 or 11.[80] A special power of search applies only to offences under s 9. Where a number of people are congregated in a public place while a breach of the peace is occurring, or where a Garda reasonably believes that such a breach has occurred or may occur, and he suspects that one or more of those people has any article to which s 9 applies[81] with him, or them, he may search a particular person. If he has no reason to suspect anyone in particular he may search them all if he considers that necessary to ascertain whether any of them has such an article with them.[82]

A District Justice or Peace Commissioner may issue a search warrant on being satisfied by a sworn information by a Garda that there are reasonable grounds for suspecting that an offence under s 12 has been or is being committed on any premises, whereupon the Gardaí may enter such premises, if need be by force, and seize anything which he reasonably believes may be required for the prosecution of such an offence, or of an offence under the Customs Acts.[83]

Note on Possession

11.14 A note on possession follows for the purpose of drawing together the disparate strands of the law so far discussed and presenting a coherent but simplified overview of this topic.

At Common Law

11.15 At common law the fact of possessing an object did not, of itself, create criminal liability.[84] Offences of possession have been subsequently created by statute. These require proof that the accused was related, in a manner proscribed by the statute, to an illicit article.[85] Possession is thus a state of affairs. The relationship between the accused and an object denoted by the word "possession" is variable dependent on the context in which it occurs.[86] Essentially, the accused must exercise

---

80   S 14.
81   See par 11.03, 11.06, 11.09.
82   S 16.
83   S. 15. The Peace Commisioner or District Justice must himself be satisfied that there are reasonable grounds for so suspecting; *Byrne v Grey* [1988] IR 31; further see par 6.37.
84   *Heath* (1810) R&R 184 158 ER 750; *Dugdale* (1853) 1 E&B 435, 118 ER 499.
85   This section of the work should be read in conjunction with chapters 9 and 10.
86   *Murphy* [1971] NI 193 at 199 CCA; Lord McDermott LCJ: "'Possession' is an ambiguous word and one which, as Lord Parker of Waddington observed in *Towers & Co. Ltd v Gray* [1961] 2 QB 351 at 361, is always giving rise to trouble. The precise meaning must depend on the context and policy of the statute using it, and no comprehensive definition is therefore possible or desirable. But in s 1(1)(a) it connotes, in our opinion, voluntary possession by actual or potential physical control, with knowledge of the nature of what is kept or controlled. Other contexts may demand less, as in *Reg v Warner* [1969] 2 AC 256. Some may demand more, as where the possession is attached to a specific purpose or some special intent. But to bring a case within s 1(1)(a) there is no need to look for any such attachment; *Sambasivam v Public Prosecutor, Federation of Malaya* [1950] AC 458, 469- 70"; *Hall v Cotton* [1987] QB 504; [1986] 3 All ER 332; [1986] 3 WLR 681, 83 Cr App R 257 DC; *United*

a sufficient degree of control over the article and must intend to exercise possessory rights over it.[87]

Personal

11.16 Possession may be actual or legal. Actual possession denotes an ideal state of affairs where the accused has complete present physical control of the property to the exclusion of others, who are not acting in concert with him. This may occur where he has the property under his manual control or where he has left it in a situation where he alone has the exclusive right or power to place his hands on it when he wishes.[88] This control will exist where the accused has an object on his person, within his "grab area", or in any other place where he can, if he wishes, exercise control over it. The element of custody will be satisfied by proof that, at the relevant time, the individual had the property in a place to which he could resort for the purpose of carrying into effect his intention to exercise control.[89]

The Australian High Court have decided in *Williams v Douglas*[90] that possession exists notwithstanding that the property is in a location where it is not beyond interference by another person. In that case the prosecution was required to prove that the accused had physical possession of gold. He had secreted it in a communal

States of America and Republic of France v Dollfus Miegs et Siesa SA and Bank of England [1952] AC 582 and 605 per Viscount Jowitt [1952] 1 All ER 572 at 581 HL.

87   Murphy, fn 86, Lord MacDermott LCJ at 199-200: ". . . the duration of a possession otherwise within this enactment is not in itself material. While a momentary possession may at times verge on the kind of offence which is little more than a bare technicality, the possession aimed at by this section cannot be measured in time, as possession for a very brief period may be just as dangerous as possession for a much longer period. The second matter concerns the voluntary element in an assumption of possession or control. The material background here is the existence of an opportunity to take into possession a firearm for which there is no appropriate certificate. This may lead to a variety of situations. For example, A finds a pistol by the side of the road, takes it up, examines it and puts it in his pocket with a view to throwing it into a river he is just about to cross. Before he gets there he is stopped by the police and the pistol is discovered. He is guilty of an offence under s 1(1)(a): he assumed control of what he knows is a firearm and he has neither duty nor excuse to justify throwing it into the river or carrying it thereto. But suppose A finds the pistol lying in an hotel bedroom as he is retiring at night, in circumstances which absolve him from responsibility for its presence. He determines to have nothing to do with the pistol and leaves it severely alone. Is he nonetheless in possession of the firearm? We think the answer must be in the negative. A has the relevant knowledge and the opportunity and ability to assume possession or control, but the necessary mental element is lacking; he does not wish or intend to take possession or assume control. Again, A on leaving the bedroom next morning takes the pistol with him with the sole object of handing it over to the police for safe custody. Has he committed an offence under s 1? This court considers he has not: like a fireman who carries a bomb from a burning house to a place of safety, he is acting as a good citizen should, and in a manner which we cannot believe Parliament intended to penalise".

88   This definition is taken from the Australian High Court decision in *Moors v Burke* (1919) 26 CLR 265 at 274. The case concerned the meaning of the expression "actual possession" in the Police Offences Act, 1915 (Victoria) s 40. Further see *Warner v Metropolitan Police Commissioner* [1969] 2 AC 256 at 309; [1968] 2 All ER 356 at 392; [1968] 2 WLR 1303 at 1349-50, 52 Cr App R 373 at 433; [1968] Crim LR 380 HL Lord Wilberforce: "Ideally a possessor of a thing has complete physical control over it, he has knowledge of its existence, its situation, its qualities—he has received it from a person who intends to confer possession of it and he has himself the intention to possess it exclusively of others".

89   Gillies, 619-20.

90   (1949) 78 CLR 521.

bathroom at the hotel where he was staying. Latham, Dixon & McTiernan JJ included within the concept of physical possession:

> . . . any case where the person alleged to be in possession has hidden the thing effectively so that he can take it into his physical custody when he wishes and where others are unlikely to discover it except by accident. . . . It seems clear enough that whoever hid [the gold] chose an effective hiding place and that when concealed there the gold was at his command.[91]

Through Another

11.17 The accused will have possession of goods where they are in the actual possession of someone over whom he has control, so that they will be forthcoming if he requires them.[92] In such a case the prosecution must prove the authority of the other party to receive the goods on behalf of the accused[93] or a common purpose between the parties in receiving the goods.[94]

Possession will also occur where the accused makes an arrangement for an article to be left in a particular location where, at some future stage, he will be able to exercise control over it.[95] Where a person gives an article into the custody of another for safekeeping he will continue to have possession of it.[96] It is not necessary to hold the article in complete security. A momentary, or fleeting, possession which is subject to termination through the interference of others is nonetheless possession.[97]

---

91   At 527; *Van Swol* (1974) 4 ALR 386 SC Vict.

92   Archbold (1922) 729 citing *Smith* (1855) Dears 559, 169 ER 845, 7 Cox 51 CCA; *Gleed* (1916) 12 Cr App R 32 CCA; *Miller* (1853) 3 Cox 353 (Ir).

93   Archbold (1922) 730 citing *Pearson* (1908) 1 Cr App R 77 CCA.

94   Archbold (1922) 730 citing *Payne* (1909) 3 Cr App R 259 CCA; *Cook* (1912) 8 Cr App R 91 CCA.

95   *Peaston* (1978) 69 Cr App R 203; [1979] Crim LR 183 CA; *Cavendish* [1961] 2 All ER 856; [1961] 1 WLR 1083, 45 Cr App R 374; [1961] Crim LR 623 CCA.

96   *Sullivan v Earl of Caithness* [1976] QB 966 at 970; [1976] 1 All ER 844 at 847; [1976] 2 WLR 361 at 363, 62 Cr App R 105 at 107 DC May J: "looking at the context of the word 'possession' in s 1 of the Act in the present case, I have no doubt that one can be in possession of a firearm even though one is at a place other than that at which the firearm physically is. To agree with the justices' decision in the present case would in my view effectively be to equate the word "possession" in s 1 with custody, and this I am satisfied would be wrong. . . . In my opinion the purpose of s 1 of the Act of 1968 and its ancillary provisions is to regulate and licence not merely those who have physical custody of firearms, or who keep them in the place in which they live, but also those who have firearms under their control at their behest, even though for one reason or another they may be kept at their country cottage, at the local shooting range or indeed at Bisley. As a matter of construction therefore, which must to some extent also be a matter of first impression, and looking at the context and what I believe to have been the intent of s 1 of the Act of 1968, it may well be, I think, that the owner of a firearm who does not at the relevant time have physical possession of it, can nevertheless be said still to be in possession of it. In the present case the defendant was at all material times the owner of the firearms. He could no doubt obtain them from his mother's flat at any time when he wanted them. She had the barest custody of them, not because she had any interest in them, but because her flat was safer than the defendant's home in Oxford. In these circumstances and on the admitted facts in my judgment the defendant was at all material times in Swalcliffe in possession . . . "; *Hall v Cotton* [1987] QB 504; [1986] 3 All ER 332; [1986] 3 WLR 681, 83 Cr App R 257 DC; Archbold (1922) 730. As to whether the bailee will also be in possession see the examples cited by Lord McDermott LCJ in *Murphy* [1971] NI 193 at 200-2 CCA.

97   *Boyce* (1976) 15 SASR 40 SC; *Turvey* [1946] 2 All ER 60, 31 Cr App R 154 CCA; *Murphy*, fn 96.

Mental Element

11.18 The accused must intend to exercise control, either exclusively or in common design with others, over the article in question. If the accused is ignorant of the existence or presence of the article he is alleged to be controlling (save in cases where the accused has made a prior definite arrangement for the delivery of an article, but has not yet satisfied himself that it has arrived, if the accused is ignorant of the existence or presence of the article he is alleged to be controlling) he is not in possession of it. In the context of receiving stolen property the Court of Criminal Appeal in England have commented:

> . . . for a man to be found in possession, actual or constructive, of goods, something more must be proved than that the goods have been found on his premises. It must be shown either, if he was absent, that on his return he has become aware of them and exercised some control over them or . . . that the goods had come, albeit in his absence, at his invitation or by arrangement. It is also clear that a man cannot be convicted of receiving goods of which delivery has been taken by his servant unless there is evidence that he, the employer, had given the servant authority or instructions to take the goods.[98]

The finding of an unlicensed firearm hidden in a person's car is not proof of his possession of it unless the prosecution prove that he knew the gun was there.[99] Of itself, presence of an article on the accused's property will not give rise to an inference of possession.[1] This principle should not be used to distort reality. There are circumstances where an inference of knowledge and control can also be drawn from the open and obvious presence of an article in circumstances where the accused's relationship to it would lead to a conclusion that he had knowledge of its presence. An inference of control can be drawn from similar factual circumstances. In some instances, despite the fact that the accused may be aware of the substance being present in such close proximity to them to indicate, in normal circumstances, control, a jury may need to be specifically directed that an intent to exercise such dominion, as opposed to an equally innocent explanation open on the facts, is necessary for a finding of guilty in relation to that element of an offence.[2]

Nature of Substance

11.19 In Australia,[3] and in England,[4] possession of a container, in which an illicit article is found to be, is possession of that article.[5] The Irish courts have yet to

---

98   *Cavendish* [1961] 2 All ER 856 at 858; [1961] 1 WLR 1083 at 1085, 45 Cr App R 374 at 378; [1961] Crim LR 623 CCA; per Lord Parker CJ.

99   *Williams* [1967] 2 NSWR 594 CCA; and see *Smith* [1966] Crim LR 558 CCC; *Ashton-Rickhard T* [1978] 1 All ER 173; [1978] 1 WLR 37, 65 Cr App R 67; [1977] Crim LR 424 CA; *Bourne v Samuels* (1979) 21 SASR 591 SC.

1   *Minister for Posts & Telegraphs v Campbell* [1966] IR 69 HC.

2   *Davis* (1990) 50 A Crim R 55 CA WA.

3   *Bush* [1975] 5 ALR 387 CCA NSW. For further authorities see Gillies, 611.

4   *Warner v Metropolitan Police Commissioner* [1969] 2 AC 256 at 309; [1968] 2 All ER 356 at 392; [1968] 2 WLR 1303 at 1349-50, 52 Cr App R 373 at 433; [1968] Crim LR 380 HL. For an explanation of the result of this extremely confusing case see Smith & Hogan, 106-10.

5   The *Warner* analysis provides a defence whereby the accused may simply possess the container where he is either (1) completely mistaken as to the nature of the contents or (2) has no opportunity to

pronounce on this issue. In England the Court of Appeal has held that if the prosecution prove that the accused knowingly had in his possession an article, which in fact fits within the definition of a firearm, then the offence of possession is committed. It has been thus held to be immaterial that the accused did not know that the article in his possession was a firearm for which a firearm certificate was required.[6] Where the statutory offence includes an ulterior element, such as an intent to endanger life, that further element would be impossible of fulfilment where the accused had no knowledge as to the nature of the article under his control.[7]

Notwithstanding that the Firearms Acts, 1925 to 1990 and the Explosives Acts, 1875 to 1883 appear to differentiate between concepts of "possession" and "knowing possession"[8] it is submitted that where a crime of possession depends on the illicit nature of an article, the accused must be, at least, reckless as to the nature of the object over which he is exercising control.[9] It cannot have been the intention of the Oireachtas to render a person liable to the stigma of criminal conviction or imprisonment who has no knowledge or suspicion that the article under his control was of a nature which, exceptionally, citizens could not lawfully exercise control over. It is submitted that a construction of the legal incidents of possession which does not include either knowledge or recklessness as to the nature of the outlawed article would be so unjust in the range of possible results it would produce, as to be in contravention of the fundamental guarantee of fairness implied in the Constitution.[10]

11.20 In the context of offensive weapons the Court of Criminal Appeal in England has held that the phrase "has with him in any public place"[11] requires the prosecution to prove knowledge.[12] It is submitted that the more personal concept of possession which this phrase implies[13] is, apart from that fact, no different in legal incident than ordinary possession.

On the balance of the authorities, it appears to be the law that where a person once has intention of control over an article but later forgets that he has it with him or under his control, he nonetheless retains possession of it.[14]

---

ascertain the nature of the contents and (3) does not suspect their illegal nature. This approach has not found favour in Australia; Gillies, 611-12. In *Waller* [1991] Crim LR 381, the *Warner* analysis that the normal inference that a person who accepts possession of a parcel accepts possession of its contents can be shaken by evidence of mistake was not accepted by the Court of Criminal Appeal. The Court applied strict liability in respect of the possession of a firearm in a black plastic bag based essentially on policy grounds.

6   *Hussain* [1981] 2 All ER 287; [1981] 1 WLR 416, 72 Cr App R 143 CA; *Howells* [1977] QB 614; [1977] 3 All ER 417; [1977] 2 WLR 716, 65 Cr App R 86; [1977] Crim LR 354 CA; *Bradish* [1990] 1 All ER 460 CA (in relation to a canister of noxious gas); further see Smith & Hogan, 120-22.

7   See chapters 9 and 10.

8   This matter is discussed in the text of chapters 9 and 10.

9   *Beaver* (1957) 118 CCC 129 SC. Liability based on criminal negligence is also a possibility in this context but there appears to be no decision to support such an analysis.

10   *King v A-G* [1981] IR 233 SC. For a further discussion see par 4.49-4.51.

11   From the Prevention of Crime Act, 1951, s 1.

12   *Cugullere* [1961] 2 All ER 343; [1961] 1 WLR 858, 45 Cr App R 108 CCA.

13   See par 11.02.

14   *Martindale* [1986] 3 All ER 25; [1986] 1 WLR 1042, 84 Cr App R 31; [1986] Crim LR 736 CA;

Joint Possession

11.21 Joint possession may occur in circumstances where the doctrine of common design is applicable. Thus two persons may possess an illegal article, though only one has it physically under his control, through acting in concert for the purpose, for example, of disposing of it.[15] Common design possession is not established by proof of mere acquiescence in the disposition of property into a place to which the accused had access.[16] There is necessary inference of either control or an intention to control from that fact.

Grave problems occur in circumstances where, ostensibly, one of a number of persons is in possession of an illicit article where the prosecution are unable to prove either a common design by some, or one, or all, to possess that article. In *Whelan*[17] the RUC raided a house in Belfast occupied by fourteen people. In a small room upstairs the three accused were found in three different beds. On searching the room the police found a revolver and some rounds of ammunition on the top of a chest of drawers. These were covered by men's clothing. The three accused were the only adult males in the house. They were questioned but denied possession of the firearm but asserted a positive defence that the police had planted the gun in an attempt to frame them. Their conviction by a jury was quashed by the Court of Criminal Appeal:

> Every argument of logic and commonsense would indicate that there was a very strong case that at least one of these men was in possession of this gun, and it is quite clear that none of them had a licence or permit to have the gun and no explanation is forthcoming as to what the gun was doing in this house. It appears to the court, however, that this is a case which could well be approached on the basis that guilt existed in the alternative, that is to say, that one, or possibly two, of these men might have been guilty, while the remaining two, or one, as the case may be, were or was innocent of the offences which have been included in the indictment and that the difficulty, in fact the impossibility, of laying the blame conclusively at the door of one accused is not a warrant for permitting or inviting the finding of guilt against each of them.[18]

11.22 This particular problem can be rectified by a statutory presumption that where an illicit article is found in or on what appears to be a person's property or vehicle, that he should be presumed, until he proves to the contrary, to be in possession of the article. No such statutory reform has been undertaken in this jurisdiction.[19]

applying *Buswell* [1972] 1 All ER 75; [1972] 1 WLR 64 CA; doubting *Russell* (1984) 81 Cr App R 315; [1985] Crim LR 231 CA; *McCallan* (1988) 87 Cr App R 372 CA.

15 *Ditroia* [1981] VR 247 SC.

16 *Hussain* [1969] 2 QB 567; [1969] 2 All ER 1117; [1969] 3 WLR 134, 53 Cr App R 448 CA; *Searle* [1971] Crim LR 592 CA; *Tansley v Painter* [1969] Crim LR 139 DC.

17 [1972] NI 153 CCA.

18 At 156-57. In *Edmonds* [1963] 2 QB 142; [1963] 1 All ER 828; [1963] 2 WLR 715, 47 Cr App R 114 the Court of Criminal Appeal made a similar decision in the context of possession of an offensive weapon. Each of the accused had been convicted of possession of a starting pistol, a piece of leaden tubing and a hammer handle under the equivalent Prevention of Crime Act, 1953, s 1(1). The Court found that by the nature of each article intent to injure (and not just to frighten) had to be proved against each person, unless joint possession of the articles had been proved.

19 For an example of statutory reform in Northern Ireland see s 7 of the Northern Ireland (Emergency Provisions) Act, 1973.

Inference

Possession may be inferred from all the circumstances linking the accused to the article in question. In particular it is relevant as to whether his actions are inconsistent with any more remote association. An inference of knowledge of the presence of an object, and thus intention to control it, may be made from evidence of actual control.[20]

Draft Indictments

11.23 There follow the appropriate forms of indictment for the offences considered in this chapter.

POSSESSION OF A KNIFE

Statement of Offence
Having a knife (or any other article which has a blade or which is sharply pointed) contrary to s 9 of the Firearms & Offensive Weapons Act, 1990.
Particulars of Offence
AB on the   at   had with him in the said public place, without good reason or lawful authority, a knife (or any other article which has a blade or which is sharply pointed).

POSSESSION OF A FLICK KNIFE

Statement of Offence
Possession of a flick knife (or an article made or adapted for use for causing injury to or incapacitating a person) contrary to s 9(4) of the Firearms & Offensive Weapons Act, 1990.
Particulars of Offence
AB on the   had with him without lawful authority or reasonable excuse, at   , a public place, a flick knife (or a   being an article, made or adapted for use for causing injury to or incapacitating a person).

OFFENSIVE WEAPON

Statement of Offence
Possession in a public place of an article intended to unlawfully cause injury, incapacitate, or intimidate, contrary to s 9(5) of the Firearms & Offensive Weapons Act, 1990.

---

20   *Williams* (1978) 140 CLR 591 at 610 (HC of Australia), Aickan J: "It is necessary be bear in mind that in possession there is a necessary mental element of intention, involving a sufficient knowledge of the presence of a drug (or other prescribed item) by the accused. No doubt in many cases custody of an object may supply sufficient evidence of possession, including the necessary mental element, but that is because the inference of knowledge may often be properly drawn from surrounding circumstances. Thus both X and Y may be charged with possession of cannabis, because on being searched each had in his pocket a cigarette packet containing, not ordinary cigarettes as marked on the packet, but 'reefers'. In each case that fact may well be prima facie evidence of possession, that is, of physical custody or control with knowledge of what is in the cigarette packet, and, if no more appeared, there would be sufficient evidence to support a conviction in each case . . ."; *Button v Cooper* [1947] SASR 286 SC.

Particulars of Offence

AB on the　　　　at　　　　, a public place, had with him an article intended by him to unlawfully cause injury to, incapacitate or intimidate a person (or CD).

BEING AN ARMED TRESPASSER

Statement of Offence

Being on a building (or part of a building or land ancillary to a building) as a trespasser and possessing a knife (or any other article to which s 9(1) of the Firearms & Offensive Weapons Act, 1990, applies, or weapon of offence contrary to s 10(1) of the Firearms & Offensive Weapons Act, 1990.

Particulars of Offence

AB on the　　　　on the building　　　　(or on any part of a building or any land ancillary to a building) being a trespasser had with him a knife (or any other article described in s 9(1) or any weapon of offence as defined in subs 10(2) and described here).

PRODUCING A WEAPON

Statement of Offence

Production of an article capable of inflicting serious injury contrary to s 11 of the Firearms & Offensive Weapons Act, 1990.

Particulars of Offence

AB on the　　　　at　　　　while committing (or appearing to be about to commit) the offence of　　　　(or in the course of a dispute or fight) produced an article capable of inflicting serious injury, being a　　　　, in such a manner as to be likely to unlawfully intimidate another person.

DEALING IN WEAPONS

Statement of Offence

Exposing for sale or hire (or manufacturing, selling or hiring or by way of business repairing or modifying) an article to which the (specify Regulations) applies contrary to s 12 of the Firearms & Offensive Weapons Act, 1990.

Particulars of Offence

AB on the　　　　at　　　　exposed for sale or hire a (specify article to which the Regulations apply).

Note: For different forms of the offences see s 12. This offence is dependent on Ministerial regulation and the articles will be specified within same in due course.

Statement of Offence

Lending an article to which the (specify Regulations) applied contrary to s 12 of the Firearms & Offensive Weapons Act, 1990.

Particulars of Offence

AB on the　　　　at　　　　lend to CD an article, being a　　　　which activity was prescribed by the (specify Regulations).

Index